American Society

Recent Sociology Titles from W. W. Norton

Code of the Street by Elijah Anderson

The Cosmopolitan Canopy by Elijah Anderson

Social Problems, Second Edition, by Joel Best

The Family: Diversity, Inequality, and Social Change by Philip N. Cohen

You May Ask Yourself: An Introduction to Thinking like a Sociologist, Fourth Edition, by Dalton Conley

The Real World: An Introduction to Sociology, Fourth Edition, by Kerry Ferris and Jill Stein

Essentials of Sociology, Fifth Edition, by Anthony Giddens, Mitchell Duneier, Richard P. Appelbaum, and Deborah Carr

Introduction to Sociology, Ninth Edition, by Anthony Giddens, Mitchell Duneier, Richard P. Appelbaum, and Deborah Carr

Mix It Up: Popular Culture, Mass Media, and Society by David Grazian

The Contexts Reader, Second Edition, edited by Douglas Hartmann and Christopher Uggen

The Society Pages: Color Lines and Racial Angles edited by Douglas Hartmann and Christopher Uggen

The Society Pages: Getting Culture edited by Douglas Hartmann and Christopher Uggen

The Society Pages: Crime and the Punished edited by Douglas Hartmann and Christopher Uggen

The Society Pages: Owned edited by Douglas Hartmann and Christopher Uggen

The Society Pages: The Social Side of Politics edited by Douglas Hartmann and Christopher Uggen

Thinking Through Theory by John Levi Martin

Doing Race edited by Hazel Rose Markus and Paula M. L. Moya

Readings for Sociology, Seventh Edition, edited by Garth Massey

Families as They Really Are, Second Edition, edited by Barbara J. Risman and Virginia Rutter

The Sociology of News, Second Edition, by Michael Schudson

The Social Construction of Sexuality, Third Edition, by Steven Seidman

Sex Matters: The Sexuality and Society Reader, Fourth Edition, edited by Mindy Stombler, Dawn M. Baunach, Wendy O. Simonds, Elroi J. Windsor, and Elisabeth O. Burgess

Gender: Ideas, Interactions, Institutions by Lisa Wade and Myra Marx Ferree

More than Just Race by William Julius Wilson

Cultural Sociology: An Introductory Reader edited by Matt Wray

To learn more about Norton Sociology, please visit wwnorton.com/soc

American Society

HOW IT REALLY WORKS

SECOND EDITION

ERIK OLIN WRIGHT

UNIVERSITY OF WISCONSIN, MADISON

JOEL ROGERS

UNIVERSITY OF WISCONSIN, MADISON

W. W. Norton & Company NEW YORK · LONDON

W. W. Norton & Company has been independent since its founding in 1923, when William Warder Norton and Mary D. Herter Norton first published lectures delivered at the People's Institute, the adult education division of New York City's Cooper Union. The firm soon expanded its program beyond the Institute, publishing books by celebrated academics from America and abroad. By midcentury, the two major pillars of Norton's publishing program—trade books and college texts—were firmly established. In the 1950s, the Norton family transferred control of the company to its employees, and today—with a staff of four hundred and a comparable number of trade, college, and professional titles published each year—W. W. Norton & Company stands as the largest and oldest publishing house owned wholly by its employees.

Copyright © 2015, 2011 by W. W. Norton & Company, Inc.

Editor: Sasha Levitt
Associate Editor: Nicole Sawa
Project Editor: Rachel Mayer
Editorial Assistants: Thea Goodrich and Mary Williams
Manuscript Editor: Chris Thillen
Managing Editor, College: Marian Johnson
Managing Editor, College Digital Media: Kim Yi
Production Manager: Ashley Horna
Media Editor: Eileen Connell
Marketing Manager, Sociology: Julia Hall
Design Director: Rubina Yeh
Permissions Manager: Megan Jackson
Composition: Jouve North America
Manufacturing: Sheridan Books, Inc.

Permission to use copyrighted material is included on p. 555.

Library of Congress Cataloging-in-Publication Data

Wright, Erik Olin.
    American society : how it really works / Erik Olin Wright, Joel Rogers. — Second edition.
    pages cm
Includes bibliographical references and index.
    ISBN 978-0-393-93885-2 (pbk.)
    1. Social values—United States.   2. United States—Social conditions.   3. United States—Economic conditions.   4. United States—Moral conditions.   5. United States—Civilization.
I. Rogers, Joel, 1952-   II. Title.
    HN90.M6W75 2015
    306.0973—dc23

                                                                            2014047605

W. W. Norton & Company, Inc., 500 Fifth Avenue, New York, NY 10110-0017
wwnorton.com

W. W. Norton & Company Ltd., Castle House, 75/76 Wells Street, London W1T 3QT

2 3 4 5 6 7 8 9 0

ABOUT THE AUTHORS

Erik Olin Wright is Vilas Distinguished Professor of Sociology at the University of Wisconsin. He is the author of many books, including *Classes, Interrogating Inequality, Class Counts, Deepening Democracy* (with Archon Fung), *Envisioning Real Utopias*, and *Understanding Class*. In 2011–2012 he was president of the American Sociological Association.

Joel Rogers is Professor of Law and Sociology at the University of Wisconsin–Madison and Director of COWS. His many books include *On Democracy, Right Turn, The Forgotten Majority,* and *What Workers Want.* A longtime activist, Rogers was identified by *Newsweek* as one of the 100 Americans most likely to shape U.S. politics and culture in the twenty-first century.

For Marcia and Sarah

CONTENTS

PART III   DEMOCRACY

CONCLUSION

This book is the product of a long friendship, the shared values and concerns that animate it, and a small convention we agreed to more than twenty-five years ago to keep that friendship well nourished. The small convention was that we would have a cup of coffee and take a walk together every Sunday morning that we were both in town. The point was simply to give us some regular time to connect with each other—on sociology department business, current events, research interests, family news, or whatever else was on our minds.

We have observed this convention with a constancy that even Kant might have admired. On most of the Sunday mornings since, rain, snow, or shine, you could have found us—fortified by coffee, usually accompanied by one of Wright's succession of dogs, sometimes by a visiting colleague—strolling around Madison's many lakes and woods, intent in conversation. During Madison's long winters when the lakes freeze over, you could have found us strolling on them. This amuses visitors from warmer climes, and is tolerated by the ice fisherman we always find there first, camped in their solitary pursuit of quiet and cold fish.

Early in the history of these walks, Rogers proposed that Wright consider joining him in teaching a large undergraduate lecture course on contemporary American society that he had developed shortly after arriving in Madison in 1987. Wright, in Madison since 1976, had never taught such a course—not because of special aversion to undergraduates, but simply because he was fully occupied with research and graduate students. But Rogers claimed he would enjoy the experience and learn from it. In the early 1990s, Wright finally gave it a try, and immediately realized that Rogers had been right. Teaching hundreds of undergraduates as a group was indeed fun, and the challenge of making complex and often controversial ideas accessible to them did sharpen his own thinking, reminding him that teaching is the best way to learn.

Since that time we have both taught this course, always jointly developing the course's content and a shared set of lecture notes that we revised together over time. We never used a textbook, but rather a collection of readings, revised each time the course was offered, that at least loosely covered the topics of the lectures. The latter contained the real guts of the course.

This way of handling the lectures and readings worked well enough but had two problems. Students often got a bit overwhelmed by processing both the lecture material and the loosely related readings. And the readings, because only loosely related, provided no real means of catch-up for students who might miss a key lecture, especially on a particularly complicated part of the argument in the course. Wright then suggested a natural solution to this problem, which was to turn our lectures into a book. We or others could, of course, always supplement this book with additional materials, but the book would ensure that the core of the course would always be available to students outside of lectures. We had no disagreements on course content, and we had gone over our detailed lecture notes time and again, so Wright thought this would be an easy task, taking only a few months of steady work.

He was wrong. All the things that make a good book different from a good lecture meant that converting our notes to narrative took longer than expected. But we eventually got it done. Because Wright wound up doing the greater share of this conversion work, we put his name first on the book, but we regard it as fully a joint product from the two of us.

The book reflects our different academic backgrounds, expertise, and practical experience.

Rogers was not trained as a sociologist. His graduate work, at Yale, Princeton, and the University of Heidelberg, was in law, political science, economics, and philosophy. The common thread in his academic work—which ranges over normative and empirical democratic theory, labor and administrative law, and American and comparative politics and policy—is democracy: how to define and measure it, what makes it work, and how to make it work better. He is also very engaged in what is sometimes called the "real world" of politics, government, business, and social movements. Rogers spends much time outside the university advising people in this world, or organizing projects to change it. He was attracted to Madison in part because of the "Wisconsin Idea" of using university research to inform democratic social experiment. He runs a center at the University that does just that. Called (first as a joke, but the name stuck) COWS (Center on

Wisconsin Strategy), it promotes "high road" (i.e., equitable, sustainable, democratic) economic development and governance. It has produced a stream of influential innovations in worker training, business and labor strategy, and local, state, and national policy.

Wright has had a more conventional academic career. He got his graduate training in sociology at the University of California, Berkeley, went straight from there to Madison, and has stayed there ever since. His research until the mid-1990s mainly involved large-scale quantitative investigations of various themes connected to social class and inequality. Since then he has organized what he calls the "Real Utopias Project," which explores a wide range of radical proposals for transforming the core institutions of contemporary society. From the start of his time in Madison, Wright has also been heavily engaged in developing a graduate program within the sociology department focusing on the analysis of class, social justice, and social change. In the mid-1980s he founded the A.E. Havens Center at the University of Wisconsin, whose mission is to foster dialogue between activists and academics and to encourage critical perspectives on contemporary social issues. Less active in the "real world" than Rogers, Wright certainly shares his colleague's democratic concerns.

These different strengths are in part reflected in different contributions to this book. From Rogers has come more of its analysis of economic and political institutions, and their practical reform. From Wright has come more of its sociological analysis of class, race, and gender. But again, the book is a joint effort, and at this point we actually find it hard to disentangle our respective contributions to it. This is a happy confusion that we blame on years of rewarding conversation on hundreds of Sunday morning walks.

Joel Rogers and Erik Olin Wright
Madison, Wisconsin
January 2010

ACKNOWLEDGMENTS

Thanks to the nearly 9,000 undergraduates at the University of Wisconsin–Madison who have, over the past twenty-five years, taken the course on which this book is based. They gave us the priceless opportunity to teach, and an ongoing trial by fire. Thanks to six students in the Graduate Program of the Department of Sociology for able assistance in final manuscript preparation: Matias Scaglione, who energetically took the lead in running down and updating sources and preparing many of the figures and tables; Pablo Mitnik, who also generated first versions of many figures and tables; and Adrienne Pagac and Edo Navot, who filled in on those rare occasions their colleagues came up short. Christina Bain and Matias Cociña provided invaluable assistance in updating the figures and tables for the second edition. And thanks to Karl Bakeman and Sasha Levitt, our editors at W. W. Norton, for their care, comments, and stalwart enthusiasm throughout.

American Society

1

PROLOGUE:
PERSPECTIVES AND VALUES

The discussion in this book revolves around three broad kinds of questions:

1. What *kind* of society is this?
2. How does it really *work*? Why is it the way it is?
3. In what ways does it *need changing*, and how can those changes be brought about?

The first of these questions is largely a matter of *description*. To know what kind of society American society is, we will have to compare it with other societies and describe its central institutions. This process will involve identifying some of the things that make the United States a very specific social world as well as the things that it shares with many other contemporary societies.

The second question, more analytical and theoretical, concerns *explanation*. Our job will be to explain a range of attributes of American society, not simply describe them. We want to open the "black boxes" of different institutions and see how they work, what consequences they have. To do this we use both empirical findings and key elements of theory drawn from sociology, political science, and economics.

The third question concerns *evaluation*. It requires coming to terms with the values, visions, and moral standards we think should be embodied in American society. Answering this question will inevitably be highly charged politically and morally because social institutions can be judged by sharply contending moral standards. What we hope to do is clarify as best we can the implications for such moral and political issues of the existing realities of American society.

Writing a book on contemporary American society, one intended primarily for people who grew up there, poses an interesting challenge. To grow up and live in a society, people have to learn a great deal about how it works, about the rules of the game, and about the nature of the society in which they live. In the ordinary course of experiencing the social world, everyone also develops theories, even if they are partial and incomplete, about why their society is the way it is. Most readers of this book are already at least amateur experts on its subject matter. They have ideas about what kind of society this is, and they have explanations for many specific questions we will explore in this book:

- Why is poverty a persistent problem in the United States?
- Why is there a consensus among the major political parties that taxes should be kept relatively low?
- Why does money seem to have so much influence in American politics?
- Why are there many fewer women than men professors, corporate presidents, and politicians?
- Why do cities find it hard to control urban sprawl?
- Why does the American military engage in military actions in so many far-flung places around the world?

Of course, having a view on something is not the same as having an accurate view. The special challenge of writing a book about contemporary American society is that we must inevitably confront strongly held beliefs by our readers, some of which we believe to be incorrect. Our task, therefore, is not simply to impart a body of information about contemporary American society, but to argue for a particular way of understanding and explaining the facts we present. This challenge poses distinct issues for the three tasks of description, explanation, and evaluation.

DESCRIPTION: GETTING THE BASIC FACTS RIGHT

The purely descriptive tasks are the easiest. People may have their "facts" wrong, or not understand their limits, or draw premature or erroneous inferences or conclusions from them. The best way to address such problems is to use only high-quality evidence and rational argument. Instead of relying on colorful anecdotes for our data, for example, we use verifiable facts, representative surveys, and other sources of reliable information. Instead of using data in an undisciplined and selective way in argument, we will do our best to make logical claims and justified inferences. We have taken this approach very seriously in writing this book and invite readers to hold us to this standard. If you see something that you think is factually wrong, or encounter a conclusion or an inference from something that you think is not rational or logical, please say so. This insistence on the best possible data and careful reasoning is essential for rational discussion. It is what distinguishes any social *science* from mere opinion or belief.

EXPLANATION: THINKING LIKE A SOCIOLOGIST

Explaining aspects of American society is much more difficult than simply describing them. The approach we adopt is broadly sociological, although we also draw on research and ideas from political science and economics. Many readers may wonder, "What is sociology?" There are many answers to this question, and we will not try to present a general review of the alternatives. Here is one way to understand this idea: The myriad of actions that we as conscious, choosing persons engage in are *governed by rules*. However, unlike the rules of nature that govern the motions of the planets, these social rules are changed by the actions they regulate. Our activities are rule governed, but our activities also produce and transform the rules that govern those activities. Sometimes the changes in social rules are the result of *deliberate* actions by people—as when we change a law; sometimes rules change as the *unintended consequence* of actions. The central task of sociology is to understand how rules generate their effects, how people respond to the rules under which they live, and how the rules change over time.

This sociological approach to understanding and explaining society may seem trivial and obvious, but it is also quite profound. And it turns out to be a very complex matter indeed to figure out how these rules work and how, out of their interactions, the social facts we observe get produced. The analysis of this book revolves around six basic aspects of the problem of understanding social rules:

1. *Rules are enforced.* There are consequences for breaking rules. If you dress badly for a job interview, you are unlikely to get the job; if you steal from a store and get caught, you get arrested. The enforcement is variable; some rules are consistently and systematically enforced, while others are loosely and erratically enforced. But to call something a social rule means that some kind of enforcement is connected to it.

2. *Rules take different forms.* There are very different kinds of rules. Among the most important types are *laws* and *social norms*. Laws are, most simply, rules whose enforcement is backed by the power of government. Social norms are much broader in application. They sometimes include morally weighty principles, like telling the truth, but they also include things with little clear moral content, like dress codes and good manners. Some of these rules are enforced by officials and authorities, while others are enforced informally. And when they are internalized, we often enforce them on ourselves. Social norms are incorporated deeply into our habits and preferences, and a significant part of their enforcement is self-administered (through guilt, shame, a feeling of awkwardness, and the like), but they are still rules.

3. *Rules are frequently not neutral.* Many rules benefit some people over others, and some kinds of rules impose real harms on some people. This idea is obvious in some contexts. In sports, the rules of a game give advantages to some sorts of people over others. Consider the height of basketball nets. But this idea is also true in society: many of the rules of the game that govern our economic, social, and political interactions give advantages to some kinds of people over others. Of course, not all rules strongly benefit some people over others. The social rules telling us to drive on a particular side of the road benefit everyone. But many important rules do serve the interests of some people over others, and understanding such rules will be a major concern of this book.

4. *Power and rules interact.* Rules are protected by power, but this power is also governed by rules. People who strongly benefit from an existing set of rules will try to defend those rules. *Social rules will tend to be stable when they confer power on the people they benefit.* This is a central problem in sociological analysis. In some situations, this point is obvious. In the American South before the Civil War, the rules of economic life enormously benefited slave owners at the expense of slaves. The Southern states enforced the rules coercively. And slave owners, who benefited from those rules, used their power to defend the rules. For a very long time, these rules were stable precisely because they conferred power on those actors who had the greatest interest in defending them.

5. *Rules can be inconsistent.* The rules that make up a society need not be coherent or consistent. Some rules contradict others, and in general it is impossible to fully follow every social rule. Societies are not like

a finely tuned machine in which all the parts must fit together smoothly for the machine to work. In many social contexts, people muddle through, coping as best they can with contradictory pressures generated by inconsistent social rules. The social norms governing the way men and women are supposed to behave, for example, are quite inconsistent with the rules governing how you get ahead in a career—and many women experience this inconsistency as a source of considerable strain in contemporary American society.

6. *Rules can change.* Because of these inconsistencies and contradictions, rules can become quite unstable. There are historical moments when rules of the game are contested, and very rare moments when they are contested in a fundamental way. More often, rules change by gradual erosion and metamorphosis.

So, to understand different aspects of social life, what we need to do is figure out the rules. We need to understand how they work, how they are enforced, how they fail to be enforced, how they fit together or fail to fit together, who benefits and who suffers, and what processes may be generating change in the rules. We will be doing all these things throughout this book.

EVALUATION: WHAT ARE THE VALUES WE CARE ABOUT?

On the most contentious issue, how to evaluate American society, the agenda of this book revolves around five core social values that most people in American society affirm in one way or another: freedom, prosperity, efficiency, fairness, and democracy. In the most general terms, here is what we mean by each of these values:

1. *Freedom*—the idea, commonly thought to be the most essential to the "American creed," that people should be able to live their lives, to the greatest degree possible, as they wish. This means people should be free from coercive restrictions imposed by others and, as much as possible, have the capacity to put their life plans into effect.

2. *Prosperity*—the idea that an economy should generate a high standard of living for most people, not just a small and privileged elite.

3. *Efficiency*—the idea that the economy should generate rational outcomes, effectively balancing costs and benefits in the way resources are used.

4. *Fairness*—the idea that people should be treated justly and that they should have equal opportunity to make something of their lives without unfair privileges and unfair disadvantages.
5. *Democracy*—the idea that our public decisions should reflect the collective will of equal citizens, not of powerful and privileged elites.

Along with valuing these things, most Americans would agree that it is reasonable to judge our institutions based on how well they achieve them. Of course, expectations about the satisfaction of these five values are not uniform across all social institutions. Most Americans, for example, expect more efficiency and prosperity from our economic institutions than from our government, and more democracy from government than from the economy. Nor are these five values the only values that people feel are important. The value of community and a sense of belonging, for example, is something that many expect of their society. The most important value for many Americans is found in religion, not secular society. The most important institution for many is the family rather than the more public institutions of the state and the economy. Some of these other values and perspectives will figure in the discussion that follows. For the most part, however, the discussion will revolve around the five values of freedom, prosperity, efficiency, fairness, and democracy.

The first three of these values play an especially important role in Part I of the book, which focuses on the capitalist economy. Our concern will be with seeing how the U.S. economy works and how well it performs in terms of freedom, prosperity, and efficiency. The analysis of inequality in Part II revolves especially around the value of fairness, although prosperity and freedom also are important. We will discuss various forms of inequality in American society today and see how consistent they are with these values. Finally, in Part III on democratic institutions, the central values are democracy and freedom.

Kinds of Disagreements

Though most Americans affirm these values, there are sharply different ideas about precisely what they mean and how well American society lives up to them. Much of the debate between the left and the right of the political spectrum, between progressives and conservatives, in fact centers on such disagreements. These disagreements tend to be of four main sorts.

First, people disagree about precisely *what is meant by each of these values.* Consider democracy. Does democracy simply mean elections of public officials and majority rule, or does it mean active involvement of citizens in political participation, public discussion, and decision making? Or take fairness: is fairness just a question of removing various forms of direct discrimination against people—for example, discrimination based on race or gender or religion—or does fairness mean that everyone really has an equal opportunity in life, which would mean drastically reducing economic disadvantages some people face?

Second, people disagree in their assessment of *the actual performance of our institutions.* Conservatives, for example, generally believe that the American-style market economy is a wonderful machine for generating prosperity and efficient, rational economic outcomes; progressives point to the high levels of poverty, irrationalities, waste, and inefficiencies generated by markets.

Third, people disagree about *the relative priority of different values.* For example, progressives and conservatives both believe in the values of freedom and fairness; but in cases of conflict between these values, progressives tend to be more attentive to fairness and conservatives to freedom. Thus, progressives are generally more willing to justify taxation of the wealthy on grounds of broader fairness; in contrast, conservatives are more likely to argue that taxes, except those necessary to protect society and enable markets to function, restrict individual freedom in unacceptable ways.

Fourth, people disagree about *how much things could really be improved.* Thus, conservatives may acknowledge that American democracy falls far short of the ideal of government of the people, by the people, and for the people, but they tend to feel that not much can be done about the situation—or, even more pessimistically, that efforts to improve things generally make them worse—whereas progressives believe that American democracy could be revitalized with appropriate institutional change.

Overall, then, conservatives tend to believe that American society measures up pretty well regarding these particular values; and where it does not, not a lot can be done to improve things. Progressives, on the other hand, are much more critical of the existing reality and feel that much could be done to improve it.

Our Views about Realization of These Values in Contemporary America

Where then do we locate ourselves in the continuum of these kinds of disagreements? We place ourselves on the left of the political spectrum. We think that American society has many great achievements and tremendous potential but falls far short of what it could be. Specifically, in terms of the five values, we believe the United States measures up nowhere near as well as it could:

- *Freedom.* Compared to most societies in the past as well as many contemporary ones, people do have a great deal of individual freedom in the United States. But real freedom is curtailed for many people by large inequalities in material conditions of life; by significant levels of poverty, especially among children; and by the excessive emphasis on using resources for private consumption rather than public goods.
- *Prosperity.* Many Americans are affluent compared to most people in the world, but the American economy is far too oriented to a narrow conception of standards of living that is preoccupied with income, wealth, and material consumption rather than the overall quality of life. True prosperity gives weight to leisure and free time rather than simply income. It places high value on public goods and collective consumption rather than simply private consumption. And it is concerned with long-term environmental sustainability rather than simply present conditions.
- *Efficiency.* The American market economy is highly productive and innovative, but it also generates pervasive irrationalities and inefficiencies because it is not subjected to sufficient social regulation. Examples we will discuss include environmental degradation, health-care failures, inadequate job training, and wasteful and inefficient transportation systems.
- *Fairness.* Although certain oppressive forms of discrimination have been reduced in recent decades, we remain a society that provides far from equal opportunity for its citizens. In particular, the levels of wealth and income inequality in the United States today generate massively unfair privileges and disadvantages that interact with continuing advantages and disadvantages linked to race and, to a lesser extent, gender.
- *Democracy.* The rules of the game of elections in the United States, especially when combined with the pervasive role of money in generating access to the political system, have profoundly undermined American democracy.

To push forward these values, then, means confronting the basic institutions of our society and trying to change them. If we really want to realize these values in practice, we must aspire to more than simply tinkering with our social institutions; we must strive for fundamental change.

This vision has deep roots in American culture. The values of freedom, prosperity, efficiency, fairness, and democracy have been a central part of both individual aspirations and collective struggles that have marked American history—even though the realization of these values has been crippled and deflected by the nature of power, property, and privilege in this society. The political perspective that animates this book does not reject American values, but rather seeks to realize the great promise for humanity and justice that is part of the American dream.

2

WHAT KIND OF SOCIETY IS AMERICAN SOCIETY?

The starting point for our exploration is to understand precisely what *kind* of a society we are talking about when we refer to contemporary American society. But first, what exactly does it even mean to ask what kind of society we live in? This sort of question has a pretty clear meaning when it comes to living organisms. Suppose you are walking through some woods and you come across a strange animal. Everyone knows what it means to wonder, what kind of a creature is this? For animals, there is a well-established set of questions you could ask: Does it have a skeleton? Does it breathe air? Is it warm blooded? These are not just random questions; they come from a highly developed scientific framework rooted in evolutionary biology that tells us what sorts of questions we need to ask in order to properly classify a strange, unknown creature within the range of variation of living things that have been studied by biologists. The same thing can be said if you come across some peculiar, as yet unknown substance and you want to know what kind of a substance it is. Chemistry has a periodic table of elements and a powerful, elegant scientific theory of how these elements combine to produce the fantastic variety of molecules that make up the physical world. After a careful chemical analysis of the substance, you will have a systematic answer to the question, what is this? Of course, it could turn out that the questions you asked were unsatisfactory and produced contradictory answers, or no answers at all, and this would provoke some rethinking of the classification menu. Discoveries of new species and new elements can lead to new understandings of the underlying logic of classification. But at least in both of these bodies of knowledge, there is a broad consensus on how to classify the things in the world.

Social science is not as developed as evolutionary biology or chemistry, and there is certainly less consensus about what are the most salient characteristics of a society that must be identified in order to answer the question, what kind of society is this? Think of the problem this way: Imagine you were dropped into another country today—Japan or Sweden, Guatemala or Nigeria. Or perhaps you were dropped into the United States in a different era—maybe 1715, 1815, or 1915. Suppose, though, that everyone talked exactly like Americans do today. How would you know that you were not in the contemporary United States? What would you look for? If you were blindfolded, what questions would you ask? Which questions would be more important than others?

This chapter explores our answers to the general question, what kind of society is this? Some of the answers may seem obvious, but they are worth noting because they help situate the United States in the world, comparatively and historically. Other answers may be less familiar. We will organize our answers under a number of quite general headings—technology, economy, inequality, politics, militarism, gender, social cleavage, immigration, culture, and violence. In upcoming chapters we provide much more detail on many of these topics, but for now it will be helpful to sketch the salient characteristics of each topic to produce a general descriptive picture of American society.

TECHNOLOGY

Many people believe that the core technology a society uses in economic production is the single most important characteristic distinguishing one society from another. If you are looking for one single piece of information that tells you something of central importance about what it means to live in any particular society—across all of human history and all the societies that have ever existed—technology is certainly a good candidate. It matters hugely whether the means of production in a society are simple hand tools or complex power-driven machines, whether food is acquired primarily through hunting and gathering or through machine-intensive and chemically enhanced large-scale agriculture.

The United States is a technologically advanced industrial society moving toward what is variously called post-industrialism, the knowledge economy, or the information society. What precisely does it mean to say that we have a high level of technological development? The main idea here is that the techniques we use to produce things are highly productive: it takes fewer inputs to produce a given amount of output than it did in the past. There was a time, not so long ago in historical terms, when nearly all people had to spend most of their time producing food so that everyone would have enough to eat. Today in the United States, less than 3 percent of the labor force has to work in agriculture to produce more than enough food for the over 300 million people who live in this country. That is what is meant by high productivity and developed technology.

As an economy becomes more and more productive, human time is liberated for various new activities. When we say that we are becoming a post-industrial society, what we mean is that most people now earn their living by producing services of various sorts rather than physical things. But of course, this is possible only because we produce physical things so productively. Human life is no less dependent on food now than it was 40,000 years ago. The difference is that human time is vastly less absorbed in the activity of producing food.

It is important to remember how recent a development this is, and how different from most of the world it is. Two empirical indicators of these changes are especially striking: the shift from rural to urban living, and the transformation of the occupations people have in order to make a living. In 1860 around 80 percent of the U.S. population was rural, and about half of

FIGURE 2.1—Trajectory of agricultural, manufacturing, and services employment and urbanization, 1800–2000

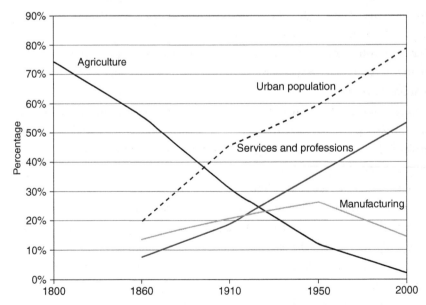

Sources: Labor force data and urban population data from *Historical Statistics of the United States Millennial Edition Online*, table Ba-A. Urban population data from U.S. Census Bureau (2004), *United States Summary: 2000*, table 18, available at www.census.gov/prod/cen2000/phc3-us-pt1.pdf (accessed July 1, 2014).

the labor force was in agriculture. This is still basically the case in the world's two most populous countries at the beginning of the twenty-first century: in India, 60 percent of the labor force works in agriculture (2003) and 71 percent of the population lives in rural areas (2007); in China, the figures are 43 percent (2006) and 58 percent (2007).[1] By the 1940s, most Americans lived in cities, and just under 20 percent of the population worked in agriculture. Today we are overwhelmingly an urban society, and less than 3 percent of Americans are employed directly in agriculture (Figure 2.1).

THE ECONOMY

When we talk about the economy, we are talking about all the ways that people produce the goods and services used and consumed in a society. Economies vary in many different ways. One of these we have already mentioned as a distinct category: technology. But a range of other important features of the American economy are also systematically shaping the kind of society we live in. What kind of economy does the United States have today? A number of features are especially salient: our economy is a type of *capitalism*, dominated by *giant corporations*, with *weak unions* and relatively *weakly regulated markets* that exist in an increasingly *globalized system of economic interactions*. Let us look at each of these characteristics in turn.

Capitalism

Sometimes people simply say that the United States has a market economy or a free market economy, but it is more precise to say that the American economy is a *capitalist* economy. For an economy to be capitalist, three things need to be true:

1. *Markets for exchange.* Production is organized for the market rather than for immediate use by the producers. This means that things are produced to be sold rather than to be directly consumed by the people who produce them or to be made freely available to others. This is the difference between growing food on a farm rather than in a family garden.

[1] CIA, *The World Factbook*, https://www.cia.gov/library/publications/the-world-factbook/ (accessed July 1, 2014); and the World Bank, *World Development Indicators 2009*, http://data.worldbank.org/indicator (accessed July 1, 2014).

2. *Private ownership and control of investment.* The firms that organize production are privately owned rather than owned by a public body like the state, a city, or a community. The private owners of these firms can buy and sell those firms in markets. As owners, they also have the freedom to dispose of their assets as they see fit. Crucially, that includes investment—assets they allocate to future economic activity.

3. *Markets for labor.* The people who work in firms are hired from a labor market to work in firms as employees; they are not themselves the owners of the firm. Of course, capitalist economies may include some worker cooperatives—firms run and owned by workers—but these are special, interesting cases of noncapitalist firms operating within capitalism. If all firms were fully owned by their employees, then the economy would no longer be an instance of capitalism.

The world has not always had capitalist economies. Until about five hundred years ago, in fact, capitalism was rather rare and occupied at most small niches in economic life. Nor has the United States always been fully capitalist. At the time of the American Revolution at the end of the eighteenth century, the new country definitely had a market-oriented economy, but it was not pervasively capitalist. Perhaps 65 percent or so of the labor force outside of the South was self-employed as small farmers who owned their farms and means of production; and in the South, many laborers were slaves.[2] Only a small minority of people earned their living by selling their labor. A hundred years later, in the period after the Civil War, capitalism was certainly well under way and constituted the dynamic force in the American economy, particularly once the process of industrialization took off. Even so, in the 1870s, over 40 percent of the labor force was still self-employed. Though slavery was abolished in the South, many ex-slaves had become sharecroppers and in many ways still operated under severe forms of direct coercion rather than as free laborers. So even though capitalism was well established in much of the country and a class of industrial workers was developing, capitalism did not yet completely pervade all aspects of American economic life.

[2]In 1800, about 70 percent of the free labor force worked in agriculture. Calculations are from data in Stanley Lebergott, *Manpower in Economic Growth: The American Record Since 1800.* (New York: McGraw-Hill, 1964, pp. 102 and 510). Consistent self-employment data are available from only 1900, but we can assume that almost all the free labor force employed in agriculture was self-employed in 1800.

By the early decades of the twentieth century, the United States had become deeply capitalist: a clear majority of the labor force owned no property and worked for wages, although until the latter decades of the century most adult women were still not in the labor force and thus were not fully integrated into capitalist economic activity. Now, in the twenty-first century, only around 11 to 14 percent of the labor force is self-employed.[3] Most people—men and women—must seek employment, get hired, and work in a hierarchal organization to obtain their living.

To understand the nature of the economy in American society, however, it is not enough to say that the economy is capitalist. Capitalism comes in many varieties. Sometimes capitalism is characterized by many small firms competing in local and regional markets. Sometimes capitalism is strongly regulated by the state. Sometimes workers in capitalism have their basic economic welfare guaranteed by an affirmative state that provides them with a strong and secure safety net. Sometimes the employees in capitalism are very well organized into collectivities called unions, so that their relationship to employers depends not just on their power as an individual person but on the collective power of the union.

The United States represents a very specific type of capitalism. In the following pages, we discuss some salient characteristics of the variety of capitalism in contemporary American society.

Gigantic Corporations

United States capitalism is dominated by huge megacorporations. Here are some striking facts:

- The top ten U.S. firms in the *Fortune* magazine list of 500 largest firms had combined revenues in 2012 of over $2.2 trillion. If these ten firms were a country, they would constitute the eighth-largest economy in the world, ranked just after Brazil (Table 2.1). The total gross domestic

[3]It is difficult to get accurate estimates of real self-employment, for a variety of reasons: many people who are technically self-employed as "independent subcontractors" are really indistinguishable from ordinary employees; government statistics often treat "incorporated" and "unincorporated" self-employed people very differently, treating the former as "employees in their own corporations"; and a significant number of people engage in off-the-books self-employment that they do not report. The low estimate here comes from the Organisation for Economic Co-operation and Development (OECD), *OECD Factbook 2011–2012: Economic, Environmental and Social Statistics*, http://www.oecd-ilibrary.org/economics/oecd-factbook -2011-2012_factbook-2011-en (accessed July 1, 2014). Estimates from social science surveys are typically closer to 12–15 percent.

TABLE 2.1—Twelve largest economies in the world in 2012

Rank		Gross Domestic Product (billions of current U.S. dollars)
1	United States	15,685
2	China	8,227
3	Japan	5,694
4	Germany	3,401
5	France	2,609
6	United Kingdom	2,441
7	Brazil	2,396
8	**Top 10 U.S. corporations**	**2,225**
9	Russia	2,022
10	Italy	2,014
11	India	1,825
12	Canada	1,819

Sources: National GDP data from International Monetary Fund (IMF), "World Economic Outlook Database, October 2012," available at http://www.imf.org/external/pubs/ft/weo/2012/02/weodata /index.aspx (accessed January 26, 2014). Fortune 500 data from money.cnn.com, "Fortune 500 Revenues," available at http://money.cnn.com/magazines/fortune/fortune500/2012/full_list/(accessed January 26, 2014).

product (GDP) of India, whose population numbers over 1 billion people, is only about 80 percent of that figure.[4]

- In the year 2000, the largest 500 corporations in the United States employed 16.3 percent of all private sector employees, yet accounted for 57 percent of total private sector profits.[5]
- America's ten largest corporations in 2012—Exxon Mobil, Wal-Mart, Chevron, ConocoPhillips, GM, GE, Berkshire Hathaway, Fannie Mae, Ford, Hewlett-Packard—each *individually* had 2012 revenues greater than the combined income of the 134 million people living in the 48 poorest countries in the world. Exxon Mobil alone had revenues greater than the combined income of 345 million people in the world's 75 poorest countries.[6]

Small firms continue to exist and play an important role in the U.S. economy, and in some situations they are particularly important for jobs and

[4]It is important to note that the revenues of a corporation are not strictly comparable to the GDP of a country, so these comparisons should be taken as only suggestive of the magnitudes involved.

[5]Lawrence J. White, "Trends in Aggregate Concentration in the United States," *Journal of Economic Perspectives* 16, no. 4 (Autumn 2002): table 8, p. 156.

[6]Sources: National GDP data from IMF, "World Economic Outlook Database, April, 2013." Fortune 500 data from money.cnn.com, "Fortune 500 Revenues." Available at http://money .cnn.com/magazines/fortune/fortune500/2012/full_list/ (accessed January 26, 2014).

local development. In 2011 there were 5.7 million firms in the United States. Just over 5.1 million of these—90 percent of the total—had fewer than twenty employees. Thirty-four percent of total employment in the United States was in companies with less than 100 employees, accounting for 29 percent of the total annual payroll of U.S. firms.[7] So, small firms are a significant part of the American economy. Still, they often depend heavily on their connections to large corporations that control most of the profits and exercise vast economic power in the American economy.

Extremely Weak Labor Unions

Sometimes politicians and employers complain about the power of "big labor" and portray labor unions as interfering with the smooth, efficient functioning of the market. In fact, based on the rights of workers, the proportion of the labor force working in unions, and the rate of union coverage, the United States has among the weakest labor movements of any developed capitalist country. In the United States in 2012, only 11 percent of nonfarm-employed wage and salary workers were unionized. This figure compares to 67.5 percent in Sweden and 20 to 40 percent in many European countries. Even more important, the United States has few "extension" laws that apply the results of bargaining between unions and employers to other workers. As a result, rates of union coverage here are just a few percentage points above our rates of union membership. In most developed countries, even those without high levels of union membership, union coverage extends to most wage and salary workers.

What exactly is a labor union? It is an association that people form so they can bargain more effectively with employers and in other ways collectively pursue their interests. Individually, an employee is usually pretty weak when bargaining with an employer. Any given worker is generally more in need of a job than the employer is in need of that particular employee. But if people join together and act collectively, they may be able to forge a better deal with employers. Although a firm may not especially need any given worker, it certainly depends upon all of its workers taken together.

Because U.S. unions are so weak, labor markets in the United States are generally much less regulated than in most developed countries and involve much more intense competition among individuals. One result of this situation is

---

[7]United States Census Bureau, "Statistics of U.S. Businesses (SUSB)," www.census.gov /econ/susb/ (accessed January 22, 2014).

that American workers have fewer rights than do those in most other developed countries. Here are just two examples:

- *Parental leaves.* In Germany, mothers get 14 weeks of maternity leave at 100 percent of their wages. In France, mothers get 16 weeks for the first two children and 24 weeks for subsequent children at 100 percent of wages, up to a maximum of about $140/day. In Sweden, mothers and fathers can share up to 15 months of paid parental leaves, paid at 80 percent of earnings for the first 52 weeks and a lower flat rate for the remaining 13 weeks, up to a maximum (in 2012) of about $71,000.[8]
- *Right to strike.* The United States is the only developed capitalist democracy in which an employer has the legal right to hire permanent replacements in a legal strike. In other countries, employers can hire temporary replacements, but striking workers have a right to get their jobs back after a strike even if they lose the strike itself.

Thus, in comparison to most other countries, U.S. labor markets operate in a quite competitive environment. American capitalists have relatively unrestricted, unilateral rights to hire and fire and are met with generally weak constraints from the organized power of workers.

Weak Public Regulation of the Economy

Americans often complain about "big government," overregulation, and high taxation. But in fact the U.S. economy is in many respects much less heavily regulated by the government than are the economies in nearly all other developed capitalist countries. This is especially the case for labor markets: employers are pretty free to hire and fire employees at will (except for some important restrictions on forms of discrimination); the minimum wage is extremely low and provides almost no real protection for workers; and government regulation of training and skills is minimal. The government also provides its citizens with many fewer direct services. Most notably, even after the passage of the Affordable Care Act in 2010, the United

---

[8]The 2014 exchange rates are used to calculate U.S. dollar equivalents. These descriptions of leave policies are from Peter Moss, "International Review of Leave Policies and Related Research 2013" (International Network on Leave Policies and Research; available at http://www.leavenetwork.org/lp_and_r_reports/, accessed July 1, 2014). This description of leave policies omits a variety of complex details in each country. For full descriptions, see the report. For a general discussion of parental leave policies in developed countries, see Janet C. Gornick and Marcia K. Meyers, *Families That Work: Policies for Reconciling Parenthood and Employment* (New York: Russell Sage Foundation, 2003), pp. 24–25.

States is the only developed capitalist country in the world in which the government does not fully guarantee universal health services or insurance for all of its citizens.

Due to the reduced role of government in the domestic economy, the government is smaller in the United States than in most other comparable countries. Consider the following facts about the U.S. state:

- *Public employment.* In the United States at the beginning of the twenty-first century, public employment is around 15 percent of the labor force. This is lower than in many developed countries. For example, in Norway, Denmark, and Sweden 25 to 30 percent of the labor force is publicly employed; in France the figure is 22 percent, and in Canada and Britain around 18 percent (Figure 2.2). Nearly all of this public employment in the United States is at the state and local levels of government (these two together accounted for about 85 percent of all

FIGURE 2.2—Government employment as a percentage of the labor force, selected countries, 2011

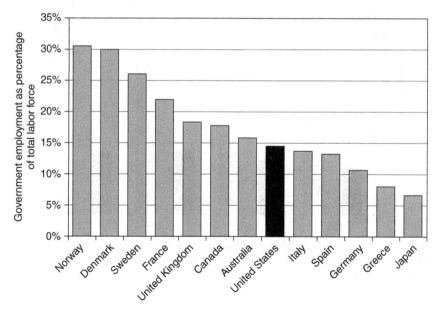

Note: Original data from: International Labour Organization (ILO) LABORSTA (database); OECD Labour Force Statistics (database). Data for Australia refer to the public sector (general government and public corporations). Data for Austria, Czech Republic, Italy, the Netherlands, and New Zealand are expressed in full-time equivalents (FTEs). Germany, Norway, Sweden, the United Kingdom: 2010 instead of 2011. Japan: 2009 instead of 2011. Greece: 2008 instead of 2011. France: 2006 instead of 2011.

Source: OECD, *Government at a Glance 2013.* Chapter 5. Public Sector Employment and Pay. Version 2—Last updated Dec. 16, 2013. http://www.oecd-ilibrary.org/governance/government-at-a-glance-2013 _gov_glance-2013-en (accessed July 1, 2014).

government employees in 2011). Furthermore, contrary to what many people think, most government growth has been at the local and state levels: from 1960 to 2011, federal civilian employment grew about 17 percent while state and local government employment increased by over 150 percent (Figure 2.3).

- *Civilian spending.* In 2012, U.S. nonmilitary spending came to about 34.5 percent of GDP. This level is much lower than Germany's (43.3 percent) or Sweden's (50.9 percent), is slightly less than Japan's (37.9 percent), and is among the lowest levels of public spending among the economically developed countries.[9]

FIGURE 2.3—Employment in federal, state, and local governments, 1950–2011

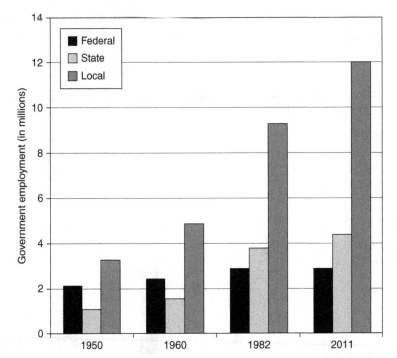

Sources: Material for 1950–2007 from http://www.census.gov/govs/apes/historical_data_2007.html. Material for 2011 from Census Public Employment and Payroll data, U.S. Census Bureau. http://www.census.gov//govs/apes/. (Both sources accessed July 1, 2014.)

[9]These figures are obtained by subtracting military spending as percentage of GDP in 2012, from total government spending as percentage of GDP for the same year. Sources: General government total expenditure as percentage of GDP from IMF (2014), "World Economic Outlook Database, April 2014," http://www.imf.org/external/pubs/ft/weo/2014/01/weodata/index.aspx (accessed May 9, 2014). Military spending as percentage of GDP from World Bank (2014), "World Development Indicators. Countries and Economies," http://data.worldbank.org/country (accessed May 9, 2014).

- *Taxation.* Taxation is also incredibly low in the United States as compared to most other wealthy countries. In 2013 the tax burden in the United
States was just over 25 percent of GDP, compared to around 36 percent in
the United Kingdom, 37 percent in Germany, 44 percent in Sweden, and
49 percent in Denmark. The United States is not a highly taxed economy.[10]

None of these facts imply that U.S. capitalism really approximates the ideal
of the free market in which the state plays almost no role. There are still
many regulations of the economy—health and safety, pollution, product
labeling, and employment discrimination, to name only a few. The point in
regard to our question, "What kind of society is this?" is that compared to
most other comparably developed capitalist societies, the American economy is situated toward the weakly regulated end of the spectrum.

Globalization

Although it is true that the United States *has* a capitalist economy, it is also
increasingly *a part of* a global capitalist economy. This integration into the
world economy can be seen from the vantage points of trade, production,
and ownership.

- *Trade.* From World War I until the late 1960s, imports plus exports
equaled about 10 percent of the total U.S. gross national product
(GNP). The United States was a very self-contained economy, producing mostly for itself and mainly consuming things that it produced. By
the end of the 1970s, total imports and exports had increased to 20 percent of the GNP; and at the beginning of the twenty-first century, the
figure was more than 25 percent. This is a major change in trade patterns. American firms are now involved in intense competition with
firms in other countries.
- *Production.* The production of almost everything involves materials
and components that are manufactured in companies from all over the
world. Production takes place, in a sense, in a global factory—the raw
materials come from different places, the parts made from those raw
materials come from other places, and all these components are assembled in still other places. Many American-made cars contain more foreign material than U.S. material. For a pair of jeans, the cloth may be made

[10]Data are from the Heritage Foundation, "2014 Index of Economic Freedom," http://www
.heritage.org/index/explore?view=by-variables (accessed July 1, 2014).

in one country, the dye in another, and the zipper in a third. Then the whole thing may be assembled in a fourth country and shipped to a fifth.

- *Ownership.* Many U.S. corporations have operations in East Asia; are these enterprises part of American society? What about Toyota factories in the United States? Which country's economy are they part of—the United States or Japan? If we subtracted those exports produced by U.S.-owned companies in Taiwan from the total exports to the United States from a country like Taiwan, the trade deficit would be drastically reduced or perhaps even eliminated. Where does the American economy end and the Taiwanese economy begin?

This increase in the intensity of global interconnectedness of economic activities is significant. Some people argue that increasing globalization even calls into question the idea that the United States is a well-bounded society. In fact, U.S. *citizenship* and *political control* are well bounded; but American *society* is not. This is one of the most important facts of social change, beginning especially in the last quarter of the twentieth century. And it profoundly affects everyone's life: the world is increasingly integrated and economically interdependent. To speak of a society as an isolated entity is increasingly problematic.

ECONOMIC INEQUALITY IN A WEALTHY ECONOMY

All capitalist societies have significant levels of economic inequality—some people are much richer than others, either because they have lots of wealth or because they have high earnings in the labor market. But capitalist societies differ in how much inequality is generated by the market. This is a complex problem; as we will see later in this book, many things come into play in producing the levels of inequality in different countries. But the bottom line is that the relatively unregulated labor markets in the United States, combined with weak labor unions and a very limited governmental role in providing its citizens with economic support, work together to generate extreme inequality. Here are some basic facts:

- The United States has the highest poverty rates and highest levels of economic inequality of any developed country, regardless of how these rates are measured.
- At the end of the first decade of the twenty-first century, around 23 percent of children were living in poor households in the United States. In most other rich countries, the figure is 5 to 15 percent (Figure 2.4).

FIGURE 2.4—Percentage of children living in poverty in 26 countries, 2009

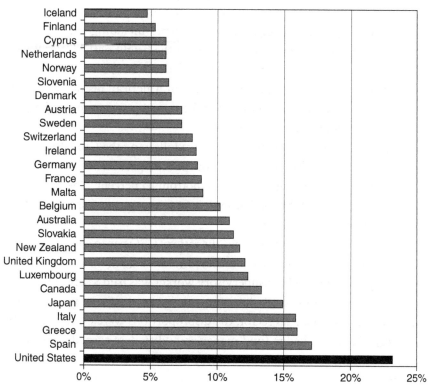

Note: The child poverty rate is the share of children living in households with income below half of household-size-adjusted median disposable income (i.e., household income after taxes and transfers).

Source: "Child poverty rate in selected developed countries, 2009," *State of Working America* (2012), Figure 7x. http://stateofworkingamerica.org/chart/swa-poverty-figure-7x-child-poverty-rates/ (accessed July 1, 2014).

- In 2010, the richest 1 percent of American households owned about 35 percent of all stocks (excluding pensions); the bottom 80 percent owned only about 8 percent.[11] The wealthiest 1 percent of households had 114 times more wealth than did the U.S. median household.[12]

- In the thirty years between 1979 and 2010, the richest 5 percent of U.S. families had their average annual income increase by $125,810— from $197,373 to $323,183 (in 2011 dollars); the poorest 20 percent had

[11]Economic Policy Institute. 2012. "Wealth groups' shares of assets, by asset type, 2010." *The State of Working America*, 12th ed. (Washington, DC: Economic Policy Institute). Available at http://www.stateofworkingamerica.org/chart/swa-wealth-table-6-6-wealth-groups-shares/ (accessed March 17, 2014).

[12]Economic Policy Institute. 2012. "Average household assets, by wealth group and asset type, 1962–2010." *The State of Working America*, 12th ed. (Washington, DC: Economic Policy Institute). Available at http://stateofworkingamerica.org/chart/swa-wealth-table-6-7-average-household-assets/ (accessed March 17, 2014).

their average income decrease by $1,854 from $17,318 to $15,464.[13] By 2007, just before the Great Recession, the top 1 percent of households received 23.5 percent of all pretax income (including capital gains), compared to only 8.9 percent in 1976. At the height of the Great Recession in 2009 this figure had dropped a little, to 18.1 percent, but by 2012 it had rebounded to 22.5. The last time in American history when this much income was concentrated at the very top was in 1928, when the top 1 percent received 23.9 percent.[14]

- In the economic recovery of 2009–2012 following the Great Recession, real income grew by 31.4 percent for the top 1 percent of families while it grew by only 0.4 percent for the bottom 99 percent. The result was that 95 percent of the total growth in real income was captured by the top 1 percent of wage earners.[15]

- In the largest U.S. corporations, the ratio of CEO pay to average worker pay rose from just under 50:1 in 1983 to 331:1 in 2013. In that year the average production and nonsupervisory worker was paid $35,239, while the CEOs in the S&P 500 index companies earned on average $11.7 million.[16] In the financial sector, the disproportions were even greater. In 2013, the top 25 hedge fund managers and traders earned on average $972 million, or more than 27,000 times as much as the average worker.[17]

---

[13]Economic Policy Institute. 2012. "Average family income, by income group, 1947–2010 (2011 dollars)," *The State of Working America*, 12th ed. (Washington, DC: Economic Policy Institute). Available at http://stateofworkingamerica.org/chart/swa-income-table-2-1-average-family-income/ (accessed March 17, 2014).

[14]Facundo Alvarado, Tony Atkinson, Thomas Piketty, and Emmanuel Saez, *The World Top Incomes Database*, http://topincomes.g-mond.parisschoolofeconomics.eu/ (accessed March 17, 2014). The corresponding figures of total share of all income earned by the top 1 percent of families excluding income from capital gains was 7.9 percent in 1976 and 9.3 percent in 2012, just below the 1928 figure of 19.6 percent.

[15]Emmanuel Saez, "Striking It Richer: The Evolution of Top Incomes in the United States (updated with 2012 preliminary estimates)," http://elsa.berkeley.edu/~saez/saez-UStopincomes-2012.pdf (accessed March 17, 2014).

[16]These data are from http://www.aflcio.org/Corporate-Watch/Paywatch-2014 (accessed July 1, 2014). The CEO pay data are for the 350 corporations in the S&P 500 index for which data are available.

[17]Nathan Vardi, "The 25 Highest-Earning Hedge Fund Managers and Traders," posted on http://www.forbes.com/sites/nathanvardi/2014/02/26/the-highest-earning-hedge-fund-managers-and-traders/ (accessed July 1, 2014).

The United States may have high levels of poverty and inequality, but by both comparative and historical standards, this is also one of the richest countries in the history of the world. The most obvious statistic for most people—one that puts the United States into a family of perhaps 15 to 20 countries in the world—is the per capita income in the United States. When adjusted for the cost of living, U.S. per capita income is at or near the highest in the world—depending on precisely how it is measured. This does not necessarily mean that the average American's quality of life is the highest in the world, or even that his or her economic well-being is the highest. Economic well-being depends not just on income but on the amount of leisure time, economic security, and other characteristics of a person's economic situation. But our average income level does mean that in terms of sheer wealth, the United States as a whole is fantastically rich.

This, then, is a crucial defining characteristic of the United States at the beginning of the twenty-first century: poverty in the midst of plenty, and tremendous inequalities in conditions of life and opportunities in the context of an extraordinarily rich society.

POLITICAL INSTITUTIONS: LIBERAL DEMOCRACY

The United States is characterized by political institutions that are generally called liberal democratic. We elect the political officials in more or less competitive elections; we have relatively secure civil liberties, including things like freedom of association, freedom of speech, and freedom of religion; and we live under the rule of law, which calls for transparency on rules of conduct and constraints on the arbitrary exercise of power. This kind of state is historically new, and it is still far from universal. It can be contrasted both with nondemocratic sorts of states and with those that extend democratic governance outside formal politics, typically through higher levels of organized citizen participation.

Among the family of liberal democracies, American democracy has a number of distinctive features. Here are some of the more important.

Winner-Take-All, Single-Member-District Elections

Electoral systems can be organized in many different ways. In some countries, for example, representatives are elected on a principle called proportional representation. In a proportional representation system, if a party wins 40 percent of the vote in an election, it gets roughly 40 percent of the seats in the representative body. In the U.S. system as well as in a few other countries, each representative is elected from a district in which only one candidate wins. This means that a party could conceivably get 49 percent of the vote in every district and end up with no seats at all in the U.S. Congress. Among other consequences of this system, it is extremely difficult to form minor parties in the United States—so difficult that we typically refer to them as third parties, in contrast to the dominant Democratic and Republican major parties.

Federalism

The United States is one of the world's federal systems, meaning that national power is explicitly shared with subnational units of government, which here we call states. Federal systems are typically contrasted with unitary states, in which the national government holds all public power.

Federalism matters for all sorts of things. It brings considerable complexity to the nature of political jurisdictions over different kinds of problems of public policy. It affords historical moments in which the states can be laboratories for new experiments in public policies. And it means that the decentralization and fragmentation of the political system can sometimes obstruct the process of forging constructive solutions to national problems.

Divided Powers and a Presidential System

The United States has what is called a divided government—one that assigns clear and separate constitutional bases for power to its legislative, executive, and judicial branches. It is also a presidential, not a parliamentary system. In most other countries, the head of state and head of government are separated. In the United States they are the same. And in the United States, the head of government is chosen by citizen election rather than, as in parliamentary systems, by the dominant party or party coalition in the legislature.

Interest Groups and Grassroots Activism

Although political power in American democracy is organized through elected government, interest groups and grassroots activism also play a particularly important role in political life. Both come in all shapes and sizes, reflecting shifting popular interests and the distribution of resources needed for any political action. The United States has historically had a quite vibrant, bottom-up tradition of local mobilization around social and political issues. It also has a particularly strong tradition of voluntary associations engaged in all sorts of civic activities, from the Rotary Club to the NAACP to the PTA.

Money in Politics

Liberal democracies always face a series of dilemmas about the role of private money in political competition. On the one hand, the principle of political equality of citizens implies that rich people, by virtue of being rich, should have no more influence in democratic politics than anyone else. On the other hand, the values of individual autonomy and free speech imply that people should be allowed to spend their money however they like, and there should be no restrictions on people's ability to express themselves. One interpretation of this idea is that people should be allowed to spend as much money as they like in support of political candidates, because this spending could be viewed as a form of speech. The United States has adopted a fairly extreme version of this principle, and thus—despite various efforts at reform—money plays a huge role in American politics. Some people argue that we have moved from one person, one vote to one dollar, one vote.

The Media and Politics

The issue of money and politics also comes into play regarding the problem of the mass media and access to political information. Although political censorship is occasionally an issue in American politics, the major problem of information for democratic vitality centers on corporate control of the mass media. Ownership of broadcast media is incredibly concentrated in a few giant corporations, newspapers in most parts of the company are run like ordinary commercial enterprises, and commercial interests generally dominate the dissemination of news and public debate.

Taken together—as we will see in the extended discussions of democracy in Part III of the book—these characteristics present a mixed picture of democratic institutions in American life. On the one hand, democratic values remain important, basic civil liberties are largely protected, regular contested elections are held, and grassroots activism is an important expression of democratic impulses. On the other hand, American political institutions give an inordinate role to money and wealth in political life, and electoral rules are designed to favor powerful established parties. Because it is affected by all these things, the basic work of any democratic government—debating issues of public concern, deciding how best to address those issues, executing whatever is decided, and doing all this in a way that reflects the interests of citizens—is also done in the United States through an unusually divided structure of formal power. John Quincy Adams once described it as "the most complicated government on the face of the earth," so making any decision, and sticking to it, is more difficult.

MILITARISM AND GLOBAL DOMINATION

In many ways, the United States has become a heavily militarized society. Regardless of what you think about the purposes for which this military might is used—whether you think it is ultimately a force for peace in the world or is among the main sources of violent destabilization and conflict—there is no doubt that one of the central characteristics of American society that distinguishes it from others is its degree of militarization. The United States spends more than ten times as much on the military as does any other country in the world. In 2003—even before the Iraq War—the United States spent 13 times more than China and over 20 times more than Russia on the military. In the 2015 fiscal year budget, the total of all military spending by the United States—including the Department of Defense budget, the military portions of other departments, and the various other supplements estimated for the Iraq/Afghanistan spending that was not included in the president's budget request—came to $786 billion. If to these we add the funding of the Department of Veterans Affairs and interest on the national debt generated by past military spending, the total increases to just over $1.3 trillion, or 45 percent of the total U.S. federal government budget.[18] Even if we exclude these expenses linked to past military activity, U.S. military spending is still more than the combined total for the next fifteen countries

[18]War Resisters League. "WRL PIE CHART FLYERS—Where Your Income Tax Money Really Goes." Available at https://www.warresisters.org/federalpiechart (accessed May 30, 2014).

on the list of highest military spenders in the world.[19] The United States has more soldiers around the world outside of its borders than do all other countries combined, and U.S. soldiers have fought in more countries than any other military in the last half century. In the last fifty years, the United States has intervened militarily in scores of conflicts and has been directly involved in trying to overthrow militarily at least a dozen governments. The U.S. economy is deeply integrated into the production of military goods, both for its own use and for export. This means that the livelihood of significant segments of the civilian population depends on the continuing strength of the U.S. military.

GENDER RELATIONS: ERODING MALE DOMINATION

American society today is in a period of dramatic transformation of gender relations. Many features of traditional forms of male domination are eroding: Until the 1920s, women could not vote in the United States. Until the 1930s, married women could not have a passport in their own name. Female adult labor force participation was only 18 percent in 1900 and 33 percent in 1950, but had grown to 50 percent in 1980 and just under 58 percent in 2012. The presence of women has increased dramatically in a wide range of previously male-dominated occupations: between 1960 and 2011, the percentage of police officers who were women increased from under 4 percent to over 17 percent; the percentage who were lawyers increased from 4 percent to 36 percent; and the percentage who were doctors increased from under 17 percent to about 36 percent.[20]

Male dominance is being undercut in various ways but has by no means collapsed. Some occupations remain highly sex segregated: over 95 percent of secretaries, dental assistants, and early education teachers are still women, but only 2.1 percent of carpenters and 1.3 percent of auto mechanics are women. Women have gained more political influence, yet they are greatly underrepresented in all levels of elected office—especially national

---

[19]Laicie Heeley, "U.S. Defense Spending vs. Global Defense Spending" (April 24, 2013), The Center for Arms Control and Non-Proliferation. Available at http://armscontrolcenter.org /issues/securityspending/articles/2012_topline_global_defense_spending/ (accessed April 9, 2014).

[20]For details, see Figure 16.3 in Chapter 16.

office. Although in 2013 nearly 90 percent of the largest 500 corporations had at least one woman on their board of directors, women still occupied only 17 percent of the actual seats.[21] And, perhaps most strikingly, even though women have made significant gains in gender equality in many public settings, within the private domain of the family they continue to do the vast majority of housework, child care, and other caregiving labor.

SOCIAL CLEAVAGE: RACIAL DIVISION

Racial inequality and racial cleavage remain a deep and serious reality of American life. For over three and a half centuries, both inequality and domination have been structured in significant ways around race in North America. The United States was founded as a liberal democratic country proclaiming equal rights for all, and yet it found a way to accommodate one of the most brutal forms of inequality of basic rights: slavery. The legacy of slavery has marked American history to the present, especially in the ways it has generated such a sharp and troubling form of racial inequality. Racism has also been deeply connected to the relationship between European immigrants to the United States (and the British colonies before the American Revolution) and Native Americans. The development and expansion of the United States depended on the displacement and destruction of Native American peoples.

This does not mean there has been no progress on issues of race and racism in the United States. The destruction of the official legal machinery of racial inequality in the 1950s and 1960s was a huge change; and since those momentous days of the civil rights struggles, educational and occupational opportunity has opened up for many African Americans. There is now a prosperous and well-educated African American middle class, and this group makes a real difference. Cultural representations of African Americans on television and film have also become less racist than in the past, often showing African Americans in a positive way. And, of course, the election of Barack Obama in 2008 constituted a profound break with racial patterns of the past. Nevertheless, racism, racial stereotyping, and potent racial discrimination remain significant and pervasive facts of contemporary American society.

[21]Catalyst, "2013 Catalyst Census: Fortune 500 Women Board of Directors," http://www .catalyst.org/knowledge/2013-catalyst-census-fortune-500-women-board-directors (accessed February 19, 2014).

IMMIGRATION

It is a cliché to say that the United States is a nation of immigrants—old immigrants, new immigrants, legal immigrants, illegal immigrants. Aside from Native Americans, everyone in the United States has ancestors who moved here—or were brought here—sometime in the last three hundred or so years. Before the twentieth century, for whites at least, there was no such thing as an illegal immigrant; more or less anyone could just come. Beginning in the 1920s, however, people needed permission to move to the United States. From the 1920s until the 1960s the rules were very restrictive, excluding almost everyone other than Europeans. Beginning in the 1960s, the rules were quite significantly liberalized. And starting in the 1980s and accelerating in the 1990s, America has seen an explosion of legal as well as illegal immigration. Today we are approaching the levels of foreign born living in the United States that existed at the beginning of the twentieth century—just over 12 percent today, compared to about 15 percent in 1910.

CULTURE

It is always difficult to make simple characterizations of something as complex as culture, particularly because all national cultures are heterogeneous and contradictory. Even so, in a somewhat stylized way, the following are some salient features of what can be broadly termed American culture.

- *Pluralism and tolerance.* The United States is characterized by a deeply diverse array of what might be called subcultures: Amish communities; urban cosmopolitans; Southern traditionalists; educated highbrows and NASCAR fans; lovers of country music, hip-hop, easy listening, and opera; and so on. By and large, this pluralism exists in a broader culture of tolerance. Most people accept this diversity as a good thing, or at least have learned to live with it. Despite the recent "culture wars" in the United States, this country surely rates as one of the most tolerant societies in the world.
- *Individualism.* The United States is generally thought to be a fairly individualistic society, one in which individual autonomy and "freedom" are considered more important than collective welfare, and in which individuals are pretty much held responsible for their own fate. It is easy, however, to exaggerate this cultural element, because many

Americans also deeply value *community* and have a strong sense of shared fate with others. Still, on the spectrum of contemporary societies it is probably fair to say that American culture is marked by higher levels of individualism than most other places.

- *Religiosity.* By every measure, Americans are among the most religious people in the contemporary world, at least if we define this term by formal beliefs and church attendance. A very large proportion of Americans profess a belief in God—upward of 90 percent, depending on precisely how the question is asked. This figure is much higher than that in any other comparably developed country. And a smaller percentage of the U.S. population believes in the scientific validity of biological evolution than do the populations in any other economically developed country: in the 2004 General Social Survey (a regular, large attitude survey of American adults), 12.4 percent of respondents agreed that human beings evolved without any divine guidance; 42 percent said that humans evolved, but with guidance from God; and another 42 percent rejected biological evolution altogether. In another question on the same survey, 54 percent said it was either definitely not true or probably not true that humans evolved from earlier species of animals. Church attendance is also higher in the United States than it is in any European country.

- *Commercialism and consumerism.* A final element of American culture is the importance of commercial forms of culture, especially consumerism, in American life. Americans save less and buy more things on credit than do people in other comparable countries. Shopping is a major recreational activity. Success in the market is a source of high status, and "keeping up with the Joneses" is a major motivation for working hard.

VIOLENCE AND REPRESSIVE SOCIAL CONTROL

Of the various attributes of American society we have proposed that are answers to the question, "What kind of society is this?" perhaps the most controversial is the idea that the United States is a violent and repressive society. The facts, however, are striking:

- *Gun murders.* In the United States in 2011, there were 31 firearm murders a day. In Great Britain the rate was 38 gun murders per year in 2010. In

Canada there were 173 gun murders in 2009, and Japan had a total of 11 in 2008.

- *Homicide.* This is the second leading cause of death among those aged 15 to 24 and the leading cause of death for black males aged 15 to 34.
- *Prisons.* In the United States in 2011, there were about 716 prisoners per 100,000 people. That is the highest in the world, ahead of Russia (481 per 100,000). The U.S. rate is four to seven times higher than in most other industrialized countries. In 2009, a shocking 24 percent of the prisoners *in the world* were in U.S. prisons, even though the United States had only 5 percent of the world's population.
- *Death penalty.* The United States is the only economically developed liberal democracy besides Japan and South Korea to have the death penalty; all other countries have abolished it. The United States takes a spot behind China, Iran, Iraq, and Saudi Arabia for the most executions in the world in 2013, sitting ahead of Yemen and the Sudan.
- *Police presence.* In 2012, the United States had almost 1.7 million police and security guards, representing over 1 percent of the labor force.

Of course, we could say many other things about American society. Other attributes could be added to classify the United States within the catalogue of contemporary societies: The United States is geographically very large (the third largest after Russia and China) and very populous (the third after China and India); Americans are highly mobile, and they move to new cities and regions to look for jobs at higher rates than do citizens in most other economically developed countries; the United States has one of the most developed university systems in the world, and by most measures the highest-quality graduate education programs anywhere; and so on. These and other things are important, but the attributes we have mentioned are especially salient for studying American society in light of its core values— freedom, prosperity, efficiency, fairness, and democracy.

Part I

CAPITALISM

In this part of the book, we will explore the nature of the American economy. This step is essential in any systematic examination of contemporary American society, both because the economy has such a big impact on people's lives and because it plays a profound role in shaping many noneconomic aspects of social life. We will enter a domain of inquiry that is usually dominated by the concepts and theories of economics, not sociology. The economy, however, is too important to leave to the economists. The discipline of economics has much to teach us—and we will draw on certain key ideas of economics in these chapters—but it also has some firmly attached blinders, so we also need a sociological analysis of the economy.

Our primary goal in these chapters is to understand how the capitalist economy in the United States really works and how well it contributes to the realization of three key values closely associated with economic institutions—efficiency, prosperity, and freedom. We will begin in Chapter 3 by explaining precisely what a capitalist market economy is and then discuss the central moral and empirical arguments in favor of capitalist markets. In Chapter 4 we will then criticize these defenses of capitalist market economies and indicate ways in which this way of organizing economic life, in the absence of effective forms of market regulation, hampers freedom, prosperity, and efficiency. Chapters 5 through 9 will then examine specific economic problems in American society—the environment, transportation, consumerism, health care, and finance—and show how the overreliance on capitalist markets in the American economy produces inefficient outcomes. Chapter 10 concludes this part by outlining a range of institutional innovations that might contribute to resolving these problems.

3

THE CAPITALIST MARKET:
HOW IT IS SUPPOSED TO WORK

The American economy is a special case of capitalism. To understand how the American economy works, we need to spend some time talking more generally about the nature of capitalism as an economic system. This in turn means we have to discuss some fairly abstract ideas and develop a number of theoretical tools, many of them from economics. These will be the main tasks of this chapter and the next.

We begin by defining capitalism as an economic system and then examining the central arguments in favor of capitalism by its defenders. Some of these arguments are philosophical, focusing especially on the relationship between capitalism and freedom. Other arguments revolve around theoretical and empirical claims about the pragmatic effects of capitalism for human well-being. These arguments mainly concern the values of efficiency and prosperity. Taken as a whole, this discussion will give us a picture of how capitalism is *supposed* to work.

WHAT IS A CAPITALIST FREE MARKET ECONOMY?

Economic life can be organized in many strikingly different ways. This is a crucial idea: history provides an enormous variety of ways of organizing economic activity—and, undoubtedly, there are many other possibilities that have not yet happened but eventually will. The first step in more precisely understanding capitalism as a specific way of organizing an economy is to get some appreciation of this broader variation.

Here are a few examples of noncapitalist economic structures:

- *Feudalism.* In feudal economies, the key economic resource is land. Different classes of people have different kinds of rights and relationships to the land. Peasants are "tied" to the land; they do not have the right to simply leave. They have the right to farm the land, but to do so they must give a certain proportion of their production to feudal lords. Sometimes this form of economy involves feudal peasants working part of the time on land directly controlled by lords and part of the time on land they control; in other situations, a certain proportion of the peasants' product is taken in the form of a rent. Unlike in market economies, farmers in feudal economies are not free to make their own choices about what to do.

- *Slavery.* In slavery, some people are the private property of other people. In some forms of slavery, this ownership is absolute; people are owned in the same sense that a farm animal can be owned. In other forms of slavery, slaves can engage in limited forms of autonomous economic activity, which give them the potential to eventually purchase their freedom. This structure is different from feudalism, in which peasants have specific kinds of rights to the land under the constraints of their obligations to lords, and feudal lords cannot buy and sell their peasants.

- *Subsistence economies.* In a subsistence economy, the means of production are owned in common by all producers and most production is simply for the direct consumption of the producers themselves. Little or no surplus is produced.

- *Simple market economy.* In a simple market economy, most producers own their own means of production and produce for their own consumption as well as for the market. There is no real labor market because people work for themselves and not for others, except perhaps as a transient status.

- *State bureaucratic socialism.* In state bureaucratic socialism, such as in the Soviet Union in most of the twentieth century, the state owns all important means of production. State officials of various sorts make the basic decisions about investment, production, technology, and so on. The economy is run through some kind of centralized planning process.

- *Other possibilities?* Many other ways of organizing the economy may be possible, but they have not been tried on a large scale. Some people have argued for the possibility of what is sometimes called market socialism. This kind of economy might be one in which firms are owned by their employees, not by capitalists, but production is still oriented toward the market. Other people have argued for a state-owned economy, but one with a highly decentralized and democratic structure, so that planning is less the business of central planners and more of citizen participants in various kinds of planning processes. Though neither of these economies may be realistic, we are quite sure that possibilities exist beyond those we have observed in history so far.

Capitalism, then, is one of the many historically variable ways that economic systems can be organized. As discussed in Chapter 2, capitalism is defined by three principal conditions: production is organized for the market; the means of production are privately owned and investment is privately controlled; and the people who use those means of production to produce goods and services—that is, the workers—are hired on a labor market to work in firms as employees. When defined in this way, capitalism is *not* identical to the idea of a market economy. To be sure, capitalism is organized through markets; but not all market economies are capitalist. In the examples we described, a simple market economy has markets and private ownership, but the producers are self-employed owners rather than employees. State-owned rather than privately owned firms can produce for a market, and that system would not be capitalism either. Slave plantations in the United States before the Civil War produced cotton for the market, but slavery itself was not a form of capitalism. Unlike all these other market economies, capitalism is that form of market economy in which production and investment are privately controlled, and the work of production is performed by employees who are hired from free labor markets.

The U.S. economy is strongly dominated by capitalism—more so than most other countries in the world. But it would be a big mistake to say that this country has a purely capitalist economy. Many aspects of production and distribution in the United States are organized in decidedly noncapitalist ways: educational services are provided by public schools; the Department of Veterans Affairs produces health-care services for a part of the population; many cities have publicly produced mass transit; churches, civic associations, and other nonprofit organizations provide a wide range of services within communities; significant aspects of the information produced and distributed through the Internet are carried out using what are called "open source" processes based on voluntary activity and nonmarket coordination; and a great deal of caregiving and meal preparation takes place within households for direct consumption. All of these are instances of noncapitalist economic activity.

A nice illustration of the difference between capitalist and noncapitalist ways of organizing economic activity is the contrast between two ways that people get access to books: bookstores and libraries. The United States turns out to have one of the best-developed public library systems in the world.

Ironically, perhaps, this system was largely founded through the philanthropy of one of the wealthiest and most powerful capitalists of the late nineteenth century—Andrew Carnegie. What are the key differences between bookstores and libraries? When you enter a bookstore in search of a book, you go to the part of the store where the book is shelved, take it off the shelf, look at its price, and then decide whether it is worth it to you to spend that amount of money to have the book. Your access to the book is governed by money: your willingness (and ability) to pay for it. In a library, you go to the shelf and see if the book is there. If it is, you take it and check it out. If it is not, you put your name on a waiting list and are notified when the book is available. Access to the book is rationed by time: your willingness to wait for it. The librarian then notes how long the waiting list is for that book and—depending on the resources of the library, the level of community support for its activities, and its policies concerning waiting lists—decides whether to order more copies of the book.

The underlying principles of a library and a bookstore are thus quite different. The basic principle of access to books in the library is "to each according to need" or interest, while the principle in the bookstore is "to each according to ability to pay." These two mechanisms have very different consequences in the world. Libraries are clearly more egalitarian in the sense that they embody an ideal of equal opportunity for all. No one is at a disadvantage because of personal resources. If bookstores were the only way of getting books, then poor people would have much less access to books. One can easily imagine libraries being used for all sorts of things besides books—movies, recordings, artwork, tools, video cameras, and so on. And indeed, some public libraries in the United States do provide some of these items. Imagine how the American economy would be different if libraries were ever to become a general, pervasive model for access to such a wide range of things.

So, the United States is definitely not a purely capitalist economy. Nevertheless, among developed capitalist countries in the world today, it is at the end of the spectrum where capitalism is strongest. And most Americans think this is a good thing. Most Americans are suspicious of government regulation, let alone public ownership; and many—perhaps most—believe that relatively unfettered markets and private enterprise are the best way of organizing economic activity.

To help us understand how the American economy works and what its problems are, it will help to lay out the central lines of defense of a free market capitalist economy and examine the basic argument underlying the skepticism about the role of government in regulating economic life. This is the task of the rest of this chapter.

ARGUMENTS FOR CAPITALISM

Defenders of free market capitalism generally make two kinds of arguments. The first is a moral argument: If you truly value individual freedom, capitalism is the most freedom-enhancing way to organize economic life. All other ways of running an economy involve more coercion of the lives of individuals in ways that violate their liberty or that put them at risk of such coercion in the future. The second is a pragmatic argument: The free market and unfettered private ownership is the most efficient way of organizing the economy. It delivers the goods. Let us look briefly at the first of these arguments and then in more detail at the second, because in the end it is the main defense of capitalist institutions.

The Moral Argument for Capitalism

The moral defense of capitalism is usually associated with the political philosophy of *libertarianism*. The basic idea is quite simple: individual freedom is the paramount social value, where freedom is mainly understood as negative freedom—the freedom from coercion by other persons or organizations. In this sense of freedom, you are "free" if no one can tell you what to do without your consent. Both you and a media tycoon have the "same" freedom of speech because no one tells you what to say. Unfettered markets are thus morally good things because in a market, buyers and sellers meet and voluntarily make exchanges without being coerced.

The moral defense of capitalism is simply a logical extension of these arguments about voluntary exchange on free markets. If people are free, then they should be allowed to use their property however they like so long as their actions do not interfere with anyone else's property rights. This means that owners of the means of production should be free to use their capital as they wish; in particular, they should be free to hire workers to use those means of production on any terms voluntarily agreed upon by the workers and employers. So long as all of the agreements are voluntary—no one is directly forced by someone else to sign a contract—this is an expression of individual freedom and autonomy. Restrictions of voluntary contracts—including restrictions governing things like working conditions, pay, rights to hire and fire, and so on—are all violations of this conception of freedom. A minimally regulated capitalism is the form of economic organization that best satisfies these moral principles.

The Pragmatic Argument for Capitalism

There are two broad pragmatic arguments for capitalism as a way of organizing economic activities: first, capitalism provides the most effective way of coordinating a complex economic system; and second, it creates powerful incentives for innovation and economic growth. The full arguments underlying these claims involve quite a lot of complex economic theory, but the basic ideas are relatively simple.

Coordination

The first pragmatic argument for capitalism centers on a crucial problem faced by any complex economic system: how to effectively coordinate the economic activities of widely dispersed people in such a way that their activities fit together reasonably well. Suppose you want to build a house. You need lumber, nails, wire, ceramic tiles, paint, carpets, and many other things, as well as a variety of tools and machines. All these inputs into your house building were themselves produced with machines and energy and many raw materials from all over the world involving tens of thousands of people engaged in laboring activity. How do you let these people know that you want a particular kind of nail and a particular variety of lumber, and that you need them on a particular date for building your house? It is an unbelievably complex matter to get all this activity even moderately well coordinated. The most basic defense of capitalism as an economic system says that a market economy based on decentralized, privately owned firms is the best way to solve this problem. How is this system supposed to work?

In a stylized way, we can think of two primary methods of solving this complex coordination problem. One solution is *planning and command*, and the other is *decentralized markets*. In a planning model, activities of individuals and firms are coordinated by a planning authority telling people what to do. This is how coordination takes place in some large organizations and corporations: there is a hierarchy of managers with various responsibilities for determining what to do, and they issue orders to subordinates that ultimately set in motion specific activities of people at the bottom. This is also, more or less, how economic coordination worked in the Soviet Union: central planners formulated plans, allocated resources to firms, and instructed those firms what to produce. Authoritative command works reasonably well in some contexts, but it has proven very problematic when applied to large and complex systems. Even apart from the problem that a system of comprehensive planning and control of a complex economy seems to violate the values of individual freedom and autonomy, the task seems impossibly complex and likely to produce massive inefficiencies.

Decentralized markets with privately owned enterprises are the principal alternative to centralized planning as a way of solving this massive coordination problem. The story about how this coordination is accomplished was first systematically elaborated by Adam Smith in his famous account of the "invisible hand" of the market. Even if, in the end, we discover that this story is far too simple and the free market does not really function in the way Adam Smith believed, it is still a remarkable account that remains the core of the pragmatic defense of capitalist institutions today.

The key idea in the theory of the invisible hand of market coordination is the notion of *prices* as a mechanism for supplying both information and incentives to people in such a way that their activities can be coordinated. Price is a pretty odd phenomenon if you think about it: you take two things, say an apple and a hammer, and a number gets assigned to each of them to tell you how many apples are worth the same as one hammer—for example, 10 apples = 1 hammer.

How, then, do prices of things work to coordinate a vastly complex system of decentralized economic activity? The conventional story is about how the interplay of supply and demand shapes the movement of prices: If, at the existing price of widgets, the number of people who want widgets is greater than the supply of widgets, then the price will rise because people who want widgets will bid the price up. This situation creates a big incentive for producers of widgets to produce more—the higher the prices go, the more profit the producers will make. Production of widgets thus increases, the supply rises, and eventually—as supply equals demand—the prices fall. Eventually no one is willing to produce more widgets at the going price, which means that the price must be pretty close to the cost of producing widgets. Economists call this condition an *equilibrium*—a situation where price and quantity remain stable because no one has an incentive to change their behavior.

This interplay of supply and demand through the mechanism of price thus leads to what economists call *allocative efficiency*—resources and activity are allocated to different purposes in such a way that the amount of different sorts of things that get produced is exactly the right amount given what people want and how much money they have. The degree of coordination this principle involves is really amazing: When you go to a store and buy a chocolate bar, you are giving information to the store owner, who automatically passes that information to the chocolate bar company in the form of new orders of candy bars; the candy bar manufacturer then communicates the information to the cocoa importer when ordering new supplies; and the importer ultimately passes this information to the farmer who is growing the cocoa beans in West Africa. Each of these actors in the chain has a personal incentive to respond to the information. So when you buy a candy bar you are, through a chain of information and incentives, communicating with a farmer in Africa.

Defenders of capitalism emphasize two important implications for the way capitalist markets accomplish this broad economic coordination. First, if capitalist markets work this way, then the underlying dynamics of the economy are driven by the preferences and behaviors of consumers. Consumers are really running the economy. They are the ones who are in command, and they have as great a power as royalty of old. The idea is referred to as *consumer sovereignty*. Producers—whether they are giant multinational corporations or small firms—have powerful incentives to respond to information given them by the consumers of their products. Producers failing to respond to that information will lose money and eventually go out of business. It is thus the final consumers of the goods and services produced by the economic system who have the most fundamental power; their preferences and choices set in motion the information and incentive system that coordinates the market. This situation is appealing because it corresponds to popular ideas about individual autonomy and freedom: apparently powerful corporations are really controlled by consumers.

The second implication is a particular (some would say peculiar) sense in which capitalist markets do more than a pretty good job in coordinating a complex system of economic activity; instead, they do an optimal job. To say that a particular way of doing things is optimal is to say it is as good as possible, and any other alternative would produce worse results. In an ideal capitalist free market, when one person makes an offer to exchange something, and if someone accepts the offer, then they both are better off; if no one accepts the offer, it is because no one could be made better off by the exchange. If you let everyone freely make exchanges, then eventually you will reach an equilibrium at which no further exchanges happen. This is a situation in which *no one can improve without someone else being worse off*. This kind of situation has a special name in economics: *Pareto optimality*, named after the Italian Vilfredo Pareto. Defenders of the free market claim that if the market is allowed to work freely, it will generate a distribution of goods that satisfies this condition of Pareto optimality.

Innovation and Growth

As many advocates of free markets stress, unfettered capitalist markets are not simply an efficient way of allocating *existing* resources. They also promote all sorts of innovations, including innovations that contribute to economic growth by improving human productivity and innovations in products that improve the quality of life. This is regarded as the real magic of capitalism: capitalist markets generate a dynamic economic system that ultimately improves the lives of people through innovation and growth. This is the key to prosperity.

There are three core reasons for this innovative dynamic: First, the market rewards people and firms financially for making the right decisions and punishes them for making the wrong decisions. In this context, *right* means "producing things people want to buy and producing them at lower cost so more people can afford them." Second, the market allows people and firms to take risks to obtain the rewards that markets potentially offer. Innovation is a gamble, and markets are one way for people to engage in gambles that potentially have significant social benefits in the form of new products and technological improvements. Third, competition among firms intensifies both of these processes: Capitalist markets put considerable pressure on firms to innovate in order to survive against competition. Over time, this means that firms that innovate successfully will tend to expand and those that do not innovate successfully will decline, thus increasing the pressure on less successful firms to adopt the best existing innovations and seek new ones. The result is that innovations tend to diffuse throughout an economic system, thus raising productivity and underwriting significant economic growth.

Risk taking is crucial here, for most innovations are the result of investing time, energy, and resources with no assurance these will generate a payoff. Of course, capitalist markets are not the only way of encouraging socially useful risk taking. Much research, for example, is conducted in academic institutions and government research institutes where risks are taken and considerable innovation occurs. These research efforts are animated not by the potential of making huge amounts of money but by desires for reputation and the opportunity to do interesting work that contributes to knowledge and public welfare. Still, capitalist markets are a powerful engine for innovation through the combination of competitive pressures and opportunities for financial payoffs through successful risk taking. Particularly because of the ways in which capitalism facilitates such broadly decentralized and diffused forms of risk taking and innovation, in which the initiative and inspiration of creative individuals get linked to financial resources of investors, capitalism has proved to be an engine of economic growth and prosperity.

ARGUMENTS AGAINST STATE INTERFERENCE WITH THE MARKET

The moral and pragmatic defense of capitalism involves not simply an affirmation of the virtues of capitalism but also a critique of the state. "The government that governs least governs best" is a standard aphorism of advocates of capitalist systems.

The moral argument against the state is simpler than the pragmatic argument and is most purely embodied in libertarian thought. Governments rule by command backed up by force. Governments are therefore inherently a threat to freedom; the sheer fact of the state implies a restriction on freedom. This does not mean that governments should be abolished—most advocates of unfettered markets are not anarchists. But they believe the role of government should be strictly circumscribed, and the burden of proof is always on those who say the government should do something. The state should be what Ferdinand LaSalle called "a night watchman state." This is a state whose role is limited as much as possible to the task of protecting property rights and the rules of the game rather than actively intervening in the economy to "solve" problems. This conception of what the state should do is minimalist and largely negative—"don't go there!" "don't tread on me!" The contrasting conception of the state can be called *affirmative*. An *affirmative state* does not put markets off-limits to intervention. A democratic affirmative state is one that deliberately uses its power, in markets and elsewhere, to improve human well-being and democratic conditions. This might take any number of forms, but a classic one involves relieving the social exclusions and material inequalities that undermine the democratic ideal of equal citizenship. Proponents of such a state think that using public power in these and other ways to further democracy is nothing to be embarrassed about. In fact, they think the whole point of democratic government is to be "of the people, by the people, for the people," not "of the market, by the market, for the market."

Although the moral argument for a limited state appeals to libertarians, this by itself would not be persuasive to many, perhaps most, people. People see many problems in American society—poverty, pollution, and inadequate health care, to name only a few—and at various times in American history, people have turned to the state for help. Opponents of a strong role for the state in a market economy have thus given considerable weight to the pragmatic argument against the state. As the aphorism popularized by Ronald Reagan proclaims, "The state is the problem, not the solution."

Two kinds of pragmatic arguments are particularly common in the attacks on state intervention. These can be referred to as the thesis of *state incompetence* and the thesis of *state malevolence.*

The state incompetence thesis suggests that government bureaucracy is inevitably clumsy and ineffective, bogged down in red tape and preoccupied with one-size-fits-all rules and regulations. Politicians and government officials may mean well, but their attempts at imposing regulations on the market almost always backfire, undermining the crucial incentives that generate efficiency in the market. Efforts at environmental protection, for example, generate endless paperwork, environmental impact studies, rigid rules that fail to take into account local conditions, and endless litigation. Even if the goals are worthy, the effects are undesirable.

The state malevolence thesis is much stronger. Here the state is viewed not just as all thumbs and no fingers, but as an iron fist. Bureaucrats strive to accumulate power either for its own sake or to serve their own career interests. Corruption is a chronic problem, not just in the sense of politicians and bureaucrats taking bribes (although this happens often enough) but in the sense of state officials protecting powerful economic actors from market competition through subsidies, tax breaks, and self-serving regulations in exchange for their political support. Either the state is captured by special interests that use the power of the state to gain special advantages, or it is an autonomous machine bent on domination for domination's sake. Perhaps the original intention of building up this machine was benevolent, seeking the means to solve real problems. But once created, this state machine becomes Frankenstein's monster—a monster that cannot be controlled by its creator. Only if the monster is slain can the full virtues of capitalism be unleashed.

It would be an exaggeration to say that most Americans fully accept these libertarian arguments against the state and for a largely deregulated free market form of capitalism. Public opinion surveys consistently indicate much more ambivalence than this. Americans typically believe in democracy and the need for a state that does much more than just enforce the rules of the game, and though Americans are strong supporters of private enterprise and market capitalism, many are skeptical about the idea that an unregulated, free-for-all market is the best for securing freedom, efficiency, and prosperity. In the next chapter we examine a range of problems, generated by market capitalism, that markets by themselves cannot solve.

4

THE CAPITALIST MARKET: HOW IT ACTUALLY WORKS

n Chapter 3, we examined the central virtues of capitalism as seen by its defenders and discussed the basic way capitalism is supposed to work. Six points were especially salient:

1. Capitalist markets are an expression of the value of individual freedom, organized around voluntary exchange between people; no one is forced by anyone to engage in any particular exchange.
2. Free markets are an extremely effective mechanism for coordinating complex economic systems.
3. Markets accomplish this remarkable result through supply, demand, and the price mechanism.
4. Free markets result in allocative efficiency: after all the trading is done, the allocation of things is Pareto optimal—no one can be made better off without someone else being made worse off.
5. Capitalist markets create incentives for risk taking and innovation, and thus capitalism is an engine of economic growth and prosperity.
6. State regulation of capitalist firms and markets interferes with the free market and undermines these virtues.

Now that we know how capitalism is supposed to work, let us look at some of the problems and dilemmas of markets and capitalism. We begin by examining the moral argument for capitalism and freedom and then turn to a range of problems with the pragmatic defense of free markets. The chapter concludes with a discussion of how intensely competitive capitalist markets can undermine a range of social values outside of the economy itself.

THE MORAL ARGUMENT:
HOW WELL DO CAPITALIST MARKETS
ADVANCE THE VALUE OF HUMAN FREEDOM?

Individual freedom is a crucial value, and it is a tremendous historical achievement that individual freedom has become a core value of American culture. Historically, this value emerged and was strengthened, if unevenly, by the spread of market relations; a good case can be made that capitalist development has further promoted this value. Nevertheless, capitalist markets affirm only a limited notion of freedom, and in certain important respects they are an obstacle to fuller realization of this value.

To understand this point, we must look more closely at the idea of individual freedom. There are two sides to the idea of freedom, sometimes referred to as negative freedom and positive freedom. Capitalism and markets have an ambiguous relationship with both of these faces of freedom.

Negative freedom means "freedom from coercion." Individuals have negative freedom when no one directly commands them to do things against their will. Individuals have autonomy to direct their own actions unless they voluntarily agree to follow orders issued by someone else. A contract embodies this ideal of freedom: Two people voluntarily agree to some kind of exchange. So long as the contract is free of force or fraud, it is an expression of negative freedom. By historical standards, capitalist markets have done a pretty good job of reducing involuntary coercion in economic life. Compare a free market economy to slavery or feudalism: in these two non-capitalist economic systems, the direct application of force is a central, pervasive feature of allocating people to tasks. In a capitalist market economy, the allocation of people to activities is the result of the self-directed choices of persons: no one is told "you must work for this employer" or "you must buy this product." In Milton Friedman's famous words, within a capitalist market people are "free to choose."[1]

Positive freedom refers to the actual *capacity* of people to do things. This is freedom *to* rather than freedom *from*. A person has greater positive freedom if he or she can do more things and has a greater capacity to act in the world. Negative freedom identifies freedom solely with the *act of choice*, whereas positive freedom identifies it with the *range of choices* a person can actually make. Capitalism has also certainly played a pivotal role in expanding the

---

[1]The expression comes from Milton and Rose Friedman in their passionate defense of capitalism, *Free to Choose: A Personal Statement* (Orlando, FL: Harvest Books, 1990).

range of choices available to many people. To appreciate this range, simply compare the vast array of consumer products available today with those in the market a hundred years ago. And further, economic growth has improved the standards of living of a significant proportion of the population by giving them access to at least a part of the expanded range of alternatives.

Regarding both the negative and positive faces of freedom, therefore, capitalism and markets can be seen as making a real contribution. And yet, in other crucial ways, capitalism also generates and enforces considerable restrictions on negative as well as positive freedom for many people. Two issues are especially salient here. First, the power relations within capitalist firms constitute pervasive restrictions on individual autonomy and self-direction. At the core of the institution of private property is the power of owners to decide how their property is to be used. In the context of capitalist firms, this is the basis for conferring authority on owners to direct the actions of their employees. An essential part of the employment contract is the agreement of employees to follow orders, to do what they are told. In most capitalist workplaces this means that for most workers, individual freedom and self-direction are quite curtailed.

One response to this situation by defenders of capitalism is that if workers don't like what they are told to do, they are free to quit. They are thus not really being dominated, because they continually voluntarily submit to the authority of their boss; they are not slaves, after all. The real freedom of individuals to quit their jobs, however, provides only an illusory escape from such domination. Without ownership of means of production or access to basic necessities of life, workers must seek work in capitalist firms or state organizations; and in all of these, they must surrender autonomy. It may be true that the agreement to work for a *particular* employer is "voluntary" in that no one is commanding it, but the decision to work for some employer is not voluntary. Capitalism, therefore, violates the value of negative freedom by making it difficult for most people to avoid being directly dominated by others in work.[2]

The second way that capitalism undermines the ideal of individual freedom and autonomy centers on the massive inequalities of wealth and income generated by capitalism. These inequalities mean that some people

[2]For a good discussion of the sense in which the employment contract, despite its apparently voluntary character, still reflects a form of unfreedom, see G. A. Cohen, "The Structure of Proletarian Unfreedom," *Philosophy and Public Affairs* 12 (1983): 3–33. For a discussion of the problematic relationship of managerial authority to individual freedom, see Robert Dahl, *A Preface to Economic Democracy* (Berkeley, CA: University of California Press, 1985).

have enormously greater capacity to act on their life plans than others do; they are in a position to actually make the choices that matter to them. Large inequalities of wealth and income mean some people have much greater positive freedom than others. Of course, we could cite many wonderful rags-to-riches stories to refute this point: some people start out with extremely limited resources and correspondingly limited options and nevertheless acquire the material conditions for expansive positive freedom. Can we say that capitalism denies people positive freedom when such opportunities exist? This is rather like observing that some people escape from prison—and undoubtedly, these prisoners are the cleverest and most committed to escaping—and then concluding that the people who do not escape are therefore not really in prison. Free markets inherently generate large disparities in resources available to people. If everyone started out in the same position with the same assets, and these differences were just the result of effort and choice, then perhaps such inequality in resources would not really contradict positive freedom. In fact, most people who accumulate great wealth started with considerable wealth and other advantages. They have greater freedom, not just more stuff, than someone born poor.

Capitalism and free markets, therefore, have contradictory effects on the value of individual freedom, whether freedom is understood in the negative or positive sense. American capitalism does relatively little to counteract these freedom-reducing processes. Employers face weak legal restrictions on their authority over their employees, and most workers have limited autonomy and self-direction in their work. Relatively despotic forms of power over individuals within workplaces are thus common. The processes of income and wealth redistribution organized by the state are also very weak, and thus little is done to secure the positive freedom of the poor and disadvantaged. American capitalism may be defended on the moral grounds of individual freedom and liberty, but it supports only a thin understanding of this important value.

PROBLEMS INTERNAL TO MARKETS: INEFFICIENCY AND MARKET FAILURES

Defenders of free markets and capitalism as a social order do not primarily defend these institutions because they embody the moral principle of maximizing individual freedom, but rather because these institutions are also supposed to promote the general welfare. Many people may concede that markets may be unfair in some ways, that real freedom is limited for many people within capitalism, but still believe that maximally free markets based on private property are the surest route to efficiency and improvements in the general welfare.

It is certainly the case that markets can be quite efficient and that private ownership of firms often delivers the goods. But this is a seriously incomplete picture. In many circumstances, markets fail; and in important instances, they do a terrible job. Our conclusion will be that if one wants to realize the values of efficiency and prosperity to the greatest extent possible, then the ideal should not be the free market of unregulated capitalism but democratically accountable markets. In the case of contemporary American society, realizing this ideal would require a dramatic revitalization of democracy and strengthening of the affirmative state.

To get to this conclusion, we need a more systematic understanding of the problems and dilemmas of capitalist markets. This task, which requires more discussion of some basic ideas and concepts in economics and economic sociology, is the focus of the rest of this chapter. Chapters 5 through 9 will then present a more empirical discussion of market inefficiency in several important domains of economic activity.

In the following sections, we examine five problems in the functioning of capitalist markets that can generate significant economic and social inefficiency:

1. Information failures
2. Concentrations of economic power
3. Negative externalities
4. Short time horizons
5. Public goods

Markets and Information

At the center of the idea that markets generate efficient allocations of resources is the problem of information. This is a simple point, embodied in jokes about used car salesmen describing vehicles as having been driven by little old ladies only on Sundays and aphorisms such as "buyers beware." Basically, the problem is that sellers on a market have strong interests in hiding certain kinds of information from buyers in contexts in which it is costly, if not impossible, for buyers to get the necessary information to make an optimal choice. Because of this severe information problem, the United

States has laws to regulate false advertising and to require that firms provide consumers with certain kinds of information *that the firms would not provide if there was a perfectly free market*. Food labeling is a good example. Laws that require nutrition information on food violate the free market. Food processors would not provide this information unless forced to do so. It costs the seller something to calculate nutritional content, assemble the data, and produce a label. Individual consumers are unlikely to have strong preferences about this information until after it is provided. And furthermore, even if there were some consumers who wanted the information, it would initially be quite costly for producers to provide this information—there are considerable economies of scale in providing the information on a wide scale rather than on a limited scale—and thus the price difference between products with and without product information would be prohibitive. As a practical matter, this information will be widely provided only when there are regulations that require it. Such regulations violate the principles of the free market.

Laws that prevent firms from false advertising violate the logic of the market as well. In a perfectly free market, firms could make whatever claims they liked about their products. If consumers felt that it was valuable for them to know the truth, then there would be a market for better information about products, and consumers could buy that information if they wanted to. If a consumer felt that the distortions of information harmed them and amounted to fraud, then they could sue the sellers in court and the threat of suits would act as a deterrent for excessive falsehood. In any case firms would not want to distort information too much or they would lose customers. Reputation matters for firms, and thus the market itself would impose constraints on distorted information.

It is possible, therefore, to imagine a free market with no government regulations on information. In such a truly free market economy, the quality of information would depend upon the preferences of consumers for good information and their ability to pay for it, the value of reputation to sellers, and the effectiveness of threats posed by private law suits for fraud. This is an imaginable world—and indeed was more or less the way American capitalism functioned in the nineteenth century—but the average quality of information consumers would get in the market would be much lower in such a world than in one with good state-enforced regulations on information. And if the average quality of information is lower, then the allocation of resources generated by such a market would be less efficient.

A special case of product information concerns product safety. Suppose there were no regulations for automobile safety standards. Carmakers would then be free to make cars with different standards of safety. If consumers valued safety, then they would be free to pay a premium for cars designed to be safe. If some consumers were risk takers and preferred a cheaper car, then they could buy a less-safe car. A libertarian might argue that this would be a better market because it would give consumers more power, more ability to choose freely their preferred mix of risk, safety, and cost. However, a major flaw in this scenario concerns information—carmakers would have large incentives to hide safety problems and characterize their cars as being safer than they really are, and consumers would have trouble weighing the technical information to make informed decisions and would find it extremely difficult to use the courts effectively in remedying the resulting harms.

This problem is not just hypothetical. The notorious cases of the Pinto automobile and its exploding gas tanks in the 1970s, the road instability of certain SUVs in the 1990s, and the ignition switch failures in the 2000s clearly show the problem of information failures in the "market" for automobile safety even in a world where safety regulations exist.[3] Ford Motor Company realized by the late 1960s that the Pinto had a design flaw that, in certain accidents, caused the gas tank to explode. Ford engineers designed a retrofit that would eliminate the problem at a cost of roughly $11 per car (in 1960s dollars). The issue, then, was whether it was worth it for the company to recall all Pintos and make the change. Ford did the math: The safety improvement would cost $11 per car and save roughly 180 lives per year. The retrofit would cost about $137 million (12.5 million Pintos × $11 per car). How much was a life worth? Ford calculated this figure on the basis of likely court costs for passenger deaths at the time and came up with an estimated $200,000 per death. After doing the math, Ford decided it was not worth making the safety change. Moreover—by fighting the court cases, insisting that these fiery deaths were due to driver error, and resisting legislative regulation—Ford could further minimize the costs of the safety problem by delaying remedies.

The same basic story was repeated in the 1990s, when certain sport utility vehicles were found to be unstable on curves and had a tendency to roll over. The manufacturers denied this was a problem, blamed drivers, and fought court cases. This event occurred in a context where considerable machinery of safety regulation was in place. Imagine how serious the safety

[3]The following account of the Pinto case comes from Mark Dowie, "Pinto Madness," *Mother Jones*, September–October 1977.

problems would become in the absence of such safety regulations and requirements for information reporting.

Concentrated Economic Power

Another premise of the defense of the virtues of free markets is that individuals and firms do not really accumulate large amounts of power in the market; instead, everyone enters into exchanges as individual, voluntary actors, making choices freely. They may have different purchasing power, which means they may have different sets of choices, but no one has the kind of power that enables them to impose their will on others.

What is power? This question has many answers, but a simple one is that power is the ability to get your way even against the objections or resistance of others. In short, this is the ability to impose your will on others. If you announce in the newspaper that you have a stereo to sell for $100, everyone who reads the ad is completely free to say no to your offer. You have no power over anyone. This powerlessness is a virtue of market exchanges, and it is why many people believe that markets are the enemy of power and domination; they are the realm of free, autonomous, voluntary action.

The problem is that free markets tend to lead to concentrations of wealth in the form of personal fortunes and, even more significantly, megacorporations. An inherent feature of market dynamics is that winners in competition will tend to become larger and larger; and when they become very large, they exert real power inside of the market (as well as in the political arena). Microsoft, Wal-Mart, Exxon Mobil, Boeing, and many other corporations are not just making things and selling them on a market; they are shaping the market through their exercise of power. A large corporation is not just a bigger version of the corner grocery store; megacorporations have the ability to make strategic choices that massively affect the lives of people and communities, the choices they face, and the kinds of lives they can lead. Microsoft is notorious in this regard: it is so big that it can force people to buy products they do not want by bundling them with their Windows operating system, and it can force computer companies to install the entire suite of programs rather than individual components. Wal-Mart forces suppliers to squeeze their workers' wages to ruthlessly cut costs. Wal-Mart is so big in many markets that suppliers simply cannot refuse to comply with its demands. Wal-Mart is not just a price *taker* that responds to the prices of products in an impersonal market; it is a price *maker* that uses power to shape prices in the market. General Motors—when it was one of the largest corporations in the world—used its power to purchase urban electric rail systems and convert them to buses, thus (as we will see in Chapter 6) expanding the potential market for automobiles. Many other examples could be given. In all these ways, concentrations of economic power undermine the efficiency-generating dynamics of markets.

The power of the large corporation is enhanced by the increasingly global character of capitalist production and markets. Large corporations have the ability to locate their facilities anywhere in the world. This means that when they face regulations they do not like or employees who demand higher wages than they want to pay, multinational corporations have the option of moving their production elsewhere. Small, local firms do not have this ability and are thus weaker in their dealings with other local actors. Because large firms have the power to use threats to get their way, they have competitive advantage over small firms. This situation again reduces the efficiency of markets.

Negative Externalities

Negative externalities are all the side effects of an activity that negatively affect others. Positive externalities are side effects that benefit others. Playing a loud boom box in a park generates negative externalities on bystanders who prefer quiet; planting flowers in one's front yard creates positive externalities for passersby who enjoy their beauty. Negative and positive externalities, therefore, are inherent features of social activity.

The problem of negative externalities is one of the most pervasive sources of inefficiency in capitalist markets. If these were just random perturbations, noise in the system, then it might be possible to think that negative and positive externalities would more or less balance each other out: the unchosen harms on people caused by negative externalities would be neutralized (in the aggregate at least) by the unchosen benefits of positive externalities. The problem is that in capitalism, negative externalities are not random deviations from a "perfect market." Rather, firms have strong incentives to engage in practices that generate them. Let us see why this is the case.

Capitalist firms do not simply produce goods and services for the market; they attempt to do so in a way that maximizes profits. Profits are basically the difference between the price at which things are sold and the costs *paid by the firm* to produce them. Therefore, a central part of maximizing profits is maximizing the difference between such costs and selling price—and one way to do this is to lower costs. But notice that only the costs actually experienced by the firm, not the total costs of production, are what matters here. In many contexts an effective way of reducing such costs faced by the firm is, in one way or another, to displace costs onto others. One way of doing this is to increase negative externalities.

The classic example of this practice is pollution. We discuss this topic in more detail in the next chapter, but the basic point is simple enough: it is cheaper for a factory to dump pollutants into a river or the air than to dispose of them in a nonpolluting way. But polluting the environment imposes costs on other people—for example, communities downstream from a source of water pollution have to spend resources to clean the water, and air pollution increases medical bills and requires homeowners to repaint their houses more often. If a firm was forced to either install technologies that would prevent the pollution or pay for all these displaced costs, then its costs of production would increase significantly. An individual firm, therefore, would be at a competitive disadvantage if it paid these costs on the basis of the moral principle that it was wrong to displace them on other people. Displacing such costs on others is therefore perfectly rational behavior for a capitalist firm engaged in profit-maximizing competition.

Another important type of negative externality centers on the investment decisions of corporations. Consider a firm that decides to move production to Mexico because it will have a higher rate of profit there than in the United States. Many firms that have moved production away from the United States did so not because those plants were losing money—they were making a profit—but because they could make higher profits elsewhere. This is a perfectly rational economic decision by the corporation, given what counts as a "cost" in their calculations. However, many significant social costs of this decision do not appear as costs to the corporation; and if the firm had to cover them, it would change its profit-maximizing strategy. For example, when a large factory moves abroad, its absence often triggers a decline in home values in the abandoned community. This situation can have a devastating economic impact on these homeowners even if they were not employees of the firm. These costs to homeowners are not included in the investment decisions of the firm owners. *If they were, plant closing would not be profitable.* To see this, suppose the plant in question were owned by all the people in the affected community rather than by an outside corporation. In that case the impact on home values of moving the factory would not be a negative externality, but a negative "internality"—it would be experienced as a cost to the people making the decision. Even if the direct production costs were lower in Mexico, in this situation it would not be viewed as a way of increasing profits.

This, then, is the important lesson about negative externalities: In making investment decisions, the owners of firms look at the costs and benefits of alternative choices, but only certain costs are counted. Some costs are displaced onto other people, so they do not appear in the bottom line of the firm. This means that the ordinary price mechanism of a competitive market cannot lead to optimal allocations, even in the restricted sense of allocative efficiency. Efficient allocations in a market happen only when prices are closely linked to the *true total costs* of producing things. But if firms can displace significant costs on others, then prices no longer reflect true costs, and allocations based on those prices are no longer efficient. Negative externalities pervasively muck up this process.

Short Time Horizons

The idea of *time horizons* refers to the length of time into the future that people take into consideration when making decisions in the present. A particularly important issue in this regard is the extent to which the interests and welfare of future generations are taken into consideration in investment and consumption decisions made today. Highly competitive free markets have the effect of shortening the time horizons of most investors. Capitalist firms compete for investments. Investors look to firms that give the highest rates of return in the relatively short term. Even investors with relatively long time horizons are concerned about the likely rates of return over a relatively short period—a decade or so perhaps—not fifty or a hundred years. This means that investors are very unlikely to consider projects that would take many decades to generate a return. The result is that investments generated through competitive markets cannot give significant weight to the welfare of future generations because this will generally not be the short-run, profit-maximizing business strategy.

The problem of energy conservation is a good example. The price of oil in the world at any given time broadly reflects the costs of extracting oil and the market demand for its products. Current market prices do not reflect the fact that in the future, the costs of extracting oil will become much more expensive due to depletion of the resource and thus it will be much more expensive to produce a given level of supply. The prices individuals face in the market when they make individual consumption choices around gasoline consumption thus do not reflect the costs to future generations. As a result, unless an individual cares a great deal about these issues, individual consumption choices will reflect only immediate personal needs. The market itself cannot solve this problem. Only through public deliberation and collective political choices can the longer-term future significantly affect present decisions and economic allocations, both in terms of broad patterns of investment and consumption.

The Problem of Public Goods

What is a public good? The simple answer is, a public good is something that benefits people even if they did not voluntarily contribute to producing it. Or, to put it slightly differently, a public good is something that, if produced, is difficult to exclude people from consuming. The classic example is national defense. Suppose national defense was paid for by voluntary contributions rather than taxes. The national defense provided by this means would benefit everyone—the people who did not contribute as well as those who did. Public sanitation and public health, public broadcasting, clean air, education, and many other things have this character. Some of these things may also provide private benefits to particular individuals: education does provide specific benefits to those who receive it, but it also contributes to higher overall economic productivity that benefits the society as a whole. And here is the problem: in general, the level of public goods provided through unconstrained free capitalist markets will be far below the socially optimal level.

A few examples will make this issue clear. Suppose that education was provided only by the market. Private firms offered educational services, and parents would buy these services for their children's education. There would be no subsidies and no public provision. In such a world, a large proportion of poor people would fail to get even minimal education. Or consider public health and sanitation. Suppose that sewers, water treatment, and human waste disposal were provided only by the market; there was no public provision of these services. This would be a disadvantage even to those who could afford those services, because poor sanitation would be a breeding ground for diseases that would affect everyone. Markets are good at producing things for which most of the benefits are captured by those who directly pay for the good or service, but not public goods whose value is diffused to a wide variety of people. Markets will underproduce public goods, and this is inefficient.

The problem of public goods is a specific example of a more general problem studied by sociologists, political scientists, and economists—the problem of *free riding* within collective actions. We will encounter collective action problems many times in this book, so it is worth spending some time explaining just what this problem is and how it relates to public goods.

The problem of collective action in regard to public goods is often explained through the analysis of a paradox called *the prisoner's dilemma*. Here is the story: Two prisoners are accused of jointly committing a crime. They are held in separate cells. They care only about their own welfare: they are purely selfish individualists. Each prisoner is told the following:

> If you confess and rat on the other person and that person remains silent, you will go free and the other person will get 10 years in prison. If you remain silent and the other person rats on you, you will get 10 years and that person will go free. If you both are silent, you each get 2 years in jail; if you both rat on each other, you each get 5 years.

These options are illustrated in the following diagram, called a payoff matrix:

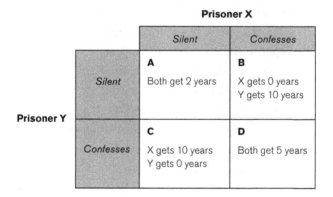

Payoff Matrix for Prisoner's Dilemma

		Prisoner X	
		Silent	*Confesses*
Prisoner Y	*Silent*	**A** Both get 2 years	**B** X gets 0 years Y gets 10 years
	Confesses	**C** X gets 10 years Y gets 0 years	**D** Both get 5 years

What should a prisoner do as a rational, selfish person? The rational thing is to confess. Here is how each prisoner reasons:

> If the other guy is silent, I get 0 years if I confess and 2 if I stay silent; if the other guy confesses, I get 5 years if I confess and 10 years if I remain silent. Regardless of what the other prisoner does, I am better off confessing. So I confess.

The other prisoner reasons (correctly) the same way and confesses; so both end up with five years in prison (cell D in the matrix above) even though, if both prisoners had remained silent, they each would have received only two years in prison (cell A). This is called a collective action failure because the two people fail to collectively coordinate their actions in a way that would have been mutually beneficial.

The underprovision of public goods has this kind of character. A good example is the problem of depletion of fishing stocks in a lake or other body of water. This is an instance of what is called the *tragedy of the commons*. A healthy stock of fish in a body of water is a public good: everyone who fishes benefits from this stock. Suppose there is a lake in which roughly 10,000 fish can be caught per year and still have the fish stock reproduced year after year. Suppose there are a thousand fishermen fishing in the lake. If everyone catches ten fish per year, the fish stock will remain stable from year to year, and all the fishermen will be able to continue to catch fish; so a sign is posted at the lake saying: "Fishing limit per fisherman, 10 fish per year." You are one of those fishermen, and you know that if you personally catch twenty fish, this amount will not significantly affect the fish stock. You figure it won't matter whether 10,000 fish or 10,010 fish are caught each year. After all, the 10,000 figure is just an estimate. So you ignore the sign and catch twenty. You are being a "free rider" on everyone else's restraint. Every other fisherman behaves the same way; so in all 20,000 fish are taken—and for the next two years, the lake has so few fish that each fisherman can catch only two per year. Now suppose you are an honest, moral person (but no one else is), so you decide to obey the sign. You catch 10 fish the first year and 2 the second and third. Everyone else has caught 20 the first year and 2 thereafter. You feel like a sucker (maybe a virtuous sucker, but a sucker nonetheless): over the three-year period, you got only 14 fish and everyone else got 24.

The number of fish caught over the three years under different combinations of choices can be illustrated in a payoff matrix like the prisoner's dilemma:

**Numbers of Fish You Catch over Three Years with
Different Patterns of Fishing
(legal limit = 10 fish/year)**

		What *you* do	
		Obey the fishing limit	Ignore the fishing limit
What *everyone* else does	Obeys the fishing limit	30	60
	Ignores the fishing limit	14	24

This is precisely what has happened in the great fishing banks in the North Atlantic: poorly regulated and policed fishing practices have led to overfishing. Each commercial fisher tries to maximize the catch, with the result that the collective resource—the fishing stock—is depleted.[4]

Here is another example that may be less familiar: the provision of skills training within capitalist firms. Firms are able to compete more effectively on world markets when they have a highly trained labor force. Workers who have what can be termed "meta-skills"—the skills needed to learn skills quickly—are especially important. Such workers can quickly adapt to new technologies and flexibly respond to production problems. Such meta-skills are often best developed within the practical settings of real production processes rather than in stand-alone schools. Every firm will be better off if there is lots of training of this general sort. But what happens in a competitive market? The owners and managers of each firm think about it this way:

> It is costly to provide such training. If every other firm provides such training but we don't, then we will save on these training costs and be able to hire workers trained at other firms by offering them a bit more money than can the firms that provided the training. Those firms won't be able to match our wage offers because they have higher costs than we do because they provided the training. We will make higher profits by poaching trained workers from the firms that train them than we can by providing the training ourselves. We will maximize our profits by free riding on other firms' efforts at training.

If every firm is maximizing profits, then every firm will make the same decision, and no one will provide the training. The result is a labor market with workers lacking adequate meta-skills. This is called the public goods problem of skill formation.

These kinds of collective action problems, which involve strong incentives to be a free rider, are difficult to solve within competitive, unregulated

[4]Peter Montague wrote in 1998, "The world's catch of ocean fish peaked in 1989 and has been declining since. In the early 1990s, scientists reported that 13 of the world's 17 major fisheries were depleted or in steep decline. Typical is the Grand Banks fishery off the shallow coast of Newfoundland in the North Atlantic. There, after 350 years of commercial exploitation, the haddock, cod, and flounder have all but disappeared and the fishery was officially closed a few years ago." From "Oceans without Fish," *Rachel's Environment & Health Weekly 587*, 26 February 1998.

markets. Because markets themselves do not produce public goods very effectively, in economic systems that rely heavily on markets—such as that in the United States—there tends to be an undersupply of public goods. This is a serious source of inefficiency, whether it is understood in narrow economic terms or broader social terms.

THE FREE MARKET AND SOCIAL VALUES

So far we have examined some ways that markets generate problems inside the economy itself—various ways that free markets fail on pragmatic grounds involving different aspects of efficiency. But capitalist free markets also have important consequences for other social institutions and values—for aspects of our lives outside of the economy as narrowly understood. And here too, weakly regulated, intensely competitive free markets of the sort that are idealized in the United States can pose serious problems.

Human activities within markets revolve around one specific dimension of human personality, values, and social interaction: *the rational pursuit of one's self-interest as a separate person*. People do act this way some of the time, in some places, under some circumstances. But humans are also characterized by solidarity, generosity, and kindness. Human beings are characterized by the search for meaning and companionship, by caring for the well-being of others and not just themselves. Even in such a rampantly individualistic society as the United States, solidarities and altruism are important. Indeed, sociologists generally argue that without such values, society would collapse: pure economic self-interest by itself cannot provide the glue for social life.

Now, here is the really important point: the specific *mix* of these human characteristics—in particular, how important is greed and competitive individualism relative to other values—is not something given once and for all by "human nature" but is shaped by our social institutions in complex ways. A crucial question for sociology and for politics is thus how our institutions either reinforce or undermine different kinds of values and traits. Or to say it even more simply, the kind of people we get in a society is not given by nature, but by the ways our institutions encourage some traits and discourage others. In our present context, the question thus becomes *what kinds of people and traits does a highly competitive, individualistic capitalist society foster?*

This turns out to be a difficult question to answer in any definitive way. The relationship between values and personality traits on the one hand and economic institutions on the other is a kind of chicken-and-egg problem: do competitive free markets foster self-interested individualism, or does self-interested individualism foster competitive free markets? The causal relation almost certainly runs in both directions: competitive markets may foster certain kinds of values and personality traits, but those traits and values, in turn, shape economic institutions. What we have, then, is a kind of system of mutual reinforcement.

We will not attempt here to sort out all the complexity of this difficult but interesting problem. What we will do is say something about the way markets act to weaken certain kinds of values and traits and reinforce others. Three issues are particularly important:

1. The erosion of community
2. The commercialization of morally salient aspects of life
3. The skills of "exit" versus "voice"

Erosion of Community

Community is one of those flexible terms in social and political discussions; it is used in a wide variety of ways for different purposes. Here we define the idea of community quite broadly as any social unit within which people are concerned for the well-being of other people and feel solidarity and obligations toward others. The value of community, understood in this way, is very close to certain core values in many religious traditions. The moral precept "love thy neighbor" is basically an expression of this idea. Although a community need not be a small geographical locale like a neighborhood, frequently communities are geographically rooted because such deep attachments and commitments are often built on direct, face-to-face interactions. One can also talk about the *degree* of community in a particular social setting, because reciprocity, solidarity, mutual concern, and caring can vary in intensity and durability. A strong community is one in which these mutual obligations run deep; a weak community is one in which they are less demanding and more easily disrupted.

Community is important both as a value in itself and because it helps people solve practical problems of social cooperation. The problems of cooperation and collective action we discussed in the analysis of public goods, for example, are easier to solve when people feel moral obligations to each other and a shared sense of community. The free-riding problem within collective action depends upon people acting strictly on the basis of their own self-interest without regard to any moral commitment to contribute to the public good. In social settings where there is a strong sense of community, free riding is less likely.

Capitalist markets are corrosive to a sense of community for two main reasons. First, intensely competitive markets reward self-interested, individualistic behavior and reinforce it as a normative ideal. The market cultivates a sense of individual responsibility, of looking out for number one, but not a sense of moral obligation to the welfare of a broader community. The market also cultivates mistrust: everyone is out to take advantage of you, to make a fast buck, so you need to be wary. Life is a competition over survival of the fittest; nice guys finish last. Buyers beware. Highly competitive markets tend to encourage the pursuit of self-interest as the overriding motivation for action, and in so doing undermine the broad value of community in society.

Second, unfettered market forces are corrosive to community solidarity because they foster high levels of inequality. Vast disparities in quality of life undermine social cohesion, breed resentments from below and contempt from above, and create a stratified social order in which people no longer feel that "we're all in the same boat." The cultural content of market competition undermines community not only by encouraging single-minded, individualistic competitiveness but also by generating poverty in the midst of plenty.

These arguments do not imply that the value of community cannot survive in a strongly inegalitarian, market-oriented society like the United States. After all, other forces are at work besides the market, and some of these help preserve a sense of moral community. Nevertheless, intense market competition threatens the values of community and makes these values more fragile and less effective.

Commercialization of Morally Salient Aspects of Life

Markets may be an economically efficient way of organizing the production and distribution of many things, yet most people feel that certain aspects of human activity should not be organized by markets even if doing so would be efficient in a technical, economic sense. Virtually everyone, except for a few extreme libertarians, believes it would be wrong to create a capitalist market for the production and adoption of babies. Even if the exchanges on such a market were voluntary, the idea of turning a baby into a commodity with a market price and selling the baby to the highest bidder is seen by most people as a monstrous violation of the moral value of human beings.

Most people object to a market in voluntary slaves—that is, a market in which you are allowed to sell yourself voluntarily into slavery. Most people also object to markets in most body parts and organs—whether the organs come from live donors, as in the case of kidneys and corneas, or from deceased donors, as in the case of hearts. Partially, this stance is based on the belief that such markets would inevitably prey on the vulnerabilities of the poor and lead to many types of abuse, but it is also due to wariness about reducing the human body to the status of a commodity with a market price attached to it. Most people also believe it would be wrong to have a free market in votes in elections, in which people could purchase votes directly from citizens, even if this would improve the welfare of both parties of the exchange. So, even in highly commercialized capitalist societies, most people believe there are moral limits to the domains in which markets should be allowed to organize our activities. Human beings and democratic rights should not be treated like commodities.

American society is one of the most commercialized in the world. Although some prohibitions on market transactions remain in force—most notably, markets are prohibited for certain kinds of recreational drugs, for sex, and for votes—commercialization has deeply penetrated many spheres of life in ways that threaten values intrinsic to those spheres. A few examples will illustrate this problem.

Child Care
Children require labor-intensive care and nurturance. This care can be provided through a variety of social organizations: the family, state-organized child-care services, various kinds of community-based child care, or for-profit, market-based child care organized by capitalist firms. The market solution to this problem does not mean that all for-profit child care will be of poor quality and harmful to the well-being of children. What it means is that the quality of the care will be a function of the capacity of parents to pay. Capitalist firms providing child-care services will be organized around the objective of maximizing profits, and meeting the needs of children will matter only to the extent that it contributes to that goal. To maximize profits, firms will have strong incentives to seek low-cost labor for the staff of child-care centers, especially for those servicing poor families. The training of caregivers will be low and the staffing ratios suboptimal in most centers. Families with lots of resources and a capacity to obtain good information about the quality of providers will be able to purchase good-quality child care, but many families will not.

The Arts

Many people regard the arts as a vital domain of human activity for exploring problems of life, meaning, beauty, and creativity. Of course, artists and performers of all sorts are often prepared to make considerable personal economic sacrifices to participate vigorously in the arts, and much arts activity takes place outside the discipline of the capitalist market. Still, the arts do need financial resources to thrive: drama needs theaters; symphonies need concert halls; and all performers and artists need to eat. If the main source of such funding is from the capitalist market, then the autonomy and vitality of the arts are threatened. Many theaters face enormous pressures to produce only those plays that will be a commercial success, rather than plays that are controversial, innovative, or less accessible. Musicians are hampered by the commercial imperatives of record deals. Writers find it difficult to publish novels when profit-maximizing strategies of publishers become oriented to producing blockbusters. A fully commercialized market for the arts thus threatens the core values of human artistic activity. This is a central reason why most countries provide substantial public subsidy of the arts. It is also why the wealthy subsidize, through philanthropy, the kinds of arts they consume—whether opera, art museums, or symphonies. These philanthropists realize that if arts organizations had to rely strictly on commercial success through the sale of tickets for performances, they would not be able to survive.

Religion and Spirituality

Religion and spirituality grapple with some of the deepest issues people confront: death, life, purpose, and ultimate meaning. All religions see these issues as transcending the mundane world of economic activity; religion is valued because of its importance in helping people come to terms with these matters. The distinctive value of religion is continually threatened by commercialization. The most notorious example, decried by many religious Christians, is the commercialization of Christmas. But perhaps even more profoundly, the commercialization of churches themselves—turning churches into profit-maximizing sellers of religion—threatens religious values.

The Value of a Human Life

Every society faces the problem of putting some kind of value on human life. In a society where highly competitive capitalist markets play a pervasive role in determining the value of things, the value of human life sometimes tends to be assimilated to market principles. After 9/11, when the U.S. government was figuring out how much monetary compensation should be given to the families of those who died in the destruction of the World Trade Center, the basic formula concerned the lost earnings of the people who died. In the Ford Pinto case, when Ford Motor Company was trying to figure out the costs and benefits of retrofitting the dangerous gas tanks, the company calculated the value of a human life in terms of the income lost because of death and the court costs they would face for wrongful death suits. This way of thinking about people flows naturally from the penetration of commercial thinking into everyday life.

Cultivation of Social Skills and Dispositions: Exit and Voice

Institutions do not just shape our values and preferences; they also significantly shape what might be called our strategic skills—our personal capacities to solve problems in particular ways. A useful way of thinking about this issue is with a contrast developed by the economist Albert Hirschman between *exit* and *voice* as two different ways of responding to an organization that does not perform as you would like.[5]

Exit means that if you don't like something, you leave, you quit, you exit. If you don't like your job, quit and get another one; if you don't like a university course, drop it and enroll in another one; if you don't like the country you live in, migrate to another; if you don't like a restaurant, go to another; if you don't like your marriage, get a divorce, and so forth. This is the way people deal with dissatisfactions in a market.

Voice, in contrast, means if you don't like something, you actively speak up, you try to change a policy, you try to improve a product. If you don't like your job, talk to the boss and fellow workers about improving conditions; if you don't like a course, negotiate with the professor to change what's going on; if you don't like the government, organize politically to change it; if you are unhappy in an intimate relationship, talk about it and try to work through the problems.

Markets encourage a style of dealing with problems through exit. Voice is difficult. It requires skills of negotiation, communication, and coalition building. This is hard. Exit is, by comparison, easy. Markets cultivate skills of exit, not of voice. The market model for getting what you want is

[5]Albert O. Hirschman, *Exit, Voice, and Loyalty* (Cambridge, MA: Harvard University Press, 1970).

shopping rather than community participation and deliberation. This model has very broad ramifications in the society at large. Consider marriage as a social institution. Finding a spouse is understood by many as a "marriage market" in which people shop for a partner. Is it any surprise that divorce is a common solution to marital dissatisfactions? If you don't like a marriage, you exit and shop for another spouse. (This is a great irony for social conservatives, who believe in both the sanctity of marriage and the unregulated competitive free market: their attack on state regulation of the market intensifies the sense of individualistic competition and exit strategies, which reinforces the idea of marriage as a competitive market.) Consider politics: Most people participate in politics as passive shoppers among political candidates, not as active participants in democratic deliberation. The political marketplace is entertaining, the media turn political conflict into a horse race, and democracy is reduced to a specialized form of consumption.

Of course, exit is an important way for people to deal with dissatisfactions, and it is an important value linked to negative freedom. The issue here is not that exit as such is undesirable, but that the dynamics of the market tend to increase the weight of exit in social problem solving, and the habits of the market tend to develop shopping skills and dispositions rather than the deliberation skills of voice. A healthy, democratic society with vibrant communities requires citizens to develop real capacities for active participation and engagement, and these are precisely the skills that the market does not reinforce.

*

This chapter has explored in general some of the ways that capitalist markets, left to their own devices, undermine certain core values they are thought to promote—especially freedom, efficiency, and prosperity. In the next five chapters, we explore these issues in more detail by examining a number of specific problems: the environment, transportation, consumerism, health care, and finance.

5

THE ENVIRONMENT

Most people are aware that we face a long list of environmental problems: air and water quality, depletion of natural resources (especially oil), toxic waste disposal, endangered species, and increasingly the threat of global warming. There is no longer much scientific debate over whether these are real problems whose solutions require some kind of collective, public response. Where people differ is in their beliefs about the underlying causes of these problems and the appropriate remedies. None of these problems, of course, are the result of some single master cause. They are all shaped by a complex array of economic, political, and cultural processes. In this chapter, we explore five important causal processes operating in contemporary American society that underlie these environmental problems: collective action failures, negative externalities, NIMBY (not in my backyard) movements, hyperconsumerism, and concentrations of corporate power. We will then look at perhaps the most pressing environmental challenge—global warming—and see how these processes play a role in both creating the problem and making it difficult to solve.

COLLECTIVE ACTION FAILURES

When economists study environmental problems, they emphasize two themes: collective action failures and negative externalities. Both of these, as explained in Chapter 4, are instances in which the actions of individuals and firms, pursuing their own interests in a strategic and rational way within markets, generate economic inefficiencies of various sorts.

In the realm of environmental issues, collective action failures are known as the tragedy of the commons. The phrase comes from the historic experience of farmers overgrazing the lands they shared in common, ultimately depleting the fertility of the land and reducing its capacity to feed livestock, but the idea refers to any depletion of a renewable resource through overuse.

In Chapter 4 we discussed an example of environmental collective action problems for capitalist firms in the depletion of the North Atlantic fishing banks through overfishing. These kinds of collective action failures also apply to the behavior of individuals. A good example for individuals is the problem of recycling. Many people rationalize their approach to the problem of recycling in the following way:

> I agree that recycling is a good thing because it will help conserve resources, and I will benefit from that. But I won't recycle, because it is too much trouble and my own wasting of resources won't really make that much difference. No one will be worse off because I don't recycle.

If everyone thinks like this, then no one will recycle and everyone is worse off. Suppose it costs you—in time, effort, and money—a total of $50 a year to recycle. If everyone recycles, in the long run you save on average $100 a year because of savings on landfills, slower depletion of resources, and so on. If everyone else recycles and you do not, your payoff is $100 because your failure to recycle is such a small part of the total. If you and everyone else recycle, your payoff is $50. If only you recycle, your payoff is negative: –$50; you have paid for the recycling, but it will have no long-term positive effect because no one else cooperates with you. If no one recycles, your payoff is $0. This is a classical free-rider problem, as illustrated in Figure 5.1.

If you are a rational, self-interested actor, your favored alternative is B; your second-best outcome is A, your third is D, and your least favored is C. If

FIGURE 5.1—Hypothetical recycling free-riding problem

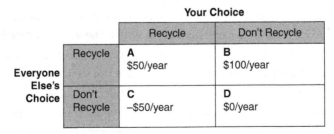

Note: The dollar amounts in the matrix are your long-term personal financial payoffs for different recycling choices.

everyone is just like you, then they will have the same preference order and would also choose B. But if everyone makes this choice, the world ends up in cell D.

This kind of behavior is certainly an element in many environmental problems: self-interested persons and firms want everyone else to be environmentally responsible and want to get a free ride on their good behavior—they want to benefit without making any personal sacrifice. This doesn't mean that they don't value a clean and sustainable environment, or even that they are unaware of environmental problems, but simply that they do not want to personally bear the costs of doing anything about it.

Solutions to this kind of collective action problem involving the environment are often relatively easy; in a prisoner's dilemma situation, the individuals involved can easily recognize that the outcome is suboptimal for their own self-interests. No one really has a vested interest in maintaining the collective action failure. In the example, if everyone has the preference ordering B-A-D-C, then each person prefers A to D—they prefer everyone, including themselves, to recycle rather than have no one recycling. Programs that make it easier for people to recycle (and so reduce the immediate time and expense they face), especially when participation is mandatory and enforced through some system of monitoring and fines, make the cooperation outcome—A—much more likely. Similarly, monitoring and enforcing fishing quotas can effectively solve the overfishing problem; and because in the long run this outcome is in the interests of everyone in the fishing industry, some system of regulation is broadly supported by fishing firms.

In the United States, many local communities have in fact adopted municipal recycling programs, supported by taxes and connected to city garbage pickup. These programs have helped stimulate a stronger market for the recycled materials, but they do not rely on market mechanisms to encourage recycling. They have resulted in a dramatic increase in recycling in the United States since the 1980s. Of course, some people might still oppose mandatory recycling on various grounds. For example, they might not believe it would work because evasion might be too easy, or they might be opposed to the government regulation on some ideological principle even though such regulations would benefit them. Still, if the only important cause of environmental problems was this kind of coordination problem among self-interested individuals and firms, the remedies would be fairly straightforward. The problem, however, is that much more is in play in solving environmental problems than simple collective action failures among rational, self-interested actors. The problem of negative externalities is also important, and because the beneficiaries of negative externalities are not themselves harmed by their own choices, they are more likely to resist regulation. And if they are also powerful, then this resistance is often effective.

NEGATIVE EXTERNALITIES

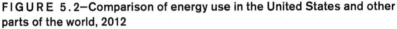

A negative externality, as explained in Chapter 4, is a negative effect of one's choices and actions on others. Like collective action failures, the problem of negative externalities concerns both the consumption choices of individuals and the production choices of capitalist firms.

An important example of environmental negative externalities caused by individuals concerns the problem of energy use. The United States contains about 5 percent of the world's population, but Americans consume about 20 percent of the world's energy (Figure 5.2). Much of this energy

FIGURE 5.2—Comparison of energy use in the United States and other parts of the world, 2012

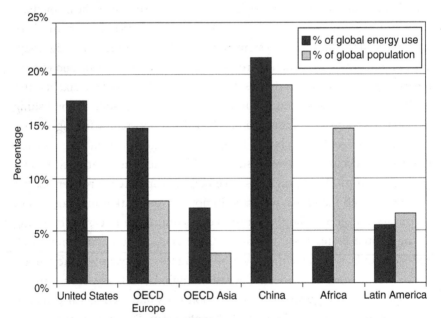

Note: Organisation for Economic Co-operation and Development (OECD) Asia is comprised of Japan, South Korea, and Australia/New Zealand; Latin America is comprised of Central and South America. In 2012, OECD Europe included Austria, Belgium, Czech Republic, Denmark, Estonia, Finland, France, Germany, Greece, Hungary, Iceland, Ireland, Italy, Luxembourg, the Netherlands, Norway, Poland, Portugal, Slovak Republic, Slovenia, Spain, Sweden, Switzerland, Turkey, and United Kingdom.

Source: International Energy Outlook, 2013. Table A1, "World Total Energy Consumption by Region," and Table A14, "World Population by Region."

consumption is of fossil fuels, and one thing we know for certain is that this resource is finite. If we continue burning fossil fuels to generate energy, eventually we will run out of this resource. The United States is a very rich country, and many people can afford to consume a great deal of fossil fuels at the current price; and so they do not give this issue much thought. They drive large, inefficient cars, leave their lights on, prefer private to public transportation, and in other ways help the United States consume more energy per capita than any other country in the world.

How is this pattern of energy consumption an example of a negative externality? The depletion of a nonrenewable resource through current consumption can be thought of as a *negative externality for future generations.* Future generations will have to pay more for fossil fuels because of the rate we are using up this resource today. As noted in Chapter 4, future generations do not participate in present choices about how to distribute the use of this resource over time. Imagine if people one hundred years from now could bid on the current price of oil: the price would surely be much higher than we see in existing markets, for it would reflect the future costs of extracting and processing a much scarcer resource. Of course, the problem of negative effects of our actions today on future generations is by no means unique to American society. It is inherent in the fact that human actions have long-term consequences. But this problem is especially acute in the United States because of the heavy reliance on market mechanisms for making long-term choices about patterns of consumption and production. Markets are simply incapable of factoring in such future consequences into present choices.

In a capitalist market economy such as the United States, environmental negative externalities are not just the result of consumers' selfishness and shortsightedness; they are also, crucially, the result of the strategic action of firms. As we explained in Chapter 4, investment decisions are made largely on the basis of profitability; effects on the environment enter into investment decisions only when they are experienced as direct costs by the investor. Thus, in general, *internal* pollution in a factory is controlled by the owner because failing to clean up oil spills on the shop floor is costly to the owner; but external pollution is another matter. In a competitive, profit-maximizing economic system, pollution is not just a random accident. There will, in general, be a tendency for the most profitable investments to be relatively polluting because they represent successful displacement of costs on others. Getting other people to shoulder some of their costs of production gives capitalist firms a competitive advantage; and thus, unless they are prevented from doing so, those firms are likely to disregard environmental negative externalities.

A few examples will illustrate this dynamic:

- *Nitrogen fertilizer and farming.* Farmers who use nitrogen fertilizers produce more at lower cost. This increases their rate of profit. Heavy use of nitrogen, however, often results in nitrogen runoff into rivers and lakes. The price of the fertilizer used by farmers does not reflect costs of the declining water quality of rivers and lakes or the costs of cleaning them up. If the price of such fertilizer to farmers fully incorporated these additional costs, then in many instances it would no longer be profit maximizing to use the fertilizer.[1]

- *Acid rain.* Coal-burning power plants in the Midwest emit a variety of pollutants into the atmosphere. Because of prevailing winds, the pollutants tend to drift eastward. Among these pollutants are sulfur dioxide and nitrogen oxides, which eventually mix with moisture and increase the acidity of rain in the eastern regions of the United States. In the United States, according to the Environmental Protection Agency, "roughly two-thirds of all sulfur dioxide and one-fourth of all nitrogen oxides come from electric power generation that relies on burning fossil fuels like coal."[2] The costs of this acid rain in the form of such things as degradation of forests and reduced longevity of exterior paints on buildings do not enter into the profit calculations of power companies.

- *Love Canal in New York.* One of the most notorious cases of environmental negative externalities generated by profit-maximizing strategies concerns the dumping of toxic waste into Love Canal near Buffalo, New York. For a period in the 1940s and 1950s, the Hooker Chemical and Plastics Corporation disposed of a variety of toxic wastes in a landfill adjoining Love Canal. The initial dumping was motivated simply by the desire to minimize the immediate costs of toxic waste disposal. It is unclear whether the decision makers actually knew the risks of this behavior, but in any event they had no incentive to figure them out. Over time, these toxic wastes leached into the surrounding area

---

[1] According to the website *Scorecard: The Pollution Information Site* (www.scorecard.org/; accessed Sept. 16, 2009), based on data reported by state governments, agricultural runoff is a principal source of impairment of water quality in rivers and streams in the United States, and the second most important source of impaired quality of lakes, reservoirs and ponds, and freshwater wetlands.

[2] www.epa.gov/acidrain/what/ (accessed Sept. 9, 2014).

and eventually polluted the adjoining canal. In the long term, this dumping imposed extraordinary private costs on people living in the area in the form of sickness, birth defects, and eventually the collapse of property values. The problems were compounded by later inaction from a government unwilling to publicly shoulder the costs of dealing with them.

The solutions to these and other examples of negative externalities nearly always require some form of public regulation that makes it more difficult for firms and individuals to displace costs on others. Where such regulations have been in place and enforced, they have generally had a significant impact on the problems they address. In the United States, the Environmental Protection Agency (EPA) is the principal government agency charged with the task of regulating various forms of pollution. Despite continual resistance by capitalist firms to such regulation, and a significant decline in enforcement budgets in the decades after 1980, the regulation of air and water pollution has had a positive effect on the air and water quality in the United States. Figure 5.3 presents data on the levels of the most common forms of air pollution from 1980 to 2010. The chart indicates about a 50 percent reduction in these pollutants. This does not mean that air quality has

FIGURE 5.3—Decline in air pollution, 1980–2012

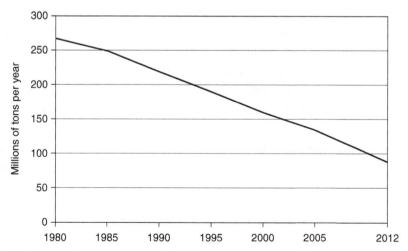

Note: Measure includes carbon monoxide (CO), lead, nitrogen oxide (NO), volatile organic compounds (VOC), particulate matter (PM), and sulfur dioxide (SO$_2$). Fire and dust are excluded because they are highly variable.

Source: U.S. Environmental Protection Agency, http://www.epa.gov/airtrends/sixpoll.html (accessed Sept. 22, 2014).

ceased to be a problem. The EPA reports that in 2012, a total of 142 million people in the United States—over half of the population—still lived in counties with air pollution above the level of the quality standards established by the Clean Air Act.[3] Still, regulations enforced against the spontaneous behavior of firms in the market have made a significant difference.

Historically, government regulation has mainly taken the form of laws and bureaucratic regulations directly enforced by the state. This situation does work pretty well for certain kinds of environmental problems, but not for all of them. More recently, a variety of new mechanisms for dealing with environmental negative externalities has been developed. For example, in some places a strategy known as "information-based monitoring" has been introduced. This is a policy of publishing the pollution levels of firms and widely publicizing a list of "bad actors." Because firms do not want their reputations tainted, they try to reduce their pollution to avoid being on the list.[4] Over time, this approach may cause firms to ratchet up their antipollution standards. Or, for another example, to reduce the emission of greenhouse gases, governments are creating "markets" in carbon emissions. The idea is that firms are allowed to emit a certain level of such gases, the level being determined by public policy goals about the aggregate level of emissions. Firms that emit less than this amount have "carbon emission credits," which they can sell to firms that emit more than the limit. If these credits are expensive enough, then this government-created market has the effect of "internalizing" the costs of the negative externality and thus creating an incentive for the firm to reduce emissions.

Both of these kinds of reforms have been touted as relying on the market to solve environmental problems and thus avoiding bureaucratic meddling by the state. This is an inaccurate way of understanding them. Both information-based monitoring and carbon trading still depend strongly on the state's capacity to gather and disseminate accurate information, create standards, and prevent cheating. Although they do use some market-like mechanisms to facilitate implementation of standards, these reforms would be ineffectual without strong state involvement. Counteracting environmental negative externalities always involves some kind of explicit intervention into the spontaneous behavior of people in markets.

---

[3] http://www.epa.gov/airtrends/sixpoll.html (accessed Sept. 16, 2009).
[4] For a discussion of this kind of policy, see Archon Fung, Mary Graham, and David Weil, *Full Disclosure: The Perils and Promise of Transparency* (New York: Cambridge University Press, 2008).

A SPECIAL KIND OF NEGATIVE EXTERNALITY: NIMBY

A special kind of negative externality occurs in the context of environmental problems; it concerns the ways in which political and economic power can be used to displace the costs of environmental problems onto vulnerable groups. This negative externality is sometimes called the NIMBY (not in my backyard) problem. NIMBY problems occur when a geographical location has to be found for something that people don't want near them: radioactive waste dumps, halfway houses for the mentally ill, fertilizer plants that process manure, and the like. Everyone agrees that we need a way of disposing of toxic wastes, but no one wants a hazardous waste disposal facility in their backyard. In such a situation, when public authorities make decisions about where to locate such facilities, they are often very responsive to pressure from powerful groups and individuals. The pressure is often backed up by rational economic arguments: a toxic waste disposal facility will adversely affect property values, so it makes economic sense to locate the facility in places away from rich neighborhoods and closer to poor neighborhoods. This solution is "cost effective" from a certain narrow economic point of view. Furthermore, it is easier to locate the facility closer to groups that are relatively marginalized politically and less likely to have effective political connections—and in many cities, this means poor neighborhoods with high concentrations of blacks and Hispanics. A 1984 report to the California Waste Management Board on "Political Difficulties Facing Waste-to-Energy Conversion Plant Siting" explicitly recommends avoiding middle- and upper-income neighborhoods for this reason:

> Certain types of people are likely to participate in politics, either by virtue of their issue awareness or their financial resources, or both. Members of middle or higher-socioeconomic strata (a composite index of level of education, occupational prestige, and income) are more likely to organize into effective groups to express their political interests and views. All socioeconomic groupings tend to resent the nearby siting of major facilities, but the middle and upper-socioeconomic strata possess better resources to effectuate their opposition. Middle and higher-socioeconomic strata neighborhoods should not fall at least within the one-mile and five-mile radii of the proposed site.[5]

[5] Cerrell Associates, Inc., "Political Difficulties Facing Waste-to-Energy Conversion Plant Siting," prepared for California Waste Management Board (State of California, 1984), p. 26. Available at http://www.ejnet.org/ej/cerrell.pdf (accessed Sept. 9, 2014). We were made aware of this document in a presentation by China Miéville at an Earth Day conference in Madison, Wisconsin, April 2014.

In the United States, many decisions of this sort are made locally. On the one hand this is a good thing, for it means that basic choices about land use are often subjected to democratic processes involving the people affected by the decision. This practice is consistent with democratic values. On the other hand, because of the significant inequalities in power within such local democratic processes, this kind of decentralized, local decision making encourages NIMBY movements against things like hazardous waste facilities. As Figure 5.4 indicates, the outcome of these processes is a concentration of hazardous waste facilities in neighborhoods with a disproportionately high minority population. In the year 2000, neighborhoods that were located within a 3-km radius of a hazardous waste facility had a racial composition of 56 percent nonwhite and 44 percent white residents. Neighborhoods that were farther than 3 km from such facilities were 70 percent white and only 30 percent nonwhite. Research indicates that these kinds of racial inequalities in environmental conditions are also likely to affect health. A study of the racial composition of census tracts in California with high and

FIGURE 5.4—Racial composition of neighborhoods with hazardous waste facilities, 2000

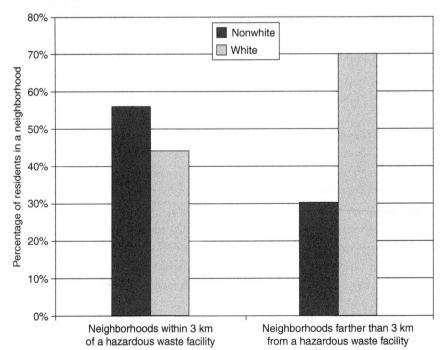

Source: Robert D. Bullard, Paul Mohai, Robin Saha, and Beverly Wright, *Toxic Wastes and Race at Twenty: 1987–2007* (Cleveland, OH: United Church of Christ, 2007).

FIGURE 5.5—Racial composition of census tracts in California by cancer risk from toxins in the air, 2000

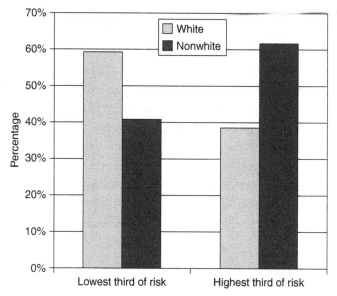

Source: Manuel Pastor, Rachel Morello-Frosch, and James L. Sadd, "The Air is Always Cleaner on the Other Side: Race, Space, and Ambient Air Toxic Exposures in California," *Journal of Urban Affairs* 27(2005): figure 2, p. 137.

low risks of cancer from toxins in the air showed that over 60 percent of residents in the high-risk tracts were nonwhite, but only 40 percent in the low-risk tracts were nonwhite (Figure 5.5).

Negative externalities are thus not simply a problem of harm to the environment caused by individuals and firms acting in their own interests and displacing costs on others. They are also the result of political processes that direct those costs toward specific groups of vulnerable people. A full social agenda for dealing with environmental issues, therefore, must concern itself with environmental injustice and environmental racism, not simply with environmental sustainability.

HYPERCONSUMERISM

An underlying engine of environmental problems is entrenched in our society and very difficult to counteract: consumerism. We will discuss this issue in much more detail in Chapter 7, when we examine shopping and consumer society. But because it is so deeply connected to environmental problems, we briefly introduce the issue here.

Consumerism is a broad term that covers a variety of senses in which an economy and a culture become oriented to consumption. Market economies have a tendency to foster consumerism—when people produce for a market, they need to find buyers of their products. Capitalism intensifies this general tendency because capitalist firms compete with each other, and their profits depend in significant ways on their ability to increase their sales. Capitalist firms, therefore, engage in all sorts of strategies to encourage people to increase their consumption, not merely buy their specific products.

Consumerism is a property of all capitalist countries, but many countries have processes in place to somewhat diminish its intensity, such as high taxes to support public goods and rules that create shorter workweeks and longer vacations. American capitalism, in these terms, is what might be called hyperconsumerist. For a host of reasons we will examine in Chapter 7, in the contemporary United States, ever increasing personal consumption is seen as a cultural ideal. This cultural ideal is ecologically disastrous: a permanent growth in consumption is a recipe for environmental devastation and is not sustainable forever.

CONCENTRATIONS OF POWER AND THE ENVIRONMENT

In the analysis of any social problem—in this case environmental problems—it is important to distinguish between the generative causes of the problem on the one hand and the obstacles to implementing an effective solution on the other. Problems and solutions need not be symmetrical: If you observe a person with a missing leg, you need to explain both how the leg was lost and why a prosthetic has not been acquired to replace it. The leg may have been lost because of an accident, but the absence of a substitute could be due to a lack of medical insurance. You might have a headache because of stresses at school, but the explanation for not getting rid of the headache might be that you lack an aspirin. The solution to a problem does not necessarily mean eliminating the cause: the cure can neutralize the effects of the cause rather than eliminate the cause itself. In the case of environmental problems, the mechanisms generating the problems in the first place may be various kinds of collective action failures and negative externalities. The principal obstacles to solving the problem, however, may be strategies of powerful actors, especially business corporations, in which they effectively use their power to block solutions. Consider two examples involving issues of energy use and development: the regulations on automobile energy efficiency and the development of alternative energy sources.

Automobiles are a central cause of the depletion of fossil fuels as well as a major source of carbon emissions influencing global warming. The energy efficiency of automobiles thus has considerable environmental importance. The distribution of efficiency levels among automobiles is the result of three main factors: the preferences and choices of individual consumers as they weigh the trade-offs among alternative properties of automobiles; the designs engineered by automakers and made available to consumers; and the regulations imposed on automakers that force them to seek appropriate innovations to meet these standards. In the United States, large automobile corporations have used their power to block higher standards because, in general, the most profitable cars to produce are not the most energy efficient. Most of the time, this strategy has had the effect of keeping the issue of government-enforced efficiency standards completely off the political agenda. But automotive efficiency standards occasionally do become an issue, as they did in 2007, and then the automobile corporations actively mobilize to block the standards or at least minimize the changes.

The role of powerful actors in obstructing certain solutions to environmental issues is particularly blatant regarding the development of alternative energy sources. Many environmentalists believe that renewable energy sources—especially wind and solar energy—should be the highest priority for energy development. Defenders of existing energy sources—especially coal, oil, and nuclear power—counter that these renewable sources are too expensive and that if they were profitable, then the market would direct investments in their direction. Their mantra is "Let the market decide." But these critics of renewable energy ignore the enormous level of direct and indirect government subsidy to other energy sources, especially oil and nuclear energy, that has resulted from the exercise of power by corporations in these sectors. It is a myth that the choice of energy alternatives is actually the result of free market mechanisms; instead, energy development has been heavily subsidized by government programs, and the distribution and magnitudes of these subsidies are the result of the exercise of power:

- The oil industry was directly encouraged by government policy, particularly through a wide range of generous tax breaks—especially for oil exploration. Every time an effort is made to close these tax loopholes, the oil industry mobilizes its opposition, claiming that these subsidies are essential for national security and a stable supply of oil.
- The nuclear industry would not exist without systematic government sponsorship. The key issue here is the rules established by the state for *limited liability for claims in nuclear accidents*. Without such rules, the

industry would not have been able to afford market-based insurance for accidents.

- In the period 1950–2006, the total amount of government subsidies directly connected to energy in the United States came to over $726 billion (2006 dollars). Of this total, 50 percent went to oil and natural gas, 13 percent to coal, 11 percent to hydroelectric power, 9 percent to nuclear power, and only 6 percent to renewable energy (wind and solar).[6] This allocation of subsidies partially reflected the power of the economic interests tied to each form of energy, not market forces.

The profile of energy use in the American economy today is thus not the result of spontaneous, impersonal operation of the market and consumer preferences; rather, it has been heavily shaped by the strategies of powerful corporations using the state to further its ends.

Occasionally, of course, the government does step in and impose new environmental regulations over the objections of powerful corporations. These regulations help define new "rules of the game" within which markets and corporations must operate. The creation of the Environmental Protection Agency (EPA) in 1970 was one such example. In the late 1960s, there was growing awareness in the United States of the need to protect the environment and a realization that the market by itself would not do this. So the EPA was created during the Nixon administration. By 1980 its activities had expanded considerably, and spending on environmental regulation amounted to nearly 1 percent of the total federal budget. Businesses objected, and in the following decades mobilized their power to undermine the agency and block its regulations. The issue was not so much that laws have been removed—although this has sometimes happened—but that their enforcement has eroded. By the early twenty-first century, the EPA accounted for only 0.4 percent of the federal budget, and by the 2012 budget, 0.35 percent (Figure 5.6). It is not enough to get effective environmental protections on the books; it is also essential to allocate adequate resources to the responsible agencies so they can actually implement the regulations and effectively monitor compliance. A central strategy of powerful business interests in blocking effective government action is to starve the regulatory machinery of such resources.

[6] Management Information Services, Inc., for the Nuclear Energy Institute, *Analysis of Federal Expenditures for Energy Development* (Washington, DC: Management Information Services, Inc., 2008), 1.

FIGURE 5.6—The Environmental Protection Agency budget as a percentage of the total U.S. federal budget

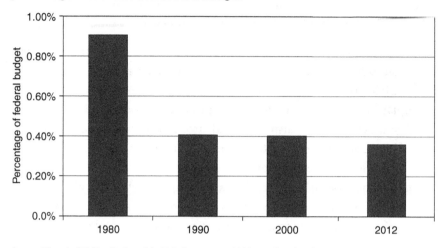

Source: *Historical Tables: Budget of the U.S. Government.* Table 4.1, "Outlays by Agency, 1962–2018."

GLOBAL CLIMATE CHANGE

Perhaps the most serious environmental challenge facing the world today is climate change. In popular discussions this problem is mainly identified with global warming—the gradual increase in global temperatures that began in the first part of the twentieth century and has been accelerating in recent decades—but the phenomenon concerns other changes in the global environment as well, in particular ocean acidification, rising sea levels, and weather pattern disruptions. In some parts of the world these transformations bring the prospect of real catastrophe and massive human suffering. This is particularly the case for poor countries in which large numbers of people live in low-lying coastal areas, such as in Bangladesh, where tens of millions of people are likely to be displaced by rising sea levels by the end of the twenty-first century. But even where the effects will not be so dire, climate change, if nothing is done, will create enormous disruptions of life and well-being.

In what follows we will first document the main trends in climate change and the underlying physical cause: the increase in carbon dioxide in the atmosphere created by human activity. We will then briefly discuss the kinds of public policies that might help to counteract these trends. This will be followed by an examination of how the five general social processes we have been discussing in this chapter help us understand the obstacles to solving the problem of climate change.

The Basic Facts of Climate Change

The basic facts of climate change are no longer in dispute among scientists. The key facts are these:

1. Global atmospheric temperatures have been rising more or less steadily since the early twentieth century. They are now roughly 1.4°F higher than they were a century ago (Figure 5.7).
2. During this same period, concentrations of carbon dioxide in the atmosphere have also increased, from roughly 290 parts per million (ppm) to around 390 ppm in 2012 (Figure 5.8). In 2014 the concentrations exceeded 400 ppm.[7]
3. Carbon dioxide is the best-known example of what are called "greenhouse gases," that is, gases in the atmosphere that absorb heat. Other greenhouse gases include methane, nitrous oxide, and ozone.

FIGURE 5.7—Global temperature rise, 1880–2008

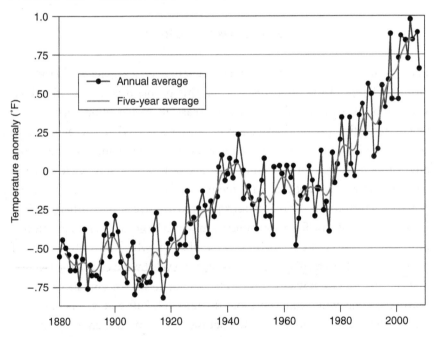

Note: The graph indicates the number of degrees Fahrenheit above or below the average temperature in the period 1880–2008 (zero on the graph).

Source: http://ete.cet.edu/gcc/?/resourcecenter/slideshow/3/1 (NASA website, Exploring the Environment: Global Climate Change). Based on an image created by Robert A. Rohde/Global Warming Art.

[7] Report from the Earth System Research Laboratory Global Monitoring Division, National Oceanic and Atmospheric Administration, http://www.esrl.noaa.gov/gmd/ccgg/trends/weekly.html (accessed April 23, 2014).

FIGURE 5.8—Global temperature rise and carbon dioxide

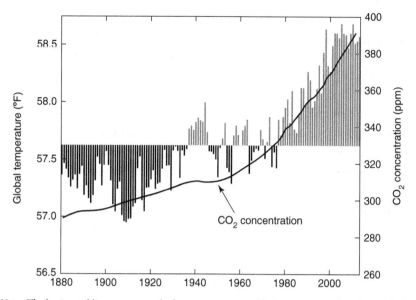

Note: The horizontal line represents the long-term average global temperature. Bars below the line indicate temperatures below that average; bars above the line show temperatures above the average. The black line shows atmospheric carbon dioxide concentrations in parts per million (scale on the right).

Sources: Original graph: U.S. Global Change Research Program (2014) "National Climate Assessment," available at https://nca3.cicsnc.org/report/our-changing-climate/observed-change (accessed Sept. 18, 2014). CO_2 concentration data: "Earth Policy Institute Atmospheric Carbon Dioxide Concentration, 2000–2013," available at http://www.earth-policy.org/data_center/C23/ (accessed Sept. 18, 2014). Global annual average temperature (as measured over both land and oceans) data: NOAA National Climatic Data Center, "Merged Land–Ocean Surface Temperature Analysis," available at https://www.ncdc.noaa.gov/data-access/marineocean-data/extended-reconstructed-sea-surface-temperature-ersst-v3b/mlost (accessed Sept. 18, 2014).

4. The rise in CO_2 in the atmosphere is to a substantial extent the result of human activity, especially the burning of fossil fuels: coal, oil, and gas. CO_2 is one of the by-products of burning carbon-based fuels, and when it is released into the atmosphere it contributes to increased atmospheric concentrations of this gas. CO_2 levels in the atmosphere also vary over time for reasons unrelated to humans; volcanic eruptions, for example, can affect atmospheric CO_2. Nevertheless, due to the enormous amount of combustion of fossil fuels over the past two centuries, there is no doubt among scientists that most of the increase in carbon dioxide in the atmosphere is the result of human activity.

The combination of these four facts—(1) global temperatures have risen over the past century, (2) CO_2 concentrations in the atmosphere have also risen during the same period, (3) CO_2 is a greenhouse gas, and (4) human activity has generated most of the increase in atmospheric concentrations of CO_2—suggests that the rise in global temperatures is, to a significant extent, the result of human-generated increases in concentrations of greenhouse gases, especially CO_2. This is referred to as *anthropogenic climate change*. While it is difficult, because of the complexity of the atmospheric system, to give a precise estimate of the magnitude of the impact of human-generated CO_2 on the global temperature, there is nearly universal agreement among scientists that it is a significant contributor. A paper in the *Proceedings of the National Academy of Sciences* published in 2010 states the following:

> (i) 97–98% of the climate researchers most actively publishing in the field surveyed here support the tenets of ACC [Anthropogenic Climate Change] outlined by the Intergovernmental Panel on Climate Change, and (ii) the relative climate expertise and scientific prominence of the researchers unconvinced of ACC are substantially below that of the convinced researchers.[8]

This central conclusion—that the human activity of generating energy by burning fossil fuels is the primary cause of increasing CO_2 in the atmosphere and this, in turn, is the primary cause of rising temperatures—underwrites a series of predictions about the future. Two of these are presented in Figures 5.9 and 5.10.

The first of these graphs shows the predicted changes over time in average global temperatures under two contrasting scenarios, a low-emission scenario and a high-emission scenario. In the low-emission scenario, drastic action is taken right now to lower greenhouse gas emission. Temperatures continue to rise because of the cumulative effects of past carbon emissions, but global warming levels off around the middle of the twenty-first century. In the high-emission scenario, where nothing significant is done to curtail the increasing concentrations of atmospheric CO_2, global temperatures keep rising rapidly into the future.

Figure 5.10 presents a similar picture for rises in sea levels. Global warming affects sea levels through two mechanisms: first, warm water has greater volume than cold water; and second, warmer summers will result in increased melting of ice at the poles, particularly since temperature increases

---

[8] William R. L. Anderegg, James Prall, Jacob Harold, and Stephen Schnieder, "Expert Credibility in Climate Change," *Proceedings of the National Academy of Sciences USA*, 107, no. 27 (July 6, 2010): 12107. Available at http://www.pnas.org/content/107/27/12107.full (accessed July 16, 2014).

FIGURE 5.9—Temperature rise scenarios

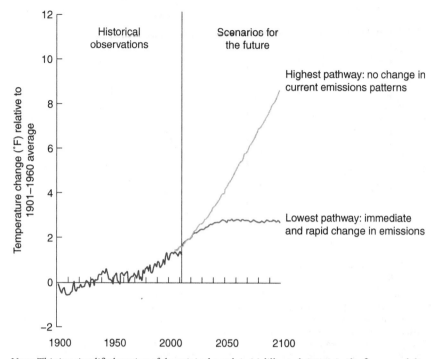

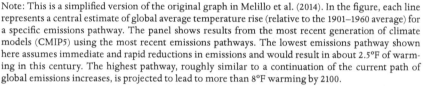

Note: This is a simplified version of the original graph in Melillo et al. (2014). In the figure, each line represents a central estimate of global average temperature rise (relative to the 1901–1960 average) for a specific emissions pathway. The panel shows results from the most recent generation of climate models (CMIP5) using the most recent emissions pathways. The lowest emissions pathway shown here assumes immediate and rapid reductions in emissions and would result in about 2.5°F of warming in this century. The highest pathway, roughly similar to a continuation of the current path of global emissions increases, is projected to lead to more than 8°F warming by 2100.

Source: Jerry M. Melillo, Terese (T.C.) Richmond, and Gary W. Yohe, Eds., *2014: Climate Change Impacts in the United States: The Third National Climate Assessment.* U.S. Global Change Research Program, 841 pp. Figure 2.4 (p. 26) doi:10.7930/J0Z31WJ2. Available at http://nca2014.globalchange .gov/ (accessed Aug. 5, 2014).

from global warming tend to be greater toward the poles than at the equator. Because of the effects of tides and other factors, the degree to which sea levels will rise will vary quite a bit around the world; the rise will be much greater in some coastal areas than in others. But if significant polar melting occurs, all coastal areas will be affected. Figure 5.10 presents scenarios for global sea rise in coming decades. If there is no significant reduction in carbon emissions and the highest-rise scenario occurs, then significant parts of coastline in certain parts of the United States will be below sea level. Figure 5.11 indicates possible effects on coastal areas in the southeastern part of the United States if there is even a one-meter increase in sea levels. Especially given the additional risks of severe flooding caused by hurricanes in

FIGURE 5.10—Global mean sea-level rise scenarios, 1900–2100

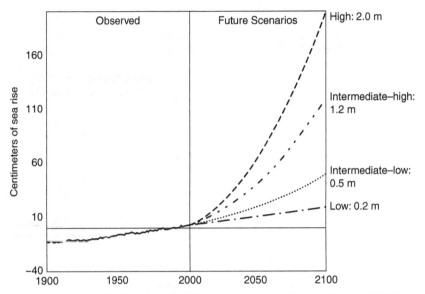

Note: Present mean sea level (MSL) for the U.S. coasts is determined from the National Tidal Datum Epoch (NTDE) provided by National Oceanic and Atmospheric Administration (NOAA). The NTDE is calculated using tide gauge observations from 1983–2001. Therefore, the mid-point 1992 is used as a starting point for the projected curves. The intermediate-high scenario is an average of the high end of ranges of global mean sea-level rise (SLR) reported by several studies using semi-empirical approaches. The intermediate-low scenario is the global mean SLR projection from the IPCC AR4 at 95% confidence interval.

Source: Adam Parris et al. 2012. *Global Sea Level Rise Scenarios for the United States National Climate Assessment*. NOAA Tech Memo OAR CPO-1. 37 pp. Figure 10 (p. 12). Available at http://scenarios .globalchange.gov/sites/default/files/NOAA_SLR_r3_0.pdf (accessed Aug. 4, 2014).

this region, such a rise in sea levels would make significant parts of existing metropolitan areas in this region uninhabitable.

Beyond rising temperatures and sea levels, climate change driven by carbon emissions poses many additional serious problems. Since warm air can hold more water, global warming is likely to generate greater rainfall in some regions as well as more frequent periods of intense rain. In the United States, heavy precipitation events (defined as a two-day total of rain that is exceeded on average only once in a five-year period) have increased every decade since the 1950s.[9] But global warming will also reduce rainfall in some regions and create more frequent droughts. In the United States this will especially affect the Southwest.[10] Warmer air is also predicted to lead to more extreme weather events like tornadoes and hurricanes. The Geophysical Fluid Dynamics Laboratory in the National Oceanic and

[9] *Federal Advisory Committee Draft Climate Assessment*, released January 11, 2013, 48. Available at http://nca2014.globalchange.gov/report (accessed Aug. 11, 2014).
[10] Ibid., 57–58.

FIGURE 5.11—Effects of sea rise on U.S. coastal areas

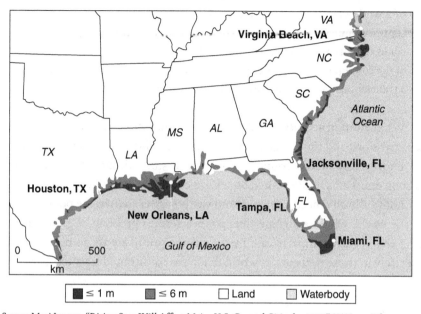

Source: Mari Jensen, "Rising Seas Will Affect Major U.S. Coastal Cities by 2100," *UANews*, February 15, 2011. Available at http://uanews.org/story/rising-seas-will-affect-major-us-coastal-cities-2100 (accessed July 16, 2014).

Atmospheric Administration (NOAA) estimates that by the end of the twenty-first century, the frequency of intense hurricanes (classified as category 4 or 5) such as Hurricane Katrina and Hurricane Sandy are likely to increase by over 75 percent compared to the period 2001–2020.[11] Globally, these changes in rainfall, drought, and air temperature will dramatically change certain natural habitats and could contribute to species extinctions. These climate changes are likely to also significantly affect the productivity of different agricultural regions. While in some specific regions they could increase productivity, these changes will be disruptive of traditional agricultural practices everywhere. Especially in the poorer regions of the world, this situation is likely to increase pressures for mass migration.

Increased CO_2 in the atmosphere also contributes to increased acidification of the oceans, threatening many forms of marine life. As reported in the *Christian Science Monitor* in 2010:

At least 19 percent of the world's coral reefs are already gone, including some 50 percent of those in the Caribbean. An additional 15 percent could be dead within 20 years, according to the National Oceanic and Atmospheric

[11] Ibid., 62.

Administration. Old Dominion University professor Kent Carpenter, director of a worldwide census of marine species, warned that if global warming continues unchecked, all corals could be extinct within 100 years. "You could argue that a complete collapse of the marine ecosystem would be one of the consequences of losing corals," Carpenter said. "You're going to have a tremendous cascade effect for all life in the oceans."[12]

While human activity throughout the world contributes to carbon dioxide emissions and thus to global warming, the contribution per person varies enormously across countries. As Figure 5.12 indicates, the per capita carbon emissions in the United States are considerably higher than in other economically advanced countries and vastly higher than in the poorer parts of the world. Climate change thus poses a serious problem of global injustice: the negative impacts of climate change are likely to be most severe precisely in those parts of the world that have contributed least to the rising

FIGURE 5.12—CO$_2$ emissions per capita, 2012

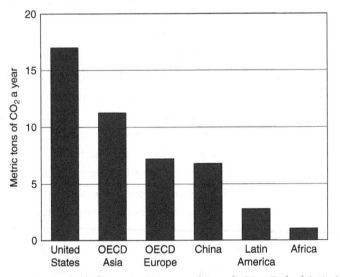

Note: OECD Asia is comprised of Japan, South Korea, and Australia/New Zealand. Latin America is comprised of Central and South America. In 2012, OECD Europe included Austria, Belgium, Czech Republic, Denmark, Estonia, Finland, France, Germany, Greece, Hungary, Iceland, Ireland, Italy, Luxembourg, the Netherlands, Norway, Poland, Portugal, Slovak Republic, Slovenia, Spain, Sweden, Switzerland, Turkey, and United Kingdom.

Source: International Energy Outlook 2013. Table A10, "World Carbon Dioxide Emissions by Region," and Table A14, "World Population by Region."

[12] Brian Skoloff, "Death of Coral Reefs Could Devastate Nations," Associated Press, March 26, 2010.

concentrations of CO_2. And since the United States has so disproportionately contributed to the problem, the United States should be at the forefront of seeking solutions. It is not.

Policies That Could Potentially Counter Global Warming

There is a wide range of policies that, if adopted, would significantly slow and perhaps eventually reverse the growth in carbon emissions in the atmosphere. Here are a few:

- A range of policies to significantly increase the costs of carbon emissions. There are many technical ways of doing this, but they all ultimately boil down to a high tax on the use of carbon-based fuels. If the price is high enough, then there would be strong incentives for investors to switch to non-carbon-based energy production and for people to use that energy when it becomes available. Such policies would need to be combined with various kinds of subsidies to ensure that low-income people are not disproportionately harmed by rising energy costs.
- Public investment in the full range of non-carbon energy sources.
- Greatly increased public funding for research on energy alternatives.
- Massive public investment in public transportation systems to make it feasible for people to switch from primary reliance on automobiles to less energy-intensive forms of transport.
- Retrofitting of buildings for energy efficiency.

All these policies are economically feasible in the sense that in a rich country like the United States, resources could be reallocated from current uses to make them possible. But all of them face significant obstacles created by the basic political economic institutions of American society.

Social Processes Underlying Climate Change and Obstructing Solutions

Let us now return to the social processes connected to environmental problems and see how each of these processes bears on the problem of climate change.

Hyperconsumerism

Perhaps the most obvious social process implicated in global warming is hyperconsumerism. As we will see in Chapter 7, consumerism connected to endless growth and the expansion of markets is an intrinsic dynamic in capitalist economies. Every firm is trying to maximize profits, and this means producing more and selling more. In the aggregate this generates economic growth, and since economic growth in a capitalist market economy is necessary for creating jobs and improving the livelihoods of ordinary people, everyone has an interest in encouraging this dynamic. Endless economic growth would not matter so much for the environment if it did not mean greater extraction of natural resources and use of fossil fuels, but it does. And so long as this is the case, economic growth and consumerism necessarily mean increasing concentrations of atmospheric carbon dioxide. Of course, there are many poor people in the world, especially in economically underdeveloped countries, who are not hyperconsumers, and for them, an improvement in basic material consumption is a necessary condition to live flourishing lives. But this is simply not the case for a majority of people in the rich countries of the world. As Naomi Klein put it, "At its core [climate change] is a crisis born of overconsumption by the comparatively wealthy, which means the world's most manic consumers are going to have to consume less."[13]

Collective Action Failures

Collective action failures figure in the problem of global warming in two different ways: at the level of individuals and their choices, and at the level of governments. First, in terms of individuals, any given person's contribution to greenhouse gas emissions is small, and drastically reducing such emissions, at least for people in rich countries, can entail considerable sacrifice. If you only care about your own advantage, you will not bother making the sacrifice even if you are convinced that global warming is caused by greenhouse gases. Your best option (given these selfish preferences) is to be a free rider. Even if you are willing to make the necessary sacrifices in order to significantly reduce your contribution to greenhouse gases, the problem will remain acute unless most people are also willing to behave in this way. And since most people do not seem willing to do so, there seems little point in your unilaterally making the sacrifice. As in many cases of collective action failure by individuals, the best solution to this problem is to change the calculation of individuals by changing the costs and benefits of their choices. This typically requires the state to take action.

[13] Naomi Klein, "The Change Within," *The Nation*, May 12, 2014, p. 20.

To deal with climate change effectively, state action is necessary. This, however, poses a second kind of collective action problem: there are many states in the world, and they are all engaged in a kind of super-game of states trying to advance their own national interests.[14] Countries can be tempted to be free riders on the sacrifices of others, especially if this gives their businesses competitive advantages in global markets. In the absence of a coherent global government to impose rules on states, it can be difficult to get high levels of compliance with efforts at raising global norms of environmental regulations. In such a situation it is especially important for the richest and most powerful countries to take the lead and set an example. The United States has consistently refused to ratify climate change treaties and adopt higher global standards.

▥ Negative Externalities

Negative externalities are at the very core of environmental problems. Particularly in capitalist economies, where profit-maximizing strategies lead firms to continually try to displace costs onto others, environmental negative externalities are a pervasive problem. In the case of climate change, however, the problem of negative externalities gets a little complicated since, ultimately, climate change will affect everyone, even those whose activities have caused the problem. Still, there are two aspects of carbon emissions that can be described as a problem of negative externalities.

First, the negative effects of global warming will be felt much more severely in the parts of the world that have not contributed to the problem: it is energy use in the developed world that has generated rising greenhouse gas concentrations, but it is the underdeveloped regions of the world that will bear the heaviest costs. At least for the moment, the benefits of carbon emissions are concentrated in one part of the world while the future costs are concentrated in another.

Still, the costs eventually will be significant even in the developed world. After all, building sea walls around Manhattan to prevent inundations from rising sea levels and hurricanes will be very costly. Increasingly severe weather events will create havoc in the United States, not just in the tropics. This leads us to the second peculiarity of negative externalities of carbon

---

[14] The idea of national interests is a pretty murky one, especially when it comes to things like global warming. Does this idea refer to the interests of all the people in a nation? To the elites? To state officials? Or what? The nature of the global collective action problem will vary depending on exactly how one answers these questions.

emissions: the time horizon of the negative effects of carbon emissions relative to the current benefits.

Time horizons play a role in all sorts of problems in human decision making. Consider the simple problem of whether to eat the extra piece of cake when you know you have a problem controlling your weight. The pleasure is immediate but the negative consequences are in the future. This is what is sometimes called the problem of "weakness of will"—not giving enough weight to the future consequences of present actions. This is partially why people often do not save enough for retirement and why they do not exercise enough to stay fit.

In the case of carbon emissions, even if carbon emissions are reduced today, it will make only a small difference in global warming in, say, the next ten years. In fact, even if we significantly cut carbon emissions immediately, global warming would continue for a while due to the cumulative effect of past emissions. To decisively change the trajectory of climate change would require quite drastic action today. This would include major new initiatives by the state to change patterns of energy use by raising the costs of fossil fuel (through taxes or other policies), subsidizing non-carbon-based energy, and making massive public investments in new forms of energy infrastructure, public transportation, and much more. All of this would cost a great deal and require significant state intervention in the market. From the point of view of profit-maximizing investors, the question then becomes: Is it worth paying these costs now for a reduction in carbon emissions and global warming in the future? Or should these costs be "kicked down the road" to be dealt with by people in the future? The key issue, then, is the relationship between the time horizon in which investors and firms calculate their profits and the time horizons in which the costs of curtailing carbon emissions today will have a sufficiently positive impact on profits in the future. If the time horizons of investors and firms were fifty years, they would all support concerted action to curtail carbon emissions. But when time horizons are only a few years long, displacing costs onto the future—what can be called a temporal negative externality—is the best option.

NIMBY Movements and Global Warming
In one sense, the fact that people in poor countries in the tropics are likely to bear the heaviest costs of global warming is an example of "not in my backyard"—wealthy people or countries make environmental choices in one part of the world with heavy long-term costs that are experienced by people in another part of the world. The difference from ordinary NIMBY

movements is that in the case of global warming, in the longer term nearly everyone will experience at least some of those costs and disruptions, so it is not exactly like siting toxic waste disposal sites in poor neighborhoods.

One way in which NIMBY movements have played a role in global warming is through protests over the siting of wind turbines. Wind turbines are one of the promising technologies for producing electricity without generating any greenhouse gas emissions. In Denmark in 2012, wind turbines generated 30 percent of the domestic electricity supply, compared to only 3.5 percent of national electricity supply in the United States.[15] Still, in the United States there has been significant growth in wind turbines in recent years. In 2012, for example, 43 percent of new U.S. electricity generation capacity was in the form of wind turbines. This growth has been impeded in some places, however, by protests over the siting of wind farms. People complain that wind farms spoil the view or that they endanger wildlife.

One of the more successful efforts at impeding wind farm development occurred in Nantucket over the Cape Wind project. The project began in 2001 with a plan to build a large wind farm off the coast of Nantucket, in Nantucket Sound. It was immediately opposed by a coalition of organizations and individuals, the Alliance to Protect Nantucket Sound. Some people supporting the alliance, like the oil billionaire William Koch, were simply opposed to government subsidies to wind energy regardless of where the turbines were located, but others were mainly opposed to the location of the wind farm. In particular, many opponents of the wind farm were wealthy landowners with property facing Nantucket Sound. While in 2014 it appears that the Cape Wind project will be able to begin construction, the efforts of the alliance delayed the project for years in court cases and other forms of protest. Like all NIMBY movements, the opponents of the wind farm have plausible arguments about negative effects. Residents of wealthy neighborhoods, after all, are correct in saying that a toxic waste disposal unit in their neighborhood would lower property values. Similarly, the homeowners and vacationers in Nantucket are correct that a wind farm would change the pristine view of the ocean.[16] Given the magnitude of the environmental problem and the need for an energy transition to carbon-

---

[15] *IEA Wind Annual Report 2012*. Available at http://www.ieawind.org/annual_reports _PDF/2012.html# (accessed July 16, 2014). USA, p. 160; Denmark, p. 78.

[16] It should be noted that what in one period is viewed as an eyesore can over time become part of the visual diversity of a landscape. When the Eiffel Tower was first built, Parisians hated it and wanted it torn down right after the World's Fair for which it was built. Now it is an iconic site of Paris.

free renewable energy, wind energy needs to be part of the solution and wind farms have to be in someone's "backyard."

Concentrations of Power

In the end, perhaps the biggest obstacle to seriously tackling the problem of climate change is the connection between power and the economic interests at stake in the transition away from a fossil fuel–based energy system. The scale of the economic interests connected to the continued exploitation and use of fossil fuels is enormous. One way of measuring the magnitude of these interests, suggested by Christopher Hayes, is to estimate the amount of wealth that the current owners of fossil fuel reserves would lose if we decided to limit the future burning of fossil fuels in order to avoid climate catastrophe:

> The Carbon Tracker Initiative, a consortium of financial analysts and environmentalists, set out to tally the amount of carbon contained in the proven fossil fuel reserves of the world's energy companies and major fossil fuel–producing countries. That is, the total amount of carbon we know in the ground that we can, with present technology, extract, burn and put into the atmosphere. The number that the Carbon Tracker Institute came up with is 2,795 gigatons. . . . Given the fluctuations of fuel prices, it's a bit tricky to put an exact price tag on how much money all that unexcavated carbon would be worth, but one financial analysis puts the price at somewhere in the ballpark of $20 trillion.[17]

That is an immense amount of wealth. Even if this is an overestimate by a factor of two or three, the magnitude is still huge. Any serious effort to shift away from a carbon-based energy system means leaving much of that wealth in the ground.[18] It is no surprise that the owners of this vast wealth resist public policies that potentially threaten its value.

---

[17] Christopher Hayes, "The New Abolitionism," *The Nation*, May 12, 2014, p. 13.

[18] In a provocative argument, Hayes argues that the magnitude of wealth that would be eliminated by a transition away from fossil fuels is of the same order of magnitude (relative to the economy of the day) as the wealth in slaves of slave owners in the U.S. South on the eve of the Civil War. Citing the historian Eric Foner, Hayes writes, "In 1860 slaves as property were worth more than all the banks, factories and railroads in the country put together." The most fundamental reason slavery was defended in the South was that such an enormous amount of wealth was invested in slaves, and slave owners would lose their wealth if slaves were freed. Wealthy people invested in fossil fuel extraction face a similar loss of wealth if we were to transition to a low-carbon energy system. Hayes, "The New Abolitionism," pp. 12–18.

Energy corporations and wealthy individuals with high stakes in fossil fuels have spent hundreds of millions of dollars opposing efforts to deal with global warming. They fund massive lobbying efforts to block legislation, fund campaigns of conservative politicians who support the expansion of fossil fuel exploitation, and engage in issue advertising on television in support of conventional energy. Most notoriously, they have vigorously promoted what has come to be known as "climate change denial," the view either that global warming does not exist or that, if it does, it is not the result of human activity. As carefully documented by Naomi Oreskes and Erik M. Conway in their book *Merchants of Doubt*, these actions repeat the strategies of the tobacco industry in opposing regulation of smoking beginning in the 1960s.[19] By the early 1960s the scientific evidence was overwhelming that smoking was a cause of cancer and other diseases. The tobacco industry mobilized a small number of scientists and doctors who were financially supported by the industry to make it seem that there was a serious controversy in the scientific community. The tactic was ultimately unsuccessful—cigarette advertising was eventually banned, health warnings were required on labels, and smoking in enclosed public spaces prohibited—but the phony "scientific controversy" funded by the tobacco industry delayed these restrictions for many years. Many people died as a result.

In a similar fashion, climate change denial is impeding political action to regulate carbon emissions. Conservative think tanks have recruited ideologically conservative scientists to challenge the scientific evidence about climate change and create the false impression that among climate scientists there is serious controversy on the core issues. As one example, the conservative foundation Americans for Prosperity, funded substantially by the oil billionaires William and David Koch, has promoted a report called *Climate Change Reconsidered*:

Unlike the United Nations Intergovernmental Panel on Climate Change (IPCC), the NIPCC [Nongovernmental International Panel on Climate Change] report finds the human impact on climate is very small and any change in temperatures that might occur in the future is so small that it will not be noticed against the climate's natural variability. . . . Climate Change Reconsidered directly contradicts the scientific claims being made by

[19] Naomi Oreskes and Erik M. Conway, *Merchants of Doubt* (New York: Bloomsbury Press, 2010).

Obama and his allies. Our team of nearly 50 scientists from 15 countries have produced a report that is more than 1,000 pages long, cites nearly 4,000 peer-reviewed reports, and finds no evidence that global warming is either man made or likely to be harmful.[20]

The Republican Party and other conservative political forces have embraced this position. In the words of Representative Steve King (a Republican from Iowa), climate change "is not proven, it's not science. It's more religion than science."[21] But what about the many scientists who argue in favor of human-generated climate change? Texas Governor Rick Perry, who is heavily supported by the oil and gas industry, dismissed them by saying, "There are a substantial number of scientists who have manipulated data so that they will have dollars rolling into their projects."[22] Or, as Ron Paul, the former Republican congressman from Texas, put it, "The greatest hoax I think that has been around for many, many years if not hundreds of years has been this hoax on the environment and global warming."[23]

If one believes the arguments of the climate change deniers, then of course there is no reason to engage in the difficult and costly process of a transition away from carbon-based energy. But even if climate change denial simply creates confusion and doubt, it makes it much more difficult to mobilize people politically to make the hard choices required if the worst effects of climate change are to be avoided. And given the power, wealth, and influence of those with the strongest economic interests in continuing on our present path, without such political mobilization the needed public policies have little prospect of being adopted.

★

The explanations for environmental problems we have examined—the free-rider problem, negative environmental externalities, NIMBY movements, hyperconsumerism, and concentrations of corporate power—all

---

[20] *Climate Change Reconsidered: The Report of the Nongovernmental International Panel on Climate Change.* Available at http://americansforprosperity.org/georgia/legislativealerts/the-debate-on-climate-change-just-changed-while-obama-wages-war-against-energy-freedom/ (accessed July 16, 2014).

[21] As reported in *The Messenger* (Fort Dodge, IA), August 9, 2013. Available at http://www.messengernews.net/page/content.detail/id/569000/King—Global-warming—not-proven—not-science-.html?nav=5010 (accessed July 16, 2014).

[22] http://thinkprogress.org/romm/2011/08/17/298288/rick-perry-big-oil-climate/ (accessed July 16, 2014).

[23] http://www.ronpaul.com/2009-11-04/ron-paul-on-fox-business-its-business-as-usual-in-washington/ (accessed July 16, 2014).

imply the need for an active, interventionist democratic state if Americans are to seriously address the environmental challenges we face in the twenty-first century. Environmental free-rider problems can be durably overcome only when individuals and firms face different payoffs for private choices, and generally this outcome requires government regulation. Environmental negative externalities are an inevitable consequence of profit-maximizing strategies unless government regulations have the effect of forcing firms to pay the costs of these externalities. Hyperconsumerism can be countered by public policies that encourage a different balance between work and leisure and between public and private consumption. And only an invigorated, affirmative state would potentially have the capacity to counter the power of corporations in obstructing environmental regulation.

One might expect that in a democracy, given the seriousness of the environmental challenges we face, the citizens would demand a strengthening of democratic authority over these issues. So long as American politics is dominated by a free market ideology proclaiming that government is the problem, not the solution, such strengthening will not occur.

6

TRANSPORTATION

Transportation is a prime example of an economic issue involving lots of public goods. Consider streets, highways, and traffic regulations. What if all streets were provided by private entrepreneurs? There would be a massive underprovision of good-quality streets, except in wealthy areas of cities. This would cause problems for everyone, including the wealthy. To have a good street system in cities and a good highway system outside of cities, therefore, we need to get together and decide collectively what to do and how to pay for it. The same is true for the provision of airports and air traffic control, rail systems, and harbors. In all cases, in one way or another, public authority is essential for the organization of an efficient transportation system. The market alone will not work.

Transportation also involves various problems of externalities, especially concerning the environment. Automobiles run primarily on nonrenewable fossil fuels, so transportation systems that rely heavily on private automobile transportation will tend to contribute more to the depletion of petroleum for future generations than will systems that rely more heavily on public transportation. Automobile traffic also contributes disproportionately to global warming though carbon emissions. These externalities also will not be counteracted by markets; they require public authority.

Still, actual systems of transportation will always involve some combination of public and private provision. The questions are, how are these combined, how are they regulated, and how much democratic control over the whole process is there?

One pivotal aspect of this general problem is the social choice between a network of publicly organized transportation options in more densely populated places and a system that promotes lower population density and relies chiefly on private cars. In this chapter, we begin by presenting a general picture of public and private transportation in American cities as compared to other places in the world. We then examine the sociological issues involved in this choice and show how public transportation is a special kind of collective action problem. This section is followed by an empirical case study of a notorious example of the problems of overreliance on private cars in a large city: the case of Los Angeles. After looking at the social costs of an automobile-based transportation system, the chapter ends with a discussion of solutions to the problem of public transportation.

URBAN TRANSPORTATION IN
THE UNITED STATES AND ELSEWHERE

Within the family of developed capitalist economies, the United States relies more heavily than any other country on the automobile for urban transportation. Figure 6.1 presents the breakdown in the percentage of all urban trips by type of transport in the United States and a number of other

FIGURE 6.1—Percentage of daily trips by public transport, bicycle, and foot, 2005–2009

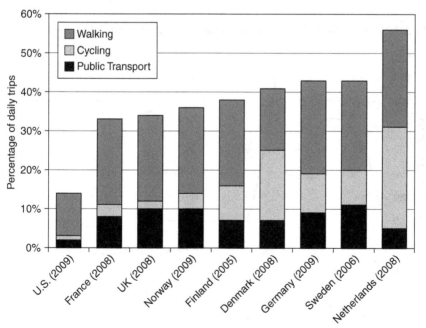

Source: Ralph Buehler and John Pucher, "Urban Transport: Promoting Sustainability in Germany," in *Lessons from Europe: What Americans Can Learn from European Public Policies*, ed. D. Kelemen (Thousand Oaks, CA: SAGE/CQ Press, 2014), figure 8.3 (p. 142).

countries. In the United States over 85 percent of all trips were taken by car, compared to 55 to 65 percent in most European countries. Public transportation accounts for 8 to 10 percent of all trips in most other developed countries; in the United States it accounts for only about 2 percent. For bicycles, the contrast is even more striking; in the United States about 1 percent of all urban trips are by bicycle, compared to 18 percent in Denmark and 26 percent in the Netherlands. This behavior cannot be attributed to climate differences, for even in Sweden 9 percent of all trips are taken by bike.

Americans did not always have such an overwhelming reliance on the automobile. Figure 6.2 shows the long-term historical trends in ridership of public transportation in the United States. In 1950, public transportation was still a major source of transportation: the average person took about 130 public transit trips a year. By 1960 this figure had declined to around 50 trips per year, and by 2010 to less than 35. When we look more narrowly at commuting rather than all urban trips, we see that not only has there been a steady decline in the use of public transportation in recent decades, but more people drive alone rather than in carpools (Figure 6.3). Automobile

FIGURE 6.2–Trend in per capita annual public transit ridership, 1900–2010

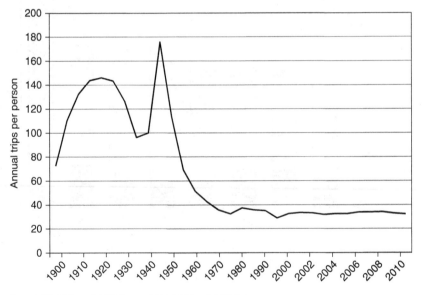

Note: 1900, 1905, and 1910 denote 1902, 1907, and 1912 data.

Source: 2012 Public Transportation Fact Book, Table 5; population estimates from the U.S. Census Bureau, Historical National Population Estimates.

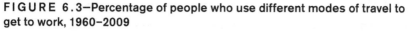

FIGURE 6.3—Percentage of people who use different modes of travel to get to work, 1960–2009

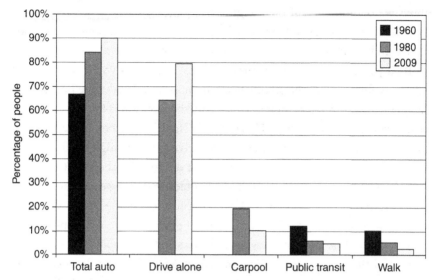

Source: 1980 and 2000 data are from *Commuting in America: Third National Report on Commuting Patterns and Trends, National Transportation Research Board of the National Academies of Sciences* (Washington, DC: Transportation Research Board, 2006), p. xiv. The 1960 data are from John Pucher and John L. Renne, "Socioeconomics of Urban Travel: Evidence from the 2001 NHTS," *Transportation Quarterly* 57, no. 3 (Summer 2003): 49–77. The 2009 data are from the United States Census Bureau American Community Survey 2010, Supplemental Table A: Means of Transportation.

use is important in all economically developed countries, but in no other country does the automobile so totally dominate the way people move around cities.

URBAN PUBLIC TRANSPORTATION AS A COLLECTIVE ACTION PROBLEM

One way of understanding the problem of public transportation is to see it as a particular kind of collective action problem. This case is especially interesting because the free-rider problem faced by individuals is strongly affected by the character of the public transportation system in which individuals make their choices. Let us consider a hypothetical example of two contrasting public transportation systems in a large city: one relies entirely on buses that share the streets with cars, and another has a developed system of light-rail or subways.

If you live in the first kind of city, you have a choice between riding the bus to work and driving your own car. Suppose the only thing you worry about is how long it will take. Figure 6.4, panel I, shows a possible payoff matrix telling you how long it will take for every combination of your choice and the choice made by most other people.

If all you care about is your time, the best option for you is B. There are relatively few cars on the streets because most people take the bus, so you can get to work in ten minutes. The second best option is for you and most other people to take the bus. This choice is significantly better than a situation in which you and most other people drive cars; the high traffic congestion with everyone driving slows everyone down. And the worst choice is to be a bus rider in a world where most people are driving cars. Your preferences are thus ranked B > A > D > C. Because everyone thinks the same way, alas—you end up with D. This is another classic free-riding problem.

We can define two interesting numbers for this table: the *free-riding bonus* and the *sucker penalty*. The *free-riding bonus* is the difference in the amount of time it takes you to get to work if most people, including you, cooperate with the collective good—taking the bus in this case—and the amount of time it takes if you drive a private car and other people take the

FIGURE 6.4—The public transportation free-rider problem under different transportation systems

		Your Choice	
		Bus	Car
Most other people's choice	Bus	**A** 25 minutes	**B** 10 minutes
	Car	**C** 1.5 hours	**D** 45 minutes

I. An inefficient public transportation system

		Your Choice	
		Light-rail	Car
Most other people's choice	Light-rail	**A** 15 minutes	**B** 10 minutes
	Car	**C** 25 minutes	**D** 45 minutes

II. An efficient public transportation system

Note: Entries in the cells are the length of time it takes to get to work under different patterns of transportation choices.

bus (i.e., A minus B). The *sucker penalty* is how much longer it takes you to get to work if you take a bus and most other people drive (C minus D). In the example here, the free-riding bonus is 15 minutes and the sucker penalty is 45 minutes. Clearly, if all you care about is minimizing your own time, you want to get the free-riding bonus and avoid—above all—the sucker penalty.

Now suppose that instead of buses, the city where you live has an extensive system of light-rail trains and subways. Now the payoff matrix looks rather different (Figure 6.4, panel II). First, the advantage of driving your car even if most other people take the train is less than the car/bus difference. Choice B is still the fastest, but not by much. The free-riding bonus has declined. Second, if you have a rail system in place and most other people drive a car, you are suddenly better off going by train. Why? Because buses compete with cars for road space, but subways and trolleys do not. (The reason the train takes longer in C than in A is that if most people take the train, more trains will be provided so they will run more frequently.) There is no longer a sucker penalty!

In actual urban transportation systems, of course, many other factors will influence the actual commuting choices people make: the density and frequency of the transportation network; the precise number of people who drive even when good rail is available; the available parking, both at commuter rail stations and at destinations; the cost of different transportation choices (public transportation fares, gas, insurance, parking, etc.). One consequence of these other complications is that in large cities with particularly good public transportation, the free-riding bonus often disappears: for many people, public transportation will be consistently quicker than private transportation (B will be greater than A).

This account of the contrast between a city with a public transportation system using only buses and one with efficient light-rail illustrates an obvious but often ignored point: The private choices people make between different kinds of transportation depend not simply on their general preferences for one kind of transportation or another, but on the practical costs and benefits they face in making those choices. And these costs and benefits, in turn, depend upon the public policies that determine the transportation infrastructure and thus the nature of the alternatives people face. The key question then becomes how we explain these public policies about the transportation choices people encounter.

One answer to this question sees these public policies for transportation as themselves the result of the preferences of citizens. This is what a democracy is supposed to do: citizens elect political representatives, who will translate the preferences of voters into policies. If public policies favor urban freeways over subways, then it is because voters prefer to drive cars rather than use public transportation. The American love affair with the car means that politicians who advocate expanded public spending on more efficient light-rail systems will tend to lose elections to politicians who argue for more freeways and better parking facilities. Thus the preferences and choices of ordinary people, acting as consumers who buy and use cars and as voters who support highways, determine the transportation alternatives faced by individuals as well as the choices they make given those alternatives. In effect, the argument goes, the transportation patterns we observe simply reflect market forces: they are reflected directly through the private consumption choices of individuals, and indirectly through individual political choices in support of those consumption decisions.

Is this a satisfactory answer? Are consumer preferences faithfully translated into the public choices about the nature of the transportation infrastructure as well the private individual choices about what transportation to use? We do not believe that the mix of forms of transportation we observe in the United States today can be explained in this way. Rather, the preferences of powerful business interests have played a pivotal role in shaping the nature of urban transit systems, thus creating constraints on the private choices individual consumers can make. A good historical illustration of this process is the fate of public transportation in the city of Los Angeles.

CORPORATE POWER AND THE AUTOMOBILIZATION OF AMERICA: THE L.A. TRANSPORTATION DRAMA

Los Angeles, California, is the iconic urban environment ruled by the automobile.[1] The metropolitan area is crisscrossed by a massive system of multilane highways. In 2011, the metro area Los Angeles–Long Beach–Santa Ana had 5,827 lane-miles of freeway, enough to cross the United States

---

[1] This account of the demise of public transportation in Los Angeles is based on research by Bradford Snell, "American Ground Transport: A Proposal for Restructuring the Automobile, Truck, Bus, and Rail Industries," Report presented to the Committee of the Judiciary, Subcommittee on Antitrust and Monopoly, United States Senate, February 26, 1974 (Washington, DC: U.S. Government Printing Office, 1974), 6–24. This report was the basis for a documentary film, *Taken for a Ride*, on the destruction of light-rail urban transit systems. For an alternative view, critical of Bradford Snell's analysis, that emphasizes local politics, see Sy Adler, "The Transformation of the Pacific Electric Railway," *Urban Affairs Quarterly* 27, no. 1 (1991): 51–86.

nearly twice. Daily vehicle miles of travel on these freeways was nearly 138 million.

It was not always this way. In the period immediately after World War II, Los Angeles had one of the best public transit systems in the country. The city had a dense network of heavily used trolley lines, and most people did not own cars. The rapid suburbanization of residential areas had not yet begun. In *Who Framed Roger Rabbit?*—a movie set in Los Angeles in the late 1940s—one of the characters, Eddie Valiant, discusses with Judge Doom the prospects of an automobile-based transportation system for the city:

> **Eddie Valiant:** A freeway? What the hell's a freeway?
>
> **Judge Doom**: Eight lanes of shimmering cement running from here to Pasadena. Smooth, straight, fast. Traffic jams will be a thing of the past. . . . I see a place where people get off and on the freeway. On and Off. Off and on. All day, all night. Soon where Toontown once stood will be a string of gas stations. Inexpensive motels. Restaurants that serve rapidly prepared food. Tire salons. Automobile dealerships. And wonderful, wonderful bill-boards as far as the eye can see. . . . My god, it'll be beautiful.
>
> **Eddie Valiant**: Come on. Nobody's gonna drive this lousy freeway when they can take the Red Car [trolley] for a nickel.
>
> **Judge Doom**: Oh, they'll drive. They'll have to. You see, I bought the Red Car so I could dismantle it.[2]

This is, more or less, what happened.

Let's go back to that time in the late 1940s. Suppose you were an automobile manufacturer—say, the president of General Motors—and you wanted to expand the market for your main product, private cars. Though you expect that the demand for cars will increase spontaneously as the economy develops and more people can afford cars, you realize there are some obstacles to the growth of the automobile market. One of these is the existence of good public transportation in many cities. So long as public transportation is efficient, inexpensive, and convenient, many people in large cities will choose not to even buy cars; and even if they own them, they will rely mainly on public transportation for most trips within the city. So what would you do? What would be a good strategy for dramatically expanding the popular demand for cars? Here is a strategy that might seem very

[2] Quoted in Alejandro Reuss, "Car Trouble: The Automobile as an Environmental and Health Disaster," in *The Environment in Crisis: Progressive Perspectives from Dollars & Sense* (3rd ed.), ed. Daniel Fireside et al. (Boston: Economic Affairs Bureau, 2005), p. 53.

attractive—especially in a place like Los Angeles, which was booming and had plenty of surrounding open land for growth: Because you control a rich and powerful corporation, you could buy up local electric public transit lines and convert these systems to diesel buses—which, incidentally, you also manufacture. To make this purchase of local transit systems seem less obvious, it would be a good idea to create a subsidiary and have it do the actual work. As part of this business plan, of course, you need to pull up the rails previously used by electric streetcars, thus making it difficult in the future to reverse the conversion from electric rail to diesel buses; you also need to destroy the old electric streetcars that are no longer needed. After this process goes on for a while, people will no longer be so keen on public transportation. The trips will take longer and be less comfortable, so ridership will decline; and with this decline, the costs of public transit will go up. Even if this strategy causes you to lose some money because you're selling fewer buses, you will make it up many times over by selling additional cars. Because of the deterioration of public transit and increasing traffic congestion, citizens will begin demanding more freeways. To be sure that these voices are heard, you should also organize a well-funded lobby for building highways. Your friends in tire manufacture, construction, and oil will be happy to join you. You will be able to argue that people are buying cars and choosing them over public transportation, so this is where public investments should be directed. Once this dynamic is set in motion, it will be self-perpetuating, producing an ever-stronger popular constituency for automobiles and less and less public support for public transportation.

This is basically what happened in Los Angeles and many other cities in the United States. It would be an exaggeration to say that all these events were fully clear to the key actors from the beginning, but a subsidiary of General Motors did buy up the electric streetcar companies in Los Angeles and convert them to bus systems and then let the bus service deteriorate as part of a strategy of encouraging private automobiles. National trends in this displacement of streetcars and light-rail transit by buses, followed by the decline in buses, are shown in Figure 6.5.

The result of these trends was that by the middle of the 1950s, there was a strong consensus among political officials throughout the United States in favor of the automobilization of transportation. This consensus combined with construction companies' interests in building freeways and real estate interests in low-density suburbanization. Over the next generation, cities effectively emptied themselves of people; urban density in 1980 was about the same as in 1940. As people invested in cars and suburban housing, a mass constituency for these policies also developed: people in suburbs

FIGURE 6.5—National trends in annual passenger trips by transit mode, 1920–2011

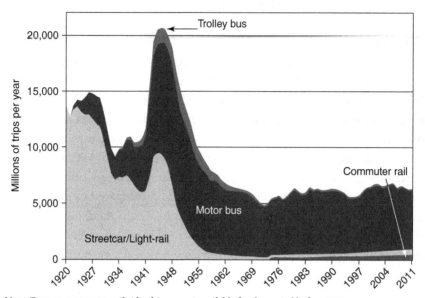

Note: Data on commuter rail ridership are not available for the period before 1973.

Source: 2013 Public Transportation Fact Book, Appendix A: Historical Tables. American Public Transportation Association Statistical Reports.

wanted more freeways. This impetus generated a particular model of urban growth: urban sprawl, degraded public transportation, the decline of central cities, and many other features of the urban environment today. The deliberate destruction of efficient public transportation systems played an important part in the process.

At the beginning of the twenty-first century, it is clear to many people that this model of urban life and transportation is undesirable and perhaps unsustainable. The reliance on private automobiles contributes significantly to global warming, traffic congestion creates an enormous waste of time, and for most people the rising cost of gasoline makes private transportation less cost-effective than a good public transportation system.

These outcomes were not the result of the operation of the "free market" governed by consumer sovereignty. Rather, they are to a significant extent the result of the exercise of private concentrations of economic power that were capable of shaping the economic environment in which individuals made their private choices. And the only way that this environment of transportation choices can be significantly transformed is through the exercise of public power to build new infrastructure and impose new rules of the game in which both individuals and corporations make their "rational" economic choices.

THE SOCIAL COSTS OF AN AUTOMOBILE-BASED TRANSPORTATION SYSTEM

If the heavy reliance on automobiles had no serious ongoing social and economic costs, then it would not be a pressing matter to reconstruct an efficient public transit system in the United States. The individual choice to drive would simply be that—an individual choice. The highly privatized automobile system of transportation, however, has significant social costs and thus is not simply a matter of private, individual concern. Most obviously, automobiles are tremendous users of fossil fuel. On a per capita basis, Americans consume vastly more gasoline than almost any other country (Figure 6.6)—over 1,500 liters per year per person compared to 300 liters or less per year per person in most other countries. Given the finite character of fossil fuel, this is a wasteful use of this valuable resource. But of course, the issue here is not simply squandering a nonrenewable resource. Burning

FIGURE 6.6—Gasoline consumption per capita, 2010

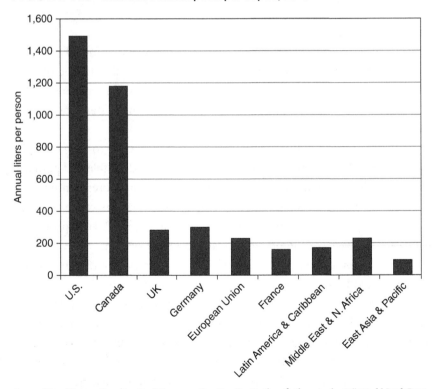

Source: "Road Sector Gasoline Fuel Consumption Per Capita (kg of oil equivalent)," *World Bank Data*, http://data.worldbank.org/indicator/IS.ROD.SGAS.PC (accessed Feb. 11, 2014).

gasoline to move people around cities contributes significantly to carbon emissions and global warming: approximately a quarter of all greenhouse gases in the United States are generated by automobiles.[3] This massive negative externality makes the private use of automobiles a matter of collective, public concern.

Even if we ignore these environmental concerns, overreliance on the automobile for urban transportation generates a huge amount of economic inefficiency in terms of time and money. Figure 6.7 presents estimates of the annual hours of delay per traveler due to traffic congestion in selected large American cities in 1982 and 2011. In every city, the situation has gotten much worse during this period. In Los Angeles in 2011 the annual delay per traveler was 61 hours, or one and a half standard work weeks. In Dallas–Fort Worth, the delays attributable to congestion increased from about 10 hours a year in 1982 to 45 hours a year in 2011, and in New York from 12 hours to 59 hours a week. The average for the fifteen largest metropolitan areas in the United States increased from 21 hours of delay in 1982 to 52 hours of delay in 2011.

Time is money. The delays due to congestion in Figure 6.7 are not simply annoying; they are expensive. If we impute an hourly cost to the time lost

FIGURE 6.7—Annual average hours of delay per traveler due to traffic congestion, 1982 and 2011

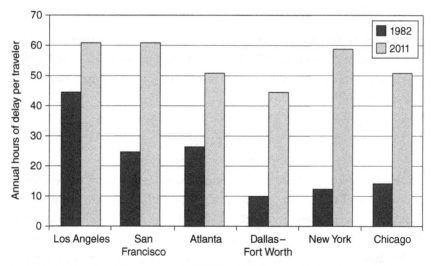

Source: David Schrank and Tim Lomax, *The 2012 Urban Mobility Report* (College Station, TX: Texas Transportation Institute, Texas A&M University System, 2012), table 1, p. 24. (http://mobility.tamu.edu/ums/)

[3] Paul Hawken, Amory Lovins, and L. Hunter Lovins, *Natural Capitalism: Creating the Next Industrial Revolution* (Boston: Little, Brown, 1999), p. 23.

FIGURE 6.8—Annual traffic congestion costs in selected large urban areas, 2011

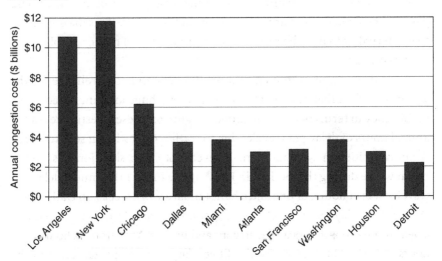

Definitions: *Travel delay* = travel time above that needed to complete a trip at free-flow speeds. The value of travel delay is estimated at $16.79 per hour of person travel. *Truck congestion cost* = value of increased travel time and other operating costs of large trucks (estimated at $86.81 per hour of truck time) and the extra diesel consumed (estimated using state average cost per gallon). *Excess fuel consumption* = increased fuel consumption due to travel in congested conditions rather than free-flow conditions. The value of excess consumption is estimated using average state cost per gallon. *Congestion cost* = excess fuel consumption + value of excess travel time.

Source: David Schrank and Tim Lomax, *The 2012 Urban Mobility Report* (College Station, TX: Texas Transportation Institute, Texas A&M University System, 2012), table 2, p. 28. (http://mobility.tamu .edu/ums/report/)

and add to that the cost of excess fuel consumption, it is possible to calculate a rough cost of congestion. The figures for the ten cities with the highest congestion costs are presented in Figure 6.8. The total for these cities comes to nearly $50 billion annually.

SOLUTIONS

Individuals making private consumption decisions can have some impact on problems of traffic congestion and the pollution and energy waste of automobile transportation. Individuals can choose to use public transportation, ride bicycles, walk, buy cars with higher energy efficiency. But to make real headway on these issues, public policy and collective, democratic regulation of the contexts for individual choices must play a major role. Here are a few things that could be done.[4]

[4] The following discussion draws heavily on Hawken et al., *Natural Capitalism* (Boston: Little, Brown and Company, 1999).

Use Taxes to Charge People the
True Costs of Driving and Parking

Gasoline in the United States is cheaper than in any other developed capitalist economy. This is not because the gas itself costs less, but because we have the lowest levels of taxation on gasoline of any comparable country. As shown in Figure 6.9, in 2012 the average tax on gas in the United States was $0.51 a gallon. In other developed countries, the typical range is between $3 and $5. One reason Americans drive so much and are willing to drive such inefficient cars is that gasoline is so underpriced relative to its true social costs. This is an example of the more general problem of the way markets underprice things that have large negative externalities: the true costs of producing and consuming gasoline are not reflected in the market price,

FIGURE 6.9—Gasoline prices and taxes in developed countries, 2012

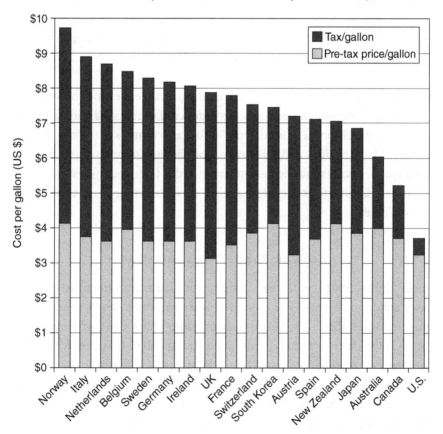

Note: Japan data are for regular unleaded gasoline as this is all that is available. Prices published in local currency and by the liter and converted to dollars per gallon. International exchange rate, 2012:Q1.

Source: International Energy Agency, *Energy Prices and Taxes*, vol. 2012, no. 1 (2012).

due to the knotty problem of the future value of the resource as well as the myriad negative externalities of its present consumption. A high gasoline tax is one way of correcting this inefficient market pricing.

Gasoline, however, is only one aspect of the underpricing problem for automobile use. Another serious problem is the underpricing of parking. Shopping malls and offices typically provide "free" parking for employees. This creates the illusion that the provision of such spaces is actually costless. Paul Hawken, Amory Lovins, and L. Hunter Lovins describe the issue this way:

> Instead of today's nearly universal U.S. practice of providing "free" parking occupying up to several times as much area as workers' office space, employers could instead charge fair market value for parking and pay every employee a commuting allowance of equal after-tax value. Workers—a third of whose household driving miles are for commuting—could then use that sum to pay for parking, *or* find access to work by any cheaper method—living nearby, walking, biking, ridesharing, vanpooling, public transit, or telecommuting. Users of alternatives could pocket the difference.[5]

Similar procedures could be adopted to charge people the true cost of using streets and highways. In London and a number of other cities, motorists are charged "congestion fees" for driving in the central areas of the city during the day. Many bridges and tollways adopt congestion pricing and reserve lanes for cars with multiple passengers in order to encourage ridesharing. More drastic measures include banning cars altogether from the central areas of cities.

Rethink Public Transportation

In the United States, with the strong ideological commitment to market-based solutions to social and economic problems, most people think public transportation should be able to cover most of its costs of production through the price of tickets. This sounds reasonable. Isn't this what "fair competition" is all about? You produce something for sale on a market, and if people want it at the price that covers costs, then they will buy it. If public transportation is heavily subsidized through taxation, many people feel that this assistance creates unfair competition with other modes of transportation,

---

[5] Hawken et al., *Natural Capitalism*, p. 42.

especially cars. And why, after all, should people who don't use public transportation be subsidizing people who do use it? Surely the users should pay.

These are familiar arguments, but they fundamentally misunderstand the complex problem of the relationship between market pricing and a public good like public transit. As we have argued, public transportation has many *positive* externalities that benefit everyone, not simply the people who directly use the service. Here is a partial list:

- Reduced air pollution, including greenhouse gases
- More efficient labor markets because it is easier for poor people to get to their jobs. This positive externality benefits employers by making it easier to hire people; it benefits the people without cars by making it easier to get to jobs. But it also benefits the society at large by contributing to a long-term reduction in poverty and thus reducing the costs of social problems associated with poverty.
- Less frequent need for house painting because of reduced particulate pollution
- Health benefits: reduced asthma and other illnesses linked to automobile-generated pollution; less obesity as people rediscover walkable neighborhoods and mixed-use (commercial plus residential plus public buildings and spaces) neighborhoods
- Less congestion on the highways for those who do need to drive

Now, suppose we could put a dollar value on all these positive externalities that would come with a massive increase in efficient public transportation. These are real economic benefits that would not happen without such investment; they represent real economic value that is being generated by the transportation service. What this means is that the costs and revenue connected to producing the service in question are not properly reflected on the balance sheets of public transportation. The balance sheet of the transportation service includes only the costs directly paid by the service—wages for transportation workers, infrastructure costs, operating costs, and so on—and the revenues they receive from tickets. None of the enormous positive economic benefits appear on the balance sheet. If the economic value of these positive, but hidden, benefits were included on the balance sheet, then we suspect there would be no need to charge consumers anything for rides in order for public transportation to be profitable. Rides could be free because even with free tickets, the sum of all the positive externalities is likely to exceed the financial costs of building and running a comprehensive public transportation system.[6] Remember also that it costs something to charge people for tickets: you need a monitoring system, cashiers, accountants, ticket machines, and so on. Part of the cost of tickets, therefore, simply covers the costs of selling tickets. These costs would be eliminated completely with a free transportation system.[7]

Of course, it could turn out that there might be reasons for charging people something to use public transportation—even if, on strict efficiency grounds, free rides would be justified. The pivotal issue here is that there are good economic grounds to use our collective resources—which we call taxes—to provide intensive and extensive public transportation and to drastically reduce the direct costs of rides to users. This use of resources should not be thought of as a subsidy in the sense of a transfer of resources to an inefficient service in order for it to survive, but rather as the optimal allocation of our resources to create the transportation environment in which people can make sensible individual choices.

Transform Land Use and Community

The problem of urban transportation is deeply connected to a much broader and more complex set of issues concerning the use of land, the character of communities, and the spatial organization of work, leisure, shopping, and residence. In the United States in the decades following World War II, cities developed around the use of automobiles; this trend created sprawling suburbs for which the automobile in turn became a necessity. Shopping is concentrated in malls and shopping districts rather than integrated into neighborhoods. With the disappearance of the neighborhood grocery store, most people need a car to go shopping for food. Zoning rules that require large plots of land for houses mean that public transportation must cope with the problem of low-density residence.

It is no easy task to undo these developments, because of the cultural expectations about housing and transportation as well as the physical

---

[6] We know of no attempt at estimating the full gambit of positive externalities—including positive externalities for future generations—of a comprehensive public transportation system, so this claim that rides should be free once all positive externalities are considered remains speculative. In any case, it is most certainly inefficient economically for ticket prices to cover most of the costs of rides on public transportation.

[7] Imagine what it would be like, for example, if we charged people for walking on sidewalks on the grounds that the users of this service should cover the costs of providing the sidewalks. This would make sidewalks more expensive, for now the "cost" of a sidewalk includes the cost of sidewalk fee enforcers and collectors.

constraints created by a given "built environment" of cities. In the long run, however, a fundamental transformation of existing patterns of land use and urban development is essential for reasons of environmental sustainability, economic efficiency, and quality of life. There is a wide range of proposals for accomplishing this transformation: drafting new rules for land use zoning that encourage higher-density residential areas; developing residential areas that are more closely integrated with commercial districts, employment centers, and recreation; and building urban transportation systems around bicycles, walking, and public transportation rather than cars. None of these developments will happen simply as a spontaneous result of market forces. They require the exercise of public power to democratically solve collective transportation problems.

7

CONSUMERISM

Consumerism is the belief that personal well-being and happiness depend largely on one's level of personal consumption, particularly on the purchase of material goods. The idea is not simply that well-being depends on a standard of living above some threshold, but that consumption and material possessions are at the center of happiness. A *consumerist society* is one in which people devote a great deal of time, energy, resources, and thought to consuming. People in a consumerist society generally believe that consumption is good—and more consumption is even better.

The United States is an example of a hyperconsumerist society. People are constantly bombarded with advertisements urging them to buy things. As shown in Figure 7.1, in the first decade of the twenty-first century, the average child aged 2–11 saw over 25,000 ads on television each year while the average adult saw 52,500. This means that children in the United States spent over a week of their lives every year (10,700 minutes) watching television advertisements; adults spent over two weeks a year in the same activity. By the second decade of the twenty-first century, exposure to advertising has, if anything, grown through the proliferation of advertising on the Internet and mobile devices. Increasingly such ads are finely tailored to personal tastes, Internet searches, and recent purchases, creating a sense of being stalked by advertisers who know your every move. Such advertisements promote not just specific products, but a vision of "the good life" and what it takes to be happy. Many people view shopping as an exciting recreational activity. People go deeply into debt to buy things beyond basic necessities: a larger house, a giant television, a fancy car. These are all the hallmarks of a society within which consumption is at the center of life.

Nothing illustrates the problem of U.S. consumerism better than the growth in the average size of new houses since the early 1980s. From the 1960s until the early 1980s, the median size of a new home in the United

FIGURE 7.1—Americans' exposure to TV ads, 2004

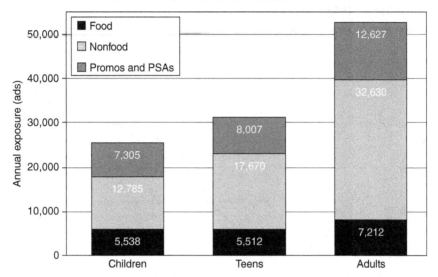

Source: Debra J. Holt, Pauline M. Ippolito, Debra M. Desrochers, and Christopher R. Kelley, "Children's Exposure to TV Advertising in 1977 and 2004: Information for the Obesity Debate," Federal Trade Commission, Bureau of Economics Staff Report (Washington, DC: Federal Trade Commission, 2007), p. ES-2.

States was around 1,500 square feet.[1] As Figure 7.2 indicates, from 1983 to 2011 the median size increased from 1,500 square feet to over 2,200 square feet. In the early 1980s, about 25 percent of all new homes were less than 1,200 square feet in size and 15 percent were over 2,400 square feet. By 2012, less than 3 percent of new homes were under 1,200 square feet and 45 percent were over 2,400 square feet (Figure 7.3). What's more, this dramatic change in the size of new homes occurred in a period when average family size was declining, so this constitutes an even greater increase in the amount of living space per person. These large new houses, of course, have to be filled with stuff. This desire also reflects hyperconsumerism: many people want bigger televisions and home theaters, exercise equipment, spacious designer kitchens, and three-car garages.

So, why is this hyperconsumerism a problem? It sounds arrogant to say to someone, "You are too preoccupied with consumption; you spend too much time shopping; you would be happier if you were less focused on

FIGURE 7.2—Growth in median size of new home construction in the United States, 1963–2011

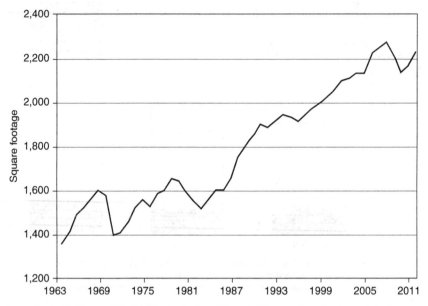

Source: Rachel E. Dwyer, "The McMansionization of America? Income Stratification and the Standard of Living in Housing, 1960–2000." *Research in Social Stratification and Mobility* (2010) and "Median and Average Square Feet by Location," *Survey of Construction Data*, Single-family detached houses only (Washington, DC: U.S. Census Bureau, 2012). Analysis provided by Rachel Dwyer.

acquiring material possessions." Aren't people the best judge of their own desires and preferences? And doesn't the free market simply translate those preferences into choices, so if people are buying huge houses, doesn't this just mean that they want big houses?

We have already identified one problem: environmental sustainability. This one is simple. The planet is incapable of supporting American-style consumption everywhere. Either we need to stop buying so many "toys," or our consumption of nonrenewable "natural capital" has to become orders of magnitude more efficient and restorative. Either, of course, would imply massive change in consumption patterns. But hyperconsumerism raises other issues as well. Toys cost money, and money takes time to earn. Many people in contemporary American society feel enormous time binds in their lives, in part because they are caught up in a work-and-spend cycle.[2] Time

[2]For a discussion of the work-and-spend cycle, see Juliet Schor, *The Overworked American: The Unexpected Decline of Leisure* (New York: Basic Books, 1992), and *The Overspent American: Upscaling, Downshifting, and the New Consumer* (New York: Basic Books, 1998). Many of the themes in this chapter are informed by these books.

FIGURE 7.3—Construction of small and big houses, 1973–2012

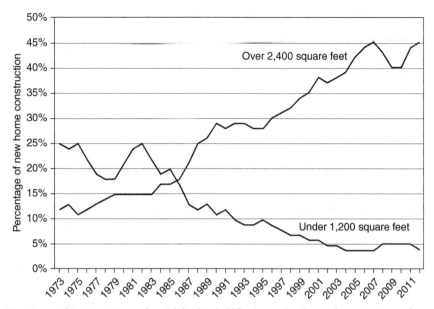

Note: In 2008 the Census Bureau changed the threshold for the smallest houses from 1,200 square feet to 1,400 square feet. The figures reported here for 2008–2012 for houses under 1,200 square feet are estimates based on the ratio of houses under 1,200 square feet to houses under 1,400 square feet for the period 2003–2007.

Source: Survey of Construction Data, Single-family detached houses only (Washington, DC: U.S. Census Bureau, 2013).

scarcity is a continual source of stress, but the cultural pressures and institutional arrangements that accompany consumerism make it difficult for people individually to solve these problems. A good case can also be made that hyperconsumerism leads to less fulfilling and meaningful lives than does a less manically consumption-oriented way of life. Research on happiness tells us something that we have always sort of known, but that competitive consumption tends to crowd out: happy people are those who feel they are interested in their work and think it is useful, feel part of a community, and have time with friends and family. Nobody on their death bed says, "Gee, I wish I had had more toys and spent even less time with my spouse, my friends, and my kids."

If people would really be better off with a less hyperconsumerist lifestyle, why then do they embrace consumerism? The basic idea here is that through various mechanisms, there is a *systematic consumption bias* in the decisions people make. If this bias were eliminated, people would in fact make different choices, consume less, and in the end be happier. The issue, then, is not really that anything is intrinsically wrong with shopping and consuming as such, but rather that the nature of the market system in which we live shapes peoples' preferences and choices excessively in favor of consumption over other values.

In the rest of this chapter, we will examine some of the critical processes in play in contemporary American society that foster this strong consumerist culture.

THE CONSUMPTION BIAS IN CAPITALIST PROFIT-MAXIMIZING STRATEGIES

Perhaps the most fundamental process that generates consumerism is the nature of profit-maximizing competition in a capitalist economy. A great virtue of capitalism is that competition among firms puts pressures on firms to innovate, and many of these innovations increase productivity over time. *Productivity* refers to the amount of inputs needed to produce a given amount of output. More specifically, increasing productivity means that it takes less laboring time to produce a given quantity of output. When productivity increases, therefore, in principle two things can happen: we could produce the same amount of things with less total labor input, resulting in more free time, or we could produce more things with the same amount of labor input. The consumption bias of capitalism involves a strong tendency for increases in productivity to lead to increased production of goods and services rather than increased free time. This may not be such a bad thing in a poor country that produces too little to provide all its citizens with adequate nutrition, housing, and other basic necessities. But when a society is already extremely rich, there is no longer any intrinsic reason for people to desire growth in average levels of consumption instead of increasing free time.

The dynamics of capitalist, profit-driven market competition, even in wealthy capitalist economies, imposes strong pressures to grow in total output, not just in productivity. From the viewpoint of profits, if productivity in a capitalist economy doubles, which option is better: doubling leisure time and keeping consumption levels constant, or doubling consumption levels and keeping leisure time constant? Capitalist economies thrive when capitalist firms make profits, and profits are made from selling goods and services. Capitalist firms, competing with each other, thus constantly attempt to increase their production and their sales. Enormous resources are devoted to this specific task, most clearly in the form of advertising and marketing strategies but also in terms of government policies that systematically facilitate expansion of output over increases in free time. In the aggregate this means that productivity growth is channeled into the continual expansion of markets, and this situation creates a tremendous bias in favor of a growth in consumption rather than leisure.

The consumption bias inherent in capitalist economies is most sharply revealed in times of economic crisis. In an economic downturn, governments attempt to stimulate the economy in various ways—by encouraging people to consume more, by reducing taxes, by reducing interest rates so borrowing is cheaper or, in some cases, by directly giving people more money to spend. In the severe economic crisis that began in 2008, economists warned that not only was consumption declining because of rising unemployment, but people were beginning to save more—and this response would only make matters worse. To get the economy back on track, it was essential that people start spending more, saving less. Because private consumption constitutes some 70 percent of the economy, reinvigorating mass consumerism was a condition for reinvigorating capitalism.

The critical point here is that these arguments by economists and policy makers are correct, *given the nature of the American economy*: for a capitalist economy to remain healthy, people must buy things in the market. If large numbers of people were to say "enough is enough" and opt for a lifestyle of voluntary simplicity by rejecting consumerism, the economy would face serious difficulties. Consumerism is therefore not simply one of many possible individual lifestyles; rather, it is a built-in tendency within capitalist economies.

ADVERTISING AND CONSUMPTION NORMS

By itself, the fact that the profits of capitalist firms in general are enhanced when increased productivity is turned into greater consumption rather than increased free time would not lead to consumerism. People also have to be motivated to want ever-higher levels of consumption. One view is that this is simply a question of human nature: we are naturally acquisitive and, when possible, will always want more stuff. Consumption, in this view, is like happiness itself—the more the better. An alternative view is that once their basic needs are comfortably met, people have no natural tendency to prefer more stuff over more free time. An incessant desire for things, therefore, requires specific social institutions that foster such preferences.

Perhaps the simplest mechanism for fostering a mass culture that under-writes consumerism is marketing. Advertising is everywhere: on television, on billboards, on smartphones, in newspapers and magazines. Corporations pay enormous sums for "naming rights" of public facilities so they can keep their brand in people's minds. Educational news programs provided free to schools contain advertisements directed at children. Marketing research devises ever more sophisticated means of reaching the public and shaping people's preferences. This effort includes intensive advertising directed at young children. Lucy Hughes, director of strategy for the large communications management company Initiative Media, has done extensive research in developing advertising strategies to exploit what she calls the Nag Factor.[3] The basic problem is simple: children don't have a lot of money to spend themselves, so how can advertisers get their parents to buy things for them? The solution is to help cultivate the art of nagging by modeling effective nagging behavior in advertisements. In an interview, Hughes reports that "the way a child nags to the parent will have an impact on whether or not the parent will buy the product."[4] Her research has demonstrated that "anywhere from 20 percent to 40 percent of purchases would not have occurred unless the children had nagged the parents."[5] So, instead of directing advertisements for children's products mainly at parents, children are targeted and shown how to nag for good results. By some estimates, spending by businesses for marketing directed at children increased from between $1 and $2 billion in 1990 to over $17 billion twenty years later.[6]

Defenders of advertising point out that advertising provides valuable information to people. Ads inform people of new products and point out the virtues of one product compared to others. If this were all that advertising did, then it might not be an important component of consumerism. But ads

---

[3]This description of advertising and nagging comes from interviews with Lucy Hughes as reported in Joel Bakan, *The Corporation: The Pathological Pursuit of Power* (New York: Free Press, 2004), pp. 119–22.

[4]Lucy Hughes, quoted in Bakan, *The Corporation*, p. 120.

[5]Ibid., p. 121.

[6]These figures come from personal communication with Juliet Schor, author of *Born to Buy: The Commercialized Child and New Consumer Culture* (New York: Scribner, 2004) and from "How Marketers Target Kids," http://mediasmarts.ca/marketing-consumerism/how-marketers-target-kids. It is difficult to accurately estimate the amount of money being spent on marketing directed toward children because many forms of marketing may be directed at both children and adults, and because a considerable amount of marketing does not take the form of advertisements.

do much more than simply transmit information: they display and reinforce certain values, constantly affirming the association between happiness and consumption, between success in life and buying things, between
sexual attractiveness and particular forms of consumption. These associations and images are part of the taken-for-granted culture that Americans
learn from early childhood and that make a life heavily oriented to consumption seem natural.

Advertising in particular, and the mass media more generally, have contributed to a gradual ratcheting up of what can be called the consumption
norms in American society. *Consumption norms* refer to the level of consumption that people see as necessary for living well. One way of thinking
about this is in terms of the basic sociological concept of a reference group.
A *reference group* is the category of people to which one refers when trying to
figure out how well one is doing or how one should behave. This idea has wide
application in sociology. Among teenagers, this concept is important in understanding such things as school achievement. Here the term often used is *peer
group*. A bright student who is part of a peer group whose members regard
academic achievement as uncool is much more likely to do poorly in school
than an equally bright kid who is part of an academically oriented peer group.

A *consumption reference group* refers to the category of people with whom
one compares oneself regarding consumption norms. Most people do not
compare themselves to Bill Gates and say, "I am doing badly because I don't
live as well as that." So the question for consumerism is, what standards of
living do people use to define *doing well*, and have they changed?

There was a time, not so long ago, when most people's consumption
norms were defined largely by people very much like themselves in their
immediate social environment. Today, consumption norms are heavily
shaped by the images people see in the mass media, especially on TV, rather
than simply by the actual standards of living of people like themselves. The
reference group for consumption is no longer defined by just "keeping up
with the Joneses next door"—a very local, neighborhood reference group—
but by keeping up with the Joneses on TV as displayed in advertisements
and sitcoms. Consider a typical commercial for television sets shown during
a football broadcast: the TVs that are advertised are not modest sets costing
a few hundred dollars, but giant flat-screen TVs hung on the wall. The
homes and apartments in most sitcoms are not the typical kind of housing
lived in by a family earning around the median income, but the living quar-
ters of affluent yuppies in fashionable apartment buildings or expensive
suburbs. Research on the impact of television has suggested that viewing

television increases people's estimates of how affluent American society is.[7] The mass media conveys a picture of consumption standards of an average, so-called middle-class lifestyle that actually corresponds to the upper end of the income distribution. The result is a large gap between what most people can afford and what they feel they should consume. Consumption norms outpace earning capacity.

CREDIT CARDS

Advertising may promote a hyperconsumerist lifestyle, and the shift upward in a typical person's consumption reference group might make people want to consume at a higher level than they can really afford, but people still need to be able to buy things. One way this problem could be solved is for people to buy their basic necessities from their earnings and then save what is left over until they have accumulated enough to purchase the wonderful forms of consumption promoted in the consumerist lifestyle. The difficulty, of course, is that a culture of consumerism fosters the desire to consume things right now. The delayed gratification of careful saving goes very much against the grain. An alternative is to devise a system in which people can easily borrow money to buy things now and pay back the loans over a long period of time. This is what consumer credit accomplishes, and nothing has fueled consumer credit more than the credit card.

Until the 1950s, credit cards were in very limited use, mostly in the form of cards issued by specific merchants or groups of merchants. In 1958 the general-purpose credit card was born when Bank of America created a bank card that eventually became the Visa card. In 1966 a group of banks joined together to create what became MasterCard. Since then the credit card industry has grown by leaps and bounds, making significant amounts of consumer credit available to nearly everyone, with minimal screening.

The basic facts about consumer debt in the United States are astounding:

- The size of the total consumer debt grew (in constant dollars) nearly three times in size from $898 billion in 1980 to $2.4 trillion in 2011.[8]

---

[7]See, for example, Thomas C. O'Guinn and L. J. Shrum, "The Role of Television in the Construction of Consumer Reality," *Journal of Consumer Research* 23 (March 1997).

[8]http://www.money-zine.com/Financial-Planning/Debt-Consolidation/Credit-Card -Debt-Statistics/ (accessed Sept. 16, 2009) and the section on "General Consumer Debt Statistics" in http://www.consolidatedcredit.org/credit-card-debt/consumer-debt-facts/#back (accessed March 17, 2014).

- Between 1970 and 2012, the percentage of families with credit cards grew from 51 percent to 73 percent; and the percentage carrying a balance on their cards, and thus paying interest on credit card debt, increased from 37 percent to 46.7 percent.[9]
- In 1968, consumers' total credit card debt was $9.45 billion (averaged over the year, in 2013 dollars). By 2013 the total averaged over $856.5 billion.[10]
- In 1989, 39.7 percent of families in the United States carried a balance on a credit card. For those families, the average balance (in 2013 inflation-adjusted dollars) was $3,312 and the median was $1,600. In 2010, the proportion of families carrying a credit card balance was almost the same (39.4 percent, with 32.7 percent owning four or more cards), but their debt was higher. Overall, the mean balance (in 2013 dollars) for those carrying a balance was $7,100 and the median, $2,777.[11]
- U.S. households received an all-time high of 7.0 billion mail solicitations for credit cards in 2006, just before the Great Recession. The numbers fell significantly, to a low of 1.5 billion in 2009, but then rose again to 4.2 billion by 2011 before falling back to 2.6 billion in 2012.[12]

Credit card companies have aggressively promoted this expansion of consumer debt. They advertise their cards by showing how pleasant life is when you use a credit card to buy what you desire and by sending unsolicited cards to millions of people a year. Even though credit card companies make money from each transaction (because merchants have to pay a fee to the credit card company) and annual fees, they make most of their earnings from interest payments. In a sense, therefore, credit card companies are

---

[9]Board of Governors of the Federal Reserve System, "Report to the Congress on Practices of the Consumer Credit Industry in Soliciting and Extending Credit and Their Effects on Consumer Debt and Insolvency" (Washington, DC: Federal Reserve, 2006), table 2, and http://www.nerdwallet.com/blog/credit-card-data/average-credit-card-debt-household/ (accessed July 21, 2014).

[10]http://www.creditcards.com/credit-card-news/federal-reserve-credit-card-report-april-2008.php (accessed Sept. 16, 2009) and "Consumer Credit: Federal Reserve Statistical Release," January 2014. http://www.federalreserve.gov/releases/g19/Current/g19.pdf (accessed March 17, 2014).

[11]Jesse Bricker, Arthur B. Kennickell, Kevin B. Moore, and John Sabelhaus, "Changes in U.S. Family Finances from 2007 to 2010: Evidence from the Survey of Consumer Finances," *Federal Reserve Bulletin* 98, no. 2 (June 2012). Available at http://www.federalreserve.gov/pubs/bulletin/2012/pdf/scf12.pdf. Federal Reserve Board, "2010 Survey of Consumer Finances Chartbook," Last updated July 19, 2012. Available at http://www.federalreserve.gov/econresdata/scf/files/2010_SCF_Chartbook.pdf (accessed May 12, 2014).

[12]Board of Governors of the Federal Reserve System, "Report to the Congress on the Profitability of Credit Card Operations of Depository Institutions," June 2013, p. 7.

particularly eager to get people to use credit cards to buy things that are more expensive than they can really afford, for these are precisely the kinds of purchases that are hard to pay off.

MARKET FAILURES IN LEISURE

So far we have examined forces that encourage a consumerist culture and enable people to buy into that culture through easy credit. Consumerism is also generated by what can be called a failure in the "market" for leisure. If we had a perfect market for leisure, then people would be able to easily choose the amount of work and leisure they preferred. This is not the case. Labor markets and employment relations in the United States are organized in a way that makes it difficult for individuals to choose a less consumerist lifestyle in favor of more free time.

Let's begin by looking at some basic facts. U.S. workers work longer hours than do workers in all other comparably developed countries. As shown in Table 7.1, Americans who worked for pay in 2012 worked, on average, 1,790 hours during the year.[13] This was more than any other economically developed country. Japan, whose workers historically have worked the highest number of annual hours, reduced the annual hours worked by 381 hours (the equivalent of over two months of 40-hour workweeks) from 2,126 in 1979 to 1,745 by 2012. In the same period, the figure for the United States declined by only 39 hours. In part this greater number of hours worked per year reflects the fact that, on average, employed workers in the United States put in longer working hours each week than do those in most other developed countries. Mandatory overtime is common, and stable, well-paid, part-time work with full benefits is relatively rare. The result is that the percentage of people who work very long hours per week in the United States is greater than in most other countries. Among dual-earner families in the United States, 30 percent of husbands work over 50 hours a week. In most other countries, the figure is in the 20–25 percent range (see Table 7.2).

---

[13]Here are several words of caution about these statistics for aggregate annual average hours worked: First, these figures are *average* hours worked per employed worker. If a country has lots of part-time workers, this number will be lower. This is one of the main reasons that the figures for the Netherlands are so low: compared to most other countries, a much higher proportion of the Dutch labor force (especially women) works part-time. These statistics are also sensitive to the demographic structure of a society: young people tend to work fewer hours per week than do people in the middle of their careers, so if a country has relatively fewer young people, this situation will show up as an increase in the mean annual hours worked. Finally, even among rich countries, countries vary in the quality of their national statistical offices.

TABLE 7.1—Annual hours worked per paid worker in the United States and other rich countries, 1979–2012

	1979	1995	2012
United States	1,829	1,844	1,790
Italy	1,859[1]	1,859	1,752
New Zealand	1,866	1,841	1,739
Japan	2,126	1,884	1,745
Spain	1,930	1,733	1,686
Canada	1,841	1,777	1,710
Finland	1,869	1,774	1,672
Australia	1,832	1,792	1,728
United Kingdom	1,813	1,731	1,654
Switzerland	–	1,704	1,636[3]
Austria	–	1,826	1,699
Ireland	1,981[2]	1,875	1,529
Sweden	1,530	1,640	1,621
Denmark	1,636	1,541	1,546
Belgium	1,670[2]	1,580	1,574
France	1,804	1,590	1,479
Germany	–	1,529	1,397
Norway	1,580	1,488	1,420
Netherlands	1,556	1,456	1,381
Average excluding U.S.	*1,793*	*1,612*	*1,525*

Notes: 1. Used 1980 data, as 1979 wasn't available.
2. Used 1983 data, the closest available to 1979.
3. Used 2011 data, as 2012 wasn't available.

Source: Organisation for Economic Co-operation and Development (OECD) statistics (accessed Feb. 16, 2014).

TABLE 7.2—Hours worked per week by men and women in dual-earner couples in selected countries, around 2000

	Mean hours worked by dual-earner couples per week	Men in dual-earner couples who work more than 50 hours/week (%)	Women in dual-earner couples who work more than 50 hours/week (%)
United States	81.2	30.3	10.2
Belgium	79.0	27.2	10.1
Italy	78.2	26.7	10.0
Finland	77.4	10.4	2.6
Canada	77.0	23.0	7.1
France	76.3	18.1	4.7
Germany	75.1	24.7	6.3
U.K.	74.3	24.3	4.0
Sweden	69.3	2.8	0.4
Netherlands	64.0	15.8	1.7

Source: Jerry Jacobs and Janet Gornick, "Hours of Paid Work in Dual Earner Couples: The United States in Cross-National Perspective," *Sociological Focus* 35, no. 2, (2002): 169–187. Adapted from Tables 1 and 3. The data are from around 2000, varying somewhat across countries.

But even more important, American workers have much shorter vacations and fewer paid holidays than do their European counterparts. As Figure 7.4 indicates, the United States is the only country in which there is no legal requirement for employers to provide paid vacation days and paid holidays to their employees. In other developed countries the legally required number of paid vacation days and holidays is in the range of four to six weeks or more. Of course, many employers in the United States do provide some paid time off even if they are not legally required to do so. But as Table 7.3 indicates, these voluntary provisions by U.S. employers are generally much less generous than the legally mandated requirements in other countries, particularly for workers in poorly paid jobs. Only about 50 percent of workers earning in the bottom 25 percent of hourly wages get any paid vacation or holidays.[14]

FIGURE 7.4–Paid vacation and paid holidays by law, OECD nations, in working days, 2013

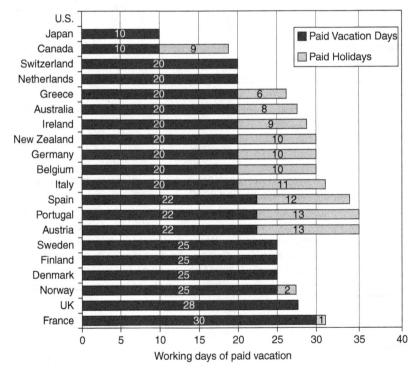

Note: Comparison assumes a five-day workweek. Data updated in September 24, 2013.

Source: Rebecca Ray, Milla Sanes, and John Schmitt, "No-Vacation Nation Revisited," *Center for Economic and Policy Research*, May 2013.

[14]Rebecca Ray, Milla Sanes, and John Schmitt, "No-Vacation Nation Revisited," Center for Economic and Policy Research, May 2013.

TABLE 7.3—Availability and generosity of actual paid annual leave and paid holidays, U.S. private sector workers, 2012

	Percent Share of Workers Whose Employer Provides:		Average Number of Days for Workers with Benefit		Average Number of Days for All Workers	
	Paid Vacation	Paid Holidays	Paid Vacation	Paid Holidays	Paid Vacation	Paid Holidays
All Workers	77%	77%	13	8	10	6
Full-time	91%	90%	13	8	12	7
Part-time	35%	40%	9	6	3	2
Bottom 25% hourly wage	49%	50%	9	6	4	3
Top 25% hourly wage	90%	91%	16	9	14	8

Source: Rebecca Ray, Milla Sanes, and John Schmitt, "No-Vacation Nation Revisited," *Center for Economic and Policy Research*, May 2013.

Perhaps these long work hours simply reflect the preferences of American workers for work and the earnings that come from work over leisure. Some data suggest that things are not quite so straightforward. As indicated in Figure 7.5, when American workers were asked in 1978 how much of *future* pay raises they would be prepared to give up in order to have more leisure time, nearly half of all people said they would give up 100 percent of a pay raise in the future for more free time.[15] Suppose that over the past fifty years or so, this preference for reduced work over pay increases had actually been followed; that is, suppose all productivity gains in the half century from 1958 to 2008 had gone into reductions of work time rather than increases in pay and consumption. If this had happened, how many hours a week would the average person have to work today? Actually answering this question is probably impossible because if people always opted for shorter hours whenever they were offered a choice of less work or more pay, the whole economy would have a different dynamic. But if we simply treat this as an arithmetic problem of using productivity increases to smoothly reduce the time of work while keeping output constant, then over the last half century the average number of hours worked per year would have been reduced by roughly 66 percent—in the form of either a much shorter workweek or much longer vacations. This would mean an average workweek of around

[15] These figures are reported in Juliet Schor, *The Overworked American: The Unexpected Decline of Leisure* (New York: Basic Books, 1991), p. 130. While these figures are from 1978, there is no reason to believe that preferences will have changed much since then.

FIGURE 7.5—Workers' attitudes toward more leisure versus higher pay

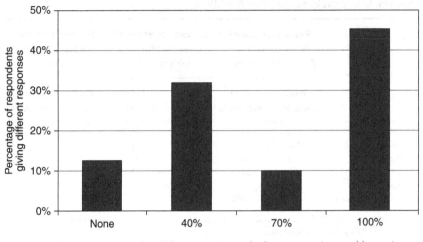

Response to question: What percentage of a future pay raise would you give up in order to have more free time?

Source: Juliet Schor, *The Overworked American: The Unexpected Decline of Leisure* (New York: Basic Books, 1991), p. 130.

15 hours or so.[16] Even if half of the productivity gains were turned into more consumption, this would still mean an average workweek of fewer than 30 hours.[17]

Even if, perhaps, people are somewhat overstating their preference for more leisure over more income, the data in Figure 7.5 do suggest that people have real preferences for more leisure time and would be prepared to forgo

[16]These estimates are based on data from the Bureau of Labor Statistics "Major Sector Productivity and Costs program" data for output per hour of nonfarm private sector businesses, which show that productivity (the amount of value produced for every hour of work) was 2.9 times greater in 2008 compared to 1958. This means that at the end of that half century, it would have been possible to produce the same amount of output as in 1958 with one-third the amount of labor input, or three times the output with the same amount of input.

[17]The preference for more leisure over future pay raises does not imply that in the future there would be a symmetrical preference for pay cuts in exchange for more leisure. If you ask people today the question, "Would you rather (a) keep your current income and work half as many hours, or (b) work the same hours and double your income?" most people would prefer to reduce their work time and keep the same income level. If, twenty years later when their income has in fact doubled, you ask them the symmetrical question, "Would you rather (a) keep your present income and work hours or (b) work half as many hours with half the income?" they would generally choose (a). Two psychological issues are in play here: first, people cannot turn productivity into leisure, so they become habituated to higher incomes and readjust their expectations about acceptable levels of consumption; and second, as a general psychological matter, people care more about losses than about gains of the same magnitude.

pay raises to gain more time. If we had a perfect market in leisure, then workers would be able to make this choice. Why don't they? If people want leisure, why do they work so hard?

For various reasons, it can be difficult for people to choose greater leisure over long hours of full-time paid work. Employers often prefer to hire fewer workers for more hours a year because it is cheaper than hiring more workers who each work fewer hours. Most jobs have some fixed overhead costs that are associated with each employee—such as paperwork costs for pay and taxation—as well as some fringe benefit costs that are not strictly proportional to the number of hours worked. This issue is particularly acute in the United States because of employer-funded health insurance. (In countries with universal health insurance provided by taxes, health insurance is no longer a work-based fringe benefit that employers have to pay.) For many jobs, employers also pay training costs associated with hiring workers; these costs may include formal training and the more subtle, on-the-job, informal learning that makes a more experienced worker more productive than a less experienced worker. The result is that in general, employers only offer reduced-hours work with large earnings penalties and greatly reduced or nonexistent fringe benefits.

Given that employers have strong incentives for creating jobs with relatively long hours, unless some countervailing power is able to counteract these employer preferences by regulating working hours, it will be difficult for workers in a "free market" to find good jobs that pay adequate wages with long vacations and moderate working hours per week. In capitalist societies, this countervailing power takes two principal forms: the labor movement and the affirmative state. In the United States, unions are weak and fragmented and generally unable to impose on employers collective forms of regulation of working hours and the work-leisure balance. Government regulation in the United States has also been weak or nonexistent. In most European countries, workers are entitled by law to 4–5 weeks of paid vacation. In the United States, there are no requirements for any paid vacations; for most jobs that include paid vacations, employers voluntarily provide only 2–3 weeks. Without strong unions and government regulation, this situation is unlikely to change.

INCREASING INEQUALITY RATCHETS UP CONSUMPTION DEMANDS

At first glance, it might seem that inequality as such would have no effect on overall pressures on consumption standards. *Inequality* refers to the economic distance between the top and the bottom, but why should it have any impact on the consumption norms of people in the middle? The economist Robert Frank argues convincingly that many kinds of consumption involve *positional goods*—goods whose subjective value depends heavily on comparisons with what other people consume.[18] Where such goods are present, increasing inequality tends to fuel what Frank calls positional arms races, much like "the familiar metaphor in which everyone stands up to get a better view, yet no one sees any better than before."[19]

Two kinds of processes underlie the salience of positional goods. The first is the psychological process in which the satisfaction one derives from owning something depends in part on one's perception of what other people own. Frank gives a vivid example of this process in a thought experiment. Consider the choice between two possible worlds: "World A, in which you will live in a 4,000-square-foot house and others will live in 6,000-square-foot houses; and World B, in which you will live in a 3,000-square-foot house and others in 2,000-square-foot houses."[20] If the only thing people cared about was their absolute level of consumption, everyone would choose World A—but this is simply not the case. Many, perhaps most people, would choose World B. This choice might be partially due to a desire to avoid envying everyone else (World A) or a desire to feel superior to everyone else (World B); but mostly, Frank argues, the choice of World B shows that the subjective meaning and value of a given size of house depends heavily on the context, on the frame of reference by which people compare themselves to others.

The second mechanism behind the consumption of positional goods is less a question of the subjective meaning or status linked to particular kinds of consumption than an indication of the ways in which people's other important interests have become linked to positional goods. Consider, again, the problem of choosing a house size—this time in the empirical context of the dramatic increase in the size of new homes being built in the United States since the early 1980s. Children's access to good schools depends to an important extent on the neighborhood where they live. As overall economic inequality increases, inequalities across neighborhoods increase,

---

[18] Robert H. Frank elaborates on the idea of positional goods in a clear and compelling way in *Falling Behind: How Income Inequality Harms the Middle Class* (Berkeley: University of California Press, 2007).

[19] Robert H. Frank, "Post-Consumer Prosperity: Finding New Opportunities among the Economic Wreckage," *The American Prospect*, March 24, 2009, 12.

[20] Frank, *Falling Behind*, 2.

and this will tend to increase inequalities in schooling. This increases pressure on middle-class people to live in more expensive neighborhoods than they can easily afford. People feel pressure to buy large, expensive houses not simply because of a consumption desire for big houses as such or because of the subjective sense of relative deprivation in living in smaller houses, but in order to move up the neighborhood hierarchy and thus gain access to better schools. The consumption norm for housing for the "middle class," therefore, is driven in part by the increasing inequality in income above the middle of the income distribution.

Of course, not every good that people consume has this positional quality. Frank gives another example in which you choose between a world in which you have four weeks of annual vacation and everyone else has six-week vacations, and a world in which you have a two-week vacation and everyone else has a one-week vacation. In this case, most people would choose the first world. This is because the length of vacations has a much less positional character than does the size of houses.

The tremendous increase in income inequality beginning in the last quarter of the twentieth century has contributed to a significant escalation in these positional arms races. Writing in 2009, Robert Frank describes the problem this way:

> Hedge fund managers need a 40,000-square-foot house and a Gulfstream jet only because their peers have them. Evidence suggests that if top earners all spent less on such things, their lives would be no less fulfilling than before. . . .
>
> For the last three decades, virtually all income gains in the United States have gone to top earners. Recipients have spent most of their extra income on positional goods, things whose value depends heavily on how they compare with similar things bought by others. . . . Additional spending by the rich shifts the frame of reference that defines what the near rich consider necessary or desirable, so they too spend more. In turn this shifts the frame of reference for those just below the near rich, and so on, all the way down the income ladder.[21]

Every economy provides both kinds of goods—positional and nonpositional. The key point here is that increasing inequality tends to increase the

---

[21] Frank, *Post-Consumer Prosperity,* 12–13.

weight of positional goods in many people's consumption basket; and this, in Frank's words, "diverts resources from nonpositional goods, causing large welfare losses."[22] This point is reflected in the example of housing. Frank explains it this way:

> When people contemplate working longer hours to buy larger houses, they anticipate additional satisfaction not only from having a larger house in absolute terms, but also from having a larger house in relative terms. For the move to appear attractive, the anticipated sum of these two gains must outweigh the loss of satisfaction associated with having fewer hours of leisure. When all make the same move in tandem, however, the distribution of relative house size remains essentially as before. So no one experiences the anticipated increase in relative house size. When the dust settles, people discover that the gain in absolute house size alone was insufficient to compensate for the leisure that had to be sacrificed to get it. Yet failure to buy a larger house when others do is not an attractive option for the individual, either. As in the familiar stadium metaphor, all stand to get a better view, but when all stand no one sees better than when all were seated.[23]

Leisure, in this example, is a nonpositional good—it is valued for its own sake—but it is displaced by the drive for positional goods through longer commuting times and longer hours of work.

The escalation of positional consumption driven by increasing inequality works its way down the income structure, having a particularly negative impact on people around the middle. At least for people at the top of the income distribution, their incomes have increased substantially as inequality has increased. People around the median of the income distribution have not seen significant increases in their income, yet they experience increased pressures for positional consumption. The result is increasing debt.

DECLINE IN PUBLIC GOODS AND ABANDONMENT OF PUBLIC CONSUMPTION BY THE AFFLUENT

In a society with very good public amenities—good public schools, good libraries, well-constructed and attractive public swimming pools, good public transportation, and so on—individuals have a readily available alternative

---

[22] Frank, *Falling Behind*, 3.

[23] Ibid., 4.

to private consumption in order to satisfy many of their needs. The erosion of the quality of public goods makes private substitutes more attractive. There are many examples:

- Private schools become more attractive because of the deterioration of public schools.
- Gated communities become more attractive because of the deterioration of policing and public safety.
- Private swimming clubs and private home pools become more attractive because of the deterioration of public recreation facilities.
- Private cars become more attractive—and more essential—because of the deterioration of public transportation.

In each of these cases, the deterioration of public goods generates a vicious cycle: as the more affluent pull out of public goods consumption, they reduce their political support for the provision of those public goods, which—because they are politically influential—leads to a further deterioration of the public goods, which leads to more people withdrawing to private, more costly substitutes. This cycle fuels consumerism—the intensified preoccupation with private consumption.

This dynamic has affected schooling in some areas of the country. In California, an antitax initiative passed in 1978, the People's Initiative to Limit Property Taxes, put a severe cap on funds available for public schools. The result was deterioration in public school quality in the period between 1970 and the 1990s. In 1970, the pupil-teacher ratio in California public schools was only 8 percent above the national average; by 1997, this number had risen to 38 percent. Some wealthy parents then began buying private substitutes for public consumption, putting their children in higher-quality private schools. In 1970 only about 13 percent of families in the top income decile in California sent their children to private schools.[24] This figure was well below the national rate outside of California of just under 20 percent. By 2000, the California figure rose to 22.6 percent while the national rate hardly changed at all; it rose to only 21.9 percent.[25] Although most

[24] The *top income decile* refers to the 10 percent of households with the highest household income.

[25] Eric J. Brunner and Jon Sonstelie, "California's School Finance Reform: An Experiment in Fiscal Federalism," *Economics Working Papers*, Department of Economics, University of Connecticut (2006), p. 20. Available at http://digitalcommons.uconn.edu/econ_wpapers /200609/ (accessed Sept. 16, 2009).

families—even relatively rich families—continued to use the public school system, the exit from the public system of significant numbers of children of influential parents reduced these families' interest in improving public education. This situation also increased the incentive for less wealthy parents, if they could afford it, to send their children to private schools.

The six factors we have reviewed in this chapter—consumption bias in capitalist markets, advertising and consumption norms, consumer credit, market failures in leisure, increasing inequality, and decline in public goods—collectively underwrite hyperconsumerist lifestyles in American society. Of course, there are always some people who reject consumerism as a way of life. There are cultural currents in the United States that embrace "voluntary simplicity" and advocate a slower pace of life with less concern for material consumption. There are people who give up well-paying jobs, leave the rat race of large urban centers, and move to rural areas. More broadly, perhaps, growing environmental consciousness means that many people are increasingly prepared to devote resources for more ecologically responsible forms of consumption, especially those involving energy use.

These countertendencies to consumerism, however, are likely to remain weak and fragmented in the absence of any serious public policies designed to reign in consumerism. One general kind of strategy for counteracting hyperconsumerism is to introduce new forms of taxation directly designed to reduce the more destructive forms of consumerist behavior. High gasoline taxes, for example, would be a way of reducing the consumption of large, low-efficiency cars. Some have proposed a progressive consumption tax to replace the current income tax as a way of creating disincentives for lavish consumption. A progressive consumption tax works like this: People are not taxed on their total income, but only on that part of their income they consume. They are not taxed on income that is turned into savings or investments, but only on that part of income turned into consumption. The tax on consumption would be steeply progressive, meaning that the rate of taxation increases with the level of consumption. Such a tax structure makes it much more expensive to turn discretionary income into lavish consumption and would thus dampen the tendency to acquire positional goods.

New forms of taxation are only part of the solution to hyperconsumerism. Without a strong effort to expand the quality and availability of public goods, privatized consumption will remain the preferred alternative for many people. Without significant reversal of the high levels of economic inequality in the United States, consumption norms will continue to ratchet upward. Without new legally enforced rules to require paid vacations on European standards and shorter workweeks, working hours will remain long and leisure time scarce. Consumerism may be an inherent tendency within capitalism, but it is still possible to move away from hyperconsumerism through a reinvigorated, democratic, affirmative state that helps create the context for more balanced patterns of public and private consumption, work, and leisure.

8

HEALTH CARE

Perhaps no domain of economic activity has generated more controversy in the United States than health care. In the advanced capitalist world, the United States is the only country within which the market plays a substantial role in the delivery of health-care services, even after the passage of the Affordable Care Act (ACA) in 2010 and its nearly full implementation in 2014. All other countries have universal, publicly supported health care in one form or another. Many people in the United States believe that private health care inherently offers people more choice and higher quality than publicly provided health care, and that market competition is the best way to control costs. Others argue that this belief is an illusion, that the peculiar character of health care as a service means that market competition will have all sorts of negative effects, and that only a publicly organized system will provide high-quality care for all.

We begin this chapter by discussing the special qualities of health care that make it so different from most other things produced for a market. We will then describe the character of the system of health care in the United States at the beginning of the twenty-first century. That account is followed by a discussion of alternative ways of organizing health-care delivery, focusing on two examples: the Department of Veterans Affairs in the United States (direct government provision) and the Canadian health-care system (universal government-provided insurance). We conclude the chapter with a discussion of why it has proven so difficult to transform the American system.

THE SPECIFICITY OF THE MARKET IN HEALTH CARE

The production and distribution of medical services is a complex social phenomenon, very different from almost anything else produced for a market. Of course, many goods and services have distinctive qualities, but generally these do not call into question the very possibility of delivering the service in a satisfactory way through market mechanisms. In the case of health care, these properties pose acute problems for a market economy. We will focus briefly on six issues.

Extraordinary Value of the Service

People in general value their health very highly, especially when life-threatening health problems exist. When people think about choices among other forms of consumption, they generally find it fairly easy to figure out the trade-offs: If I buy this more expensive car, how will this affect my budget for new clothing or vacations? In the case of health, people are willing to pay a great deal for cures. If the price goes up and a person can pay for it, they will do so. This is especially the case when their lives or the lives of people they love are at stake: how much income would you give up to save your life or the life of your child? It is thus not surprising that in the United States medical expenses are the leading cause of consumer bankruptcy. People would rather risk bankruptcy than forgo critical health care.

Ethical Issues in Distribution of Health Care

Almost everyone believes that people should not be denied basic medical care because they cannot afford it. Virtually everyone feels that this should be the case for children, who are not responsible for their poverty. Should children of rich people have access to higher-quality care and get better doctors and more comprehensive, advanced treatments than do poor children? Should a poor child have to wait in a crowded hospital emergency room while a rich child goes to a pleasant urgent care facility? Most people would say that such situations are unfair, even if they are reluctant to do anything about them. Most people also feel that when it is necessary for certain kinds of treatments—like heart transplants—to be rationed, they should not be rationed by price and ability to pay. Should hearts and kidneys be auctioned off to the highest bidder? Most people recoil at such a market solution to the problem of distributing life-saving organs; they believe instead that organs should be distributed on the basis of medical need and prospects for benefiting from the treatment.

When it comes to the distribution of health-care services to adults, there is less universal agreement among Americans that health care is a basic human right and that inequalities in access to health care are unfair. If some adults go bankrupt due to health-care costs, then this situation may be regrettable, but—libertarian defenders of markets would say—it is not the state's responsibility to cover these costs. Still, most people feel that at least basic health care (even if not all treatments) should be accessible to everyone. Health care goes along with food and shelter as consumption goods that are close to a human right, and thus there is general consensus to have a mechanism for paying for medical care for people who cannot afford it. There are many alternative ways of doing this: charity from doctors or the public; direct government provision for people below a certain income level in the forms of hospitals and clinics for the poor; direct government provision of health care for everyone; government insurance for which only the poor are eligible; universal government insurance for everyone; and government subsidies for private insurance. The fact is that health care has to be rationed one way or another, and the ethical problem is how this rationing should be done—by ability to pay or ability to wait.

Another issue in the ethical distribution of health care concerns the priorities for research on new medications and treatments for diseases. From an ethical viewpoint, the amount of research effort and funds devoted to any given health problem should depend in significant ways on the seriousness of the disease and the number of people whose lives would be helped by prevention and treatment. In a market-based system, however, research and development will be directed toward the profitability of the treatment once developed—and this outcome depends significantly on the wealth of the people who get the disease. The result is that far more research goes into diseases and health conditions of people in rich countries than in poor countries. The most notorious example is the low level of research on malaria, which kills tens of millions of people a year. A report by the Bill & Melinda Gates Foundation in 2005 found that

> total spending on research and development for the disease amounted to US$323 million last year [2004]. That represents about 0.3 percent of total research and development investments. . . . However, malaria is responsible for 3 percent of all the lost years of productive life caused by all diseases worldwide. . . . Lost years of productive life is a standard measurement of a disease's impact on society. By contrast, diabetes gets about 1.6 percent of the total money spent on medical research, while it accounts for 1.1 percent of all the productive years of life lost to disease. In other words, the disease

burden to society is about one-third of that of malaria, but it gets nearly six times more money in research and development funding.[1]

Information Costs

Most consumers of health care find it extremely costly, if not impossible, to acquire the necessary information to make informed decisions as consumers. How do you really get high-quality information on the relative competence of different doctors or clinics or hospitals? Hospitals receive public ratings, but they are hard to interpret and often quite misleading. A given doctor may exude self-confidence with a warm and engaging personal style and yet be much less competent than a much less personally appealing doctor. How can most people really figure out which doctor is better? And what about alternative treatments? To be sure, lots of good information can be found on the web about alternative treatments for any given disease, but lots of bad and misleading information also can be found. How can an ordinary person sort out all this information? And think how much harder it is to sort out good from bad information in the context of the worry and anxiety that accompany a serious illness. For all these reasons, people almost always rely on experts, especially on their doctors, to give them information about their health conditions and what to do about them. And though it is desirable for patients to be active participants in making choices about their health care and to learn about illnesses and treatments, realistically for most people these things will play a secondary role to listening to the advice of their physicians.

There are, of course, information costs involved in really learning about the quality of other goods and services that are important to people. Consider the notorious information problem of buying used cars when the salesman says they were driven only on weekends by little old ladies. It is difficult to get reliable information on financial advisors, as reflected in the extraordinary scandal involving Bernie Madoff's Ponzi scheme. It is in the nature of markets that actors in exchanges have incentives to hide information when it is to their advantage. But the information problems people face in making choices about health care are particularly salient because the stakes

[1] Emma Ross, "Report Highlights Low Level of Malaria Research Spending," The America's Intelligence Wire, October 31, 2005. Available at http://chealth.canoe.ca/channel_health _news_details.asp?news_id=16147&channel_id=143 (accessed Oct. 15, 2009).

are so high and the information so technically complex. This is why everywhere, even in the market-dominated health-care system of the United States, health-care services are heavily regulated.

The Market for Health versus the Market for Treatment

Consumers want to be *healthy*, not to consume medical treatments. From the consumers' viewpoint, prevention is much more important than treatment, but from the viewpoint of profit-maximizing producers of health care, treatment is much more lucrative than prevention. The folk saying is "an ounce of prevention is worth a pound of cure"; but if you are selling things, you would rather have people buy a pound of cure than an ounce of prevention. This means that in a market-oriented system dominated by profit-maximizing investors, there will be a significant underproduction of preventive measures and a strong emphasis on expanding the market for expensive treatments.

A good example of this mismatch between the priorities of consumers (health) and the priorities of sellers (treatment) was the crisis in availability of flu vaccines in 2007. Flu shots are an example of preventive medicine: you take a shot to prevent an illness, not to treat an illness. Drug manufacturers do not make much money on the flu vaccine, so only a few facilities are devoted to producing it. When, in 2007, one of these facilities had to be shut down because of contamination, the result was a worldwide shortage in flu vaccine. More generally, because profit-maximizing firms can make more money in treating illness, they are unlikely to devote a lot of resources to disseminating health-promoting knowledge and encouraging healthy lifestyles.

Supply Creates Demand in Health Care

In most markets, the consumer's demand for a good or service is what generates the supply: producers see what people want and then increase production (supply) to satisfy these desires (demands). In health-care services, the causal relationship between supply and demand often works in the opposite direction: the existence of a medical technology tends to generate a demand for its use in medicine. For example, when a group of doctors or a hospital purchases expensive technology like a CAT scan, to pay for the equipment they then need to use it in treating patients. This situation generates a strong pressure to increase the use of the technology. This does not mean, it should be said, that the invention and diffusion of CAT scan machines is not an advance in medical treatment. But when the purchase and use of such technologies is governed by market principles, on the whole there will be a tendency for unnecessary treatments and tests to occur because of the incentive for using them.

Competition among Providers Generates Overinvestment

In a competitive market for health-care services, every hospital wants to have the latest, most advanced technologies because they improve an organization's ability to recruit patients. This means, for example, that every hospital wants to have a CAT scan or the facilities needed for open-heart surgery. Instead of figuring out the optimal level of investment in these advanced, expensive technologies relative to other kinds of medical facilities for a particular geographical region, all the hospitals acquire the expensive technologies in their competition for patients. Instead of competition lowering costs and generating efficiency, it raises costs by generating massive duplication and waste.

Taken together, these six factors show that the delivery of health-care services is quite different from the market for shoes or cars or entertainment. Different countries have responded to this set of issues in different ways, but among the countries with developed economies, only the United States relies significantly on market mechanisms in the health-care sector. In the next section, we will see exactly how this system works.

THE SYSTEM IN THE UNITED STATES

At the beginning of the twenty-first century, health care is one of the most complex economic sectors in the United States. Even though in the United States the market plays a much bigger role in the delivery of health care than in any other economically developed country, it would be a mistake to think of the American health-care system as a free market system. Rather, the U.S. system should be regarded as a kind of incoherent patchwork of different ways of organizing health-care services. The system has developed haphazardly over many decades, during which the state became heavily involved in health care along with nonprofit organizations, groups of doctors, and capitalist firms operating within markets. Most recently, in 2010, the system was modified by the ACA, which added a range of new government initiatives to expand health-care coverage. In the following subsections, we will lay out the basic components of this system and discuss some of its consequences.

How Health Care Is Provided

In describing how health care is provided, we must make a distinction between the *organizational form through which the service is produced* and the *mechanism through which people gain access to the service.* The main organizational forms in the United States include private doctors' offices organized as individual or group practices; nonprofit clinics and hospitals; for-profit hospitals run by capitalist corporations; health maintenance organizations (HMOs), which include both primary-care physicians and hospitals; and government-run clinics and hospitals, organized by cities, counties, states, and the federal government. Access to these services is controlled through a variety of processes involving private payment, various kinds of insurance, and government rules of personal eligibility:

1. *Direct private payment for medical services.* At one time in history, people got access to medical services simply by paying for it out of pocket on a fee-for-service basis. This is the purest market-based form of delivering health services: the service is offered on a market, and when you need it, you buy it. Because in the case of serious illness, these expenses can far exceed most people's ability to pay (except for the very wealthy), most people prefer having some kind of health insurance rather than relying on good luck and their ability to pay.

2. *Employer-provided insurance.* This has been the core of the health insurance system in the United States since the 1950s. Sometimes employer-provided insurance takes the form of a general health insurance policy that enables the insured person to see any doctor or go to any hospital; but more often, employer-provided insurance is connected to HMOs. HMOs are usually large organizations that include hospitals, clinics, doctors, and a range of other health-related services. A well-known example is Kaiser Permanente in California. When an employer provides HMO insurance, employees have access to the health-care providers within the HMO; employees cannot use the insurance to pay for health care by nonparticipating doctors or hospitals without HMO permission. Generally this kind of insurance comes with various forms of co-payment—the insured person pays a

relatively small out-of-pocket fee for a given service. Even after the full implementation of the ACA, around 55 percent of the non-elderly population is covered by employer-provided insurance.

3. *Government-provided insurance.* Two principal government insurance programs are paid for through taxation in the United States: Medicare provides fairly comprehensive health insurance for the elderly, and Medicaid provides health insurance for the very poor. Because Medicaid is administered by each state, the quality of service and the level of income used to qualify vary enormously across the states. In 2014, in 14 states, in order for parents of dependent children to be eligible for Medicaid, their household income had to be less than 50 percent of the poverty line; in 26 other states, parents in households with incomes well above the poverty line were eligible. This means, for example, that in Alabama, parents in a family of three with a family income above $3,221 would be ineligible for Medicaid, whereas in Minnesota, Connecticut, and a few other states, the threshold was $50,000 or more.[2] In 23 states, childless adults, no matter how poor, were completely excluded from Medicaid eligibility; in 27 states and the District of Columbia, the threshold for Medicaid eligibility for poor childless adults is household income of 138 percent of the poverty line (or even higher in some cases).[3] Following the passage of the ACA in 2010, federal funding for Medicaid was expanded considerably to potentially include many more families well above the poverty line. However, due to a Supreme Court decision in 2012, state governments were given the option to decline this additional federal support. As a result, in many states where the Republican Party controlled state policy, this expansion was refused—even though 100 percent of the costs of this expansion were covered by federal funds for three

---

[2] The Alabama figure comes from "The Coverage Gap: Uninsured Poor Adults in States That Do Not Expand Medicaid," Table 1, Issue Brief by the Kaiser Family Foundation, April 2, 2014. Available at http://kff.org/health-reform/issue-brief/the-coverage-gap-uninsured-poor-adults-in-states-that-do-not-expand-medicaid/ (accessed April 7, 2014). The Minnesota and Connecticut figures come from the National Conference of State Legislatures website at http://www.ncsl.org/research/health/medicaid-eligibility-table-by-state-state-activit.aspx (accessed April 7, 2014).

[3] "Where Are States Today? Medicaid and CHIP Eligibility Levels for Children and Non-Disabled Adults as of April 1, 2014," Kaiser Family Foundation report, January 13, 2014. Available at http://kff.org/medicaid/fact-sheet/where-are-states-today-medicaid-and-chip/), (accessed August 11, 2014).

years, and 90 percent of the costs would be covered by federal transfers thereafter.[4]

4. *Individually purchased private health insurance.* Until the ACA went fully into effect in 2014, many people purchased health insurance through the ordinary private health insurance market. Small employers rarely offered health insurance as a fringe benefit; and increasingly, larger employers had ceased to offer this benefit. In many firms, part-time workers were not eligible for health insurance. Self-employed people and unemployed people also do not have access to employer insurance. Before 2014, in all these cases, people had to turn to the private health insurance market for health insurance. This coverage was often very expensive, generally in the $5,000–$10,000 range annually for a single person, and often had high co-payments and large deductibles. In many cases, it was simply impossible to buy private insurance: insurance companies had the right to refuse to insure someone on the basis of preexisting medical conditions. Companies often refused insurance even when the condition was relatively minor.

5. *Government-subsidized, privately purchased insurance.* The ACA is an attempt at reducing problems in the private health insurance market. It introduces a new element to the complex configuration of the health-care system in the United States: direct public subsidies for the purchase of insurance by individuals on the private health insurance market. The ACA contains five central provisions: First, as discussed above, the ACA underwrites a significant expansion of the already existing federal health-care program for the poor, Medicaid. Second, it creates a new rule that private health insurance providers cannot refuse to insure people with preexisting medical conditions or charge them higher premiums because of those conditions. Third, the act includes a requirement—called the "individual mandate"—that virtually everyone has to buy health insurance or pay a fine. This element is essential if the rule requiring insurance companies to insure

---

[4]As of May 2014, twenty states had decided not to move ahead with Medicaid expansion: all the states in the South except for Arkansas and Kentucky, as well as Alaska, Idaho, Kansas, Maine, Montana, Nebraska, Oklahoma, South Dakota, Wisconsin, and Wyoming. Four other states were still considering expansion: Pennsylvania, Indiana, Missouri, and Utah. "Where the States Stand on Medicaid Expansion," the Advisory Board Company, *Daily Briefing,* May 28, 2014. Available at http://www.advisory.com/daily-briefing/resources /primers/medicaidmap (accessed July 21, 2014).

people with preexisting health problems is to be viable, since without the individual mandate some people would wait until they got sick before buying insurance. Just imagine if this were the case for fire insurance: you cannot allow people to wait until their house is on fire to get insurance and then also require insurance companies to insure them.[5] Fourth, the ACA creates a list of basic provisions of coverage that must be included in all insurance policies in the private insurance market. For example, before the ACA, in many states, health insurance companies refused to include coverage for pregnancy in their individual health insurance policies; now pregnancy must be covered. Finally, and perhaps most significantly, the act creates a system of income-based subsidies to help people pay the premiums of health insurance policies in the private market.[6] To put into operation this element, a new kind of marketplace for the purchase of private health insurance has been introduced—online health insurance exchanges—designed to enable consumers to easily compare the provisions and prices of different plans and find out the level of subsidy for which they are eligible.

6. *Direct government-provided health care.* Access to government-run health-care services is generally governed by strong eligibility criteria. The most important of these services are linked to the military—military hospitals serve active duty soldiers, and the Veterans Affairs hospital system serves military veterans. The VA hospitals constitute a form of socialized medicine: the state does not simply provide insurance for people to go to private doctors; it directly organizes the service itself. As we will see at the end of the chapter, this is accomplished in a relatively cost-effective way without sacrificing quality.

7. *Pro bono services provided by doctors and hospitals.* The final way that people get access to health-care services is through the charity of doctors and hospitals providing free health care to people who do not have insurance and cannot afford to pay. In principle, no one is

---

[5] When there is a rule that insurance companies cannot refuse to insure someone with a preexisting health condition, then the absence of a rule requiring healthy people to buy health insurance creates what is called an "adverse selection" problem. If only already sick people buy health insurance, then health insurance premiums would have to be incredibly high in order for the companies to cover their costs.

[6] While these are the most central provisions of the act, there are many other details; for example, children are allowed to stay on parents' health insurance policies until age twenty-six, and businesses above a certain size are required to offer health insurance.

refused admission to an emergency room or denied medical care for life-threatening conditions. Care is supposed to be provided without first screening patients for their ability to pay. The result is that in many instances the costs of this care have to be absorbed by hospitals and doctors, which ultimately means higher insurance premiums and out-of-pocket expenses for everyone else. Reducing the need for such pro bono services, especially by emergency rooms in hospitals, was one of the rationales for the ACA.

Taken together, these six elements constitute a complex hybrid system of public and private institutions. Passage of the ACA has increased the public role in some very specific ways; but it is not, as some of its critics insist, a government "takeover" of the health-care system. At its core, the ACA is a government program that relies heavily on the private insurance market but imposes new rules that make access to that market fairer and insurance purchased in that market more affordable to lower-income people. Even before the ACA, health insurance markets, like all other kinds of insurance markets, were regulated by the government. What have changed are the specific rules of this regulation and the introduction of significant subsidies to make policies more affordable to low- and moderate-income people. The system remains heavily shaped by private corporations and market processes.

Figure 8.1 shows the Congressional Budget Office's estimates of the expected impact of the ACA on how people get access to health care in the United States.[7] The graph compares the estimated percentage of the non-elderly population in 2024 that would receive health care through different sources if the ACA had not been implemented with the percentage that is expected to receive care through each source because of the ACA. As the figure indicates, the overall distribution of how people get access to health care is not projected to change dramatically as a result of the ACA. In 2024, if the ACA had not passed, the Congressional Budget Office (CBO) estimates that 57.8 percent of people would receive health insurance through employer-based coverage; with the ACA, the CBO estimates that this number will decline to 55.8 percent. The biggest change is in the percentage of people without any insurance—that figure is expected to be cut nearly in

---

[7]Congressional Budget Office, "Updated Estimates of the Insurance Coverage Provisions of the Affordable Care Act, April 2014."

FIGURE 8.1—Estimates for 2024 of the distribution of the non-elderly population across alternative sources of funding for health care

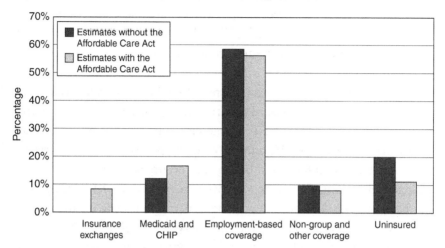

Source: Congressional Budget Office, "Updated Estimates of the Insurance Coverage Provisions of the Affordable Care Act, April 2014," Table 2.

half by 2024—but still the CBO predicts about 8–11 percent of the non-elderly population will be without health insurance.[8] This means that even after the ACA has been fully operating for a decade, it will still fall short of a universal health insurance system.

Arguments in Defense of a Market-Driven System

In every other developed capitalist economy in the world, people have decided that it is a bad idea to allow markets a large role in determining access to medical care. Every other country has some kind of universal system organized by the government and paid for by taxes. In the United States, even after the passage of the ACA, the market still plays a very large role. It remains a market-based system, even though the regulations of the market have increased and subsidies to purchase insurance on that market are now available for lower-income people.

Two kinds of arguments in favor of competitive markets in health care have dominated the discussion in the United States. The first is simply the general pro-market argument applied to health care: the market allows

---

[8]The 11 percent figure includes unauthorized immigrants who are not eligible for any publicly supported insurance programs; the 8 percent figure is for U.S. citizens only.

freedom and choice; if the government provides universal health-care insurance, it will ration health-care services; this approach will result in long waiting times for doctor's appointments and necessary surgery and reduce the ability of individuals to choose their own doctors and treatments. Bureaucrats in Washington, conservatives insist, will make these decisions for you.

The second argument involves a special kind of issue called the moral hazard problem. A moral hazard is a situation in which there is no incentive to worry about costs because someone else is paying the bill. Insurance sometimes creates a moral hazard by enabling people to engage in riskier behavior. The moral hazard in health care occurs because, it is argued, if you have insurance, you will tend to overuse medical services since you do not have to pay each time you go to the doctor. In private insurance, this problem is mitigated because the insurance companies will be worried about such overuse and will impose co-payments and other controls to counter it. But in government insurance, these incentives will disappear. If no one has an incentive to make responsible choices, then this situation will lead to a massive overuse of the medical care system: people will consume more medical care than they need, and doctors will order more tests than are necessary. Because both doctors and patients face no direct costs for doing so, they will overspend, imposing costs on others—taxpayers in this case—because the government assumes all the risk in paying for health care.

The proposed solution to this moral hazard problem in health care is a good dose of market competition that involves individuals paying more of medical costs and health-care providers competing with one another to reduce costs. In short, the argument goes that *markets impose responsible behavior on people by making them bear the costs of their choices.* Such a market solution should lower usage of medical services, which in turn will result in lower spending on medical care. This is why the main proposal for health-care reform by strong pro-market conservatives promotes the idea of health savings accounts: the money people put into these accounts will be exempt from taxes and then used to pay for medical bills. This solution implies that in a sense we have too much insurance now rather than too little.

Both of these arguments in favor of market competition in health care are flawed. The first argument incorrectly assumes that a system of government payment for health care requires strong government control over the autonomy of doctors and the choices of patients. As we will see in the discussion of the Canadian system at the end of this chapter, this does not have to be the case: the government can pay the bills and negotiate prices and yet allow as much freedom of choice as in a market. Furthermore, in the U.S. health-care system as currently organized, choice is heavily limited for most people: employer insurance often requires employees to sign up with a specific HMO, and within that HMO they are assigned doctors and cannot go outside of the HMO without permission. People often have to wait a long time for appointments to see specialists. Most fundamentally, the existence of a market does not guarantee freedom of choice and short waiting times unless you have the resources required by that market.

The second argument—that universal insurance guaranteed by the government generates massive moral hazard problems—is greatly exaggerated as an issue in medical care. The problem in health-care systems is that people tend to go to the doctor only when they are very sick; this behavior ultimately costs the system more than does going to the doctor too often. Most people do not want to overconsume medical services, regardless of who is paying. When they face high deductibles, co-payments, and other direct expenses that reduce the moral hazard, they may indeed wait longer to see a doctor; but in the end, delaying treatment often makes their health condition worse and more expensive to treat.

Still, there is a moral hazard problem in health care—for example, of doctors ordering unnecessary tests because an insured patient does not directly have to pay for them. However, it is probably impossible to completely eliminate such problems so long as insurance plays an important role in health care, and this will certainly be the case no matter how the insurance is provided—by the government or by private insurance companies. The most we can hope for is to minimize moral hazard problems through more coherent efforts at cost control within health-care delivery organizations.

Performance of the U.S. Health-Care System

In 2014 the health-care system in the United States is in a period of considerable flux due to the implementation of the ACA. It will take years before we can assess the full impact of the reforms and evaluate the extent to which they have improved the overall performance of the system. What follows, therefore, will of necessity be mainly a discussion of the performance of the American health-care system just before the implementation of the ACA. To the extent that the ACA alters the dynamics of the system as a whole, then some of these problems may be reduced in the future. However, since the

ACA remains a system deeply connected to market forces and continues to rely heavily on employer-provided health insurance benefits, private insurance, and privately provided health care, it is also reasonable to anticipate that the differences that existed before the ACA between the performance of the U.S. health-care system and more comprehensive systems will remain in the future.

The fact that the United States has a complex, hybrid structure of health-care services that combines market and government processes is not necessarily a problem. Indeed, one might think that each of the elements in this system might counteract the flaws in the other. A pure state-based system might be plagued by government inefficiencies and bureaucratic rigidity, which market competition might alleviate. A pure market-based system might generate unacceptable gaps and inequalities in access to health care, which the government system could alleviate. So, it *could* be that the

FIGURE 8.2—International comparisons of total health expenditure per capita, 2012

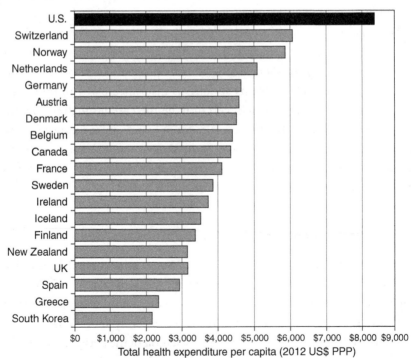

Note: Data for Spain and New Zealand are from 2011. The figures are expressed in "purchasing power parity" (PPP) dollars. This means that spending in national currencies is converted to U.S. dollars by adjusting the official exchange rates to take into account the general cost of living differences.

Source: "OECD Health Data 2014. Main Indicators." Available at http://stats.oecd.org/Index .aspx?DataSetCode=SHA (accessed Sept. 22, 2014).

complexity of the multipronged approach to providing health care in the United States makes it better than other, less pluralistic approaches.

That, however, does not seem to be the case. For starters, Americans spend more on health care than do people in any other country, both in absolute dollars and as a percentage of national income. In 2012, Americans spent about $8,400 per capita yearly on health care, which comes to 16.2 percent of the gross domestic product (GDP). Compare this health-care cost with those for other economically advanced countries (Figures 8.2 and 8.3): In 2012, when the United States spent about $8,400 per capita on health care, no other country spent more than $6,100 per capita, and most other developed countries were in the $3,000–$4,500 range.[9] Based on percentages of

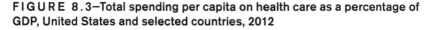

FIGURE 8.3—Total spending per capita on health care as a percentage of GDP, United States and selected countries, 2012

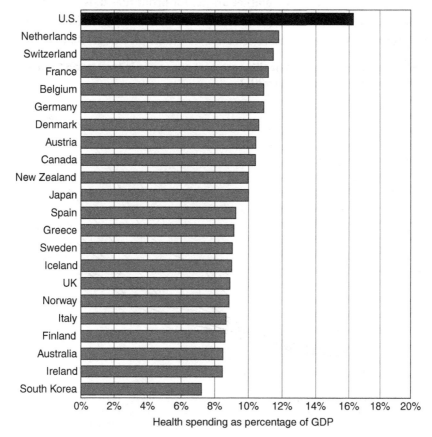

Note: Data for New Zealand, Spain, Japan, and Australia are from 2010.

Source: "OECD Health Data 2014. Main Indicators." Available at http://stats.oecd.org/Index .aspx?DataSetCode=SHA (accessed Sept. 23, 2014).

9 "OECD Health Data 2014," http://stats.oecd.org/Index.aspx?DataSetCode=SHA (accessed August 31, 2013).

GDP, our nearest rival in 2012 was the Netherlands, which spent just under 12 percent of its GDP on health care; most other countries were in the 9–11 percent range. What's more, as indicated in Figure 8.4, the growth rate of spending on health care has been much more rapid in the United States than other countries.

Proponents of market competition in health care argue that competition should force health-care providers to reduce costs to attract customers, but that simply has not happened. This outcome is actually not so surprising, for various reasons. First, as already noted, due to the peculiar character of health care, competition can raise costs as hospitals compete with each other by buying expensive equipment, which they then want to use to recover costs. Overuse of expensive technologies and duplication of facilities combine to raise the aggregate cost of health-care services. Contrary to what defenders of the free market argue, for-profit hospitals are *not* more efficient than nonprofit hospitals. They may be more *profitable*, but this is mainly because they are more selective in whom they treat; they refuse to

FIGURE 8.4—Growth in health-care cost per capita in the United States and selected countries, 1960–2011

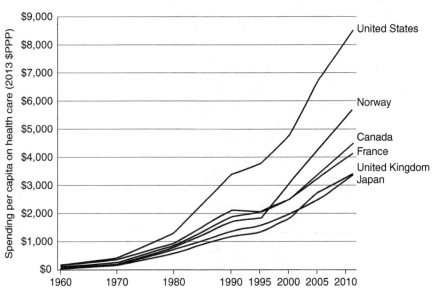

Note: Data in 1960–1990 were adjusted from 2004 to 2013 dollars, reflecting the 23 percent inflation over that period, as calculated using Consumer Price Index (CPI) data from the Bureau of Labor Statistics. Last data available for Japan are 2010. The 2011 data point for that country has been linearly extrapolated.

Source: 1960–1990 data: National Center for Health Statistics, *Health, United States, 2007, with Chartbook on Trends in the Health of Americans* (Hyattsville, MD: NCHS, 2007), table 120, p. 374. 1995–2011 data: OECD, "OECD Health Data 2012—Frequently Requested Data," available at http://stats.oecd.org /Index.aspx?DataSetCode=SHA (accessed May 20, 2013).

treat uninsured poor people. Profitability and efficiency are not the same thing.

Second, the complexity of the system—particularly the enormous variety of insurance plans, each with specific rules and procedures—increases administrative and paperwork costs of medicine tremendously. As indicated in Figure 8.5, in a study of eleven economically developed countries, the per capita cost of health insurance administration was more than twice as much in the United States than in any other country. Furthermore, the complexity of the systems means that both patients and doctors have to spend a great deal of time sorting out issues connected to insurance coverage. As shown in Figure 8.6, 54 percent of primary care physicians in the United States report that the time they spend on insurance coverage issues is a major problem. This is more than twice as high as the figure reported for most other countries.

Third, the highly fragmented system of financing health care in the United States makes it very difficult for providers to negotiate with the large pharmaceutical companies for lower prices for medicines. When Congress finally agreed to include prescription drugs in Medicare coverage for the elderly, drug companies explicitly blocked the government from

FIGURE 8.5—Spending on health insurance administration per capita, 2011

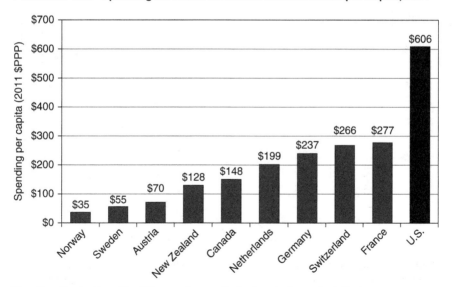

Note: Spending is adjusted for differences in cost of living (purchasing parity dollars).
Source: Cathy Schoen, Robin Osborn, David Squires, and Michelle M. Doty, "Access, Affordability, and Insurance Complexity Are Often Worse in the United States Compared to 10 Other Countries," *Health Affairs* 32 no. 12(2013): 7. Available at http://content.healthaffairs.org/content/32/12/2205 .abstract (accessed Aug. 11, 2014).

FIGURE 8.6—Effects of insurance complexity and restrictions on patients and doctors

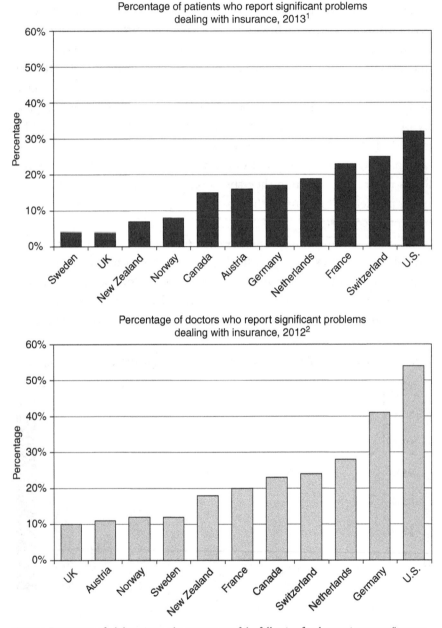

Percentage of patients who report significant problems dealing with insurance, 2013[1]

Percentage of doctors who report significant problems dealing with insurance, 2012[2]

Notes: 1. Percentage of adult patients who report one of the following for the previous year: "spent a lot of time on paperwork or disputes for medical bills or insurance"; "insurance denied payment or did not pay as much as expected."

2. Percentage of primary care physicians reporting that insurance restrictions pose a *major* time concern.

Source: Cathy Schoen, Robin Osborn, David Squires, and Michelle M. Doty, "Access, Affordability, and Insurance Complexity Are Often Worse in the United States Compared to 10 Other Countries" *Health Affairs* 32 no. 12(2013): 7. Data from 2012 and 2013 Commonwealth Fund Health Policy Surveys.

negotiating lower prices. As a result, drug costs in the United States are significantly higher than in other countries where government-organized health care is able to control such costs.

Now, it is not completely obvious that spending 17 percent of American national income on health care is too much. After all, the United States is a very rich country whose people certainly value their health, so perhaps the comparison with other countries reveals that other countries are spending too little, not that the United States is spending too much. A key issue, then, is what do Americans get from this high level of spending?

Unfortunately, in many respects the American health-care system does not compare favorably with other countries in terms of what it actually delivers. First, consider access. Every other developed capitalist country guarantees universal health-care coverage to all its citizens. The United States is the only country without some form of universal health care. As already noted in Figure 8.1, according to the Congressional Budget Office, while the ACA will reduce the percentage of non-elderly adults without health insurance, current estimates are that 23 million U.S. citizens will remain uninsured in 2024. There are a number of reasons that people will remain uninsured under the provisions of the ACA. Some people, of course, will simply refuse to participate in programs for which they are eligible. But a significant proportion of the anticipated uninsured lives in states that have chosen not to expand Medicaid coverage for low-income people. In the original design of the ACA, a key provision was expanding Medicaid coverage to everyone up to 133 percent of the poverty line. The government subsidies for privately purchased insurance by individuals on the insurance exchanges were designed to make premiums affordable to people above that level. This plan was derailed when the Supreme Court ruled that states could opt out of the Medicaid expansion. As a result, there will remain many poor people who will not be covered by Medicaid and also cannot afford the government-subsidized insurance premiums. According to Colin Gordon, a historian who specializes in health-care policy, the refusal by nearly half of all states to expand Medicaid "will leave two-thirds of poor blacks, two-thirds of single mothers, and half of all uninsured low-wage workers ineligible for Medicaid and therefore unable to afford coverage offered by the insurance exchanges."[10]

The United States relies heavily on private insurance provided by employers, but in recent years the percentage of people covered by

---

[10] "The Irony and Limits of the Affordable Care Act," *Dissent*, October 15, 2013.

workplace-based insurance has declined. This is true at all income levels, but the declines have been especially sharp for people just above the poverty line. Let us define four categories of people with respect to poverty: the *poor*, whose income falls below the poverty line; the *near poor*, whose income is 100–199 percent of the poverty line; *moderate income people*, whose income is 200–399 percent of the poverty line; and the *affluent*, whose income is above 400 percent of the poverty line. As indicated in Figure 8.7, among the poor, the percentage of people with workplace-based health insurance declined from 32 percent to 16 percent between 1984 and 2010; among the near poor, the decline was from 70 percent to 35 percent. Even among moderate-income people there was some decline, from almost 90 percent to 71 percent. Before passage of the ACA, these declines in the percentage of people covered by workplace-based insurance would not have been made up for by any public programs for health insurance; as a result, in 2011 roughly 40 percent of the poor and the near poor had no health insurance at all (Figure 8.8).

It is not surprising that so many people lacked insurance in a system in which public insurance was available only for the elderly and the poor before the ACA went into effect in 2014, and private insurance companies were free to deny people coverage. Private insurance companies, after all,

FIGURE 8.7–Percentage of people under age 65 who get private health insurance through their workplace by economic status: 1984, 2000, and 2010

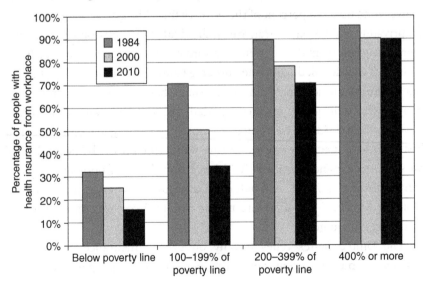

Source: National Center for Health Statistics, *Health, United States, 2011, with Chartbook on Trends in the Health of Americans* (Hyattsville, MD: NCHS, 2011), table 138, p. 414.

FIGURE 8.8—Economic status and health insurance, 2011

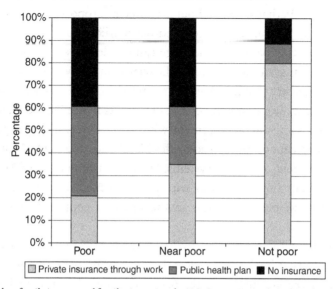

Note: Based on family income and family size, using the U.S. Census Bureau's poverty thresholds. *Poor* persons are defined as those below the poverty threshold; *near poor* persons have incomes of 100% to less than 200% of the poverty threshold; and *not poor* persons have incomes of 200% of the poverty threshold or greater. The "unknown" poverty status response has been excluded. The respondents with unknown poverty status in 2011 totaled 11.5 percent.

Source: Robin A. Cohen and Michael E. Martinez, "Health Insurance Coverage: Early Release of Estimates from the National Health Interview Survey, January–March 2011," tables 4, 5, and 6. Available at http://www.cdc.gov/nchs/data/nhis/earlyrelease/insur201109.htm (accessed July 22, 2014).

are profit-maximizing businesses. If you are in the business of insuring people against medical risks, your ideal customer is a healthy young person who is unlikely to use the insurance. Above all, you would like to avoid insuring anyone with a known, serious health problem. Typically, insurance companies therefore refused to insure people who had preexisting conditions; or, if they were willing to provide insurance, they excluded coverage for those conditions. Insurance companies also liked to deny payment for conditions that they claim were a prior condition, even if the patient was unaware of the condition when purchasing the insurance. Sometimes people who had purchased private insurance in the market and paid premiums for many years found that when they got sick, it became impossible to renew their insurance after the policy ended. These kinds of practices by insurance companies meant that if people on employer-provided health insurance developed cancer or had a heart attack or some other serious illness and then lost their job, they generally found it impossible to buy insurance on the private market. These are some of the issues meant to be solved by the ACA.

What about the length of time it takes to get an appointment when you are sick? Perhaps, even though a higher proportion of Americans were without insurance, the competitive market aspects of the system would ensure that patients on average can get doctor appointments more quickly than in systems with much heavier control by public authorities. Figure 8.9 indicates that this does not seem to be the case. In a 2011 study by the Commonwealth Fund, 59 percent of patients in the United States were able to get a same-day appointment with either a doctor or a nurse compared to 75 percent or more in countries like France and the UK with much more government-controlled systems. In addition, 37 percent of Americans report that they had difficulties with access to medical care due to cost, compared to 22 percent or less in the other 10 countries in the study (Figure 8.10).

What about the quality of American medical care and, above all, its impact on actual health outcomes? There may be problems with health insurance coverage, but the quality of care could still be sufficiently good to more than compensate for insurance problems. And, after all, most of the uninsured do get some kind of health care when they have an emergency. So, perhaps despite the problems of access and high aggregate cost, the quality of health care in the United States could be relatively good compared to other comparable countries.

The first point to make here is that the best hospitals and doctors in the United States do in fact provide excellent medical care. Indeed, this is one reason why wealthy people from around the world often come to the

FIGURE 8.9—Access to doctor or nurse when sick across countries, 2011

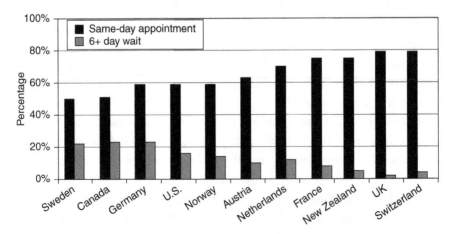

Source: 2011 Commonwealth Fund International Health Policy Survey of Sicker Adults.

FIGURE 8.10—Percentage of people who experienced cost-related access barriers to health care

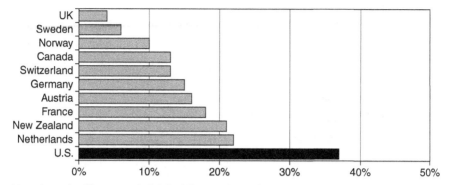

Note: Cost-related barriers included the following: did not fill/skipped prescription, did not visit doctor with medical problem, and/or did not get recommended care.

Source: Cathy Schoen, Robin Osborn, David Squires, and Michelle M. Doty, "Access, Affordability, and Insurance Complexity Are Often Worse in the United States Compared to 10 Other Countries," *Health Affairs* 32 no. 12 (2013): 3.

leading American hospitals for treatment. With their cutting-edge technologies and highly trained doctors, such facilities are undoubtedly among the best in the world. Nevertheless, in evaluating the system as a whole, the central issue is not the quality of the very best facilities, but how well the system delivers adequate medical care for the society as a whole.

Linking the characteristics of the health-care system to health outcomes is a complex matter because so many other things also affect health; nevertheless, available data suggest that health outcomes in the United States also do not compare favorably with most other countries. Figures 8.11 and 8.12 rank the United States with other comparable countries on two important indicators of health outcomes: infant mortality and life expectancy. On both of these measures, the United States fares worse than other wealthy countries. In the case of infant mortality, the United States ranks thirty-sixth among the 195 countries in the United Nations: the U.S. rate is 5.9 infant deaths for every 1,000 live births. This compares to rates of around 3–4 for many European countries. For black infants, the rates in the United States are comparable to some third world countries—they fall between the rates for Panama and Jamaica. In overall life expectancy, the United States ranks thirty-second among the countries in the United Nations—just below Portugal and just ahead of Bahrain. Although these dismal figures for infant mortality and life expectancy are not simply the result of problems with the health-care system, inadequate access to health care is a critical contributing factor.

FIGURE 8.11—Infant mortality rates, United States and selected countries, 2013

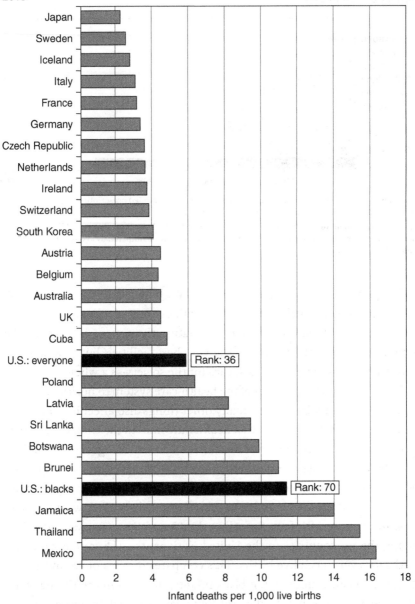

Note: American statistics on African Americans are from 2011.

Source: Cross-national data are from the Central Intelligence Agency, *The World Factbook, 2013*, "Country Comparisons—Infant Mortality Rates." The U.S. data on African Americans are from Table A, "Deaths, age-adjusted death rates, and life expectancy at birth, by race and sex; and infant deaths and mortality rates, by race: United States, 2011," in *National Vital Statistics Reports* 61, no. 6 (October 10, 2012).

One final consequence of the strong presence of markets within the American health-care system is the preoccupation with medical treatment of disease rather than public health and preventive medicine. The United

FIGURE 8.12—Life expectancy at birth, United States and selected countries, 2013

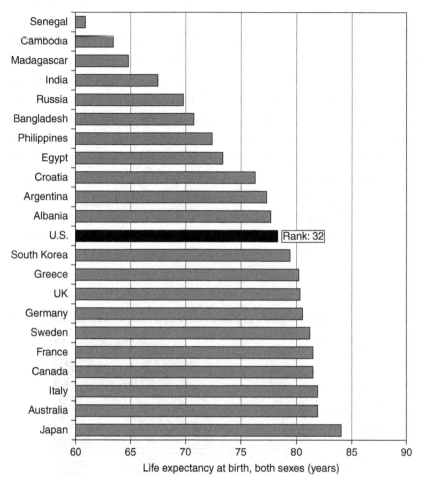

Note: Rankings come from the 193 countries listed by the United Nations.
Source: Central Intelligence Agency, *The World Factbook, 2013*, "Country Comparisons—Life Expectancy at Birth."

States is the only country that does not provide universal, free vaccinations of children. When an attempt was made to provide federal funding for universal vaccination of children in the mid-1990s, it was seen as controversial. It was strongly opposed by drug companies and ultimately failed to pass through Congress. The United States also does not provide free prenatal care for pregnant women, even though research indicates that $1 of prenatal care ultimately reduces medical costs for postnatal care by $3. A market-based logic of health-care provision does not encourage prenatal care; as we noted earlier, when people have to pay for their own medical care (either outright or through co-payments), most people go to the doctor only when something hurts or seems to be going wrong. The only way to make prenatal care widely used is for it to be free, and this means that it must be paid by taxpayers.

Because of these various problems—high cost of medical care, inequalities in access, insecurity of insurance coverage, weak preventative care—many Americans, consumers as well as doctors, are dissatisfied with the health-care system. The level of people's satisfaction with their institutions is difficult to compare across countries because satisfaction and dissatisfaction depend on people's expectations. Nevertheless, it seems that people's level of satisfaction with their health-care system is lower in the United States than in other countries, and much lower than in many. As Figure 8.13 indicates, in 2013, 27 percent of Americans felt that the American health system "has so much wrong with it that we need to completely rebuild it," compared to 4 percent in the United Kingdom and 12 percent or less in most other countries. Only 25 percent of Americans feel the system works well

FIGURE 8.13—Overall views of health-care systems, eleven countries, 2013

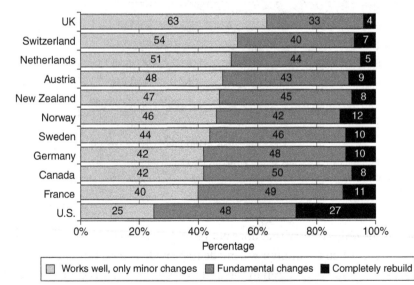

Note: On the survey, the question options were worded as follows:
"On the whole, the system works pretty well and only minor changes are necessary to make it work better."
"There are some good things in our health care system, but fundamental changes are needed to make it work better."
"Our health care system has so much wrong with it that we need to completely rebuild it."

Source: Cathy Schoen, Robin Osborn, David Squires, and Michelle M. Doty, "Access, Affordability, and Insurance Complexity Are Often Worse in the United States Compared to 10 Other Countries" *Health Affairs*, 32, no. 12 (2013): 7. Data from Commonwealth Fund Health Policy Survey in Eleven Countries.

and needs only minor changes, compared to 40 percent or more in all other countries.[11]

It is one thing for people to feel dissatisfied with the status quo and another thing to propose a workable alternative that actually improves overall performance of the system. In the next section, we examine two models for a more efficient, equitable health-care system: the U.S. Veterans Health Administration and the Canadian single-payer health-care system.

HEALTH-CARE ALTERNATIVES

Veterans Affairs Health-Care System

The Veterans Health Administration (VHA), established after World War II as part of the Department of Veterans Affairs, is a system of direct health care provided to U.S. military veterans. These hospitals are run by the federal government, and their doctors are employees of the government. It is not fee-for-service medicine paid for by private insurance. It is a direct government system. As recently as the 1980s, the VHA was a mess: the hospitals were deteriorating, morale was low, efficiency was down, and quality was uneven. Given the general turn to privatization, there was a lot of pressure to scrap the VHA altogether and give the veterans vouchers for buying health care on the free market. This approach more or less describes Medicare: the elderly select their health care on the open market and pay for it through the Medicare public insurance system. The dismantling of government-run hospitals for veterans seemed like the natural thing to do.

Instead, what happened was a major internal reorganization of the VHA—with new technology, new procedures for quality control, new systems of cost containment. How do things look after the reforms?[12] In 2003, the *New England Journal of Medicine* published a study comparing veterans' health facilities with the more market-oriented Medicare on a wide variety of quality measures. The study concluded, "As compared with the Medicare fee-for-service program, the VA performed significantly better on all 11

[11]This strong dissatisfaction with the American health-care system in 2013 is not simply a reflection of the hostile reaction of some people to the health-care reforms passed in 2010. In a 2008 survey asking the same questions, an even higher number of Americans—33 percent—felt that the system needed to be completely rebuilt.

[12]The following account of VA hospitals comes from an article by Phillip Longman, "The Best Care Anywhere," *Washington Monthly*, January/February 2005, 38–45.

similar quality indicators for the period 1997–1999. In 2000, the VA outper-
formed Medicare on 12 of 13 indicators."[13] A second study comparing the VA
and Medicare, published in 2011 by the *Annals of Internal Medicine* at
Harvard Medical School, showed that cancer care provided by the VHA for
men 65 years and older is at least as good as, and by some measures better
than, Medicare-funded fee-for-service care obtained through the private
sector.

Several factors could account for the high quality of VHA care. "Care in
the VHA is much better coordinated than most other settings," said
Nancy Keating, an associate professor at Harvard Medical School. As she
explained,

> The VHA has a good, integrated medical record. Their doctors all work
> together and communicate more effectively. There are no incentives for the
> overuse of cancer treatments because VHA physicians are not rewarded
> financially for prescribing more drugs or procedures. The VHA also mea-
> sures quality across a wide range of conditions, so there is a culture of qual-
> ity improvement.[14]

The National Committee for Quality Assurance (NCQA), an organization
that provides information about health-care quality for business, ranks
health-care plans on 17 different performance measures. Phillip Longman,
reporting on the NCQA evaluations, wrote,

> Winning NCQA's seal of approval is the gold standard in the health-care
> industry. The winner in 2005 was not Johns Hopkins or the Mayo Clinic or
> Massachusetts General. In every single category, the VHA system outper-
> forms the highest-rated non-VHA hospitals.[15]

Contrary to what most Americans believe, at least in the domain of
health care the public sector seems better able than the private sector to
provide consistently high-quality care while controlling costs. There are a
number of reasons for this. First, the size of the VHA generates large

[13]Ashish K. Jha et al., "Effect of the Transformation of the Veterans Affairs Health Care
System on the Quality of Care," *New England Journal of Medicine* 348, no. 22 (May 2003):
2218–2227.

[14]"VHA vs. Medicare: And the Winner Is . . .," *Harvard Gazette*, June 6, 2011. Available at
http://news.harvard.edu/gazette/story/2011/06/vha-vs-medicare-winner-is
-%E2%80%A6/.

[15]Longman, "The Best Care Anywhere."

economies of scale in purchasing all sorts of inputs into production. This is especially important in the VHA's purchase of drugs at a reduced cost by negotiating significant discounts from large pharmaceutical companies. Second, the VHA has much lower administrative overhead costs than any other health system in the United States. This is also, partially, due to economies of scale—a single system of paperwork serves a very large organization. But it is also because the VHA does not have to deal with a wide variety of insurance programs. Third, the VHA system has strong incentives for preventive medicine because of the lifetime link between the VHA and the patient; this lifetime connection also facilitates medical record keeping and health monitoring. Private health companies do not have incentives for doing this. Here is an example from the report by Phillip Longman:

> Suppose a private managed-care plan follows the VHA example and invests in a computer program to identify diabetics and keep track of whether they are getting appropriate follow-up care. The costs are all upfront, but the benefits may take 20 years to materialize. And by then, unlike in the VHA system, the patient will likely have moved on to some new health-care plan. As the chief financial officer of one health plan told Casalino [a professor of public health at the University of Chicago]: "Why should I spend our money to save money for our competitors?"[16]

More generally Longman writes, "Investing in any technology that ultimately serves to reduce hospital admissions, like an electronic medical record system that enables more effective disease management and reduces medical errors, is likely to take money straight from the bottom line."[17]

Of course, there is no guarantee that a system of direct state delivery of medical services will perform well. After all, until the VHA was reorganized and modernized in the 1990s, its hospitals were, by most accounts, not doing a good job. There needs to be effective and committed leadership and meaningful political support for public initiative. When such political support is lacking, then public systems run into trouble. This is precisely what happened to the VHA in the era of the wars in Afghanistan and Iraq.

Reports documenting the outstanding performance of VHA hospitals were all based on data compiled before the impact of the long wars in Iraq and Afghanistan. To deal effectively with the enormously increased demand

[16] Ibid.

[17] Ibid.

for services as a result of these wars, the VHA would have had to expand dramatically. While funding did increase, actual facilities and staffing did not expand sufficiently to deal with the rapidly increasing numbers of veterans in need of care. The result, in 2014, was a political uproar over long waiting times for veterans to get appointments and the practice in at least some VHA hospitals of covering up the problem by falsifying data in official reports. These were indeed very serious problems, resulting in deaths of people on waiting lists. Phillip Longman characterized the problem this way:

> Overwhelmingly, the failures of the VA in recent years have not been about the quality of health care for those who get covered. Instead, they've mostly been about the excessive waiting times and excessive red tape that vets must go through to establish eligibility.[18]

Long waiting times and restrictive eligibility screening are to a substantial extent the result of understaffing relative to patient needs. As one veteran put it, "It's frustrating and infuriating that there are so many dedicated doctors who work for the VA but it seems impossible to get to them. . . . They're serving too many people."[19] So, while direct, publicly provided health care can deliver high-quality medical services, it is also vulnerable to politically motivated budget constraints.[20]

The Canadian Health-Care System

Until the early 1970s, the Canadian health-care system was very much like that in the United States. Most health care was provided on a fee-for-service basis paid for by various forms of private insurance, often connected to employment. There was no national program and no universal guarantee of health care. In 1971 Canada enacted the Canadian National Health Insurance System, now commonly referred to as a single-payer system.

---

[18] Quoted by Robert Pear in "History and Context of an Embattled Department of Veterans Affairs," *New York Times*, May 21, 2014.

[19] Abby Goodnough, "Many Veterans Praise Care, but All Hate the Wait," *New York Times*, June 1, 2014.

[20] As of mid-2014, the precise causes of the failure in the VA to keep up with the increased number of veterans needing its services have yet to be determined. While Republicans have blocked some legislation to increase facilities and staffing, VA budgets have increased during the Middle Eastern wars, and in some years not all of the budget that was approved was actually spent, so the problem is probably not only lack of funding.

The system involves a close working partnership between the Canadian federal government and the provincial governments. The plans are actually run at the provincial level with substantial subsidies from the federal government. The federal government provides grants covering about 40 percent of total costs to provinces on the condition that they provide a health-care program satisfying these core conditions:

- It is universal, available to all citizens.
- It is comprehensive, covering all necessary medical services.
- It is portable in the sense that it recognizes the health-care systems of other provinces and will provide care to any Canadian citizen in the province.
- It is fully accessible to all—there are no special limits and no supplementary charges.
- It is publicly administered and mostly does not allow doctors or hospitals who receive payment from the government program to also receive funds from private insurance or other private forms of payments. This is why the system is referred to as "single payer." This single payer negotiates fees and total budgets for hospitals, clinics, and doctors. In recent years the system has been somewhat modified, allowing health-care providers in some circumstances to operate outside of the single-payer system and accept privately paying patients; but it is still the case that overwhelmingly the payment for health-care services is done directly by the government.[21]

Within this system, the actual provision of health-care services can be organized in a wide variety of ways. Individual doctors can open up offices as solo practitioners. Doctors can form group practices of various sorts. Grassroots organizations can create community clinics. Hospitals can be run by churches, nonprofit organizations, or local governments. Individual patients chose their doctors or groups. The national government does not directly run these services. What it does is pay the bills on an agreed-upon fee schedule that is negotiated annually.

---

[21] Beginning in the 2000s, there has been some erosion of the single-payer condition in the Canadian system. In 2005 the Canadian Supreme Court ruled that people in Quebec—and by extension the rest of Canada—have a right to purchase private insurance as a supplement to the public insurance. This ruling has not, as of 2014, led to a major shift to private insurance.

How does this system work in practice? First it must be said that there is rationing on the basis of medical need in Canada, and sometimes this means longer waits than would occur for some people in the United States. There is less diffusion and duplication of CAT scans, for example, in Canada. They are located in fewer hospitals, whereas in the United States competition for patients has the result that most hospitals acquire such technologies. Even though the overall satisfaction with the Canadian system is higher than in the United States, these longer waits for some procedures do lead to complaints, and sometimes wealthy Canadians come to the United States to get quicker service. Some of these problems of waiting times and rationing are the result of budgetary decisions by political authorities and could be remedied by increased budgets. But it is also important to recognize that all medical systems have to ration medical services in one way or another: by denying access through the policies of private insurance companies, by rationing access through ability to pay, or by applying government policies. It could be argued, therefore, that the form of rationing that comes with the single-payer system does result in a lower "quality" health-care system *for some people*, because individuals are unable to so easily buy better care or quicker service in the system.

This rationing, however, does not mean that these waiting times necessarily have adverse effects on real health outcomes. Indeed, in some situations the existence of a waiting list can actually improve health outcomes because it forces doctors to be more concerned about placing those in greatest need at the top of the list, and this practice can result in reducing unnecessary surgery. In the United States, heart surgeons have considerable incentives to perform coronary bypass surgeries, a certain proportion of which are medically unnecessary. If there was a waiting list, the more ambiguous cases would be placed lower on the list and alternative therapies would be tried. Some of these people, in the end, would not need surgery. In any case, there is no evidence that the modest delays sometimes caused in the Canadian system adversely affect health outcomes.

A second consequence of the Canadian single-payer system is that Canada has much more uniform medical services across regions and across classes. There is relatively little difference in the quality of medical care received by the rich and the poor.

Third, in Canada the availability of health insurance does not enter into employment decisions. In the United States, people are very concerned about health benefits with jobs. Many people are reluctant to leave a job they dislike in order to get new training or to look for a better job because they fear being without insurance. Health insurance costs are also a major problem for many employers because this expense significantly raises their costs of production. These rigidities are absent in Canada.

Fourth, as already noted in Figure 8.5, the administrative costs for medical care are much lower in Canada than in the United States.

Fifth, in Canada patients don't have to deal with the hassles of paperwork that plague the U.S. health-care system. In the United States, even if you have good insurance, the amount of paperwork involved in getting sick is overwhelming, especially for long, complex illnesses involving different doctors, hospitals, and clinics. This complexity is increased when people create health savings accounts to cover deductibles and co-payments. Patients using these accounts have to keep track of all expenses, get proper documentation, and submit complicated forms to the appropriate agencies. In Canada, patients face none of these headaches. They go to a doctor, get treated, and that's it. The doctor submits the bill to the single-payer system and gets paid according to the negotiated fee structure.

These characteristics of the Canadian system create a great irony: Canadians have socialized universal insurance, but doctors there are less hassled by the state and by bureaucracy than doctors in the United States. Government programs actually result in a leaner and simpler bureaucracy than do more market-oriented programs! And what's more, individual consumers of health care actually have greater freedom of choice in Canada than in the United States. People are not forced to join a specific health plan that pays only for specific doctors, but can choose any doctor who has available slots in his or her clinic.

OBSTACLES TO TRANSFORMATION

Given the broadly superior performance of the Canadian single-payer system as well as most other nationally organized universal systems, the real puzzle is why it has proven so difficult to create some system of universal national insurance in the United States. One common answer to this question is American individualism and the cultural opposition to government programs in the United States, and the generally conservative policy preferences of average Americans. Public opinion undoubtedly plays some role in obstructing universal health care, but a more important factor is the power of organized forces with a stake in the existing institutional structure. Three interest groups are especially important: organized physicians, the insurance industry, and pharmaceutical corporations.

The American Medical Association (AMA), the professional association of doctors, has been militantly opposed to anything that smacks of socialized medicine. Colin Gordon writes, "In the 1940s the American Medical Association fabricated a quote from Lenin—'socialized medicine is the keystone in the arch of the socialist state'—to punctuate its Cold War campaign against public health insurance."[22] In 1989 the AMA committed $2.5 million to tell Americans the "facts" about the Canadian system, emphasizing the complaints about the system and ignoring the high level of overall satisfaction with the system as voiced by both patients and doctors. During the early 1990s, the AMA raised the specter of big government making health decisions for all Americans, depriving them of freedom of choice.

Though the AMA is strongly hostile to state-run universal health programs, ordinary doctors are more receptive. For example, a 2007 opinion poll by Indiana University's Center for Health Policy and Professionalism indicated that 59 percent of physicians supported the idea of federally funded national health insurance, and a 2009 opinion poll by Mount Sinai School of Medicine indicated that "nearly three-quarters of physicians supported some form of a public option, either alone or in combination with private insurance options."[23] Yet, it also seems physicians generally believe that their colleagues are less in favor of a significantly more expansive role for the government in financing health care. In a 2004 study of physicians in Massachusetts, 63.5 percent indicated that they preferred a single-payer, publicly financed health insurance system over a system based on managed-care private insurance or a fee-for-service system, but only 51.9 percent of the respondents believed that most physicians would support a single-payer system.[24] A similar discrepancy between the views of physicians and their perception of their colleagues' beliefs was found in earlier studies: a study in the 1960s on physicians' attitudes toward Medicare when it was first introduced found that "70 percent of private practitioners in the State of New York were in favor of it, but only 26 percent thought most of their colleagues

---

[22] "The Irony and Limits of the Affordable Care Act," *Dissent*, October 15, 2013.

[23] The Indiana Poll is reported in Aaron E. Carroll and Ronald T. Ackerman, "Support for National Health Insurance among U.S. Physicians: 5 Years Later," *Annals of Internal Medicine* 148, no. 7 (2008): 566. The Mount Sinai School of Medicine Poll was reported on National Public Radio, "Poll Finds Most Doctors Support Public Option," by Joseph Shapiro, Sept. 14, 2009. Available at http://www.npr.org/templates/story/story.php?storyId=112818960.

[24] Danny McCormick, David U. Himmelstein, Steffie Woolhandler, and David Bor, "Single-Payer National Health Insurance: Physicians' Views," *Archives of Internal Medicine* 164 (2004): 300–304.

were in favor of it."[25] In a 1973 national study of physicians' general attitudes toward National Health Insurance,

> Three-fourths (74%) of the physicians interviewed thought that most of the doctors they knew personally were opposed to 'some form of national health insurance'. . . . Yet when asked about their own attitudes, more than half (56%) were in favor of some form of NHI.[26]

What these studies show is that doctors' beliefs about the opinions of other doctors are shaped by the AMA, and because the AMA so stridently opposed national health insurance, most doctors believe that this must be the dominant view among doctors. In fact, the AMA's opposition is rooted in interests and preferences of the elite strata of doctors, but because of their visibility and power they are able to define the "public opinion of doctors" as a whole.

The other powerful sources of opposition to national health insurance are the private insurance companies and large pharmaceutical companies. Commenting on the prospect of a Canadian-style single-payer system in the United States, Carl Schramm, a spokesman for the Health Insurance Association of America, stated: "We'd be out of business; it's a life and death struggle."[27] In the discussions in 2009 leading up to the introduction of the legislation for the ACA, many people felt that a much better reform would have been "Medicare for all." One way of accomplishing this would be to reduce eligibility age for Medicare by one year every year until eventually everyone was covered. In effect this would have gradually converted the U.S. system to something like a single-payer system. This option was strongly opposed by the insurance industry and as a result was never seriously pursued. A second idea was to include a "public option" that people could choose instead of private insurance. This would have forced private insurance companies to compete with publicly provided insurance and given citizens an open choice about the kind of plan they preferred. A public option provision was initially included in the legislation, but again, it met

[25]John Colombotos and Corrine Kirchner, *Physicians and Social Change* (New York: Oxford University Press, 1986), p. 28.

[26]Ibid., 27–28.

[27]Quoted in Theodore R. Marmor and Jerry Mashaw, "Canada's Health Insurance and Ours: The Real Lessons, the Big Choices," in *National Health Care: Lessons for the United States and Canada*, ed. Jonathan Lemco (Ann Arbor: University of Michigan Press, 1994), p. 70.

with such strong opposition from the insurance industry that eventually it was dropped.

Pharmaceutical companies also strongly opposed greater public involvement in regulating—let alone directly providing—health-care services. Large pharmaceutical companies are among the most profitable corporations because of their ability to charge high prices on patented drugs. They successfully blocked the idea of negotiated lower prices for the Medicare drug plan passed in 2003. In Canada the single-payer system has forced drug companies to lower their prices, and the VHA in the United States has also been able to negotiate lower prices than the open market. The pharmaceutical companies oppose any unified national system for paying for health care because of the threat this would pose to their ability to demand such prices.

So long as these private interests are able to dominate the public debate over health care and influence the policy options that politicians are prepared to put on the table, the prospects for a universal health-care system capable of controlling costs and providing high-quality care for all are dim.

9

FINANCE

One of the general messages of our analysis of the American economy is that while markets are a necessary and important part of all complex economies, in many situations markets generate considerable harms if they are not effectively regulated. We have looked at this problem in some detail for the environment, transportation, and health care. In this chapter we pursue this same broad problem for finance.

Because the workings of financial systems are relatively unfamiliar to most people, we will begin with a brief discussion of the central purposes of financial systems and a tour of the basic concepts needed to understand them. We will then look in a little more detail at one specific financial institution: banks. A full account of a financial system would include discussions of many other institutions as well, including insurance companies, stock markets, venture capital firms, commodity futures markets, private equity firms, and much more. We will focus on banks because they play such a central role in the financial system and because failure in their regulation was a major cause of the financial crisis of 2008. The discussion of banks will be followed by an empirical examination of the historical trajectory of finance in the United States since the middle of the twentieth century and the causes of the crisis at the end of the first decade of the twenty-first.

WHAT A FINANCIAL SYSTEM DOES

Three things are at the heart of financial systems: money, investment, and credit. We might begin by asking: Why do we need money? What is the point of investment? What is so great about credit? We have familiar sayings about these issues: Money is the root of all evil; but also money makes the world go 'round. A penny saved is a penny earned. And, as Polonius warned his son Laertes in Shakespeare's play *Hamlet*, "neither a borrower nor a lender be."

Why do we need money? For millennia humanity did without proper money. When things needed to be exchanged, people bartered. In families things are shared without money. But it is pretty easy to see why money is useful once social life becomes reasonably complex: it enables people to buy things without needing to have some specific useful object that a seller wants in exchange. In a market, money makes the world go 'round because it makes all sorts of transactions much simpler. This doesn't answer the question of what kind of money we have, or even what it is—just what it does and why it is important.

Investment is a very general idea about all the ways we use our current resources not for consumption today but to enhance things in the future. This is by no means an idea restricted to modern market economies. In any society where some resources that could be consumed now are used in ways to increase future benefits, we can speak of investment. When people devote time and energy now to increase their skills, they are investing in future productivity. When business owners buy machines to increase output, they are investing in future profits. When workers put aside some of their earnings in retirement accounts, they are reducing their current consumption in order to generate a stream of income from those investments when they retire. Investment, then, is a way of using resources in the present to enhance resources in the future.

What about credit? Let's imagine a world in which there was no way to get a loan. There is money and investment, but no banks or similar institutions. Suppose you have a project that requires $100,000 of capital and will generate $10,000 in income a year once it is in place. Suppose that out of your own income from your existing work, you can save $5,000 a year. Now, if there were no banks or other institutions for getting loans, it would take you twenty years to save the money you need for the project. With a bank that is willing to give you a loan at, say, 5 percent annual interest, you can start the project right away and pay the interest on the loan with the $5,000 a year that, in the absence of a credit market, you would have put in savings for the project. In this way, credit is of absolutely fundamental importance for economic growth and investment. If all investment were to come out of people's own savings—or for firms, out of their own profits—then many worthwhile and productive projects simply would not happen, and many others would take much, much longer to get off the ground.

Credit is, in a sense, a way of bringing anticipated resources from the future into the present to increase what we can do now.

What money does, then, is make complex coordination of exchange much simpler; what investment does is use resources today to improve our capacities in the future; and what credit does is make investments quicker and easier. All of these are crucial for any complex economy, and this is why all modern economies have institutions built around money, investment, and credit. As it turns out, like other topics we are examining in this book, the actual institutions that organize and regulate money, investment, credit, and other elements of a financial system vary in significant ways across time and place, and this variation can have a significant impact on people's lives. In particular, financial systems vary in the extent to which they underwrite broad prosperity and security for all or primarily benefit the wealthy.

A PRIMER ON BASIC CONCEPTS

In talking about how financial systems work, we first need to define a few basic concepts. Even though some of these will be familiar, it will still be useful to formally define them.

Money

Money is generally defined as a *medium of exchange*, that is, some kind of object or record that can be used as payment for goods and services.[1] In its simplest form it is a physical object—say a gold coin—with an intrinsic value that is recognized by everyone engaged in exchange. In prisons, sometimes cigarettes become a currency in this way: they have an intrinsic value, they can be accumulated, and other goods and services can be denominated in terms of numbers of cigarettes. Some forms of money serve highly specialized purposes. Frequent flyer miles function as a special kind of money, denominated in miles of travel, that enables people to buy airline tickets. Ordinary currency, in contrast, can be used to buy anything that is for sale.

At one time, the money issued by governments was generally backed by gold. This meant that although the money in circulation that was being

---

[1] To the idea that money is a medium of exchange, full definitions of money add two other ideas: money is a *store of value*, and money is a *unit of accounting*.

used to buy things might have been made of paper, the paper money could always be exchanged for the equivalent value in gold. Such a currency system is usually referred to as the gold standard. This turned out to significantly constrain the ability of governments to issue money when needed, especially in times of economic crisis or other emergencies. As a result, eventually all countries abandoned the gold standard and adopted monetary systems based on what is called *fiat money*. Fiat money is issued by a government but is not backed by the value of any physical object like gold. The value of such fiat money depends entirely on the expectations of people that it will be accepted in exchanges by others. One way of thinking about this is that fiat money is backed by the overall wealth and productivity of a country and the faith that people have in the government issuing the money.

Assets

An asset, in the context of finance, is anything of value that is a potential source of income, either because it can be sold for money or because it generates an ongoing stream of income. Some assets, like a home, can also be something you use while you own it. Others are simply financial assets that are being owned because they will be profitable. If you buy an asset, hold it for a period of time, and then sell it for a gain, the difference between the purchase price and selling price is called a *capital gain*.

Stocks, Bonds, and Securities

Stocks and bonds are the most familiar examples of what are called *securities*— financial instruments that can be bought and sold. A stock—also called a share—is an ownership stake in a corporation. If a corporation has 1 million shares, and you own 10,000 of them, then you own 1 percent of the corporation. This gives you a claim on the corporation's assets and earnings, along with the people who own the remaining 99 percent of shares. Owning stock also often gives the owner voting rights in choosing the boards of directors of the firm.[2]

A bond is a particular kind of loan. Organizations that issue bonds are borrowing money from the person who purchases the bond. Unlike stockholders,

[2]There are two principal kinds of shares in corporations: common stock gives their owners voting rights for the board of directors on the basis of one share, one vote; preferred stock does not give the owner voting rights, but has some advantages with respect to the receipt of dividends.

who own a piece of a corporation, bondholders do not own part of the organization; they have merely lent the organization money. Many different kinds of organizations issue bonds, such as corporations; local, state, and national governments; school districts; and banks. While there is a lot of technical language connected to bonds, basically the buyer of a bond earns an interest rate on the bond in exchange for lending the organization money. The bondholder can also make money by selling the bond if it appreciates in value.

Leverage

Leverage refers to the act of borrowing money to buy an investment asset rather than buying the asset exclusively with your own money. Suppose you buy $100,000 of stocks with your own savings and then a year later, you sell them for $200,000. You have made capital gains of $100,000. That is a tidy profit of 100 percent. But suppose you borrowed $90,000 at 10 percent interest per year, and used only $10,000 of your own money to buy the $100,000 of stocks. When you sell the stocks for $200,000 a year later, you pay back the $90,000 loan plus $9,000 in interest. This gives you a profit of $91,000 (i.e., $200,000 minus the $90,000 loan and $9,000 interest and your original $10,000 investment), but now it is a 910 percent profit on your original $10,000 personal investment. By borrowing money for the initial investment, you increased your rate of profit from 100 percent to 910 percent. This is the purpose of leverage: the more you borrow in order to buy assets, the higher the profit you will make *if the asset goes up in price.*

What happens if the asset price goes down? Suppose you borrowed $100,000 from a bank to buy stocks—thinking that their price would rise to $200,000—and instead they decline to $50,000. Your assets are now worth less than the money you borrowed to buy them. You could sell the stocks, but you would still owe $50,000. The time comes to pay back the loan. You can't. You declare bankruptcy. And the bank is out $50,000. This is the sort of thing that produces a financial crisis.

Speculation

Speculation describes a particular kind of economic activity: buying some kind of asset purely because of the belief—or hope—that it will rise significantly in price in the future. This involves taking risks, because you never really know the future. In the 2000s lots of people bought homes not because they needed a place to live, but because they saw the prices of houses rising rapidly and they wanted to buy now and sell later at a higher price. When this activity occurs fairly rapidly, it is called "flipping" houses.

When people buy stocks in corporations, they potentially earn income through two different processes: First, as a part owner of the corporation, they receive an annual dividend—a small piece of the firm's profits. And, second, if the value of the stock itself goes up over time, they can sell the stock and receive capital gains. The second of these processes is an instance of speculation.

Speculative Bubbles

When people buy assets in the hope that they will rise in value, it can happen that the price rise accelerates as more and more people begin bidding up the price of assets. Prices get higher and higher, but in spite of these high asset prices, people continue to buy the asset so long as they have confidence that the prices will continue to rise in the future. The key here is confidence in future price rises. Such high asset prices become unsustainable when people begin to lose confidence that the high price will continue indefinitely. This is referred to as an asset bubble: bubbles cannot expand forever without bursting.

There have been many historical episodes of bubbles: a bubble in the value of tulips in Holland in 1636, investments in the South Sea Company in the nineteenth century, the stock market bubble and crash in the 1920s, the dot.com bubble in the 1990s, and the housing bubble in the 2000s.[3] Often it is not clear while it is happening whether a rapid rise in the price of a type of asset is a bubble or simply reflects an increase in the real demand for the asset. Housing prices can rise, for example, because of increasing demand for houses by people who want to live in a particularly desirable place. If, however, the price rise is not grounded in increases in the real economic value of the underlying asset (what is sometimes called "economic fundamentals"), then at some point some people will begin to suspect that this rise in prices cannot go on forever. They will then sell their stake, wanting to get out while the going is good. If others interpret this action as a sign that it is time to sell, then a panic can ensue—a rapid, mass exodus from

[3]For a history of bubbles and financial crises, see Charles P. Kindleberger and Robert Z. Aliber, *Manias, Panics and Crashes: A History of Financial Crises*, 6th ed. (New York: Palgrave Macmillan, 2011).

holding the asset. Prices plummet; there are lots of sellers and few buyers. The value of the asset crashes. The bubble has burst.

BANKS

With these concepts in hand, let us now look at one critical component of financial systems—banks—and see how they work. Looking at this one critical institution will reveal some of the key issues in how the U.S. financial system works and what has caused its failures.

There are many kinds of banks: small, locally owned community banks; credit unions; large national commercial banks with branches in many cities; investment banks that underwrite the sale of corporate bonds, stock offerings, and a wide range of esoteric forms of investment; central banks run by governments; and others. Like the financial system as a whole, the institutional landscape even within banking is highly differentiated and complex.

Two of these kinds of banks are especially important: commercial banks and investment banks. The first of these are the kinds of banks most people know: banks where people and businesses have savings and checking accounts, and where they go for loans.[4] Investment banks, on the other hand, are banks that deal directly in capital markets in a variety of ways. Unlike commercial banks, they do not have depositors with savings accounts but instead get their capital from investors and loans from other banks. They are particularly important in helping corporations raise capital by underwriting new stock offerings and the sale of corporate bonds.[5] They often play an important role in facilitating mergers and acquisitions of corporations. And unlike traditional commercial banks, they also directly buy and sell all sorts of securities for their own accounts. This means that they directly engage in speculative activity—buying assets in the hope of selling them at a higher price.

While there has always been a distinction between these two kinds of banking activities, before 1933 there was not a sharp distinction in the

---

[4] The banks where individual persons do their banking are also referred to as "retail banks." The broader term *commercial banks* also covers banks where businesses put their deposits and get loans.

[5] When a bank "underwrites" the initial sale of stocks to the public, it signs a contract with the company guaranteeing the sale of a certain number of stocks at some minimum price within a specified period. This is a way of telling the public that the bank has confidence in the value of the company and is thus willing to back the company with its own resources.

United States between types of banks based on these activities. A given bank could engage in both clusters of financial transactions. It is easy to see why bankers liked this: it enabled them to flexibly use money from depositors not simply to make loans but also to directly invest in securities. In general, investing in securities involves more risk than making loans, since borrowers typically put up collateral to get a loan and interest rates are calibrated to reflect the riskiness of the loan. Allowing banks to use deposits to make speculative investments, therefore, inherently means that those deposits are exposed to greater risk.

This interpenetration of the two kinds of banking was a key cause of the financial crash of 1929. Investment bankers invested heavily in the stock market, and when the stock market crashed this threatened the solvency of the banks, which eventually triggered panic among depositors, accelerating bank failures. For this reason, as part of the New Deal, the Glass-Steagall Act of 1933 was passed. This act rigidly separated commercial banking from investment banking by prohibiting any bank from engaging in both kinds of banking activities. This was especially important since the banking reforms of 1933 also created the Federal Deposit Insurance Corporation (FDIC) to provide federal insurance for bank deposits, and it was important to prevent banks from using those insured deposits for speculative investments. This is what "FDIC insured" means. The repeal of the Glass-Steagall Act in 1999, among other factors, set in motion the dynamics that culminated in the financial crisis of 2008.

Let us now look more closely at how these two kinds of banks work.

In ordinary commercial banking, people and businesses deposit money in a bank account and then use that money as a ready reserve to pay bills and withdraw cash for various purposes. Most bank deposits are immediately accessible to the depositor. They are what are called "liquid assets"— a person does not have to wait to get access to them. The bank pays the depositor interest, usually at a fairly low rate, in exchange for holding those funds.

The bank then lends out that money to other people or organizations that want to use it for various purposes, say to expand a business or buy inventory, or buy a house or car. Some of these loans are very short term: due to the timing of cash flow from its sales, a business needs a short-term loan to meet payroll obligations, or a construction firm needs to buy raw materials to build a house before the home buyer pays for the house. Other loans are long term. Among the most important examples of long-term loans are home loans, or mortgages. The bank is able to make money on these transactions because the interest rates on loans are greater than the interest rates on deposits. That difference in rates is called a *spread*.

When banks lend out money they are, in effect, "creating" money in the economy—increasing the amount of money in circulation. Here is how that works: One person deposits $1,000 into a bank. Suppose the bank is required to keep 10 percent of all deposits as a capital reserve. The bank then lends out $900 to someone. The original depositor still owns the $1,000 deposited and can withdraw it at any time, but now a second person has $900 to use. So there is now $1,900 in the economy, whereas before there was only $1,000. The borrower then buys a couch for $900, and the store puts this revenue in an account in a bank, which then lends out 90 percent of this deposit, $810, to someone else. Now there is $2,781 in the economy: the original $1,000 deposit, the $900 owned by the store that sold the couch, and the $810 by the new borrower. And so on.

Banks get money to lend out in other ways besides from depositors. They can also borrow money from other banks. They can sell bonds to people who are in effect lending the bank money and then lend out this money at higher rates to people who borrow from the bank. They can sell shares in the bank to people who want to invest directly in the bank. And, if they are a federally charted bank, they can borrow money from the Federal Reserve Bank.[6] This turns out to be a pretty important part of the whole banking system; this is the way that the government can infuse money into the economy. The government can lend money to banks at relatively low rates, which the banks then lend to people and businesses to use for various purposes. This "federal funds" rate—the interest rate at which the Fed lends to banks—is also the main way the Federal Reserve Bank can influence the interest rates in the economy at large: the cheaper it is for banks to acquire money from the Fed, the lower the interest rates they can charge for the loans they in turn make.

There is always some risk attached to making a loan, since the borrower may default on the loan and not pay it back. This is why it is important for banks to look carefully at the creditworthiness of the people and businesses seeking loans, assess the risks involved, and charge an appropriate interest rate: the higher the risks, the higher the interest rate should be.

---

[6]The Federal Reserve Bank is the government-run central bank of the United States. Its responsibilities include shaping the money supply and interest rates in the United States through a variety of policies; regulating banks; working to maintain the stability of the entire financial system by reducing "systemic" risks; and providing a range of financial services, especially to commercial banks (banks with deposits) and the U.S. government.

A bank can go bankrupt if it makes lots of stupid loans and doesn't get paid back, or perhaps even if it makes sensible loans and then some catastrophe occurs that results in too many loan defaults. The potential for a bank to fail because of defaults on loans can, in the right circumstances, trigger a problem called *a run on the bank.* Here is how this can happen: A fundamental aspect of banking is that banks do not keep most of their depositors' money in their vaults; they lend out most of the money. What banks keep is called a capital reserve. The smaller the reserve required by the government's regulatory rules, the more can be lent out and the more money the banks can make. But what happens if suddenly all the depositors wanted their money out of the bank? Suppose depositors were afraid that the bank was going to go bankrupt. Perhaps the bank was making very sensible loans, but other banks were failing and depositors panicked. Thinking that their bank also was going to fail, they line up to take out their deposits. But the bank has only 10 percent of the deposits in the bank, and whereas depositors have the right to withdraw their deposits "on demand," the bank cannot instantly call back the loans it has made.

When this kind of run on the bank occurs, a perfectly sound bank could collapse. What is more, because banks are interconnected—they make loans to one another—the failure of one bank can trigger failures of others. The cumulative cascading effect of such failures constitutes a financial "panic" in which the entire economy becomes deeply disrupted. This is an important aspect of what happened in the Great Depression in the United States in the early 1930s.[7]

What is the solution? One solution is for the government to insure bank deposits. This is what the U.S. federal government did in the 1930s in response to the banking crisis of that era when it created the Federal Deposit Insurance Corporation (FDIC). Bank deposits are now insured up to $250,000. Even if a bank collapses, the depositors get their money back. In the financial crisis of 2008, no depositor of $250,000 or less in a bank account insured by the FDIC lost a penny.

---

[7]The Great Depression also critically involved a stock market crash. These two dimensions of the Depression—the stock market crisis and the collapse of banks—were deeply interconnected because in the mid to late 1920s, many people had borrowed heavily from banks in order to invest in the stock market. This helped fuel the stock market bubble. When the stock market bubble burst, not only did investors lose their investments, but they also defaulted on the loans used to purchase the stocks, and this in turn contributed to the financial panic in the banking sector.

Unfortunately, deposit insurance, while solving the problem of runs on banks, contributes to a new, potentially serious problem: knowing that the depositors are insured, banks may be willing to make riskier loans. This is another example of what in Chapter 8 we referred to as a moral hazard problem: insuring people or an institution against certain kinds of risks may increase the willingness of people to engage in risky behavior.[8] This problem becomes even more serious if the banks become so big that their collapse would threaten the stability of the entire economy. This is often called the problem of becoming "too big to fail" (TBTF). Because of the intense interconnections among large financial institutions, the collapse of a gigantic financial institution can generate ripple effects that pose potentially serious threats to the economy as a whole. Governments are thus very reluctant to let very large financial institutions collapse, and so when large banks run into serious trouble, governments often rescue them through bailouts. A bailout functions very much like insurance: in effect it means that if a high-risk strategy pays off, the bank reaps the rewards, but if it fails, someone else has to pay. When the government pays in the form of a bailout, taxpayers ultimately bear the cost.

So, if deposit insurance and the prospects of bailouts encourage risky behavior by banks and other financial institutions, and such risky behavior potentially threatens the stability of the economic system as a whole, wouldn't it be better to refuse bailouts and end government insurance of deposits? Banks, like ordinary people, should have to pay the costs of their own mistakes, it is often said. This could be a reasonable conclusion if bank failures harmed only the people who made the risky investments, but that simply is not the case. This seems very much like a "damned if you do, damned if you don't" situation: if the government refuses to bail out large financial institutions when they run into trouble, many innocent bystanders are harmed; if the government does bail out those institutions, this only encourages them to engage in the same behavior that led to the need for a bailout in the first place.

This picture is complicated enough, but it only gets more complex when we add investment banks to the story. When people talk about the centers of power on "Wall Street," part of what they are talking about are investment banks like JPMorgan Chase and Goldman Sachs. Investment banks make their money in two principal ways: through fees from clients for various kinds of financial transactions, and through their own direct investments.

[8] See p. 154.

Investment banks receive fees for all sorts of transactions in which they act as financial intermediaries for clients. Suppose a new corporation that is not yet listed on a stock market wants to become a shareholder company by selling stock to the public. An investment bank will be called in to underwrite the initial public offering (IPO) of the stock.[9] Similarly, if an existing corporation wishes to issue new stocks or bonds, an investment bank will act as the intermediary, organizing all the details of the sale. Investment banks also play this role for mergers and acquisitions. On all such transactions, investment banks receive fees regardless of whether the investment itself ultimately pays off for their clients.

Investment banks also make money by directly investing their own capital. They may, for example, not simply underwrite the sale of stock by a corporation to the public; they may also hold such stock in their own investment portfolio. Investment banks, in short, make money both through fees charged to clients and through speculation.

Because investment banks directly engage in speculative activity, they are vulnerable to the risks that typically accompany speculation: they can acquire securities in the expectation that these assets will increase in value, only to see the value of those assets fall. The potential risks of speculation will be intensified if the bank itself borrows heavily to finance its acquisition of those securities in the first place. Investment bankers will generally have an incentive to do so, since the rate of return on a successful investment is higher if the investment involves borrowed money (see the discussion of leverage earlier in this chapter).

In normal times, investment banks generally have sufficient capital reserves to deal with the inevitable ebb and flow of investment outcomes. But in situations where there are financial bubbles, investment banks can become precarious if they have borrowed heavily to fuel their investment strategy. When bubbles burst and the securities held by the bank collapse, then the bank may not be able to repay these loans, thus jeopardizing the solvency of other banks. As in the case of runs on commercial banks by depositors, the intense interconnections of banks means that the failure of a giant investment bank can trigger cascade effects that generate instability and even crisis in the financial system as a whole.

The only viable way to avoid these threats to financial stability posed by both commercial and investment banking is to systematically regulate the financial sector to ensure that banks and other financial institutions act

[9]See note 5.

responsibly in the public interest. If this regulation is effective and fair, then a finance system can broadly advance the goal of prosperity for all. Let us now turn to the development of the U.S. financial system in the late twentieth century and the financial crisis of the early twenty-first century.

The U.S. Financial System

To understand the financial crisis that began in 2008, it will be helpful to look at certain longer-term trends in the U.S. economy. In particular, we need to understand what is sometimes referred to as the *financialization* of the U.S. economy.

In a very rough way, economic activity can be divided into two sorts: activity directly involved in producing the goods and services people consume—cars, computers, food, education, health care, haircuts—and activity that involves, in one way or another, purely financial transactions—borrowing and lending, buying and selling stocks and bonds, speculating on highly specialized markets like the market for mortgage-backed securities, and so on. Sometimes it is hard to tell which of these activities is taking place, but it is still possible to broadly distinguish between activities in what economists call the real economy and activities within the purely financial economy. Profits are made in both kinds of activities in a capitalist economy. An automobile company like General Motors can make profits by producing and selling cars to consumers and also by loaning money to consumers to help them purchase cars. In the housing sector, construction companies make profits by building houses; banks make profits from the interest payments on mortgages sold to home buyers.

The striking thing about the trajectory of American capitalism in the last half of the twentieth century is a sharp shift from a system in which profits were overwhelmingly being generated through the production and distribution of goods and services—the real economy—to a system in which profits increasingly came from purely financial transactions. Figure 9.1 indicates the long-term trajectory of the financial sector's profits as a share of total domestic corporate profits in the post-WWII period from 1947 to 2013. From the end of WWII through the 1970s, financial profits fluctuated mostly in the 10–15 percent range of total corporate profits, averaging 13.8 percent for the entire period. Beginning in the early 1980s this figure rose sharply, reaching a high in 2002 of over 37 percent of profits in the economy. Financial profits have been at or above 25 percent every year of the twenty-first century except during the worst period of the financial crisis.

FIGURE 9.1—Financialization of the American economy, 1947–2013

Source: From U.S. Department of Commerce Bureau of Economic Analysis (BEA), National Income and Product Accounts (NIPA) Tables. Table 6.16, "Corporate Profits by Industry" (last revised April 30, 2014); and Table 1.1.4, "Price Indexes for Gross Domestic Product." Available at http://www.bea.gov/iTable/index_nipa.cfm (accessed May 14, 2014).

This shift in the weight of finance in the share of corporate profits corresponds to a second shift in the American economy: the relationship of wages and salaries in the financial sector to wages and salaries in the rest of the economy. As shown in Figure 9.2, until the early 1980s, the growth in annual wages and salaries in the finance sector was only slightly above that of the rest of the private sector and grew at pretty much the same rate. Then, quite abruptly, annual earnings among employees in finance began growing much more rapidly than in the rest of the economy, so that by the first decade of the twenty-first century annual earnings in finance were twice that of the rest of the private sector.

FIGURE 9.2—Real average annual compensation (wages and salaries), finance sector vs. rest of the private sector, 1947–2012

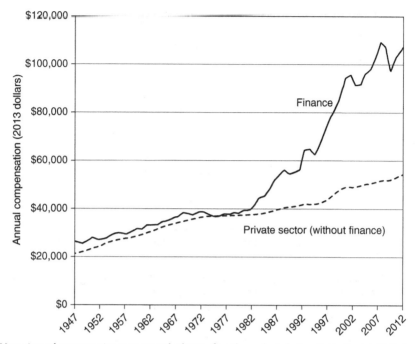

Note: Annual compensation is wages and salaries of employees by industry, divided by total full-time equivalent employees in that industry. Finance excludes real estate and insurance industries.

Source: Authors' calculations based on data from U.S. Department of Commerce Bureau of Economic Analysis (BEA), NIPA Tables. Table 6.3, "Wages and Salaries by Industry" (last revised Aug. 7, 2014); Table 6.5D, "Full-Time Equivalent Employees by Industry" (last revised Aug. 7, 2014); and Table 1.1.4, "Price Indexes for Gross Domestic Product" (last revised April 30, 2014). Available at http://www.bea.gov/iTable/index_nipa.cfm (accessed May 15, 2014).

A third trend is connected to these first two: the degree of regulation and deregulation of the financial sector. Thomas Philippon and Ariell Reshef have developed an index of financial deregulation; the higher the value of the index, the *less* regulation there is of finance.[10] Figure 9.3 indicates the changes in this index over the course of the twentieth century.

At the beginning of the century, there were very few restrictive regulations on banks and other financial institutions. Serious regulation began in the 1930s in the aftermath of the Great Depression. Most notably, the Glass-Steagall

[10]For details on the construction of the index, see Thomas Philippon and Ariell Reshef, "Wages and Human Capital in the U.S. Financial Industry: 1909–2006," National Bureau of Economic Research working paper No. 14644, January 2009, p. 33.

FIGURE 9.3—Historical changes in levels of financial regulation and deregulation, 1909–2006

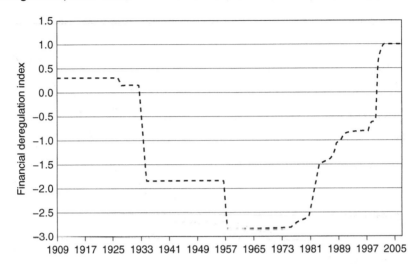

Note: The deregulation index is derived from four different kinds of financial regulation. The lower the value of this index, the higher the level of financial regulation.

Source: Thomas Philippon and Ariell Reshef, "Wages and Human Capital in the U.S. Financial Industry: 1909–2006" (NBER Working Paper No. 14644, 2009).

Act of 1933 rigidly separated commercial banking from investment banking, imposed restrictions on interest rates, and created a variety of other provisions that restricted the activities of financial institutions. These regulations were designed both to protect the economic interests of ordinary people by insuring their deposits and to increase the stability of the financial system as a whole by reducing the likelihood that a bank will collapse. In the 1950s a second wave of regulations imposed restrictions on the relationship between banks and insurance companies and tightened up restrictions on banks headquartered in one state with branches in another.

By the end of the 1950s, regulation of finance in the United States was at its high point (and thus in Figure 9.3, *de*regulation was at the minimum). Banks, especially large banks, did not like these restrictions and did their best to undermine them. Even if these regulations helped prevent financial instability in the system as a whole, they clearly constrained the profitability of financial institutions. Bankers did their best to get around the restrictions when they could and worked politically to change the rules in their favor. Many arguments were used against these regulations of the financial sector: the rules reduced competition and thus were inefficient; they impeded financial innovation; they reduced the amount of credit available; they made U.S. banks less competitive than their European rivals. But more than anything, the regulations hampered the profitability of the financial sector and thus harmed the material interests of wealthy investors in finance; this was the central motivation for the efforts at deregulation.

The first significant weakening of the restrictive rules governing finance occurred in the late 1970s around issues of caps on interest rates and the regulation of pension funds. This was followed in 1980 by the Depository Institutions Deregulation and Monetary Control Act, which eliminated a number of important restrictions on the economic activities of savings and loan institutions, a specialized kind of bank for home mortgages.[11] Until this time, S&Ls, or thrifts, were tightly regulated financial institutions devoted almost exclusively to financing residential homes. They were universally considered safe and sober institutions. Their deregulation in 1980 resulted in a rapid intensification of the speculative behavior of these banks, culminating in what came to be known as the S&L crisis: over 1,000 S&Ls out of a little over 3,000 failed in the late 1980s and early 1990s. Because the deposits in these banks were insured by the government, the crisis directly cost taxpayers around $130 billion (in 1995 dollars, or about $200 billion 2014 dollars).

The late 1970s was the beginning of what later became known as the era of "neoliberalism," the broad doctrine that markets work best when they are only lightly regulated and that the government provision of goods and services should be broadly replaced by private market provision. The election of Margaret Thatcher in Britain in 1979 and Ronald Reagan in the United States in 1980 brought this ideology to the center of political power, accelerating efforts to privatize government functions and eliminate government regulations that interfered with the private pursuit of profits. As a result, deregulation accelerated in the 1980s.

In the 1990s the strong restrictions on investment activities of commercial banks were initially relaxed. Finally, in 1999, the Financial Modernization Act repealed what was left of the Glass-Steagall Act. The Financial Modernization Act was quickly followed by the Commodities Futures Modernization Act of

---

[11] The regulations that were eliminated or relaxed included accounting standards, rules governing the size of loans that were permitted given the value of a property, and the levels of net worth savings and loan companies (S&Ls) were required to have in order to operate. For an analysis of the role of deregulation in the S&L crisis, see FDIC, *History of the Eighties— Lessons for the Future* (Federal Deposit Insurance Corporation, 1997), Chapter 4, "The Savings and Loan Crisis and Its Relationship to Banking," available at http://www.fdic.gov/bank/historical/history/167_188.pdf (accessed July 28, 2014).

2000, which opened up even more arenas for only lightly regulated specula-tive activity. By the first decade of the twenty-first century, according to Philippon and Reshef, the American financial system was less tightly regu-lated than it had been at the beginning of the twentieth century.

This process of ending the elaborate system of financial regulation that had developed from the 1930s through the 1950s was enthusiastically sup-ported by both the Democratic and Republican parties; it was not a partisan issue. Both parties embraced the neoliberal idea that markets could be largely self-regulating and that government interference should be mini-mized. Both parties systematically served the needs of Wall Street. The earliest significant deregulation—the removal of many restrictions on S&Ls—occurred at the end of the Carter administration. The Reagan administration deepened the ideological position that deregulation of the financial sector was a basic political objective. Some of the key changes in regulation, especially reducing the supervision of banks and allowing commercial banks to engage in speculative investments, occurred in the 1990s during the Clinton adminis-tration. Obama, in the aftermath of the financial crisis, remained friendly to Wall Street, supporting only modest new regulations that did not challenge the core interests of large financial institutions. The financialization of the American economy has bipartisan support in government.

Of course, it can never be the case that a financial system is completely *un*regulated. There are always rules, but the new rules in play by the year 2000 allowed for much more freewheeling risk taking and what is called "financial innovation" than had been the case three decades earlier. This meant that the opportunities for profit in the financial sector increased rap-idly. And with this, financial institutions could increase the pay of some seg-ments of their labor force in order to attract people who were especially skilled at aggressively exploiting these opportunities. The result was both the rapid expansion of the financial sector (Figure 9.1) and a rise in the earnings of many people working in the sector (Figure 9.2). As indicated in Figure 9.4, the changes in relative earnings in the financial sector compared to other sectors closely track the changes in the degree of regulation and deregulation of financial institutions.[12]

---

[12] This close association, of course, by itself does not prove that deregulation caused the rapid growth of profits in the financial sector and the divergence of wages in that sector from the rest of the economy. Nevertheless, since bankers had been pushing for such dereg-ulation for years, arguing that regulations hurt their profits, there is little doubt that remov-ing restrictive regulations on the strategies of banks significantly contributed to these changes in the fortunes of the financial sector.

FIGURE 9.4—Relative financial wage and financial deregulation, 1909–2006

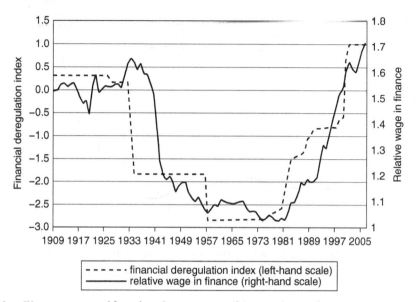

Note: Wages are computed from the industry accounts of the United States, from Kuznets (1941), and from Martin (1939). The relative wage is the ratio of financial to non-farm private wages.

Source: Thomas Philippon and Ariell Reshef, "Wages and Human Capital in the U.S. Financial Industry: 1909–2006" (NBER Working Paper No. 14644, 2009).

Deregulation also contributed to rapid growth in the size of financial institutions. Size matters both because of the TBTF problem and because of the power that financial institutions accumulate once they become enormous. Many of the previous restrictions on banking practices were also, in practice, restrictions on the size of banks. If a bank cannot have branches in states outside of the state where it is headquartered, and if commercial banking and investment banking are rigidly separated, then this also limits how large banks can get.

Elimination of restrictive rules on banking in the last quarter of the twentieth century meant not only that profits overall in the financial sector grew, but that the size of the largest financial institutions grew rapidly as well. Figure 9.5 shows the total assets of the three largest U.S. banks as a percentage of total commercial banking assets. This figure hovered around 10–15 percent of total assets for over half a century from the mid-1930s to the early 1990s. The concentration of banking then began a steady rise, accelerating dramatically after the Glass-Steagall restrictions on commercial and investment banking were removed. By the eve of the financial crisis, over 40 percent of all commercial banking assets were owned by the

FIGURE 9.5—Changes over time in concentration of banking, 1946–2007

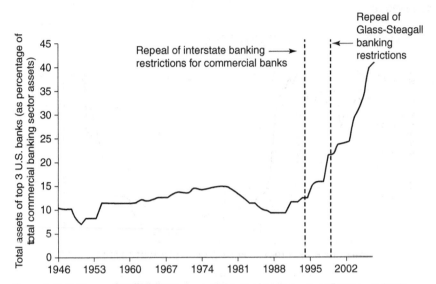

Source: A. G. Haldane and R. M. May, "Systemic Risk in Banking Ecosystems," *Nature* 469 (2011): 351–355. doi:10.1038/nature09659.

three largest banks: JPMorgan Chase, Bank of America, and Citigroup. These banks had become absolutely gigantic, dwarfing nearly all other enterprises in the economy.

One way of getting a sense of the scale of these large banks is to compare their size to the total income generated annually by the entire U.S. economy, the gross domestic product (GDP). Figure 9.6 shows the growth in the size of the six largest banks, defined by their total assets, as a percentage of U.S. GDP. In 1995 the assets of the six largest banks were the equivalent of less than 20 percent of GDP. By 2009 this had risen to just over 60 percent of GDP. In 2009, GDP in the U.S. was about $14.5 trillion. The six largest banks had assets worth over $8.5 trillion.

The dismantling of the regulatory apparatus of finance was defended on the grounds that this would encourage financial innovation and make financial markets more efficient. There is little doubt that deregulation spurred innovation. A wide variety of novel financial innovations were created or refined in this new environment, including such things as mortgage-backed securities, credit default swaps, collateralized debt obligations, and much more. Deregulation also encouraged the emergence of what has been called the "shadow banking system," new kinds of institutions that look a lot like specialized investment banks but are officially exempted from whatever remaining regulations monitor the behavior of

FIGURE 9.6—Total assets of six "too big to fail" banks, 1995–2009

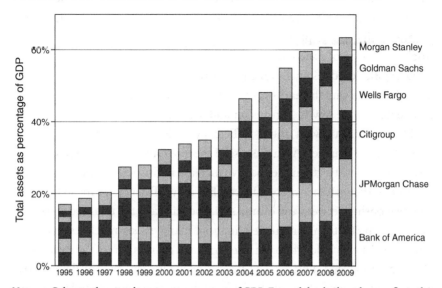

Notes: 1. Columns show total assets as a percentage of GDP. For each bank, the column reflects the "total assets" line from the bank's annual balance sheet. Data comes from each company's annual reports. 2009 is at end of the third quarter.

2. These are conservative estimates of the actual size of the banks: from an economic standpoint, the balance sheets exclude several assets that should be counted, like many derivatives contracts.

3. Most of these banks were involved in mergers during the period considered in the graph. For each bank, before the merger, the authors use the asset size of the larger pre-merger entity. (This information was provided by the authors through personal communications, May 2014.)

Source: Simon Johnson and James Kwak, *13 Bankers: The Wall Street Takeover and the Next Financial Meltdown* (New York: Pantheon Books, 2010), Figure 7-1, "Growth of Six Big Banks." Data update provided by the authors.

banks. These new institutions are specifically geared toward augmenting the wealth of already very wealthy people. Perhaps the most well-known of these shadow-banking institutions are hedge funds, defined by the website Investopedia as follows:

> An aggressively managed portfolio of investments that uses advanced investment strategies such as leveraged, long, short and derivative positions in both domestic and international markets with the goal of generating high returns (either in an absolute sense or over a specified market benchmark). Legally, hedge funds are most often set up as private investment partnerships that are open to a limited number of investors and require a very large initial minimum investment. . . . In the U.S., laws require that the majority of investors in the fund . . . must earn a minimum amount of money annually and have a net worth of more than $1 million.[13]

[13]http://www.investopedia.com/terms/h/hedgefund.asp.

Deregulation also encouraged a range of technological innovations in finance, including the use of powerful computers with automated trading programs that make profits by buying and selling enormous volumes of stocks a fraction of a second earlier than other brokers.[14]

Deregulation does encourage innovation. It also increases profits in the financial sector and the earnings of at least some of the people who work in that sector, as we saw in Figures 9.1 and 9.2. Financial profits soared in the neoliberal age. But what about "efficiency"? Here we enter a much more contentious set of issues. As in the case of the environment, if efficiency simply means "profitability," then the massive increase in financial profits necessarily means that the system is more efficient. But if by efficiency we mean the optimal relationship between the overall social benefits and the total social costs of a certain activity, then deregulated financial markets look much less efficient. Above all, if we include economic insecurity and crisis as part of the social costs of an institution, and consider the extreme inequality generated by deregulated financial institutions, then the deregulated financial system created in the last decades of the twentieth century looks far from efficient.

The Financial Crisis of 2008

With this general background about the development of the U.S. financial system in the last decades of the twentieth century, we can now look more closely at the financial crisis of 2008. At the heart of the crisis was the accumulation of interlocking debt among extremely large financial institutions engaged in increasingly risky investments using esoteric financial instruments—and all of this was happening in the context of weak regulation of financial markets. A detailed account of the crisis involves lots of highly technical issues in the operation of financial markets, but there is a fairly straightforward story of the underlying dynamic at work that centers on the housing market, mortgages, and a highly leveraged speculative process that became linked to a housing bubble.[15]

---

[14]For a discussion of high frequency trading (HFT), see Michael Lewis, *Flash Boys* (New York: W. W. Norton & Company, 2014), and Nick Bauman, "Too Fast to Fail: Is High-Speed Trading the Next Wall Street Disaster?" *Mother Jones*, January/February 2013.

[15]This account of the 2008 crisis draws on the following sources: Carmen Reinhart and Kenneth Rogoff, *This Time Is Different* (Princeton, NJ: Princeton University Press, 2009); Simon Johnson and James Kwak, *13 Bankers: The Wall Street Takeover and the Next Financial Meltdown* (New York: Pantheon Books, 2011); and Mensie D. Chinn and Jeffry A. Frieden, *Lost Decades: The Making of America's Debt Crisis and the Long Recovery* (New York: W. W. Norton & Company, 2011).

Very few people can save enough money to buy a $220,000 home, which was more or less the median price for a home in the United States in 2014, so they borrow the needed funds from banks on various terms. Mortgages can be for fifteen years or thirty years; they can have fixed interest rates or variable rates; they can require large or small down payments; they can sometimes involve public subsidies to make a loan more affordable to certain categories of people (for example, GIs after WWII). These different terms enable mortgage lenders to carefully tailor the loans to the financial situation of the borrower. Mortgage lending is thus essential to enable large numbers of people to own homes when they otherwise could never afford to do so.

Once a financial institution has made a mortgage loan to a home buyer, it can hold that mortgage and earn profits from the interest payments, or it can sell the mortgage to other investors who treat mortgages as an asset. This system serves a positive function by enabling the mortgage-originating institution to make more mortgage loans than it otherwise could. But it also opens the door for a much more speculative dynamic in the mortgage market.

Here is how that happened in the run-up to the 2008 financial crisis: These buyers of mortgages bundled them together, combining high-risk and low-risk mortgages into complex financial instruments called mortgage-backed securities. Then, to add another layer of complexity, other financial institutions were willing to sell insurance policies to these investors based on the value of these mortgage-backed securities—basically insuring them against a fall in the value of these packages of bundled mortgages. Other investors made bets on the future values of these bundled assets, predicting that the assets would rise or fall. What is more, to increase the rate of profit on these speculative investments, investors took out loans to buy the securities, creating layers upon layers of actors engaged in interconnected, leveraged speculative investments. On all these transactions fees were paid, and so there was a built-in incentive for people deeply engaged in these financial processes to keep the supply of these securities flowing.

In the early 2000s these general dynamics intensified. Housing prices were going up. Some people were getting loans to buy houses, thinking that they could sell the houses later at much higher prices. Others were buying houses thinking that because of future price rises, they would rapidly accumulate equity in their homes. (Home equity is the difference between the value of the house if it were sold and what the homeowner still owes on the mortgage.) Home equity is a form of wealth that enables homeowners to take out additional loans—called home equity loans—to increase their consumption or pay for college tuition or cover an emergency health crisis.

Sellers of mortgage loans had an incentive to provide the loans and then sell the mortgage on the secondary market to financial institutions that create the complex mortgage-backed securities. The banks and other mortgage-lending institutions actually making the original mortgage loans in the first place got a fee for every mortgage they sold to a home buyer and another fee when they sold the mortgage on the secondary market. Since the originating banks sold these mortgages to other institutions, they had little incentive to worry about the longer-term risk of default. Because of deregulation, some of the largest financial institutions in the country were also in the business of both creating these initial mortgages and then packaging them for the secondary market.

As the process started heating up, mortgage lenders began issuing mortgages to people who really couldn't afford them, often selling these mortgages in highly deceptive ways by misrepresenting the longer-term costs faced by the home buyer seeking the loan. This is the famous problem of subprime mortgages: mortgages are sold to people with insufficient income to pay for the interest in the long term. So, to get such people to take out loans, lenders offered them mortgages with low initial monthly payments; however, after a period, the payments were scheduled to rise rapidly. The homeowners with subprime mortgages also often thought that once their houses appreciated in value, they would be able to refinance them at a lower, more affordable interest rate because then the asset would be more valuable. As long as housing prices kept rising, this looked like a safe bet.

Meanwhile, the investors who bought the mortgages from the initial mortgage lender sold them in the form of mortgage-backed securities. The institutional investors that bought these mortgage-backed securities saw them as a fairly safe investment. On the one hand, since the mortgage-backed securities contained both high-risk and low-risk mortgages, the bundles seemed to be a way of balancing risk. On the other hand, with housing prices continually rising it appeared that even if the original borrowers defaulted on their loans, this would not pose a serious problem. The foreclosed properties would be worth more than the loan, and thus when they were eventually sold, the loans would be repaid.

As this process continued, all sorts of other actors got into the game: insurance companies insuring these financial instruments; developers taking out large loans to build huge tracts of new houses and condos; other investors borrowing money to buy mortgage-backed securities; unions, city governments, and school districts buying mortgage-backed securities as investments for their pension funds. The result was a complex array of interlocking debts—leveraged in sophisticated ways to maximize profits. This all worked fine, so long as prices kept rising.

Figure 9.7 shows the long-term trends in housing prices from 1901 to 2013. In this graph, housing prices are adjusted for general price inflation and are given an index value of 100 in the year 2000. For the half century from 1947 to 1996, housing prices were relatively stable, fluctuating between 80 percent and 100 percent of the price level in the year 2000. Then, beginning in the late 1990s, housing prices began a rapid rise, reaching 160 percent of their 2000 value by 2006. Clearly, this was a housing bubble. The price rise was not driven by any underlying real increase in the value of houses or the costs of producing them; it was driven by the way financial institutions organized speculative investments in the credit market for housing. When prices started declining, the whole structure of interconnected debt began to unravel. And when the bubble burst, some very large financial institutions suddenly found themselves unable to pay their debts.

FIGURE 9.7—Real housing prices in the United States, 1901–2013

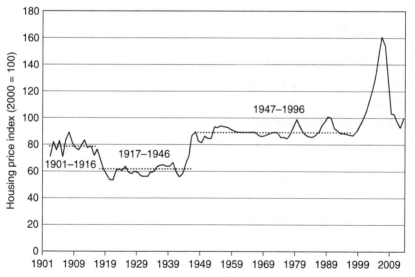

Note: Real housing prices are indexed to year 2000 = 100. Starting in 1953, data correspond to prices during the first quarter of each year. House prices are deflated by GNP deflator.

Source: Robert J. Shiller, *Irrational Exuberance*, 2nd ed. (Portland, OR: Broadway Books, 2005), Figure 2.1. Updated data available online at http://www.econ.yale.edu/~shiller/data.htm (accessed May 15, 2014).

Things came to a head in the fall of 2008 when a large and respected Wall Street investment bank, Lehman Brothers, failed. Lehman Brothers was heavily involved in all sorts of derivatives markets, including mortgage-backed securities. Its investments were also heavily leveraged—that is, it had borrowed heavily from other banks to increase its rate of profit. Many of its assets dropped in value as housing prices began declining in 2007, and by mid-2008 its assets were basically worthless. When it could not repay loans that were due in September 2008, it collapsed. Because it could not repay the loans it had gotten from other banks, and because of its size, its collapse threatened the solvency of those other financial institutions. And since the institutions most connected to Lehman Brothers also had debts, if they collapsed this could trigger a domino effect.

The ramifications of Lehman Brothers defaulting on its loans were intensified by the array of new financial instruments that were linked to the mortgage-backed securities—collateralized debt obligations, credit default swaps, and other esoteric devices. Almost immediately, Lehman Brothers' bankruptcy helped push the American International Group—an extremely large insurance company that also invested heavily in speculative markets—over the brink. Very quickly, a full-blown panic was threatening the stability of the entire financial system. Many other giant banks were in extremely precarious positions. Credit markets froze up as banks refused to make loans to anyone—including longtime, stable clients—because they feared not being repaid and needed cash to repay their own debts as they came due. This situation in turn jeopardized the ordinary day-to-day functioning of businesses, which were then unable to get loans for ordinary business operations like purchasing inventory or paying employees.

As the sense of crisis mounted, the government faced a stark choice: let these banks fail and risk a complete financial collapse on the scale of the Great Depression of the 1930s, or use taxpayer money to bail them out. Simon Johnson, former chief economist at the International Monetary Fund, and James Kwak describe the "too big to fail" problem this way:

> Certain financial institutions are so big, or so interconnected, or otherwise so important to the financial system that they cannot be allowed to go into an uncontrolled bankruptcy; defaulting on their obligations will create significant losses for other financial institutions, at a minimum sowing chaos in the markets and potentially triggering a domino effect that causes the entire system to come crashing down.[16]

[16] *13 Bankers*, p. 201.

Faced with these potential calamities, the government bailed out the banks.[17]

Even with the bailout of the banks, the financial crash had devastating consequences. Most immediately, the bursting of the housing bubble meant that millions of people saw the equity in their homes disappear. Many homeowners in the hardest-hit states—Arizona, Florida, Nevada, and California—found themselves "under water," meaning that the value of their homes had fallen below the size of their mortgages.

Three things then happened. First, those homeowners who had planned to refinance their homes to lower interest rates once their home equity had increased (because of anticipated price rises) were not able to do so. Second, many people who had purchased subprime mortgages with low introductory interest rates suddenly faced jumps in their interest payments even though the value of their homes had declined. And third, as the recession got worse and people lost their jobs, many people could no longer afford their monthly mortgage payments. The result was a rapid increase in home foreclosures (Figure 9.8), which rose from around 2 foreclosures per 1,000 owner-occupied dwellings at the beginning of 2005 to a peak of 7.5 foreclosures per 1,000 owner-occupied dwellings in 2009. Between September 2008 and April 2014, there were approximately 5 million completed foreclosures across the country.[18]

The depth of the financial crisis was also reflected in the overall disruption of the economy. Figure 9.9 indicates the magnitude and duration of employment losses in every recession since 1981. Two things are striking about this figure. First, it has taken longer in each successive recession for employment levels to return to pre-recession levels: 27 months in the 1981 recession, 30 months in the 1990 recession, 45 months in the 2001 recession,

---

[17] The total magnitude of the bailout is extremely hard to calculate for a variety of reasons. The most visible form of bailout was the Troubled Asset Relief Program (TARP), which authorized a total of $700 billion to purchase "toxic" assets (assets that had lost most of their value) and provide equity to financial institutions. In the end, not all of this money was used for this specific purpose. Other forms of government support for distressed financial institutions, especially actions done through the Federal Reserve, were much less visible. In any case, the total sums involved were huge—by many estimates, in the trillions of dollars—but much of this was ultimately paid back.

[18] This estimate comes from the March 2014 National Foreclosure Report by CoreLogic (NYSE: CLGX), a leading global property information, analytics, and data-enabled services provider. Available at http://www.corelogic.com/about-us/news/corelogic-reports-48,000 -completed-foreclosures-in-march.aspx (accessed July 28, 2014).

FIGURE 9.8—Foreclosures per 1,000 owner-occupied dwellings, 2000–2011

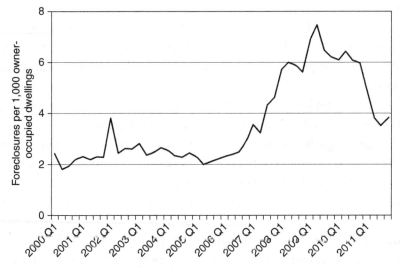

Note: The data are reported quarterly. Thus 2000 Q1 means "first quarter, of the year 2000."

Source: Economic Policy Institute (EPI) analysis of Reserve Bank of New York's "Quarterly Report on Household Debt and Credit" and Current Population Survey (CPS) data. *State of Working America*, 12th ed. Available at http://stateofworkingamerica.org/chart/swa-wealth-figure-6m-foreclosures-1000-owner/ (accessed May 19, 2014).

FIGURE 9.9—U.S. recession employment losses: indexed job loss for last four recessions

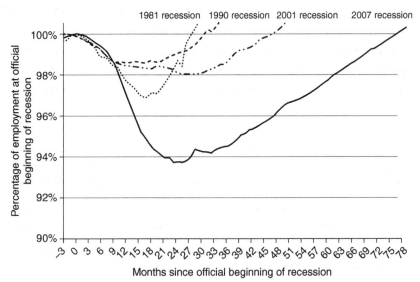

Note: Official start dates of recessions are July 1981, July 1990, March 2001, and December 2007.

Source: EPI analysis of CPS data. Available at http://stateofworkingamerica.org/charts/job-loss-in-prior-recessions/ (accessed May 16, 2014).

and 76 months—over six years—in the Great Recession that began in December 2007. And second, the magnitude of the employment loss was vastly greater in the financial crisis of 2007–2009 than in the earlier recessions. One consequence of this is that the number of people who remained unemployed for very long periods was much greater in the 2008 Great Recession than in other recessions since the end of World War II. Figure 9.10 indicates the average duration of unemployment for each recession since 1948. In no previous recession did the peak average duration of unemployment go much above 20 weeks. In the Great Recession, the peak was over 40 weeks. In April 2014, there were still 3.5 million people who had been unemployed for over 27 weeks.

Not everyone suffered as a result of the Great Recession. In particular, the financial sector itself rebounded very quickly in spite of the fact that its risk-taking strategies were at the center of the financial crisis in the first place (Figure 9.11). While undoubtedly some people lost fortunes because of the crash, the sector as a whole fared very well. Even in 2009, in the midst

FIGURE 9.10—Average duration of unemployment in the United States (weeks), 1948–2013

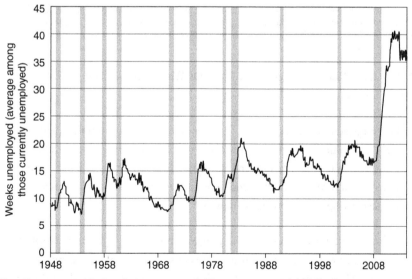

Note: Data are monthly. Population 16 years and older. Recessions are highlighted.

Source: Bureau of Labor Statistics, Labor Force Statistics from the Current Population Survey. Table A-12, "Unemployed persons by duration of unemployment." Available at http://www.bls.gov /webapps/legacy/cpsatab12.htm (accessed May 22, 2014). Recession dates from the National Bureau of Economic Research, "US Business Cycle Expansions and Contractions." Available at http://www .nber.org/cycles.html (accessed May 22, 2014).

FIGURE 9.11—Finance profits recovered quickly after the Great Recession

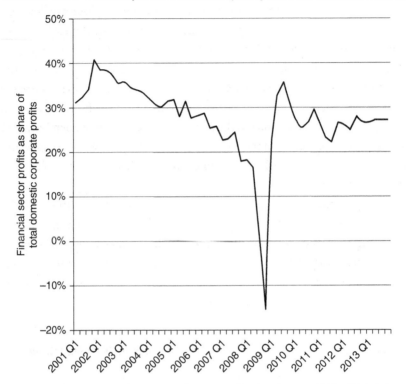

Source: Bureau of Economic Analysis, National Income and Product Accounts Tables. Table 6.16, "Corporate Profits by Industry" (last revised April 30, 2014), and Table 1.1.4, "Price Indexes for Gross Domestic Product." Available at http://www.bea.gov/iTable/index_nipa.cfm (accessed May 14, 2014).

of the Great Recession, according to the *Wall Street Journal*, U.S. financial institutions paid record bonuses:

> The surge in bonuses comes barely a year after the government bailed out the U.S. financial system amid the worst economic crisis in generations. This year major U.S. banks and securities firms are poised to pay their employees a record amount in compensation and benefits—about $145.85 billion, according to the Journal's analysis.[19]

As indicated in Figure 9.12, the average bonus for Wall Street employees never dipped below $100,000, and in 2013 rose to over $160,000 per person. The total of these 2013 bonuses—$26.7 billion—comes to more than the combined annual earnings ($15 billion) of all 1,085,000 full-time minimum-wage

---

[19] *Wall Street Journal*, January 14, 2010, "Banks Set for Record Pay." Available at http://online .wsj.com/news/articles/SB10001424052748704281204575003351773983136 (accessed July 28, 2014).

FIGURE 9.12—NYC securities industry average bonus, 1985–2013

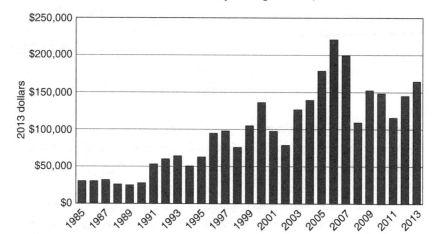

Note: The 2013 estimate was derived by the New York Offices of State Comptroller (OSC) from personal income tax withholding collections. Historical bonuses are OSC estimates using data from the NYS Department of Labor's Quarterly Census of Employment and Wages (QCEW) series.

Source: Thomas P. DiNapoli, "Wall Street Bonuses Went Up in 2013" (News from the Offices of the New York State Comptroller, March 12, 2014). Available at http://www.osc.state.ny.us/press /releases/mar14/031214.htm. Original data available at http://www.osc.state.ny.us/press/releases /mar14/av_bonus_chrt.pdf (accessed May 23, 2014). CPI-U data available at http://stats.bls.gov/cpi /cpifiles/cpiai.txt (accessed May 23, 2014).

workers in the United States.[20] In that same year, the twenty-five highest-earning hedge fund managers earned $24.3 billion, nearly as much as the total bonuses of all Wall Street employees.[21] The deregulated U.S. financial system is clearly an efficient system for enhancing the wealth of the wealthiest people in society, but it does little to improve the security and well-being of the average person and deepens the precariousness of the most vulnerable.

Prospects for Change

In the immediate aftermath of the financial crisis of 2008 and the Great Recession there was considerable talk, both among policy makers and the broader public, about the need to substantially strengthen the regulation of the financial sector in order to protect consumers from abusive lending

[20] Sarah Anderson, "Wall Street Bonuses and the Minimum Wage," Institute for Policy Studies, March 12, 2014. Available at http://www.ips-dc.org/reports/wall_street_bonuses_and _the_minimum_wage (accessed July 28, 2014).

[21] Forbes, "The 25 Highest-Earning Hedge Fund Managers And Traders," 2/26/2014. http:// www.forbes.com/sites/nathanvardi/2014/02/26/the-highest-earning-hedge-fund -managers-and-traders/ (accessed July 28, 2014).

practices and prevent the kinds of behaviors that pose risks to the economy as a whole. The result, passed in the summer of 2010, was the Dodd–Frank Wall Street Reform and Consumer Protection Act. This is an enormously complex piece of legislation, consisting of sixteen major sections (called "titles") and dozens of subsections. According to one estimate, once fully implemented the act explicitly requires the specification of around 250 separate rules.[22]

On paper, the Dodd–Frank Act gives the impression of being a demanding overhaul of the regulatory framework for the U.S. financial system. The preamble to the act states that its purpose is

> to promote the financial stability of the United States by improving accountability and transparency in the financial system, to end "too big to fail," to protect the American taxpayer by ending bailouts, to protect consumers from abusive financial services practices, and for other purposes.[23]

To accomplish these goals, the act created, among other things, a Bureau of Consumer Financial Protection, designed to protect consumers from abusive and predatory practices of financial institutions; new procedures for the "orderly liquidation" of insolvent banks; new rules for transparency and accountability of some types of Wall Street firms; and new forms of supervision of institutions that potentially posed "systemic risk." If all these agencies and procedures had been given the powers and mandates needed to fully accomplish the stated objectives of the act, then this would indeed have been a major transformation of the relationship between the state and the financial system. That, however, is not what happened.

The stated goals of Dodd–Frank have not been realized, for two basic reasons. First, even in the initial legislation that Congress passed, there were significant gaps in the effort to solve some of the key problems in the financial system. It is true that the preamble to the act makes note of the dangers of "too big to fail" institutions, but none of the act's provisions seek

---

[22] There is some ambiguity in deciding how many distinct rules are mandated by the law, since many "rules" may have many specific parts. The estimate of around 250 comes from Davis Polk, "Summary of the Dodd-Frank Wall Street Reform and Consumer Protection Act, Enacted into Law on July 21, 2010" (Davis Polk & Wardwell, LLP). Available at http://www.davispolk.com/dodd-frank/ (accessed Aug. 21, 2014).

[23] Text of H.R. 4173, https://www.sec.gov/about/laws/wallstreetreform-cpa.pdf.

to break up excessively large financial institutions.[24] Nor did the act propose to reinstitute the separation of commercial and investment banking that had helped stabilize the American financial system from the 1930s through the 1990s, although there are provisions to impose some constraints on this interpenetration. And while the act proclaims an end to bailouts, there is no real provision to prevent their necessity. If the largest, systemically important financial institutions once again got into trouble, they would have to be bailed out to avoid catastrophe, just as in 2008. So, even though the act did embody some real reforms of the system of financial regulation, these absences significantly weakened its potential impact.

Second, and equally important, as in any complex regulatory context, much of the effectiveness of actual regulations depends on the way the abstract purposes of laws-on-paper are turned into concrete rules. Legislation itself generally only states the purposes of new rules, but the actual specification of rules is left up to relevant regulatory agencies. This transformation of statutes into functioning rules involves public hearings, lobbying, technocratic policy making, and informal behind-the-scenes negotiations. All of this opens a space for powerful interests to undermine the rules themselves. Writing in mid-2013, Arthur Wilmarth, a leading legal expert on financial regulation, stated the problem this way:

> The financial industry has pursued a three-front campaign that has blocked the fulfillment of many of Dodd–Frank core reforms. First, the industry's aggressive lobbying efforts have persuaded regulatory agencies to delay or water down regulations mandated by Dodd–Frank. Second, industry trade groups have filed lawsuits to strike down completed rules. Third, the industry helped to elect a Republican majority in the House of Representatives in 2010 and again in 2012, and Republican leaders have introduced numerous bills to repeal or weaken key provisions of Dodd–Frank. . . . As soon as Congress passed Dodd–Frank, the financial industry unleashed a massive lobbying campaign to undermine the ability of federal agencies to issue rules to implement the statute. Due in large part to the success of that

[24]Gestures were made to deal with the TBTF problem by announcing the intention to more closely monitor and regulate what were called systemically important financial institutions (SIFI)—banks and nonbank financial institutions that were large enough to pose systemic risks. The problem is that when financial institutions become as large as these SIFIs, it is impossible to effectively regulate them in ways that eliminate their risks to overall financial stability.

campaign, federal agencies failed to adopt more than three-fifths of the 279 rules whose issuance was required by June 2013.[25]

The magnitude of the lobbying effort by the finance industry to shape the rule-making process for the Dodd–Frank finance reform law is staggering. Writing in March 2013, Haley Sweetland Edwards reported that

> since the passage of Dodd–Frank, the industry has spent an estimated $1.5 billion on registered lobbyists alone—a number that most dismiss as comically low, as it doesn't take into account the industry's much more influential allies and proxies, including a battalion of powerful trade groups, like the U.S. Chamber of Commerce, Business Roundtable, and American Bankers Association.[26]

This funding results in extraordinary levels of direct contact between these lobbyists and regulatory agencies:

> According to the Sunlight Foundation, the top twenty banks and banking associations met with just three agencies—the Treasury, the Federal Reserve, and the CFTC—an average of 12.5 times per week, for a total of 1,298 meetings over the two-year period from July 2010 to July 2012. JPMorgan Chase and Goldman Sachs alone met with those agencies 356 times. That's 114 more times than all the financial reform groups combined.[27]

Groups supporting financial reform cannot possibly compete with these forces. By one estimate, groups supporting the finance industry send 20 times more lobbyists to Capitol Hill than do reform groups.[28] As Bart Chilton, a Democratic commissioner at the U.S. Commodity Futures

---

[25] Arthur E. Wilmarth Jr., "Turning a Blind Eye: Why Washington Keeps Giving in to Wall Street," 81 *University of Cincinnati Law Review* (2013), pp. 1289, 1296–97. Available at http://scholarship.law.uc.edu/uclr/vol81/iss4/4.

[26] Haley Sweetland Edwards, "He Who Makes the Rules," *Washington Monthly*, March/April 2013. Available at http://www.washingtonmonthly.com/magazine/march_april_2013/features/he_who_makes_the_rules043315.php (accessed July 28, 2014).

[27] Ibid.

[28] Gary Rivlin, in "How Wall Street Defanged Dodd-Frank," *The Nation*, May 20, 2013, reports that the top 5 finance industry groups sent 406 registered lobbyists to Capitol Hill compared to only 20 by consumer protection groups defending Dodd-Frank.

Trading Commission reported, "For every one hundred meetings I have, only one of them is with a consumer group or citizens' organization."[29]

Still, one might ask: why don't the officials making these regulations simply resist these pressures and make rules that fully serve the broader public interest? In principle they could, but some very strong forces encourage the policy makers in these regulatory agencies to accommodate the views and interests of the financial sector. First, the key people involved in making these rules within regulatory agencies are political appointees, and the direct influence of Wall Street on both Democratic and Republican parties is substantial. As Wilmarth puts it, "The financial industry's political clout discourages regulators from imposing tougher restraints on financial institutions. Regulators who dare to challenge the industry encounter intense 'pushback' from industry trade groups and their political and regulatory allies."[30]

Second, many regulators actually believe the conventional wisdom of the neoliberal era in which government regulation is viewed with suspicion. Specifically in the case of finance, many experts in regulatory agencies continue to believe that excessive government regulations could impede the efficient allocation of capital and the ability of American banks to compete with foreign rivals.

Finally, there is the problem of the "revolving door": many experts who spend time working in government regulatory agencies hope to eventually get jobs in finance, and many others begin their careers in finance and then do a stint in regulatory agencies. While this does not mean that these regulatory officials are literally being bribed by finance, in many instances their personal financial interests are closely connected to being favorably regarded by Wall Street.

Given these forces at work, there are limited prospects for a deep reform of the American financial system and its regulatory framework in the near future. But if the opportunity for such reform were to occur, what are the most important things that should be done? What would need to be done to ensure that financial institutions were subordinated to the needs of society rather than society held hostage to the needs of finance? This is an especially complex arena for policy innovation, but as a start, we would suggest the following.

---

[29] Quoted by Haley Sweetland Edwards in "He Who Makes the Rules."

[30] Arthur E. Wilmarth Jr., "Turning a Blind Eye," p. 1293.

First, the parts of the Dodd–Frank Act that are concerned with consumer protection and systemic risk should be fully and rigorously implemented. This means strong rules combined with adequate monitoring and effective enforcement capacity. The idea of such provisions already has broad support in the United States. What is lacking is the political will to translate the idea into the kinds of rules and powers that would make a substantial difference.

Second, it is essential to deal seriously with the "too big to fail" problem. The mega banks and gigantic financial institutions need to be broken up. The issue here goes beyond their potential danger to the stability of the economy. The issue is also the political power wielded by institutions with such enormous financial power.

Third, we need to strengthen financial institutions that are more deeply connected to the real economy and more oriented toward community development rather than simply augmenting the wealth of already wealthy people. This means revitalizing privately owned community banks that are rooted in local and regional economies. It means removing many existing restrictions on the lending capacity of the nation's vast network of not-for-profit credit unions. And it also likely means creating public banks whose mission is the public interest and economic development, not speculative investment.

Only one such public bank exists in the United States at present, the Bank of North Dakota. This bank was founded in 1919 to provide reliable and affordable credit to the people of the state and foster economic development that would benefit them—exactly what we would want any bank to do. In its annual report for 2013, the BND defined its vision this way: "Bank of North Dakota is a financial services leader in North Dakota, fostering growth and economic well-being for the state and its citizens, using a partnership approach."[31] In recent years this publicly owned bank, in a politically conservative state, has been directly involved in affordable housing initiatives and child care issues; it has created a pilot program to allow physicians in rural areas to consolidate student loans; and it has developed a program to help rural residents obtain mortgages.[32] Nothing, other than political obstacles created by powerful forces opposed to such innovation, is stopping the creation of such banks throughout the United States.

[31] Bank of North Dakota, "Stronger Together. Annual Report 2013," p. 5, at http://banknd .nd.gov/pubs/annualreport13/index.html (accessed July 28, 2014).

[32] Ibid., p. 6.

A financial system in the United States that provided rigorous regulation of financial institutions in the interests of consumers and citizens, curtailed the power of large financial institutions, and contained a vibrant sector of publicly owned and public-interest banking would be a system very different from what we have today. It would also contribute to a very different pattern of development of the American economy into the future. We refer to this approach as building a high-road economy, which is the subject of the next chapter.

10

BUILDING A HIGH-ROAD ECONOMY

I n the United States at the beginning of the twenty-first century, many people believe that free markets, largely unregulated by the state, are the best way to organize an economy. Beginning in the last quarter of the twentieth century, politicians of both parties have argued that low taxes are essential for a healthy economic environment and that government regulations hinder energetic entrepreneurs and are thus harmful to prosperity. The economic crisis that began in 2008 and the slow recovery in the years that followed may signal a change in this faith in the free market and hostility to government. However, conservative politicians still proclaim, in the words of Ronald Reagan, that "government is not the solution to our problem; government is the problem."

In previous chapters we looked at some of the problems with free markets in particular domains of economic life: generating negative externalities on the environment; undermining an efficient transportation system; intensifying consumerism; creating a high-cost health-care system with great inequalities in access; and producing an unstable and inequitable financial system. But the question still remains: how well do deregulated, free markets perform at the core of economic life itself? This is the bottom line for many people: do weakly regulated free markets and capitalist enterprises "deliver the goods" of prosperity, opportunity, and reasonable economic security for most people?

We begin this chapter by analyzing how well American capitalism has really performed in the lives of most people in recent decades. We then lay out a contrast between two broad ways of organizing a developed capitalist economy, which we will refer to as "low road" and "high road." We will argue that the erosion of the affirmative state through the deregulation of capitalist markets has put the American economy on the low road, and the only way to change routes is to rehabilitate an affirmative state capable of providing a range of vital public goods and imposing constraints on the strategies of powerful actors within markets. We conclude the chapter with a discussion of the obstacles to accomplishing this task.

THE ECONOMIC RECORD

From the end of World War II until the early 1970s, average real weekly earnings for private production and nonsupervisory employees—over 80 percent of all private sector wage and salary employment—rose by over 60 percent from $387 per week in 1947 to $633 per week in 1973 (in 2011 dollars; Figure 10.1).[1] This increase in earnings was evenly distributed throughout

FIGURE 10.1—Average real weekly earnings of private production and nonsupervisory workers, 1947–2011

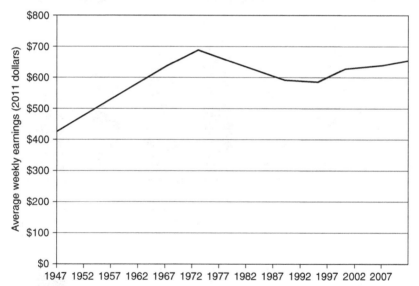

Note: Data is available for years 1947, 1967, 1973, 1979, 1989, 1995, 2000, 2007, and 2011. Lines between marks are linear interpolations. Figures are for private production and nonsupervisory employees who account for more than 80 percent of private wage and salary employment.

Source: "Hourly and weekly earnings of private production and nonsupervisory workers, 1947–2011 (2011 dollars)" *State of Working America, 12,* Table 4.3. Available at http://www.stateofworkingamerica .org/chart/swa-wages-table-4-3-hourly-weekly-earnings/ (accessed October 4, 2014).

[1]"Hourly and Weekly Earnings of Private Production and Nonsupervisory Workers, 1947–2011 (2011 dollars)," *The State of Working America,* 12th ed. (2012), Table 4.3. Before the early 1970s it is not possible to calculate *median* earnings, which is generally a better indicator of economic conditions for the average person (the person in the middle) than is mean earnings because the latter is affected by skewness in the earnings distribution.

the economy: during the thirty-two years from 1947 to 1979, the average incomes of families in the bottom fifth of the income distribution increased by 122 percent, in the middle fifth by 113 percent, and in the highest fifth by 99 percent (top panel of Figure 10.2).

Things changed dramatically during the 1970s. Beginning in the middle of that decade and intensifying during the 1980s, earnings stagnated. The average weekly earnings of private production and nonsupervisory employees declined from $633 in 1973 to $541 in 1995, and even by 2011 had risen to only $655 (in 2011 dollars). Median household income did continue to rise, but at a much slower pace (Figure 10.3). The rise that did occur was due largely to the increased employment levels of married women. Median hourly real wages for men were virtually identical in 1973 and 2011 ($22.03 in

FIGURE 10.2—Change in family income by income group, 1947–2012

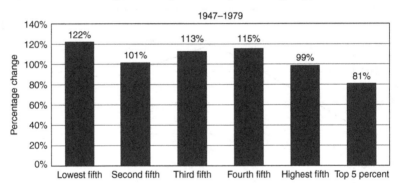

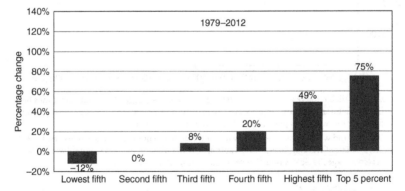

Note: Figures correspond to growth in average real income for families within each income group.

Sources: Authors' calculations based on data from U.S. Census Bureau, Current Population Survey, Annual Social and Economic Supplements. Average income for years 1966–2012 from Table F-3, "Mean Income Received by Each Fifth and Top 5 Percent of Each Fifth and Top 5 Percent of Families, All Races: 1947 to 2012," average income for 1947 calculated from Table F-2, "Share of Aggregate Income Received by Householder—Families by Median and Mean Income: 1947 to 2012." Available at http://www.census.gov/hhes/www/income/data/historical/families/ (accessed June 3, 2014).

FIGURE 10.3—Median family income, 1947–2010

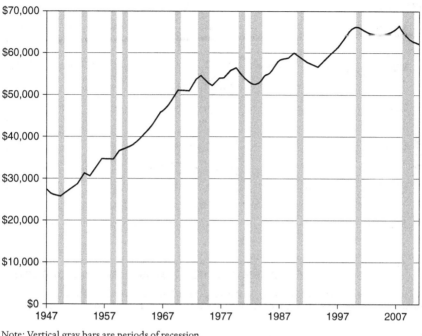

Note: Vertical gray bars are periods of recession.

Source: "Real Median Family Income, 1947–2010," *The State of Working America*, 12th ed. (2012), Figure 2A.

1973 and $22.05 in 2011, in constant inflation-adjusted dollars), but within households this stagnation in wages was compensated for by women's increased real hourly wages and increased participation in the labor force (Figure 10.4).

Not only did earnings stagnate during the last quarter of the twentieth century, but the growth that did occur was heavily concentrated at the top of the earnings distribution (bottom panel of Figure 10.2). From 1979 to 2012, incomes of families in the bottom quintile of the income distribution actually declined by 12 percent; incomes of families in what might be thought of as the broad "middle class"—from the second to the fourth quintile of the distribution—grew very modestly over this thirty-two-year period (between no growth and 20 percent). Only families at the top of the income distribution saw their family income grow substantially: 49 percent for the highest fifth of the distribution, and 75 percent for the top 5 percent of families.

Underlying this dramatic change in the performance of the American economy after the 1970s was a sharp divergence of the growth rates of productivity and total employee compensation—the sum of wages, salaries,

FIGURE 10.4—Median real hourly wages for male and female employees, 1973–2011

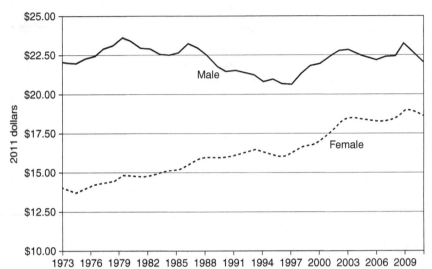

Source: "Change in Hourly Productivity, Real Average Hourly Compensation, and Median Compensation, 1973–2011," *The State of Working America*, 12th ed. (2012), Figure 4V.

health care, pensions, and other nonwage benefits. *Productivity* is a measure of the amount of economic value generated *per* unit of input, typically denominated by hours of labor. This value is a function both of the absolute value of the thing produced (its quality, distinctiveness, etc.) and of the efficiency of that production (how much nonrenewable energy, depreciating capital stock, or other inputs were used in production). Growth in productivity is the most important source of new wealth in any economy. People learning how to make new things or offer new services, or how to make or offer them better and faster or with less waste, is the essence of economic progress.

The core implicit "social contract" in any capitalist economy is that the workers doing this learning and making should share in this new wealth. Capitalists get more profits, but workers get increased compensation, both at about the rate of productivity growth. When employee compensation grows at a slower rate than productivity, that implicit contract is violated; a disproportionate amount of the extra value being created by rising productivity is going to owners of capital rather than workers.

As Figure 10.5 indicates, until the early 1980s, the growth of both average compensation and median compensation closely tracked productivity growth. In the 1980s, these rates began to diverge. This divergence is revealed in a particularly stark way by comparing rates of growth of productivity and

FIGURE 10.5—Trends in productivity and compensation, 1973–2011

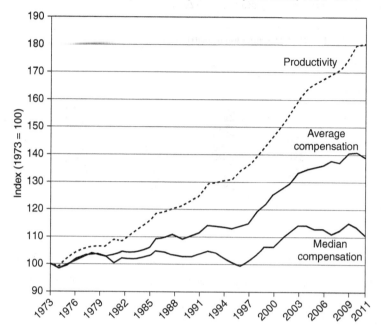

Note: Setting all the values at 100 in 1973 is a way of showing their relative change over time. For example, the index value of productivity of 150 in 2001 means that productivity in 2001 was 150 percent of the level in 1973 (i.e., productivity had increased 50 percent during that period).

Source: "Cumulative Change in Hourly Productivity, Real Average Hourly Compensation, and Median Compensation, 1973–2011," *The State of Working America*, 12th ed. (2012), Figure 4V.

compensation during periods of economic expansion (Figure 10.6): In the economic expansion from 1975 to 1979, median compensation grew at about 1 percent a year and productivity at just under 1.5 percent a year. In the expansions of the 1980s, 1990s, and mid-2000s, this gap between productivity growth and compensation grew considerably. Finally, in the economic expansion during the two years after the Great Recession, productivity growth was a healthy 1.75 percent, but median compensation actually declined.[2]

What happened to the income generated by all of this productivity growth? Figure 10.7 gives a partial answer: It went to the very top of the

[2] As the economic expansion continues, compensation likely will stabilize and perhaps rise slowly.

FIGURE 10.6—Annual growth in productivity and compensation during periods of economic expansion, 1975–2011

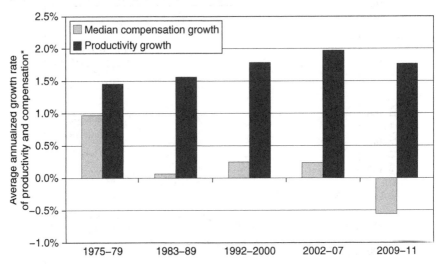

*"Average annualized growth rate" is the total percentage change in a period divided by the number of years in the period.

Source: "Cumulative Change in Total Economy Productivity and Real Hourly Compensation of Selected Groups of Workers, 1995–2011," *The State of Working America,* 12th ed. (2012), Figure 4A.

FIGURE 10.7—How income growth is distributed during economic expansions, 1949–2012

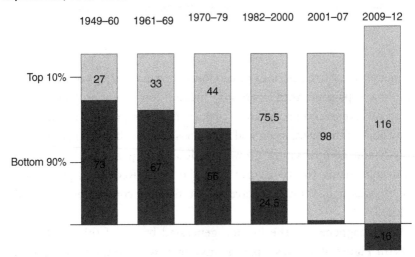

Note: Figures are the averages across the economic expansions in each period: three periods of expansion in 1949–60, one in 1961–69, two in 1970–79, and one in each of the other periods.

Source: Adapted from Pavlina R. Tcherneva. Calculations based on data from Thomas Piketty and Emmanuel Saez and N.B.E.T reported in the *New York Times,* Neil Irwin, "The Benefits of Economic Expansion are Increasingly Going to the Richest Americans," September 26, 2014.

income distribution. From the end of World War II through the 1970s, in every economic expansion, between 55 percent and 80 percent of income growth went to earners in the bottom 90 percent of the income distribution. This declined to 20–27 percent in the 1960s and 1990s. In the expansion of 2001–2007 only 2 percent of income growth went to the bottom 90 percent. And in the economic expansion of 2009–2012 following the financial crisis of 2008, the income of people in the bottom 90 percent actually declined; the top 10 percent therefore received over 100 percent of the income growth in this period. We have moved from a world in which the fruits of economic growth were broadly dispersed in the population to one in which the gains from growth are concentrated at the top. Clearly something fundamental has changed since the 1950s and 1960s.

The general deterioration of the connection between economic growth and broad prosperity is related to a significant change in the nature of the jobs being created in the American economy. Jobs are the main way that most people acquire their standard of living, so it matters quite a bit where in the economy job growth is occurring. During periods of economic expansion, are jobs being created mainly in the middle of the economic structure? At the top? At the bottom? It would be nice to chart the trajectory of the job creation over time in terms of a full range of measures of the quality of work: pay and benefits, job security, meaningfulness of the work, social benefits from different kinds of jobs, and so on. This is simply not possible. However, we can investigate how the patterns of job growth over time have changed in terms of the earnings associated with different kinds of work. Here is the basic strategy:[3] Using data for the American labor force, we can define different kinds of jobs as specific kinds of *occupations* within *economic sectors*. Truck drivers in the medical services sector, secretaries in durable manufacturing, and accountants in the insurance sector are examples. The number of categories varies for different periods because of changes in the way data about the labor force are gathered, but since the 1980s it is possible to classify over 2,000 types of jobs in about 100 occupations and 23 sectors.

This list of job types is then rank-ordered based on the median hourly earnings of people in these jobs, and this rank-ordered list grouped into what we call *job-quality quintiles*: the highest quintile represents the 20 percent of

[3]For a more detailed discussion of the methods used here, see Erik Olin Wright and Rachel Dwyer, "Patterns of Job Expansion and Contraction in the United States, 1960s–1990s," *Socioeconomic Review* 1 (2003): 289–325.

the employed labor force in the best-paying types of jobs, the lowest quintile represents the 20 percent in the worst-paying types of jobs, and so on. We are interested in where job growth occurs among these five job-quality quintiles during periods of employment expansion, and where job declines occur in periods of contraction.[4]

Since the end of World War II, the two most sustained periods of job expansion in the United States occurred in the 1960s and the 1990s. The pattern of job growth in these two periods, however, was dramatically different. Figure 10.8 presents the net change in the number of jobs in each job-quality quintile in the 1960s and the 1990s. In the 1960s, there was strong growth of jobs in the middle of the employment structure and weak growth at the bottom. This pattern of job growth can be described as job upgrading.

In the 1990s the pattern of job growth was polarized—weak growth in the middle and strong growth at the tails. In the 1980s, job growth was fairly

FIGURE 10.8—Patterns of job growth in the 1960s and 1990s

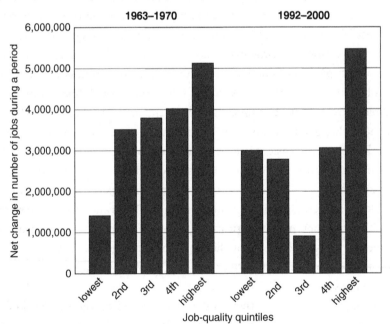

Source: Erik Olin Wright and Rachel Dwyer, "Patterns of Job Expansion and Contraction in the United States, 1960s–1990s," *Socioeconomic Review* 1 (2003): 289–325, figure 3, p. 304.

[4]This strategy of analysis is different from simply looking at changes over time in income distribution or earnings distribution across *persons*. Here we are looking at the way the distribution of *types of jobs* changes over time, where we are indexing job types by one salient characteristic: the amount of earnings they typically generate.

evenly dispersed across all five quintiles. This new pattern emerged first during the employment contractions of the early 1990s, when job decline was strongest in the middle of the employment structure (Figure 10.9). The pattern has continued during the contraction of the early 2000s, in the relatively weak job expansion in the period 2002–2007, and even more intensely in the Great Recession, when job loss was especially concentrated in the second and third quintiles of the employment structure—the heart of the middle class. In the period following the Great Recession, the feeble overall job growth is once again stronger at the tails of the distribution than in the middle. Overall, then, in the period since around 1990, job creation in the middle of the employment structure has been weak compared to the tails, and when recessions occur, job loss in the middle has also been especially significant.

The pattern of employment polarization in Figure 10.8 is at least in part linked to changes in the distribution of jobs across economic sectors. Of particular importance is the steady decline in manufacturing employment since the 1970s (Figure 10.10). The rise in manufacturing jobs in the 1950s and 1960s is one of the reasons that employment in the middle quintiles also expanded in this period. The decline in manufacturing employment from over 25 percent of all jobs in 1970 to less than 10 percent by 2011 is one of the

FIGURE 10.9—Patterns of job growth and decline, 1990–2013

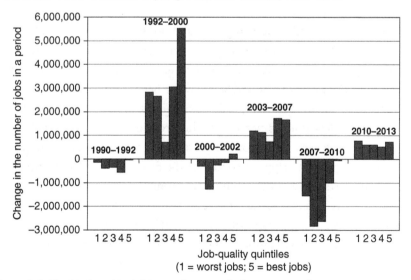

Source: Erik Olin Wright and Rachel Dwyer, "Patterns of Job Expansion and Contraction in the United States, 1960s–1990s," *Socioeconomic Review* 1 (2003): 289–325. Additional calculations for the periods beginning in 2000 provided by Matias Scaglione and Rachel Dwyer from *Current Population Survey*, outgoing rotation files.

FIGURE 10.10–Manufacturing employment in the U.S., 1910–2020

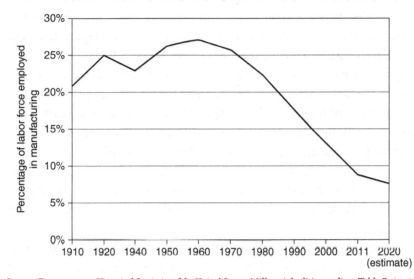

Sources: For 1910–1990: *Historical Statistics of the United States*, Millennial edition online, Table B1652-669. For 2000–2020: *The State of Working America*, 12th ed. (2012), Figure 5b. http://stateofworkingamerica .org/chart/swa-jobs-figure-5b-distribution-employment/

main reasons that job growth in the middle has been so weak from the 1990s on.[5] This situation has been particularly harmful to people without university degrees, since in the decades after World War II manufacturing was the main sector in which people with only a high school education could find reasonably well-paying jobs.

This decline in manufacturing is bound up with another critical, long-term trend in the American economy since the late 1970s: the increasing imbalance of international trade (Figure 10.11). From the end of World War II until the 1970s, the United States was a net exporter. Nearly all these exports were manufactured products. Exports and imports combined accounted for less than 15 percent of the gross domestic product (GDP). Beginning in the early 1970s, both imports and exports began to rise; by the late 1970s, imports outstripped exports. By the first decade of the twenty-first century, imports and exports combined accounted for 25–30 percent of GDP, and our negative trade balance for several years exceeded 5 percent of GDP.

This massive and rapid growth of trade deficits since the 1970s is linked to the growing financialization of the economy discussed in the preceding

[5]For a discussion of the connection between the decline of manufacturing and the weakness of middle-income job growth, see Wright and Dwyer, "Patterns of Job Expansion and Contraction in the United States, 1960s–1990s," *Socioeconomic Review* 1 (2003): 289–325.

FIGURE 10.11—Imports, exports, and trade balance in the United States as a percentage of GDP, 1947–2014

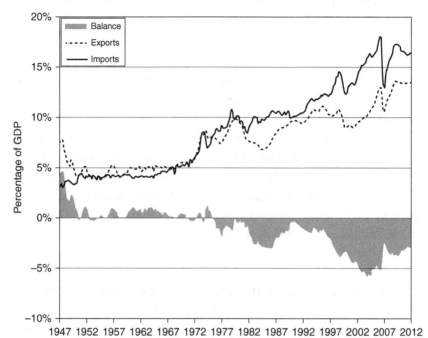

Notes: Series for real imports, exports, and balance of trade includes goods and services. Quarterly data are seasonally adjusted and expressed in current prices and current dollars. 2014 data end in Q1.

Source: Calculations based on trade data from the U.S. Department of Commerce, Bureau of Economic Analysis, NIPA Table 4.1, "Foreign Transactions in the National Income and Product Accounts," and Table 1.1.5, "Gross Domestic Product." Available at http://www.bea.gov/iTable/index_nipa.cfm (accessed: June 19, 2014).

chapter—the shift from an economy in which profits were largely being generated through the production and distribution of goods and services to a system in which profits increasingly came from purely financial transactions. Much of this financialization of the economy was bound up with rapidly rising consumer debt, especially in the form of mortgages, as well as public debt generated by large government deficits. This growing public and private debt was to a significant extent financed by flows of capital from those countries like China that accumulated large dollar reserves due to our trade imbalances. This situation enabled Americans to consume more than they produced for an extended period of time; but as we know, this imbalance eventually became unsustainable.

These are all long-term trends reflecting the general performance of American capitalism in the last part of the twentieth century and the beginning of the twenty-first. None of them specifically concerns the sharp 2008–2009 economic crisis. Even without the added problem of the economic disruptions generated by the financial crisis, the economic trajectory for average people in the United States since the 1970s has yielded at best very modest improvement and, for many people, none at all.

Many factors have come into play in explaining these trends. Our central thesis is that this mediocre long-term performance of the economy for the lives of most Americans is to a significant extent due to the absence of effective state involvement in the creation of key public goods and the regulation of critical aspects of the capitalist economy.

To further understand this thesis, next we will contrast two different paths of economic development, two different roads that modern capitalist economies can take. Joel Rogers has called these alternatives the high road and the low road. Our basic argument can be summarized in a slogan about what needs to be done: Close off the low road, pave the high road, and help firms and workers stuck on the first to roll along to the second.

COMPARING HIGH- AND LOW-ROAD CAPITALIST FIRMS

Capitalist firms vary in all sorts of ways: by the markets they serve, the technologies they use, the wages and benefits they pay, and so on. Here we want to draw a contrast between two broad types of firms within economically advanced capitalism, based on their competitive strategy. We will refer to them as low-road and high-road firms.

In sociology, this kind of contrast involves what are called ideal types. An *ideal type* is a stylized description of something in a pure form, a kind of perfect model of some idea or principle. The real world is almost always much messier. In physics, for example, a frictionless plane is an ideal type— a plane in which one specific property, friction, has been reduced to an extreme value, zero. No real plane ever has zero friction, but this ideal type helps clarify certain kinds of problems. Similarly in our analysis, most firms will not be perfect examples of either high-road or low-road characteristics; but, nevertheless the contrast will help us understand some of the dilemmas and constraints in the American economy today.

Table 10.1 lays out the basic contrast between low-road and high-road firms. The key idea underlying the high and low metaphor is that the first type of firm is organized in such a way that it generates a large number of high-skill, well-paying jobs, whereas the other primarily generates low-skill, low-wage jobs. The metaphor applies both to individual firms and their strategies, and by extension to the broader economy within which they function. A low-road economy is one in which low-road firms

TABLE 10.1—High-road and low-road capitalist firms

	Low-road firms	High-road firms
Competitive strategy	Primarily price reduction	Primarily quality (uniqueness, performance)
Product market	Mass goods, homogeneous products	Diversified, high-performance goods and services
Jobs	Very specialized	Multitask
Skill level and scope	Low, narrow	High, wide
Training	Limited, job specific	Extensive, including meta-skills
Job autonomy	Low	High
Incentives	Punishment, fear of being fired	Promotions, future job prospects, pay raises, bonuses
Hierarchy	Rigid differentiation of managers and workers; many managerial layers	Low differentiation of managers and workers; few layers
Wages	Relatively low wages	Relatively high wages
Environment	Low concern, if any	Higher concern via attention to production waste and concern for community quality
Attachment to place	As little as possible	Higher, given dependence on institutional infrastructure

predominate; a high-road economy is one in which high-road firms do. The table outlines the various characteristics of firms that point in these two directions. More detailed descriptions of each characteristic follow.

Basis of Competition among Firms

Firms compete with one another in many different ways. One important contrast is between competition based on the *price* of what is produced and competition based on the *quality*[6] of what is produced, the extra money gained from a product's distinctiveness or superior performance.

Of course, all firms compete on both price and quality, but one or the other is often particularly important to the strategies of firms. In low-road capitalism, the key thing firms compete over is price. They are therefore constantly pressured to reduce costs so that prices can be lower. This process typically begins by reducing the price of inputs over which the firms have the most control, namely the cost of their own employees. In high-road capitalism, competition is primarily over the efficient production of quality goods. Firms are less worried about final costs per se. They are more

---

[6] Businesses generally use the term *quality* in a narrow way to refer to the consistency in the attributes of a product. We are using it in the ordinary sense of desirability and level of performance of a product.

concerned with producing the best (or the better), rather than the cheapest, in ways that most efficiently use all their inputs: the "human capital" of their workers, the "physical capital" of their technology and machines, and the "natural capital" of raw materials and the environment. The firms bet that customers are willing to pay a premium for goods and services that perform better and more precisely meet their needs; they also bet that they can make money by reducing their own waste.

Nature of the Product Market

In a stylized way, the goods and services produced by capitalist firms for a market can be divided into two broad types: mass markets for essentially identical goods, and more diverse markets for differentiated goods. This contrast is not identical to, but has a certain observed affinity with, the distinction between competition over price and quality. In mass markets for homogeneous products, the main way that customers distinguish among firms is on the basis of price; in markets for more customized products with distinctive properties, quality plays a bigger role. In general, low-road firms aim at the first kind of product market, mass commodity production; high-road firms aim at the second, at more diversified and higher-performing products.

Jobs

In low-road firms, jobs are typically organized around narrow sets of tasks, often highly routinized, within a prescribed division of labor. In high-road firms, jobs typically involve many different kinds of tasks, and, most important, these tasks change or are frequently combined in new ways. Essentially, workers are expected to be able to learn and to do new kinds of things in new ways. In high-road firms, where the emphasis is on innovation in improving product performance or distinctiveness and wringing as much market revenue as possible out of all inputs, new ideas are tried all the time.

Skill Level and Scope

Frederick Taylor, a famous industrial engineer at the beginning of the twentieth century, said that the ideal workplace would consist of jobs in which workers could be "trained gorillas"—the skills would be so rudimentary that anyone could be snatched off the street and perform the tasks with almost instant learning. These kinds of low-skill jobs characterized the assembly lines of mass production. Of course, the trained gorilla image is an exaggeration, but low-road capitalism is built around highly routinized jobs that require relatively low levels of skills to perform. Most retail trade and food services jobs, which have shown enormous growth since the 1970s, are of this character. High-road capitalism, in contrast, relies primarily on high levels of skills—especially intellectual skills, although some high-road jobs require high levels of manual skills as well. These jobs are not highly routinized, and they involve lots of problem solving.

Training

The difference between low skill and high skill corresponds to a sharp contrast in the nature of training in low-road and high-road firms. In low-road firms, training is tightly linked to the requirements of specific jobs in specific firms. Workers in low-road jobs may get training, but their training does not give them much job mobility because the skills are not very relevant to jobs in other firms. The jobs in high-road capitalism require what can be called *meta-skills*—the skills to learn skills. These are highly portable skills, transferrable across jobs and employers. The training process in low-road capitalism is mainly short-term training provided by the employer for the narrow, specific tasks in that specific firm. High-road capitalism requires more lifetime training and retraining that is provided through various kinds of partnerships between employers and public institutions.

Job Autonomy

Job autonomy refers to the extent to which people in their work are able to direct their own activities, make choices, figure things out, and control their time. Job autonomy is generally very circumscribed in low-road jobs. People are closely supervised by bosses who give them specific instructions and carefully monitor their compliance. In high-road capitalism, job autonomy is high, considerable responsibility and initiative is expected of employees, and monitoring is much looser. Workers do not feel that they always have a boss breathing down their necks.

Incentives

In low-road capitalist firms, work effort is mainly elicited by negative sanctions, especially the fear of being fired for not working hard enough or well enough. In high-road firms, work effort is much more linked to positive incentives like prospects for promotions, future raises, bonuses, or greater authority. Often there are demarcated career ladders. Even when this is not so much the case, workers have expectations that if they are responsible and work creatively, they will be able to move to better jobs. This is one way that firms share productivity gains with individual workers.

Hierarchy

In low-road firms, there is a rigid differentiation of managers and workers. Managers make the decisions and issue orders; workers follow those orders. There are many layers of managers, and authority is organized through top-down commands with little participation from below. High-road firms have relatively low differentiation among workers, supervisors, and managers. Managerial hierarchies are relatively flat, and there are many occasions for easy interaction and dialogue between managers and nonmanagerial employees. Authority is not exercised exclusively as top-down command and control, but in a manner that involves much more bottom-up participation. This is not to say that firms are really democratic, but they are organized in such a way that ordinary workers play a more active role in collective deliberations and problem solving.

Wages

Wages for most employees in low-road firms are generally much lower than in high-road firms. This is because of the lower levels of labor productivity but also because the strategies of low-road firms are so relentlessly linked to cost cutting. Competitive firms are not interested in productivity per se; their central goal is profits. And those can always be increased by sweating labor.

Environment

Low-road firms are classic producers of negative environmental externalities. High-road firms tend to be better for the environment for several reasons. First, and most important, they tend to be much more attentive to wresting value from inputs and reducing any waste. This applies not just to human and physical capital, but to natural capital as well. Second, within limits, high-road firms tend to favor stricter environmental regulations because they are typically better able to meet them than are their low-road competitors. Third, high-road firms tend to rely more on high-quality public goods to support their competitive strategy. They rely on support from the state for these things and wish to maintain good relations with it. Fourth, environmental quality is important to the sort of highly qualified workers and managers they wish to attract. These kinds of employees are people with labor market options. They want to live in healthy communities, not waste dumps, and generally prefer to associate with firms that are contributing to, not debasing, those communities. Finally, high-road firms commonly compete in part on their reputation for being more responsible corporate citizens than their low-road competitors. That reputation would be hurt if their greater concern for workers, the environment, and community was shown to be a sham.

Attachment to Place

High-road firms tend to be more attached to particular places than are low-road firms. They rely on specific places to furnish the better-prepared workers they want and the demanding customers that keep them sharp. High-road firms are rooted in locations that provide the myriad public goods on which they rely, the learning opportunities they seek for themselves outside the firm, and other elements of what is sometimes called *institutional infrastructure*. Low-road firms also need basic infrastructure—communications systems, transportation systems, and sources of energy—but are typically much less dependent on such institutional infrastructure that is supplied in particular places.

In the stylized contrast between these two models of firms, all the traits line up together. American capitalism today, of course, reflects much more heterogeneity than this. Certainly, some firms overall have a high-road character and others have a low-road character: Google has many of the high-road characteristics; Wal-Mart is a low-road firm. A given corporation may have some departments with high-road characteristics—highly skilled workers, participatory norms, meta-training, and the like—while other departments are characterized more by the logic of cost cutting and low-skill jobs with only job-specific training. And some jobs may have some but not all of the high-road properties. Still, as a broad generalization one can say that in the last quarter of the twentieth century, low-road strategies have played a particularly strong role in the development of the U.S. economy.

Most people, if given a choice between high- and low-road capitalism and asked which is a better world, would rather work in a high-road firm and live in a capitalist economy dominated by such firms. On almost every dimension, the quality of life and work would seem better in such an economy.

If most people would prefer a high-road economy, then why does the American economy have so many low-road firms? The simple answer is that capitalist firms are not in the business of building better societies, but making a bigger profit. Although the high road may clearly be preferable for the society, it may not be clearly preferable for individual firms. Getting onto and maintaining position on the high road is often expensive and almost always complicated. If easy money is available at low cost and with less hassle, many firms will take it.

Take skills and training as one example. Suppose you are a business owner and have a choice between two production processes, one requiring minimal labor skill—meaning you can find the necessary labor almost anywhere—and one requiring higher initial skill and continuous learning. The second choice implies a higher cost of initial labor but also ongoing investment in workers. And though they are potentially much more productive, educated workers are harder to deal with—at least if *deal with* means "bossing around"—because they know more and have options in the labor market. If both types of production processes are equally profitable, most firms will naturally take the first. Capitalist firms, after all, are not first and foremost concerned with the value or quality of products, but with the profit for their owners.

At least initially, globalization can encourage this low-road choice. The entry of billions of very low-paid workers into the global labor market puts downward pressure on wages in rich countries while opening up a new supply of labor for employers in poor countries. Employers look immediately to start rolling back domestic labor costs, or structuring production in ways that can take advantage of this new labor supply. This means that firms will generally avoid making the kinds of investments needed to get on the high road, for example in worker training. We can see this in education trends in the United States, which is unique among developed nations in actually going backward in the secondary education of its workforce. And, of course, we see it in the bifurcated pattern of job generation we observed in Figure 9.8 for the 1990s and 2000s: many good jobs, few middle-class jobs, lots of lousy jobs.

Now, in the long run this seems like a hopeless strategy: the wage differences between rich countries and poor countries are so huge that firms in rich countries cannot realistically compete globally through a low-wage, low-skill strategy. Furthermore, in the aggregate, a low-wage strategy of competition erodes the buying power of consumers within the rich countries, and in the long run this too weakens those economies. Over time, therefore, it would seem that the low road is likely to be a bad strategy for capitalists, not just for their employees.

This conclusion obviously leads to the critical question of what it would take to change directions. To answer that question, we first examine three obstacles to change—three processes that make it difficult to move from the low road to the high road. We then briefly show how a reinvigoration of the democratic affirmative state might help overcome these obstacles.

OBSTACLES TO MOVING FROM THE LOW ROAD TO THE HIGH ROAD

The core economic structures of a society are almost always difficult to change in any significant way. One reason for this difficulty might be thought of as simple inertia: there are established ways of doing things; people have habits and interconnected sets of expectations; and people are mostly resistant to change. But for particular problems of institutional transformation, specific obstacles also get in the way of beneficial changes; clarifying these obstacles may help identify ways of removing or at least mitigating them. The following are three obstacles to changing American capitalism in ways that would move us from the low road to the high road: transition costs, collective action failures in training, and deficits in worker organization.

Transition Costs

Any significant change in strategies and structures of firms involves added costs. Managers must learn new ways of doing things; new training programs are costly and take time to integrate into a system; significant changes in technologies may be needed to be a successful high-road firm. Together, these costs of transformation constitute a significant obstacle to major change. This barrier is especially acute when the time horizon of investors—the length of time in which they calculate their rates of return— is shorter than the time it takes to realize the economic gains from the organizational and strategic changes in the firm.

This transition cost problem is illustrated in Figure 10.12. The figure tracks the ability of firms in a country like the United States to compete internationally over time. If firms stay on the low road, their ability to compete declines gradually. If they adopt high-road practices, then eventually their ability to compete significantly improves. The problem is the transition trough—the length of time in which the transition costs outweigh the competitive gains. If investors are always looking for the highest short-run rates of return, then they are unlikely to be patient enough to accept this transition trough. They will either preemptively block the decision to

FIGURE 10.12–The transition cost problem

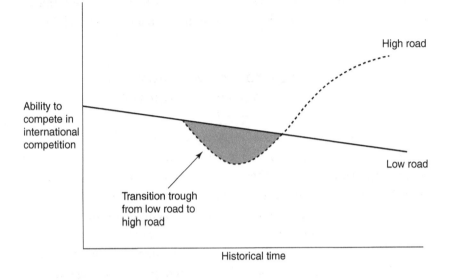

attempt the transformation, or they will pull out their investments if it occurs.

Collective Action Failures in Training and Skill Formation

A collective action failure in training is an example of the free-riding collective action problem we discussed in Chapter 4. The kinds of skills that are most central to high-road capitalist firms are flexible meta-skills developed through various types of general training rather than narrow, job-specific skills. These meta-skills take time to produce and are easily portable from one employer to another. Thus individual employers are often hesitant to provide extensive general training, both because of its cost and because employees can always leave. Due to these risks of providing good general training, employers have incentives to provide only the narrow, job-specific training consistent with the low-road option. Overcoming this collective action failure requires some form of active coordination among firms and some mechanism to discourage free riding.

Deficits in Worker Organization and Participation

Deciding how to overcome the obstacle posed by deficits in worker organization and participation is a much more controversial issue. In the United States, capitalist firms are generally hostile to unions. Conservative commentators portray unions as bullies that interfere with the efficient functioning of the market. This view is consistent with strong free market ideology: If you don't like your job or your working conditions, then you should quit. If you want to earn more money, then you should acquire more skills; this is your responsibility. Due to the political strength of the interests that hold these views, labor law in the United States has been quite unfavorable to unions, resulting in one of the lowest rates of unionization among economically advanced countries.

It might seem that weak unions would make it easier, not harder, for firms to make the necessary transformations to move from low-road to high-road strategies. After all, if unions were strong, employers and managers would have to negotiate such reorganizations with organized labor, and this would make the transformations more difficult.

In fact, strong unions facilitate high-road capitalism. First, the presence of strong labor organization makes movement down the low road more difficult. A strong union can prevent drastic wage reduction and in other ways reduce the incentives for capitalist firms to seek low-road solutions to competitive pressure. Second—and ultimately, perhaps, even more significant—high-road capitalism requires stable cooperation and trust between labor and management. High-road capitalism involves much more complex relations between employees and employers than does low-road capitalism. In the latter, managers issue commands and workers do what they are told. High-road capitalism requires active, creative participation by employees and the willingness of managers to let employees engage in ongoing problem solving within the firm. This relationship requires mutual trust and a belief by workers that employers will not unilaterally defect from collaborative practices. Strong working-class organization, within firms and within the labor market, potentially can play a strong role in creating the conditions for such trust and predictability by reducing the vulnerability of workers and imposing constraints on capitalists.

This argument is grounded in a specific view about the relationship between the degree of organization and participation of workers and the competitiveness of capitalist firms. Many people think there is a simple, inverse relationship between worker organization and the competitiveness of firms: the stronger the workers' organizations, the less competitive the firms in which they work. We believe, in contrast, that the relationship looks more like the graph in Figure 10.12: As the power and organization of employees in a firm increases from very low levels, worker organization initially interferes with the profit-maximizing strategies of firms. But once workers become strong enough to forge robust relations of cooperation, worker organization and participation become an asset, not a liability.[7]

Even more important than relations within firms is the extent of worker power in the broader society. The first goal of the union movement is to "take wages out of competition" between firms—to establish industry-wide norms of compensation and enough union power to forestall employer attempts to benefit by breaking with those norms. Once such power is established, productive cooperation between labor and capital is in the interest of both sides. Unions want to keep their employers healthy; employers want to get the most from the workers they cannot pay less.

As illustrated in Figure 10.13, the United States in the second decade of the twenty-first century lies somewhere to the left of the low point. This shows why, when competitive pressures increase, employers intensify their anti-union stance; improving their position by moving further up the left-hand part of the curve is easier than moving toward the right-hand part of

FIGURE 10.13—Worker organization and high-road capitalism

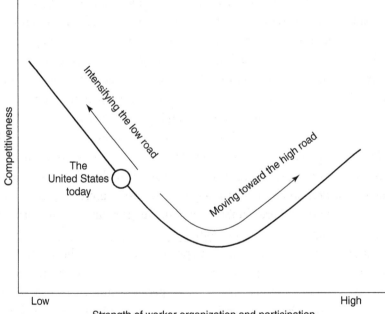

[7] For a more extended discussion of this curvilinear relationship between the strength of unions and the interests of employers, see Joel Rogers, "Divide and Conquer: Further 'Reflections on the Distinctive Character of American Labor Law,'" *Wisconsin Law Review* 13 (1990): 1–147, and Erik Olin Wright, "Working-Class Power, Capitalist-Class Interests, and Class Compromise," *American Journal of Sociology* 105, no. 4 (2000): 957–1002.

the curve because small moves in the rightward direction reduce the competitiveness of firms. Movement to the high road requires crossing the trough, which constitutes another obstacle to getting on the high road.

CLOSING OFF THE LOW ROAD, HELPING TO PAVE THE HIGH ROAD

If the United States is to move in the direction of the high road, how should we think about the process of overcoming these obstacles? The basic idea is pretty simple: public policies of various sorts need to be adopted to make it more difficult for firms to pursue low-road strategies, in effect closing off the low road. Other policies need to be adopted to make it easier for firms to adopt high-road strategies; we can call this, with some sense of the environmental irony, paving the high road. And, inevitably, during transition, steps need to be taken to enable workers and firms now stuck on the first to get on the second. Let's say a bit more about the kinds of policies that would advance these goals.

Closing Off the Low Road

Closing off or discouraging the low road basically means using public policy or private action to raise the standards of firms. One example is setting wage standards. People commonly think of living-wage guarantees as good for poor people, and indeed they are. Ensuring decent wages at the bottom of the labor market helps the working poor and tends to push up wages generally. But wage increases also have an important productivity effect. By making labor cost more, employers have more incentive to make it more productive. Better jobs also lead to workers sticking around longer, and they pick up additional skills in doing so.

The United States has largely abandoned efforts at such wage-led redistribution or productivity growth. Take minimum wages, a central part of the U.S. wage standard effort. A higher minimum wage would tend to discourage low-road practices, but we've let it fall. As Figure 10.14 shows, in terms of real purchasing power, the minimum wage in the United States reached its peak in 1968 at over $10.00 per hour in inflation-adjusted 2014 dollars. This amount declined (with various ups and downs) to just under $6.00 by 2006, the lowest value of the minimum wage in real purchasing power since 1950. In 2007, 2008, and 2009, increases in the minimum wage were enacted so that by 2009, the level had risen to $7.25 (equal to $7.87 in the 2013 inflation-adjusted dollars in Figure 10.14). This level, however, was still well below the minimum wage of the late 1960s of $10.71 (2013 dollars).

These figures are particularly astonishing given the fantastic growth over the same period in overall wealth and productivity in the United States. If the U.S. minimum wage had kept up with the growth of productivity in the United States since 1968, it would have been $21.72 in 2012.[8] Even if it had grown only as fast as half the average earnings of production workers in the private sector (which grew more slowly than productivity), it would now be about $10.00.[9] In fact, the minimum wage has lagged so far behind the over-all growth in the American economy that it has become largely (not entirely) irrelevant in labor markets. As late as 1980, some 15 percent of hourly work-ers were paid the minimum wage. By 2013, that figure had fallen to around 4.5 percent of hourly workers.

Another way that wages rise is through worker bargaining with employ-ers in labor markets. Here, especially for less educated workers, it is

FIGURE 10.14—The real value of the minimum wage, 1960–2013

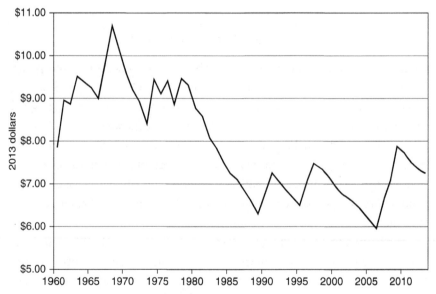

Source: Minimum wage values from U.S. Department of Labor, "History of Federal Minimum Wage Rates Under the Fair Labor Standards Act, 1938–2009." Available at http://www.dol.gov/whd /minwage/chart.htm (accessed June 3, 2014). Data have been inflated to 2013 dollars by using data from Bureau of Labor Statistics, "CPI for All Urban Consumers (CPI-U) 1982–84 = 100 (Unadjusted)." Available at http://data.bls.gov/cgi-bin/surveymost?bls (accessed June 3, 2014).

[8] John Schmitt, "The Minimum Wage is Too Damn Low," Center for Economic and Policy Research, issue brief, March 2012, p. 1.

[9] Ibid.

important that individual workers be able to bargain with employers as a group. They simply lack the labor market position, as individuals, to negotiate with employers on their own. In the United States, as in most countries, the best means of collective bargaining is through independent worker organizations, or unions. As we will see in more detail in Chapter 22, however, American labor law makes it particularly difficult for workers to form unions.

It is possible, however, to imagine raising the minimum wage much further and connecting it to the rest of the labor market by indexing it to inflation or setting it to some constant share of the median wage, or even indexing it to economy-wide productivity growth. Changes in labor law could make it easier for workers to join with other workers in collective bargaining with employers. It is also possible to imagine imposing higher environmental standards on employers, and conditioning any subsidies to them on performance, with clawbacks of those subsidies if they did not perform.[10] The United States might also require employers to provide worker training or pay into a federal fund that did this. All these sorts of policy steps would make it more difficult to pursue the low-road option. They would effectively close it off.

Paving the High Road

Encouraging higher wage and other standards, and facilitating collective bargaining, would be some of the sticks needed to drive employers toward the high road. What about carrots?

A first answer to this question is that closing off the low road would, for many firms, be carrot enough. Relief from competition from low-road firms would immediately benefit already-existing high-road firms as well as those wanting to get on the high road. It would give them some breathing room. At present, such "good" firms often pay the cost of "bad" ones. All else being equal, firms that pay their fair share of taxes and offer their workers decent wages and health benefits, for example, are at a competitive disadvantage with firms that do none of these things. As if that's not bad enough, however, they often wind up subsidizing the very firms that are unfairly outcompeting them.

A firm that fails to pay its taxes still insists on police protection and basic infrastructure, which taxes pay for. Even though the firm pays its workers

---

[10] A *clawback* is a provision in a government subsidy that requires repayment if certain conditions are not met.

too little even to owe taxes, those workers still want the same sort of basic infrastructure. They want decent schools for their kids, care at the emergency room or public clinic when the kids get sick, and maybe even a safe park for the kids to play in. As economists are fond of saying, "There is no free lunch." If some public good or service costs money, somebody is paying for it. Low-road firms, by externalizing those costs to the rest of society, are the ultimate free riders.

But if eliminating the low-road competitors is not enough, there are other things that society can do to make the high road more accessible for firms. What high-road firms need most, it turns out, is the institutional infrastructure we talked about before. They need decent schools and training systems whose costs they can share with other firms. They need help making sure their remaining collective action problems are solved through partnerships with their competitors in producing specialized public goods of concern to all the firms involved. They need modernization services that alert them to new technologies to improve productivity. They often need help in getting through that transition trough. And, of course, they need markets for their goods. These can come from other firms or individual consumers. But they can also come from government, especially a government that uses its purchasing power to upgrade standards by requiring, for example, better wages and benefits, improved health or environmental practices, more open and accountable management, and so forth.

Many other economically developed countries recognize and do all these things. They have long since decided to take the high road, and they recognize that it is the only way they will prosper in a global economy with many low-wage producers. Those countries invest in public goods—education, advanced transportation, and communications infrastructure. They reduce all kinds of waste—of energy, people, and nonrenewable physical resources. And they make sure that, for their effort, they capture some of the resulting productivity gains.

We know such a high road is perfectly possible under capitalism, because other capitalist democracies are pursuing it. If Americans genuinely want an economy that provides broad prosperity and stability in the twenty-first century, then the United States must also begin the difficult task of closing off the low road, paving the high road, and helping workers or firms stuck on the low road get onto and stay on the high one.

Part II

INEQUALITY

The next six chapters explore the problem of fairness and inequality in American society. Inequality is central to moral concerns in thinking about social institutions. Nearly everyone thinks that certain kinds of inequality are unfair. In contemporary American society, for example, few people would defend inequalities in legal rights based on race or gender or religion. Yet there are other kinds of inequalities that most people feel are just facts of life and are not of any general moral concern. There are great inequalities in physical strength among people, and while this may matter in some contexts, few people see this inequality by itself as morally troubling. And, of course, there are inequalities whose moral standing is deeply contested. Consider the following:

- In 2013, the average chief executive officer (CEO) in the United States earned about 313 times the salary of the average nonmanagerial employee.
- Women made up nearly 45 percent of the labor force in 2012 but only about 4 percent of the CEOs of the largest U.S. corporations.
- Young African American men are 7.5 times more likely to be in prison than are white men of the same age.
- Roughly one out of five children in the United States lived in poverty in 2014.
- The probability of a manual worker's son becoming a professional worker is about 40 percent that of the son of a professional.

The claim that each of these facts is an example of an unjust inequality is contested to varying degrees, resulting from disagreements over the underlying explanation of the specific inequality. If the explanation for why women are less represented among top managers is simply that they freely choose other kinds of career paths, then many people would conclude that there is nothing unfair about the inequality of outcomes; if young African American men commit seven times more serious crimes than young white men do, then their disproportionate imprisonment might not be viewed as reflecting an injustice; if the children of manual workers are less academically talented or motivated, then many people would feel that there is nothing unfair in their having a lower chance of becoming a professional. But the contested quality of judgments about the fairness of inequality may also depend upon underlying philosophical views. Many people would argue that it is unfair for a CEO to earn three hundred times the salary of an ordinary worker, even if this pay differential is the result of free market competition and meritocracy, and that it is unfair in a rich society for children to live in poverty regardless of why their parents lack adequate income.

In this part of the book, we will explore the kinds of inequalities in contemporary American society that raise moral issues of fairness and injustice. We begin in Chapter 11 by clarifying what we mean by fairness and its relationship to the problem of social and economic inequalities. Chapter 12 then explores a particularly salient concept in the analysis of economic inequality—class. Chapter 13 examines the empirical patterns of poverty, wealth, and inequality in the United States today and discusses the alternative explanations for these patterns. In Chapter 14, we look at possible remedies to both extreme inequality and poverty in the United States. In Chapters 15 and 16, we shift our attention from economic inequalities to inequalities rooted in what sociologists call ascriptive characteristics—characteristics that a person is born with. Chapter 15 examines racial inequality in the United States, briefly charting its historical development and variations and paying particular attention to the deep connection between racial inequality and class. Chapter 16 explores the dramatic transformations of gender relations since the middle of the twentieth century and the forms of gender inequality that still pose challenges today.

11

THINKING ABOUT FAIRNESS
AND INEQUALITY

I n most societies there are certain broadly shared beliefs about what is socially just and unjust, what is fair and unfair. Here is the basic problem: We observe some empirical case of social inequality—some people are better off than others, or they have more fulfilling lives than others, or they are healthier than others. These are observations. And we ask: Is the observed inequality just or fair? Does the inequality violate some principle of justice? Now, some inequalities are simply cases of bad luck. When one person gets hit by lightning and another does not, there is a dramatic inequality in their fates. And there is a sense, of course, in which one could say (as kids do): that's not fair; the person who got hit by lightning didn't deserve it. Such expressions reflect a deep moral intuition that most people have: *people should get what they deserve and deserve what they get*. This is why when someone gets struck by lightning we say, "That's so unfair, they didn't deserve that."

When we talk about a *social* injustice—not just the unfairness of bad luck—we mean there is an inequality that is unfair *and that could be remedied* if our social institutions were different. Something *could in principle* be done about it. When we say that it was a social injustice for African Americans to be denied admission to all-white universities before the end of racial segregation in America, we mean that it was not just bad luck to be born black and thus denied admission, but that this grossly unfair inequality in educational opportunity could have been remedied by a change in social institutions. This does not mean, of course, that it was *politically possible* to remedy that injustice in the 1920s or 1930s. Racial segregation was always a profound social injustice, as was slavery before it, but the social forces supporting segregation were so powerful and cohesive that until the 1950s and 1960s they were able to successfully repress struggles against segregation and maintain those institutions. The claim that an inequality is unjust, therefore, can be seen as an indictment of the way in which existing configurations of power block the social changes needed to reduce or eliminate the inequality in question.

Discussing problems of social justice quickly becomes complicated because a diagnosis of injustice really requires two judgments: first, a *moral judgment* that an inequality is unfair, and second, a *sociological judgment* that this unfairness could be remedied by a social change. It's not fair that some children are born with physical disabilities—they don't deserve it. But their condition is not by itself necessarily a social injustice.[1] It becomes a social injustice when there are things we could do to minimize the effects on people's lives of the unfairness of such bad luck and we fail to do so. The lack of curb cuts in sidewalks is an injustice for people in wheelchairs. The lack of affordable prosthetic limbs is an injustice for amputees. Ensuring that curb cuts exist requires a change in rules governing urban planning. Ensuring that everyone who needs a prosthetic limb can afford one requires a change in the rules governing access to medical services. Both of these examples constitute social changes. And because remedies like these involve changes in the uses of resources, they almost inevitably trigger resistance and conflict from those who stand to lose from the social change.

When an inequality is also an injustice—that is, an unfair inequality that could be remedied—we can expect a set of power relations to be operating in the situation that block the necessary remedies. Injustices do not continue just because of some law of inertia; they continue because people are unwilling to pay the costs to remedy the injustice, and they have sufficient power to avoid doing so. This combination of inequality, injustice, and power is what we will call *oppression*.[2]

In this chapter, we focus on the moral dimension of inequality and try to clarify what we mean when we say that an inequality among people is unfair. In later chapters we will talk about remedies.

---

[1]Being born with a disability could itself be a social injustice if the disability was also the result of a social injustice, such as a pregnant woman's lack of access to good prenatal medical care.

[2]Words like *oppression* have considerable emotional bite, for they are laden with moral judgments. Some sociologists argue that such terms should be kept out of sociological analysis. In this view it is fine to use descriptive terms like *racial inequality* and perhaps even racial *domination*—because defining a group as dominant does not inherently imply a moral condemnation. But a term like *oppression* should be avoided because it invokes inherently contested moral stances. We feel that coming to terms with the moral issues bound up with inequalities—and thus making a judgment about the justice or injustice of existing social arrangements—is an essential part of social science, and thus words like *social justice* and *oppression* are needed to make these judgments explicit.

THE JUSTICE AND INJUSTICE OF INEQUALITIES:
FAIR PLAY VERSUS FAIR SHARES

Consider, first, an easy case: Two farmers each have identical plots of land for gardens. Each farmer has the same time and resources available for growing vegetables. One works hard, the other does not; and at the end of the summer, one has lots of produce and the other has little. Most people would say there is nothing unfair in this inequality. To be sure, something could be done about it—the tomatoes could be redistributed. But most people would say *that* act would be unfair: the lazy gardener would then have a summer of leisure plus an equal amount of tomatoes as the farmer who worked hard all summer. This situation would be an injustice to the hardworking farmer.

Most examples of inequality we observe in a society like the United States are not so simple. Let's examine three additional cases, one of which almost everyone would consider an example of injustice, one of which most people would not, and one of which would be a source of disagreement:

Case 1. A police chief will hire only personal relatives—sons, daughters, cousins—as police officers.

Case 2. The owner of a small shop is willing to have only his son or daughter become a co-owner of the store.

Case 3. In the United States—one of the richest countries in the world— millions of people, children and adults, live in desperate poverty.

In the first case there is a consensus—at least in liberal democratic capitalist societies—that it is unfair for a public official to hire only family members. Nepotism is widely considered unfair. In the second case there is also little disagreement. The owner of a small shop has the right to decide who will be a co-owner of the business. As long as the shop owner is the legitimate owner of the business and acquired it in a legitimate way, then most people would say there is nothing unjust in deciding that only family members can become co-owners rather than someone else who might be more qualified.

For the third case, however, there is a lot of disagreement. Many people believe there is nothing unjust about having lots of poor people in a rich country; it is unfortunate, but not necessarily unjust. The argument usually goes something like this: The United States is a land of opportunity, and even if it is not exactly true that everyone has *equal* opportunity, nevertheless there is *ample* opportunity for anyone who works hard to make it. Like the lazy farmer who ends up with little produce at the end of the summer, poverty is largely the fault of those who are poor. And besides, as libertarians like to argue, the rich and successful have a right to what they have earned through their own efforts, and it would be an injustice to force them to help the poor. On the principle of "two wrongs don't make a right," it is unfair to take from the rich to give to the poor *even if* the poverty itself is unfair.[3]

Other people argue that poverty in the midst of plenty represents a deep injustice. Although there may be some cases of poor people who have squandered their resources and opportunities, most poor people do not bear full responsibility for their condition of poverty, and certainly poor children bear no responsibility for their deprivations. Much of the inequality in contemporary American society is the result of injustices in the ways our institutions and rules are organized rather than the outcome of lazy or irresponsible behavior within a fair process. What is more, if there is a problem of self-destructive behavior in poor communities—what some sociologists call a *culture of poverty*—this is largely the result of the despair and alienation generated by the objective deprivations, disadvantages, and lack of opportunities people face in those communities. These are quite sharply polarized views. They underlie many of the political disagreements about what, if anything, should be done to reduce poverty.

Why does it matter whether you think some form of inequality is unjust? It matters because when people feel something is unjust, they are more likely to support efforts to change social institutions. People are often willing to do things that go against their own personal interests when they think it is necessary for justice. Many affluent people, for example, believe that it is unjust in a rich country for poor children to be hungry and that therefore it is a good thing to use taxes to pay for food stamps and health care for poor children, even though these affluent people pay the taxes. So, the stakes can be quite high in deciding who deserves what, what kinds of inequalities are justified, what kinds violate principles of justice, and what should be done to redress an injustice.

Let us now look more closely at different ways of understanding what it is that renders an inequality a matter of injustice. A useful contrast between

---

[3]The libertarian argument acknowledges that it might be morally desirable for the rich to help the poor, but that forcing them to do so would nevertheless be a violation of their rights. The most influential contemporary elaboration of this view is by Robert Nozick in *Anarchy, the State, and Utopia* (New York: Basic Books, 1974).

two ways of thinking about the fairness of what people get is captured by the expressions *fair play* and *fair shares*.[4]

In the fair-play conception, inequalities are fair so long as the rules by which people compete for valued goods are fair. The key metaphor is of a sporting competition. In sporting events there are winners and losers, and the losers have no complaint as long as there is an equal playing field, no cheating, and a fair umpire. In the world at large, if there is no discrimination and no artificial barriers to each person's pursuit of happiness, then high levels of inequalities of outcomes are fair and just. Or, to use another common way of expressing this idea, so long as there is something approximating *equal opportunity*, inequality of *results* is not a moral problem.

In the fair-share view of equality and inequality, everyone is entitled to a share of society's resources sufficient to live a dignified, flourishing life. *Sufficient* means having enough to be able to participate fully in the exercise of rights and liberties, to be able to exercise personal freedom and develop one's talents. Particularly in a rich society, everyone has a basic human right to good health care, decent housing, and adequate nutrition. It is not enough that there is a fair competition for these valued goods; the losers in that competition still deserve a fair share of society's bounty.

Both principles are deeply embedded in American life, but fair play is the dominant view. Most Americans believe that so long as everyone has equal opportunity, then inequalities in what people earn don't really matter. Michael Jordan and Bill Gates deserve their high incomes because they didn't cheat to get what they got; they worked hard and competed fairly. They get what they deserve and deserve what they get.

Still, for many people there is a niggling sense that by itself, fair play in the distribution of income and other valued goods is not an entirely satisfactory principle. Although suffering because of "bad luck" is consistent with a fair-play doctrine—after all, many athletes lose competitions because of random bad luck—it seems a little harsh to treat bad luck in life the same way we treat bad luck in a football game. In addition to the ideal of equal opportunity, therefore, many—perhaps most—Americans also feel that everyone has at least a right to have their basic needs met, and at least some Americans believe that everyone has a right to live above the poverty level. Inequalities *above* that level may be justified on the basis of fair play, but

[4]The use of the contrast between fair play and fair shares as a way of understanding the moral dimension of inequality comes from William Ryan, *Equality* (New York: Pantheon, 1981).

everyone has the right to live above poverty; thus the fair-shares principle should prevent inequality from pushing people below poverty.

Even if one rejects fair shares as a general argument for redistribution, there is another fundamental problem with fair play as the exclusive moral principle governing acceptable inequality. This concerns the fate of children. So long as children are raised in families, then large inequalities in the life circumstances of parents profoundly undermine equal opportunity for children. At first glance it seems that fair play and fair shares are radically different ideas: the former concerns the fairness of opportunity to acquire income and says nothing about the actual distribution; the latter says nothing about the process of acquiring income and focuses only on the fairness of the shares people acquire. In reality, however, these two principles interact, especially in the lives of children: if we want children to have remotely equal opportunities in life, then we cannot allow any children to grow up in conditions of dire poverty and large inequalities. Thus if you are really serious about the fair-play idea of equality of opportunity, then you also have to consider the problem of the distribution of outcomes—fair shares—as a means for achieving even rough equality of opportunity—fair play. The implication of this argument is pretty radical: high levels of inequality in income and wealth undermine the principles of fair play itself.

COMPLICATIONS: DEFENSES OF UNJUST INEQUALITY

Even if you decide that having poor children in a land of plenty is unjust because it violates the principles of both fair play and fair shares, this position does not necessarily imply that it would be justified to redistribute wealth and income to remedy the situation. Two sorts of reasons might be given to defend maintaining unjust inequalities: First, the means needed to rectify the injustice may themselves violate some other important value; and second, redistributing income may be a bad idea for pragmatic reasons.

The Problem of Conflicting Values

At the center of the idea of fair play is equality of opportunity. And in contemporary American society, that means equality of access to education. To ensure that all children have even approximate equality of educational opportunity, however, would require putting significant restrictions on what parents are allowed to do for their children. Specifically, rich parents would not be allowed to send their kids to expensive private schools or pay for expensive private tutoring for standardized exams, because such actions would give their kids an unfair advantage. So long as parents are free to spend whatever they like on their children, they can purchase advantages that violate equality of opportunity. The principle of fair play, therefore, would justify imposing such restrictions on parents. But we also place a high value on parents being able to help their children—both because we value the parent-child nurturance relationship and because we value people's freedom to choose how they spend their money, and giving special help to your child is such a choice. So, to truly rectify the unjust inequality of educational opportunity conflicts with other important values. When such conflicts of values occur, it is always difficult to manage the trade-off, to balance the compromise between the two values.[5]

If, on balance, someone decides that the values of freedom of choice and parental autonomy to help their children are so much more important than fair play, then that person is stuck with the unpleasant fact of supporting the perpetuation of a social injustice. However, the injustice of this inequality of opportunity doesn't itself magically become just simply because some other value—parental autonomy and freedom to spend one's money—is seen as more important. Defenders of property rights (i.e., the right to do with one's money what one chooses), therefore, should honestly admit that their strong support of these rights generates an injustice.

The implication of this conflict of values is that the distribution of income and wealth that results from these unjust unequal opportunities would itself be unjust. This, then, strengthens the arguments for redistribution based on the principles of fair shares because under these conditions, the shares that go to the children of wealthy adults are clearly unfair *by the very criterion of fair play*. The ironic result of these conflicting values is thus the following: *if* you believe strongly that parents should have the right to give special advantages to their children, then you should also support some redistribution of income to counteract the unfairness of the resulting income distribution.

[5]For a careful discussion of parental rights and how these can sometimes clash with other values, see Harry Brighouse and Adam Swift, *Family Values: The Ethics of Parent-Child Relationships* (Princeton, NJ: Princeton University Press, 2014).

The Pragmatic Issue: Is Inequality Good for Society?

A pragmatic argument for something is an argument that focuses on practical consequences and conditions rather than strictly on moral issues. In addition to conflicting values, many people argue that inequalities—even if unfair—should not necessarily be significantly reduced, because *the poor may be made worse off by redistributing wealth or income to them.* In the extreme case, it can be imagined that if we redistributed wealth in a significant way, the economy would collapse—in which case the poor would starve. Remember, in the end a social injustice is an unfair inequality *that can in principle be eliminated.* Well, if the poor would be made much worse off by significantly reducing an inequality, then perhaps it would be better to leave it in place. This is the standard pragmatic defense of inequalities that might otherwise be suspect. This, of course, sounds like a self-serving ideology of privileged people. Still, it cannot be dismissed.[6]

What is the argument behind this pragmatic defense of inequality? The key idea is that inequalities are deeply connected to incentives. There are two forms of the argument, one concerning the incentives of poor people and the second the incentives of more affluent people.

The incentive argument for poor people argues that if income is redistributed to the poor, they will have less incentive to work hard and responsibly to improve their lives. Why work hard if you can avoid poverty without working? Redistribution therefore will permanently lock poor people at the bottom of the socioeconomic hierarchy. This situation will be especially bad for poor children, who will be raised in families without a strong work ethic or motivation for self-improvement. So, even if it is unfair for children to be poor because they bear no responsibility for their poverty, redistribution will ultimately make their lives worse.

The incentive argument for people who are more affluent goes like this: people need incentives to be productive, to work hard and invest. If people work hard and invest, they produce more. Such activity energizes the economy and leads to economic growth, which ultimately benefits the poor. This is the essential argument of what has come to be known as trickle-down

---

[6]One form of this argument is embodied in the arguments for justice of the most influential political philosopher of the second half of the twentieth century, John Rawls. Rawls argues for what he calls the difference principle, which is roughly the following: a level of inequality in income is just if it is the case that any reduction of the degree of inequality would worsen the condition of the worst off. The goal is to maximize the minimum level of income, or what is called maxi-min.

economics: cutting the taxes of high earners will make them increase their effort and invest more, which increases economic growth in ways that benefit everyone—a rising tide raises all boats. The causal connections in this argument are illustrated in Thesis 1 below:

Thesis 1: Inequality → incentives → people are motivated to work harder and invest more → enhanced productivity and prosperity → ultimately benefits the poor.

By itself this thesis merely states that *some* level of inequality is needed to give people the incentive to work hard and invest, but it says nothing about how much inequality is needed to produce this effect. Defenders of existing levels of inequality in the American economy therefore make a second argument: whatever level of inequality is spontaneously generated by market interactions generates the necessary incentives to get people to invest as much as can be profitably invested and to work as hard as is economically efficient. Because all transactions in the market are voluntary, no employer will make a wage offer unless the employer thinks doing so is profitable. So if high wages are offered as an incentive to some people, it is because of the productivity that this employment will generate. The same logic applies to investors. Because investors always have the option of consuming their capital rather than investing it, and because investments are voluntary, the levels of inequality generated by capital investments exactly reflect the incentives needed to get people to invest. This implies a second thesis:

Thesis 2: Reducing inequality below the level generated by free markets → reduces incentives to work hard and invest → reduces productivity and economic growth → harms the poor.

If this thesis were true, it would be a powerful argument against efforts to reduce inequality. Even if those inequalities were judged to be unfair, the remedies would not make life better for those at the bottom. The unfairness would not constitute a social injustice.

Critique of the Pragmatic Defense of Inequality

The pragmatic defense of market-generated inequality rests on two important assumptions. The first is that the incentives needed to get people to work and invest are not themselves affected by the level of inequality in a society. Economists call this the problem of endogenous preference formation.

Suppose that the amount of income needed to get people to work or invest depends upon cultural standards and expectations, and that these in turn are shaped by the level of economic inequality in a society. If this is the case, then high levels of economic inequality will tend to foster cultural frameworks and norms in which individuals at the top require greater incentives. CEOs in the United States are not notably more talented or hardworking than their Japanese or German counterparts, but they earn fantastically higher salaries at least in part because of the cultural expectations and norms that have evolved over time in the United States.

The second assumption of the pragmatic defense of market-generated inequality is that the power of actors plays no role in how much they earn through the market. In a "free" market, no one exercises power over anyone; no firms or individuals exercise power in the market. In the language of economists, there are no "monopoly rents" in the earnings of people in the labor market or in the profits of firms. If people have real power, then they are in a position to extract extra income by using threats of various kinds. CEOs and other high executives are able to raise their incomes in part because of the power they wield within firms. The earnings of workers in some industries are pushed down because of the weakness of unions to protect their interests when bargaining with employers. On the other hand, people with scarce talents and credentials also can use the bargaining power of their skills to acquire greater income than would be needed as an incentive to get them to use their talents and skills productively. In all of these cases, the levels of inequality in the resulting income distributions would be greater than what is needed simply to provide people with the necessary incentives to work and invest.

Of course, people who are in a position to use their power to extract high income are likely to defend their high incomes in terms of necessary incentives. Privileged elites will always say that they "need more" to be motivated to work hard, to produce, to save, to invest. They will fight against tax increases directed against the rich on the grounds that this will destroy the incentive to invest, and as a result everyone will be worse off. Such claims are often—perhaps usually—self-serving rationalizations masking the simple desire to preserve privilege and advantage.

The level of inequality in a society, therefore, is not a simple function of the technically required incentives needed for market efficiency, but of a much more complex process through which threats and bluffs backed by power shape a range of economic practices that generate unequal earnings. These unequal earnings in turn shape the cultural expectations and norms that become embodied as preferences and incentives. These complex processes are ignored by the simple pragmatic argument for inequality.

A Pragmatic Argument against High Inequality

It is important not to think that pragmatic arguments about inequality always support the status quo. There are also strong pragmatic arguments *against* high levels of inequality. Excessive inequality can have all sorts of undesirable practical consequences. Two considerations are particularly important here: the impact of inequality on the costs of social control and the impact of inequality on democracy.

First, high levels of inequality can be costly to a society in a variety of ways. High inequality fosters resentment and conflict. It undermines community and erodes a sense of common fate and mutual obligation among people. This situation in turn fuels crime and social disorder, which negatively affect productivity and economic efficiency. Social conflict and disorder are costly because of their directly destructive effects as well as the social control costs needed to contain them: police, prisons, security guards, and so on. These drains on the economy are all linked to inequality. The social resentment and erosion of a sense of social solidarity generated by inequality also undercuts general values of cooperation and mutual obligation, thus reducing productivity within work itself. Where inequalities and competition are intense, more managers and supervisors are needed to ensure work discipline—and this, again, reduces economic efficiency. There is, finally, compelling empirical evidence that high levels of inequality undermine average levels of health and well-being in a society, not just the well-being of people at the very bottom.[7]

The second critical effect of high levels of inequality concerns its impact on democracy: high inequality concentrates material resources in the hands of elites in ways that enable them to have a vastly disproportionate influence in political life, both at the local level and at higher levels of the political system. Furthermore, because high inequality erodes the sense of everyone being in the same boat—we are all in this together—the influence of wealthy elites on state policy tends to serve their interests over those of the broader

---

[7]A thorough discussion of the impact of inequality on average health and well-being using a wide variety of indicators can be found in Kate Pickett and Richard Wilkinson, *The Spirit Level: Why Greater Equality Makes Societies Stronger* (New York: Bloomsbury Press, 2010).

public. We will explore these issues in Part III of the book, when we discuss democracy.

CONCLUSION

Few subjects are more fraught with controversy than the problem of the justice or injustice of social and economic inequalities. It is difficult to calmly discuss these matters, because powerful interests are at stake. If a person decides that it is a profound injustice that nearly 15 million children are poor in the United States in the second decade of the twenty-first century, then it is difficult to defend doing nothing about the situation. And doing something serious about poverty and inequality inevitably means that at least some of the privileges and advantages of people who manage to do well under the existing rules of the game will be reduced.

Now, not everyone who has advantages that may be reduced by remedies to injustice will actively oppose the remedy. People's moral commitments to social justice can be strong enough that they support public policies and social changes that challenge injustice even if they themselves do not gain from such changes. But many people in such a situation oppose changes to existing arrangements out of narrow self-interest. They use power to defend their interests and thus turn an injustice into a form of oppression. This, of course, is a morally uncomfortable position. Rarely do people in such a situation forthrightly say: "I know this is a violation of moral principles of fairness and justice, but I am rich and oppose policies that will help the poor because I don't want to pay for them." Most people, it seems, feel a need to justify the defense of their advantages on moral grounds, and so their self-interest gets dressed up in moral language of one sort or another. And because these rationalizations involve a certain amount of persuasiveness, many people come to genuinely believe them.

12

CLASS

I n Chapter 11 we explored the moral question of what it means to say
that an inequality is unfair. In this chapter, we examine the problem
of alternative ways of thinking sociologically about one domain of
inequality—class. In the following chapters, we will explore the empirical
problem of inequality in America and discuss how it has changed over time.

Class, like many concepts in sociology, is a hotly contested idea. There is
not even an agreed-upon definition of *class*, let alone a consensus on the best
theory of class. All approaches to class see it as a way of thinking about economic inequalities, but they use the word *class* in very different ways.[1]

The various approaches to class among sociologists fall into three broad
categories. The first identifies class with the attributes and material conditions of life of individuals. The second sees class as mainly about the ways in
which social positions give some people control over economically valued
resources of various sorts while excluding others from access to those resources.
And the third sees class as, above all, involving the ways in which economic
positions give some people control over the lives and activities of others. We can
call these three approaches the *individual attributes* approach to class, the
opportunity-hoarding approach, and the *domination and exploitation* approach.

CLASS AS INDIVIDUAL ATTRIBUTES
AND MATERIAL CONDITIONS OF LIFE

Both for sociologists and the lay public, the principal way that most people
understand the concept of class is in terms of individual attributes and
life conditions. People have all sorts of attributes, including sex, age, race,

[1] For a thorough discussion of alternative approaches to class, see Erik Olin Wright, ed.,
Approaches to Class Analysis (Cambridge: Cambridge University Press, 2005). Parts of
this chapter are taken from Erik Olin Wright, "Understanding Class," *New Left Review* 60
(November–December 2009).

religion, intelligence, education, geographical location, and so on. Some of these are attributes people have from birth; some are acquired, but once acquired are very stable; and some are quite dependent on a person's specific social situation at any given time and may change accordingly. These attributes are consequential for various things we might want to explain, from health to voting behavior to child-rearing practices to income and wealth. People also can be characterized by the material conditions in which they live: squalid apartments, pleasant houses in the suburbs, or mansions in gated communities; dire poverty, adequate income, or extravagant wealth; insecure access to health services or excellent health insurance and access to high-quality services.

Class, then, is a way of talking about the connection between individual attributes and these material life conditions: class identifies those economically useful attributes of people that shape their opportunities and choices in a market economy and thus their material conditions of life. Class should neither be identified simply with the individual attributes nor with the material conditions of life of people, but with the interconnections between these attributes and conditions.

The key individual attribute of class in contemporary American society within this approach is education, but some sociologists also include somewhat more elusive attributes like cultural resources, social connections, and even individual motivations. All these things deeply shape the opportunities people face and thus the income, type of housing, and quality of health care they are likely to get. When these different attributes of individuals and material conditions of life broadly cluster together, then these clusters are called classes. Within this approach to the study of class, the term *middle class* identifies people who are more or less in the broad middle of the American economy and society: they have enough education and money to participate fully in some vaguely defined "mainstream" way of life. *Upper class* identifies people whose wealth, high income, social connections, and valuable talents enable them to live their lives apart from so-called ordinary people. *Lower class* identifies people who lack the necessary educational and cultural resources to live securely above the poverty line. And finally, *underclass* identifies people who live in extreme poverty, marginalized from the mainstream of American society by a lack of basic education and skills needed for stable employment.

In the individual attributes approach to class, the central concern of sociologists has been to understand how people acquire the attributes that place them in one class or another. Given that most people acquire economic status and rewards mainly through employment in paid jobs, the central thrust of most research was on the process by which people acquire the cultural, motivational, and educational resources that affect their occupations in the labor market.

Skills, education, and motivations are, of course, important determinants of an individual's economic prospects. The missing ingredient in this approach to class, however, is any serious consideration of the *inequalities in the positions themselves* that people occupy. Education shapes the kinds of jobs people get, but what explains the nature of the jobs that people fill by virtue of their education? Why are some jobs "better" than others? Why do some jobs confer on their incumbents a great deal of power while others do not? Rather than focusing exclusively on the process by which individuals are sorted into positions, the other two approaches to class analysis begin by analyzing the nature of the positions into which people are sorted.

CLASS AS OPPORTUNITY HOARDING

The idea of opportunity hoarding is closely associated with the work of the early-twentieth-century sociologist Max Weber.[2] The idea is that for a job to give its occupants high income and special advantages, it is important that the incumbents of those jobs have various means of excluding people from access to the jobs. Sociologists also refer to this concept as a process of *social closure*: the process whereby access to a position becomes restricted or closed off to some people. One way of doing this is by creating requirements for filling the job that are costly for people to meet. Educational credentials often have this character: high levels of education generate high income in part because there are significant restrictions in the supply of highly educated people. Admissions procedures, tuition costs, risk aversion to large loans by low-income people, and so on all block access to higher education for many people, and this situation benefits those with higher education. If a massive effort were made to improve the educational level of those with less education, the resulting increased supply of highly educated people would lower the economic value of education because its value depends to a significant extent on its scarcity.

[2] Among contemporary American sociologists, the term *opportunity hoarding* was used most explicitly by Charles Tilly, especially in his book *Durable Inequality* (Berkeley: University of California Press, 1999).

Someone might object to this description of educational credentials by arguing that education also affects earnings by enhancing a person's productivity. Economists argue that education creates "human capital," which makes people more productive, and this is why employers are willing to pay them higher wages. Though some of the higher earnings that accompany higher education reflect productivity differences, this is only part of the story. Equally important are the ways in which the process of acquiring education excludes people through various mechanisms and thus restricts the supply of people for these jobs. A simple thought experiment shows how this works: imagine that the United States had open borders and let anyone with a medical degree or engineering degree or computer science degree anywhere in the world come to this country and practice their profession. The massive increase in the supply of people with these credentials would undermine the earning capacity of holders of the credentials, even though their actual knowledge and skills would not be diminished.

Credentialing and licensing are particularly important mechanisms for opportunity hoarding, but many other institutional devices have been used in various times and places to restrict access to given types of jobs: color bars excluded racial minorities from many jobs in the United States, especially (but not only) in the South until the 1960s; marriage bars and gender exclusions restricted access to certain jobs for women until well into the twentieth century in most developed capitalist countries; and religion, cultural style, manners, and accent all have constituted mechanisms of exclusion.

Perhaps the most important exclusionary mechanism that protects the privileges and advantages of people in certain jobs in a capitalist society is private property rights in the means of production. Private property rights are the pivotal form of exclusion that determines access to the "job" of employer. The capacity of owners to acquire profits depends on their defense of this exclusion. If workers attempted to take over a factory and run it themselves, they would be violating this process of social closure by challenging their exclusion from control over the means of production. Within both Weberian and Marxian traditions of sociology, the core class division between capitalists and workers can therefore be understood as reflecting a specific form of opportunity hoarding enforced by the legal rules of property rights.

Exclusionary mechanisms that shape class structures within the opportunity-hoarding approach do not operate only in the most privileged parts of the class structure. Labor unions can also function as an exclusionary mechanism by protecting the incumbents of jobs from competition by outsiders. This does not mean that on balance unions contribute to increasing inequality. They may also act politically to reduce inequalities; and they may effectively reduce inequalities generated by other mechanisms of exclusion, especially mechanisms connected to private ownership of the means of production. Still, to the extent that unions create barriers to entry to certain jobs, they do create a form of social closure that raises the material conditions of life for insiders.

Sociologists who adopt the opportunity-hoarding approach to class generally identify three broad class categories in American society: capitalists, defined by private property rights in the ownership of means of production; the middle class, defined by mechanisms of exclusion concerning the acquisition of education and skills; and the working class, defined by its exclusion from both higher educational credentials and capital. The segment of the working class that is protected by unions is seen either as a privileged category within the working class or, sometimes, as a component of the middle class.

The critical difference between the opportunity-hoarding concept of class and the individual attribute concept of class is this: In the opportunity-hoarding view of class, the economic advantages people get from being in a privileged class position are causally connected to the disadvantages of people excluded from those class positions. In the individual attributes approach, advantages and disadvantages are simply outcomes of individual conditions. To state this more simply, in the opportunity-hoarding conception, the rich are rich in part *because* the poor are poor; the rich do things to secure their wealth that contribute to the disadvantages poor people face in the world. In the individual attribute approach, the rich are rich because they have favorable attributes, the poor are poor because they lack these attributes, and there is no systematic causal connection between these facts. Eliminating poverty by improving the relevant attributes of the poor—by improving their education, cultural level, and human capital—would in no way harm the rich. In the opportunity-hoarding approach, in contrast, eliminating poverty by removing the mechanisms of exclusion potentially undermines the advantages of the rich in the existing system.

CLASS AS DOMINATION AND EXPLOITATION

The most controversial way of thinking about class is as a mechanism of domination and exploitation. This approach is associated most strongly with the Marxist tradition of sociology, but some sociologists more influenced by Weber also emphasize domination and exploitation in their conception of class.

Domination and, especially, *exploitation* are contentious words in sociology because they tend to imply a moral judgment, not simply a neutral description. Many sociologists try to avoid such terms. As with the term *oppression*, we feel that these terms are important and accurately identify certain key issues in understanding class. Both domination and exploitation refer to ways in which people control the lives of others. *Domination* refers to the ability to control the *activities* of others. *Exploitation* refers to the acquisition of economic benefits from the laboring activity of those who are dominated. Therefore, all exploitation implies some kind of domination, but not all domination involves exploitation.

In relations of domination and exploitation, it is not simply the case that one group benefits by restricting access to certain kinds of resources or positions. In addition, the dominating and exploiting group is able to control the laboring effort of another for its own advantage. Consider these classic, contrasting cases: In the first case, large landowners seize control of common grazing lands, exclude peasants from gaining access to this land, and reap economic advantages from having exclusive control of this land for their own use. In the second case, the same landlords seize control of the grazing lands and exclude the peasants, but then they bring some of those peasants back onto the land as agricultural laborers. In this second case, besides gaining advantage from controlling access to the land, the landowner also dominates and exploits the labor of the farmworker. This is a stronger form of interdependency than in the case of simple exclusion, for here there is an ongoing relationship between the *activities* of the advantaged and disadvantaged persons, not just a relationship between their *conditions*. Domination and exploitation are forms of structured inequality that require continual active cooperation between dominators and the dominated, exploiters and the exploited.

Within the domination and exploitation approach to class, the central class division in a capitalist society is between those who own and control the means of production in the economy—capitalists—and those who are hired to use those means of production—workers. Capitalists, within this framework, both dominate and exploit workers. Other kinds of positions within the class structure get their specific character from their relationship to this basic division. Managers, for example, exercise many of the powers of domination, but they are also subordinated to capitalists. CEOs and top managers of corporations often develop significant ownership stakes in their corporations and therefore become more like capitalists. Highly educated professionals and some categories of technical workers have sufficient control over knowledge (a critical resource in contemporary economies) and skills that they can maintain considerable autonomy from domination within work and thus significantly reduce, or even neutralize, the extent to which they are exploited.

In both the opportunity-hoarding and domination-exploitation approaches to class, power plays an important role. In both of these approaches, the inequalities in income and wealth connected to the class structure are sustained by the exercise of power, not simply by the actions of individuals. The inequalities generated by opportunity hoarding require the use of power to enforce exclusions, and the inequalities connected to exploitation require supervision, monitoring of labor effort, and sanctions to enforce labor discipline. In both cases, social struggles that would challenge these forms of power would potentially threaten the privileges of people in the advantaged class positions. To repeat what we already have said: these advantages causally depend upon the mechanisms of exclusion and exploitation that impose disadvantages on others.

CLASS IN AMERICA TODAY

Sociologists have generally tended to base their research on one or another of these three approaches to class, but there really is no reason to see them as mutually exclusive. Instead we can see the reality of class as being generated by the complex interactions of the different mechanisms identified within each approach. One way of combining the three approaches is to see each of them as identifying a key process that shapes a different aspect of the American class structure:

1. The domination and exploitation approach to class identifies the fundamental class division connected to the capitalist character of the economy: the class division between capitalists and workers.
2. The opportunity-hoarding approach identifies the central mechanism that differentiates middle-class jobs from the broader working class by creating barriers that in one way or another restrict the supply of people for desirable employment. The key issue here is not mainly *who* is excluded, but simply that mechanisms of exclusion are sustaining the privileges of those in middle-class positions.

3. The individual attributes approach identifies a key set of processes through which individuals are sorted into different positions in the class structure or marginalized from those positions altogether. Opportunity hoarding identifies exclusionary processes connected to middle-class jobs. The individual attributes approach helps specify what it is in the lives of people that explains who is excluded.

These three processes operate in all capitalist societies. The differences in class structures across countries are produced by the details of how these mechanisms work and interact.

Economic systems differ in how unfettered are the rights and powers that accompany private ownership of the means of production, and thus in the nature of the basic class division between capitalists and workers. As we have discussed in earlier chapters, the United States has long been characterized as a capitalist economy with among the weakest public regulations of capitalist property. This weak regulation is reflected in a number of critical facts about the United States: a very low minimum wage, which allows for higher rates of exploitation than would otherwise exist; low taxation on high incomes, which allows the wealthiest segments of the capitalist class to live in extraordinarily extravagant ways; weak unions and other forms of worker organization that could act as a counterweight to domination within production. The result is that among developed capitalist countries, the United States probably has the most polarized class division along the axis of domination and exploitation.

The United States has historically had one of the largest middle classes. This reflects, to a significant extent, its early expansion of higher education, a key mechanism of opportunity hoarding that underwrites the middle class. For a long time, access to higher education was very open and relatively inexpensive, so that people with few resources could attend universities. The United States has also been characterized by a multitiered higher-education system—with community colleges, junior colleges, liberal arts colleges, universities, and public and private institutions—that made it possible for people to enter higher education later in life and to move from one tier to another. People could screw up as young adults, but if they got their act together, they at least had the possibility of going back to school, getting a credential, and gaining access to middle-class employment. This large and diverse system of higher education helped support the creation of a large number of middle-class jobs. This accessibility of higher education was complemented, in the decades after World War II, by a relatively strong labor movement that was able to mute competition for jobs in the core of the American economy that did not require higher education. The labor movement enabled unionized workers in those jobs to acquire income and security similar to that of the credentialed middle class.

Now, it was never the case—contrary to popular rhetoric—that the United States was overwhelmingly a middle-class society. Most jobs in the American employment structure did not gain advantages from exclusionary credentials, and the labor movement never organized more than about 35 percent of the nonmanagerial, private sector labor force. Furthermore, in recent decades at least some of these processes of middle-class exclusion have eroded: the labor movement has precipitously declined since the 1970s; many kinds of middle-class jobs have become less secure, less protected by the credentials associated with employment; and the economic crisis of 2008 has intensified the sense of precariousness of many people who still think of themselves as being in middle-class jobs. Thus, although it is still certainly the case that higher education—and increasingly, advanced academic degrees—play a central role in creating access to many of the best jobs in the American economy, it is much less clear what the future prospects are for a large and stable middle class.

Finally, the American class structure has been characterized by a particularly brutal process through which individual attributes relevant to the fate of individuals in the class structure are formed. The U.S. educational system is organized in such a way that the quality of education available to children in poor families is generally vastly inferior to the quality of education for children of middle-class and wealthy families. This deficit in publicly provided education for the poor is intensified by the extreme deprivations of poverty in the United States due to the absence of an adequate safety net and supportive services for poor families. The rapid deindustrialization of the American economy and the absence of comprehensive job training for people displaced by deindustrialization mean that a significant number of people find themselves without the kinds of skills needed for the current job structure. As a result, the class structure in the United States is characterized by the highest rates of poverty and economic marginality of any comparable country.

Taking all these processes together yields the following general picture of the American class structure at the beginning of the twenty-first century:

- An extremely rich capitalist class and corporate managerial class, living at extraordinarily high consumption standards and having relatively weak constraints on their exercise of economic power. Among developed capitalist countries, the American class structure is the most polarized at the top.

- A historically large and relatively stable middle class, anchored in an expansive and flexible system of higher education and technical training connected to jobs requiring credentials of various sorts, whose security and future prosperity are now uncertain.
- A working class that once was characterized by a relatively large unionized segment with a standard of living and security similar to those of the middle class, but that now largely lacks these protections.
- A poor and precarious segment of the working class, characterized by low wages and relatively insecure employment, subjected to unconstrained job competition in the labor market and receiving minimal protections by the state.
- A marginalized and impoverished part of the population, without the skills and education needed for jobs above poverty, living in conditions that make it extremely difficult to acquire those skills. Among developed capitalist countries, the American class structure is the most polarized at the bottom.

13

PERSISTENT POVERTY
AND RISING INEQUALITY

P eople are generally interested in economic inequality for two somewhat independent reasons: First, income inequality is deeply connected to poverty, and poverty is a moral concern due to the deprivations and suffering associated with it. Second, inequality is associated with concentrations of income and wealth among elites. For many people, this situation also seems undesirable—both because of the unfair advantages such income often represents and because of the power such concentrations of wealth confer on the rich.

In this chapter we will look at both aspects of inequality, although we give more attention to poverty. We begin with a broad empirical sketch of patterns of poverty, wealth, and inequality in the United States. This section is followed by a discussion of two alternative explanations of persistent poverty in contemporary America: the "blame the victim" and "blame society" approaches. The chapter concludes with a discussion of the principal social structural processes that contribute to rising inequality, persistent poverty, and high concentrations of wealth and income at the top in the United States today.

FACTS ABOUT POVERTY
AND INEQUALITY IN AMERICA

In this section, we examine three clusters of facts about poverty in the United States: comparisons with other countries, trends in poverty rates over time, and the racial component of poverty in America.

Perhaps the most striking fact is that the United States has by a considerable margin the highest rate of poverty among all the developed capitalist economies (Figure 13.1).[1] The figures are especially disturbing for children, for whom the poverty rate in the United States is 3 to 4 times greater than in many European countries (see Figure 2.4 in Chapter 2). Much of this difference across countries is directly attributable to public policies. Figure 13.2 calculates two child poverty rates across countries: the first rate is based on household income *before* taxes and income transfer payments from government programs, and the second is based on household income *after* taxes and transfers. Before taxes and transfers, the child poverty rate in the United States in 2009 was 25.1 percent, which is the same as Canada and slightly less than Australia (28 percent) and the United Kingdom (33 percent). These are the child poverty rates based on the income households earn in the market. The picture is completely different after taxes and transfers. The poverty rate among children in the United States declines only slightly, from 25.1 percent

FIGURE 13.1—International comparison of poverty rates among wealthy countries, 2010

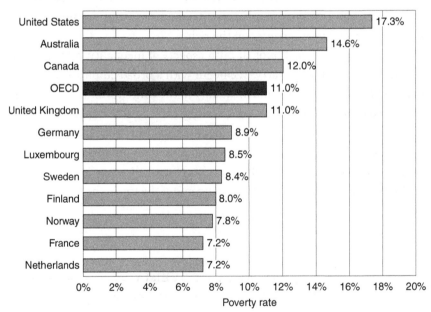

Note: The poverty line is defined as 50 percent of the median household disposable income, after taxes and transfers.

Source: "Production and Income—Income Inequality and Poverty—Poverty Rates and Gaps," *OECD Factbook 2011: Economic, Environmental and Social Statistics.*

[1] In international comparisons, the standard definition of poverty is a household income less than 50 percent of the national median. This level of income is also called *relative* poverty because it defines poverty relative to the median standard of living in a country. Because countries vary so much in their costs of living, this measure is generally considered much more reliable for comparative analysis than is absolute poverty as defined by a poverty line.

FIGURE 13.2—International comparisons of child poverty rates before and after taxes and transfers, 2009

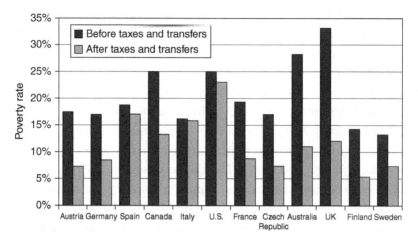

Note: The poverty line in both cases is defined as 50 percent of the median disposable income (i.e., income after taxes and transfers).

Source: Figure 8 and Figure 8A: "Child Poverty Rates Before Taxes and Transfers (market income) and After Taxes and Transfers, Selected Countries," in *The League Table of Child Poverty in Rich Nations* (Florence, Italy: UNICEF Research Center, 2012), Report Card 10.

to 23.1 percent, whereas in the United Kingdom it drops to 14 percent and in Australia to 11 percent. Our first general observation, then, is that poverty rates are very high in the United States compared to those in other economically developed countries, and to a significant extent this difference is the result of public policies rather than simply the "natural" functioning of the market.

Some people may be inclined to dismiss these observations because they are based on relative poverty measures rather than some absolute poverty line. After all, it is sometimes pointed out, people whose income is half of the median income in the United States today nevertheless have higher income than did Americans living at the median just after World War II.[2] Two comments on this observation: First, the quality of life a person can obtain from a given amount of income depends in significant ways on cultural standards, not just on some absolute level of consumption. It really does matter for economic well-being if a person is unable to participate in the mainstream standard of living of a society, and this is the situation for

[2] The median income for all families in 1947 (using constant 2013 dollars) was $27,651. In 2013, it was $63,815. Figures from *The State of Working America*, Figure 2A: "Real median family income, 1947–2013 (2013 dollars)," available at stateofworkingamerica.org/chart/swa-income -figure-2a-real-median-family/ (accessed Oct. 15, 2014).

people whose income is less than half of the median. Secondly, there is strong evidence that high levels of relative poverty are harmful to people beyond the simple fact of the poor having low income relative to prevalent social standards. A good example is the relationship in rich countries between levels of relative poverty and health. Figure 13.3 shows the relationship between the child poverty rate and the mortality rate among children under age five in thirty-five rich countries. Although this chart does not prove that a high rate of relative poverty contributes to higher infant mortality, the strength of the association is strongly consistent with this interpretation.

Our second cluster of observations concerns change in poverty rates over time within the United States. For this analysis, we will use the official U.S. poverty line as the basis for defining the poverty rate. It is, of course, problematic to define a specific absolute threshold below which a person is identified as poor. The basic idea is to define an income level above which it

FIGURE 13.3—Relationship between child poverty rate and mortality rate among children under age 5 in 35 high-income countries

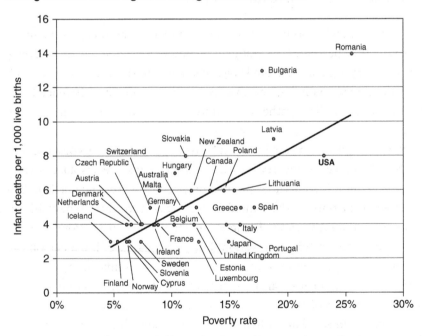

Note: Poverty data are from 2009; child mortality data are from 2010. Poverty line is 50 percent of median disposable household income.

Source: Poverty data are from Figure 1B: "A League Table of Relative Child Poverty, 35 Economically Advanced Countries," in *UNICEF, Report Card 10: Measuring Child Poverty, New League Tables of Child Poverty in the World's Rich Countries* (Florence, Italy: UNICEF Innocenti Research Center, 2012). Child mortality data are from "MDG 4: Child Health: Under 5 Mortality by Country," *Global Health Observatory Data Repository, World Health Organization*. http://apps.who.int/gho/data/node.main.525 (accessed May 24, 2013).

is possible to have adequate nutrition, housing, clothing, and other basic necessities. The problem is that the notion of necessities is heavily influenced by cultural norms and social expectations rather than simply by technical or biological considerations. This is one reason that in international comparisons, poverty is generally defined relative to a country's median income rather than by some absolute level of income. In any case, in our analyses within the United States, we will follow the standard convention of using the official government poverty line as the criterion for poverty. In 2014, for a single person, the poverty line was $11,670; for a family of four, it was $23,850.

On the basis of the official poverty line, poverty rates for children (Figure 13.4) and for adults (Figure 13.5) declined sharply in the 1960s in the wake of new government programs directed at poverty reduction. Since then, poverty rates among children have fluctuated depending on market conditions and changes in public policy. In 2011 the poverty rate for children under six years of age stood at just over 15 percent, a full 10 percentage points higher than at its low point in 1969. Poverty rates for adults 18–64 have also risen since the early 1970s, from a low of 8.3 percent in 1973 to 13.7 percent in 2011. If we look at extreme poverty—the percentage of the poor who are living at less than half of the official poverty line—the upward trend is even more dramatic (Figure 13.6). In 1976, around 28 percent of the poor lived in

FIGURE 13.4—Poverty rate among children, 1959–2013

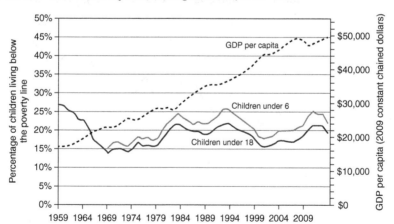

Note: *Poverty rate* is defined as the percentage of children in age group living in households below the official poverty line.

Sources: Poverty rates: U.S. Census Bureau, *Current Population Survey, Annual Social and Economic Supplements*, Table 20: Poverty Status of Related Children Under 6 Years of Age: 1969 to 2012," Table 3: "Poverty Status of People, by Age, Race, and Hispanic Origin: 1959 to 2013." Available at http://www.census.gov/hhes/www/poverty/data/historical/people.html (accessed Oct. 14, 2014). GDP per capita: Bureau of Labor Statistics, National Income and Product Accounts (NIPA) Tables, Table 7.1: "Selected Per Capita Product and Income Series in Current and Chained Dollars." Available at http://www.bea.gov/iTable/index_nipa.cfm (accessed Oct. 14, 2014).

FIGURE 13.5—Poverty rate among adults, 1959–2013

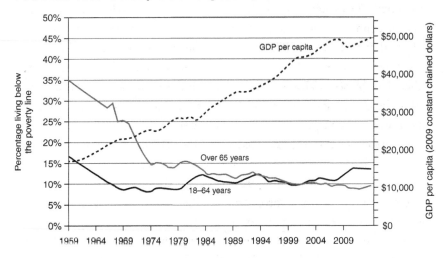

Note: *Poverty rate* is defined as the percentage of people in an age group living in households below the official poverty line. Data for 1960–1965 is a linear interpolation between data points 1959 and 1961.

Sources: Poverty rates: U.S. Census Bureau, *Current Population Survey, Annual Social and Economic Supplements*, Table 3: "Poverty Status of People, by Age, Race, and Hispanic Origin: 1959 to 2013." Available at http://www.census.gov/hhes/www/poverty/data/historical/people.html (accessed October 14, 2014). GDP per capita: Bureau of Labor Statistics, National Income and Product Accounts (NIPA) Tables, Table 7.1: "Selected Per Capita Product and Income Series in Current and Chained Dollars." Available at http://www.bea.gov/iTable/index_nipa.cfm (accessed Oct. 14, 2014).

FIGURE 13.6—Percentage of the poor in extreme poverty, 1975–2011

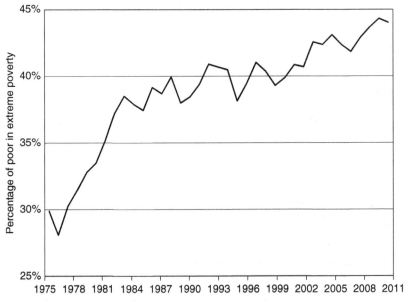

Note: *Extreme poverty* is defined as below half of the official poverty line.
Source: The State of Working America, 2011/2012, figure 7G.

extreme poverty. By 2011, the figure was 44 percent. This rise in poverty rates and the rates of extreme poverty occurred even though the per capita gross domestic product—a measure of the overall wealth of the United States—more than doubled in the period from the early 1970s to 2007. The United States is therefore not simply a very rich country with high levels of poverty; it is a rich country in which increasing wealth since the early 1970s has not resulted in any reduction of poverty.

Another aspect of changes in poverty in the closing decades of the twentieth century concerns the spatial distribution of poverty. Two things should be noted here. First, with respect to the regional distribution of poverty, in the 1960s and earlier the poverty rate in the South was much higher than in the rest of the United States (Figure 13.7). In 1969 the overall poverty rate in the South was 18 percent, whereas in the other regions of the country it was 8–10 percent. By 2007 the rate in the South had declined to 16 percent and in the other regions had risen to 13–14 percent. At the beginning of the twenty-first century, poverty is a widespread national phenomenon, not something concentrated in a specific region of the country. Second, before the 1960s poverty was especially acute in rural areas and small towns (Figure 13.8). Even in 1969 it was still the case that poverty rates in nonmetropolitan areas

FIGURE 13.7—Poverty rates across regions: 1969, 1987, 1997, and 2011

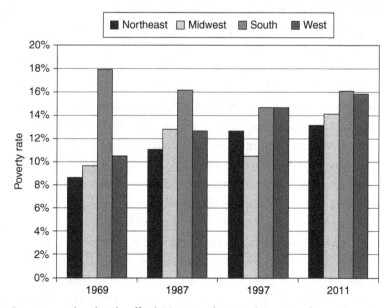

Note: Poverty rate is based on the official U.S. poverty line in each time period.

Source: U.S. Census Bureau, *Current Population Survey, 2012 Annual Social and Economic Supplement* POV40. http://www.census.gov/hhes/www/cpstables/032012/pov/POV40_000.htm (accessed May 20, 2013).

FIGURE 13.8—Poverty rates in central cities, suburbs, and nonmetropolitan areas, 1959, 1969, 1989, 2007, 2012

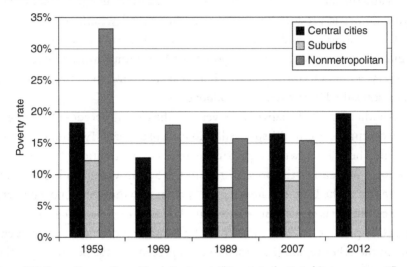

Source: U.S. Census Bureau, Current Population Reports, "Poverty in the United States: 1959 to 1968"; "24 Million Americans—Poverty in the United States: 1969"; "Poverty in the United States: 1988 and 1989"; and U.S. Census Bureau, Current Population Survey, Annual Social and Economic Supplements, Table 3: "People in Poverty by Selected Characteristics, 2011 and 2012."

were nearly 50 percent higher than in central cities. This is no longer the case: poverty in nonmetropolitan areas is about the same as it was in the late 1960s and has risen in the central cities, so that in 2012, central city poverty rates were slightly higher than those outside of metropolitan areas.

Our final set of observations about poverty concerns its connection to race. We will discuss this topic further in Chapter 14. For now, it is sufficient to note the dramatic difference in poverty rates across different racial categories (Figure 13.9). In 2011, 27 percent of African Americans and 25 percent of Hispanic Americans lived below the poverty line, compared to only 10 percent of whites. Race and poverty clearly are closely linked. However, two things are important to note about this connection. First, the *disproportion* in poverty rates among African Americans compared to whites has declined over this period: In 1973, the poverty rate among African Americans was 4.2 times greater than it was among whites. By 2011, this ratio had declined to 2.8 (Figure 13.10). Second, even though poverty rates remain much higher among African Americans and Hispanics than among white Americans, it is still the case that over 40 percent of poor people in the United States are white. In 2011, 42.2 percent of the people living below the poverty line were white, 21 percent were African American, and 28.2 percent were Hispanic. These figures run counter to the widespread belief that poverty is overwhelmingly a problem of minority communities. Poverty is an American

FIGURE 13.9—Poverty rates by race and ethnicity, 1973–2011

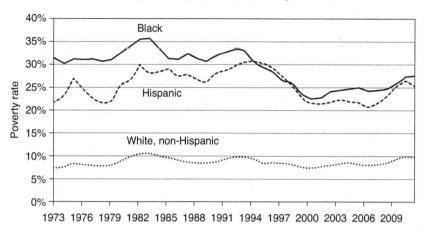

Source: The State of Working America, 2011/2012, figure 7C.

FIGURE 13.10—Ratio of black to white poverty rates, 1973–2011

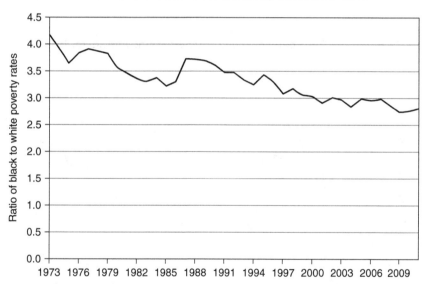

Source: The State of Working America, 2011/2012, figure 7C.

problem that disproportionately affects African Americans and Hispanics, but it affects millions of white Americans as well.

Though poverty is certainly the most salient moral issue linked to economic inequality, it is not the only reason to study inequality. Inequality also matters because of the way it concentrates resources, advantages, and power at the top of the distribution relative to the middle. As we saw in Figure 10.2 in Chapter 10, in the quarter century after World War II all income strata experienced roughly the same rates of growth in income—about 3.5 percentage points a year. Since that time, the rate of income growth has been much higher at the top of the income distribution than at the bottom or the middle. Figure 13.11 looks at the inequality generated by the top of the distribution over a much longer period, 1913–2012. This trajectory over time is sometimes called the great U-turn. Before World War II, people in the top 10 percent of the income distribution earned between 40 percent and 45 percent of all the income earned in the United States. This figure dropped precipitously in the early 1940s and stayed around 33 percent for over three decades. Then, beginning in the late 1970s and accelerating in the 1980s, the income share of this top group increased sharply and reached 40 percent by the early 1990s and 50 percent by 2012, higher than the previous peak of 49 percent in 1928.

The top decile is certainly an extremely privileged category. On closer inspection, however, the real growth in income inequality in the United States in the last decades of the twentieth century was actually driven by

FIGURE 13.11—Top 1 percent and top 10 percent income share, 1913–2012

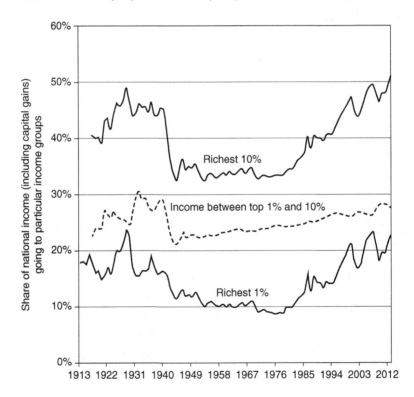

Source: Calculated from *The World Top Incomes Database,* http://topincomes.g-mond
.parisschoolofeconomics.eu

fantastic increases in income in the top 1 percent of households. As indicated in Figure 13.11, in 2012, over a fifth of all income earned in the United States went to the richest 1 percent of the population, more than double its share of national income in the early 1970s. In contrast, people in the next 9 percent of the income distribution only increased their share from around 24 percent to around 28 percent. This growth in the concentration of income shares at the very top of the distribution is shown in a different way in Figure 13.12, which presents the ratios of the average household income of people in different income strata from 1979 to 2009. Three ratios are presented in the figure. The 50:20 ratio is the ratio of the average income of people in the middle quintile (which is almost exactly the same as the overall median income) to the average income of people in the bottom quintile.[3] This is a

FIGURE 13.12—Ratios of household income between different income strata, 1979–2010

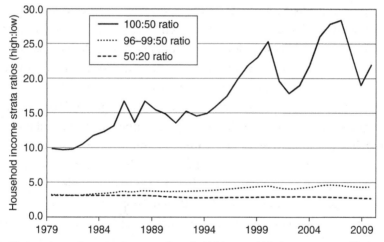

Note: These ratios are between the *average* household income within income groups. The average income of the middle quintile is very close to the median income because the income distribution *within* the middle quintile is not very skewed.

50:20 ratio = the ratio of the *average* household income in the middle quintile to the *average* household income in the bottom quintile.

96–99:50 ratio = the ratio of the *average* household income of households in the 96th–99th percentiles to the *average* household income in the middle quintile.

100:50 ratio = the ratio of the *average* household income of households in the top percentile to the *average* family income in the middle quintile.

Source: Congressional Budget Office, 2013, "The Distribution of Household Income and Federal Taxes, 2010." Supplemental data, Table 3: "Number of Households, Average Income, and Shares of Income for All Households, by Before-Tax Income Group, 1979 to 2010." Supplemental material available at http://www.cbo.gov/sites/default/files/44604_Average TaxRates_Supplemental.xlsx.

[3] The middle quintile of an income distribution includes everyone from the 40th to the 60th percentile in the distribution. The median of the whole distribution—the 50th percentile— is close to the average income in this group because income distribution within the middle quintile will be fairly symmetrical around the midpoint.

measure of how much inequality there is between the middle and the bottom of the income distribution. The 96–99:50 ratio is the ratio of the average household income of people in the 96th–99th percentiles (i.e., the 4 percent of the population just below the top 1 percent of the income distribution) to the average household income of people in the middle. And finally, the 100:50 ratio is the ratio of the average household income of the top 1 percent of households (the 100th percentile) to the middle. Figure 13.12 shows that the first of these ratios, the ratio of people in the middle to the people at the bottom, does not change at all in the period 1979–2010. The second ratio changes a little, indicating a modest increase in the degree of inequality between the middle of the income distribution and the 96th–99th percentiles. The real action, however, is in the ratio of average income of people in the top 1 percent of the income distribution to people in the middle. In 1979, the average income of people in the top 1 percent was 10 times that of people in the middle of the distribution. This figure increased to 15 times greater in the course of the 1980s and into the 1990s and reached over 25 times greater in 1999 and again in the mid-2000s. Even after the financial crash, the ratio of income of the top 1 percent to the middle remained almost 22:1. The overall increase in levels of inequality in the United States at the end of the twentieth century is clearly driven by the extremely rapid increase in income among the very richest Americans.

One final set of data will complete our statistical portrait of inequality in America: inequality in wealth. Income is defined as the *flow* of money a person has available over a given unit of time; in contrast, wealth is a *stock*, the amount of money and other assets that someone owns at any given moment. Wealth takes many forms. For most people, the primary form of wealth is home ownership. When people buy a home, usually they take out a loan (a mortgage), and their wealth consists of the difference in the value of the home and the amount they owe on the loan. This form of wealth is called home equity. As the home owners pay off the loan over time, and as the value of the home increases based on the market for houses (assuming, of course, that home prices are increasing), their equity in the home increases, and thus their wealth increases. Other forms of wealth include savings; investments in stocks, bonds, and other financial instruments; real estate other than owner-occupied houses; and many other things. A person's net worth is the difference between the value of all these assets—both financial assets and nonfinancial assets—and whatever debts a person has. Financial wealth is the difference between the value of financial assets and debts.[4]

Wealth in the United States is distributed much more unequally than income. Figure 13.13 indicates the percentage of all household income, household net worth, and household net financial assets that go to the top 1 percent of households, the next 9 percent, and the bottom 90 percent. In the case of income, the bottom 90 percent of households get a little over 50 percent of all

FIGURE 13.13—Distribution of household income and wealth, 2010

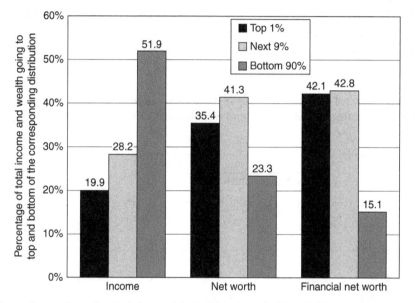

Sources: Income shares data (including capital gains) from Facundo Alvaredo, Tony Atkinson, Thomas Piketty, and Emmanuel Saez, "The World Top Incomes Database" at http://topincomes. parisschoolofeconomics.eu/ (accessed Oct. 15, 2014). Data are based on tax tables. Wealth data from Edward N. Wolff, 2012, "The Asset Price Meltdown and the Wealth of the Middle Class," NBER Working Paper Series No. 18559, Table 2: "The Size Distribution of Wealth and Income, 1962–2010." Data are based on the Survey of Consumer Finances.

[4]Net worth corresponds to marketable wealth, defined as "the current value of all marketable or fungible assets less the current value of debts. Net worth is thus the difference in value between total assets and total liabilities or debt. Total assets are defined as the sum of (1) owner-occupied housing; (2) other real estate; (3) demand and savings deposits, certificates of deposit, and money market accounts; (5) government bonds, corporate bonds, and other financial securities; (6) the cash surrender value of life insurance plans; (7) the cash surrender value of pension plans, including IRAs, Keogh, and 401(k) plans; (8) corporate stock and mutual funds; (9) equity in unincorporated businesses; and (10) equity in trust funds. Total liabilities are the sum of (1) mortgage debt, (2) consumer debt, including auto loans, and (3) other debt such as educational loans" (Wolff 2012, p. 8). Consumer durables (cars, TVs, furniture, etc.), as well as the value of future Social Security benefits and private pension plans, are excluded. Financial wealth, which can be thought of as non-home wealth, "is defined as net worth minus net equity in owner-occupied housing (the primary residence only)" (Wolff 2012, p. 9).

income, and the top 1 percent of households get about 19 percent of all income. That is a disproportionate share, to be sure, but it is nothing like the disproportion for overall wealth and financial assets: the net worth of the top 1 percent accounts for about 35 percent of all wealth and 42 percent of financial assets ("non-home assets"). For the bottom 90 percent of households, the corresponding figures are 23 percent and 15 percent. If we convert these into ratios of average wealth at the top and bottom of the distributions, the average net worth of people in the top 1 percent is about 137 times greater than the average net worth of people in the bottom 90 percent of the U.S. population, and the average net financial assets of people in this tiny group at the top is 251 times greater than the average person in the bottom 90 percent (see Figure 13.14).

FIGURE 13.14—Ratios of mean income and wealth of households at the top to the bottom of the income and wealth distributions, 2010

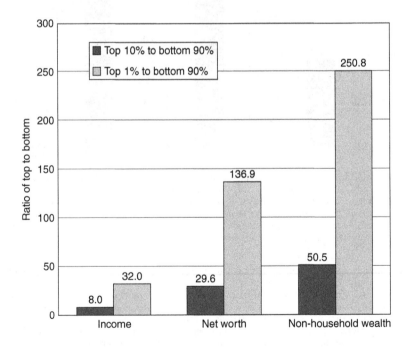

Sources: Mean income data (including capital gains) from Piketty and Saez, "Income Inequality in the United States, 1913–1998," *Quarterly Journal of Economics* 118, no. 1 (February 2003): 1–39. Tables and figures updated to 2012 by Emanuel Saez at http://elsa.berkeley.edu/users/saez/ (accessed March 10, 2014). Mean wealth data for top 1 percent of households from Wolff, *The Asset Price Meltdown and the Wealth of the Middle Class*, NBER Working Paper Series No. 18559, table 2. Data are based on the Survey of Consumer Finances. Mean wealth data for top 10 percent and bottom 90 percent was provided by Edward Wolff (personal communication, March 18, 2014).

EXPLAINING PERSISTENT POVERTY

In both the scholarly literature and popular discussions about poverty, it is possible to distinguish three broad ways of explaining poverty in the United States. The first of these explanations, sometimes referred to as "blame the victim,"[5] emphasizes how poverty is generated by a range of flawed attributes of the poor. The second is referred to as "blame society" and focuses on the way social structures and institutions generate poverty. The third straddles this contrast by examining how various kinds of deficits in the attributes of the poor, especially inadequate skills and abilities, are generated by the social conditions in which they live.

Blame the Victim

The reasoning behind blaming the victim is pretty simple and intuitive: some people are poor and others are not, even though they come from the same social background. Indeed, it is easy enough to find cases of adult siblings from the same family in which one sibling is poor and the other has a steady, well-paying job. So, if two people come from the same origins and face more or less the same opportunities, and only one of them is poor, then surely there must be some difference between them that explains their different fates. The explanation for being poor, the reasoning goes, must lie in some flaw within poor people, not in the social system in which they live. And the solution to poverty, therefore, must be to somehow change the person, not the society.

Once you decide that the central explanation for poverty lies in the qualities of poor people, the next step is to sort out the many different specific causal processes that could be at work. For example, one theory of poverty that used to be quite popular, but now is generally not given much credibility among social scientists, is that poor people are generally genetically inferior to the nonpoor. The most common version of this view identifies intelligence as the key issue: the poor have deficits in the genes that affect IQ. Such views were once particularly strong in discussions of poverty that linked poverty to race, but they occasionally still resurface. As recently as the 1990s, Richard Herrnstein and Charles Murray argued in their notorious

---

[5] The phrase "blame the victim" was coined by William Ryan in his book *Blaming the Victim* (New York: Vintage Books, 1976).

book *The Bell Curve* that genetic deficits in intelligence are a central explanation for the high poverty rates among black people in America.[6]

One version of the blame-the-victim theory of poverty remains quite influential. In this version, the deficit within poor people is identified as psychological dispositions closely connected to culture. As a result, this explanation for poverty is sometimes referred to as the "culture of poverty" thesis. The key idea here is that poor people have a distinctive pattern of cultural values that makes it difficult to delay gratification and plan for the future. They don't save. They have difficulty controlling their impulses—for sex, for immediate pleasure, for anger, for obeying the law. The anthropologist Edward Banfield popularized this perspective in his study of poverty in Puerto Rico in the 1950s. He wrote that poverty is explained by "the existence of an outlook and style of life which is radically present-oriented and which therefore attaches no value to work, sacrifice, self-improvement, or service to family, friends or community."[7] These attributes may come from adaptations to past discrimination, or they may come from other sources; but once the person is inculcated with those attributes, they are hard to change. They become internalized psychological dispositions that are transmitted intergenerationally in an endless cycle of persistent poverty.

Blaming the poor for their poverty remains a popular way of understanding poverty, in part because it provides explanations that do not threaten those with privilege. Poverty in the midst of plenty is a deeply disturbing fact of contemporary American society, and people with stable jobs and good incomes feel a need to justify their advantages. The most painless way to do this is to believe, if only vaguely, that the poor are somehow unworthy. This stance is never fully convincing, especially because children cannot be seen as deserving to be poor. Still, it reduces the moral pressure on the middle class and the wealthy to take seriously the problem of changing institutions to eliminate poverty.

Blame Society

The second alternative general approach to explaining poverty can be referred to as "blame society." Although of course there may be some specific individuals who are poor and remain poor because of their personal

---

[6] Richard Herrnstein and Charles Murray, *The Bell Curve* (New York: Free Press, 1994). Social scientists have thoroughly attacked this book for its serious methodological flaws. See, for example, Claude S. Fischer et al., *Inequality by Design: Cracking the Bell Curve Myth* (Princeton, NJ: Princeton University Press, 1996).

[7] Edward Banfield, *The Unheavenly City Revisited* (Boston: Little, Brown, 1974), p. 87.

attributes, mostly the poor are not very different from others when it comes to motivations, preferences, hopes, and aspirations. Indeed, many poor people work incredibly hard, patching together a number of low-paying jobs that barely meet basic needs. The most important causes of poverty, the argument goes, lie in the rules of the game and power relations of society, not in the internalized cultural characteristics of poor people.

Consider the core psychological issue raised in the culture-of-poverty thesis: the problem of delayed gratification and impulse control. Is it really true that, in general, poor people suffer from an inability to delay gratification whereas middle-class and rich people do not? Credit card consumerism in the middle class is profoundly present-oriented. Many middle-class people, as we saw in Chapter 7 on consumerism, accumulate large credit card debts and pay exorbitant interest rates because they want things now and are unwilling to save. William Ryan, in his book *Blaming the Victim*, reports the following research that bears directly on the problem of whether poor people generally have more difficulty in delaying gratification than do more affluent people: as a reward for completing a task, children from different race and class categories were given the choice of getting one Hershey candy bar immediately or two the following week. In the experiment, Ryan says,

> [This promise] was either kept or not kept. When the experiment was repeated this was the only factor that differentiated between those who chose immediate gratification and those who chose to delay. Class and race were *not* related to delay. Those who had experienced a broken promise were the ones—not unsurprisingly—who were not willing to delay and therefore risk another disappointment. . . . The situational variable, then, rather than class affiliation, determined the ability to delay.[8]

Or, think about another issue that is often seen as characteristic of the culture and dispositions of the poor: an amoral attitude toward social norms and crime. Do the poor really differ from the middle class or the rich all that much on these dimensions? A significant proportion of "respectable" wealthy people cheat on their taxes. The media frequently cover scandals of a rich person being nominated for a high political appointment only to have the appointment fall apart when it is revealed that the person "failed" to pay all

[8] William Ryan, *Blaming the Victim* (New York: Vintage Books, 1976), p. 133; reporting research by S. Miller, F. Riesmann, and A. Seagull, "Poverty and Self-Indulgence: A Critique of the Non-deferred Gratification Pattern," in *Poverty in America* (rev. ed.), eds. L. Ferman, J. Kornbluth, and A. Haber (Ann Arbor: University of Michigan Press, 1968).

his or her taxes. Why do sophisticated, wealthy people who can easily afford to pay their taxes—and even hire professional accountants and lawyers to make sure they do not make "mistakes"—still cheat on their tax payments? The answer is pretty simple: they do so because they think they can get away with it. The resulting theft adds up to orders of magnitude more than the property theft by the poor: in 2011 the total economic loss from property theft (burglary, larceny-theft, and motor vehicle theft) was estimated to be somewhere around $15.1 billion (in 2011 dollars), compared to over $270 billion from tax fraud in 2013.[9] Even if some of this underpayment of taxes was simply due to errors, not deliberate cheating, the tax-cheating total would still be vastly greater than that for property theft. If one adds to tax cheating the other kinds of corporate fraud that wealthy elites commit—think of the Enron scandal or the insider trading scandals on Wall Street, for example— the disparity between the magnitude of theft by the rich compared to theft by the poor grows even larger. It is hardly surprising, of course, that executives in a large corporation or prominent politicians would never consider robbing a convenience store, although they are happy to steal from the public by cheating on their taxes, padding expense accounts, or cooking the books of a corporation. The difference in patterns of theft by the rich and by the poor, therefore, is really much more a function of the opportunities people face than of their character or moral values.

This, then, is the central thesis of the social explanations of poverty: *Circumstances of people across classes and economic conditions vary much more than values and personalities.* Plenty of poor people and rich people have problems with impulse control, anger management, and willingness to delay gratification, but these traits have very different consequences for people's behavior and lives because of the circumstances in which they act. This is not to say that the experience of poverty has no impact on psychological states and dispositions of people to behave in particular ways, but simply that the most important difference between the poor and the rest of a society is the character of opportunities and circumstances they encounter, not their inherent attributes, personalities, or values.

[9] Crime statistics from "Crime in the United States: 2011," a publication by the FBI. http://www.fbi.gov/about-us/cjis/ucr/crime-in-the-u.s/2011/crime-in-the-u.s.-2011/property -crime/property-crime. The tax-cheating estimates come from http://www.statisticbrain .com/how-many-people-cheat-on-taxes/.

Education, Skills, and Poverty

The most popular explanation in policy circles for poverty—that poverty is the result of deficits in education—blurs the distinction between blaming the victim and blaming society. This explanation clearly identifies a social cause of poverty: the American school system fails to provide decent education for poor people. One of the goals of the No Child Left Behind legislation in 2001 was to remedy this deficit by holding schools accountable, closing bad schools, and in other ways reducing the educational achievement gap between children of middle-class families and poor families. The educational deficit explanation, therefore, identifies failed institutions as a central problem. Nevertheless, this explanation for poverty also embodies some aspects of the blame-the-victim approach to poverty; the failed educational system is still seen as generating poverty because of the way it shapes a particular attribute of poor people—in this case, their human capital or skills.

The claim that poor people generally lack marketable skills may be completely accurate, but it does not adequately or completely explain why they are poor. Having little education explains poverty only because of certain features of the social environment in which the person lives, and this broader social context must also be part of the explanation for poverty. Or, to make the point in a slightly different way: explaining why particular people are poor is not the same as explaining the level of poverty itself. This idea can be clarified by thinking of an entirely different example: the way grades in a class are distributed to students.[10] Suppose a really nasty professor has a terrible grading curve, so that in a class of 20 students, only one A and two Bs are given, and everyone else gets a C or less. At the end of the semester, Mary gets the A; John and Melissa get the two Bs; and George, among others, gets a C. Now, if you ask the question, "Why did Mary get an A?" it may well be that she was smarter, worked harder, studied more than anyone else in the course, and had more knowledge of the material. And why did George get a C? He didn't have good study habits and didn't know as much. But surely this reasoning seems to miss the actual process at work here: the real explanation lies in the power structure of the university that allowed a dictatorial, mean-spirited professor to create these rules of the game. If the power structure was different and students could vote on the grading curve, then there would be less "grade poverty" in the class. Explaining why a particular person gets a poor grade, in short, is not the same as explaining why there are so many poor grades in the class.

[10] This example comes from Alan Garfinkel, *Forms of Explanation* (New Haven, CT: Yale University Press, 1981).

In the case of economic poverty, of course, creating and maintaining the rules of the game is much more complicated than the process described in the grading curve example. Nevertheless, the fact that low skills and limited education result in poverty still depends on the rules of the game through which jobs are created and income is distributed. Under alternative rules of the game, for example, the government could directly create reasonably well-paying jobs that do not require high levels of education or skills. Such jobs could begin to deal with the many important needs that are not adequately met through the market economy: public infrastructure is crumbling, bridges need to be repaired, home-care services for the elderly need to be provided, buildings need to be retrofitted for energy conservation, after-school programs in central cities need to be expanded, and so on. Many jobs to meet these needs would not require high levels of skills or education. The fact that there are not many above-poverty-level jobs for people with relatively low education is thus as much the result of public policies for creating such jobs as it is a result of the low skills themselves. Furthermore, even apart from the problem of the weak public commitment to creating adequately paying jobs for everyone, public policies could do a great deal to alleviate poverty through more generous programs of publicly subsidized housing, income support, and other forms of income redistribution. None of this implies, of course, that lousy education for poor children is not a serious problem and a form of injustice. Equal opportunity is a fundamental value and an essential aspect of fairness. Even so, poverty in a rich society does not simply reflect a failure of equal opportunity to acquire a good education; it reflects a social failure in the creation of sufficient jobs to provide an adequate standard of living for all people regardless of their education or levels of skills.

SOCIAL STRUCTURAL CAUSES OF INEQUALITY AND POVERTY IN AMERICA

Saying that inequality and poverty are to be explained mainly by social processes is only the first step in an analysis. What remains to be elaborated are the specific social causes operating to generate specific patterns of inequality.

We will approach this problem by discussing three kinds of inequalities generated within a capitalist market economy:

1. Inequalities generated through *exclusion from labor markets* (i.e., inequality between the stably employed labor force and marginalized categories of people)

2. Inequalities generated *within labor markets* (i.e., inequality between well-paid workers and badly paid workers)
3. Inequalities generated through *non*-labor-market income (i.e., inequality between wealthy and nonwealthy individuals)

If we want to sort out the causes of overall economic inequality within the United States, we need to look at the social processes that determine each of these inequalities.

Marginalization: The Problem of Acute Poverty

Marginalization refers to a situation in which a person is, through one mechanism or another, unable to get access to the necessary means to acquire a basic livelihood. In developing countries, marginalization is an acute problem: Landless peasants leave rural areas for the city and are unable to find stable, paid work. They live in shantytowns and eke out a marginal existence in various ways: as scavengers in refuse dumps, street vendors, as informal day laborers, and so on.

In the United States, marginalization occurs because of the mismatch between distribution of skills in the population and distribution of jobs in the economy. This mismatch has intensified in recent decades due to the decline of manufacturing. Heavy industry, relying largely on manual labor, was once a good source of employment for people with limited education. Much of the work was unskilled or semiskilled, and in any case, many of the skills needed in the more skilled jobs were learned on the job rather than in school. The rapid deindustrialization of America beginning in the 1970s destroyed those kinds of jobs.

Marginalization in the contemporary American economy is generated by the lack of good employment for people with low or outmoded skills and low education. This is not, as we have already stressed, just a problem of inadequate skill formation; *it is equally a problem of inadequate job creation.* Some people argue that the problem of acute poverty could be solved by dramatically improving education for the poor, giving everyone the knowledge and skills needed to compete effectively in the high-tech, information economy. Improving education, of course, would be a very good thing, but it would not completely solve the problem of marginalization. No matter how effective the educational system is, not everyone will acquire the knowledge and skills needed for stable, well-paying jobs in the high-tech sectors of the market economy. And even if everyone could acquire such knowledge-intensive skills, there is no guarantee whatsoever that increasing the supply of people with these skills would generate the necessary number of jobs that require those skills.

Inequalities within Labor Markets

The second source of economic inequality occurs among people with stable employment. Two issues are particularly important here: First, since the late 1970s a dramatic increase in inequality has occurred at the top of the pay scale, especially among managers in corporations and professionals. Second, large numbers of jobs in the American economy pay only poverty-level wages. This situation is referred to as the problem of the so-called working poor. Figure 13.15 shows the trends in real hourly wages of male and female workers at the 20th percentile from 1973 to 2011. The horizontal line in this figure shows the wage level for a full-time worker needed to bring a family of four above the official poverty line. At no time during this period were wages of female workers at the 20th percentile sufficient to do this; for male workers at the 20th percentile, their wages hovered just above the poverty level in the 1970s, but since then their wages have been well below

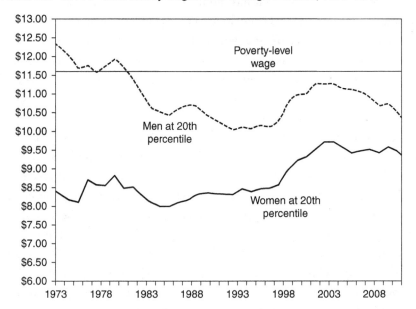

FIGURE 13.15—Real hourly wages of low-wage workers, 1973–2011

Note: Poverty-level-wage workers are defined as those earning at or below the wage a full-time, full-year worker would have to earn to give a family of four enough income to reach but not exceed the poverty threshold ($11.06 per hour in 2011).

Source: The State of Working America, 12th edition, Tables 4.5 and 4.6.

it. Taken together, the escalation of pay at the top of the labor market and the continued existence of large numbers of badly paid jobs at the bottom generates very high levels of overall earnings inequality within American labor markets.

The two most common explanations for the increased earnings inequality within the paid labor force since the 1970s center on technological change and globalization. The argument goes like this: Due to the rapidity of technological change in the last quarter of the twentieth century, particularly in information technologies, high education and technical skills have become much more valuable to employers. As a result, the inequality between skilled and unskilled and between the highly educated and less educated has increased. This increase occurred precisely in the period when international competition also increased. Thus American firms were increasingly involved in competition with low-wage foreign producers, and this competition put downward pressure on less skilled jobs. The combination of the effects of globalization on the wages of low-skilled workers and technological change on the wages of highly educated workers generated the dramatic increase in overall earnings inequality.

Technological change and globalization certainly contributed to rising inequality, but they do not adequately explain the magnitude of either the level of inequality in earnings in the United States or the degree to which it has increased. Empirical research on this issue indicates that, at best, the effects of these two processes on increasing inequality are modest.[11] Rapid technological change and increasing global competition since the 1970s characterize all developed capitalist economies, from Sweden to France to Japan to the United States. Yet in some of these countries, earnings inequality has changed hardly at all over this period—and in none of them are the levels of poverty and inequality as high as in the United States.

We want to emphasize two other, interconnected processes that have played a particularly important role in the United States: the decrease in government regulation of labor markets, and the increase in competition within labor markets. In all labor markets in capitalist societies, people with high levels of education, skills, and talents are generally paid more than people with low skills and education, but the degree of inequality associated

---

[11] A good overview of this research can be found in Lane Kenworthy, "Inequality and Sociology," *American Behavioral Scientist* 50 (2007): 584–602; and Martina Morris and Bruce Western, "Inequality in Earnings at the Close of the Twentieth Century," *Annual Review of Sociology* 25 (1999): 623–57.

with this universal association depends on other institutional features of the labor market. Specifically, we need to understand the institutional processes through which wages are connected to jobs and jobs are filled by people. Imagine the following two systems of linking wages to jobs and people:

1. *Intense individualized competition.* In this system, people in the labor market are constantly bidding against everyone else for jobs and earnings. There is continual jockeying around; employers lower and raise wages as they compete for employees, and employees are constantly looking for new jobs that offer higher wages. There are no effective minimum-wage rules, so employers pretty much pay what market forces allow. Employers can hire and fire, promote and demote employees without significant restrictions imposed by government or by organized labor. Employees are continually evaluated according to their "merit" relative to other employees, and their pay is adjusted accordingly. Individuals make individual employment bargains with their employers; labor unions play no role in the process.

2. *A labor market governed by rules that dampen competition.* Employees are governed by employment contracts that make it difficult for employers to fire workers or lower their wages. Wages are partially based on seniority rather than intense individual competition and continual performance evaluation. Workers have high job security, and thus employers have to seek ways of forging stable cooperation and productivity improvements among the existing workforce, rather than continually looking for "better" workers. Unions support wage rules that reduce wage spread, and the government imposes significant constraints on employers' pay policies, especially through a high minimum wage. Collective bargains dominate the employment relationship rather than individual deals.

The first of these systems generates much greater wage inequality than does the second because it both pulls down wages at the bottom of the labor market and pulls up the earnings of people at the top of the labor market. No actual society can be considered a pure example of one or the other of these systems, but the United States is the closest to the first type of labor market of any of the developed capitalist countries. If anything, since the 1970s the United States has moved closer to the competitive labor market model.

For a number of reasons, the deregulation of labor markets and the intensification of competitiveness within labor markets will tend to escalate inequality in earnings. First, the constant upward and downward adjusting of pay as people compete for jobs leads to a greater spread of earnings over time. An employee's early success in intense competition tends to generate cumulative gains over time because it acts as a signal to other employers about the employee's desirability. In a complementary way, failure in a labor market—for example, losing one's job—acts as a negative signal even if the failure was not under the person's control. There are always winners and losers in market competition, but in weakly regulated markets with high-stakes competition, the consequences of winning and losing tend to cumulatively intensify overall inequality.

Second, in certain labor markets competition takes the form of what Robert Frank has called *winner-take-all competitions*.[12] A winner-take-all market is one in which very small differences in performance generate big differences in pay. This market is like the Olympics, in which the gold medal winner of a race receives all the fame and fortune, even though the difference between first and second place may be only a hundredth of a second. Although true winner-take-all markets that result in a single winner are rare, many labor markets for high-paying jobs have some features of those markets: corporations are prepared to pay enormous salaries for people they consider to be the "stars" in particular fields. This situation tends to ratchet up the salaries at the top of the pay scale, particularly when the competitive market expands from local to regional to national and even international arenas. To the extent that labor markets become more like winner-take-all competitions, overall earnings inequality within those markets will increase.

A third way that competition can be intensified or muted is through social norms that define acceptable kinds of behavior in the market. Is it acceptable for an upper-level manager in a firm to be constantly on the look-out for higher pay in another firm, or are managers expected to display real loyalty to their present corporation? Does jumping from firm to firm to increase one's pay indicate healthy ambition, or a lack of commitment? In the mid-twentieth century, corporations had fairly strong norms—informal rules and expectations—that held managerial salaries in check. In 1967, the economist John Kenneth Galbraith wrote that "management does not go

---

[12] Robert H. Frank and Philip J. Cook, *The Winner-Take-All Society: Why the Few at the Top Get So Much More Than the Rest of Us* (New York: Penguin Books, 1996).

out to ruthlessly reward itself—a sound management is expected to exercise restraint. . . . There are few corporations in which it would be suggested that executive salaries are at a maximum."[13] Managers and executives were expected to act in the best interests of their corporation "in accordance with accepted canons of behavior" rather than constantly trying to maximize their personal gain.[14] Managers and executives in corporations were still well paid, but the norms and expectations of the era kept their salaries somewhat in check. Beginning in the 1970s and accelerating in the 1980s those norms disintegrated, particularly for the top leadership of large corporations. The dramatic rise in the salaries at the very top, in turn, tended to pull up salaries of managers in lower tiers. By the end of the century, in many corporate settings not moving from job to job was seen as an indicator either that one's work must be unsatisfactory in some way or that one lacked competitive drive.

These changes in norms of behavior and earnings have also occurred within the professions, not just in corporate hierarchies. Pay for professors in American universities has traditionally been governed by a combination of seniority rules, academic rank, and merit pay. Professors who published a lot and had strong academic reputations received merit pay increases, but professorial rank and seniority were equally important in determining salaries. Since the 1970s, "playing the market" has become an additional powerful force in determining faculty pay. Deans at some universities explicitly tell faculty members that if they want a pay increase, they need to get an outside offer from another university; the current university then makes a retention offer. As a result, high-profile professors with no serious intention of leaving their university often seek outside offers simply to trigger a bidding war between universities. This practice can sometimes lead to fantastic pay increases of 100 percent or more. In the past, such behavior was viewed as quite disreputable. The social norms that dampen market competition in academic labor markets have clearly weakened.

Increased competitiveness, tendencies toward winner-take-all markets, and weakening social norms that dampen income-maximizing strategies have all had particularly important effects on increasing inequality at the top of the earnings distribution. The decline of government regulation of low-wage labor markets and the virtual collapse of the union movement have especially harmed workers at the bottom of the labor market. The most obvious form of this deregulation is the destruction of an effective

[13] John Kenneth Galbraith, *The New Industrial State* (Princeton, NJ: Princeton University Press, 2007; originally published 1967), p. 146.

[14] Ibid., p. 151.

minimum wage, as we described earlier in Chapter 9. This decline in the legal minimum wage has led directly to a gradual decline in the wages for many low-wage jobs—not just for minimum-wage jobs themselves, but for jobs paying just above the minimum wage whose pay scales are pegged to the minimum wage. Economists have estimated that wages in roughly the bottom 11 percent of jobs are directly affected by the level of the legal minimum.[15] Other forms of government deregulation of low-wage labor markets include lax enforcement of workplace regulations, which have allowed an increase in sweatshops in some cities; the increasing employment of illegal immigrants who are often paid below the minimum wage; and an extremely hostile stance by employers and the government toward labor unions. All of these factors have the effect of keeping wages at the bottom of the labor market low and thus increasing the distance between the bottom and the top in the distribution of earnings.

Wealth Inequality

Economic inequality is not simply the result of earnings inequalities generated through paid employment; it is also generated by inequalities in wealth. Wealth, as we saw in Figures 13.13 and 13.14, is much more unequally distributed than is earnings. Near the end of the twentieth century, there was a significant increase in the diffusion of financial assets and home ownership in the American population: home ownership rates increased (at least until the housing market crash in 2008), and more people owned at least some stocks, particularly in the form of mutual funds in retirement accounts. Yet this increased wealth diffusion did not result in any reduction in the overall inequality of wealth. Three processes in the economy have reinforced wealth inequality.

First, inequality in labor market earnings itself contributes to inequality in wealth because people with high labor market earnings are in a much better position to use some of their earnings for investments in wealth-generating assets than are people with more modest earnings. The fantastic rise in employment earnings at the high end of the labor market has allowed well-paid professionals and corporate managers to turn surplus earnings into investments of various sorts.

Second, as we discussed in Chapter 9, since the 1970s the character of the American economy has undergone a dramatic process of financial

---

[15] For estimates of the spillover effects of minimum wages, see Alan Manning, *Monopsony in Motion* (Princeton, NJ: Princeton University Press, 2003).

deregulation, which opened up a wide range of new strategies for financial speculation without any meaningful supervision. Wealthy people were in a much better position to take advantage of these new opportunities than were people without financial assets. Wealth begets wealth. Although a considerable amount of this wealth was destroyed in the financial crash of 2008, the financial sector of the economy quickly recovered and these losses were recouped.

The third process that reinforced wealth inequality concerns the change in the relationship between productivity growth and wage growth since the 1970s (see Figures 10.5 and 10.6). Before the 1980s, there was a rough correspondence between the growth of labor productivity—how much value people produced per hour of labor—and the growth of hourly wages. Since around 1980, this correspondence has largely disappeared: there has been considerable growth in labor productivity in the economy, but hourly earnings have remained quite stagnant. What this means is that an increasing portion of the economic value created by the increased productivity was going to owners of assets rather than to the producers themselves. There is considerable debate over the precise mechanisms through which capital owners have been able to accomplish this, but at least part of this comes from the decline of union power combined with the increased global mobility of capital assets, which has enabled the owners of corporations to keep wages down.

In this period since the 1970s, the United States has thus experienced three significant economic shifts, all of which reinforce inequality of wealth. Earnings inequality has increased dramatically, creating in the upper tiers of the earnings distribution much more discretionary income that can be invested in wealth; profits have shifted from sectors that actually produce goods and services to the financial sector; and income has shifted from the people doing the work in the economy to those owning assets.

Back to the Questions of Ideals and Reality

It is one thing to chart the changes in levels of inequality in the United States and provide the outlines of an explanation for these trends. It is another to pass judgment on these distributions. Often it is thought that because Americans have strong beliefs in "rugged individualism," they don't really object to high levels of inequality. They may value fairness, of course, but they don't really care about inequality.

A study by Michael I. Norton and Dan Ariely explored this issue by asking a random sample of people what they thought would be the ideal distribution of wealth in the United States and what they thought the actual distribution looked like.[16] The results of their study are presented in Figure 13.16. In this experiment, it was explained to respondents that in a perfectly equal world, each 20 percent of the population would own exactly 20 percent of the total wealth of the society. Respondents were then asked to indicate what they thought the ideal distribution of wealth across these quintiles would be for the United States. The average response is indicated in the lower panel: the poorest 20 percent of the population would get about 10 percent of the wealth, while the richest 20 percent would get a bit over 30 percent of the wealth. This means that the ideal ratio between the top and bottom quintiles would be around 3:1. Respondents were then asked to indicate what they thought was the actual distribution in the United States. The average response is presented in the middle panel of the figure. On average, respondents thought the poorest fifth of the population owned only 3 percent of total wealth while the richest fifth owned 59 percent, or about 20 times more. The reality, as indicated in the top panel, is dramatically more unequal than most people think: the bottom fifth owns only 0.1 percent while the wealthiest fifth of the population owns 84 percent of all wealth.

FIGURE 13.16—Ideal, perceived, and actual wealth inequality in the U.S.

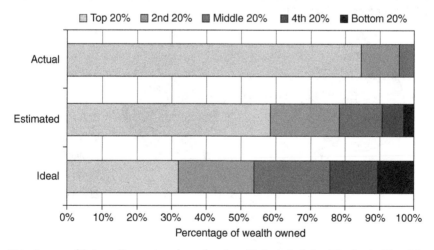

Note: Because of their small percentage share of total wealth, both the "4th 20%" value (0.2%) and the "Bottom 20%" value (0.1%) are not visible in the "Actual" distribution.

Source: Michael I. Norton and Dan Ariely, "Building a Better America—One Wealth Quintile at a Time," *Perspectives on Psychological Science* 6 (2011): 9–12, p. 11.

---

[16] Michael I. Norton and Dan Ariely, "Building a Better America—One Wealth Quintile at a Time," *Perspectives on Psychological Science* 6 (2011): 9–12.

So, while it is true that Americans are not in favor of an absolutely equal distribution of wealth, most people's vision of the ideal distribution is still vastly more equal than the reality of the United States in the twenty-first century. In fact, the ideal of most Americans actually looks a lot like the reality of Sweden. In a second part of their research, Norton and Ariely asked people to make choices between paired sets of wealth distributions: one was perfectly equal, 20 percent of the wealth going to each fifth of the population; one was the actual distribution in the United States; and the third was the actual distribution in Sweden (the people in the study were not told that these distributions corresponded to any specific countries). They were asked, for each pair, in which country they would like to live if given the choice. Figure 13.17 presents the results: 92 percent of the respondents preferred the Swedish distribution to the American distribution, and a surprising number preferred complete equality. This does not mean, of course, that these people would automatically support the social and economic policies needed to generate such distributions of wealth, but it does indicate that in terms of core values, Americans are much more egalitarian than is typically thought. This suggests that there might eventually be support for public policies that move us in that direction, which is the topic of the next chapter.

FIGURE 13.17—Preferences for three wealth distributions: Sweden, United States, and perfect equality

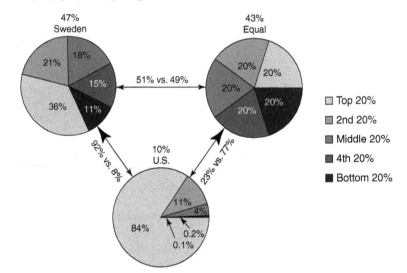

Note: Respondents were asked to choose between pairs of wealth distributions without knowing that two of them corresponded to any real countries. The pie charts depict the percentage of wealth possessed by each quintile; for instance, in the United States, the top quintile owns 84 percent of the total wealth, the second highest 11 percent, and so on.

Source: Norton and Ariely, "Building a Better America," *Perspectives on Psychological Science* 6 (2011): 9–12; Figure 1, page 10.

14

ENDING POVERTY IN AMERICA

P overty in the midst of plenty is an indisputable fact of American life. Nearly everyone feels that in a country as rich as the United States, this situation poses a moral challenge, particularly in the case of children living in poverty. Americans may endorse a strongly individualistic ethic by which people should be responsible for their own well-being, and many may feel that redistribution of income from rich to poor is somehow a violation of the right of people to do what they like with their own money. Yet it still seems unjust, even to many ardent individualists, when children suffer due to the poverty of their parents. Because children are clearly not responsible for their own plight, most people believe that something should be done.

Something should be done, but what? Before the 1960s, the most significant program directly designed to reduce poverty in the United States was old-age pensions provided through Social Security. Social Security was an extraordinarily successful program. It began very modestly in the 1930s as a New Deal reform; by the end of the twentieth century it had almost eliminated acute poverty among the elderly, particularly after medical care for the elderly was added in the 1960s. There were also some programs directed toward children, but these were badly funded and grossly inadequate by any reasonable standard.

As part of the Great Society agenda of the 1960s, the United States initiated a major effort at tackling the problem of poverty. Lyndon Johnson declared a War on Poverty and launched a range of new initiatives. The most important of these, called Aid to Families with Dependent Children (AFDC), was a dramatic expansion of an earlier program that dated from the 1930s. AFDC was a moderately generous program of income transfers targeted to families with children. When combined with food stamps, medical assistance, and various kinds of housing subsidies, it had a significant impact on the standard of living of poor children even if it fell far short of eliminating poverty itself. This was the program that came to be known as welfare.

AFDC was passed in the last period of vigorous liberal reform in the twentieth century. By the 1980s, when conservative politics were in the ascendancy, welfare programs like AFDC were under concentrated attack on the grounds that they perpetuated rather than relieved poverty. The argument was pretty simple: By giving "handouts" to poor people, welfare programs encouraged dependency rather than autonomy and responsibility. AFDC, the argument went, gave single women incentives to have children outside of marriage in order to get welfare payments, and thus the system also undermined the family. Because it had no time limits and no work requirements, AFDC fostered a culture of passivity and irresponsibility. And on top of this, conservatives argued, welfare was riddled with fraud by "welfare queens" who drove Cadillacs and lived better than many hardworking wage earners. Liberals were also unhappy with the program. Some thought the programs were too stingy and still left children in poverty. Others felt that the specific structure of the programs had certain perverse effects, called poverty traps: to qualify for welfare programs, you had to earn below a certain level of income and would lose your benefits if you earned above that threshold, so the programs created a disincentive for people to incrementally improve their income from employment. Unless you could get a good-paying job, you were better off not working.

By the 1990s, support for the AFDC kind of welfare had virtually disappeared. This situation led to two principal developments during the decade. First, there was a significant expansion of a second kind of income support program, the Earned Income Tax Credit (EITC), designed to help the working poor rather than people outside of the labor force. The EITC is a refundable tax credit given to working families with children whose annual earnings fall below a certain level. Unlike AFDC, it is available only to people in the paid labor force and is thus not subject to the central criticisms of traditional welfare. Second, in 1997 AFDC was eliminated and replaced by a new program—the Temporary Assistance for Needy Families program (TANF), established by the Personal Responsibility and Work Opportunity Act. Unlike the program it replaced, TANF assistance was available only for limited time periods. Recipients were required to attempt to find employment, and various provisions of the act attempted to encourage marriage.

The act, in the words of President Clinton, may have "ended welfare as we know it," but it has not ended poverty. As we noted earlier (see Figures 13.4 and 13.5), the poverty rate has changed hardly at all since the late 1960s.

It is true that the number of people receiving welfare payments from the government has declined dramatically since the end of AFDC: in 1995, just before the enactment of TANF, 4.7 million families received AFDC payments; in 2010, only about 2 million received any support from TANF (Figure 14.1). But this shift away from government transfers has not resulted in significant improvements in the economic conditions at the bottom of the income distribution; it just means that a smaller proportion of poor families have access to income supports. As indicated in Figure 14.2, in the two-year period 1996–1997, 64 percent of families with children in poverty accessed cash assistance; in 2009–2010, the figure was only 27 percent.[1]

In the rest of this chapter, we explore various ideas about what could be done to significantly address the problem of poverty and economic inequality in the United States. We begin by briefly discussing the concept of welfare and making the argument that in the United States today, the main

FIGURE 14.1—Number of families receiving cash-assistance welfare benefits, and number of families with children in poverty, 1978–2010

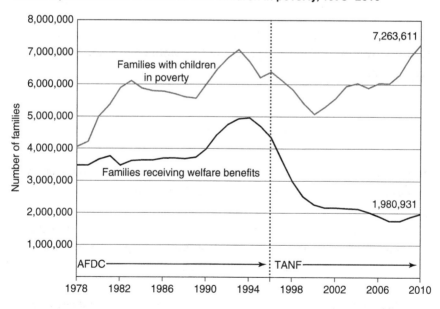

Source: Danilo Trisi and LaDonna Pavetti, "TANF Weakening as a Safety Net for Poor Families" (Center on Budget and Policy Priorities, 2012).

[1] Danilo Trisi and LaDonna Pavetti, "TANF Weakening as a Safety Net for Poor Families," Center on Budget and Policy Priorities (March 13, 2012), at http://www.cbpp.org/cms/index.cfm?fa=view&id=3700.

FIGURE 14.2—Percentage of families with children in poverty receiving AFDC/TANF benefits

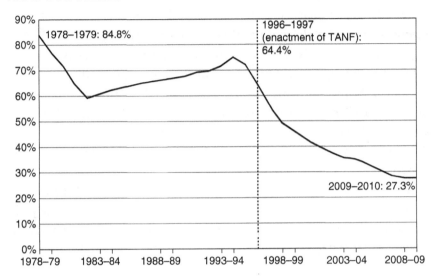

Source: Danilo Trisi and LaDonna Pavetti, "TANF Weakening as a Safety Net for Poor Families" (Center on Budget and Policy Priorities, 2012).

recipients of welfare are middle-class and wealthy people, not the poor. We then examine a number of proposals that would significantly affect poverty and inequality.

THE PROBLEM OF WELFARE

In the United States, *welfare* has become a dirty word. But what exactly is welfare? Here is one way we might define the core idea:

> Welfare policies are any government subsidy to a particular group of people to provide them with certain kinds of material advantages that they would not have if things were just left to the market.

When defined in this way, welfare has two main forms: *direct targeted government spending*, such as nutrition programs for poor children, public housing, income grants, tuition subsidies for university students, and government bailouts of failing corporations and large banks; and *tax subsidies*, such as home mortgage deductions, tax breaks for corporations, tax deductions for charitable contributions, and the earned income tax credit. Many people do not realize that tax deductions and tax credits are a form of government transfer for private purposes. Consider the home mortgage tax deduction. If you pay $10,000 per year in interest payments on a home mortgage and are in the 35 percent tax bracket (i.e., your income is such that you are paying 35 percent in taxes on any additional income), then your income taxes to the government would be reduced by $3,500. This situation is exactly the same as the government transferring $3,500 to you to reduce your interest payments from $10,000 to $6,500.

Once welfare is understood in this broad way, it is clear that most welfare spending in the United States goes to the middle class and the rich. Let us look briefly at some important examples.

University Students in Public Institutions

All college students in public institutions are recipients of massive welfare payments because the tuition they are charged generally covers well under half the cost of their education.[2] The rest comes from a variety of other sources, including endowments, but much of the cost of higher education is a subsidy from taxpayers. This kind of welfare spending raises significant social justice issues. After all, most taxpayers never went to college, and the average college graduate will earn considerably more than the median income of all people. In effect, less-advantaged taxpayers are providing welfare payments to middle-class students so that they can earn higher incomes later in life.

Homeowners

The home mortgage interest payment tax deduction constitutes a massive subsidy to homeowners.[3] What's more, because the magnitude of the subsidy is a function of both the size of the mortgage (the more expensive the

[2] Average tax subsidies for higher education have declined in the last decades, so net tuition paid by students has increased as a proportion of total education and related costs. This trend has continued in the last few years. In 2005, the net tuition portion of education and related costs in public four-year universities (bachelor's degree) averaged 41 percent, with students spending an average of $4,759 (in 2010 dollars); in 2010, this figure increased to 45 percent, averaging $5,746. In public community colleges (associate's degrees), median net tuition covered 29 percent of total education and related costs in 2005, and 34 percent in 2010. These figures come from the Delta Project's Trends in College Spending Online database at http://tcs-online.org/Home.aspx (accessed March 17, 2014).

[3] The federal tax subsidy for homeowners includes a few other things besides the mortgage interest deduction, especially local property tax payments.

house, the greater the subsidy) and the income tax rate paid by the home-owner (the richer the homeowner, the higher the percentage deduction for the interest payments), this particular form of welfare payment is highest for the most affluent homeowners. In 2010, from the $304 billion in existing housing tax subsidies, 56 percent went to homeowners with incomes of $100,000 or more (corresponding to the richest 18 percent of homeowners), while only 14 percent went to homeowners making $50,000 or less.[4] This subsidy is clearly a form of welfare for the affluent. Moreover, this subsidy is vastly greater than public assistance for housing for the poor. The budgetary authorization[5] for federal housing assistance for economically disadvantaged persons declined from $56.4 billion (in constant 2004 dollars) in 1976 to $29.2 billion in 2004; during the same period, the tax subsidy on mortgages to homeowners increased by 260 percent from $33.2 billion to $119.3 billion.[6]

Farm Subsidies

One of the most durable forms of welfare spending in the United States is agricultural subsidies. This expenditure averages more than $30 billion per year. Farm subsidies include substantial payments for tobacco farmers producing a crop that harms the health of Americans. Cotton farmers receive huge direct subsidies that give them a competitive advantage against cotton farmers in poor countries. There are also myriad forms of indirect subsidies, such as inexpensive water for rice farming in arid regions of California. From 1995 to 2012, 75 percent of all farm subsidies went to the wealthiest 10 percent of farmers. The average farm payment to this wealthy group in this period was $32,043 per year, while the average payment to farmers in the bottom 80 percent was only $604 per year.[7]

---

[4] Authors' calculations, based on data from Robert Carroll, John F. O'Hare, and Phillip L. Swagel, "Costs and Benefits of Housing Tax Subsidies," *The Pew Charitable Trust*, 2011), p. 3.

[5] *Budgetary authorization* refers to the amount of money that has been authorized in the federal budget to be spent for a particular purpose. In the case of large infrastructure projects that take many years to complete, the budget authorization will typically be considerably larger than the actual outlays in any given year.

[6] Cushing N. Dolbeare, Irene Basloe Saraf, and Sheila Crowley, "Changing Priorities: The Federal Budget and Housing Assistance, 1976–2005," *National Low Income Housing Coalition* (October 2004), available at http://nlihc.org/sites/default/files/cp04.pdf (accessed Sept. 16, 2009).

[7] http://farm.ewg.org/region.php?fips=00000.

Corporate Welfare

The examples of government welfare for corporations are endless. Here are some from the politically conservative Cato Institute's "Handbook for the 105th Congress"[8]:

- Commerce Department's Advanced Technology Program ($200 million a year) gives research grants to consortiums of some of the nation's largest high-tech companies. Those grants allow private companies to use taxpayer dollars to help them develop and bring to market profitable new products.
- The Export-Import Bank ($700 million a year) uses taxpayer dollars to provide subsidized financing to foreign purchasers of U.S. goods. Its activities include making direct loans to those buyers at below-market interest rates, guaranteeing the loans of private institutions to those buyers, and providing export credit insurance to exporters and private lenders.
- The Energy Department's Energy Supply Research and Development Program ($2.7 billion a year) aims to develop new energy technologies and improve on existing technologies. Its activities include applied research and development projects as well as demonstration ventures in partnership with private sector firms.
- Overseas Private Investment Corporation ($70 million a year) provides direct loans, guaranteed loans, and political risk insurance to U.S. firms that invest in developing countries.

Libertarians like those associated with the Cato Institute object to all these subsidies because they oppose any use of taxation that goes beyond the most minimal needs of public order and the protection of private property. We, on the other hand, believe that many of these forms of government welfare may be entirely justified. It is probably good public policy to facilitate home ownership, and the mortgage interest tax deduction is one way of doing this. University education is in part a public good, and tax subsidies are certainly justified. Even corporate welfare and agricultural subsidies may serve useful public purposes in some circumstances, helping to overcome market failures, solve prisoner's dilemmas, reduce negative externalities of various sorts, improve the lives of people and communities. Such programs may be good public policy, but they are still welfare that

[8] Available online at http://www.cato.org/cato-handbook-policymakers/cato-handbook -congress-policy-recommendations-105th-congress-1997 (accessed Sept. 16, 2009).

benefits primarily the more affluent. And the total spent on such programs is vastly more than the transfers to the poor that fall under what is usually called welfare. As critics of the inequalities of these subsidies have sometimes said, this is "socialism for the rich, capitalism for the poor."

SOLUTIONS TO POVERTY AND EXCESSIVE INEQUALITY

Current discussions for reducing poverty have focused mainly on the issue of education and skill formation. As we explained in our discussion of high-road capitalism, we too feel that a transformation of the institutions of skill formation is an important element of moving toward high-road capitalism. Certainly any serious political project for ending poverty will include life-long education, beginning with high-quality preschool and continuing through higher education, vocational education, and flexible periodic skill formation and retraining. Nevertheless, we feel that poverty and excessive inequality cannot be effectively dealt with by education alone, both because there is no guarantee that the increased supply of educated labor will automatically generate sufficient numbers of appropriate jobs needing such educated workers, and because acquiring the skills and education for good-paying jobs will not be a sensible strategy for everyone.

Still, we believe that it is entirely feasible to *completely* eliminate poverty in America. To do so would require a significant reduction in the overall levels of inequality, and this means reducing the incomes of people at the top of the income distribution. Poverty can be eliminated in a rich society, but eliminating poverty while leaving intact the power and privileges of the wealthy is not plausible.

In the following subsections, we examine three clusters of programs and social changes that we believe would do much for eliminating poverty. The first of these involves partially decoupling the real standard of living of all people from their personal income; the second involves partially decoupling paid employment from the capitalist market; and the third involves partially decoupling income from earnings. We briefly discuss the first two of these strategies for eliminating poverty and then examine the third in more depth.

Partially Decouple Standards of Living from Earnings

Let us define in a general way a standard of living above poverty. It entails having adequate and nutritious food, comfortable shelter, good health care, decent clothing, opportunities for recreation and entertainment, reasonable transportation, and sufficient income to be a full participant in the social life of a community. That definition is admittedly vague, because words like *adequate* and *comfortable* and *reasonable* leave much room for interpretation. Nevertheless, for our purposes, this definition is precise enough.

How much income a person needs to live above poverty defined in this way depends to a significant extent on how many components of this standard of living a person needs to purchase with his or her income and how much is provided through other means. The clearest example is health care: If everyone is publicly provided good-quality health insurance that includes doctor visits, hospitalization, medications, nursing care, dental care, and all other necessary health-care services, then they need less income in order to live above poverty. If public transportation is well designed and cheap, and if cities have well-designed bike paths, then people have less need for cars; or at least in many families, only one car would be needed. If communities have good parks, community centers, public swimming pools, libraries, ice-skating rinks, community concerts, and so on, then people need to spend less money for recreation. If university education, vocational training and retraining, technical training and community colleges, and other forms of lifelong education are free or heavily subsidized, then people need less income to deal with the uncertainties of jobs and the labor market. If good-quality, publicly funded child care is available for all, then people need less income to cover those costs.

Taken together, all these things constitute what some people call the *social wage*. The social wage plus labor market earnings plus income derived from wealth (savings, investments, etc.) determine a person's standard of living. The greater the social wage, the smaller the burden there is on labor market earnings to raise a person above the poverty line. One critical social change to reduce poverty, therefore, is increasing the social wage.

Partially Decouple Paid Employment from the Capitalist Market: Publicly Created Jobs

The social wage will never be enough to constitute an adequate standard of living. People will still need money to buy things on the market. For the foreseeable future, the labor market and paid employment will be the main way most people get their income; but as we noted in Chapter 13, there is little reason to believe that private capitalist firms will ever spontaneously provide enough jobs of the right kind. One solution is for a significant number of jobs paying reasonable wages to be created directly by public initiative. These jobs need not all involve direct employment by the state; publicly *created* jobs can be organized by community groups, nonprofit organizations, and other associations in what is sometimes called the social economy.[9] Such organizations can be effective in providing all sorts of services that meet human needs, but they often have great difficulty in acquiring the financial resources needed to provide those services as well as a living wage for the service workers. Publicly funded and subsidized social economy jobs on a large scale could help solve this problem.

Partially Decouple Income from Earnings: Unconditional Basic Income

The final proposal departs much more fundamentally from the basic organization of American capitalism. The idea of expanding the social wage and publicly funded and subsidized jobs would be a significant change in the United States, but both of these efforts would build on already familiar elements in the economic system. Decoupling the income needed to purchase the basic necessities of life from earnings acquired in labor markets would constitute a much more fundamental break with existing ways of organizing things. Although we believe this proposal has no chance of being adopted in the United States any time soon, we still think it is an important idea and it might become politically feasible sometime in the future. It would have a range of positive effects if it were implemented, and so it is worth thinking about in some detail.

This proposal is called *unconditional universal basic income*, or *basic income* for short.[10] The idea is quite simple: All citizens are given a monthly income sufficient to live at a no-frills level above the poverty line. Everyone receives the basic income—it is universal, it is given unconditionally, and it entails no work requirements or other conditions. People as wealthy as Bill Gates receive the basic income along with everyone else. It is a citizen right, just

[9] For a discussion of the social economy and the ways that it might provide for good and meaningful employment of relatively less skilled people, see Erik Olin Wright, *Envisioning Real Utopias* (New York: Verso, 2010), ch. 7.

[10] For a thorough discussion of the idea of basic income, including a range of commentaries and criticisms, see Bruce Ackerman, Anne Alstott, and Philippe van Parijs, *Redesigning Distribution: Basic Income and Stakeholder Grants as Cornerstones for an Egalitarian Capitalism*, The Real Utopias Project, Vol. V, ed. Erik Olin Wright (New York: Verso, 2005).

as free public education is a right for children and free health care is a right for everyone in most countries. Parents are the custodians of the basic income given to their children (which could be at a lower level than for adults). Basic income grants replace all other cash transfer programs of the welfare state—unemployment insurance, food stamps, cash payments for poor families, social security pensions, and so on—but not the kinds of government programs embodied in the social wage (education, health care, etc.). It is paid for out of general income taxes, so of course rates of taxation have to be increased. For high-earning people, taxes will rise by more than the basic income, so those people will be net contributors. Although the basic income is sufficient to live on, most people will want some discretionary income; there is no disincentive to work, because the rate of taxation on low labor market earnings will continue to be relatively low.

The basic income proposal contrasts sharply with existing income transfer programs designed to reduce poverty. Nearly all those programs are *means tested*, given only to people whose income falls below some threshold. Basic income is a universal program given to everyone. At first glance, it might seem that means-tested programs that are targeted to the poor would provide more resources for the people who need them most. This expectation generally turns out not to be the case. The problem with means-tested programs is that by identifying a specific, well-demarcated category of beneficiaries, means-tested programs create a sharp division between those who receive the benefits and those who do not. Universal programs build bridges across groups, creating large potential coalitions in support of funding the program and symbolically affirming the idea that the program reflects a universal right, rather than charity. Targeted programs isolate recipients, symbolically stigmatizing them as needy, dependent persons incapable of being responsible adult citizens. Due to these characteristics, universal programs tend to provide more rather than less funds for the poor. As it is sometimes said, programs targeted to the poor are usually poor programs.

The idea of unconditional universal basic income runs against the grain of the political and economic views of most Americans. It seems to reward laziness and undermine individual responsibility. And besides, many people will argue, it would simply be too expensive: even a rich country like the United States could never afford to give everyone, unconditionally, an above-poverty basic income. We will discuss these objections in a moment, but first let us look at some potential benefits of a basic income system if it were implemented and if it were affordable.

First, and most important in the context of the discussion of this chapter, basic income eliminates extreme poverty without stigma because the grant is universal. No child will live in poverty if an unconditional universal basic income guarantees everyone an adequate standard of living.

Second, if a well-funded, basic income were in place, it would tend to make unpleasant work more costly. In the existing labor market, badly paid jobs are often also the least pleasant. A basic income would make it harder for employers to recruit workers for unpleasant, boring, physically taxing jobs. Either such jobs would become better paid or employers would feel pressure to get rid of unpleasant work through work reorganization and technical change. Basic income, therefore, is likely to create a bias in economic change toward labor-humanizing innovations.

Third, unconditional basic income can be seen as a way of supporting a wide range of nonmarket economic activities as well as enabling people to engage in market-oriented activities in new ways. For example, a problem in the performing arts is that for people to be actively engaged in the arts, they have to eat; and it is often extremely hard for people to generate a basic income through their artistic activities. Many artists, actors, musicians, writers, and dancers therefore need to work at low-paying "day jobs" so they can earn just enough to be able to do their artistic work. An unconditional basic income would liberate them from this constraint. Similar problems confront people engaged in community activism of various sorts, nonprofit services, caregiving for children and the elderly, and many other activities that generate considerable social benefits. All these areas would expand if the people engaged in these activities did not have to use them for generating income to meet their basic needs.

The same argument applies to the formation of worker-owned cooperatives. One way of organizing production for a market is through firms that are entirely owned by the people who work in them. Worker-owned cooperatives, however, are often hard to form and unstable because workers find it difficult to get the capital they need for their business in ordinary credit markets and because they need to generate income to live on right from the start. They cannot afford to start the business and wait several years before generating income. An unconditional basic income would make it easier to get loans for the cooperative business because the basic income would make the business more viable and thus more creditworthy, and it would give the worker-owners the necessary time to get the firm going. Basic income would also make it much easier for small farmers to thrive without needing subsidies specifically targeted to agriculture. The problem with existing farm subsidies such as price supports for crops is that they benefit large corporate farms much more than small family farms, even though they are typically justified politically as a way of helping family farmers. Unconditional basic income directly supports the standard of living of small farmers, making it easier for them to sustain their farms, but does not provide tax subsidies to corporate farms.

Finally, basic income can be seen as guaranteeing what Philippe van Parijs, the leading theorist of basic income, has called "real freedom for all."[11] Real freedom exists when people have the actual capacity to make critical choices and act on them, to put their life plans into effect. In a world without basic income, wealthy people with assets have this freedom because they can choose whether they want to work for pay, and the children of rich parents have this freedom because their parents can provide them with the necessary resources to make such choices. A basic income would give such real freedom to everyone. Most crucially, people would have a real choice about whether to enter the labor market and work for pay. All people, not just wealthy people, would have the freedom to exit the labor market—to care for children, be an artist, work as a community organizer.

These consequences of a basic income are attractive to many people. But will it work? Is it actually feasible? Critics of unconditional basic income typically raise two practical objections: First, if there were a basic income above the poverty line, then so many people would stop working for pay that not enough income would be generated to provide the necessary taxes to fund the system. The basic income would collapse because tax revenues would plummet due to the lack of labor supply. Second, basic income would be so expensive that the tax rates would have to be extremely high; high taxes, in turn, would generate massive disincentives to invest and to work. Again, the basic income would collapse, this time due to a lack of investment.

These are empirical questions, and it is difficult to know exactly how people would react if a basic income were in place. Estimates have been made of the total cost of a basic income; and at least in those European welfare states that already provide something close to a basic income through a patchwork of targeted and means-tested programs, the increased net cost is not all that great. Remember, the basic income replaces lots of existing

---

[11] Philippe van Parijs, *Real Freedom for All: What (If Anything) Can Justify Capitalism?* (Oxford, UK: Clarendon Press, 1995).

income support programs, and it is also much cheaper to administer than other programs because of its simplicity. Even in the United States, which at the beginning of the twenty-first century has among the lowest aggregate rates of taxation among developed countries, the estimates of the tax increases needed to fund a basic income suggest that the tax rates would not cripple the economy.[12] Nevertheless, we do not know how people will react to a basic income; so many people might exit the labor force that it just would not work. Its viability can ultimately be tested only in practice.

Even if we suppose that a basic income would work, many people will have doubts about its desirability. To many it will just seem wrong to give everyone money to live on regardless of their behavior or contribution to society. Paid work at least demonstrates that you are doing something useful for someone besides yourself. Basic income allows people to be lifelong couch potatoes without contributing anything. This prospect just seems unfair to those people who do the work that generates the taxes that pay for the basic income.

These are indeed serious moral objections that certainly cannot be dismissed. We have two responses. The first rests on van Parijs's arguments for real freedom for all. In the United States, rich people are able to do nothing without contributing anything to society, and yet they are allowed to keep their wealth. Basic income merely extends this "right to be lazy" to everyone; or, to say this more positively, it extends the real freedom to make choices over work to everyone. The second response has a more pragmatic character. Many values are in play regarding inequality and poverty as well as the alternative policies for dealing with these issues. All solutions to problems involve trade-offs. To be sure, the idea that some people will live off the basic income and contribute nothing to society is distasteful. The problem is that requiring people to work or make social contributions as a condition for receiving the basic income creates huge monitoring problems and opens the door for scams, deception, and other perverse effects. These problems, in turn, would raise the costs of basic income by requiring lots of monitoring, investigating, and legal actions against fraud. It is possible, therefore, that the other good things about basic income—eliminating poverty in a rich society, especially for children; raising the price of unpleasant work and generating a bias in technical change that will reduce such work;

[12] See, for example, the estimates by Irvin Garfinkel, Chien-Chung Huang, and Wendy Naidich, "The Effects of a Basic Income Guarantee on Poverty and Income Distribution," in Ackerman et al., *Redesigning Distribution*.

opening up the possibilities for more nonmarket, socially valuable activities; and providing basic, real freedom for all—are compelling enough to outweigh the undesirable aspects of basic income. Such issues are similar for virtually all policies: almost never does a public policy perfectly embody a salient social value without having any negative effects whatsoever. The political task, therefore, is to weigh the trade-offs rather than reject a policy simply because it involves trade-offs.

Left to its own devices, capitalism inherently generates high concentrations of income and wealth at the top of the economic structure and high levels of serious economic deprivation at the bottom. This is what markets do: they reward the winners and punish the losers, and over time this dynamic cumulatively generates high levels of economic inequality. There is no reason, however, that capitalism must be left to its own devices. A wide array of public policies are available that can significantly counteract these tendencies. In some developed capitalist countries, as we have seen, the adoption of such policies has dramatically reduced poverty, especially among children, and has done so without significantly harming the economy. The continuing tragedy of extreme poverty in the United States alongside the extraordinary affluence of the rich is not the result of some law of nature, but of the political failure to adopt the kinds of policies that would solve the problem.

15

RACIAL INEQUALITY

Race and racial inequality have powerfully shaped American history from its beginnings. Americans like to think of the founding of the American colonies and, later, the United States, as driven by the quest for freedom—initially, religious liberty, and later, political and economic liberty. Yet, from the start, American society was equally founded on brutal forms of domination, inequality, and oppression that involved the absolute denial of freedom for slaves. This is one of the great paradoxes of American history—how could the ideals of equality and freedom coexist with slavery? We live with the ramifications of that paradox even today.

In this chapter we explore the nature of racial inequality in America, from its historical variations to the contemporary realities. We begin by clarifying precisely what we mean by race, racial inequality, and racism. We then briefly examine the ways that racism harms many people within racially *dominant* groups, not just racially oppressed groups. It might seem a little odd to raise this issue at the beginning of a discussion of racial inequality, for racial inequality surely is more damaging to the lives of people within the oppressed group. We do this because we feel this issue is one of the critical complexities of racial inequality, and it needs to be part of our understanding even as we focus on the more direct effects of racism. This topic is followed by a more extended discussion of historical variations in the forms of racial inequality and oppression in the United States. The chapter concludes with an exploration of the empirical realities today and prospects for the future.

This chapter focuses primarily on the experience of racial inequality of African Americans, although in the more historical section we briefly discuss specific forms of racial oppression of Native Americans, Mexican Americans, and Chinese Americans. This focus on African Americans does not imply that the forms of racism to which other racial minorities have been subjected are any less real. And certainly the nature of racial domination of these other groups has also influenced the character of contemporary American society.

WHAT IS RACE?

Many people think of races as "natural" categories reflecting important biological differences across groups of people whose ancestors came from different parts of the world. Because racial classifications are generally tied to observable physical differences between people, the apparent naturalness of race seems obvious to most people. This conception reflects a fundamental misunderstanding about the nature of racial classifications. Race is a social category, not a biological one. Racial classifications generally use inherited biological traits as criteria for classification; nevertheless, how those traits are treated and how they are translated into the categories we call races is defined by social conventions, not by biology.

In different times and places, racial boundaries are drawn in very different ways. In the United States, people are considered black if they have any African ancestry. This extreme form of binary racial classification reflects the so-called one-drop rule that became the standard system of racial classification in the United States after the Civil War. Imagine how different the meaning of race would be in the United States if the one-drop rule were reversed: anyone with any European ancestry would be classified as white. In Brazil, in contrast to the United States, racial classifications are organized on a more continuous spectrum. In the United States, all East Asians are considered a single racial category; in East Asia, on the other hand, Chinese, Japanese, Koreans, and Vietnamese are considered separate races. The United States Immigration Commission in 1911 considered people of Irish, Italian, Polish, and English descent to be distinct races, and the 1924 Immigration Act passed by Congress restricted immigration of what were termed inferior races from Southern and Eastern Europe. In Germany under the Nazis, Jews were considered a distinct race, not merely a religious group or an ethnic group. In Africa today, Tutsi and Hutu have sometimes been regarded as distinct races. Racial classifications are thus never simply given by biological descent, even if they always invoke biology; they are always constructed through complex historical and cultural processes.

Racial *classifications* do not logically imply racial *oppression* (i.e., a social injustice backed by power). Consider how ethnic distinctions are sometimes experienced: to be of Irish or Swedish or Italian descent in America today is to share a certain cultural identity, and perhaps to participate in certain cultural practices as well, but these identities do not imply any forms of oppression involving these categories. Ethnic difference can be just that: differences. Racial classifications could in principle be simply a way of noting physical differences of various sorts that are linked to biological descent. However, in practice racial classifications are almost always linked to forms of unjust economic and social inequality, domination, and exclusion, as well as to belief systems that assign superior and inferior statuses and attributes according to race. Indeed, as a sociological generalization we can say that racial classifications become salient in people's lives primarily to the extent that they are linked to forms of socioeconomic inequality and oppression.[1] The term *racism* designates this intersection of racial classification with oppression.[2]

RACISM AND THE LIVES OF WHITE AMERICANS

To study race in American society, then, is to investigate the ways in which racial classifications are linked to historically variable forms of oppression. At the moral core of such an analysis is an understanding of the ways that racial oppression harms the people in the racially oppressed category. Nevertheless, it is a mistake to think of racism as something that negatively affects only the lives of African Americans, Native Americans, Asian Americans, Hispanic Americans, and other racially defined "minorities." Racism has profoundly shaped American society and politics in ways that adversely affect the lives of many white Americans as well, particularly the lives of working-class and poor whites.

Racism harms disadvantaged groups within the white population in two principal ways. First, racism has repeatedly divided popular social and political movements, undermining their capacity to challenge prevailing forms

---

[1] Once a racial category becomes historically rooted and part of people's daily lives, it can also become an ethnicity—a category of people with shared historical experience, cultural practices, and identities. This fusion of race and ethnicity adds to the complexity of race as a form of social division.

[2] The word *racism* is sometimes used more narrowly to refer simply to beliefs and ideologies that have a racist content. We use the term in a more encompassing way to include the social relations as well as the systems of belief that link forms of socioeconomic injustice to racial classifications.

of power and inequality. Ruling elites have often used race as part of a strategy of "divide and conquer" to protect their class interests. Numerous examples can be cited:

- In the 1880s and 1890s, a radical political movement of workers and small farmers—the Populists—emerged in the Midwest and the South. For a time it appeared that black tenant farmers and white farmers in the South might be able to make common cause against large landowners and Southern elites. At its height the Populist movement appeared to pose a potentially serious challenge to the dominant political parties of the period and even to the interests of dominant classes. Racial conflict eventually tore apart the agrarian unity of the Populists and contributed to the decline of the movement overall.

- Throughout the late nineteenth century and the first part of the twentieth century, employers used racial minorities as strikebreakers in industrial strikes. This tactic significantly weakened the ability of unions to win strikes and contributed to deep resentments against blacks and other minorities within the white working class.

- In the late 1960s and early 1970s, in response to the civil rights movement, the Republican Party under Nixon adopted what came to be known as the "Southern Strategy," in which racial fears were deliberately used to get white working-class voters to switch political allegiance from the Democrats to the Republicans. Many scholars credit this strategy with ushering in an era of conservative politics that ultimately significantly harmed the economic interests of white workers by weakening unions, lowering the minimum wage, and reducing job security.

- Research on wage inequality has demonstrated that in those cities and regions of the United States where the black-white wage difference is the greatest, it is also the case that the wages of white workers are the lowest and inequality among whites is greatest.[3] This finding suggests that racial divisions within the working class weaken the ability of workers as a whole to bargain for higher wages with their employers. White workers, in the long run, would be better off economically if there was less inequality and more solidarity between white and black workers.

[3] See Michael Reich, *Racial Inequality: A Political-Economic Analysis* (Princeton, NJ: Princeton University Press, 1981).

In the absence of racial divisions and racial conflict, popular social forces would in general have been stronger and more capable of influencing political parties and challenging dominant class interests.

The second way that racism has negatively affected the interests of less-advantaged segments of the white population is by undermining universalistic aspects of the welfare state. Universal programs apply to all people. They are contrasted with targeted programs that apply only to special, designated groups. In general, as we noted in our discussion of poverty, universalistic programs tend to be better funded than targeted programs and more robustly improve the life conditions of people at the bottom of the class structure. In the critical period in the 1930s when the American welfare state was initially created through the New Deal, Southern Democrats strongly opposed universalistic policies because of the ways such policies would benefit black Americans as well as white Americans.[4] Despite widespread poverty in the South, Southern Democrats were extremely conservative on social welfare issues and effectively blocked the possibility of national universalistic programs because of racism. For example, in the legislation that set the basic framework for labor law and the rights of unions, these Democrats insisted on including provisions that would effectively exclude most black labor from union rights; Social Security initially excluded domestic workers and agricultural labor for the same reasons. Universal health insurance was off the table at least in part because of opposition to universalism. Many such exclusions of the New Deal have since been eliminated, but they nevertheless helped create a type of welfare state averse to the kind of universal programs that we see in most developed capitalist democracies. Racism played an important role in producing this outcome, which has harmed the interests of the majority of whites.

THE HISTORICAL TRAJECTORY OF RACIAL OPPRESSION

As we have just explained, racism may harm significant segments of the racially dominant group in American society. Nevertheless, racism is above all a form of domination that harms the racially oppressed groups. These harms have been a core part of American history, and not merely of distant

---

[4] For a discussion of the role of the racial politics of Southern Democrats in shaping the New Deal, see Ira Katznelson, *Fear Itself: The New Deal and the Origins of Our Time* (New York: Norton, 2013).

history. It is hard to overstate this point: only in the most recent past has the classical liberal idea of equality before the law been extended to include racial minorities, and even today, in many critical respects, such equality remains more promise than reality.

In this section, we explore historical variations in the distinctive forms of racial oppression in the United States. This will, of necessity, be a highly simplified and stripped-down historical account. Its purpose is to help give specificity to the current problem of racial inequality in American society by seeing what has changed and what remains. We focus on five primary forms of racial oppression that have occurred in U.S. history: genocide and geographical displacement, slavery, second-class citizenship, noncitizen labor, and diffuse racial discrimination. These forms constitute an overlapping historical sequence in which various racially defined groups are the primary subjects of different forms of racism in different historical periods.

Genocide and Geographical Displacement

When European settlers came to North America, they encountered an indigenous population that effectively controlled the most important economic resource of the time: land. From very early on, the central ways of dealing with the inevitable conflicts over this resource were genocide and displacement, first by the British colonies and later by the U.S. government. The nineteenth-century folk saying attributed to General Phil Sheridan, "The only good Indian is a dead Indian," reflects the moral monstrosity of these policies. Such sentiments were not on the margins of American culture; they were echoed by prominent figures. In a speech in 1886, Theodore Roosevelt stated, "I suppose I should be ashamed to say that I take the Western view of the Indian. I don't go so far as to think that the only good Indians are the dead Indians, but I believe nine out of every ten are, and I shouldn't inquire too closely into the case of the tenth. The most vicious cowboy has more moral principle than the average Indian."[5]

Most often the land was simply confiscated by force, and the indigenous inhabitants were driven off or killed. Occasionally, Native American tribes formally ceded land through treaties in the aftermath of military defeat. When treaties occurred, they guaranteed the native people making the treaty certain rights in exchange for the agreement. Often these rights were subsequently ignored.

[5] Thomas Gossett, *Race: The History of an Idea in America* (New York: Oxford University Press, 1997), p. 238.

Such displacements were claimed to be justified on the grounds that the native people were uncivilized "savages" and did not really "own" the land because they were often nomadic or seminomadic; they had no permanent settlements and did not permanently cultivate particular pieces of land. But even where Native Americans were agriculturalists and did have such settlements, there was little hesitation in forcibly evicting them from the land. The removal of the Cherokee Nation from the Southeastern United States by Andrew Jackson in the 1830s is the best-known instance. The Cherokees had deliberately adopted a policy of assimilation into American ways of life: they lived in settled communities, practiced extensive farming, and even owned slaves. Despite the Cherokees' efforts, Andrew Jackson used the military power of the federal government to force the Cherokees and the other Native American peoples of the Southeast to move west of the Mississippi.

By the end of the nineteenth century this displacement was complete, and Native Americans were largely confined to bounded geographical spaces called Indian reservations. The precise legal standing of these reservations has varied over time, but generally they have been accorded semi-sovereign status with at least some rights of self-government. In the twenty-first century, Native Americans are no longer required to live on Indian reservations. They are now full American citizens and can move freely about the country. Nevertheless, the lives of many Native Americans are still deeply marked by the legacy of the severe forms of racial oppression and geographical isolation to which they were historically subjected. As a group, they are among the most economically deprived segments of the American population, particularly when they live on reservations.

Slavery

Everyone knows that most people with African ancestors living in the United States today are the descendants of people who were the property of white Americans. Everyone knows this, but it is easy to lose sight of what it really means. Human beings were *property*: They were owned in the same sense as a horse can be owned. They could be whipped and branded and in other ways physically harmed with virtually no legal restrictions. The killing of a slave by a slave master was almost never punished. The rape of slaves was a common practice. Slave owners were free to split up families and to sell the children of slaves.

The fact that slave owners had absolute power over their slaves, of course, does not mean that all slave masters ruthlessly abused their slaves. Many slave owners accepted a paternalistic ideology in which slaves were regarded as children for whom they had moral responsibility, and certainly some slave owners tried to live up to that ideal. More importantly, slave owners were businesspeople for whom slaves were an important investment, and the value of that investment needed protection. Just as farmers have an incentive to be sure their horses are well fed and not overworked to the point of threatening their health and productivity, so slave owners had incentives to take care of their investments in the bodies of their slaves. Particularly after the international slave trade was banned at the beginning of the nineteenth century and thus the price of slaves increased, slave owners took measures to keep the value of their investments from deteriorating. As a result, by the time of the Civil War the calories consumed and material standard of living of American slaves was not very different, and perhaps even a little higher, than that of poor peasants and unskilled workers in many parts of Europe.

Some scholars have argued on the basis of these facts about improving standards of living of slaves in the nineteenth century that slavery was not as oppressive as often thought.[6] This claim minimizes the impact of such radical and complete unfreedom and the deep, symbolic degradation of slavery. By its nature, the social structure of slavery meant that significant physical brutality was ubiquitous despite the modestly improving standard of living of slaves and the ideology of paternalism. Because slavery was a lifetime condition, slaves had very little positive incentive to work hard. The prosperity of slave owners depended on the effort of their slaves, so this meant that slave owners had to rely heavily on negative incentives—force and the threat of force—to extract such effort. As a slave owner in Arkansas stated, "Now, I speak what I know, when I say it is like 'casting pearls before swine' to try to *persuade* a negro to work. He must be *made* to work, and should always be given to understand that if he fails to perform his duty he will be punished for it."[7] Even slave owners who sincerely believed in their paternalistic responsibilities to care for their slaves justified this harsh treatment on the grounds that the childlike nature of their black slaves meant that force was the only thing they understood.

The pervasive domination and exploitation of slavery was accompanied by pervasive forms of resistance by slaves. The most common form of resistance

---

[6] The best-known defense of this view is by Robert Fogel and Stanley Engerman, *Time on the Cross: The Economics of American Negro Slavery*, 2nd ed. (New York: W. W. Norton, 1995).

[7] Quoted by Kenneth Stamp in *The Peculiar Institution: Slavery in the Ante-Bellum South* (New York: Knopf, 1975), p. 171.

occurred in the mundane activities of the slave plantation: poor work, occasional sabotage, passivity. Runaway slaves were a chronic problem, and political conflict over how to deal with slaves who escaped to the North was one source of the tension that led to the Civil War. Occasionally there were violent slave revolts; though rare, they fueled an underlying fear of blacks among whites in the South and contributed to the massively repressive and violent apparatus of the slave state.

Slavery came to be restricted to the South over the course of the nineteenth century, but it would be a mistake to see this form of racial oppression as exclusively affecting the South. The economy of the North was deeply linked to Southern slavery in the colonial period, particularly through the notorious "triangular trade": slaves were purchased in Africa with European goods, they were sold in the Caribbean and North America, and the profits were used to ship tobacco, rum, and cotton back to Europe. Some have argued that the direct and indirect profits from this trade were the single most important source of capital accumulation in the colonies, including in New England.[8] At the time of the Constitutional Convention, slaves were owned by Northerners as well as Southerners, and many of the founding fathers were slave owners. In the early years after the revolution, slavery was still legal in a number of Northern states. In New York there were still 10,000 slaves in the 1820 census, and significant numbers of slaves were reported as late as the 1840 census in New Jersey. Right up to the Civil War, the Northern economy continued to be linked to slavery through textile manufacturing. Even after slavery was outlawed in the Northern states beginning in the late eighteenth century, the North collaborated with the South in allowing escaped slaves to be captured and returned to the South, particularly after the *Dred Scott* decision of the U.S. Supreme Court.[9] And though it was true that in the years leading up to the Civil War abolitionist sentiment grew steadily in the North, many people in the North were perfectly content to let slavery continue in the South.

By the time of the Civil War, nearly 4 million slaves were living in the United States—accounting for about 13 percent of the total U.S. population. In the fifteen states where slavery was legal, just over one in four white

[8] See, for example, David Eltis, *Economic Growth and the Ending of the Transatlantic Slave Trade* (New York: Oxford University Press, 1987).

[9] In the *Dred Scott* decision of 1856, the Supreme Court ruled that an escaped slave remained the property of the original slave owner even if the slave managed to get to a state where slavery was illegal, and thus it was legal for the slave owner to recapture the slave.

families were slave owners.[10] This figure is higher than the proportion of families who hired maids and servants in the non-slave states.[11] In Mississippi, 49 percent of households owned slaves in 1860.[12] Though most of these Southern slave-owning families owned just a few slaves, these percentages mean that the direct experience of owning another person of a different race was widespread in the South. For the white population in the antebellum South, the racial oppression of blacks was not simply part of the social environment in which they lived; it was a significant part of their daily routines.

Slavery ended with the Civil War a century and a half ago, but of course its impact did not disappear simply because this form of racialized class relations had been destroyed. Slavery contributed to an especially pernicious and durable form of racist beliefs that continues to influence American culture today. Slavery posed a deep cultural problem for the United States after the American Revolution: How could a country founded on the principles of "life, liberty, and the pursuit of happiness" accommodate slavery? How was it possible to reconcile the devotion to liberty and democracy with the treatment of some people as the property of others? The solution to this deeply contradictory reality was the elaboration of racial ideologies of degradation and dehumanization of blacks as intellectually and morally inferior and thus not worthy of treatment as full persons. The attribution of intellectual inferiority meant that blacks were seen as lacking intellectual capacities for rational action; thus, as in the case of children, choices should be made on their behalf by responsible adults. The attribution of moral inferiority supported the view of blacks as inherently dangerous, ruled by passions, both aggressive and sexual, and thus incapable of exercising liberty. These beliefs constituted the core of the racist culture forged under slavery. And though such beliefs were increasingly challenged in the last decades of

---

[10] According to Gavin Wright, a leading authority on slavery, "As of 1860, in the cotton-growing areas approximately one half of the farms did not own slaves; for the South as a whole, the percentage of slave-owning families declined from 36 in 1830 to 25 in 1860." Gavin Wright, *The Political Economy of the Cotton South* (New York: W. W. Norton, 1978).

[11] In the 1860 census, in the non-slave states, 506,366 people were classified as private household workers (housekeepers, laundresses, and other). The population of the non-slave states in 1860 was 19,410,197. Because, on average, households at that time consisted of about 5.3 people, this means there were approximately 3,640,000 households in the non-slave states in the United States in 1860. The maximum percentage of these households that could have employed a private household worker was 14 percent, if (implausibly) no household employed more than one such worker.

[12] These figures come from 1860 census data reported on "The Civil War Home Page" at http://www.civil-war.net/pages/1860_census.html (accessed Sept. 16, 2009).

the twentieth century and are no longer seen as respectable, they continue to influence race relations to the present.

Second-Class Citizenship

Slavery was abolished after the Civil War, but this did not mean a complete dismantling of legally enforced racial oppression. On paper, the Fourteenth Amendment to the U.S. Constitution, ratified in 1868, guaranteed equal protection of the law and full rights to all citizens. The Fifteenth Amendment, passed two years later, explicitly specified these rights applied to all people regardless of race or color. If these amendments had been taken seriously and rigorously enforced, then racial oppression could not have taken the form of second-class citizenship.

Second-class citizenship refers to a situation in which some categories of citizens have fewer rights than others. This can take the form of either an official, legally defined denial of some rights or a less formal, practical denial of rights. Laws that prohibit people who have been convicted of felonies from voting are an example of legally defined second-class citizenship that is still common in the United States today.[13] Police practices that target certain groups of people for stricter law enforcement, or judicial practices that systematically impose stiffer sentences on particular categories of people, are examples of unofficial second-class citizenship. Public policies that treat some categories of citizens as more worthy of respect than others can also be seen as creating a kind of second-class citizenship. Margaret Somers has argued that the public disrespect of poor African Americans reflected in the abandonment of the people left behind in New Orleans during Hurricane Katrina is a striking example of the denial of their full recognition as equal citizens.[14]

---

[13] In the United States today, there is considerable variation across the fifty states in the political rights of ex-prisoners. According to *The Sentencing Project* (http://www.sentencing project.org/), 35 states prohibit felons from voting while they are on parole; 30 of these states exclude felony probationers as well. In most states, once a person has completed a prison sentence and parole, all their rights are restored and they become full citizens once again. Two states deny the right to vote to all ex-offenders who have completed their sentences. Nine others disenfranchise certain categories of ex-offenders and/or permit application for restoration of rights for specified offenses after a waiting period (e.g., five years in Delaware and Wyoming, and two years in Nebraska). Not surprisingly, the harshest rules denying political rights to ex-prisoners can be found in the Southern states.

[14] Margaret Somers, *Genealogies of Citizenship* (Oxford, UK: Cambridge University Press, 2008).

Official second-class citizenship became the pivotal form of racial oppression in the United States, especially in the South, in the decades following the Civil War. The emancipation of slaves in the South posed a serious problem for large landowners who had previously relied almost entirely on slave labor for their incomes. Most slaves wanted to become small farmers, and there were moments when the promise of "forty acres and a mule" seemed to open the possibility of former slaves becoming a yeoman class of independent farmers. For this dream to have become a reality, however, widespread dispossession of large Southern landowners of their land would have been necessary. And despite having just waged the Civil War, in which large Southern landowners almost universally supported the Confederacy, the federal government was loath to violate the rights of private property owners to this extent. As a result, few ex-slaves were in a position to acquire land.

Large Southern landowners thus retained possession of the land, but they no longer owned the labor to work the land. In terms of the concept of class we discussed in Chapter 12, the landowners effectively hoarded the economic opportunities represented by land, but they no longer had complete control over a supply of labor to exploit. What these landowners needed, then, was a new system to tie ex-slaves to the land that would give planters effective control over their labor. In the decades following the Civil War, Southern planters experimented with different arrangements and finally settled on a system called sharecropping. *Sharecropping* is a form of agriculture in which tenant farmers pay rent to landowners in the form of a certain percentage of the total crop grown on the land. The profitability of landowning depends on what that percentage is, and this in turn depends on the bargaining power of the tenant farmers. It is of considerable advantage to landowners, therefore, to have a politically weak and economically vulnerable population available to be tenant farmers. This is what the denial of full political and legal rights to blacks in the South accomplished. This new form of racism, which came to be known as Jim Crow, played a central role in consolidating the new agrarian social order in the South by the end of the nineteenth century.

The rules of racially based, second-class citizenship in the South had a number of key components. The most obvious, of course, were the laws that effectively denied blacks the right to vote. Typically these took the form of literacy tests that were much more strictly enforced against blacks than against whites; but at various times and places in the South, other devices were used to accomplish this black disempowerment. Harsh vagrancy laws in the South were also used to prevent blacks from seeking better employment. Although officially such laws did not have a racial character, their application was directed primarily against blacks and significantly impeded their movement. These kinds of directly repressive laws were reinforced by a wide range of segregationist laws that excluded African Americans from white schools and universities, barred them from white hotels and restaurants, and relegated them to segregated facilities in public transportation. And lurking in the background of all these forms of legal segregation was widespread legal and extralegal violence directed against blacks. The Ku Klux Klan was tacitly supported by the state and allowed to terrorize black communities. Lynchings, the most extreme form of such violence, were a common event in parts of the South from the 1880s through the first decades of the twentieth century (Figure 15.1). Violence against blacks was not simply tolerated by state authorities in the South; it was official state policy. Legally enforced public violence against blacks is revealed starkly in the statistics on executions for rape by race in the period before the 1960s (Figure 15.2). In the United States from 1930 to 1960, between 5 and 25 black men—nearly all in the South—were executed annually for rape; for whites the numbers were never more than four, and in most years zero or one.

In 1900 roughly 90 percent of the black population in the United States lived in the South, mainly in rural areas. In the North, African Americans were not denied the right to vote, but it would be incorrect to see second-class citizenship as exclusively a Southern problem. Even though there were generally laws prohibiting school segregation in Northern states (except in Indiana, the one Northern state that allowed local school districts the legal option to officially segregate their schools), in practice many school boards in the North enforced racial segregation. The landmark Supreme Court case against school desegregation—*Brown v. Board of Education*—was a case brought in Kansas, not a Southern state. Laws against interracial marriage were present in thirty-six states in the 1920s and were still in place in nearly half the states in the 1950s. The federal government itself supported segregationist principles, in both the civil service (after Woodrow Wilson imposed segregation in the civil service in 1913) and in the military until Harry Truman desegregated the armed forces in 1948. During the New Deal, some of the landmark federal legislation—for example, Social Security and labor rights laws—explicitly excluded coverage of types of jobs that were predominantly filled by blacks. Thus, although the most restrictive forms of second-class citizenship for African Americans occurred in

FIGURE 15.1—Lynchings of blacks per year, 1882–1956

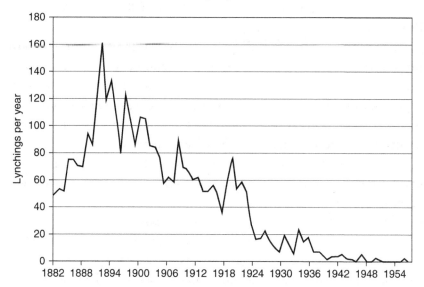

Source: University of Missouri–Kansas City School of Law, http://www.law.unkc.edufaculty/projects /ftrials/shipp/lynchstats.html (accessed Sept. 16, 2009). Data from the Archives of Tuskegee University.

FIGURE 15.2—Executions for rape by race in the U.S., 1930–1964

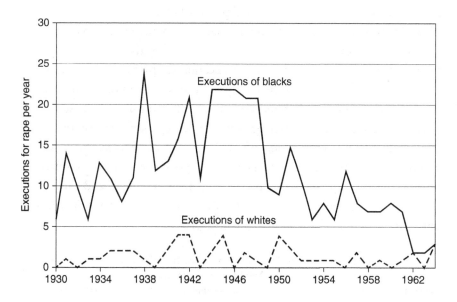

Source: U.S. Department of Commerce (Bureau of the Census), *Historical Statistics of the United States, Colonial Times to 1970* (Washington, DC: U.S. Government Printing Office, Series H 1155–1167, 1975).

the South, the problem was national. Until the 1960s, racism in the United States was a system of explicit legal denial of equality to people based on their race.

Just as slavery was met with resistance by slaves and political opposition by abolitionists, the legalized segregation of second-class citizenship also met with resistance from African Americans as well as white supporters of civil rights. Such opposition to segregation was often met with extreme forms of violence. Lynching of blacks was a common occurrence in the South, and rarely were perpetrators punished. Efforts at passing national antilynching laws failed. Segregationist laws and practices were maintained by violence and terror through the first decades of the twentieth century.

After World War II, things began to change. A number of factors were important. First, the United States had just fought a war against the Nazis; due to the extreme racist ideologies of the Nazis, state-supported racism had been significantly discredited. Secondly, in the context of the Cold War and the effort by the United States to be the "leader of the free world," the racist legal institutions of second-class citizenship were an international embarrassment, particularly given American efforts to gain influence in the newly independent ex-colonies of Africa and Asia. Third, during the 1930s and 1940s there had been large-scale migration of African Americans to the North, where they became a more important voting bloc; thus the issue of civil rights could more easily be translated into national politics. Finally, due to mechanization of agriculture and other economic changes, sharecropping had sharply declined in the South beginning in the 1930s, so that by the mid-1950s it was no longer a central element of the Southern economy. This meant that one of the crucial economic reasons for the highly coercive system of racial domination in the South no longer mattered very much.[5] Taken together, these factors meant that even though the struggles against segregationist laws in the South continued to be met with strong, often violent resistance by Southern whites and their state governments, the civil rights movement gained considerably greater national support than it had earlier. By the late 1950s and early 1960s the federal government began to back these efforts, which resulted in the landmark civil rights legislation of the mid-1960s.

---

[5] For an excellent discussion of the importance of the decline of sharecropping for the eventual destruction of segregation, see David James, "The Transformation of the Southern Racial State: Class and Race Determinants of Local-State Structures," *American Sociological Review* 53 (1988):191–208.

Segregationist laws were eliminated in the 1960s, but legacies of these legal forms of second-class citizenship still exist today. In some parts of the United States a variety of rules concerning voter registration, for example, have the practical effect of reducing the rate of voter registration among African Americans. Most notorious are rules that permanently prevent people convicted of felonies from voting, even after they have fully served their time in prison and on probation or parole. Such rules do not explicitly link disenfranchisement to race; however, they were initially passed, usually at the end of the nineteenth century, as part of the effort of excluding African Americans from the electorate. And they continue to create a lower tier of citizenship closely connected to race because of the much higher rates of imprisonment of African Americans than of whites. Registration rules that require government-issued voter IDs and that raise the costs of voting for poor people also disproportionately affect African Americans. Again, these rules are not officially framed in racial terms, but they have systematic racial effects and the support for such rules is at least in part due to racial hostility. Police practices continue to target racial minorities, especially young African American men, and courts continue to give harsher punishments to African Americans. A young black man driving a car in a white suburb is much more likely to be stopped by police for questioning than is a white man. This is sometimes jokingly referred to as a DWB offense—driving while black. Equally important, a wide range of public policies—from the location of toxic dumps to the funding of education—continue to implicitly assign greater value to the well-being and interests of some citizens over others. As in the case of police practices, such policies are never explicitly framed in racial terms. In these and other ways, vestiges of state-backed second-class citizenship continue to play a role in the structure of racial inequality in the United States.

Noncitizen Labor

The fourth form of racial oppression in American history involves the linkage between race and legal citizenship status. As everyone knows, the United States is a country of immigrants. Aside from Native Americans, everyone who lives in the United States is descended from people who came to North America from other continents sometime in the last few centuries. Starting in the middle of the nineteenth century, some categories of these immigrants were denied legal access to citizenship status. The first instance of this was the importation of Chinese "coolie" labor on the railroads. Large numbers of poor Chinese were brought to the United States by labor recruiters as a source of cheap labor to work on building the railroads in the West and on other large-scale infrastructure projects. Anti-Chinese feelings were generated by the repeated use of Chinese labor as a way of cutting wages of native-born white workers and breaking strikes. Eventually political mobilization against Chinese immigrants led to the Chinese Exclusion Act, which blocked the further immigration of nearly all Chinese and made those Chinese already in the United States permanent aliens, prohibited from obtaining U.S. citizenship. In 1924 other severe restrictions on immigration were enacted, especially focused on prohibiting legal immigration from Asia, Africa, and Latin America. For forty years, until immigration reform in 1965, legal immigration to the United States was almost entirely white.

In the twentieth century, the most important category of racialized noncitizen labor was Hispanic, especially from Mexico. In the period from the early 1940s until 1964, a formal "guest worker program" for Mexican labor existed. The program, generally called the *bracero* (Spanish for "day laborer") program, involved bringing Mexican workers to the United States on contracts to work mainly in agricultural jobs on a seasonal basis without the prospect of becoming citizens. Since the 1970s an increasing flow of illegal immigrants (also called undocumented workers), again particularly from Latin America, have provided a cheap source of labor for American employers. These undocumented workers, who lack full citizenship rights, are particularly vulnerable to extreme forms of exploitation because they cannot join unions or defend themselves in court for various kinds of abuse—from mistreatment on the job and violations of safety conditions to wage violations.[16]

Not all undocumented workers are racial minorities. Canadians and white Europeans are also working in the United States without

---

[16] For a thorough documentation of violations of workplace regulations by employers of undocumented immigrants, see the report by Annette Bernhardt, Siobhan McGrath, and James DeFilippis, *Unregulated Work in the Global City: Employment and Labor Law Violations in New York City* (New York: Brennan Center for Justice, New York University, 2007). The report documents the following violations: wage and hour violations, health and safety violations, workers' compensation violations, retaliation and violation of the right to organize, independent contractor misclassification, employer tax violations, discrimination, and trafficking and forced labor.

legal status. Nevertheless, the intersection of illegal status with race is especially salient because an identifiable racial minority who is an illegal worker is likely to be much more vulnerable. Pressures on employers not to hire illegal immigrants, and on the government to deport them, contribute to more diffuse hostility toward the racial minorities associated with illegal immigration.

Diffuse Discrimination

In a certain sense, all forms of racism involve racial discrimination—that is, treating people differently by virtue of their race. Here we use the term more narrowly to refer to situations in which such discriminatory action is not directly backed by the legal powers of the state. These situations include a wide range of specific practices: employers not hiring or promoting someone on the basis of race, landlords renting only to people from certain racial groups, banks making it more difficult for racial minorities to get loans, salespeople in a store treating African American customers differently from white customers, and so on. Often this kind of private discrimination is difficult to detect because it occurs informally, behind the scenes in the interpersonal encounters and decisions made in everyday life. In contemporary American society, many such behaviors are in fact illegal. They are also very hard to prove, so laws against private discrimination are usually difficult to enforce. Half a century after the passage of civil rights legislation abolishing segregation and guaranteeing voting rights for African Americans, racial discrimination is still a reality in the United States.

Though most white Americans probably regard private acts of discrimination as undesirable, whites generally believe that racial discrimination is largely a thing of the past and that it no longer significantly affects people's lives. Figure 15.3 presents responses by whites and African Americans from 1985 through 2008 to a survey question concerning the importance of discrimination in explaining black-white differences in jobs, income, and housing. For both blacks and whites, the percentage saying that these differences were mainly due to discrimination has declined over time. Yet most blacks still respond yes to this question, compared to only 30 percent of whites. White Americans generally reject the idea that continuing forms of discrimination really constitute a form of oppression requiring serious public

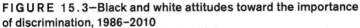

FIGURE 15.3—Black and white attitudes toward the importance of discrimination, 1986–2010

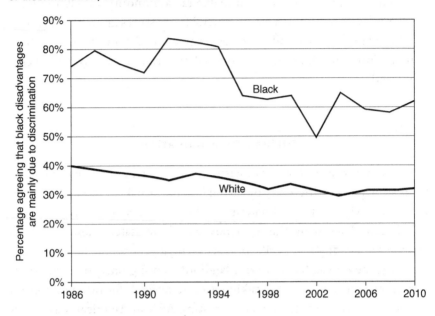

Note: Survey question asked, "On the average (negroes/blacks/African Americans) have worse jobs, income, and housing than white people do. Do you think these differences are mainly due to discrimination?" Percentage who responded yes.
Source: General Social Survey.

policy for its elimination: If African Americans are disproportionately poor, it is because of their behavior and culture, not because of discrimination. If they drop out of school more than whites, it is because of peer pressure and lack of motivation. If young African American men are in prison at six times the rate of young white men, it is because they proportionately commit more crimes. Most white Americans believe that discrimination at most plays a marginal role in any of these conditions.

It is, of course, difficult to get evidence demonstrating precisely how much of the racial inequality we observe is the result of discrimination. We will not attempt to solve this problem here.[17] What we will do in the next section is provide evidence for the continuing importance of discrimination affecting the lives of racial minorities in the United States today.

---

[17] Sometimes social scientists try to get a handle on this problem by examining all of the measurable factors that might affect forms of racial inequality and then treating the amount of inequality left "unexplained" as being the result of direct discrimination. This research strategy is not very convincing, because the results are highly sensitive to how well different factors are measured.

CONTINUING REALITIES OF RACIAL DISCRIMINATION
IN THE TWENTY-FIRST CENTURY

The realities of racial relations in the United States at the beginning of the twenty-first century are the result of the civil rights movement, the dismantling of the apparatus of legal segregation in the 1950s and 1960s and subsequent erosion of many of the cultural and economic supports of racial domination. As we discuss here, racial discrimination remains a significant problem, but it must be understood against the background of extraordinary progress since the 1950s.[18]

Consider the transformations of cultural representations of African Americans. By the 1980s the media began to routinely display positive images of African Americans in television programs like *The Cosby Show*. Black sports stars, singers, and actors had become celebrities within the white population as well as among African Americans. By the 1990s, African Americans began to appear regularly in advertisements sentimentally depicting people in middle-American families, laughing, loving, working, playing. African Americans also began to appear in television programs in roles traditionally filled only by whites—doctors, lawyers, scientists—and in story lines in which race as such was not a central focus. In a popular 2003 movie, *Bruce Almighty*, the black actor Morgan Freeman played God. Books endorsed by Oprah Winfrey became instant best sellers.

Consider the transformation of the economic situation of African Americans. In 1954 the median annual income for black men was 49.8 percent of the median for white men, and the median income for black women was 54.2 percent of the median for white women. In 2012 the comparable figures were 69.8 percent for black men and 91.7 percent for black women.[19]

---

[18] The most influential discussion of the erosion of the structures of racial domination since the 1960s is William Julius Wilson's *The Declining Significance of Race* (Chicago: University of Chicago Press, 1978). Wilson's argument has sometimes been mischaracterized as the emerging insignificance of race, but that is not his claim. Rather, he argues that the lives of disadvantaged African Americans are increasingly shaped by brutal class realities that are rooted in urban economic structures and dysfunctional labor markets rather than directly in forms of racial exclusion and domination.

[19] In the years just before the financial crisis of 2008, the ratios of black:white median annual income reached its highest point: the median annual income of black men was 74 percent of the median for white men in 2006, and the median income for black women was 99.4 percent of the median for white women in 2002. Data are from U.S. Census Bureau—Income. Historical Tables: People. https://www.census.gov/hhes/www/income/data/historical /people/ (accessed March 26, 2014).

The education gap between blacks and whites has narrowed significantly (Figure 15.4): in 1957 whites twenty-five years and older had a high school graduation rate over twice as high as that for blacks—43.3 percent versus 18.4 percent; by 2012 the black rate was nearly the same as the white rate— 85 percent compared to 88 percent. A similar pattern occurs for college degrees: in 1957, just before the major breakthroughs of the civil rights era, 11 percent of whites between the ages of twenty-five and twenty-nine had completed four years of college, compared to 4 percent of blacks; just over half a century later, in 2012, the figures were 31.3 percent and 21.2 percent. The occupational distributions of blacks and whites have also become much more similar since the middle of the twentieth century (Table 15.1). In 1950 only 2 percent of black men in the labor force and 1.3 percent of black women were in managerial jobs, compared to 12 percent of white men and 5 percent of white women. Among men, therefore, blacks were about one-fifth as likely to be managers as whites; among women, blacks were about one-fourth as likely. By 2012, the percentage of black men in the labor force who were managers had risen to 7.6 percent, just over half the percentage for white men; the percentage of black women in managerial jobs had risen to 9.2 percent, about three-fourths of the figure for

FIGURE 15.4—Black and white education levels, 1957–2012

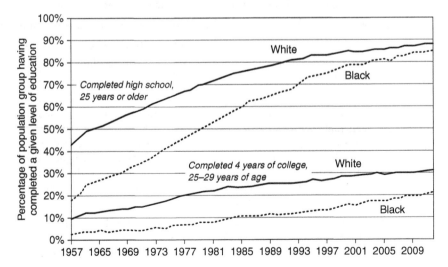

Source: "Table A-2. Percent of People 25 Years and Over Who Have Completed High School or College, by Race, Hispanic Origin and Sex: Selected Years 1940 to 2012" *Current Population Survey, Social and Economic Supplements.*

TABLE 15.1—Occupational distributions within race and gender categories, civilian labor force, 1950–2012 (percentage)

	1950	1960	1970	1980	1990	2000	2012
White Men							
Managerial	11.9	11.9	12.7	12.4	13.3	13.6	14.2
Professional and Technical	6.8	9.1	11.2	13.2	15.2	16.4	17.1
Administrative Support	7.5	7.2	7.4	6.6	6.5	7.4	7.3
Skilled Manual	12.1	13.4	13.4	12.6	11.0	10.6	8.6
Construction, Transport, Extractive	21.0	20.9	20.3	22.4	21.1	20.2	20.1
Unskilled Manual	13.5	13.5	12.2	9.4	7.4	6.6	5.3
Services and Sales	12.2	14.3	16.4	18.5	21.2	21.3	23.1
Farm	15.2	9.7	6.5	4.9	4.3	3.9	4.3
Total	100.0	100.0	100.0	100.0	100.0	100.0	100.0
Black Men							
Managerial	2.1	1.7	3.4	5.0	6.1	6.6	7.6
Professional and Technical	2.0	2.8	4.3	7.0	8.5	9.8	11.5
Administrative Support	3.3	5.0	7.5	8.7	9.7	10.9	10.9
Skilled Manual	3.9	5.2	8.5	8.7	8.0	8.6	6.5
Construction, Transport, Extractive	34.5	35.4	30.6	29.6	27.4	25.1	23.3
Unskilled Manual	13.8	15.8	18.0	14.6	10.6	9.4	7.0
Services and Sales	15.2	18.1	19.7	22.2	26.2	26.6	30.5
Farm	25.1	16.0	8.0	4.1	3.4	2.8	2.7
Total	100.0	100.0	100.0	100.0	100.0	100.0	100.0
White Women							
Managerial	4.9	3.8	4.9	7.0	10.9	11.2	12.2
Professional and Technical	13.1	12.4	13.4	15.9	18.9	22.9	25.6
Administrative Support	29.2	31.9	32.5	30.4	28.0	25.6	21.9
Skilled Manual	2.2	4.2	1.6	1.9	1.7	1.9	1.7
Construction, Transport, Extractive	1.1	0.9	1.7	3.4	3.1	2.5	2.3
Unskilled Manual	19.3	14.1	14.0	8.8	5.9	4.4	2.5
Services and Sales	26.4	30.7	30.8	31.3	30.5	30.6	32.7
Farm	3.8	2.2	1.2	1.3	1.1	1.0	1.1
Total	100.0	100.0	100.0	100.0	100.0	100.0	100.0
Black Women							
Managerial	1.3	1.0	2.3	4.0	6.9	8.0	9.2
Professional and Technical	6.1	6.9	9.1	13.0	14.6	17.2	19.3
Administrative Support	3.9	6.5	17.5	23.7	24.6	23.9	20.8
Skilled Manual	1.1	1.9	1.4	1.9	1.8	2.0	1.6
Construction, Transport, Extractive	1.9	1.5	2.1	4.5	3.8	3.4	3.3
Unskilled Manual	16.3	13.7	16.7	12.9	9.6	7.0	3.7
Services and Sales	58.3	58.1	47.5	38.9	38.1	38.2	41.9
Farm	11.2	10.4	3.4	1.1	0.6	0.4	0.3
Total	100.0	100.0	100.0	100.0	100.0	100.0	100.0

Source: Analysis by Matías Cociña of microdata samples from the Census of population 1950, 1960, 1970, 1980, 1990, and 2000; and microdata samples from the American Community Survey (ACS) 2012, which is the last available data. Variables are used as harmonized by Steven Ruggles, J. Trent Alexander, Katie Genadek, Ronald Goeken, Matthew B. Schroeder, and Matthew Sobek. *Integrated Public Use Microdata Series: Version 5.0* [Machine-readable database]. Minneapolis: University of Minnesota, 2010. Data downloaded from https://usa.ipums.org/usa/ (accessed August 13, 2014).

white women. A roughly similar pattern occurred for other higher-status and desirable occupations.

Consider the transformation of the political role of African Americans. In 1964 there were only 103 black elected public officials in the United States. By 1970, after the main legislation of the civil rights era had been passed, this figure had increased to 1,469. In 2013 there were over 10,500 black elected officials, or about 2 percent of all elected officials. Of these, 641 served in state legislatures, 42 in the U.S. House of Representatives, and 3 in the U.S. Senate. The rest were city and country elected officials.[20]

And the most stunning development of all: the election of Barack Obama as president in 2008. Forty-three percent of white voters voted for a black president. This outcome would have been utterly unthinkable just a few decades earlier.

These are all significant developments. They are not simply superficial, cosmetic changes; they constitute a profound erosion of the structures of racial domination and oppression. An erosion, yes, but not an elimination. In the next section we focus on the incomplete transformation of racial inequality by examining continuing socioeconomic disadvantages of African Americans and certain other racial minorities. We then examine the various forms of discrimination that underwrite these disadvantages. The chapter concludes with a discussion of the problem of affirmative action and the politics of racial equality in the twenty-first century.

Stagnation in the Erosion of Racial Inequality

Some of the figures we have just cited clearly demonstrate the incompleteness of the social transformation of racial inequality and oppression. It is true that in the four decades following the voting rights bill of 1964, black elected officials increased from virtually none to almost 2 percent of all elected officials; however, African Americans constitute about 13 percent of the population, so this is still a large underrepresentation. Occupational distributions among whites and blacks are more similar today than in the 1950s, but there are

[20] The 1964 figure comes from an article by Don Sneed, "Has Anything Changed in 20 Years?" *Chicago Tribune*, July 2, 1988. The 1970 figures come from *The 2010 Statistical Abstract of the United States*, available at http://www.census.gov/compendia/statab/2010/cats/elections /elected_public_officials–characteristics.html (accessed August 13, 2014). The figure for total elected officials in 2013 of 10,500 is based on the number for 2011 in the Black Elected Officials Roster prepared by the Joint Center for Political and Economic Studies. The figures for specific offices in 2013 were provided by the Joint Center for Political and Economic Studies.

still significant gaps among desirable jobs. Furthermore, much of the convergence in distributions occurred in the 1960s and 1970s. Since the 1980s, progress has been much slower. Figure 15.5 illustrates this progress for a number of desirable occupations. For example, the ratio of the percentage of black men in

FIGURE 15.5—Changes in the underrepresentation of African Americans in desirable occupational categories

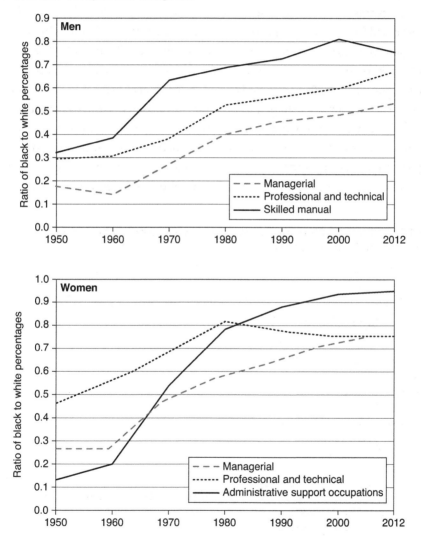

Note: The numbers indicate how likely, within a given gender category, it is for a black compared to a white to be in a given occupation. Thus, 1.0 means that, within a given gender category, it is just as likely for a black to be in a given occupation as for a white; 0.3 means that, within a gender category, the percentage of a given occupation among blacks is only 30 percent the percentage among whites.

Sources: See Table 15.1.

managerial jobs to white men in managerial jobs increased from 17.6 percent to 40.3 percent between 1950 and 1980, and then increased only to 53.5 percent by 2012; for black women, their percentage in managerial jobs relative to white women increased from 26.5 percent in 1950 to 57.1 percent in 1980 and then to 75.4 percent in 2012. In professional and technical jobs the relative percentage of black women actually declined from 1980 to 2012, from 81.8 percent to 75.4 percent.

In terms of economic standing, median income for black families increased from around 50 percent of the median for white families in 1947 to 60 percent in 1967, but it has not changed much since (Figure 15.6). The ratio of black to white wealth, as indicated in Figure 15.7, has improved slightly from the early 1980s to the early 1990s but has declined since then. As of 2010, this was actually slightly lower than it had been three decades earlier.[21] Finally, as we saw in Chapter 13, although the difference in poverty rates among blacks and among whites declined between 1973 and 2000, poverty rates among blacks remain much higher than among whites. Poverty rates for black children remain especially high (Figure 15.8): in 2011, 43 percent of

FIGURE 15.6—Black median family income as a percentage of white median family income, 1947–2010

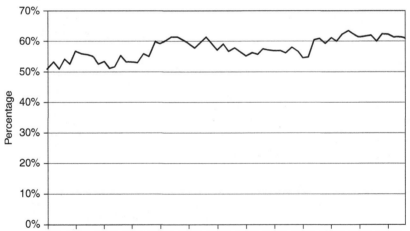

Source: "Black median family income, as a share of white median family income, 1947–2010," *The State of Working America, 2012,* Figure 2D.

---

[21] Racial disparities in financial wealth, which exclude home equity, are even greater than disparities in overall net worth: Black median financial wealth reached a peak of 3 percent of white median financial wealth in 2001, only to decline to well under .5% in 2010. Wolff, Edward N. 2012. "The Asset Price Meltdown and the Wealth of the Middle Class." NBER Working Paper Series 18559, http://www.nber.org/papers/w18559 (accessed April 16, 2014).

FIGURE 15.7—Median net worth by race, 1983–2010

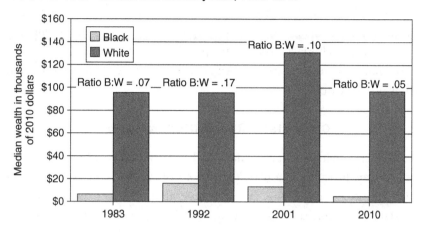

FIGURE 15.8—Child poverty rates by race, 1979–2011

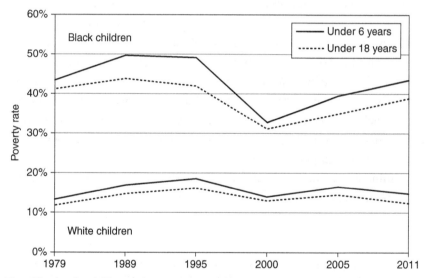

Note: The data for children under age six were unavailable for 2005. The figure reported here is for 2003.

Source: The State of Working America, 2006/2007, Table 6.3; and *The State of Working America, 2012,* Figure 7D.

black children under age six lived below the poverty line, compared to 15 percent of white children.

Taken together, these figures reveal a stark reality in the United States today: tremendous progress has been made in ending racial injustice, but the economic inequalities between blacks and whites remain substantial. The causes for this situation are complex. Some of the inequalities are without doubt simply "legacies" of past injustices. If up to a particular point in time the inequalities were due to legally enforced forms of oppression, and then those legal forms were destroyed, it would still take an extended period of time for the inequalities to disappear *even if* there was no ongoing discrimination. This fact has led many people to believe that discrimination is no longer a significant issue in American life. As we shall see, however, that is not the case.

Contexts of Racial Discrimination

Racial discrimination remains a daily and pervasive fact of life in the United States today. It occurs in a wide variety of institutional contexts and takes many forms. Here we will focus on several contexts of discrimination: mundane micro-interactions, "driving while black," housing, credit markets, employment, education, and the criminal justice system.

Mundane Micro-interactions

Perhaps the most pervasive form of discrimination occurs in the context of ordinary, daily interactions on the street, at work, in stores, or in class-rooms. This kind of discrimination is often difficult for an outside observer to detect, but it can be acutely felt by the person being subjected to it. A Gallup poll conducted in 1997 reported that about half of black respondents said that in the previous month they had experienced at least one form of such discrimination in daily interactions, and according to a 2012 *Newsweek/Daily Beast* poll, 74 percent of blacks have personally felt they were being discriminated against because of their race.[22] Here are some well-documented forms that this discrimination can take:[23]

---

[22] Survey by Gallup Organization, January 4–February 28, 1997. Reported by Christopher Doob in "On Race, Americans Only Talk a Good Game; For Whites, Confusion," *New York Times*, November 19, 1997. The *Newsweek/Daily Beast* poll is reported at http://www.thedailybeast .com/articles/2012/04/07/newsweek-daily-beast-poll-finds-majorities-of-americans-think -country-divided-by-race.html (accessed August 12, 2014).

[23] These examples are drawn mainly from the following sources: Devah Pager and Hana Shepherd, "The Sociology of Discrimination: Racial Discrimination in Employment, Housing, Credit, and Consumer Markets," *Annual Review of Sociology* 34 (2008): 181–209; Joe R. Feagin, "The Continuing Significance of Race: Antiblack Discrimination in Public Places," *American Sociological Review* 56, no. 1 (1991): 101–16; and William A. Smith, Walter R. Allen, and Lynette L. Danley, "'Assume the Position . . . You Fit the Description': Psychosocial Experiences and Racial Battle Fatigue among African American Male College Students," *American Behavioral Scientist* 51 (2007) 551.

- In stores, black customers are more likely than are white customers to be monitored and treated with suspicion by store employees concerned about shoplifting. This is not simply the case for teenagers, but also for middle-class, well-dressed African Americans.
- White people walking on city streets frequently cross the street when there is a black man behind them or to avoid passing a black man.
- Many middle-class blacks report the experience of having to wait longer to be served in restaurants than do white customers who arrive after them.
- In a study of black male college students at elite, historically white universities, the research participants reported many incidents of surveillance by campus police in which they were treated with suspicion and asked for their IDs.
- It takes, on average, longer for a black man to get a taxi than it does for a white man. This can happen even when the man is well dressed and clearly affluent. A famous incident was reported in the *New York Times*: "But the actor Danny Glover was not laughing last month when several taxis declined to pick him up in Manhattan, presumably because Mr. Glover is black and stands 6 feet 4 inches tall. In lower Manhattan, the actor was forced to hide in the shadows while his daughter did the hailing. The driver had to be cajoled into unlocking the doors."

Any given incident may seem petty, but cumulatively these kinds of interactions constitute a stream of lived experiences that communicate denigration and a lack of social respect. Psychological research shows that these kinds of experiences can have a significant impact on morale and self-esteem. In perhaps the best-known experiment on the impact of discrimination and denigration, Jane Elliott, then a schoolteacher in Iowa, subjected students in her elementary class to systematic discrimination on the basis of eye color: brown eyes were superior, blue eyes inferior. After two days of this treatment, the blue-eyed group performed much more poorly on a simple math test than did the advantaged group. When the same experiment was conducted using adults, the results were the same.[24] The experience of repeated social disrespect generates forms of stress, anxiety, and self-doubt that significantly undermine performance.

[24] Jane Elliott's experiments are presented in two documentary films: *Eye of the Storm* and *A Class Divided*. For a discussion of these films, see a review by Anthony J. Cortese in *Teaching Sociology* 15, no. 4 (1987): 450–52.

"Driving while Black"

One of the best-documented forms of ongoing discrimination is traffic stops by police for the "offense" that is ironically called DWB—driving while black. A report by the Leadership Conference on Civil Rights provides systematic evidence that this practice is widespread:[25]

- Under a federal court consent decree, traffic stops by Maryland Police on Interstate 95 were monitored. In the two-year period from January 1995 to December 1997, about 70 percent of the drivers stopped and searched by the police were black, while only 17.5 percent of overall drivers—as well as speeders—were black.

- In Volusia County, Florida, in 1992, nearly 70 percent of those stopped on a particular interstate highway in Central Florida were black or Hispanic, although only 5 percent of the drivers on that highway were black or Hispanic. Moreover, minorities were detained for longer periods of time per stop than were whites, and 80 percent of the cars that were searched after being stopped had nonwhite drivers.

- A study of traffic stops on the New Jersey Turnpike found that 46 percent of those stopped were black, although overall only 13.5 percent of the cars had a black driver or passenger, and there was no significant difference in driving patterns of white and nonwhite motorists.

- A Louisiana State Police Department training film specifically encouraged the department's officers to initiate pretextual stops against "males of foreign nationalities, mainly Cubans, Colombians, Puerto Ricans and other swarthy outlanders."

- In 1992, as part of a report by the ABC news program *20/20*, two cars—one filled with young black men, the other with young white men—navigated the same route, in the same car, at the same speed through L.A. city streets on successive nights. The car filled with young black men was stopped by the police several times during the drive; the white group was not stopped once, despite observing police cars in their immediate area no less than sixteen times during the evening.

- A July 2008 *New York Times*/CBS News poll asked a national random sample of adults, "Have you ever felt you were stopped by the police

[25] *Justice on Trial: Racial Disparities in the American Criminal Justice System* (Washington, DC: The Leadership Conference on Civil Rights, 2000), 2. The sources for each of these examples are given in the report.

because of your race or ethnic background?" Sixty-six percent of black men responded affirmatively, compared to only 9 percent of white men.

This kind of racial profiling subjects many innocent people to the humiliating experience of being hassled by the police for no good reason. It also contributes to the disproportionate arrest of young black men for nonviolent drug crimes, because these racially motivated traffic stops are frequently accompanied by searches that result in arrests that otherwise would not have occurred.

Housing

Housing segregation is a reality in the United States. In northern cities in the 1980s, on average over 80 percent of people would have had to move to different neighborhoods in order for their city to have random housing patterns.[26] In 1990 the levels of segregation were as high as they had been at the beginning of the twentieth century.[27] Although research indicates that since 1980 residential segregation has declined slightly, most American cities remain highly segregated along racial lines. This pattern of segregation is the result of four interconnected factors.

First, there is certainly some historic inertia from past practices. Until the civil rights era, in many cities real estate agents would simply refuse to show blacks houses in white neighborhoods. Until the 1974 Equal Opportunity Credit Act, redlining (the practice of banks not making loans to people in certain parts of cities) was legal in the United States, and this factor certainly contributed to housing segregation. Even with no further discrimination, these past practices would account for some of the existing segregation of American cities.

Second, a certain amount of self-segregation also occurs. African Americans may buy houses in predominantly black neighborhoods because it is more socially comfortable, less of a struggle, less likely to involve hostile interactions with neighbors. Although self-segregation does not directly involve discrimination in the housing market as such, nevertheless it reflects the ongoing realities of racial hostility. According to Lincoln Quillian, "On surveys, most

[26] Douglas S. Massey and Nancy A. Denton, *American Apartheid: Segregation and the Making of the Underclass* (Cambridge, MA: Harvard University Press, 1993), p. 63.

[27] Pager and Shepherd, "The Sociology of Discrimination," p. 188.

Whites say they prefer neighborhoods that are less than 30% Black. . . . African Americans, on the other hand, strongly prefer neighborhoods that are 50% Black. These surveys suggest that Blacks prefer much more integrated neighborhoods than do Whites, but not entirely White neighborhoods."[28]

Third, housing segregation is generated by what is known as *white flight*—the tendency for whites to move out of a neighborhood once a few black families move in. White flight need not indicate that most whites are averse to living in a neighborhood with some black residents, but simply that they do not want to live in a neighborhood with many black neighbors. The reasons for these preferences are varied: For some it is directly a question of racist attitudes, but for many the issue may be more about concerns for long-term housing values. Even if many white homeowners have no personal problem at all with living next to African American families, they may worry that increasing black residency will depress home prices; and given that homes are for most people their only form of wealth, this concern may lead them to move. As a result, once African Americans begin moving into a previously all-white neighborhood, there can be a cascade of white exits.[29] Even though the "tipping point" for white flight may have changed—there was a time when having a single black family on a block could trigger an exodus of white families—white flight remains a continual problem in the segregation of neighborhoods in many cities.

Finally, there is strong evidence that active discriminatory practices continue to exist in housing markets. This ongoing discrimination is best demonstrated by what are called housing audit studies. In this kind of research, home buyers of different races, but with identical credit ratings and income, go to real estate agents for help in buying a house. The key issue is whether, and in what ways, these prospective home buyers receive

---

[28] Lincoln Quillian, "Why Is Black-White Residential Segregation So Persistent? Evidence on Three Theories from Migration Data," *Social Science Research* 31 (2002): 199.

[29] This kind of cascade was first systematically analyzed by the economist Thomas Schelling. Suppose there is a distribution of preferences within an all-white community about how many black residents are acceptable. Some white residents say they will leave if any blacks move into the neighborhood, some will leave if there are 3 percent blacks, and for others the thresholds are 5 percent, 10 percent, 20 percent, and so on. Depending on the distribution of such thresholds, a single black moving into a neighborhood can set in motion a cascade of exits, so eventually the entire neighborhood shifts from all white to all black. See Thomas Schelling, "A Process of Residential Segregation: Neighborhood Tipping," in *Racial Discrimination in Economic Life*, ed. A. Pascal (Lexington, MA: D.C. Heath, 1972), pp. 157–84.

differential treatment on the basis of race. Devah Pager and Hana Shepherd summarize the results of a series of large housing audit studies by the U.S. Department of Housing and Urban Development:

> The study results reveal bias across multiple dimensions, with blacks experiencing consistent adverse treatment in roughly one in five housing searches and Hispanics experiencing consistent adverse treatment in roughly one out of four housing searches (both rental and sales). Measured discrimination took the form of less information offered about units, fewer opportunities to view units, and, in the case of home buyers, less assistance with financing and steering into less wealthy communities and neighborhoods with a higher proportion of minority residents.[30]

Credit Markets

We have already shown that as a category, white Americans are much wealthier than African Americans: whites have greater savings, they own more stocks, they have greater equity in their homes. Because assets that can be used as collateral play an important role in getting loans, this wealth difference would be expected to directly translate into racial differences in the credit market. In addition to this situation, however, there is good evidence that African Americans face discrimination in acquiring loans. Again, audit studies are the clearest evidence for this practice. Black testers with the same credit histories, wealth, and income as white testers are

> less likely to receive a quote for a loan than are white testers and . . . are given less time with the loan officer, are quoted higher interest rates, and are given less coaching and less information than are comparable white applicants. . . . In two audit studies in which creditworthy testers approached subprime lenders, whites were more likely to be referred to the lenders' prime borrowing division than were similar black applicants. Further, subprime lenders quoted the black applicants very high rates, fees, and closing costs that were not correlated with risk.[31]

Similar problems exist in credit markets for small business loans.

---

[30] Pager and Shepherd, "The Sociology of Discrimination," p. 188.

[31] Ibid., p. 190.

■ *Employment*

Employment discrimination is difficult to demonstrate because hiring decisions are made in private. Large-scale statistical studies attempt to compare the probabilities of people of different races holding a given kind of job, adjusting these probabilities for a long list of characteristics—age, education, skills, test scores, gender, and so on. Generally, even after applying a long list of controls, these studies find that whites are advantaged relative to blacks. Critics of such research, however, can always say that some unmeasured, salient characteristic of the people explains the racial gap.

This is why audit studies of hiring are valuable, for they make it possible to more carefully control for individual characteristics other than race. In one well-known study, racially identifiable names were used as the way to signal race to prospective employers. As the title of the published paper from the research asked, "Are Emily and Greg more employable than Lakisha and Jamal?"[32] Résumés that were otherwise substantively identical were sent to employers to see how they would react to the different names. The callback rate for white names was 50 percent higher than for black names. Even more surprisingly, this difference increased with the level of qualifications of the résumés—the racial gap in callbacks increased with skill level.

In a second study, Devah Pager trained black and white male testers to apply in person for entry-level, low-wage jobs in Milwaukee, Wisconsin.[33] Half of the testers had résumés indicating that they had served eighteen months in prison for a nonviolent drug offense, and half did not. In other respects the résumés indicated equal education and job experience. The study thus involved four "types" of people: white felons, black felons, white non-felons, and black non-felons. Again, the empirical question is, how different across these categories are the rates at which the applicants were called back for an interview? Figure 15.9 presents the results: 34 percent of the whites without prison records received callbacks, compared to 17 percent of the whites with prison records, 14 percent of the blacks without records, and 4 percent of the blacks with records. In other words, in the labor market a white male with a prison record and a black male without a prison record have roughly the same disadvantages.

---

[32] Marianne Bertrand and Sendhil Mullainathan, "Are Emily and Greg More Employable than Lakisha and Jamal? A Field Experiment on Labor Market Discrimination," NBER Working Paper 9873 (Cambridge, MA: National Bureau of Economic Research, 2003).

[33] Devah Pager, *Marked: Race, Crime, and Finding Work in an Era of Mass Incarceration* (Chicago: University of Chicago Press, 2007).

FIGURE 15.9—The effects of race and criminal record on employment

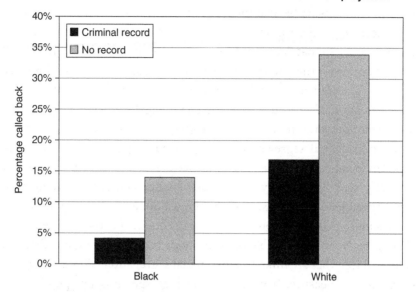

Note: The graph presents the percentage of job applicants to entry-level unskilled jobs who were called back for an interview depending upon their race and criminal record (nonviolent drug conviction).

Source: Devah Pager, *Marked: Race, Crime, and Finding Work in an Era of Mass Incarceration* (Chicago: University of Chicago Press, 2007).

These studies unequivocally indicate that active discrimination exists in labor markets. This does not mean that the employers in question personally dislike African Americans, or even that they believe people of one race are somehow inferior to another. Much of this discrimination is probably what economists call *statistical discrimination*. Employers believe that the average black worker will be less capable or reliable than the average white worker. This view need not be due to the employers' belief in the inherent intellectual inferiority of blacks. It can be because they believe the quality of schooling of the average black worker is inferior to that of the average white worker. The important point is the employers' belief that the average member of one racial category is less desirable as an employee than the average member of another category. Because it is difficult and costly to get accurate information about the actual reliability and competence of any given individual, employers rely on these perceived group differences to make individual hiring decisions. This strategy is perfectly rational and economically efficient, even if it is morally unjustified and harmful. The result is discrimination.

Education

Education has always been at the heart of conflicts over race. The key civil rights decision by the Supreme Court in the 1950s was over racial segregation in schools. In that decision, *Brown v. Board of Education* (1954), the Court rejected decisively the doctrine of "separate but equal" education for black and white children, arguing that *separate* was inherently unequal.

More than half a century after the end of legal segregation, schools in many American cities remain sharply segregated, largely as a by-product of extreme residential segregation. This problem is particularly evident in large American cities, where the confluence of race and poverty means that inner-city schools typically have much higher concentrations of poor minority students than do suburban schools. Equally troubling, however, is not simply the racial concentration of schools, but the differences in funding between the schools of many poor black children and those of white children that are linked to this spatial segregation. This is not a simple matter to measure. If we look at average spending per pupil across school districts within states, weighted by the number of students in different racial and ethnic groups, then it seems that on average most states show no difference in the per-pupil spending on black and white children.[34] This method assumes, however, that within districts all students receive the same per capita funding. This is simply not the case. A study of within-district spending on specific schools in Baltimore, Cincinnati, and Seattle "indicated district funding differences for high- and low-poverty schools ranging from $400,000 to $1 million."[35] These discrepancies were explained this way:

> Districts often allocate a certain number of staff to a school, rather than giving schools a per student amount for staff compensation. As teachers gain experience, they often take advantage of seniority rules to move to more affluent schools where students are perceived as easier to teach. . . . This can lead to more experienced teachers clustering at low-poverty schools with vacancies at schools serving underserved populations filled by new teachers. As a result, new teachers (who have much lower salaries than experienced teachers) work disproportionately in schools in the poorest neighborhoods. Because of the large range in staff pay, schools with the

[34] Kim Rueben and Sheila Murray, "Racial Disparities in Education Finance: Going Beyond Equal Revenues" (Washington, DC: Tax Policy Center, Urban Institute, and Brookings Institution, Discussion Paper No. 29, November 2008), p. 5.

[35] Ibid., p. 7.

highest needs within a district often receive substantially less funding because they employ the least experienced teachers.[36]

As a result, even though spending per pupil may be roughly equalized across districts within a state,

> resources (including experience and qualification levels of teachers) vary dramatically across schools serving high- and low-income (and white and nonwhite) students. Schools serving low-income students typically have a larger percentage of inexperienced and non-credentialed teachers, and the variation in teacher qualifications is greater in large urban districts than in the state as a whole.[37]

The national per-pupil spending between blacks and whites also masks very large discrepancies between wealthy white suburban school districts and urban districts with high concentrations of poor black students.[38] Figure 15.10 illustrates this discrepancy for wealthy suburban schools and urban schools in New York and Chicago in 2010–2011. This large funding gap is partially the result of lower property values and thus less tax resources as these factors intersect patterns of housing segregation and discrimination. School funding, however, is never such a simple matter; it also depends on the balance of political forces over how schools should be funded. As long as schools are funded substantially by local property taxes, wealthy communities will have better-funded schools than will poor communities. The unwillingness of state legislatures to fundamentally rethink the way schools are funded and create a genuinely uniform, egalitarian structure of funding is partially the result of ideological commitments to local control, but it is also shaped by the racial and class implications of creating more universalistic principles. However, even if the underlying motives of politicians and voters are not themselves shaped by racial considerations, the effect is serious discrimination in the opportunities for good-quality education of black children.

---

[36] Ibid., p. 8.

[37] Ibid.

[38] The issue here is that schools are considerably cheaper to run in small towns and cities than in large cities—not because the quality of education being provided is lower, but because the cost of living is lower and thus salaries and other expenses are lower. Black children are concentrated in large cities where costs of living and teacher salaries are higher. On a statewide level, high-spending white suburban districts are counterbalanced by lower-spending white school districts in smaller cities and towns, thus making it seem that overall per capita spending on black and white children is about the same.

FIGURE 15.10—Per-pupil education spending in core cities and wealthy suburbs, New York City and Chicago areas, 2010–2011

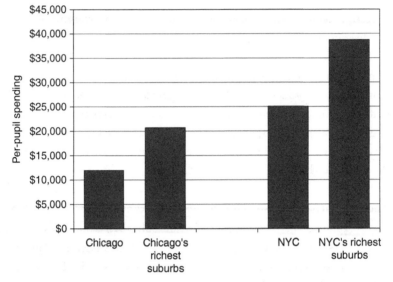

Notes: (1) All figures are per-pupil total spending in 2010/11 dollars. Total spending includes both instructional spending and noninstructional spending. (2) *Richest suburbs* are defined as the highest-spending 5 percent of districts in New York and in Illinois. These turn out without exception to be districts in relatively close proximity to New York City and Chicago, respectively, and are thus designated the rich suburbs in the graph. (Analysis provided by Edo Navot.)

Source: National Center for Education Statistics, U.S. Department of Education, Institute of Education Sciences, "Common Core of Data" for academic year 2010–11, *Data sheet: "School expenditure per pupil."* http://nces.ed.gov/ccd/elsi/expressTables.aspx (accessed August 25, 2014).

Criminal Justice

Of all the domains in which we have discussed the persistence of discrimination, the criminal justice system is perhaps the most difficult to nail down. Here is the problem: it is easy enough to demonstrate that African Americans are arrested for criminal activity, convicted, and sent to prison at much higher rates than are whites, but it is more difficult to demonstrate that racial discrimination inside of the criminal justice system is directly implicated in each of these disparities. African American men have nearly seven times the rate of imprisonment of white men, but theoretically this could simply be because they commit proportionately seven times as many crimes. Racism could still be implicated in shaping the social and economic conditions that lead to such criminal behavior, but racial discrimination inside of the criminal justice system would not be a significant factor. We will first look at the basic data on racial disparities, and then examine the problem of discrimination.

Figure 15.11 presents imprisonment rates by race in 2010. Overall, the rate for blacks is 2.2 percent (2,207 prisoners per 100,000 people), 5.8 times greater than the white rate of 0.38 percent. The racial disproportion is even greater among men—especially young men between ages twenty-five and twenty-nine, for whom the imprisonment rate among blacks is 8.9 percent, 6.2 times greater than the 1.4 percent rate for white men in the same age group. If the rates that occurred in the last quarter of the twentieth century were to persist into the future, the lifetime probability of an African American man spending time in prison would be 32 percent, compared to 11 percent for all men (Figure 15.12).

These incarceration rates reflect the outcome of the process through which people move through the criminal justice system. This process has four principal steps: first, an offender needs to be arrested; second, an arrested person needs to be charged and prosecuted or released without charge; third, a prosecuted person need to be tried and convicted or acquitted;

FIGURE 15.11—Incarceration rates by race and age, 2010

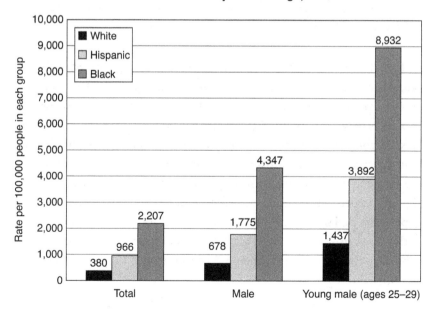

Source: Peter Wagner, "Incarceration is not an equal opportunity punishment," Prison Policy Initiative (2012). http://www.prisonpolicy.org/articles/notequal.html (accessed March 24, 2014).

FIGURE 15.12–Lifetime chances of being sent to prison

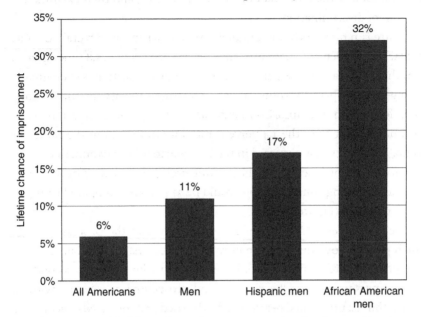

Note: These estimates of the lifetime chance of imprisonment are based on the rates of imprisonment for different groups of people during the last quarter of the twentieth century. Of course, if these rates were to change significantly, then these estimates would need to be revised.

Source: Thomas P. Bonczar, "Prevalence of Imprisonment in the U.S. Population, 1974–2001," Bureau of Justice Statistics Special Report NCJ 197976 (August 2003), available at http://bjs.ojp.usdoj.gov /content/pub/pdf/piuspo1.pdf (accessed August 13, 2014).

and fourth, a convicted felon needs to be sentenced to prison or probation. Figure 15.13 shows the percentage of African Americans at some of these steps for drug offenses. The proportion of regular users of illegal drugs who are black is very close to the proportion of the population as a whole who are black: In 2012, blacks were roughly 13 percent of the U.S. population and about 14 percent of regular drug users in 2011. When we look at the percentages for people within the criminal justice system, the picture is entirely different: 32 percent of people arrested for drug offenses, 41 percent of the people convicted of drug crimes, and 43 percent of the people sent to prison for those offenses in 2011 were black.[39] Blacks clearly have a much higher probability than do whites of being sent to prison if they are arrested for drug offenses.

[39] The figure for drug offense convictions is for 2008, the most recent year for which that information is available.

FIGURE 15.13—Black share of drug use and punishment, 2011

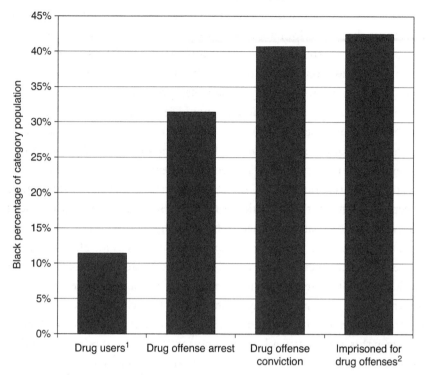

Notes: (1) Data for drug users are for 2012. (2) Percentage for imprisonment for drug offenses calculated over white, black, and Hispanic population only.

Sources: Drug use: drugwarfacts.org. "Drug Use Estimates." http://www.drugwarfacts.org/cms /Drug_Usage#Demographic (accessed August 22, 2014). Drug offense arrest: Snyder, H. and Mulako-Wangota, J., Arrest Data Analysis Tool at www.bjs.gov. Bureau of Justice Statistics, Washington, D.C. http://www.bjs.gov/index.cfm?ty=datool&surl=/arrests/index.cfm# (accessed August 23, 2014). Drug offense convictions: Carson, Ann E. and Daniela Golinelli. 2013. "Prisoners in 2012—Advance Counts," Bureau of Justice Statistics. http://www.bjs.gov/content/pub/pdf/p12ac.pdf (accessed August 23, 2014). Imprisoned for drug offenses: Carson, Ann E. and Daniela Golinelli. 2013. "Prisoners in 2012. Trends in Admissions and Releases, 1991–2012," Table 8. http://www.bjs.gov /content/pub/pdf/p12tar9112.pdf (accessed August 23, 2014).

These data certainly show large racial disparities throughout the process that leads to incarceration. Racial discrimination of various forms could play an important role in generating these disparities at every step of the process: racial biases and racial profiling by police could lead to disproportionate surveillance and arrests of blacks, racial biases during the processing of arrests could lead to more prosecutions of blacks, racial biases within court proceedings could lead to more convictions, and racial biases in sentencing could lead to more incarceration. But it is not easy to get solid, unequivocal statistical evidence for the magnitudes of such possible effects of racial bias. And even with good data, it is often very difficult to draw solid inferences about discrimination and bias from the results. Here is one illustration of the interpretative problem: Studies of racial bias in sentencing generally include some measure of the "prior record" of offenses of a convicted felon. It seems perfectly reasonable, after all, that a person with a longer record of criminal convictions should receive a harsher sentence. On this basis, it is assumed that if a black defendant and a white defendant who are convicted of the same crime with the same prior record get the same sentence, then no racial bias was involved in sentencing. This result would not, of course, rule out biases at earlier stages in the process; but at the stage of sentencing itself, there would be no bias. However, if significant racial biases are found in patterns of arrest, filing charges, prosecution, and conviction, and on average they generate longer prior records for blacks than for whites, then the sheer fact that prior records are treated in the same way for blacks and whites itself embodies a racial bias. The judge in the courtroom who hands out the sentence may personally not be racially biased in any way, but the basis on which the sentence is made could still embody a racial bias.[40]

Given this kind of difficulty, it is important to be cautious in interpreting the results of statistical analyses of convictions and sentencing, and it should not be surprising that the results of different studies are inconsistent. A comprehensive review of this research, published in 2000, characterizes the problem this way:

> Critics of the sentencing process contend that crimes by racial minorities are punished more harshly than similar crimes by equally culpable whites. Other scholars challenge this assertion. They contend that the harsher sentences imposed on racial minorities reflect the seriousness of their crimes and prior criminal records as well as other legally relevant factors that judges consider in determining the appropriate sentence.

---

[40] The problem of interpretation here is similar to some issues in assessing the relationship between test scores and admissions to academic programs. Suppose, for example, that middle-class students who take the SAT test have all taken expensive private courses on how to do well on the test, and these courses on average raise test scores by 100 points, while poor students never get such special training. If an admissions committee at a university treats the scores of these students identically, a good argument can be made that this treatment of test scores constitutes a class bias in admissions. A score of 1400 for the middle-class student *means* "1300 + a Kaplan course," whereas the same score for a poor student means "1400." The same can be said about prior criminal records for black and white defendants.

The findings of more than 40 years of research examining the effect of race on sentencing have not resolved this debate. Some studies have shown that racial/ethnic minorities are sentenced more harshly than whites, even after crime seriousness, prior criminal record, and other legal variables are taken into account. Other studies have found either no significant racial differences or that blacks are treated more leniently than whites. Still other research has concluded that race influences sentence severity *indirectly* through its effect on variables such as bail status, type of attorney, or type of disposition, or that race *interacts* with other variables and affects sentence severity only in some types of cases, in some types of settings, or for some types of defendants.[41]

Still, despite these problems and inconsistencies, this review concludes that the preponderance of evidence suggests racial biases within the criminal sentencing:

The findings of these studies suggest that race and ethnicity do play an important role in contemporary sentencing decisions. Black and Hispanic offenders—and particularly those who are young, male, or unemployed—are more likely than their white counterparts to be sentenced to prison; in some jurisdictions, they also receive longer sentences or differential benefits from guideline departures than do similarly situated white offenders. There is evidence that other categories of racial minorities—those convicted of drug offenses, those who accumulate more serious prior criminal records, those who victimize whites, or those who refuse to plead guilty or are unable to secure pretrial release—also are singled out for harsher treatment.[42]

In some special instances, clear and unequivocal evidence of racism within the criminal justice system can be found. One of these we have already noted: the research on systematic police biases in disproportionately stopping black motorists. Because the offense in these cases is easy to observe—speeding or erratic driving—it is possible to directly measure the extent to which police treat black and white motorists differently. The evidence is unequivocal: though they were not more likely to speed than were white drivers, black drivers were much more likely to be stopped and questioned by the police.

---

[41] Cassia C. Spohn, "Thirty Years of Sentencing Reform: The Quest for a Racially Neutral Sentencing Process," *Criminal Justice* 3 (2000): 429. (Internal references have been deleted from the passage.)

[42] Ibid., pp. 481–82.

A second powerful piece of evidence comes from a study of the death sentences in murder convictions. In this research, photos of convicted murderers in death penalty states were obtained, and people unconnected with the research were asked to rate the photos in terms of how stereotypically "black" they looked. The defendants were then divided into two categories: those who closely fit the stereotype of a black appearance and those who less closely fit the stereotype. The question then was whether these two groups of convicted murderers differed in the likelihood of getting a death sentence. The analysis adjusted these likelihoods for six nonracial factors that are known to strongly affect death sentences, including aggravating and mitigating circumstances, the severity of the murder, and various personal characteristics. The results are striking (Figure 15.14): when the victim is white, 57.5 percent of the black defendants whose appearance more closely fit the black racial stereotype were given the death sentence compared to only 24.4 percent of black defendants whose appearance fit that stereotype less well. When the victim was black, there was no difference in the percentages of these two categories receiving the death sentence.

Beyond the question of the forms of possible racial discrimination within the internal operation of the criminal justice system, one other critical problem of racial bias has powerfully affected the rate of incarceration of African American men during the last two decades of the twentieth century: the "war on drugs" and the targeting of minority communities for drug-related

FIGURE 15.14—Black racial stereotypes and the death sentence

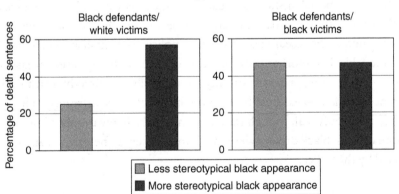

Source: Jennifer L. Eberhardt, Paul G. Davies, Valerie J. Purdie-Vaughns, and Sheri Lynn Johnson, "Looking Deathworthy: Perceived Stereotypicality of Black Defendants Predicts Capital-Sentencing Outcomes," *Psychological Science* 15, no. 5 (2006): 383–86.

arrests. The war on drugs was a centerpiece of the get-tough-on-crime poli-cies championed by conservative political forces beginning in the 1970s and gaining ascendancy in the 1980s. A strong belief in the effectiveness of highly repressive strategies in combating crime and disorder is a hallmark of con-servative politics. In the last quarter of the twentieth century, all aspects of a repressive response to crime increased: prison sentences became more likely for convictions; sentences became longer, particularly for repeat offenders; parole violations were more harshly punished; judicial discretion for mitigating circumstances was reduced. The result was a rapid, massive increase in the prison population in the United States (Figure 15.15). In the half century before 1980 the incarceration rate was relatively stable, hovering

FIGURE 15.15—U.S. incarceration rates and total number of inmates. Sentenced inmates in prisons (1925–2012) and total population in custody in jails and prisons (1980–2011)

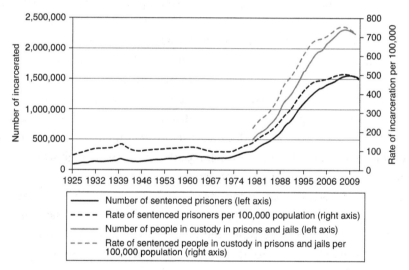

Note: Rates for prison and jail inmates are not reported in the original series for years prior to 1990. The series is thus imputed for 1980–1989 by dividing the data on number of people in custody series by the population total. The population total is implicit in the sentenced prisoners series and can be obtained by dividing the number of sentenced prisoners by the rate of sentenced prisoners, times 100,000.

Source: "Sourcebook of Criminal Justice Statistics Online." http://www.albany.edu/sourcebook/, Table 6.13.2011 "Number and rate (per 100,000 U.S. residents) of persons in custody of state and federal prisons and local jails, U.S. 1985, 1990–2011"; Table 6.1.201 "Adults on probation, in jail or prison, and on parole, U.S. 1980–2011"; Table 6.28.2012 "Number and rate (per 100,000 resident population in each group) of sentenced prisoners under jurisdiction of state and federal correctional authorities on December 31, by sex, U.S. 1925–2012." Earlier version of graph from Bruce Western, *Punishment and Inequality in America* (New York: Russell Sage Foundation, 2006), p.13.

around 100 prisoners per 100,000 population. This rate changed dramatically around 1980, rising rapidly to well over 500 prisoners per 100,000 by the early 2000s. If jail inmates are added to this calculation, the total incarceration rate increased from around 200 to over 700 in this same period.

The law enforcement policies that fueled this rise in the prison population affected all categories of crime, but the increased severity of punishment was most dramatic for offenses connected to the war on drugs. In the 1980s, arrests for drug offenses rose by 125 percent, over four times as much as for other crimes. Even more critically, the rate of prison admissions per arrest for drug crimes increased much more rapidly than for other crimes (Figure 15.16): In 1980, only 2 out of every 100 people arrested for a drug crime were sent to prison. This figure increased fivefold to 10 prison admissions for every 100 arrests in 1990. In comparison, for violent crimes in this period, the increase was from 13 to 17 prison admissions per 100 arrests; for property crime, the increase was from 6 to 10 admissions. As a result, the incarceration rate for drug offenses soared from 8 prisoners per 100,000 population in 1980, to 59 in 1990, to 86 in 2001, and then to 101 in 2010—more than 12 times the rate in 1980. By comparison, incarceration rates for property crimes in 2010 were only 2.7 times greater than three decades earlier and incarceration rates for violent crimes four times greater.[43]

In principle, this increased repressiveness of the criminal justice system directed against drug use need not have disproportionately affected blacks. After all, the black population does not use drugs at higher rates than does the white population. Research on self-reported drug use by high school students from 1980 to 2000 consistently shows significantly higher rates of use among white students than among black students, and studies of hospital emergency room visits for drug-related emergencies indicate that "whites had roughly twice to three times the number of drug-related emergency room visits than blacks."[44] So, if the law enforcement efforts were strictly a response to drug activity, then the impact would not have been so focused on blacks and other minorities.

Figures 15.17 and 15.18 show the disproportionate impact of the war on drugs on African Americans. The graph in Figure 15.17 shows that in the

---

[43] Data from Bruce Western, *Punishment and Inequality in America* (New York: Russell Sage Foundation, 2006), chap. 1; and from "Correctional Populations in the United States, 2010" (Washington, DC: Bureau of Justice Statistics).

[44] Western, *Punishment and Inequality in America*, p. 47.

FIGURE 15.16—Indicators of increasing intensity of punishments for drug offenses

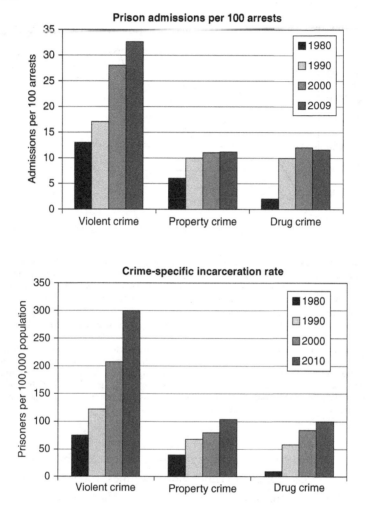

Note: Prison admissions data are from 2009.

Source: 1980–2000 data are from Bruce Western, *Punishment and Inequality in America*, p. 45. 2010 data: Arrest data are from *Crime in the United States: 2010* (U.S. Department of Justice, Criminal Justice Information Services Division); prison population and admissions data are from *Correctional Populations in the United States, 2010* and *Prison Admissions, 2009* (Washington, DC: Bureau of Justice Statistics).

mid-1970s, the black-white ratio for drug arrests was less than 2:1. Beginning around 1980, this inequality rose rapidly, so that by 1990 the ratio was over 4:1. This increased inequality in arrest rates, combined with the general increased likelihood of prison sentences for drug convictions, led to a strong rise in racial inequality in imprisonment for drug crimes. Figure 15.18

FIGURE 15.17—Arrests for drug offenses, 1965–2012

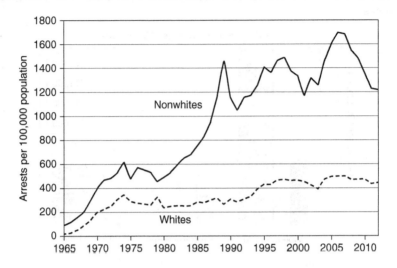

Note: In order to calculate the ratio, the FBI provides the population coverage of their crime data. The coverage data are not available after 2001. We thus impute the population coverage by using the average coverage for previous years. From 1995 to 2001 the U.S. population covered by the Uniform Crime Reporting (UCR) statistics averages 74.14 percent, which is the rate we use for 2002–2012.

Source: 1965–1992 series: Federal Bureau of Investigation. 1993. "Age-Specific Arrest Rates and Race-Specific Arrest Rates for Selected Offenses 1965–1992." https://www.ncjrs.gov/pdffiles1/Digitization /148356NCJRS.pdf (accessed June 12, 2014). 1993–2001 series: Federal Bureau of Investigation. 2003. "Age-Specific Arrest Rates and Race-Specific Arrest Rates for Selected Offenses 1992–2001." http:// www.fbi.gov/about-us/cjis/ucr/additional-ucr-publications/age_race_arrest93-01.pdf (accessed April 21, 2014). 2002–2012 series computed by the authors using data on "Total Arrests, Drug Abuse Violations" from the FBI, http://www.fbi.gov/about-us/cjis/ucr/ucr-publications#Crime (accessed April 21, 2014); data on total population by race from the Census. Earlier version of graph from Western, *Punishment and Inequality in America*, p.46.

presents trends in racial disparities in prison admissions for new sentences for four broad categories of crime: violent crimes, robbery and burglary, theft, and drug offenses. In the early 1980s, the black rates of new prison admissions for all these categories were around seven times the rates for whites. In the second half of the 1980s, as the war on drugs intensified, the rate changed dramatically for drug offenses—the rate of black admissions to prison rose to nearly twenty times the white rate by the early 1990s. This increase was largely the result of two factors: changes in laws that imposed harsh mandatory sentences on certain kinds of drug offenses, most notably on offenses connected to drugs commonly used in minority communities (e.g., crack cocaine), and policing practices that targeted drug enforcement on minority communities.

FIGURE 15.18—Black-to-white disparity in prison sentences by offense group

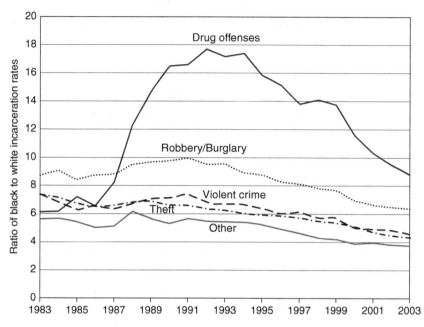

Source: Calculated by Pamela E. Oliver from National Corrections Reporting Program. States with full NCRP data only.

Cocaine, heroin, and certain other illegal drugs are, of course, a serious problem. Their use and the violence associated with their distribution can have a devastating impact on individuals and communities. There are, however, a variety of possible collective responses to this problem. Instead of mass incarceration of people convicted of nonviolent crimes associated with illegal drugs, large-scale resources could have been put into residential and community drug treatment programs in combination with serious job creation and urban revitalization projects. The fact that the war on drugs targeted minority communities and included arrest and prison at the center of the policy reflected a political strategy, not simply a natural response to a pressing social problem. "Law and order" has always been a slogan of conservative political forces because it reinforces fear, and fear tends to push people in a politically conservative direction. The politics of fear undermines political efforts at social and economic justice. In the historical context of the United States in the 1970s and 1980s, the war on drugs combined classic law-and-order themes with fears rooted in racial threats. The result was a set of highly repressive policies that significantly contributed to the increasing disproportion of blacks in American prisons. These policies embody racial bias even if, at the final stage of the process, when a judge imposes a prison sentence, race plays no direct role in the decision.

PROSPECTS FOR THE FUTURE: THE POLITICS OF RACIAL EQUALITY

The situation of race in America at the beginning of the twenty-first century can be characterized by three central features:

1. Considerable real progress has been made in the decades since the civil rights victories of the 1960s on many aspects of racial inequality. These gains have led to the emergence of a solid black middle class of educated workers, professionals, and owners of small businesses, as well as a significant presence of African Americans within the corporate, cultural, and political elite.

2. Discrimination continues to exist, both in mundane social interactions and in the major institutional contexts in which lives and opportunities are formed. These discriminatory practices harm people, they violate values of fairness, and they block the further advance of racial equality. They affect all African Americans— including the wealthy and middle class—even if the consequences are most damaging for the poor.

3. Acute poverty and economic marginalization continue to characterize the lives of many African Americans and certain other minority groups. The intersection of the sharp deprivations generated by economic marginalization and continuing discrimination underwrites racial oppression in the United States today, as reflected in the devastating rates of incarceration of young black men. The mass incarceration of poor young black men in turn deepens their marginalization from the labor force and stable employment. As a broad generalization, compared to the middle of the twentieth century, at the beginning of the twenty-first century race has become less salient and life defining within the educated middle class and elite; but race continues to intensively reinforce the deprivations and disadvantages of acute poverty.

Any serious political project attempting to address these issues must deal directly with the problems of both economic deprivation and continuing discrimination. We have already discussed ending poverty in Chapter 14. That chapter describes an array of proposals designed to reduce economic inequality and eliminate poverty; those policies would also have a large impact on economic aspects of racial inequality, particularly if combined with a shift away from mass incarceration as a way of dealing with crime. Such policies might also indirectly reduce the impact of the various forms of diffuse racial discrimination in American society, but they do not directly address racial discrimination itself.

How, then, should we think about policies that might counter ongoing discrimination? One remedy, of course, is the courts—at least for those contexts in which discriminatory behavior is technically illegal. The examples of housing, lending, and employment discrimination we have just discussed mostly reflect behaviors that violate legal prohibitions on discrimination. So, one solution is for the targets of such discrimination to sue the discriminator.

In most situations, this solution is simply not possible in practice. Hiring decisions are made behind closed doors. The rejected candidate has no way of knowing who the other candidates were, what their relative qualifications were, and so on. After all, in the Milwaukee audit study, 69 percent of whites without prison records also did not get a callback, so on what basis could a black applicant make the claim of discrimination? Even in cases where the discrimination is more blatant, as happens sometimes in discrimination over promotion or pay, it is extremely difficult and costly for an individual to bring a suit against an employer. In the discrimination that takes place in real estate offices and lending institutions it is equally hard, if not impossible, to prove discrimination.

The principal alternative to using the courts to counter discrimination has been a set of policies known as affirmative action. *Affirmative action* refers to a family of policies that give some kind of preference in a context of scarce resources to a traditionally disadvantaged category of people. The main contexts in which such policies have been implemented are admission to higher education and hiring and promotions in jobs, but rules that require a certain proportion of contracts by cities to be issued to minority businesses would also constitute a form of affirmative action. Many specific devices are possible. The simplest is a quota system in which, for example, a certain proportion of the students admitted to a program are required to be

African American or other groups that were historically discriminated against. More complex systems allocate points to a wide variety of criteria relevant to admissions: test scores, interviews, extracurricular activities, special talents, economic disadvantage, and so on. Race could be one criterion in such a list. This is not a quota system, but a system for giving some weight to race. A third strategy is to adopt selective admissions criteria that are anchored in some condition highly correlated with race, but not race itself. Extra admissions points, for example, can be given to a student who comes from a school with a high poverty rate, because the students in such schools will be disproportionately minorities. But regardless of the specific mechanism, all of these are devices that would enable more African Americans and other historically disadvantaged groups to be admitted.

Many people strongly object to affirmative action on the grounds that it is "reverse discrimination"; contrary to what is often thought, opinion polls consistently indicate that most Americans support at least some forms of affirmative action. In a 2013 Gallup poll, for example, in response to the question, "Do you generally favor or oppose affirmative action programs for racial minorities?" 58 percent of all respondents and 51 percent of whites said that they favored such programs. This is broadly in the range of Gallup poll responses in recent years. The ambivalence toward affirmative action programs, however, is revealed when people are asked more specifically about affirmative action for admission to universities. Sixty-seven percent of all respondents, and 75 percent of white respondents, say that admission to college or university should be based "solely on merit even if that results in few minority students being admitted." Even among African Americans, there was almost an even split between respondents who said that admission should be based solely on merit (44 percent) and those who said that race should be considered (48 percent).[45]

The fact of the matter is, basically no viable alternative to some form of affirmative action exists if we want to counter the pernicious effects of certain forms of discrimination. Affirmative action policies create real incentives for employers and admissions officers to accept the additional costs needed to overcome statistical discrimination based on race and actively seek out the best minority candidates they can find. It is expensive for organizations to gather high-quality information on applicants and actively

[45] Jeffrey M. Jones, "In U.S., Most Reject Considering Race in College Admissions," GALLUP Politics (July 24, 2013). http://www.gallup.com/poll/163655/reject-considering-race-college-admissions.aspx.

recruit people from outside of spontaneous networks. In the absence of affirmative action, in many contexts it is cheaper just to treat individuals on the basis of group characteristics. Affirmative action undermines the incentives that sustain that kind of discrimination.

The first African slaves were brought to the American colonies in 1619. Blacks have thus been a part of what was to become the United States for nearly four hundred years. During 245 of these years they were slaves, subordinated in brutal and dehumanizing ways. This period was followed by a century of legalized discrimination that ended fifty years ago.[46] So, for 345 out of almost 400 years—over 80 percent of American history—African Americans have been subjected to legalized, state-enforced oppression justified through virulent racist ideologies. It is hardly surprising that racial discrimination continues to operate and that economic inequalities associated with race have not yet disappeared. The spontaneous action of actors in the market will not be sufficient to eliminate these inequalities. For this to happen, collective, public action is necessary against the economic marginalization associated with racialized poverty as well as against the effects of ongoing racial discrimination.

[46] This temporal breakdown of the experience of African Americans is modified from S. Plous, "Ten Myths about Affirmative Action," in *Understanding Prejudice and Discrimination*, ed. S. Plous (New York: McGraw-Hill), pp. 206–12.

16

GENDER INEQUALITY

The transformation of gender relations since the beginning of the twentieth century is one of the most rapid, profound social changes in human history. For the more than seven thousand years of human history since settled agriculture and early states emerged, male domination has characterized the gender relations of these societies and their successors. Even at the beginning of the twentieth century, men and women were generally viewed as occupying sharply different roles in society: a woman's place was in the home as wife and mother; the man's place was in the public sphere. Men had legal powers over the lives of their wives and children, and though wife beating was never strictly legal in the United States, its practical legal status was ambiguous and perpetrators of domestic violence were rarely punished. To be sure, articulate critics of patriarchy—rule by men over women and children—had emerged by the end of the eighteenth century, and the movement for the right of women to vote was well under way by the end of the nineteenth century. Nevertheless, at the beginning of the twentieth century, the legitimacy of patriarchy was taken for granted by most people and backed by religious doctrines that saw these relations as ordained by God.

By the twenty-first century, only a small minority of people in the United States still hold the view that women should be subordinate to men. Though all sorts of gender inequalities continue to exist, some of them quite resistant to change, they exist in a completely different context of cultural norms, political and social rights, and institutionalized rules. Male domination has not disappeared, but it is on the defensive and its foundations are crumbling.

In this chapter, we explore the realities of gender relations in the United States at the beginning of the twenty-first century. We begin by defining the concept of gender in sociological terms and explain what it means to talk about gender inequality and the transformation of gender relations. This section is followed by a broad empirical description of the transformations of gender in America since the middle of the twentieth century, and an explanation of those transformations. This discussion gives us an opportunity to explore a central general sociological idea in the analysis of social change: how social change is the result of the interplay of *unintended changes* in the social conditions that people face and *conscious, collective struggles* to change those conditions. The chapter concludes with a discussion of the dilemmas rooted in gender relations in the world today and what additional changes are needed to move people closer to full gender equality.

GENDER, NATURE, AND THE PROBLEM OF POSSIBLE VARIATION

At the core of the sociological analysis of gender is the distinction between biological *sex* and gender: *sex* is a property of the biological characteristics of an organism; *gender* is socially constructed, socially created. This is a powerful and totally revolutionary idea: we have the potential capacity to change the social relations within which we live, including the social relations between biologically defined men and women. Sometimes in the media, one hears a discussion in which someone talks about the gender of a dog. In the sociological use of the term, dogs don't have gender; only people living within socially constructed relations are gendered.[1]

This distinction raises a fundamental question in sociological theory about what it means to say that something is "natural." Gender relations are generally experienced as natural rather than as something created by cultural and social processes. Throughout most of history, for most people, the roles performed by men and women seemed to be derived from inherent biological properties. After all, it is a biological fact that women get pregnant and give birth to babies and have the ability to breastfeed them.

---

[1] There are peculiar circumstances in which animals could be said to have a socially constructed gender. In the spring of 2009 a female horse, Rachel Alexandra, won the Preakness Stakes, one of the premier horse races in the United States. This horse was the first filly in eighty-five years to win this race. News headlines about the race included things like the MSNBC website banner, "You go, girl! Filly wins Preakness Stakes thriller." Commentators before the race talked about Rachel Alexandra being able to "run with the boys." Because cultural representations are one aspect of "constructing" gender relations, this is an instance in which an animal's sex is being culturally represented as gender.

Men cannot do this. It is a biological fact that all women know that they are the mothers of the babies they bear, whereas men know that they are the fathers of particular children only when they are confident that they know the sexual behavior of the mother. It is a small step from these biological facts to the view that it is also a fact of nature that women are best suited to have primary responsibility for rearing children, and because of this they should be responsible for other domestic chores.

The central thesis of sociological accounts of gender relations is that the biological facts by themselves do not determine the specific form that social relations between men and women take. This thesis does not imply, however, an even stronger view—that gender relations have nothing to do with biology. Gender relations are the result of the way social processes act on specific biological categories and form social relations between them. One way of thinking about this is with a metaphor of production: biological differences rooted in sex constitute the raw materials that, through a specific process of social production, get transformed into the social relations we call gender.

This way of thinking about sex and gender leaves entirely open the difficult question of what range of variation in gender relations is stably possible. This is a critical question if one holds to a broadly egalitarian conception of social justice and fairness. From an egalitarian point of view, gender relations are fair if, within those relations, males and females have equal power, equal autonomy, and equal opportunity. This is what could be termed *egalitarian gender relations*. This view does not imply that all men and all women do exactly the same things, but it does mean that gender relations do not generate unequal opportunities and choices for men and women.

The sociological problem, then, is whether it is possible to have a society within which deeply egalitarian gender relations predominate. We know from anthropological research that in human history taken as a whole, there is enormous variation in the character of social relations between men and women. In some societies at some points in history, women were virtually the slaves of men, completely disempowered and vulnerable. In some contemporary societies, they must cover their faces in public and cannot appear outside the home without being accompanied by an appropriate man. In other times and places, women have had considerable autonomy and control over their bodies and activities. So, one thing is for sure: we can observe enormous empirical variation.

It is much less clear what sorts of variation are *possible*, and what sorts of possibilities that have not yet occurred could nevertheless be stable over time. For example, in all societies women have historically had primary responsibility for early infant care; no society has displayed prevalent social norms backing the principle that fathers should be as involved as mothers in the care of babies. As a generalization from this empirical observation, therefore, we might conclude that strongly egalitarian norms about parenting of babies are not possible. Such a conclusion would be unjustified. Because this observed universal has occurred in a world characterized by certain specific economic, political, and cultural conditions, the empirical universality of this "fact" does not mean that it is simply a natural reflection of biological imperatives. Until the very recent past, for example, birth control was relatively ineffective; now it is reliable. Until the last 150 years or so, most people had to spend most of their time producing food. This is no longer true. Until recently, because of relatively high infant mortality, women needed to have many children so that some would survive to adulthood. For most people, having adult children was essential if they hoped to have anyone to take care of them when they were old. Again, this is no longer the case in economically developed countries like the United States. Most of these changes have occurred only in the last few generations. Also, until the recent past, no governments were organized on popular-democratic principles, and no cultures valued individual autonomy and liberal rights. All of these are historically novel developments of the past few centuries. What we do not know, then, is what new forms of gender relations might become possible and stable given these dramatically altered economic, cultural, and political conditions. In particular, we do not know whether fully egalitarian gender relations are possible under the dramatically altered material and cultural circumstances of the United States and similar countries in the twenty-first century.

Furthermore, *even if* we decided for some reason that it was indeed "natural" for women to specialize in taking care of infants, this would not actually resolve the question of whether it was *desirable* for there to be a cultural norm telling women that they should do most of the caregiving, or whether egalitarian norms could never become dominant. Just because something is natural—in the sense of reflecting some underlying biological human characteristics—does not mean it is desirable and untransformable. It is perfectly natural for a person to die from smallpox: our biological system is such that this infection often kills us. No one feels that this makes it undesirable to develop vaccines. Human beings are naturally omnivorous—we have the necessary enzymes to digest animal products—and in all societies before "civilization" intruded on people in the form of settled agriculture, people were indeed omnivores; this does not settle the question of whether it is possible and desirable to be a vegetarian. So, the sheer "naturalness" of inegalitarian aspects of gender relations—even if this could somehow be convincingly demonstrated—does not prove that egalitarian relations are impossible, let alone undesirable.

A final issue involved in thinking about possible transformations of gender relations concerns variations among men and among women in underlying biologically rooted dispositions. It *may* be that because of genes and hormones, men are on average more aggressive than women and, on average, have stronger instinctual proclivities to dominate; and that women, because of genes and hormones, are on average more nurturant and have stronger dispositions to engage in caregiving activities. However, regardless of the "natural" dispositions of the *average* man and woman, it is also equally certain that the distribution of these attributes among men and among women overlaps tremendously. Many women are more aggressive than the average male, and many men are more nurturant than the average female. It is also virtually certain that whatever behavioral differences between genders are generated by genes and hormones, society and culture exaggerate these differences because of the impact of socialization and social norms on behavior. One thus cannot take the simple empirical observation of the existing differences in distributions of these traits between genders and infer anything about what is the "true" biological difference under alternative conditions.

This general point about the relationship between the distribution of underlying biological dispositions in men and women and the distribution of manifest behaviors of men and women under existing social relations is illustrated graphically in Figure 16.1. This figure illustrates the distribution of time spent taking care of babies and young children by mothers and by fathers in two-parent households under two hypothetical conditions. The graph at left represents this distribution in a society like the United States, where strong cultural norms affirm that taking care of infants is more the responsibility of mothers than of fathers. The graph at right represents the hypothetical distribution of such behaviors in a society whose norms say that it is as good for fathers as for mothers to take care of infants. In the first case girls are socialized to believe they should take care of babies, and the prevailing norms are critical of mothers who hand off that responsibility to others. In the second case both boys and girls are taught that it is a good thing for both fathers and mothers to do intensive caregiving, and the prevailing norms create no pressures for mothers to take on this responsibility more than fathers.

FIGURE 16.1—Hypothetical distributions in alternative worlds of child-care provision by men and women living in households with children

(a) Existing distribution of child-care labor among men and among women with children

(b) Hypothetical distributions of child-care labor among men and among women with children in a world with no gendered norms of appropriate child-care responsibility and no gender-specific costs to doing child care

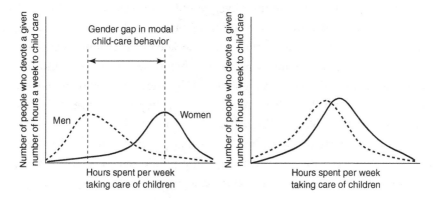

In this second, hypothetical world, it could still be the case that mothers on average do spend more time in infant care. Even if there was no cultural pressure on them to do so, the underlying biologically rooted dispositions could lead, on average, to some gender differences in the average time spent on this task. We do not know how big the gender gap in caregiving of infants would be, because it is not possible to do the experiment. But what we know virtually for certain is that the gap would be smaller than it is in the world in which we live today.

These observations on gender, nature, and the possibilities of much more egalitarian relations than currently exist constitute the theoretical background for the rest of this chapter. In the following sections, we describe the empirical changes that have occurred in recent decades and explore the conditions that would make further changes toward gender equality possible in the future.

THE TRANSFORMATION OF GENDER RELATIONS IN AMERICA

What follows is a brief descriptive tour through some of the major changes in patterns of gender inequality during the last decades of the twentieth century. The simple story is that despite tremendous gains in the direction of greater equality, significant inequalities remain.

Legal Rights

It is hard for most people alive today to really understand how it could be possible that before 1920, women in the United States did not have the right to vote. This disenfranchisement of women was justified on many grounds: women were not as rational or intelligent as men; they were not really autonomous, and the men in their lives would control their votes; like children, they were ruled by their emotions. Consequently, women were not really full political citizens until the third decade of the twentieth century. Even then, it would be many more decades before women's social and economic rights were the same as men's. Until the 1930s, married women were not allowed to travel on their own passports; they had to use their husband's. Until World War II, formal and informal "marriage bars" were in place in many parts of the United States that prohibited married women from many clerical jobs and from teaching public school. One historian described the logic of marriage bars for teachers this way:

> Prejudice against married women as teachers derived from two deeply rooted ideas in American society: first, that women's labor belongs to their husbands, and second, that public employment is akin to charity. School authorities doubted that women could service their families and the schools without slighting the latter.[2]

It was not until the passage of the Civil Rights Act in 1964 that discrimination against women in jobs, pay, and promotion was made illegal. Even though in the 1970s a constitutional amendment to guarantee equal rights for women—the Equal Rights Amendment—failed to pass the required number of states, by the end of the twentieth century, virtually all legal rules differentiating the rights of men and women had been eliminated. The last significant vestige of legally enforced inequality in rights between men and women in the United States—the military's ban on women serving in combat—was lifted in early 2013.

Labor Force Participation

In 1920 only about 5 percent of married women with children were in the paid labor force. By 1950 this figure had only risen to just over 10 percent; 90 percent were stay-at-home moms (Figure 16.2). Even when the youngest child reached school age, over 70 percent of married women were still full-time

---

[2] Eric Arnesen, *Encyclopedia of U.S. Labor and Working-class History* (Boca Raton, FL: CRC Press, 2006), p. 1359.

FIGURE 16.2—Labor force participation rates of married women with children, 1880–2011

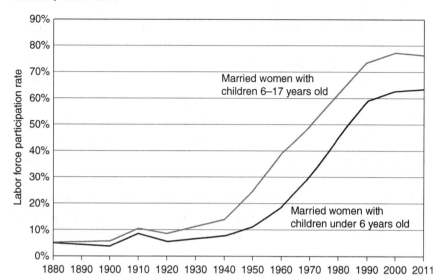

Sources: For women with children 1960–2009: *The 2012 Statistical Abstract of the United States*, Table 599: "Employment Status of Women, by Marital Status and Presence and Age of Children: 1970 to 2009," http://www.census.gov/compendia/statab/2012/tables/12s0599.pdf (accessed March 31, 2014). For all women, 1960–2000: Bureau of Labor Statistics, "Labor Force Statistics from the Current Population Survey." Original data value. http://www.bls.gov/webapps/legacy/cpsatab1.htm (accessed March 31, 2014). For 1880–1950: *Historical Statistics of the United States*. Millennial Edition Online. Table Ba425–469: "Female Labor Force Participation Rate, by Race, Marital Status, and Presence of Children: 1880–1990 [Census estimates]." http://hsus.cambridge.org/ (accessed March 31, 2014). Data for married women with children (two categories) 2010–2011 provided directly by the Bureau of Labor Statistics.

homemakers. This was clearly the cultural standard, at least for white women. For black women the norm was always weaker, although it was still the case in 1950 that 64 percent of black women with children over age six did not work in the formal paid labor force.

By the beginning of the twenty-first century, the situation had dramatically changed: Over 60 percent of mothers with children under six and nearly 80 percent of mothers with children in school were now in the paid labor force. Continuous labor force participation, with only brief interruptions for the birth of a child, had become the new cultural norm. This is an extraordinarily rapid change in the relationship between women and the labor market—more rapid, for example, than the change in employment patterns that occurred during the Industrial Revolution.

Occupational Structure and Earnings

The dramatic increase in female labor force participation has been accompanied by a significant change in the economic opportunities of women in terms of the occupations women fill as well as the earnings they receive.

In certain occupations that were previously almost entirely male, women have made substantial headway (Figure 16.3). In 1930, only 1.5 percent of police officers, 1.5 percent of architects, 2.4 percent of lawyers, and 5.1 percent of doctors were women. By 1960 these figures had increased modestly to 3–7 percent across these categories. By 2011, the change was dramatic: women represented 17.4 percent of policemen, 27.2 percent of architects, 35.7 percent of physicians, and 35.6 percent of lawyers. It will, of course, take many years for the proportion of women in a traditionally male occupation to approach 50 percent even if all barriers to women disappeared and half of all new entrants to the profession were women, because it takes time for all the men who entered the system under the earlier conditions to retire. One critical issue for the future of the gender composition of a profession, therefore, is the rate of increase of women who enter the professional training program. This, too, is happening: In the 1949–1950 academic year,

FIGURE 16.3—Percentage of people in selected traditionally male professions who are women, 1930–2011

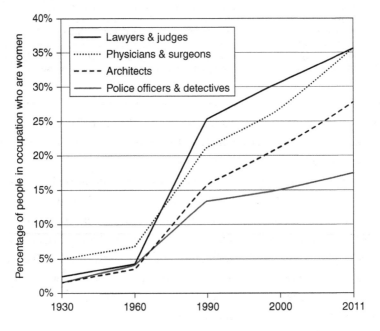

Source: IPUMS Census samples, 1950–2011 (variable: OCC1950).

7.2 percent of students in medical school and 2.8 percent in law school were women. These figures increased to 7 percent and 9 percent in 1969–1970 and then took off, reaching 47 percent for both professions in 2011–2012 (Figure 16.4).

These are real and important reductions in the gender segregation of certain important occupations. It would be a mistake, however, to conclude that the occupational structure as a whole has become degendered. Many occupations remain heavily dominated by one gender or another. Table 16.1 presents a selection of occupations that are heavily sex typed as either male or female. In 2013 it was still the case that 94 percent of secretaries, 98 percent of kindergarten and preschool teachers, and 96 percent of dental assistants were women. Among iconic male occupations, in 2013 women constituted only about 6 percent of airline pilots and less than 2 percent of carpenters and auto mechanics.

FIGURE 16.4—Gender compositions of enrollments in medical school and law school, 1949–2011

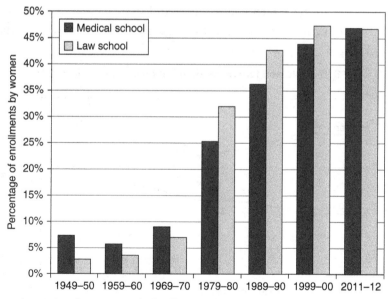

Sources: Association of American Medical Colleges, Table 26: "Total Enrollment by U.S. Medical School and Sex, 2008–2012," available at https://www.aamc.org/data/facts/ (accessed September 2, 2014); and American Bar Association, "First Year and Total J.D. Enrollment by Gender 1947–2011," http://www.americanbar.org/content/dam/aba/administrative/legal_education_and _admissions_to_the_bar/statistics/jd_enrollment_1yr_total_gender.authcheckdam.pdf (accessed May 23, 2014).

TABLE 16.1—Examples of highly sex-typed jobs that have changed little, 1970–2011

	Percentage of people in occupation who are women				
	1970	1980	1990	2000	2013
Secretaries	98.1	98.8	98.6	96.5	94.4
Registered nurses	97.8	96.2	94.7	92.8	90.1
Dental assistants	98.6	97.9	97.1	96.8	95.7
Kindergarten and preschool teachers	98.3	96.7	98.1	98.1	97.8
Carpenters	1.6	1.9	1.9	2.0	1.6
Airplane pilots and navigators	1.6	1.6	3.8	4.2	5.5
Automobile mechanics	1.6	1.4	2.1	2.1	1.8

Source: IPUMS Census samples, 1950–2011 (variable: OCC1990).

Women have also made significant progress in earnings: the relative pay of women increased from 63 percent of male median hourly earnings in 1973 to 84 percent of male earnings in 2012 (Figure 16.5). Much of this gain comes directly from the increased labor market participation of women, because years of experience and continuity of employment in the labor market result in higher pay for both men and women. And some gain probably reflects efforts to eliminate pay discrimination against women. Still, even when

FIGURE 16.5—Male and female median hourly earnings, 1973–2011

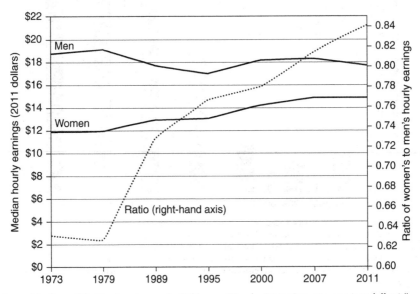

Source: The State of Working America, 2011/12, Table 4.22: "Gender Wage Gap, 1973–2011 (2011 dollars)."

you control statistically for experience levels, education, skills, and other factors, a pay gap remains between men and women.

Much of this gender gap in pay (after statistical controls) reflects the large differences in pay that continue to exist for jobs that are identified with women compared to jobs associated with men: parking attendants typically earn more than preschool teachers, for example. It is a difficult task to sort out exactly why such stereotypically female jobs generally earn less than stereotypically male jobs. Some of this earnings gap may be due to what economists call overcrowding: if women are highly concentrated in certain jobs, either through discrimination or self-selection, then there will tend to be an oversupply of people competing for such positions and thus the wages will be bid down. In this view, the lower pay for women simply reflects the supply-and-demand dynamics of markets. Many sociologists, in contrast, argue that wages are shaped by cultural expectations and norms about appropriate pay, not simply by the supply-and-demand conditions of markets.[3] Jobs associated with women are traditionally devalued, and the kinds of skills those jobs require are deemed less valuable than the kinds of skills associated with male jobs. More specifically, skills connected to care-giving and nurturance are undervalued in markets. Much of the gender gap in pay between male and female jobs is linked to these cultural standards.

Power

Gender inequality in the extent to which women occupy positions that confer significant power is more difficult to assess than inequality in pay or in occupational distributions. One indicator is presence of women on boards of directors and top managerial positions in large corporations. In 2012, only 16.6 percent of the seats on boards of directors of Fortune 500 firms were held by women, 14.3 percent of the corporate officers in those firms were women, and 4.2 percent of the CEOs were women (Figure 16.6). These figures certainly show a significant underrepresentation of women, but they also mark a significant improvement over the past.

More difficult to ascertain is the extent to which the underrepresentation reflects systematic barriers and discrimination faced by women today. At least some of this underrepresentation of women at the top of

---

[3] An influential statement of this perspective can be found in Paula England, *Comparable Worth: Theories and Evidence* (New York: Aldine, 1992).

FIGURE 16.6—Women in corporate management, 1995–2013

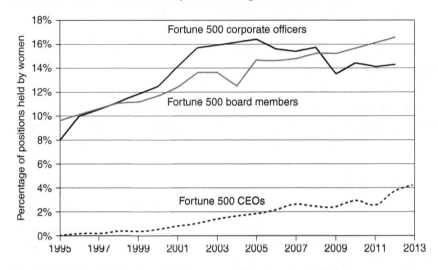

Note: Published data on Fortune 500 female corporate officers are not available for 2001, 2003, and 2004, so data points for these years are interpolated.

Source: Catalyst Quick Take: Women in U.S. Management and Labor Force (New York: Catalyst, 2013).

managerial hierarchies is simply the historical legacy of the virtual absence of women from lower levels of the management structure twenty-five years ago, because women need to be in the pipeline of promotions to make it to the top by the end of their careers. How much of the rest of the under-representation is the result of gender-specific barriers and discrimination faced by women—especially the strong barriers referred to as the glass ceiling—and how much of it reflects the ways in which women themselves may choose not to compete in those hierarchies because of their personal priorities is an extremely difficult empirical question. It is particularly difficult because, of course, the choices women make may themselves be conditioned by the experience of barriers. If the barriers make managerial careers for women more difficult, women may decide that such a career is not worth the fight and thus "select themselves" out of the competition.

What about women in positions of political power? Figure 16.7 presents the percentage of elected officials in the U.S. Congress, state legislatures, and statewide elective offices. In 1979, only 3 percent of people in Congress (House of Representatives and Senate combined) were women, and only around 10 percent of people elected at the state level were women. By 2013

FIGURE 16.7—Women elected officials, 1979–2013

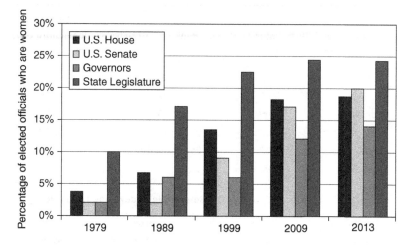

Sources: "Women in Elected Office 2013" and "History of Women Governors," Center for American Women in Politics, Rutgers University, 2013. "Women Representatives and Senators by Congress, 1917–Present," drawn from the *Biographical Directory of the United States Congress*. http://history.house .gov/Exhibitions-and-Publications/WIC/Historical-Data/Women-Representatives-and-Senators-by -Congress/ (accessed May 23, 2014).

women constituted nearly a quarter of all people elected at the state level and just under 19 percent of people in Congress. This is certainly progress, but it still puts the United States well below most other economically developed democracies. As indicated in Table 16.2, the United States ranks twenty-first among developed democracies in the proportion of women in the national legislature. Sweden is first with 44.7 percent. Other Northern European countries are all above 39 percent. Even among the English-speaking countries, which are generally lower than other European countries, only Ireland has a lower proportion of women in the national legislatures than does the United States.

Transformation in Family Structure

The period since the end of World War II has also witnessed a dramatic and rapid change in the nature of family structure and the composition of households. At midcentury, almost 80 percent of all people lived in households in which there was a married couple. This meant that many adult children lived with their parents until getting married, or they lived on their own for only a short period. This was clearly the cultural standard. Other household forms were either deviant or transitional. By 2012, only

TABLE 16.2—Women in national legislatures: international comparisons

Rank	Country	Women in legislature (%)*	Rank	Country	Women in legislature (%)*
1	Sweden	44.7%	19	Israel	21.7%
2	Finland	42.5%	20	Greece	21.0%
3	Iceland	39.7%	**21**	**U.S.**	**17.8%**
4	Norway	39.6%	22	Korea	15.7%
5	Denmark	39.1%	23	Ireland	15.1%
6	Netherlands	38.7%	24	Japan	7.9%
7	Belgium	38.0%			
8	Spain	36.0%			
9	Germany	32.9%	**Selected less-developed countries**		
10	New Zealand	32.2%		Senegal	42.7%
11	Switzerland	29.0%		South Africa	42.3%
12	Portugal	28.7%		Costa Rica	38.6%
13	Italy	28.4%		Argentina	37.4%
14	Austria	27.9%		Mexico	36.8%
15	France	26.9%		Poland	23.7%
16	Australia	24.7%		Chile	14.2%
17	Canada	24.7%		India	11.0%
18	United Kingdom	22.5%		Brazil	8.6%

*Data are for lower house in two-chamber legislatures.

Source: "Women in National Parliaments, Situation as of April 1, 2013," Inter-parliamentary Union. http://www.ipu.org (accessed May 23, 2013).

half of all households consisted of a married couple. Households of a single person living alone increased from under 10 percent of all households in 1940 to 33.5 percent in 2012. The remaining households consisted of cohabiting unmarried couples (including same-sex couples), households headed by a single parent, and households of single people with roommates (Figure 16.8). In the half century following the end of World War II the single, monolithic cultural model of household composition had largely disappeared and was replaced by a much more heterogeneous array of forms.

These changes in the distribution of types of households reflect important changes in family structures and marriage patterns over the same period. In the last half of the twentieth century, in a variety of ways, marriage has become a less central and stable institution in many people's lives. In 1960, only 7 percent of women aged 30–34 had never married. By 2010 this figure had increased to over 30 percent (Figure 16.9).

FIGURE 16.8—Distribution of household types, 1940–2013

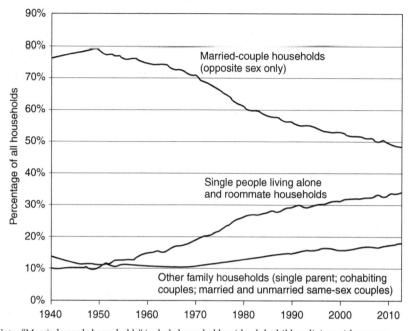

Note: "Married-couple households" include households with adult children living with parents.

Source: Census Bureau. *Households*, Table HH-1: "Households, by Type: 1940 to Present." http://www.census.gov/hhes/families/data/households.html (accessed April 4, 2014).

FIGURE 16.9—Percentage of women aged 30 to 34 who have never married, 1880–2010

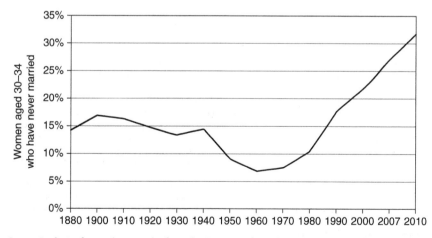

Source: Analysis of microdata samples from the Censuses of Population 1880 and 1900–2010 and the American Community Survey (2001–2007), as harmonized in S. Sobek, M. Ruggles, et al., *Integrated Public Use Microdata Series: Version 4.0* [Machine readable database] (Minneapolis, MN: Minnesota Population Center [producer and distributor], 2008). Data downloaded from http://usa.ipums.org/usa (accessed April 4, 2014).

For those who choose to marry, marriages have become much less durable: In the early twentieth century, there were fewer than 100 divorces for every 1,000 marriages. By the 1950s, this figure had increased to roughly 250 divorces for every 1,000 marriages; and in the late 1970s and early 1980s, the figure hovered around 500 (Figure 16.10). This very high rate of divorce in the 1970s and 1980s leads demographers to estimate that eventually somewhere between 45 and 50 percent of

FIGURE 16.10—Divorce rate in the United States, 1867–2011

Note: Data for 1999 were linearly imputed through linear interpolation.

Sources: Authors' calculations from marriage and divorce totals; 1867–1967 from U.S. Department of Health, Education, and Welfare, 1973, "100 Years of Marriage and Divorce Statistics. United States, 1867–1967," Table 1. Data for 1968–1978 from National Center for Health Statistics (NCHS), 1982. "Annual Summary of Births, Deaths, Marriages, and Divorces: United States, 1981," (all data accessed June 12, 2014). Marriages for 1979–1985 from NCHS, 1990, "Advance Report of Final Divorce Statistics, 1987," *Monthly Vital Statistics Report* 38(12, supplement 2). Divorces for 1979–1985 from NCHS, 1988, "Advance Report of Final Marriage Statistics, 1985," *Monthly Vital Statistics Report* 37(1, supplement). Data for 1986–1987 from NCHS's *Monthly Vital Statistics Report* 36(13). Data for 1988–1989 from NCHS's *Monthly Vital Statistics Report* 38(13). Data for 1990–1991 from NCHS's *Monthly Vital Statistics Report* 40(13). Data for 1992–1993 from NCHS's *Monthly Vital Statistics Report* 42(13). Data for 1994–1995 from NCHS's *Monthly Vital Statistics Report* 44(12). Data for 1996–1997 from NCHS's *National Vital Statistics Report* 46, no. 12 (1998). Data for 1998 from 1996–1997 from NCHS's *Monthly Vital Statistics Report* 47, no. 21 (1999). Data for 2000–2011 from Center for Disease Control and Prevention, "National Marriage and Divorce Rate Trends," (all data accessed June 12, 2014).

marriages in this period will end in divorce.[4] Along with this decline in marriage, an increasing number of children are born to single mothers. Between 1940 and 1960, less than 5 percent of all births were to unmarried women. The percentage rose steeply beginning in the 1960s, reaching 33 percent by 2000 and 40 percent by 2011 (Figure 16.11). The result of these trends—more divorces and more births outside of

FIGURE 16.11—Percentage of births to unmarried mothers, 1940–2011

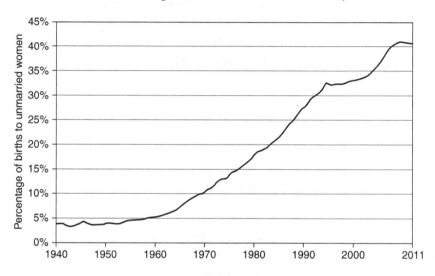

Source: "Non-marital Childbearing in the United States," *National Vital Statistics—Births*. http://www.cdc.gov/nchs/data_access/vitalstats/VitalStats_Births.htm (accessed May 20, 2013).

[4]Lynne Casper and Suzanne Bianchi, *Continuity and Change in the American Family* (Thousand Oaks, CA: Sage, 2002), p. 25. Though it is easy to count the number of divorces in any given year, it is much more difficult to estimate the proportion of marriages that eventually end in divorce because for a given cohort of marriages, this percentage constantly increases over time until everyone in the cohort has died. The estimate of the percentage of marriages that end in divorce is therefore a projection into the future based on trends to the present. It is possible, however, to make broad comparisons across cohorts, such as the following: "14% of white women who married in the 1940s eventually divorced. A single generation later, almost 50 percent of those who married in the late sixties and early seventies have already divorced [by the early 1990s]." Amara Bachu, *Fertility of American Women: June 1994* (Washington, DC: U.S. Census Bureau, September 1995), p. xix, table K. Cited in Maggie Gallagher, *The Abolition of Marriage: How We Destroy Lasting Love* (Washington, DC: Regnery Publishing, 1996), p. 5.

marriage—is that in 2012, only 55 percent of children aged 15–17 were still living with two biological parents.[5]

These trends in family formation and family structure are complex and contradictory. Some of the childbirth by unmarried women occurs in stable families of cohabiting heterosexual and lesbian couples who either choose not to get married or who cannot legally marry. A certain proportion of single parenthood is deliberate, reflecting a conscious choice by women who want to have a child to do so on their own. Some divorces, even when there are children in the family, may be the best resolution of a bad marriage. But certainly divorce also can be very disruptive to the lives of children, and single parenthood, especially under difficult economic conditions, can be enormously stressful. In any case, our central point here is not to pass judgment on these specific developments but to emphasize how decisively the United States has moved from a society overwhelmingly dominated by a single model of the family to a much more heterogeneous array of family forms.

Domestic Division of Labor within the Family

The family is one of the pivotal sites where gender relations are produced and reproduced. It is a central place where children first learn about the roles connected to gender, and where power relations built around gender are located. Patriarchy as a historically central form of gender relations means literally "rule by the father" and was firmly based in male domination inside of families. Gender relations are formed not only within the intimate relations of the family; they are constructed within the public sphere as well. But a good case can be made that the family constitutes the most fundamental arena within which these relations are forged.

A central aspect of gender relations within families is the division of labor over domestic tasks. In what has come to be known as the traditional American family, the wife was a full-time homemaker—particularly when children were living in the family—and the husband was the breadwinner. As a full-time homemaker, the wife/mother did virtually all the housework and most of the child care, except for some recreational activities.

[5] U.S. Census Bureau, *Current Population Survey, Annual Social and Economic Supplement* (2012), table Fam1.B, http://www.childstats.gov/americaschildren/tables/fam1b.asp?popup=true.

Husbands did many home repairs, took care of the car, and did certain heavy outdoor tasks like lawn mowing and snow shoveling. Although it was never the case that all families followed this model of male-breadwinner and female-homemaker, it was certainly the dominant American ideal in the middle of the twentieth century and the practical reality for most households.

At the beginning of the twentieth century, the average woman between the ages of 18 and 64 did around 46 hours of domestic work in the home per week while the average man did only about 4 hours.[6] At the middle of the century, this division of labor in the home was still pretty much intact. The roles of women outside the home, however, began to change rapidly in the decades after 1950 through increases in the labor force participation rates of married women and, increasingly, through changes in their occupational roles and relative earnings. Initially these changes in the public roles of women were not reflected within the division of labor in the home. As shown in Figure 16.12, between 1965 and 1975 men hardly increased their involvement in housework labor at all, while women decreased their involvement quite a bit. The initial effect of increased labor force participation of wives and mothers was messier houses. But then, between 1975 and 1985, men did gradually begin to do more. The increase is especially dramatic for ordinary housework. In 1965, mothers spent 19 times more time in core housework chores—cooking, meal cleanup, housecleaning, and laundry—than did fathers. This figure declined only modestly to 13.8 times more than did fathers in 1975, but the change occurred entirely because mothers on average decreased the amount of time they spent cleaning house— from an average of around 32 hours a week to 24 hours a week. In both periods, fathers typically spent less than 2 hours a week on routine housework. By 2005 the ratio had declined to 3.3:1, but this time much of the change came from a doubling of fathers' housework labor. This is still far from an equal sharing of housework, but it reflects some real movement in that direction. Full-time working mothers still do a second shift at home, and they have less free time than their husbands, but the disparity has begun to decline.

[6] Valerie A. Ramey, "Time Spent in Home Production in the 20th Century: New Estimates from Old Data," NBER Working Paper 13985 (Cambridge, MA: National Bureau of Economic Research, April 2008).

FIGURE 16.12—Time spent per day on different kinds of household labor for mothers and fathers in homes with children

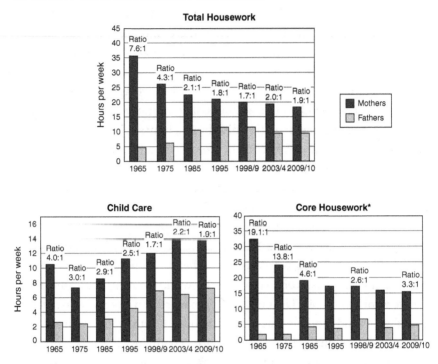

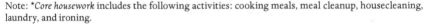

Note: *Core housework* includes the following activities: cooking meals, meal cleanup, housecleaning, laundry, and ironing.

Source: Suzanne M. Bianchi, Liana C. Sayer, Melissa A. Milkie, and John P. Robinson, "Housework: Who Did, Does or Will Do It, and How Much Does It Matter?" *Social Forces* 91, no. 1, (2012): 55–63.

Sexuality

Sexuality has an extremely complex relationship to gender relations in general and gender inequality in particular. Some scholars have argued that historically, a central motive for male domination centered on the problem of female fertility: the only way men could guarantee that they were in fact the fathers of their children was to control the bodies of the women who were to be mothers of those children. Controlling female sexuality and fertility was therefore a central component of the social processes that generate male domination. The continuing controversies in American society over the availability of certain forms of contraception—and, above all, abortion—reflect this age-old issue of the social processes used to control biological reproduction.

Sexuality is also tied to inequality in gender relations through sexual violence. Sexual violence both outside and inside of marriage is a central feature of male domination in many societies, including the contemporary United States. It expresses the unequal power relations between men and women, and it helps to reinforce that inequality because the greater vulnerability of women to such violence inhibits their easy movement in public spaces.

Social attitudes and treatment of homosexuality are also bound up with gender relations insofar as men and women having sexual relations with members of their own sex violates a core element of the social norms regulating male-female relations. Certainly many people view the idea of same-sex marriage as a direct threat to a conventional understanding of how families should be structured around traditional, inegalitarian forms of gender roles.

Like the other trends we have discussed, the transformation of social norms and legal rules around sexuality has been dramatic since the middle of the twentieth century. Part of this change is anchored in technological changes, especially the invention and widespread dissemination of the birth control pill, which made women's control over their own fertility much easier and reliable and opened the door—some people believe—for the so-called sexual revolution. Equally important were changes in laws regarding availability of birth control and the fairly rapid change in social norms about their visibility and accessibility. Even in the case of abortion—the most contentious aspect of control over female fertility—most people in the United States believe that women should have the right to choose. In 2009, only around 20–25 percent of people believed that abortion should be illegal in all cases, and a clear majority believes it should be legal in most or all cases.[7]

The transformations in sexual norms, however, go far beyond simply the issues of birth control. Sexual violence and sexual abuse have become much more heavily condemned and controlled since the middle of the twentieth century. Until the mid-1970s, rape was defined as a crime only if the perpetrator was not a spouse. By the first decade of the twenty-first century, half of the states in the United States had completely removed the marital exemption from rape laws; the remaining states treated it as a crime, but one of lesser severity than rape outside of marriage. Sexual abuse of

---

[7] http://www.pollingreport.com/abortion.htm (accessed February 28, 2014).

children has also become a much more salient issue, particularly in the aftermath of the repeated child abuse scandals by priests. Sexual harassment in workplaces, schools, and other public places—at once regarded by many men as at worst coarse behavior—is now acknowledged as a form of serious intimidation of women that generates real harms.

Perhaps the most dramatic transformation of sexual norms concerns homosexuality. After all, sexual violence and abuse of children were always thought of as reprehensible; what has changed is the visible public attention these are given. In the case of homosexuality, the prevailing attitudes, norms, and laws have changed in fundamental ways. In the 1950s homosexuality was a criminal offense in all states in the United States under the rubric of sodomy laws, even if the statutes were only erratically enforced. Police periodically raided gay bars, and being revealed as a homosexual was grounds for losing a job. Homosexuality was broadly regarded as immoral and shameful, and most homosexuals had to remain "in the closet" to avoid stigma and ostracism.

In 1961 Illinois became the first state to repeal its sodomy law. By 2003 such laws had been repealed throughout most of the United States, except for Southern states and a few others. In 2003 the Supreme Court ruled that such laws were unconstitutional, and that the state cannot restrict the right of adults to engage in consensual sexual activity.

By the beginning of the twenty-first century, laws criminalizing homosexuality had been ruled unconstitutional, and the public acceptance of homosexuality as simply a variation of human sexuality had become fairly widespread. Discrimination in employment and housing against homosexuals is broadly viewed as illegitimate; and as of 2010, in many states such behavior is illegal under antidiscrimination statutes. Even in the military, the awkward "don't ask, don't tell" policy adopted during the Clinton administration has been dropped and all formal restrictions on homosexuality eliminated.

On the most high-profile, hot-button issue for gay rights—the legalization of same-sex marriage—by 2009 a majority of the public favored giving all of the substantive rights associated with marriage to same-sex couples under the rubric of civil partnership, even if a majority still opposed the use of the word *marriage* to designate these legal arrangements; by 2014 a clear majority supported legalizing same-sex marriage itself (Figure 16.13). Among younger cohorts the most recent polls indicate that a sizeable majority favors full legalization of such marriages while

FIGURE 16.13—Trends in public support for same-sex marriage

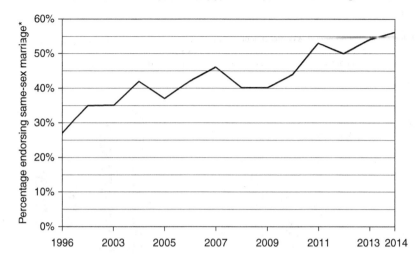

*The precise wording of questions varies somewhat across polls. A typical question is, "Do you think marriages between same-sex couples should or should not be recognized by the law, with the same rights as traditional marriages?" (Gallup poll, wording used 2006–2013).

Sources: 1996: Gallup and Time/CNN; 1998/1999: Gallup; 2000: CNN/USA *Today*/Gallup; 2002: CNN/USA *Today*/Gallup and Time/CNN; 2003: ABC/*Washington Post*, Gallup, and CNN/USA *Today*/Gallup; 2004: ABC/*Washington Post*, Gallup, and CNN/USA *Today*/Gallup; 2005: ABC/*Washington Post*, and Gallup; 2006: ABC/*Washington Post*, and Gallup; 2009: ABC/*Washington Post*; 2011, 2012 and 2013: Gallup; 2014: CBS News/New York Times Poll.

only 30 percent of people 65 and older do so. In Minnesota, a ballot proposition to define marriage as only between a man and a woman was defeated in 2012; in that vote, over 70 percent of voters ages eighteen to twenty-four and 60 percent of voters ages twenty-five to twenty-nine supported legalized same-sex marriage. Similarly, in a vote in favor of same-sex marriage in Maryland in 2012, 70 percent of voters ages eighteen to twenty-nine voted yes, compared to only 36 percent of voters ages sixty-five and older (Figure 16.14). Given these sharp differences in attitudes by age group, it seems very likely that eventually same-sex marriage will become legal in the United States as the older generations that still harbor homophobic views die. By 2014, this has already happened in ten Western European countries—Belgium, Denmark, France, Luxembourg, Netherlands, Norway, Portugal, Spain, Sweden, and the United Kingdom—and most others have formalized full civil unions with all legal rights of marriage. Same-sex marriage is also legal in New Zealand, South Africa, Iceland, Brazil, Uruguay, Argentina, and Canada.

FIGURE 16.14–Support for same-sex marriage in different age groups, 2012

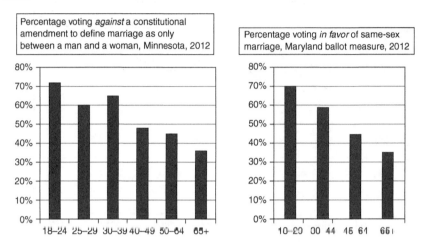

Sources: CNN Politics. *2012 Election Center: Races and Results for Minnesota*. http://www.cnn.com /election/2012/results/state/MN (accessed November 18, 2012). CNN Politics. *2012 Election Center: Races and Results for Maryland*. http://www.cnn.com/election/2012/results/state/MD (accessed November 18, 2012).

Given the salience of issues involving sexuality in religion and culture, and given how restrictive the dominant cultural norms were in the middle of the twentieth century, these changes are indeed striking. They constitute substantial gains in individual autonomy and self-determination, and they are also intimately connected to the transformation of gender relations in an egalitarian direction.

EXPLAINING THE TRANSFORMATION OF GENDER RELATIONS

How do we explain these patterns in gender relations? How do we account for the trajectory of changes in gender relations we are living through? The answer to this question focuses on the ways the massive changes in the American economy opened up new opportunities in the paid labor force for women, and on how, as women took advantage of those opportunities, their actions undermined certain traditional patterns of gender relations. These processes in turn opened a space for collective action by women's groups to challenge the rules of the game that discriminated against women and created barriers to their advancement; the success of those challenges in turn accelerated the movement into the labor force and the erosion of some aspects of traditional gender relations.

Underlying this account are three different kinds of processes at work that interact first to erode the basis for traditional gender relations and then to make possible their transformation:

1. In the second half of the twentieth century there were increasing inconsistencies in the interests of men, especially powerful men, in defending male domination.
2. What can be called a crisis of female domesticity made it more difficult for women to be full-time housewives and mothers.
3. The capacity for women to struggle against male domination increased.

These processes created the context in which collective struggles, especially those organized by women, against the established rules of the game could achieve significant gains.

The Problem of the Interests of Men

Inequalities of power and privilege do not continue out of sheer momentum; they require considerable social energy and resources to be reproduced. If, over time, the interests of powerful people become less tied to a particular form of oppression, they are likely to devote less energy and fewer resources to sustain that inequality; and this decline in salience makes the oppression in question more vulnerable to challenge. In the case of gender inequality, the interests of men in general—and elite, powerful men in particular—in maintaining certain aspects of male domination and gender inequality weakened over time.[8] This does not mean that men ceased to be sexist. They have all sorts of attitudes and beliefs that impeded, and continue to impede, gender equality. The key idea here is that many men also had interests that weakened their stake in male domination.

[8] The argument presented in this section concerning the importance of the weakening of coherent interests among men in male domination comes from the work of Robert M. Jackson, *Destined for Equality: The Inevitable Rise of Women's Status* (Cambridge, MA: Harvard University Press, 1998).

A good example of this dynamic is the economic interests of employers in capitalist firms, particularly as their need for highly educated, literate labor increased. Increasingly in the period after World War II, because of technological change and the growth in importance of the service sector in the economy, employers needed to find a new source of educated labor for white-collar jobs. Women were an obvious and largely untapped potential source of such labor. But to get women into the labor force, the barriers to their participation had to be eased. Once women were in the labor force, employers had interests in promoting talented employees, giving them more responsibilities, and so on. Now, employers were also overwhelmingly men and generally had sexist attitudes, and these attitudes continued to interfere with the most efficient hiring and promoting practices, particularly when sexism also allowed employers to pay women less than men. For these reasons, male employers were rarely at the forefront of actively challenging sexism. Nevertheless, their interests in maximizing profits for their capitalist firms and their interests as men in maintaining traditional gender relations often cut in opposite directions. This increasing incoherence of their interests undermined men's determination to defend sexist practices when those practices came under challenge. Robert Jackson explains the erosion of women's subordination this way:

> The driving force behind this transformation has been the migration of economic and political power outside the household and its reorganization around business and political interests detached from gender. . . . Gender inequality declined because modern society transferred social power from people committed to preserving men's advantages to institutions and people whose interests were indifferent to gender distinctions. . . . While prejudices against women still ruled many actions of men with power, *their institutional interests repeatedly prompted them to take actions incompatible with preserving gender inequality.*[9]

The Crisis of Female Domesticity

Changes in the interests of men within the public sphere are only part of the story. A second powerful cluster of processes are also at work in the radical transformation of gender relations: processes that have eroded the stability

---

[9] Jackson, *Destined for Equality*, p. 2. (Italics added.)

of the traditional role for women in the private sphere and therefore affect the interests of women with respect to gender relations. These processes have been described by Kathleen Gerson as generating a crisis of female domesticity in the United States.[10]

The American family in the 1950s can be seen as embedded in a systematic structure of interconnected, reinforcing social supports for female domesticity. This system has five main elements:

1. *Stable marriages.* Stable marriages gave women a long time horizon in forming their expectations about the support that will be provided by their husbands and sense of security in these relations. This situation encourages economic dependency of women on men and reinforces the sense of the motherly role as natural. Particularly in a world where most families had at least three or four children and mothers were not expected to work for pay while children were living in the home, this marital stability encouraged an ideal of lifelong domesticity for married women.

2. *Blocked work opportunities.* When labor market opportunities for women are fairly restricted, domesticity becomes a more attractive practical alternative than when lots of interesting and well-paid work opportunities are available.

3. *The family wage.* The family wage is the principle that the earnings of the male breadwinner should be sufficient to support a family. In the United States, the ideal of the family wage became the norm from the end of the nineteenth century until the middle of the twentieth. Especially if income is rising over time, the household feels reduced pressure for the wife to earn income. The family wage was never a universal reality in the United States—in many poor families, wives always had to bring in some income—but for middle-class women, the family wage was a reality in the 1950s.

4. *Cultural and social supports for domesticity.* The sheer fact that being a full-time mother and housewife was such a common choice added credibility and support to the choice. Women were not isolated as homemakers, because most women were homemakers; this made the task of being a homemaker much easier. Housewives had many neighbors in the same position who could help out and validate the choices being made. This was the "normal" way for married women

[10] Kathleen Gerson, *Hard Choices* (Berkeley: University of California Press, 1986).

to live their lives, and being statistically normal contributed to the view of this situation as also being normative (viewed as desirable).

5. *Cultural sexism.* Sexism as a cultural force also contributed to stabilizing female domesticity. The aphorism that "a woman's place is in the home" was backed by a wide range of beliefs about women and their competences: women are naturally nurturant and gentle, best suited for the role of mothers and homemakers; they lack men's competitive drive and resilience, which are needed for successful careers; men need a supportive wife to take care of them and stand behind them; and so on.

This was a real system: a coherent, interconnecting set of social forces that reinforced each other and sustained the pattern of gender relations in which women were very disproportionately housewives and men breadwinners. At its height, this system constituted a kind of self-sustaining equilibrium.

Beginning in the 1960s and accelerating in the 1970s, every one of these elements eroded:

1. *The decline of permanent, stable marriage.* Less stable marriages meant that women could no longer count on the lifelong financial support of a husband, so it was important for them to obtain skills and maintain their earning power. Economic dependency became an increasingly risky strategy once divorce rates rose.

2. *The expansion of work opportunities.* Rapid changes in the labor market for women meant that the viability of alternatives to domesticity was increasing, even if these opportunities were still more restricted than those of men. The demand by employers for female labor increased dramatically in the post–World War II period.

3. *The decline of the family wage.* Stagnation of male wages, especially since the early 1970s, meant that women felt increasing economic pressures to work to sustain family income. This decline in the family wage was partially the result of the rapid decline in the labor movement, which had long backed the principle of the family wage, but it was also due to the general deregulation of labor markets that began in the 1970s.

4. *Erosion of supports for domesticity.* The cultural supports for the full-time housewife role began to erode in the 1960s. By the 1990s, in many

communities full-time housewives were a small minority; as a result, women in this role were much more socially isolated and, to some extent, less valued.

5. *Cultural antisexism.* Strong criticisms of cultural sexism became an important force beginning in the 1960s. This change is reflected in language, schoolbooks, advertising, and the mass media. The cultural attack on sexism is still partial and incomplete, but to an unprecedented extent, the images and role models of women in traditionally male roles of all sorts have become commonplace. Advertisements portray female construction workers; TV shows have female police detectives as well as publicly visible and powerful female corporate executives and politicians. The development and cultural dissemination of images of men in traditional female roles is much weaker, but nevertheless the idea that men can effectively and lovingly take care of babies is no longer a strange idea. As a small indicator of this cultural change, today at most American airports the men's restrooms have diaper-changing stations.

Taken together, these forces mean that the taken-for-granted, self-reinforcing model of female domesticity has collapsed. And with that collapse, the interests of women in transforming gender relations also have changed.

Capacities for Challenge

The change in the interests of many men, linked to changing economic conditions, contributed to a weakening of male resolve to maintain traditional forms of male domination; the erosion of the culturally dominant model of female domesticity led many women to see that their interests would be advanced by challenging male domination. The actual transformation of the rules of the game that back gender inequality, however, required collective action and struggle. What eventually came to be known as the women's movement was key to this transformation. The struggles took many forms: Court cases against specific forms of discrimination against women were brought by individuals and organizations. Women's political organizations were established to lobby for legislative change and play an active role in shaping political agendas. The Democratic Party took on equal rights for women as a central policy objective, even if there was uneven enthusiasm for actively pursuing this agenda. Women's caucuses and networks were formed within professional organizations and academic disciplines to pressure for changes in internal policies and priorities. Women's studies programs were established in universities, and there was a proliferation of serious academic journals that focused on gender. Sexist language and practices were challenged in public meetings and institutional practices. At times there were significant public demonstrations, but more often the challenges took the form of arguments within meetings where institutional decisions were made.

The trajectory of these challenges was by no means smooth. There were major defeats, such as the failure of the Equal Rights Amendment to the U.S. Constitution. Frequently the demands of women were mocked, and feminism as the articulated way of talking about gender relations and male domination was often caricatured and denounced. Nevertheless, the cumulative effect of these challenges over time has been to fundamentally shift the terms of public discussion about gender. Overt defenders of male domination are on the margins of the public debate and have virtually no chance of rolling back the major institutional and legal changes that have occurred. There is also virtually no chance that the major social structural changes concerning gender inequality will be substantially reversed. The United States is unlikely ever to return to a social pattern of high fertility and large families, with a predominance of stable lifetime marriages in which most married women are full-time housewives and women no longer aspire to challenging careers in the public sphere. The issue now is not whether a regime of unequivocal male domination can be reinstated, but how much further we can go in eliminating the remaining forms of gender inequality.

PROSPECTS FOR FURTHER TRANSFORMATION: REMAINING CRITICAL TASKS

In the United States at the beginning of the twenty-first century, men and women both have complex and sometimes contradictory interests in pushing forward the frontiers of gender equality. Although most women benefit from greater gender equality, certainly some women experience increasing equality as a threat that imposes costs on them because it would further erode the historic protections of women that accompanied their economic dependency on men. For women who, for whatever reasons, embrace the ideal of lifelong female domesticity and really want to be full-time housewives and mothers, the decline of this cultural ideal and the accompanying social supports for such a life is harmful.

In pretty obvious ways, many men have something to lose from further advances in gender equality. Certainly men have some privileges in the workplace and at home that are undermined by gender equality: when the obstacles to women entering professions and managerial positions are removed, competition for these jobs increases. Some men, undoubtedly, would have gotten better jobs if women dropped out of the race. If true pay equity existed in the wage structure of jobs, the wages of some men would decline. Because of resource constraints, gender equality in the funding of sports at universities means a reduction in funding for some traditionally male sports. At many universities, some intercollegiate men's sports had to be dropped altogether. And if gender equality within the division of labor in the home were to increase to the point that men shared equally in the time-consuming burdens of domestic tasks, then the leisure time of many married men would decline. But it is also true—and this is an important yet often neglected point—that in certain important ways, men potentially have much to gain from deeper and more robust forms of gender equality in American life.

In a world of real gender equality, men would have a richer array of life choices for parenting and work. The dominant models of masculinity make it difficult for many men to play a full and active role in caregiving activities within the family. It is difficult for men to interrupt their careers to take care of small children. The dominant models of masculinity also promote intense forms of competitiveness that make many men miserable; in working excessively long hours, they often lose sight of more important things in their lives. Further advances toward gender equality will potentially involve a significant restructuring of the rules that govern the relationship between work and family, and this change would give both men and women greater flexibility and balance in their lives. So, while men do have things to lose from a full realization of the ideal of gender equality, they also have potentially important things to gain.

In moving more fully in the direction of gender equality, perhaps the key problem that needs to be solved is the gendered division of labor within the family.[11] As we have seen, even after the major changes that have occurred in the participation of women in the labor force, women still spend considerably more time doing domestic labor—housework and child care—than do men. This situation is itself a source of gender inequality insofar as it means that married men with children have more free time than do married women with children, at least if the women also work full-time in the labor force. There is no inherent reason that spouses should do exactly the same things in the household, but from the viewpoint of egalitarian conceptions of fairness, they should share equally in the burdens of domestic responsibilities—and this means that however the labor is divided, the spouses should end up with the same amount of free time. This is not the case in most families.

The inequalities in the gender division of labor, however, have an impact far beyond simply the specific problem of free time available to men and women within families. The division of labor at home also deeply affects inequalities in the labor market and employment. The greater domestic burdens that, on average, married women have compared to married men act as a significant constraint on the kinds of jobs they can seek in the labor market. It also affects the attitudes of employers toward prospective women employees, married or not.

It is one thing to demonstrate that the gender division of labor within the family constitutes one of the central social processes impeding further advances toward gender equality, but it is another thing to do something about this problem. Public policy can directly intervene in public forms of gender inequality in all sorts of ways: by developing legal rules against discrimination, changing the funding formulas for university programs, adopting affirmative action policies, and so on. But it is basically impossible and undesirable to directly intervene in the domestic division of labor. The idea of a law mandating equal housework for men and women is ludicrous, and the vision of housework police monitoring how couples share tasks is monstrous. So if we are to move toward a more equal sharing of the time burdens of family life, the process will have to occur through indirect means that change the incentives men and women have regarding these

---

[11] For a wide-ranging discussion of the link between the gender division of labor within the family and the broader problem of gender inequality, see Janet Gornick and Marcia Meyers, *Gender Equality: Transforming Family Divisions of Labor*, Vol. VI in the Real Utopias Project (New York: Verso, 2009).

tasks—and, perhaps, that also affect the balance of power of men and women within these domestic relations as they negotiate over domestic responsibilities.

Three policies are particularly relevant here: pay equity; publicly provided, high-quality child-care services; and egalitarian paid parental leave.

Pay Equity

We can think about the problem of gender equality in pay within the labor market in two different ways: equal pay for *identical* work, or equal pay for *equivalent* work. The first of these prohibits paying different salaries to male and female nursery-school teachers who have the same seniority and responsibilities. But this approach allows for truck drivers and parking attendants to be paid more than nursery-school teachers.

The second sense of equal pay says that two jobs with equivalent levels of skills and responsibilities should be paid the same. This principle, also known as comparable worth, poses a much more complex problem because it requires comparing very different kinds of jobs and assessing their skill and responsibility characteristics. Equal pay for equivalent work would go much further in eliminating gender inequality in labor market earnings because it would directly undermine the strong tendency for jobs that are associated with "women's work" to be less valued than traditionally male jobs. In particular, this tendency has underwritten the low wages of various types of caregiving jobs.

Beyond simply improving the wages of workers in many traditionally female jobs, paying jobs on the basis of comprehensive comparable worth has two potential consequences. First, in the long run this change is likely to lead to a decline of sex segregation of occupations. Many more men would eventually want to be day-care workers if those jobs paid as much as being a postal worker or a bus driver. Lower pay is not the only reason men stay away from traditionally female jobs, but it is surely one of the reasons. Second, and particularly important for the issue of the division of labor within families, strong forms of comparable worth would go a long way toward equalizing the average earnings of men and women, and this in turn would affect the domestic conditions of negotiation over household tasks. One reason men do less work in the home is that they earn more in the labor market. This inequity has important symbolic effects, making it seem that a husband's time is more "valuable" than that of his wife. If husbands and wives earned roughly the same, then they would enter into negotiations over housework on more equal footing.

We do not want to oversimplify the complex process by which people navigate the many trade-offs and dimensions of their intimate lives. Much more is in play here than simply the power resources people bring into a relationship. Men and women have habits and dispositions that shape their expectations regarding family relationships, and they have emotional vulnerabilities and needs that affect the outcomes of conflicts over housework and child care. Still, within this complex process, a shift in the external resources a person can bring into the family plays a role, and public policies over pay equity can affect this aspect of the problem.

Publicly Supported, High-Quality Child-Care Services

Another public policy that could significantly affect the gender division of labor within families concerns the availability of affordable child-care services, including early infant day care, preschool programs, and after-school programs. A fully developed system of such services would include day-care facilities within workplaces, neighborhoods, and schools. The only way such services will be both affordable for most families and of high quality is for them to be heavily subsidized. Without such services, the responsibility for providing caregiving to children falls entirely on the family, and in practice this generally means mainly on mothers. This burden of responsibility in turn undermines the kinds of jobs women with families can seek and the hours they can work, and it makes it more difficult to move toward an equal sharing of responsibilities within the family.

Paid Parental Leave

The final policy that would have a potentially important impact on the gender division of labor within the family is paid parental leave for family caregiving responsibilities. Parental leave can be used at the birth of a child or to tend for a sick family member.

Among all economically developed countries, the United States has by far the most limited legally required provisions for parental leave (Figure 16.15). In the United States there is no legal right for any *paid* family caregiving leave; only two weeks of unpaid leave are required, and even that policy applies only to businesses employing more than fifty workers.

FIGURE 16.15—Legally required paid parental leave in 20 countries, 2011

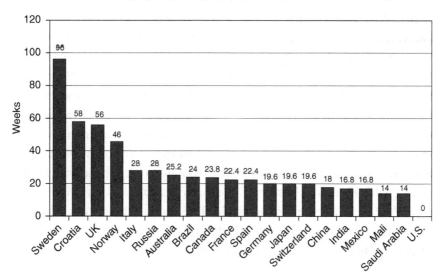

Source: International Labour Organization report, *Maternity at Work: A Review of National Legislation*, 2nd ed. (New York: United Nations Statistics Division).

All other developed countries, and even many relatively poor countries, have provisions for some level of legally required paid family caregiving leaves. In Sweden, for example, families are entitled to 480 calendar days of paid child-based leave per couple. Of these 480 days, the first 390 are paid at 80 percent of the person's salary and the rest at 180 Swedish kroners (about $28 in 2014) per day, which is about 18 percent of average wages. Mothers are also entitled to fourteen weeks of paid maternity leave, beginning seven weeks before birth. The 480 days of paid leave can be divided by mothers and fathers in whatever way they choose, except for a sixty-day quota that is reserved for each parent. As might be expected, mothers take a much greater amount of leave than do fathers, but fathers have been slowly increasing the amount of leave they take.[12] Few other countries are as generous in their paid parental leave policies as Sweden, but every rich country provides at least some leave, and nearly all countries provide leave for fathers as well as mothers.

These kinds of requirements regarding paid family leave make it easier for families to juggle the demands of paid work and family responsibilities in a

[12] This description of Swedish parental leave policy comes from Rebecca Ray, Janet C. Gornick, and John Schmitt, *Who Cares? Assessing Generosity and Gender Equality in Parental Leave Policy Designs in 21 Countries* (Washington, DC: Center for Economic Policy Research, 2009).

more balanced way. The policies do not, however, necessarily do much to change the gender division of labor within families, because when generous paid parental leave is available, women are much more likely to take advantage of it than are men. Janet Gornick and Marcia Meyers have proposed a different format for this leave that would encourage greater gender equality in its use.[13] Instead of allocating, as in Sweden, the paid leave to *families*, the leave should be allocated to individual spouses on a use-it-or-lose-it basis. For example, in the Swedish case this would mean that at the birth or adoption of a child, mothers and fathers each would be allocated six and a half months of paid leave at 80 percent of pay. Employers would be required to keep the seniority clock ticking while a leave was being taken, so that men (and, of course, women too) would not feel they were losing out in their career advancement while on leave. Over time, with such individualized leave, it would be expected that men would begin to take leave more extensively.

These three policies—pay equity; high-quality, publicly funded child care; and paid parental leave—would help change the environment in which men and women grapple with the difficult issues of transforming gender relations. A skeptic of these kinds of policy proposals might argue that the cultural norms regarding appropriate roles for mothers and fathers are too deeply ingrained for these kinds of policies to have much of an impact. Unless the policies are highly coercive, men will simply not take much advantage of paid leave; and though pay equity and good child care might be desirable in their own right, they will have little impact on what happens inside of families because of men's resistance to them. There are indications, however, that unmarried young men and women in the United States today are strongly disposed to more egalitarian relationships.

Sociologist Kathleen Gerson has done intensive research on how young men and women think about the way they want to live their lives when they form families. She identifies three different ideal models of family relations held by the subjects of her research:

1. *A neo-traditional model* involving a permanent bond with an intimate partner in which one partner specializes in breadwinning and the other in caretaking (even if both hold paid jobs)

---

[13] See Gornick and Meyers, *Gender Equality*.

2. *A broadly egalitarian model* involving a lasting bond with an intimate partner, a search for personal balance between work and family, and a commitment to flexible, egalitarian sharing of earning and caring

3. *A self-reliant model* emphasizing self-reliance whether single, cohabiting, or married, and a belief that it is important not to rely on a partner for breadwinning or caretaking even if one happens to be in a long-term relationship

The participants in Gerson's study were then asked which of these ideals would be their first choice. Those who picked the egalitarian model as their ideal were also asked what their fallback position would be if they were unable to have their ideal. The results are extremely revealing about ideals and dilemmas at this point in the transformation of gender relations (Figure 16.16). There was very little gender difference in the stated ideals: over two-thirds of the young men and young women in the study endorsed the egalitarian family model. The fallback positions of young men and women,

FIGURE 16.16—Family ideals and fallback positions of young men and women

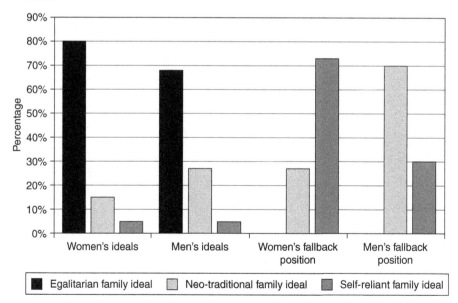

Source: Kathleen Gerson, *The Unfinished Revolution: How a New Generation Is Reshaping Family, Work, and Gender in America* (New York: Oxford University Press, 2009).

however, were completely different: 73 percent of women who preferred the egalitarian family said that if this ideal was not possible, they would prefer the self-reliant model over the neo-traditional model; in contrast, 70 percent of men chose the neo-traditional family model as their fallback position.

These preferences suggest that if young families lived and worked in an environment with strong supports for egalitarian relations, then in a significant proportion of these families men and women might collaborate in forging more egalitarian relations. Ultimately it is in the micro-settings of everyday life, where men and women live their lives within gender relations, that deeper forms of egalitarian relations will be created. This will certainly be a protracted process. Children born at the beginning of the twenty-first century already live in a dramatically transformed world of gender dynamics as compared to the world of their grandparents. These children will bring to the intimate relationships they create as adults much more egalitarian expectations about the appropriate roles for men and women than those held in the past. With these expectations and, perhaps, greater institutional supports for equal sharing of domestic burdens, they may also be able to further erode the inequalities linked to gender that are rooted in the intimate settings of the family.

Part III

DEMOCRACY

In the first part of this book, we explored how the American economy works. The central theme of our investigation was that even though a capitalist market economy may be efficient in many ways and may be an effective engine of economic growth and technological innovation, it also generates important inefficiencies and creates many problems that it cannot solve by itself. In one way or another, these problems can be countered only by an affirmative state in which the government acts to correct the pathologies of markets.

In the second part of the book, we examined the value of fairness and the problems of inequality—especially economic inequality, but also racial and gender inequality. The central theme was that the extremely high levels of economic inequality and poverty in the United States today pose serious challenges to principles of fairness. Again, these problems will not self-correct simply by the actions of individuals and the market; a collective response through a democratic process is required if fairness is to be achieved.

So, the themes of these first two parts bring us to democracy—the main tool we have for solving collective, common problems. Our task will be to examine how American democracy works, and why in many instances it fails to redress the kinds of problems we have identified in our study of the market and inequality.

We begin this discussion in Chapter 17 by clarifying exactly what we mean by *democracy* and by examining the difficult problem of building democracy in a society whose economy generates high concentrations of private power. In Chapter 18, we explore the dilemmas of political representation within American democracy and discuss how the specific rules of the game of electoral competition shape the kind of representation that becomes possible. Elections are the very core of democracy; however, as we shall see, due to the role of money in politics as well as the rules of electoral competition, elections in the United States fall far short of democratic ideals. Chapter 19 explores the attack on taxation and the affirmative state in American politics. The American Revolution was triggered by the issue of taxation–"no taxation without representation"–and to this day taxation is a central axis of political conflict. Taxes are essential to a democratic society, for they are the way we as a society can collectively allocate social resources between public and private purposes. In this chapter we explore the nature and purpose of taxation and the political assault on taxation.

The quality of democracy, of course, depends not just on the mechanics of representation but also on the extent to which citizens have access to high-quality information about political issues as well as the capacity to effectively process that information in making collective choices. The relationship between democracy and the corporate domination of the media is the central theme of Chapter 20.

Chapter 21 deals with the problem of militarism and empire in American democracy. The military always has a potentially ambiguous role in a democracy. On the one hand, the military is critical for national defense. On the other hand, when the military becomes connected to militarism and empire, it distorts national priorities and undermines democracy by fueling a politics of fear.

We conclude our exploration of democracy with two chapters that focus on the issue of mass participation in democratic life. In Chapter 22 we examine the labor movement as a critical basis for getting citizens involved in democracy and discuss how the hostile legal and economic environment for unions in the last decades of the twentieth century undercut this role. In Chapter 23 we explore various new kinds of initiatives by citizens to revitalize democracy from below.

17

DEMOCRACY: HOW IT WORKS

Democracy means "rule by the people." This is an extraordinary idea, a truly revolutionary ideal in the history of human affairs. Imagine: power should be vested in the people—not a hierarchy, not a king, not an elite, but the people. In most complex societies for most of human history, this notion would have been viewed as absurd. Government of the people, by the people, and for the people—the ideal is inspiring, revolutionary, emancipatory. But the reality is often ugly, cynical, manipulative. Instead of political equality and popular empowerment, democracy can become a game dominated by the power of elites. Rule by the people becomes largely a symbolic sideshow while the real exercise of political power occurs behind the scenes.

Most Americans are convinced that they live in a profoundly democratic society. Indeed, many believe that the United States is the most democratic society on earth. Some truths are lurking behind these claims: the United States has fairly competitive elections for many public offices; civil liberties are at least loosely protected; public officials are generally constrained by the rule of law and prevented from arbitrarily exercising their power. Life would be very different under a Fascist police state or a military dictatorship. So, the democraticness of American democracy is not an empty ideal. Nevertheless, we will argue in this chapter that the democratic character of American political institutions is much more contradictory and limited than this popular image.

DEMOCRACY AS A VALUE

Before exploring the problem of the contradictions and constraints facing American democracy, we need to more precisely define the ideal of democracy itself. What does *democracy* really mean? What is the core principle we really want to accomplish?

Democracy as an ideal, we believe, is embedded in a broader value concerning individual autonomy and power:

> All people should have broadly equal access to the necessary means to participate meaningfully in decisions over things which affect their lives. This includes both the freedom of individuals to make choices that affect their own lives as separate persons, and their capacity to participate in collective decisions which affect their lives as members of a broader community.[1]

This conception explicitly connects the problem of individual liberty with the problem of democracy. These issues are deeply connected because both embody the idea that people should control as much as possible the decisions and conditions that affect their lives. Freedom is the capacity to make choices over one's own life; democracy is the capacity to participate in the effective control over collective choices that affect one's life as a member of a wider society. Of course, the line of demarcation between these two ideas is often ambiguous because many actions of individuals have, as we saw in earlier chapters, externalities that affect the lives of others, particularly when those individual choices are viewed cumulatively. The decision to drive an SUV affects other people through carbon emissions and the depletion of petroleum resources. The decision to build a large house in a suburb affects other people through urban sprawl. The decision to buy expensive private education for one's children affects other people by changing the conditions for competition to enter the best universities. Should these decisions be viewed as purely private decisions and thus in the domain of individual freedom and autonomy, or are these public decisions because of their effects on other people as members of a society? There is no simple answer to this question, because these decisions have both public and private dimensions.

A central problem of a democracy is, therefore, how to balance these considerations, how to take into account the social externalities of the choices people make as separate individuals while at the same time allowing individuals to make meaningful choices over their own lives. One possible balance is to decide to ignore many of the social externalities of private choices on the grounds that all things considered, tolerating negative effects

---

[1]This particular formulation comes from Erik Olin Wright, *Envisioning Real Utopias* (New York: Verso, 2010), chapter 2. For a more extended discussion of democracy, including the principle of democratic legitimacy by which we think democratic institutions should be judged, see Joshua Cohen and Joel Rogers, *On Democracy* (New York: Penguin, 1983). We draw on their analysis of the workings of capitalist democracy throughout this chapter.

on others is better than interfering with individual choice. This is the balance that creates strong private property rights and blocks intrusive forms of democratic interference with the acquisition and use of private property. Another possible balance is to impose many restrictions on individual choices through various kinds of regulations—zoning rules for cities, taxes on large cars, limitations on private education—on the grounds that the harmful effects of these externalities are themselves a violation of other people's individual liberty. This is always a difficult issue, but at least in a democracy, in principle the people who are deciding how to work out this balance are the same people being affected by such decisions.

In a democracy, then, the general idea that people should control the decisions that affect their lives is applied to the context of decisions that affect their lives as members of society:

> In a democracy, decisions that affect our common fate and common interests should reflect the collective will and choices of equal citizens rather than of powerful elites.

This is a demanding ideal, for it says more than simply that we have regular elections and basic political freedoms and rights; it says that political institutions are designed to require decisions affecting our communities and collective destiny to be made in ways that are truly subordinated to the will of ordinary citizens. There are two key parts to this definition:

1. *Decisions that affect our common fate and common interests* . . . Democracy concerns a particular subset of all the decisions people make: those decisions that affect our common fate and common interests. This principle implies that it is possible to make a rough distinction between decisions that affect only the individual persons making the choice and decisions that affect a broader community. This condition also means that the robustness of a democracy depends upon the extent to which issues of collective concern are in fact included within collective decision making. A narrow scope for democratic decision making undermines democracy itself. In these terms, the general trend—beginning in the early 1980s—in the United States toward privatization of state functions and deregulation of market activities constitutes a reduction in democracy.

2. *. . . should reflect the collective will and choices of equal citizens rather than of powerful elites.* The notion of a "collective will" is an especially

elusive one. Individuals have minds and motivations, and thus we all have an intuitive sense about what is meant by *individual* will. The precise meaning of the idea of a *collective* will is less transparent. In an ideal sense, what we mean is a broad consensus reached through the open deliberation of people making a collective decision. The will is collective insofar as it is the result of a collective process of genuine deliberation and consensus formation. That is the ideal. In practice a full consensus is rarely possible, so the issue is more a question of collective decisions coming out of open debate by those affected by the decision.

The idea of "equal citizens" means that everyone has not only equal political *rights* to participate in democratic processes but also equal *access* to the practical means of political participation. The first of these considerations is much easier to realize than the second, although in the United States it took almost two centuries of protracted struggles—from the founding of the country to the 1960s—to accomplish anything close to equality of formal citizenship rights. The second of these conditions—equal access by citizens to the practical means of political participation—is much harder to achieve and remains a distant ideal in contemporary American society.

This ideal of democracy can be undermined in many ways:

- Important issues of collective concern may be excluded from the arenas of democratic decision making.
- Citizens may have very unequal access to the political process, due to either official discrimination or inequalities in politically relevant resources and capacities.
- The process by which citizens form their opinions on political issues may be heavily manipulated by elites and other powerful actors, so that even if the citizens have meaningful access to political processes, they do not really participate as autonomous persons.
- The electoral rules of the game may give advantages to some kinds of interests over others.
- The internal organization of the bureaucratic machinery of the state may give special access to certain groups of citizens and elites in shaping the implementation of public policy.
- Politicians and state officials may have sufficient autonomy and power that they use the state in pursuit of their own interests. Public policy in

practice, therefore, may reflect the will and collective choices of political officials more than of equal citizens.

- The private exercise of power outside the political realm may block or undermine public decisions.

Of course, each of these threats to democracy is a matter of degree. Thus we can talk about the extent to which any given political system is democratic, not simply whether it is or is not democratic. Political institutions should be judged by the ways in which they advance or thwart movement toward the democratic ideal.

In the rest of this chapter, we explore a number of core problems in the actual functioning of democratic institutions in the contemporary United States. We begin by stating what should be a noncontroversial claim about the relationship between public and private power in American democracy: private property removes decisions of collective importance from democratic decision making. This proposition forms the basis for a more elaborate discussion of the two kinds of constraints on democracy in a capitalist economy, which we refer to as the *demand constraint* and the *resource constraint*. These general considerations will form the backdrop for our more detailed discussions of particular aspects of democracy in the chapters that follow.

THE CORE PROPOSITION: PUBLIC AND PRIVATE POWER IN CAPITALIST DEMOCRACY

Underlying our exploration of American democratic institutions is a simple proposition: *Many decisions that are of momentous importance to society as a whole and that have deep public ramifications are made as private decisions by capitalist firms and wealthy individuals.* The proposition states that in a capitalist democracy, the basic decisions over the allocation of investments and how they are used are made by private owners on the basis of their own self-interest. This allocation of power to individuals and firms is called private property. This claim should not be viewed as controversial. It is an almost trivial observation of how a democratic capitalist society works, but still it is of fundamental importance if we are to understand the limits and possibilities for democracy in America.

Of course, there are public rules that impose constraints on how people spend their money and what they can do with their private property, but the underlying premise of all such rules is still that individuals have the right to do with "their" property as they see fit and that the rules should interfere as little as possible with such rights. Many such decisions have a large impact on other people and broader communities who have no say at all in the decisions. Here are some examples:

- Decisions to close a factory and move production abroad can have a devastating impact on the people in a region, including many people who do not work in the factory. For example, the home values of everyone in an area can drop precipitously when a large factory closes. Decisions to close factories are not simply the effect of the operation of impersonal market forces beyond anyone's control. Frequently a factory is closed not because it is unprofitable, but because the rate of profit would be higher in another location. If the people affected most by the decision—the employees—owned the factory, they would not close it, because they would weigh the costs and benefits very differently. In American society, as it exists, such decisions are made on the basis of a private calculation of costs and benefits to owners without regard to the effects on others.

- Decisions to invest in certain lines of production rather than others—for example, large inefficient automobiles rather than smaller energy-efficient vehicles—have big effects on the environment and cities. Even if these decisions are made in response to consumer demand for big cars, nevertheless these are still private decisions made on the basis of each person's private evaluation of their own interests. And yet these decisions have big public ramifications.

- The choice of technologies, work organization, the skill structure of jobs, and other aspects of the production process have large effects on the lives of people who work within firms, and yet these people are rarely part of the decision-making process. Decisions to introduce labor-saving technologies and to fire workers have a large impact on the families of those workers and on the larger community in which they live, but again, these are legally defined as managerial decisions made on behalf of the owners of private property and need not in any way be responsive to the interests of the affected workers.[2]

---

[2] For an extended defense of why a commitment to democracy entails the right of workers for strong representation on the board of directors of corporations, see Robert Dahl, *A Preface to Economic Democracy* (Berkeley: University of California Press, 1986), especially chapter 4, "The Right to Democracy within Firms." Dahl's central argument is that the reasons defenders of democracy use to oppose political dictatorships in the state also apply to the workplace: in both cases, people have the right to be empowered to participate in decisions that deeply affect their lives.

These are perfectly ordinary, legal business decisions, the kinds of decisions that get made every day. They are considered private matters, but they massively shape the fate of communities, our collective dilemmas and futures, and thus these private decisions violate the fundamental principle of democracy. People may disagree about what is a desirable balance between the democracy and the powers linked to private property. Some people argue that even the limited restrictions we currently have on private property are undesirable because a more unfettered capitalism would be a more efficient capitalism; others argue that the existing balance between public regulation and private power is far too skewed toward the private. But regardless of one's views on what constitutes the optimal balance, by allocating so much power to private actors in the form of private property rights, extensive decisions of great concern for the public fall outside the realm of public, democratic decision making.

This core proposition—that in a capitalist democracy many decisions with large public consequences are made privately—provides the foundation for understanding the constraints on American democracy. In what follows, we distinguish two broad types of constraints that impinge on democratic institutions: the *demand constraint* and the *resource constraint*.[3] In assessing any political process, two kinds of questions need to be explored: What do people want? What kinds of power do they have to get what they want? The demand constraint refers to *restrictions on the goals of politics*, on what people can realistically demand from the government; the resource constraint refers to the *different capacities different actors have* for accomplishing their goals.

THE DEMAND CONSTRAINT

What explains why certain demands get raised in the political system and others don't? Why is such a narrow range of issues so actively debated in the political arena? In particular, why are political demands generally so mild, so unthreatening to the system as a whole? Why, most of the time, do people limit their political demands to things that are compatible with the central economic interests of business corporations?

The basic argument is this: so long as most important economic decisions are made through the exercise of private power—that is, so long as the economy remains capitalist—*the welfare of everyone depends upon the welfare*

---

[3] The language and analysis of the demand constraint and resource constraint are from Cohen and Rogers, *On Democracy*.

of capitalist firms. Because owners of capital control investments, and investments are so important for the overall health of an economy, the satisfaction of the interests of owners is a necessary condition for the satisfaction of all other economic interests in the system. The rules of the game for a capitalist democracy ensure that, in general, the only demands that get raised are those compatible with capitalist interests and a good business climate.

This argument can be elaborated through six steps:

1. If the basic interests of capitalist firms are not stably secured, then capitalist firms will not make adequate profits.
2. If capitalist firms do not make adequate profits, then owners of capital will reduce their investments in capitalist firms.
3. If investments decline, then there will be a decline in production.
4. If there is a decline in production, then there will be a decline in jobs and wages.
5. If there is a decline in jobs, income, and production, then there will be a decline in tax revenues available to the state.
6. A decline in taxes means that the capacity of the democratic state to pursue all its goals declines. The state is dependent upon income generated in the capitalist economy for whatever it does. Any political demand that requires state spending, therefore, ultimately must be consistent with the process that generates the revenues for that spending.

Taken together, this connected chain of cause and effect means that political demands within a capitalist democracy are broadly constrained to be consistent with what is good for capitalist firms. Of course there will still be sharp debates about what is in fact good for the profitability of firms. Some people will argue that government programs to reduce pollution will ultimately be good for firms by creating a healthier natural environment; others will argue that the regulations will harm firms because the regulated firms will face higher costs than do firms in other countries. But everyone, on whatever side of the debate, will ultimately have to worry about the policy's real effects on the vitality of the economic environment for profit making.

One consequence of the state's deep dependence on the private capitalist economy is that the interests of business appear to be in the "general interests" of society rather than merely the "special interests" of a particular class of people. There is a certain irony here. The political demand for lower taxes on business is defended as being in the interests of everyone; the demand for higher wages for workers is attacked as reflecting the special interests of unions. The saying, "What is good for General Motors is good for the country," therefore expresses a certain real truth: so long as America has a capitalist economy, it is critical for its corporations to be profitable.[4] This point implies that people will have a strong tendency to limit their demands to those that are consistent with a "good business climate." Every potential policy confronts the question, how will this affect business? This issue imposes significant constraints on the character of demands that have any political traction for improvements of health care, child care, the environment, energy, transportation, poverty. In each case, a pivotal axis of contention will be over the effects of such policy on the vitality of business. A sure way for a demand to be marginalized is for people to believe that it will be bad for business.

Furthermore, because of competition and pressures from investors, the time horizons for most capitalist firms tend to be fairly short term, and thus the priority given to a healthy business climate and the interests of firms also tends to shorten the time horizons of political demands. Reforms that are actually beneficial to capitalists as a whole in the longer term but costly in the short term are thus generally resisted by the business community. For example, suppose a reform of health insurance from the current mixed government and employer-based system to a single-payer system was proposed. On the one hand, this system would save money for most capitalists in the long run by restraining the long-term rise in health costs; but on the other hand, it would increase costs in the short term because of the universal health insurance coverage of all citizens. Such reforms are generally opposed by business. Similarly, reforms that would have a serious impact on global warming or energy conservation are likely to increase costs on capitalist firms in the short term, even though they would have long-term benefits for capitalism as a whole. Again, such reforms are likely to be opposed by capitalists. Knowing these things, political actors are less likely to voice demands for such reforms in the first place.

The demand constraint on politics thus narrows political demands in two ways: first, it forces all political actors to be concerned with maintaining a healthy business climate; and second, it shortens the time horizon in which even the business climate is treated. The result is a pervasive

[4] The saying is an accurate statement of the meaning, if not the precise wording, of Senate testimony in 1953 by the then president of General Motors, Charles Wilson, who said, "For years I thought what was good for the country was good for General Motors, and vice versa."

preoccupation with short-term economic issues in political conflicts. This does not mean, of course, that people are interested only in money or never think about the future. People value many things other than money—art, justice, spiritual salvation, and nature, to name only a few. But even if people value these things, they still need material resources to pursue them. Even artists need to eat and have a roof over their heads, so they have an interest in a healthy capitalist economy and thus a concern for the short-term interests of capitalist firms.

THE RESOURCE CONSTRAINT

The demand constraint imposes limits on *what people are likely to demand*, but it does not dictate unique outcomes. Even given the pressures toward short-term economic interests, political demands can be more or less short run; more or less favorable to different categories of people; and, in particular, more or less favorable to the interests of capitalists. There is also often considerable ambiguity on precisely what the effects of any given policy will be, so even quite contrasting policies can all lay claim to being good for the economy. Furthermore, capitalists—like everyone else in a bargaining situation—often politically ask for much more than they actually need to make adequate profits. Bluffs and threats are a key part of political conflicts in a democracy, and so exactly which policies are adopted depends on the outcomes of political struggles among contending groups, not simply on abstract considerations of what kinds of policies will be good or bad for business.

This is where the *resource constraint* comes into play: in the political struggles that take place within capitalist democracies, ordinary citizens operate under severe resource constraints in having their interests translated into public policy. The most straightforward examples are instances in which money and wealth directly shape the outcomes of political processes:

- In all capitalist democracies, bribes and corruption influence public policy in various ways. All things considered, the United States probably has somewhat less corruption than do many other capitalist democracies; nevertheless, the direct use of bribes to influence both the passage of laws and the details of their implementation is a significant reality at every level of the political system. Corporations and wealthy individuals are in a much better position to influence government action in this way than are workers, the poor, and other categories of ordinary citizens.

- Even if we discount bribery, well-financed lobbying backed by wealthy corporations and individuals plays a significant role both in legislation and in the details of the actual implementation of public policy.
- Campaign contributions are another source of resource constraint: As we will see in Chapter 18, when elections are privately funded and the constraints on private funding are weak, the wealthy and organizations representing the wealthy are in a much better position than ordinary voters to influence the selection of candidates and the outcomes of elections.
- Control over mass media is another critical form of resource constraint. Freedom of speech is a formal right in the sense that everyone has the same freedom to express their ideas. But different social categories have vastly unequal access to the means of disseminating their ideas. Whose "free speech" is likely to be heard more loudly—an unemployed worker or a media magnate like Rupert Murdoch?

In each of these examples, people with limited wealth and money have distinct disadvantages in directly influencing political outcomes. Money talks. Still, in a democracy, numbers talk also. Elites and wealthy individuals are a small proportion of the total population. If public policy is drastically biased in favor of the rich and powerful, why don't ordinary citizens just get together and elect politicians who will serve their interests? They greatly outnumber elites, so they would win every time in a game of numbers, and that is what democracy is supposed to be.

The problem is that the resource constraint fundamentally undermines the ability of citizens to act collectively. To understand how this works, we have to return to a theme we explored in our discussion of the market: the free-rider problem.

The Resource Constraint and the Free-Rider Problem

As noted earlier, the central issue in the free-rider problem is that in many situations, people can personally benefit from the collective actions of others without directly participating in and bearing the costs of those collective actions. A worker who does not participate in a strike will still get a wage raise if the strike succeeds. A person who does not recycle will still get the benefit of an improved environment if everyone else recycles. Because a real cost is involved in contributing to the "public good" that results from collective action, and because each person's own participation makes so little difference to the outcome, many people are tempted to sit on the sidelines and let other people pay these costs. That behavior is called *free riding*.

How does the free-rider problem affect democracy, and how is it linked to the resource constraint? Here is the central issue: Democracy requires very high levels of robust cooperation among people. This is sometimes called *mobilization:* mobilization for political campaigns, voting, protests. People have to be willing to join together for political purposes, and costs are always associated with such participation. The free-rider problem makes political mobilization difficult. And—here is the crucial point—it is generally easier for wealthy people, people with lots of resources, to solve this problem or at least reduce its negative impact on their interests.

Let us look at the political free-rider problem for ordinary citizens: The empirical efficacy of *individual* participation in many political contexts is very low for most people. In most forms of political mobilization, the likelihood of success of the political action in question is not greatly affected by any given individual's participation. Elections, especially for important offices, are virtually never decided by one vote. One person more or less at a demonstration does not change the impact of the demonstration. One letter more or less from an ordinary citizen to a politician is not going to change a vote on legislation. From the simple viewpoint of one's own time and effort, for most citizens the answer to the question, "Is my effort in this political cause likely to affect an outcome that I care about?" is almost always no. If most people decide to participate in political mobilization only when their individual participation will clearly make a difference, then most people will abstain.

In the case of wealthy elites and corporations, the problem looks quite different. Individual corporations and wealthy individuals can participate in many ways in political activity for which their individual contribution significantly affects the outcome. When the executives in a large pharmaceutical corporation ask themselves, "Is the effort—and especially the money—our corporation can contribute to a political cause that is in our interests likely to affect the outcome?" the answer is often yes. The individual contribution of a corporation to a lobbying effort or to a political campaign of a sympathetic candidate can potentially affect the outcome significantly. This makes the cost-benefit calculation much simpler: Individual effort has more than a negligible impact on the outcome. It also makes coordinated contributions easier because each contributor sees a tangible benefit from contributing.

Here is another way of framing this contrast between elites and ordinary citizens: For elites, political influence depends mainly on their *willingness to pay*. For ordinary citizens, the most critical forms of participation are time and effort. Their political influence depends mainly on their *willingness to act*.[5] For rich individuals and powerful corporations, financial contributions to political campaigns generally do not significantly reduce their own levels of consumption or investment—they have plenty of discretionary resources to use for this purpose. For ordinary people, active participation always implies a decision to use scarce resources—time and effort—in one way and not another. The willingness to act involves much tougher problems of collective action, cooperation, and coordination than does the willingness to pay. This contrast between the way resources impinge on the process of political participation for powerful and wealthy political actors— both individuals and corporations—and for ordinary citizens is the fundamental issue of the resource constraint in capitalist democracies.

Information and the Problem of Rational Ignorance

Another critical way that the resource constraint undermines democracy concerns the problem of information. Good-quality information is critical for any democratic process. If citizens are to participate in the exercise of political power in an effective and meaningful way, then they need to have good information relevant to the problems being confronted in the political arena. This is one reason that in democratic political systems, freedom of speech is considered such an important right and a free press such an important institution.

The problem is that high-quality information is often costly to obtain. It takes time and effort to distinguish reliable from unreliable information, and in many instances it takes considerable training even to know how to go about this task. This is one reason, for example, for the existence of

[5] This contrast between willingness to pay and willingness to act comes from Claus Offe and Helmut Weisenthal, "Two Logics of Collective Action: Theoretical Notes on Social Class and Organizational Form," in *Political Power and Social Theory*, Vol. 1, ed. Maurice Zeitlin (Stamford, CT: JAI Press, 1980), pp. 67–116.

specialized services that provide certain kinds of information to people. *Consumer Reports*, one such service, is a nonprofit organization that tests consumer products and publishes easily accessible evaluations and ratings of different brands. Particularly when a consumer is purchasing an expensive product, this service offers an inexpensive way to make decisions based on high-quality information.

In the instance of consumer choices in the market, people have a fairly significant incentive to get good information. After all, that information will affect not only the choice they make, but the actual outcome of that choice. In the case of political information, the issue is not so simple. It is true that having good-quality information could affect the choice an individual citizen might make in the voting booth; however, that individual's own vote has in practical terms no effect on the outcome of the election (because elections are virtually never decided by one vote), so *getting good information will not affect the outcome itself.* When most citizens ask themselves, "Is the benefit of having good information worth the costs of acquiring it?" the answer will therefore be no—at least if the motivation for getting good information is actually affecting the political outcome.

There are, of course, other motivations, and they can be quite important. Many people are curious about the world and want to have good information about what is going on. This is the hallmark of the social category called intellectuals: they enjoy knowledge for its own sake and value high-quality information not simply because it makes for more rational choices, but because it contributes to their knowledge of the world. For information about social and political issues, however, most people are not serious intellectuals in this sense. Thus they have little incentive to seek out high-quality information about politically important issues, because such information is costly to obtain. The result is that for most people most of the time, the information they acquire on political issues is limited to the information available at zero cost—namely, information provided through the mass media, especially television.

Consider, for example, the question of health-care reform. There are many conflicting views about the nature of the problem and the optimal solutions. To really sort out the issues and come to a well-informed opinion about what would be the optimal policy for the United States requires a lot of effort. Is it worth the trouble? Time is scarce; people care about many things for which getting good information will have tangible effects. Is it worth sorting through all the arguments, searching out the most respected and reliable scholars and experts on the issues, and using this information to make up one's own mind? For most people, even those whose lives will be most affected by a change in the health-care system, getting good information on this political issue will in no way affect the outcome. It does not really matter how important the political decision is to them and how much difference a "right" decision will make in their lives. What matters in information acquisition is whether the value of the right decision, given the microscopic probability that a well-informed (or ignorant) individual will make any difference in the outcome, is greater than the cost of being well informed. It almost never is. So, unless they value being well informed for its own sake, it will not be economically rational for most people to invest their own time in acquiring that information. It is economically rational to be ignorant, or limit your information acquisition to the information that can be acquired for "free."

For elites and powerful corporations, in contrast, it is often worth getting high-quality information about political issues, the alternatives being debated, and the nature of government regulations and policies. It is worthwhile for health insurance corporations to have precise information about the nature of proposed legislation on health care and its expected impact on their interests, and to have good information about the likely behavior of different politicians regarding these issues. Furthermore, given the enormously high stakes of the policy issues and given their ability to influence the outcomes, it is worth spending large sums of money to influence the terms of the debate. In particular, it is worth spending a lot of money providing "free" information to the public about the effects of alternative health-care reform proposals. This is done most obviously through advertising campaigns, like the notorious campaign against health-care reform in the early 1990s, but it is also done through "talking heads" commentaries on news programs and talk ratio. In these and other ways, elites are able to influence how issues are framed in public discussions.

In short, it makes sense for powerful groups to spend lots of money to provide free information—or, more precisely in many contexts, misinformation—to citizens, and for most ordinary people to consume only such free information. Or, to put the matter in starker terms: *It is rational for most people to remain ignorant about political matters.*

Rational ignorance is another example of a collective action problem: Most citizens have an interest in having elections decided on the basis of good-quality information because good information increases the chances of electing candidates who best serve their interests. If all citizens paid for good-quality information on political issues, then this would improve the quality of electoral competition and increase the likelihood of the interests of most citizens being effectively represented. But for any given voter, whether or not they themselves spend the time and money for good information will not affect the outcome of elections. If most citizens behave this way, then elections will be based on poor-quality information—sound bites, political propaganda, advertisements by wealthy interest groups, and so on.

All capitalist democracies confront the problem of the demand constraint and the resource constraint on democratic politics. This is inherent in the basic structure of these societies. Nevertheless, the degree to which these constraints reduce democracy varies. In all capitalist democracies, the centrality of private ownership to the functioning of the economy excludes important issues from direct democratic decision making and constrains the kinds of political demands citizens can realistically make. Citizens in all capitalist democracies face resource constraints in organizing politically, and "rational ignorance" is an issue everywhere. Yet, depending on how the political system is organized, how the rules of the game are structured, how the rights of private property are regulated, and many other things, these constraints on democracy may be very narrow or relatively lax. In the chapters that follow, we will examine a range of issues that shape the distinctive character of these constraints in American democracy.

18

ELECTIONS AND VOTING

Elections are at the very core of democracy. While an ideal democracy includes important forms of direct participation by citizens in many aspects of public decisions, the most basic constraint on oppressive state authority that we have is the fact that we elect the decision makers and can get rid of them if we dislike what they do. Any evaluation of democracy in America must include a careful examination of its electoral system and how it works.

In this chapter we explore two broad themes about voting and elections in American democracy. The first concerns an important theoretical puzzle about democratic elections: why do people bother voting in the first place? Given that a single vote almost never decides large elections, on the face of it voting might seem to be a waste of time: doing something that has no practical effects. Answering this question will help us get a sense of some of the conditions that strengthen or undermine the vitality of electoral politics.

The second theme concerns the problem of how deeply democratic are elections in the United States. In the transition to democracy within authoritarian regimes, the catchphrase "free and fair elections" is often invoked in assessing how democratic a society really is. Some countries hold regular elections in which a single candidate receives 99 percent of the vote, but we do not consider this result the slightest bit democratic. But what precisely do we mean by *free and fair*? An election might be unfair in obvious ways— stuffing the ballot box, faking the numbers, preventing people from voting by intimidation or simply excluding them from the voter lists. Until the 1960s in the South, most African Americans were blocked from voting through various devices. The most notorious were the infamous literacy tests requiring potential black voters to show a thorough knowledge of the U.S. Constitution (for example) before they could be registered, whereas white voters had much less demanding tests. This process, by any standard, was unfair.

Fraud, intimidation, and illegal exclusions are obvious ways to render elections less democratic. Although these kinds of processes do happen in the United States—for example, in the 2000 presidential election when the state of Florida purged its voter lists of felons in such a way that many non-felons, mostly black, were illegitimately denied the right to vote—fraud and repression of voters are not generally the most important issues in the United States. We will focus instead on three crucial features of our electoral system that undermine the fairness and democratic nature of elections: (1) representation rules, (2) the boundaries of electoral districts, and (3) campaign finance.

WHY DO PEOPLE BOTHER VOTING?

During election campaigns, people are encouraged to vote by claims that every vote matters, but this slogan is plainly false. *Voting* matters and the *aggregate* of all votes matter, but each single vote as such does not matter, at least in the sense of really influencing the outcome of the election. It takes time and effort to vote, and in some places a lot of time and effort, so why do people do it?

If people really behaved like simple, self-interested, rational actors making cost-benefit calculations in the way that is described in the prisoner's dilemma, then virtually no one would bother voting. However, even in low-turnout national elections in the United States, somewhat more than 50 percent of eligible voters do vote, which means that something else is going on. People make many choices on the basis of what they believe is the morally right thing to do, and on their more general sense of their efficacy as a citizen, rather than on the basis of a simple cost-benefit analysis of what's in it for them. People are moral beings, not just self-interested actors, and many people see voting as a duty. This sense of moral obligation can take different forms.

One possibility is that when people recognize that they care about the outcome of the election—they believe that one candidate or party will be better than another—they then feel it would be wrong to be a free rider on the efforts of others. Norms against free riding are quite pervasive in all societies, even in a highly individualistic, market society like the United States. Not doing one's fair share or not pulling one's weight is broadly viewed as a violation of social norms in situations in which one is benefiting from some process of cooperation. Elections are one example. People may also believe in civic obligation and see voting as a strong duty that comes from membership in a community. In this case the issue is not simply that it is unfair to be a free rider on other people's efforts, but that it is a violation of one's identity as a citizen not to vote.

The fact that people vote, then, reflects the presence of important morally infused motivations. The vitality of popular participation in elections thus depends significantly on the way a society nurtures or undermines these kinds of civic identities and moral sentiments.

How does the United States fare in these terms? Table 18.1 indicates the average voter turnout rates in elections for the lower legislative houses from 1945 to 2013 for the United States and selected other capitalist democracies that had at least ten free elections in this period. (Figures for the United States are only for elections in presidential years. In off-year elections, figures for the United States are 10–15 percentage points lower.) Of the 31 countries in the table, the United States ranks 29th with an average turnout of only 47.5 percent; 19 countries had average turnouts above 70 percent; and 10 countries had turnouts above 80 percent. What's more, the longer-term trends in the United States do not point to a reversal of this low voter turnout. In off-year congressional races, the rate has declined from an average of 45.3 percent in the period 1950–1970 to 36.9 percent in the elections of 1990–2010. In presidential elections, even with the enthusiasm of Obama supporters in the 2008 and 2012 elections, voter turnout was still below the levels of the 1950s and 1960s (Figure 18.1). By comparative standards, we have an extremely apathetic electorate. Only 55 percent of voters vote even in high-profile presidential elections, and less than 40 percent vote in off-year national elections. In state and local elections the turnout figures are even worse, often falling below 10 percent.

A variety of factors come into play in explaining this low level of voter participation in the United States. One often-discussed issue is that in most places in the United States, voter registration procedures are much more difficult than in other democratic systems. Typically in the United States, people have to register to vote in special venues like county courthouses weeks before elections, and every time they move to a new address, they have to register again. The eight states that offer same-day voter registration at the polls—Idaho, Iowa, Maine, Minnesota, New Hampshire, North Dakota, Wisconsin, and Wyoming—have significantly higher voter turnout than does the United States as a whole: In the 2012 election, the turnout was about 68 percent for those states compared to 60 percent for the country overall. This finding suggests that the voter registration rules in other states

TABLE 18.1—Average voter turnout, 1945–2013, national parliamentary elections: Selected countries with at least 10 elections since 1945

Country	Compulsory vote	Number of elections	Parliamentary election turnout (%)—Average
Italy	No	18	89.4
Iceland	No	20	88.3
Belgium	Yes	21	85.3
Australia	Yes	27	83.9
Denmark	No	25	83.6
New Zealand	No	23	83.5
Sweden	No	20	82.6
Austria	No	21	82.4
Netherlands	No	21	81.7
Greece	Yes	21	80.1
Norway	No	18	78.7
Israel	No	20	78.2
Germany	No	18	77.7
Finland	No	19	76.7
Portugal	No	14	76.5
Turkey	Yes[1]	13	75.3
Spain	No	11	74.6
Ireland	No	18	73.6
UK	No	17	72.2
Japan	No	25	68.9
South Korea	No	13	68.6
Costa Rica	Yes	17	66.7
Canada	No	22	65.4
Venezuela	No	13	63.8
France	No	18	63.7
Luxembourg	Yes	16	61.9
India	No	15	61.4
Mexico	Yes	23	49.3
United States	No	34	47.5
Switzerland	No	17	46.6
Colombia	No	23	36.9

Note: For Turkey, No until 1977, Yes after.

Source: Authors' calculations based on data from International IDEA Unified Database. Available at http://www.idea.int/uid/search-adv.cfm (accessed April 7, 2014).

FIGURE 18.1–Voter turnout rates in U.S. national elections, 1948–2012

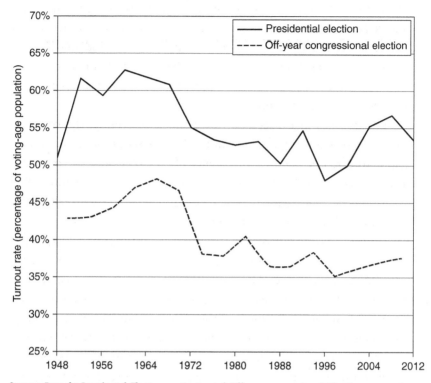

Sources: *Data for Presidential Elections, 1948–1980, and Off-year congressional Elections, 1950–1982, are from Michael P. McDonald and Samuel L. Popkin, "The Myth of the Vanishing Voter," American Political Science Review 95, no. 4 (2001), table 1. Data for Presidential Elections, 1984–2012, and Off-year congressional elections, 1986–2010, are from United States Elections Project, http://elections.gmu.edu/voter_turnout.htm (accessed Nov. 18, 2013).*

contribute to the depressed voter turnout rates. Still, even a rate of 68 percent falls well below that of nearly all other democracies.

In addition to cumbersome voter registration rules, beginning in the early 2000s the Republican Party initiated new impediments to voting in a number of states in the form of a requirement that voters show a government-issued identification card at the polls. For people with a driver's license, this poses no special burden. But for people without a driver's license, the requirement imposes significant costs in time and effort in order to be able to vote. This especially affects young people, the poor, central city dwellers, and minorities. The stated justification for requiring official photo identification at the polls is to prevent voter fraud, but there is simply no evidence that voter fraud is a significant problem anywhere in the United States. The real motivation for these laws is to reduce voting by social and demographic groups likely to vote for liberal and progressive candidates.

This partisan motivation is often revealed in the details of photo ID laws. In Texas, for example, student identification cards issued by universities are not allowed but gun registration cards are. As of 2014, five states have passed and implemented strict photo ID requirements—Georgia, Indiana, Kansas, Tennessee, and Texas—and five other states have passed but not yet implemented such requirements—Arkansas, Mississippi, North Carolina, Pennsylvania, Virginia, and Wisconsin.[1]

Aside from rules that directly create obstacles to voting, the very low level of voter turnout suggests that in the United States the sense of civic obligation to vote is low, for in the absence of civic obligation the individualistic cost-benefit calculation on voting strongly favors staying home. The question then becomes why civic obligation is generally so weak in the United States. We would stress a number of contributing factors.

First, some important elements in American culture run directly counter to values of collective responsibility and civic obligation: consumerism stresses the importance of private consumption over public goods; individualism stresses the importance of autonomously pursuing one's own life goals rather than being a member of the collective; and privatism emphasizes the superiority of private solutions to social problems over public initiatives. Within American history there is also an important strand of civic and even communitarian values, but these have been relatively marginalized beginning in the last decades of the twentieth century.

Second, since the 1970s, the constant attack on big government and the zealous praise of the virtues of the market have undermined many people's identification with the government and belief in politics. If, as Ronald Reagan said, "government is not the solution to our problem; government is the problem," then to many people politics will seem a largely irrelevant, even discredited activity. People with strong moral commitments toward the welfare of others are more likely to be drawn to participation in nonpolitical community service activities, often connected to churches rather than to politics. These kinds of morally driven service activities have the advantage of producing a tangible, positive effect from each person's participation—unlike voting, in which the positive effect comes from the collective aggregation of individual acts.

---

[1] In January 2014, as reported on the website of the National Conference of State Legislatures, a "state judge struck down Pennsylvania's strict photo ID requirement, saying that it would place an unreasonable burden on voters who do not currently have photo IDs. An appeal to the state Supreme Court is expected." http://www.ncsl.org/research/elections-and-campaigns/voter-id.aspx (accessed March 6, 2014).

Third, the very high levels of economic inequality in the United States erode the sense of community, of everyone being in the same boat together. And with that erosion comes a weakening of the sense of mutual obligation that is the core of civic obligation. This eroding sense of community reinforces efforts to seek private solutions to collective problems: gated communities in the face of urban poverty and crime; private schools in the face of deteriorating public education.

Finally, the role of money in politics and the recurrent stream of political scandals at all levels of government have led to a significant erosion of trust in government and politicians since the 1960s. Corruption breeds cynicism, and cynicism breeds apathy. But even aside from pure corruption, the importance of corporations and money in politics leads many people to feel that politics is not their affair, that it is rigged in favor of elites, and their interests do not count. People feel alienated and disconnected from the political system because it is so unresponsive to their needs.

Taken together, these factors mean that a significant proportion of citizens do not feel a strong sense of civic obligation to participate in electoral processes. This doesn't mean, of course, that all nonvoters lack civic motivations altogether, and it certainly doesn't mean that they lack moral commitments. It does mean that for many people, voting is not seen as a meaningful way of expressing moral commitments and civic obligations. The result is low turnout and a relatively apathetic democracy.

THE RULES OF THE ELECTORAL GAME

In Chapter 1, in our discussion of what it means to study something sociologically, we emphasized the importance of understanding the way our social activities are *governed by rules*. This is a very general idea applicable to all social contexts, but there is probably no better example than elections. Elections are one way of accomplishing a critical task that is faced in all complex social organizations: how to select the people who will make decisions that are binding on everyone. There are many ways of doing this. For example, in privately owned corporations, the owners of the corporation (the shareholders) choose the governors of the corporation. Private property rights confer on people the right to make binding decisions on the people who use that property, and when those rights are dispersed among many people in the form of shares, then—usually on the basis of one share, one vote—these owners collectively decide who will direct the business.

Election by all members of an organization is another way of choosing decision makers.

Though all democratic states share the general principle that political leaders are elected, there is enormous variation in exactly how each political system translates this general idea into concrete rules governing the actions and strategies of its people. Democratic elections are such a good illustration of the general sociological idea of rule-governed activity precisely because the variation in these rules is so clear and the consequences of this variation so important. In the rest of this chapter, we focus on three clusters of rules of the game that shape American democracy and affect its ability to support the ideals of democracy as rule by the people: representation rules for legislative elections, rules governing the boundaries of electoral districts, and rules governing financing elections.

Representation Rules

It is not enough to say that in a democracy people vote for candidates, these votes are counted, and the winner is elected. This description is far too vague to actually define the way an election is organized. What defines winning? What happens if no one gets a majority? How many candidates can you vote for? Do you vote for specific candidates or for parties? A full specification of an electoral system requires answering these and many other questions. Answering these questions is critical because different electoral rules generate very different dynamics of political competition with very different long-term effects on democratic life. This is a really interesting idea: that when you design an electoral system, the technical rules you adopt can generate dramatically different long-term patterns. Some electoral rules make it almost impossible for new political parties to become successful; others lead to massive fragmentation of the political system into tiny, unstable parties. Studying this sort of thing is what political scientists do. Here we will sketch only the most fundamental features of the representation rules in American elections and discuss how they reduce democracy.

Basic Structure of U.S. Elections: Single-Member Districts with Plurality Voting

In the United States, most elections are governed by rules referred to as single-member district elections with plurality voting, also called first past the post (FPP) single-member district election. Here is how it works: Within an electoral district, a number of candidates run for a single seat. Whoever gets the most votes wins. End of story. If you have three candidates, one could get 34 percent, and the other two 32 percent, and the candidate with 34 percent wins. This is the way we elect people to Congress in almost all states, and it is the process used in nearly all elections to state legislatures and local political offices.

The major consequence of a single-member district plurality voting system is a strong tendency for two political parties to dominate the political system, or what is called a two-party duopoly. In this kind of political system, it is extremely difficult for third parties to play a sustained, important role because third-party candidates have to confront the chronic problem of people's fear of wasting their vote on a third party.

Suppose that three candidates are running from three parties in an election—the Democratic Party, the Republican Party, and the Independent Party. You really like the Independent Party candidate, but you despise the Republican. The opinion polls indicate that about 35 percent of the electorate supports the Democratic Party candidate, 40 percent supports the Republican, and 25 percent the Independent. You much prefer the political positions of the Independent to those of the Democrat, but you really dislike the political positions of the Republican Party. What should you do? You fear that if you (and other people like you) vote for the Independent Party, your vote will help the Republican get elected. So, despite your preference, you end up voting for the Democratic Party. Most people who support the Independent share your worries and also vote for the lesser of two evils, so the Democratic Party candidate is elected. The final tally was 55 percent Democrat, 40 percent Republican, and 5 percent Independent. This outcome hardly reflects the true political sentiments of the electorate. The Democrat is elected with a strong "mandate," and the political position of the Independent Party is marginalized.

This kind of scenario is not simply a theoretical possibility. In the 2000 presidential election, the Green Party ran Ralph Nader as a third-party candidate opposed to both the Republican Party and the Democratic Party. Many people who actually supported Nader's positions nevertheless voted for Al Gore because they feared the consequences of a Bush victory. Despite this fear, in one key state—Florida—Nader received 95,000 votes or 2 percent of the total. Bush won (after hotly contested irregularities in the vote count) by roughly 500 votes. It is true that if Nader had not run in Florida, some of those 95,000 voters would not have bothered to vote, because no candidate represented their views. Still, many of them would have voted, and in that case those voters would have voted strongly for Gore over Bush. The Green Party was widely criticized after the election for being a spoiler; though there are arguments for both sides of this issue, the net effect on the fate of the Green Party was to reduce its political standing.[2]

The monopoly of power by two major political parties has many consequences. Most obviously, it tends to put on the political margins social interests that are not represented by the two dominant parties. It is very hard for a new political party to be taken seriously, for it to gradually increase its standing in the political system. Typically, new parties start small and then gain credibility, first by getting limited representation in local elections and eventually by getting representation at higher levels of the system. If all levels of the political system are organized as FPP single-member districts, then this process is blocked from the start. This problem is particularly serious if, as we will soon see, both of the dominant political parties also rely heavily on financial contributions from elites for elections. This common dependency of both dominant parties on the support of the wealthy means that neither party is likely to adopt policies that are strongly opposed by corporations and the capitalist class. A privately financed two-party system, therefore, reinforces the resource constraint faced by popular social forces (discussed in Chapter 17).

The Historical Consolidation of the System

Although the United States has basically had one version or another of single-member district FPP elections since its inception, in the nineteenth century the system functioned very differently in ways that created much greater space for third parties. Specifically, in the nineteenth century, states allowed what was known then as fusion voting. This meant that contending parties could "share" or jointly nominate selected candidates, and the votes cast on any nominating party's ballot line counted in that candidate's total against rivals. As a contemporary instance of what this system might look like, suppose there is a Republican Party nominating someone named Bush and a Democratic Party nominating someone named Gore. With

---

[2]Defenders of the Nader candidacy in the 2000 election argue, with some force, that it is unfair to say Nader caused the Bush victory, because if Gore had run a more progressive and populist campaign, Nader would not have taken 95,000 votes in Florida. This may be true, although it is always hard to know such things; a more populist campaign by Gore would also have lost him some "swing votes" from people wavering in the center. Even if this were the case, it is still true that if Nader had not run, Gore would have easily won Florida.

Gore's consent, a minor party—let's say a Green Party—could also nominate Gore. In a fusion voting system, the votes cast for Gore on either the Democratic or Green Party ballot line would count in his contest with Bush. Let's say this was done and Gore lost to Bush (35–48) on just the Democratic/Republican lines but still won overall (52–48) due to the 17 percent of the vote he got on the Green Party ballot line.

A couple of things have happened in this example, besides Gore winning the election. First, Green Party members have been able to vote their values without wasting their votes. They have helped decide a national election not by being spoilers, but by contributing to an electoral majority, and they have done so without changing their partisan color. Second, Gore now knows that he would not have won this election without the Greens. He owes them something: a seat or two in the cabinet and a stronger environmental vision. Third, the Democratic Party now knows that they need some working agreement with the Greens. In return for Green support at the top of the ticket, they might throw their support to the Green nominee at the bottom of the ticket. And so on. In essence, fusion permits a distinct American answer to the question that is elsewhere answered by proportional representation: how to give real weight to minority electoral sentiment.

Throughout the post–Civil War period, fusion candidacies appeared up and down the ballot across America in almost every election. The Grangers, Free Soilers, and other minor parties of that era all depended on the tactic, as did one of the most famous third party in American history—the People's Party, also known as the Populists. Populism was a mass-based popular mobilization against large corporations and banks during the long deflation of the American currency that followed the Civil War. Populists forged an alliance between small farmers and workers, especially in the Midwest and, at least for a time, parts of the South. The Populist Party gained strength because it could endorse Democratic Party candidates in elections where there was a sympathetic Democratic candidate, and the votes would be counted as "People's Party" votes. This strategy was critical to creating space for the party to gradually increase its popular support and influence. It also meant that in some instances, it was the Democratic Party that cross-endorsed the Populist candidate. Through this strategy, the Populists elected people to state legislatures and the U.S. House of Representatives, and they even elected some governors and senators.

The high-water mark for the Populist Party was the tumultuous election of 1896, in which William Jennings Bryan ran as both the Democratic Party and Populist Party candidate. Although the pivotal issue of the campaign was the attack on the gold standard—which Populists believed was a key source of the power of bankers and large corporations against farmers and workers—many Populists also called for nationalization of the railroads, strong regulations of banks and corporations in the interests of the wider public, and promotion of other, more "commonwealth" forms of ownership, insurance, and finance. The elite political establishment and the capitalist class were terrified by the Populists, seeing them as potentially a real threat to their power. The American economy had just witnessed a terrible panic in 1893, and people had little confidence in its future stability. As it turned out, this upsurge in radicalism dissipated in the years after 1896; but at the time, the ruling class did not know if this was the peak or merely the opening gambit of accelerating movement.

After the election of 1896, the political establishment was not about to sit by passively and see what happened next. There was a general realization that the rules of the game needed to be changed to make the founding of political movements like the Populists more difficult in the future. A key component of the reforms was to make fusion elections illegal in most places in the United States, precisely because abolishing fusion was a way to prevent third parties from gaining any credibility. Fusion is still legal in a few U.S. states, but throughout the second half of the twentieth century it was commonly practiced only in New York. There, it still had an effect. Republicans like Ronald Reagan and Democrats like John F. Kennedy owed their success in New York presidential politics to votes cast on the lines of other parties that nominated them. The socially liberal Republican senator Jacob Javits owed his career to steady cross-endorsement by the Liberal Party. And Rudolph Giuliani won the New York mayoralty, defeating Democrat David Dinkins, largely because the same Liberal Party endorsed him.

In the 1990s a national attempt was made to resurrect the fusion idea as a way of opening up more political space for third parties. The New Party, with the core slogan "A Fair Economy, a Real Democracy, a New Party," was a social-democratic political party formed by a group of activists disaffected with the Democratic Party. The New Party organizers realized that third parties had virtually no chance of seriously contesting elections unless the rules of the game changed, and because fusion was once a legitimate part of American politics and would not require a major overhaul of the machinery of elections, they decided to challenge the prohibitions of fusion.

The grounds were fairly straightforward. Under the First Amendment right to freedom of association, previous law had established two principles of party freedoms: one was about autonomy, the other about freedom from abusive monopoly. The autonomy principle held that any political party should be allowed to nominate "the standard bearer of its choice." Assuming the person wanted their nomination, parties could nominate any qualified candidate they desired. The antimonopoly principle, declared in prior litigation over the right of a minor party, was more complicated. The Supreme Court had long recognized that America's single-member district, plurality voting system strongly inclined it toward two-party dominance. The Court had also often noted the virtues of a two-party versus a multiparty system. But it held that the particular two parties in that duopoly, at any given time, had no right to abuse their de facto monopoly on state legislative power to discriminate against minor parties or to establish rules that would have the effect of such discrimination.

The prohibition against fusion, the New Party argued, fundamentally violated both the autonomy and antimonopoly rules. But in 1997 the Supreme Court ruled 6–3 in *Timmons v. Twin Cities Area New Party* against the New Party, holding that it was perfectly constitutional for the two major existing parties to pass laws with the intent of limiting competition. This ruling was a remarkable setback not only for the New Party but the First Amendment. Over the previous two hundred years, the Court had been very careful to say no such thing.[3]

Alternative Rules

There are many alternative rules of the game for choosing political officials in popular elections, and many variations in the details of any particular type of rules. Two general kinds of alternatives have been particularly important in discussions of how the American system of electing its officials might be made more democratic.

The first alternative is *proportional representation* (PR). In a PR system, electoral districts are represented by multiple elected officials rather than a single official. In the simplest form of PR, each party has a rank-ordered list of candidates, and the voters vote for the party, not directly for individual candidates. The party wins a proportion of the seats roughly equal to the proportion of votes. For example, if there are six representatives from a district and a party gets 33 percent of the vote, then the top two people on its list get elected. In such a system, every party that receives votes above some minimum threshold gets representation in the legislature.

---

[3] One of us, Rogers, was the lead attorney for the New Party and chair of it at the time.

Proportional systems have many variants and details. Some systems dispense with geographical districts altogether: the legislature is selected from the entire geographical area of its jurisdiction on a proportional basis. Other systems combine representatives from geographical districts with at-large representatives. One particularly interesting form of PR allows voters to vote for specific candidates on different party lists. Through a complex procedure, the ultimate distribution of elected officials reflects the proportional support for the different parties, but the specific elected candidates are chosen by the voters rather than by the parties themselves.

A second alternative to single-member districts with plurality voting is called instant runoff voting (IRV). In an IRV system, elected officials are still tied to a specific geographical district, but they need a majority of votes—not a plurality—to win. One way of doing this would be to have two rounds of elections: the first round has many candidates; then, in the second round, the top two face each other. This procedure has the problem that if the first round contains many more than three candidates, the top two could themselves represent only a small proportion of the preferences of voters. It also takes more time, effort, and resources to organize two rounds of voting. An alternative, then, is a single election in which voters rank-order as many of the candidates as they want to from their most to least preferred. Everyone's first choices are then tallied. If no candidate gets 50 percent of the votes cast, then the candidate with the fewest first-rank votes is eliminated and the second choices of those voters are added to the remaining candidates' tallies. This procedure is continued until someone gets 50 percent of the votes. This rank-order system simulates a much more expensive and cumbersome system involving multiple rounds of elections in which one candidate is eliminated after each round.

In both PR and IRV systems, third parties have much more room to maneuver because voters have much less reason to fear that their vote for a minor party will inadvertently help a party they dislike. In an IRV system, voters who liked Nader in the 2000 U.S. presidential election could have ranked Nader first and Gore second, knowing that their vote could not contribute to a Bush victory. Both IRV and PR would therefore considerably increase competition among parties. More people would feel their ideas and interests were given political voice, and they would thus be more likely to feel connected to the political process.

There is a third, more radical transformation of the existing electoral rules of the game that we both find attractive. It is worth thinking about because of the way it more deeply embodies the core idea of government of the people and by the people. Suppose that in legislative elections all candidates in an electoral district who received above a certain minimum threshold of votes were elected, but when they sat in the legislature they would cast as many votes as they received in the election rather than simply a single vote as an elected official. This means that if in a legislative district there were, for example, two candidates and one received 45,000 votes and the other 55,000, they would both be elected. When they voted in the legislature on bills, their vote would have different weight exactly proportional to their popular support: one would cast 55,000 votes and the other 45,000. In the legislature, of course, elected officials would form coalitions, effectively pooling their weighted votes. Every representative would still represent citizens in a specific geographical location, but it would also be the case that every voter would have a representative in the legislature directly representing their preferences.[4]

Electoral Districts

No major overhaul of the basic electoral rules of representation in American elections is likely to occur in the near future, so for now Americans are stuck with single-member district FPP elections. But even here, there are ways to make the system more or less unfair. One pivotal problem is gerrymandering, the strategy for drawing the boundaries of electoral districts in such a way as to give advantages to one party or another.

An example is given in Table 18.2. Suppose you have a state with 6.3 million voters and three electoral districts. Suppose 4 million are Democrats and 2.3 million are Republicans. And suppose the Democrats are geographically more concentrated than the Republicans. It might be possible to draw boundaries in such a way that the three districts would have equal populations—as required by the principle of one person, one vote—while at the same time creating a single district with a high concentration of Democrats.

There are a number of strategies in drawing district boundaries to give advantage to one party or another. In *packing*, lines are drawn to pack as many of your opponent's voters as possible into a single district; *cracking* splits your opponent's supporters into two or more districts to dilute

---

[4] Of course there would be lots of additional details needed for such a system to work well. For example, some minimum threshold would be needed to avoid the legislative assembly getting too large and unwieldy; voters could then designate a second or even third choice on the ballot who would receive their votes if their preferred candidate fell below the threshold needed to get elected. This system could allow for political parties to run candidates and for individuals to run as independents.

TABLE 18.2—Illustration of effects of gerrymandering on an election

District number	Democrats	Republicans	Winner in election
1	2 million	100,000	Democrat
2	1 million	1.1 million	Republican
3	1 million	1.1 million	Republican
Total	**4 million**	**2.3 million**	**1 Democrat, 2 Republicans**

support; and *gerrymandering* is the process of drawing electoral district boundaries in very odd shapes to accomplish electoral goals. These strategies are illustrated in Figure 18.2.

U.S. history provides many examples of this kind of gerrymandering of electoral districts. Some of the most egregious examples in the 2012 congressional elections are shown in Figure 18.3.[5] In most, but not all, states, the responsibility for redrawing congressional district boundaries every ten years falls to the state legislatures. In the 2010 elections, the Republican Party gained control of a number of state legislatures and governorships in states that are usually closely balanced between Republicans and

FIGURE 18.2—Illustration of the process of gerrymandering

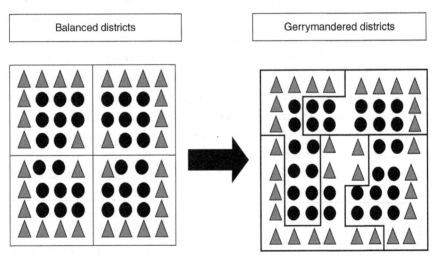

Note: Redrawing the balanced electoral districts in this example creates a guaranteed 3-to-1 advantage in representation for the circle voters. Here, 14 triangle voters are *packed* into the lower left district and the remaining 18 are *cracked* across the three other districts.

[5] District boundaries are redrawn every ten years after the decennial census in order to ensure that there are more or less the same total number of voters in each district. Thus, boundaries were redrawn in 2011 following the 2010 elections. Those new electoral district boundaries were then in effect for the 2012 elections.

FIGURE 18.3—Examples of gerrymandering in 2012 election

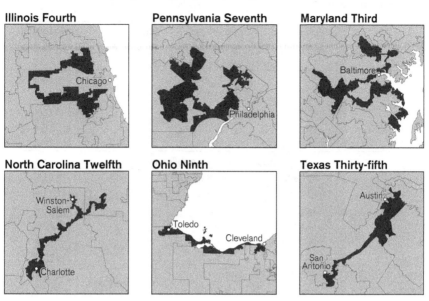

Source: Reid Wilson and Steven Shepard. 2012. "Drawn and Quartered: The decennial redistricting process is just about over. Who's been helped? Who's been hurt? And who's been eviscerated?" The National Journal. March 29, 2012. Available at http://www.nationaljournal.com/member/magazine /drawn-and-quartered-20120329 (accessed May 2, 2014).

Democrats. In some instances the Republican-controlled legislatures seized this opportunity to redraw congressional district boundaries so that Democratic voters would be heavily packed into a few districts, thus reducing their overall impact on the election of members of Congress.

As Table 18.3 indicates, this strategy was especially successful in Pennsylvania. In Pennsylvania overall, Democratic candidates for Congress received 50.7 percent of the vote while Republican candidates received 48.4 percent. Since there are 18 congressional seats in Pennsylvania, one might have expected that nine or ten of these seats would be held by Democrats. Because of gerrymandering, however, Democrats won only five of these eighteen elections. The average margin of victory for the five Democrats who won their districts was 52.6 percentage points (i.e., a vote of 76.3 percent for the Democratic candidate and 23.7 percent for the Republican), while the average margin of victory for the thirteen Republicans was only 18.7 percentage points. An example in Pennsylvania is the Seventh Congressional District, pictured in the upper center of Figure 18.3. This is exactly what packing and cracking are meant to accomplish: concentrate as many Democratic voters as possible into as few districts as possible. Of the

TABLE 18.3—Results of gerrymandering in Pennsylvania in the 2012 congressional election

	Democratic candidate	Republican candidate	Other party candidates	% margin (% Dem−% Rep)
	Districts won by Democrats			
PA-1	235,394	41,708		69.9%
PA-2	318,176	33,381	4,829	79.9%
PA-13	209,901	92,918		38.6%
PA-14	251,932	75,702		53.8%
PA-17	161,393	106,208		20.6%
	Districts won by Republicans			
PA-3	123,933	165,826	12,755	−13.8%
PA-4	104,643	181,606	17,734	−25.3%
PA-5	104,725	177,740		−25.8%
PA-6	143,803	191,725		−14.3%
PA-7	143,509	209,942		−18.8%
PA-8	152,859	199,379		−13.2%
PA-9	105,128	169,177		−23.3%
PA-10	94,227	179,563		−31.2%
PA-11	118,231	166,967		−17.1%
PA-12	163,589	175,352		−3.5%
PA-15	128,764	168,960		−13.5%
PA-16	111,185	156,192	17,404	−15.8%
PA-18	122,146	216,727		−27.9%
Total votes	2,793,538	2,667,365	52,722	2.3%
Percentage	50.7%	48.4%	1.0%	

Democrats won their districts on average by: 52.6%

Republicans won their districts on average by: 18.7%

Source: Calculations based on data from official election returns website, state of Pennsylvania, at http://www.electionreturns.state.pa.us/Default.aspx?EID=27&ESTID=2&CID=0&OID=11&CDID=0&PID=0&DISTID=0&IsSpecial=0&PageRefID=1.

2.8 million Democratic voters in the Pennsylvania congressional election in 2012, 1.17 million (42 percent) lived in just five of the eighteen congressional districts. Nationally, in 2012, if the party composition of the U.S. House of Representatives had faithfully reflected the overall popular vote for Democratic and Republican candidates, the Democratic Party would have won a majority of seats.[6]

[6] While in the 2012 elections gerrymandering especially helped Republicans, when Democrats control state legislatures, they also manipulate district boundaries for their advantage. Good examples are Maryland's Third Congressional District and Illinois's Fourth Congressional District, pictured in Figure 18.3.

With some special exceptions (like using gerrymandering to eliminate the possibility of racial minorities getting elected), gerrymandering is entirely legal in the United States. Because in most states electoral districts are drawn by state legislatures, this means that once a particular party has strong control of the legislature, it can draw district boundaries in such a way as to consolidate its power and prevent challenges. This clearly violates any principle of democracy as giving all citizens equal access to the political process.

Money and Politics

Money plays a direct role in politics in two principal ways. First, money plays a critical role in lobbying the legislators as well as administrative agencies responsible for translating legislation into specific rules and regulations. Legislators have limited staffs to study problems, work out policies, and acquire information. Well-funded lobbyists representing wealthy interest groups and corporations are in a position to provide vast amounts of information to legislators. The same is true for administrative agencies, which often rely on trade associations for various sorts of data crucial to the formulation of regulations. Groups without much money are sometimes able to effectively mobilize people for successful lobbying efforts, but money gives lobbyists a tremendous advantage. It is one of the important ways that the resource constraint operates in democratic politics.

But money also matters, crucially, at the heart of the democratic process: the election of people to public office. It costs an enormous amount to run for national public office, and this necessity transforms the fundamental process of democratic competition. Almost always, the candidate who raises the most money wins. Although candidates still need to get votes, they have to chase dollars before chasing voters. Thus an enormous amount of politicians' time and energy is spent raising funds; of necessity, this means that politicians must in one way or another try to appeal to the interests of potential donors. Sometimes this effort crosses the line into outright corruption, where there is a direct quid pro quo between donations and political favors. More generally, the need to acquire campaign funds simply creates a general disposition to act in ways favorable to the interests of large donors.

The Nature of the Problem

If the reliance of politicians on monetary contributions from rich donors undermines democracy, then the solution might seem pretty straightforward:

put serious, systematic constraints on how much money people can give to politicians, and provide a good system of public finance of elections.

Unfortunately, in a crucial decision in 1976, *Buckley v. Valeo*, the Supreme Court basically ruled that restrictions on spending amounted to restrictions on free speech: governments are prohibited from regulating individual candidates' spending from their own pockets or overall amounts spent on campaigns or limit "independent expenditures," particularly "issue ads" in favor of a candidate paid for by independent bodies. The reasoning was pretty simple: limiting spending is the equivalent of limiting the ability to speak, and the Supreme Court argued such limits were therefore an unconstitutional restriction on the First Amendment guarantee of freedom of speech. Certain kinds of limits on direct individual contributions to specific candidates were still allowed, but there are many ways of getting around such limits, and they have not proven to be an effective way of constraining the influence of wealthy donors on the political process. Since 1976, each attempt by Congress to legislate some kind of campaign finance reform has basically failed to solve the problem.

Because of the existing system, candidates without strong financial networks or personal fortunes cannot run for office. The Senate is filled with millionaires. In 2011, according to the nonpartisan research organization Center for Responsive Politics, 65 percent of the members of the Senate were millionaires, and the median net worth of all U.S. senators was $2.5 million. A number of senators are so rich that they can run their campaigns entirely out of their own pockets: Herb Kohl, a Wisconsin senator from 1989 to 2013, proudly proclaimed that he was "nobody's senator but yours" because he was so rich that he did not need financial contributions.

Candidates generally get most of their money from wealthy individuals and corporations. In 2012, half of 1 percent of the adult population contributed $200 or more to political campaigns. The vast majority of these donations come from elites. A study of congressional elections published in 2003 reported that of the individual donors to congressional elections, 52 percent were business executives, 17 percent attorneys, 13 percent medical professionals, and 11 percent in education and media occupations. That leaves less than 10 percent of donors from all other occupation groups.[7] As the study notes,

[7] Peter Francia, Paul Herrnson, John Green, Lynda Powell, and Clyde Wilcox, The Financiers of Congressional Elections: Investors, Ideologues, and Intimates (New York: Columbia University Press, 2003), table 2.4.

if the donor pool looked like America, one might not care that a small number of donors provide so much of the funding for congressional candidates. But the donor pool clearly looks like an "upper class choir." Contributors to House and Senate campaigns are overwhelmingly rich and well-educated, and they are also overwhelmingly middle-aged white men.[8]

Plenty of evidence points to a strong correlation between the votes of politicians and their sources of funding. The 213 members of Congress who voted to spend almost half a billion dollars more on B-2 stealth bombers received on average nearly $2,100 from the contractor; the 210 members who voted against it got, on average, only about $100.[9] This, of course, does not prove an explicit quid pro quo. These 213 members of Congress could be people who would have voted for these kinds of policies even if there were no contributions from contractors. And, of course, contractors are more likely to contribute money to reelect politicians whom they know will vote for their interests for ideological reasons even in the absence of a direct campaign contribution. More generally, the fact that interest groups give large sums of money to sympathetic politicians does not prove that those politicians *change* their votes to get the money: the NRA is going to give money to gun supporters to help them get elected, but this does not prove that these candidates support the NRA *because* they get money from them. Still, as former longtime U.S. Representative Barney Frank said, "We are the only human beings in the world who are expected to take thousands of dollars from perfect strangers on important matters and not be affected by it."[10]

What Can Be Done?

The dominant approach to campaign finance reform can be called the patchwork option: adopting specific measures to deal with specific aspects of the problem. The McCain-Feingold reform of 2002 is a good example. This law was designed to reduce particular kinds of abuses, but it did not really tackle the central issue. Even after the initial proposal was weakened to deal with objections, it still had great difficulty getting passed. The reform imposed some constraints on soft money—money contributed for

---

[8] Ibid., 27.

[9] Ken Silverstein, "US: The Northrop Grumman B-2 Boondoggle," *Multinational Monitor*, September 1, 1997, at http://www.corpwatch.org/article.php?id=7831 (accessed Sept. 16, 2009).

[10] Quoted by Paul Taylor, "Lobbyists' Success at Raising Funds Proves Costly," *Washington Post*, August 2, 1983, A2.

open-ended purposes to parties—but it did not fundamentally break the link between private wealth and political influence. And then, in 2010, even these relatively weak restrictions were scaled back when the Supreme Court ruled, in *Citizens United v. Federal Election Commission*, that all restrictions on the political spending of corporations in candidate elections was an unconstitutional violation of their "free speech."

A more promising line of reform is represented by measures like the Maine Clean Elections Act, passed as a citizen initiative in 1996 and first applied in 2000. A similar act was passed in Arizona. Here is how the official website of the state of Maine describes the act:

> The Maine Clean Election Act (MCEA) established a voluntary program of full public financing of political campaigns for candidates running for Governor, State Senator, and State Representative. Maine voters passed the MCEA as a citizen initiative in 1996. Candidates who choose to participate may accept very limited private contributions at the beginning of their campaigns. . . . To become eligible, candidates must demonstrate community support through collecting a minimum number of $5 checks or money orders payable to the Maine Clean Election Fund.[11] After a candidate begins to receive MCEA funds from the State, he or she cannot accept private contributions, and almost all goods and services received must be paid for with MCEA funds.[12]
>
> Maine Clean Election Act (MCEA) candidates may receive matching funds based on their opponents' contributions and expenditures, and independent expenditures made by third parties. The purpose of matching funds is to ensure that a candidate participating in the MCEA will not be greatly outspent by private campaign funds of a non-participating opponent or by independent expenditures.
>
> To determine whether a MCEA candidate is entitled to matching funds, the Commission will add the opponent's contributions or expenditures (whichever is greater) plus the independent expenditures made in favor of the opponent or against the MCEA candidate. If that sum is more than the amount of the initial distribution received by the MCEA candidate, he or she will receive matching funds.[13]

[11] The minimums are 50 qualifying contributions for House candidates (at least $250), 150 qualifying contributions for Senate candidates (at least $750), and 3,250 qualifying contributions for gubernatorial candidates (at least $16,250).

[12] See MCEA, http://www.maine.gov/ethics/mcea/index.htm.

[13] See MCEA, http://www.maine.gov/ethics/mcea/matchfunds.htm.

The program is entirely voluntary, so it puts no caps on private spending and thus does not violate the constitutional restrictions mandated by the Supreme Court. Even so, it has effectively marginalized private spending from Maine elections because candidates who accept public funding have a potent argument against candidates who rely on private money. The very phrase "clean elections" implies that a candidate who refuses the clean money from the public must be using "dirty" money. In the 2010 general election, 77 percent of the legislative candidates participated in the MCEA.

Statutes for public financing, like the MCEA, work extremely well in small states with relatively small populations where the stakes in running for political office are relatively modest. It is less certain that this would be a satisfactory model for national elections. Furthermore, because the Maine system funds all candidates equally regardless of whether they are candidates of major parties with large followings or fringe extremist parties, in some ways it violates the egalitarian norms of democracy. In a truly egalitarian democracy, each voter would have equal influence in the funding process; but in the Maine system, each *candidate* gets equal funding. The result is that voters of small, marginal parties have much greater per capita funding of their political organizations than do voters of larger parties. If the Maine system was expanded to a national program, then small, marginal political parties would receive hundreds of millions of dollars of public funding.

Bruce Ackerman, law professor at Yale Law School, has developed a provocative proposal for comprehensive campaign finance reform that avoids these problems while still being consistent with the strictures of *Buckley v. Valeo*.[14] The basic idea is simple: At the beginning of every year, every citizen would be given a special kind of debit card. Ackerman dubs it a patriot card, but we prefer to call it a democracy card. He proposes putting $50 on each card. With 220 million people above the age of 18, the cards would cost a total of roughly $10 billion per year. The funds on the card can be used exclusively for electoral campaigns: to contribute to a candidate for a specific electoral campaign or to a political party that participates in elections.[15] However—and this is the pivotal condition that makes this a deeply

---

[14] Bruce Ackerman, *Voting with Dollars* (New Haven, CT: Yale University Press, 2004). The exposition of Bruce Ackerman's arguments presented here draws heavily from Erik Olin Wright, *Envisioning Real Utopias* (New York: Verso, 2010), chapter 6.

[15] Although the democracy card proposal is specifically directed at financing elections, a modified version of the proposal could allow funds to be used for other forms of political action—referenda, lobbying, social movements. The central issue is creating a mechanism by which inequalities generated in the economic sphere are less easily translated into inequalities in financial resources for actors in the political sphere.

egalitarian proposal—any candidate or party accepting funds from democracy cards cannot accept any funds from *any* other source. But why should candidates and parties opt for this restriction? Why not still court the fat cats and rely on private funding?

There are two reasons why private funding from wealthy individuals and organizations is likely to be drastically reduced under a well-financed democracy card system. First, if the funding level of the democracy cards is high enough, it will swamp other sources of funding. There simply will be much more money to be had through the democracy card "political market" than the private funding market; and because the two sources of funding cannot be mixed, most candidates will find it easier to raise funds from voters. Good money will drive out bad money. Second, once the system is in place and becomes part of the moral climate of political life, using private funding itself is likely to become a political issue. Candidates who rely on the democratic mechanism of seeking funding from equally endowed citizens will have a potent weapon to raise against candidates who seek funding from corporations and wealthy individuals. We have already seen this happen in the much more limited clean elections funding in Maine and Arizona.

The democracy card would set in motion a very different kind of electoral process. In effect, all elections would have essentially two phases: first, a phase in which candidates and parties attempt to recruit democracy dollars from citizens; and second, a phase in which parties and candidates would use those dollars in electoral competition. Of course, under current conditions electoral politics also have these two phases. Electoral campaigns in any democratic system require financial resources, so the question is whether the mechanisms available for providing these funds are consistent with democratic principles of political equality. Under the existing rules of the game, the first phase is a radically inegalitarian process: wealthy people and corporations are the major players in the game of recruiting funding. What the system of democracy cards does is restore a strong notion of political equality to both phases of the electoral process. In addition to one person, one vote in the casting of ballots, there is now one person, one card in the funding of elections. The mechanism therefore provides public funding for electoral politics based on a simple egalitarian principle—each citizen has exactly the same capacity to contribute financially to political activity—but it is citizens, not the state, who decide on the actual allocation of these funds to different political causes.

A well-designed system of public financing of electoral campaigns through a system of democracy cards would largely remove private money from the political process. It would increase the involvement of ordinary citizens in all phases of electoral politics and thus deepen the political equality and efficacy of citizens.

Democracy is not simply a question of free and fair elections. It also entails an open and vibrant media system, opportunities for active citizen participation in public deliberation and decision making, transparent policy making by public officials, and much more. Nevertheless, elections are at the very heart of a system of democratic accountability of public power. The central features of the design of electoral institutions in the United States—the rules of representation, the procedures for drawing electoral districts, and the permissive rules governing private money in electoral campaigns—all systematically undermine its democratic potential.

19

TAXATION AND THE ATTACK
ON THE AFFIRMATIVE STATE

In many discussions of democracy, democracy gets its essential meaning from a contrast with dictatorship: in democracies the political leadership is accountable to the people through elections and the rule of law; in dictatorships the political leadership rules without such constraints. This framing of the problem is valid but incomplete. A democratic society is also one in which people have the power through their political institutions to make collective decisions over matters of public concern. Democracy is thus a question of the scope of public authority, not simply of the way that authority is exercised. A society is less democratic when the public domain is severely narrowed and decisions with large collective ramifications are made privately. This claim implies, as we argued in Chapter 17, that we can make a meaningful distinction between matters of public concern and private matters. This is certainly a difficult and hotly contested task, but whatever else *public* might mean, it includes the provision of a wide range of public goods and the regulation of the market in ways that minimize its negative externalities. To do these things, the state needs resources. In a capitalist society, in which most of the economy is organized through privately owned enterprises and most income is earned through market activity, these resources are acquired through taxation.

This chapter explores the problem of taxation and the uses to which taxes are put by the democratic state. Taxation might seem to be a dry, technical topic of concern mainly to specialists. This view would be mistaken. Taxation is at the very core of how a democratic capitalist society like the United States works. Taxation raises fundamental questions about the prospects for democracy and the conditions for fairness in societies where so much power is vested in private property and the market.

We begin by exploring different ways of understanding the idea of taxation and the problem of what it means for a tax system to be fair. We then look at taxation in the United States, examining a number of myths about the tax system. The chapter concludes with a discussion of antitax politics and the assault on the affirmative state.

WHAT IS TAXATION?

There are two sharply different ways of thinking about taxation:

1. Taxation is the public taking resources *from* the private.
2. Taxation is *the division of the economic pie* between private and public shares.

In the first of these views, the economic pie is produced by private firms and individuals, and then the state comes in and coercively takes part of this pie for public purposes. In the second, the economic pie is the result of complex cooperation among people in both public and private spheres and then a set of rules are established to divide the pie among different purposes.

Taxation as the Public Taking from the Private

In the most common view of taxation, the public sphere takes resources from the private. Here's how the story goes: People work and earn an income through various activities. Some get their income in the form of a wage. Some get their income as a return on investments. Some get it by owning a business, employing others, and making a profit. Some people win the lottery, and others play poker in Las Vegas. The important thing is that regardless of how people earn their livelihood, this income is their personal, private property. If you earn it, it is yours and you have a right to it. The government then takes some of your income away from you for public purposes in the form of taxes. The tax level may be the result of democratic decisions, but even so, the government has taken something that was yours away from you through taxes. And something is always a bit suspect about this. Somehow this feels like an abridgement of your freedom, your liberty. Maybe on balance this is still acceptable, but only on balance. The burden of proof is on the state to justify its need for *your* money. Indeed, some people like to call the point in the year where they have earned enough to pay all their taxes as freedom day: up to that point, they have been working for the government; after that point, they are working for themselves.

The extreme libertarian version of this understanding of taxation proclaims that *taxation is theft*. Grover Norquist, the conservative political analyst who played an influential role in the antitax movements beginning in the 1980s, explained that the state should not help the needy "because to do that, you would have to steal money from people who earned it and give it to people who didn't. And then you make the state into a thief. . . . Taxation beyond the legitimate requirements of providing for justice is theft."[1] So long as you yourself did not personally agree to the things taxes are being used for—even if they were decided democratically—then the taxes you are paying are being coercively taken from you, and this makes it equivalent to theft. Most people do not agree with this rhetoric, but they still accept the core intuition that what you earn is rightfully yours, and this intuition suggests that there is always something suspect about taxation.

Taxation as the Division of Total Income between Public and Private Shares

An alternative way of thinking about taxation is to see taxation as a practical way of dividing up the total pie between private uses of income and public purposes. The "total pie" consists of all the goods and services produced in a society. It is the result of our combined, interdependent, collective effort within a complex matrix of institutions, both public and private. It is a genuinely social product. It is part of our collective heritage from the efforts and ingenuity of past generations. We collectively inherit this society and all of its accumulated knowledge and productive capacity, and together—through a complex process of cooperation—we produce the pie. If you tried to produce your own income in isolation from this social context and social cooperation, your standard of living would plummet. No one is responsible for being born into a highly productive, advanced industrialized society capable of producing so much. If Bill Gates had been born a peasant in medieval England, he would not have become a multibillionaire. This is not to say there is no meaning to the idea that individual effort matters and that individuals bear some responsibility for what they contribute to this total pie. But the deeper reality is that each person's contribution is so dependent on the complexities of interdependence, social cooperation, and interactions that it is an illusion to think that we can meaningfully

[1] From an interview with Alain de Botton in the 2004 television adaptation of his book *Status Anxiety*, available at http://alaindebotton.com/tv-audio/ (accessed Sept. 3, 2014).

identify how much a given person produces and how much comes from those collective interactions in a given social environment.

Since we have a total social product, we have to devise rules for dividing it up for different purposes. In these terms, what we call capitalism and democracy are particular ways of organizing these rules for social cooperation and allocation. In this distinctive form of society—capitalist democracy—the social rules are such that most of the production of goods and services is organized through privately owned firms separate from state institutions. Within this kind of society, this division between private economic activity and public state functions is defended on the grounds of efficiency. Given this division, some mechanism needs to be devised to get resources to the state for public purposes. Taxation is the main device by which we organize this crucial public choice—how much of total social income to give to people for their private allocations and how much to use for public purposes. *Private consumption is just as much a deduction from public purposes as the public use of resources is a deduction from private consumption.*

If you think about taxation this way, then the resulting division of resources between public and private purposes may be desirable or undesirable, efficient or inefficient, conducive to human flourishing or harmful; but there is no meaning to the claim that people somehow really and truly "own" their income independently of the rules that govern these processes. In this way of conceiving taxation, it is still perfectly reasonable to say that taxes are too high—or too low—because the consequences of the division of total income between public and private uses may be undesirable or inefficient. If too much goes to public purposes, for example, people may not have much private incentive to work hard and invest; if too much goes to private purposes, all sorts of important public goods may deteriorate. Too little spending on bridges increases the likelihood they will collapse. Too little spending on cleaning up toxic waste means that people's health may deteriorate. Too little spending on schools may mean the labor force will be unprepared for new technologies. And so on. These practical consequences of incentives and public goods provide a basis for criticizing levels of taxation, but this does not mean that there is anything inherently unjust about high taxation.

It should be clear to everyone that in the United States, the first of these two conceptions of taxation dominates most people's views of the matter. This understanding is reflected in much of the political rhetoric concerning taxes and tax cuts: as antitax conservative politicians are fond of saying: "You know better how to spend *your* money than do bureaucrats in Washington." A tax cut lets you keep more of "your money." Most people just assume that it makes sense to see taxes as a way for government to take something that belongs to you.

Which of these views is "correct"? This question is difficult to fully resolve. Answering it carefully would involve subtle philosophical issues about the nature of rights, private property, social justice, and other matters as well as methodological discussions about the way outputs are generated by the interplay of cooperation, individual action, and social institutions. We endorse the second understanding of taxes, but we will not try to defend that view here.

Regardless of one's final judgment about which of these understandings of taxation is more adequate, there is a different set of questions we can answer more simply: Who really benefits from a particular view of the problem? In whose interests is it to insist that taxation is a form of legalized theft? Is this understanding more in the interests of the rich and powerful? Average citizens? The poor? Whatever else one might say about these issues, one thing is clear: people who are well positioned to acquire a high income from private transactions in the market have an economic interest in making strong claims about their rights to that income and treating taxation as a coercive infringement.

THE LOGIC OF INCOME TAXES

Now, suppose we decide that taxation is legitimate—that in a democratic society, it is right and proper for the democratically elected government to decide that a significant part of the total social product will be used for public purposes. Because the economy is itself organized in a capitalist manner—that is, as a privately run economy—getting resources for these public purposes means that in one way or another, income has to be taxed. In this section, we start by looking at the theoretical problem of what it means to say a tax system is fair; then we look at the U.S. income tax system.

Alternative Understandings of Tax Fairness

Taxes are gathered in many different technical ways. There are property taxes, corporate profits taxes, sales taxes, income taxes, payroll taxes. There are also fees charged for various government services; these can be kind of a quasi-tax. For example, in a society in which nearly everyone needs a car to get around, car registration fees are a kind of tax on driving a car, even though you pay the fee only if you have a car. In Chapter 7 on consumerism, we briefly discussed the idea of a progressive consumption tax as a specific way of dampening excess consumption. We won't discuss the pros and cons of these alternative kinds of taxes here. All these taxes are ultimately taxes on income, whether they are technically a direct income tax or some other kind of tax, because they have the effect of diverting a certain amount of income from private to public uses. The issue we will address is the underlying principles that make this division fair or unfair.

What is the fairest way of imposing taxation? We have to allocate resources to public purposes, but how should we distribute the burdens of paying for those resources? Here are three main ideas regarding what would be fair:

- Everyone pays the *same tax*. This is called a poll tax. For example, every person could pay $5,000 a year in taxes regardless of the level of their privately earned income.
- Everyone pays the *same proportion* of their privately earned income as a tax. This is called a flat tax.
- Everyone has the *same burden*. Everyone should experience the taxes they pay as an equal sacrifice from the standard of living that they can generate through the private capitalist market.

Few people think the first of these proposals is fair because poll taxes affect the living conditions of the poor vastly more than they affect the rich. In certain times and places, poll taxes were important. The ability to pay the poll tax was a condition for full citizenship. But in no contemporary capitalist society is a poll tax or a head tax an important form of taxation.

The second and third principles inspire much greater debate. Some political conservatives argue in favor of a flat tax on the grounds that it treats everyone equally: everyone pays the same proportion of their privately acquired income as taxes. Treating everyone the same seems like a fair principle; after all, even with a flat tax the rich will still pay the most in taxes. If 100 people are earning $30,000 a year and 10 people are earning $300,000 a year, and everyone pays 10 percent of their income in taxes, those 10 people will still provide half of all revenues to the state. Or, to put it slightly differently: each rich person in this example pays for 5 percent of the costs of running the state while each lower-income person pays only 0.5 percent of those costs.

The third option treats the problem of fairness as a question of the real burden experienced by each person. The underlying idea sees contributions the way we would evaluate many ordinary situations of cooperation among people. Think of a situation in which a group of people of different ages and strengths are unloading a truck. How much should each person carry? The usual way people would answer this is to say that everyone should expend the same effort and experience the same burden from the task. Clearly, this means that strong people should carry heavier loads.

What does "equal burden" mean in the case of taxation? Let us compare a person who earns $10,000 a year with a person who earns $100,000 a year. A flat rate tax means that each person pays the same proportion of their earnings as taxes. Suppose the tax rate was 10 percent a year. The poorer person would then pay $1,000 in taxes and the rich person $10,000. Is this fair?

The third concept of tax fairness would ask whether in this case both of these people are making an equal sacrifice for the public good. The way to think about this is to ask the question in a slightly different way. Suppose the person who earns $10,000 got a pay raise of $1,000, resulting in a new income of $11,000 per year. This would mean that he or she would pay $100 more in taxes if the flat tax rate were 10 percent. Now suppose the rich person earned $1,000 more. How much of this $1,000 would cause the equivalent "pain" or sacrifice for the rich person as would the $100 in taxes deducted from the poor person's extra income? Surely we don't think that $100 matters as much to the rich person as it does to the poor person, do we? Perhaps $100 for the poor person has the same bite as $800 would for the rich person. This means that to equalize the sacrifice, the rich person would have to pay 80 percent taxes on that additional $1,000.

The tax paid on the additional $1,000 of income in our example is what is meant by the *marginal tax rate*. The word *marginal* here refers to the tax rate on additional income given the level of income one already has. Economists like to talk about the marginal utility of income. "Utility" is the economist's way of talking about the satisfaction one gets from something. The *marginal* utility of income thus refers to how much additional satisfaction a person gets from earning additional income, given the level of income that person already has. Once income reaches a certain level, the marginal utility of additional income begins to decline—that is, less and less additional satisfaction is gained from each additional dollar earned. In terms of the equal burden principle of tax fairness, the implication is that the marginal tax rate has to increase as income increases so that every person, regardless of income, will experience the same "disutility" (loss of satisfaction) from paying taxes. This is called a progressive income tax.

Now, it could be that a marginal 80 percent tax rate on incomes above a certain level would not be politically feasible because of the power of the rich. They would put up such a fuss at this marginal tax rate—and use their power to turn that fuss into political pressure—that it simply could not be adopted. Or it might be the case that at the equal burden level of taxation the rich person would stop working for that additional $1,000, and thus the 80 percent marginal tax rate might be inefficient. But this response by the rich does not mean that the tax is unfair; efficiency and fairness are two different things. For a tax system to be fair in a society in which people receive very different incomes from the private market economy, the real burden represented by those taxes should be shared equally. And this means that tax rates should increase steeply with income.

U.S. Progressive Income Tax: How It Works

To clarify the logic of a progressive tax system, it will be helpful to quickly run through the mechanics of the U.S. federal income tax system. Table 19.1 presents the marginal tax rates for U.S. federal income taxes in 2014. In this table, *tax bracket* refers to a category of tax rates, based on income level,

TABLE 19.1—An illustration of the U.S. income tax brackets, 2014 tax rates

Bracket 1—10% on income from $0 to $9,075
Bracket 2—15% on income over $9,075 but not over $36,900
Bracket 3—25% on income over $36,900 but not over $89,350
Bracket 4—28% on income over $89,350 but not over $186,350
Bracket 5—33% on income over $186,350 but not over $405,100
Bracket 6—35% on income over $405,100 but not over $406,750
Bracket 7—39.60% on income $406,750 and above

Example: A person who has $100,000 in taxable income will pay total income taxes of $21,175.75, which implies an overall tax rate of just over 21% as a result of paying taxes within the first four tax brackets as follows:

Income bracket	Income earned in this bracket	Tax rate within brackets	Tax due
1	$9,075	10%	$907.50
2	$27,825	15%	$4,173.75
3	$52,450	25%	$13,112.50
4	$10,650	28%	$2,982
Totals:	$100,000	21.0%	$21,175.75

within a progressive tax system. Tax brackets define the cutoff values at which income beyond that point is taxed at a higher rate. In 2014 there were seven tax brackets, the highest being on incomes above $406,750 for a single person. In the example in the table, a person who has a taxable income of $100,000 would pay a total tax of $21,175, for a total tax rate of 21 percent. This figure is the result of combining the taxes for the income earned in each of the first four tax brackets.

Complexities in the Tax System

Once a society decides to use a progressive income tax of the sort represented in Table 19.1, its policy makers immediately face a host of problems that need solving. The first and most basic question is, what should be included as taxable income? Should it be every penny a person earns? Or should we allow a person to deduct certain kinds of costs from this total income before calculating the tax? Some deductions seem completely obvious. One family has five children and has total household gross income of $40,000 per year; another is a single person who also earns $40,000 per year. Should they both pay the same tax? The equal burden idea suggests that the family with five children should pay less, and this means trying to figure out how much should be deducted from the $40,000 of that family. The deduction from total income that simply reflects the number of people supported by the income is called personal exemptions. The U.S. tax code also includes what is called a standard deduction, which is meant to reflect a certain amount of income that should not be taxed at all in every household. In 2014 the personal exemption was $3,950, and the standard deduction was $6,200. This means, in effect, that for a single person the actual income tax rate would be 0 percent if earnings were less than $10,150.

Once deductions are allowed, however, a door is open for a new kind of policy. It is now possible to create incentives for people to do things by allowing them to take tax deductions for certain kinds of costs. These deductions, in effect, become a form of disguised government spending. Consider charitable deductions. Suppose you earn $200,000 and you give $10,000 to a charity. If your marginal tax rate was 33 percent, you would normally have paid $3,300 in taxes on that $10,000 if you had kept that income and spent it on personal consumption. When you give the $10,000 to the charity, the government reduces your taxes by $3,300. So in reality, it costs you only $6,700 to donate $10,000. In practice, the government has spent $3,300 in taxes for the charity of your choice! This is exactly the same as if the government had a procedure whereby you received no tax deduction for charitable contributions, but the government would pay a charity a direct subsidy for every dollar you gave the charity based on your income tax bracket: if you sent $6,700 to the charity, the government would send it $3,300. This is why such policies are referred to as *tax expenditures*: the government is subsidizing private charities through the use of the tax code.

Housing is another important example of tax expenditures. One way to encourage people to buy homes is to allow them to deduct their mortgage interest payments from their income. The more expensive the house, the bigger the mortgage interest payment, and thus the bigger the deduction. The tax system, in effect, not only subsidizes private home ownership— which might be a good public policy—but also subsidizes rich people more than everyone else. A person with taxable income of $50,000 a year and $10,000 a year in interest payments on a mortgage will get a tax subsidy of $2,500 (because of a marginal tax rate of 25 percent). A person with an income of $500,000 a year and $50,000 a year in interest payments will receive a subsidy of $17,500 (because of a 35 percent marginal tax rate). What's more, if you compare these tax subsidies for private housing with direct subsidies for public housing for the poor, as noted in Chapter 14, the United States provides vastly more subsidy for private homes of middle- and upper-income people than it does for public housing for the poor. In 2004, tax subsidies for homeowners were about four times greater than all subsidies combined for housing for the poor. These payments to homeowners must be considered real subsidies; they just take an indirect form.

These deductions are often called *tax loopholes*—ways in which people can reduce their tax liability and legally avoid paying taxes. Some tax loopholes increase the fairness of the system—especially the deductions for having children and paying health-care expenses. Others may be good public policy, such as the charity deductions or the mortgage deductions, because it is probably a good thing to encourage private charity and home owning. But many of these loopholes end up being clever devices for rich people to dramatically reduce their income tax obligations and sometimes even avoid paying taxes altogether. The tax code contains many complex mechanisms for calculating the depreciation of various kinds of assets, profits and losses from investments, and various costs of doing business. With clever accountants and tax lawyers, these devices make it possible for many very wealthy people, especially those whose income is derived from investments and businesses, to virtually avoid paying any income taxes at all. The specific ways in which tax policy and rules are created in the United States—through a political system in which money plays a large part in electing politicians—have encouraged the massive proliferation of all sorts of special provisions in the tax code that end up creating tremendous complexity and special privileges.

Levels of Taxation and Fairness of Its Burden

Few issues in American politics are more contentious than taxation. Every time a new public program is proposed (with the exception of military spending), conservatives object on the grounds that it will raise taxes, which will dampen investments and harm our ability to compete with other nations. Defenders of government programs are referred to as tax-and-spend liberals. The image created is that Americans are heavily taxed, that these taxes cripple American business, and that in any event most of these taxes are spent on wasteful endeavors.

What is the reality of taxation in the United States? The first thing to note is that compared to other developed capitalist countries, aggregate rates of taxation are quite low in the United States. Table 19.2 indicates the total taxation as a percentage of GDP in rich countries in 2012. In the United States, just over 24 percent of our total GDP was paid in taxes in 2012. Roughly, this means that about three-quarters of national income is

TABLE 19.2—Total tax revenue as percentage of GDP, 2012

Denmark	48.0	Spain	32.9
Belgium	45.3	Estonia	32.5
France	45.3	Portugal	32.5
Italy	44.4	Poland*	32.3
Sweden	44.3	Israel	31.6
Finland	44.1	Canada	30.7
Austria	43.2	Japan*	28.6
Norway	42.2	Slovak Republic	28.5
Hungary	38.9	Ireland	28.3
Netherlands*	38.6	Switzerland	28.2
Luxembourg	37.8	Turkey	27.7
Germany	37.6	South Korea	26.8
Slovenia	37.4	Australia*	26.5
Iceland	37.2	**United States**	**24.3**
Czech Republic	35.5	Chile	20.8
United Kingdom	35.2	Mexico*	19.7
Greece	33.8	**OECD–Average****	**40.5**
New Zealand	32.9		

*Data are for year 2011. **Average calculated using latest available data for each country.

Source: Organization for Economic Co-operation and Development (OECD), *Revenue Statistics 1965–2010*, 2012 edition. Available at http://stats.oecd.org/Index.aspx?DataSetCode=REV (accessed Sept. 15, 2014).

allocated to private consumption and investment and one-quarter to public purposes. In Canada, a country in many ways similar to the United States, the figure for 2012 is almost 31 percent—a little below the average for all developed countries. In eight rich countries the figure is over 40 percent. These are all prosperous capitalist countries with a high standard of living for their citizens. Corporations are privately owned, and they attract investments the same way they do in the United States—by offering acceptable rates of return. Yet over 40 percent of the economic pie goes to the state through taxes to be used for public purposes, compared to less than 25 percent in the United States. Clearly, there is nothing fundamentally incompatible with having a much higher rate of taxation than in the United States and still having a well-functioning capitalist economy.

What about the fairness of the tax burdens in the United States? We do have a progressive income tax that is at least nominally consistent with the equal-burden principle. On the other hand, a number of taxes clearly fall more heavily on lower-income people. Sales taxes are flat rate taxes on purchases, and because the poor consume a much higher proportion of their income than do the rich, this tax is a higher proportion of their income. Social Security taxes are also regressive. In 2014, the Social Security tax of 6.2 percent was paid only on the first $117,000 of earnings. This means that a person who earns $30,000 a year would pay a tax of 6.2 percent, but a person who earned $300,000 would have an effective Social Security tax rate of only 2.3 percent. This tax, like the sales tax, constitutes a much greater burden on low-income people than on high-income people. It doesn't even come close to an equal-burden principle of tax fairness.

The unfairness of the tax system is particularly striking for local and state taxes. Figure 19.1 shows the U.S. average state and local taxes as a share of family income for non-elderly married couples. For the richest 1 percent of families, state and local taxes average 5.6 percent of their family income.[2] For the lowest 20 percent, the figure is 11.1 percent.

What about the rates of taxation on labor market earnings and rates of taxation on returns to investments? From the viewpoint of individuals, income is income regardless of its source: however you get it, you can spend it as you wish. The tax system, however, treats income very differently depending on its source. A family with a net household income of $400,000 per year pays a marginal tax rate on earnings of 35 percent. This means

[2] This is the figure after what are called *federal offsets*—reductions in federal taxes because some state and local taxes are treated as tax deductions for federal income tax purposes.

FIGURE 19.1–State and local taxes for rich and poor, 2010

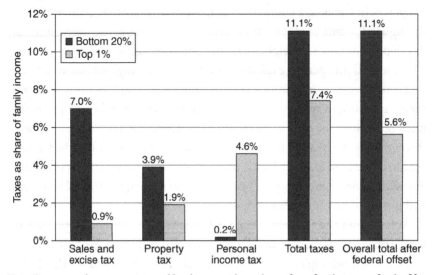

Note: Figures are the average state and local taxes paid as a share of 2010 family income for the fifty states and the District of Columbia. The federal offset comes from reductions on federal income taxes due and tax deductions for local and state taxes.

Source: Institute on Taxation and Economic Policy (ITEP), *Who Pays? A Distributional Analysis of the Tax Systems in All 50 States*, 4th ed. (Washington, DC).

that if they earned an additional $100,000, they would pay $35,000 in additional taxes. If they sold some long-term investments and made a $100,000 profit on the sale, they would be taxed at a rate of only 15 percent on this additional income. This kind of tax is called the *capital gains tax*. Because income from capital gains goes disproportionately to wealthy individuals, this sort of tax again violates the equal-burden principle of fair taxation.

Overall, then, we can say the following about taxation in America: First, the United States is not a heavily taxed nation. In dividing up the fruits of the collective productive efforts of Americans, less than a quarter is allocated to public purposes through taxation.[3] Because this amount is so much less than that allocated by most other comparable countries, it suggests that given the constraints created by living in a capitalist economy, there is considerable room for the expansion of taxation—for shifting the balance between public goods and private consumption—if there were a political will to do so. Second, the distribution of burdens in the American tax system falls far short of the ideal of equal sacrifice. Not only does the United States have the most unequal distribution of income of any developed

[3] The amount of actual state spending is somewhat greater than this because some state spending is paid for out of borrowing rather than directly by taxes.

capitalist country, but the beneficiaries of this unequal distribution do not pay their fair share of the taxes needed to fund the public goods and state regulations that sustain their advantages.

THE ATTACK ON THE AFFIRMATIVE STATE

Taxation is the way the state gets its resources in a capitalist society. Democracy depends crucially on what the state does with those resources. The unfairness of a tax system would be of less concern if what the state did with those resources was counteract the inequalities and deprivations generated within the market and promote collective welfare through the provision of public goods.

The *affirmative state* is the term we use to describe a state that plays an energetic and positive role in the society by solving collective problems and advancing public purposes.[4] This role includes a wide range of things: providing education; building infrastructure like roads and sewers; providing health care, public safety, subsidies for the arts and recreation, large support for scientific research and technological development; and so on. The affirmative state also involves regulations of various kinds of activity for the public good: regulation of pollution, health and safety in the workplace, food quality, truthful advertising, and many other things.

In the twentieth century, the affirmative state went through episodes of sometimes dramatic expansion; during other episodes, it came under concentrated attack. The two biggest episodes in the United States for the expansion of the affirmative state in the twentieth century were the New Deal in the 1930s and the Great Society in the 1960s. In both of these periods of reform, the affirmative state was expanded because of popular democratic mobilization—the union movement was especially important in the 1930s and the civil rights movement in the 1960s. These popular mobilizations led to dramatic expansions of the government's role in society and, accordingly, a shift in the division of the total pie between private consumption and public purposes.

---

[4] This is not the conventional term used to describe the array of state policies and programs that we include in this expression. We feel that *affirmative state* is more appropriate than *welfare state* because the latter term has come to have a quite narrow meaning involving reduction of risk and services for the poor. We also prefer *affirmative state* to *interventionist state*, because the term *interventionist* does not imply the kind of positive role for society as a whole that we envision.

The period beginning in 1980 witnessed a relentless attack on the affirmative state, an attack that tried to undo the popular gains of the previous half century and create a world in which democratic power played a much more marginal role in social affairs. Although the attack has been partially successful, it has seriously undermined state capacity to deal with the challenges of the twenty-first century.

Arguments against the Affirmative State

Well before coming to power with the Reagan election in 1980, conservative foundations and political analysts had been elaborating a series of arguments against the affirmative state. Four have become particularly central to the ideological justification of policy initiatives against the affirmative state beginning in the 1980s: taxation is fundamentally illegitimate, government deficits and debts are a deep threat to prosperity, government officials have mostly malevolent goals, and governments are incompetent even when officials have good intentions.

The attack on the legitimacy of taxation is particularly important, both because it has a certain real appeal to many voters who want to keep more of "their" money and because delegitimizing taxes is an indirect way of undermining the state's capacity to do anything. Grover Norquist argued that the key purpose of massive tax cuts is primarily to "starve government." As he put it in a frequently cited quip: "I don't want to abolish government. I simply want to reduce it to the size where I can drag it into the bathroom and drown it in the bathtub."[5] Accomplishing this goal requires the constant reiteration of the idea that taxation is oppressive, that taxes are too high, that the government is taking your money away from you. This attack on taxation has been hugely successful, to the point that few politicians believe it is feasible to say in a straightforward way: "There are desperately important problems our society faces that can only effectively be solved through public action, and this requires resources. The only responsible way to provide these resources is through fair taxation. Taxes are too low in America." Even President Obama, when acknowledging in 2009 the need for new taxes to fund initiatives such as health-care reform, felt compelled to say he would raise taxes on only the wealthiest 5 percent of Americans and that most people would get a tax cut.

[5] Norquist made this statement in a report on National Public Radio, *Morning Edition*, May 25, 2001. Available at http://www.npr.org/templates/story/story.php?storyId=1123439 (accessed Sept. 16, 2009).

Closely connected to the attack on taxation is the argument that government deficits and debt are intrinsically a deep threat to prosperity. It often happens that government budgets are not "balanced"—that revenues acquired through taxation are not sufficient to cover all the spending planned in the budget. This is a particularly pressing issue when levels of tax revenues decline sharply in a period of economic recession similar to the one the United States experienced in the period 2008–2010. When this happens there are three main alternative courses of action: taxes can be raised to cover the additional spending, the government can borrow money by issuing bonds, or spending can be cut.

The preferred solution of opponents of the affirmative state is to cut programs. The problem is that many government programs are very popular. Therefore, to make cuts in these programs politically acceptable, it is essential to convince the public that the other two solutions to deficits—borrowing or raising taxes—are either morally undesirable or economically not possible. We have already discussed the largely successful effort to delegitimize taxation. The attack on borrowing was more difficult because it does not so directly impinge directly on people's pocketbooks. Two key arguments are made. First, conservatives argue that government borrowing crowds out private investment by raising interest rates and redirecting people's savings from profitable investments in markets to government bonds. Second, government debt—the cumulative result of borrowing over time—will saddle future generations with intolerable levels of interest payments to service the debt. If you believe either of these arguments, then when deficits occur either because of economic downturns or because of tax cuts, then the only option is to cut spending and programs.[6]

The third prong of the attack on government involves characterizing government officials and those politicians who support a more expansive view of government programs as mainly motivated by power for its own sake. Big government, the argument goes, does not have the interests of the country at heart, or even of the people who vote for politicians who support big government. Bureaucrats within an affirmative state, conservative critics argue, are concerned only with accumulating power "in Washington"

---

[6] There is a grain of truth to both of these arguments: In times of rapid economic growth, high levels of government borrowing could impinge on private investment, and if debt levels rise too high relative to the productive capacity of an economy, this could generate a significant debt burden for the future. The validity of these arguments depends entirely on the context. Neither is plausible in the United States in the second decade of the twenty-first century.

and imposing their values and priorities on everyone else. At its core, they are arguing that big government is an instrument of oppression.

The final line of attack challenged the competence of government to do anything well. The private market solution to problems and market provision of services is held up as efficient and responsible; government provision is portrayed as incompetent and wasteful. Because firms within the market are driven by competition, good solutions thrive and bad solutions disappear. Government programs are immune from competition, and thus ineffective and wasteful programs continue out of inertia (buttressed by the self-interest of bureaucrats). Government regulations for the public good are denounced as heavy-handed bureaucracy mired in red tape that causes more harm than good. Even when the original purposes for a government bureaucracy are laudable—improved air quality, good education, better public transportation—government simply cannot deliver the goods. The combination of government malevolence and government incompetence means that even if various kinds of problems are generated by imperfections of the market, government failures will almost always be worse than market failures.[7]

All these attacks resonated with the public, particularly in the absence of well-organized, visible, and articulate voices countering the arguments. Of course most people would rather pay lower taxes; so unless they are reminded that critical public purposes depend on taxation and are convinced that these public goods will actually be provided, then they are likely to be receptive to antitax arguments. With respect to government malevolence and incompetence, there are certainly examples of bad regulations and bureaucracies that interfere unnecessarily with business. To prevent businesses from polluting, for example, excessive paperwork may be imposed to track the disposal of toxic materials. And many politicians and bureaucrats are certainly more concerned with advancing their careers and increasing their power than with advocating for the public good. It is always possible to find such examples. The question is whether such government failures should indict the very idea of government regulation and government provision of public goods, or whether what is needed is reform and

---

[7] The Nobel Prize–winning economist Milton Friedman, for example, acknowledges that negative externalities are a significant problem within markets and that within some kinds of markets, firms have a tendency to develop monopolistic power. Still, he argues, these market problems may not justify government intervention if such intervention is doomed to fail. If the cure is worse than the disease, it is better to just leave things alone.

revitalization of democratic governance. Should the problems of the democratic affirmative state be dealt with by a retreat from democracy or a deepening of democracy? The answer, by leading political forces in the United States from the last decades of the twentieth century to the beginning of the twenty-first, was a narrowing of democracy.

Taken together, these attacks crystallized into a doctrine of the appropriate role for the state that came to be known as *neoliberalism*: basically, the idea that "free" markets, unimpeded by government regulations and government programs, do a much better job of solving almost all problems than do states.[8] Although states do have a legitimate role in providing for national defense and protecting private property rights—and thus neoliberals support a strong (and expensive) national defense and police and prisons to combat crime—other activities of the state should be kept to a bare minimum. The full force of neoliberalism has never been put into place, but it has defined the basic terrain of political debate over the role of government and public policy from the 1980s.

In the course of the 1980s, this conservative economic doctrine became linked to a range of cultural themes that were salient to social conservatives—especially opposition to abortion and to homosexual rights, support for an expanded role of religion in public life, and the protection of rights to own and carry guns. This alliance between neoliberalism and social conservatism was not really comfortable, for the neoliberal economic position was rooted in libertarian desires for a largely passive, nonintrusive state, whereas social conservatives wanted the state to intrude into private life by prohibiting abortions, restricting the rights of homosexuals, controlling pornography, and promoting religion. None of these positions fit with libertarian ideas. Furthermore, many social conservatives are working-class people adversely affected by neoliberal economic policy and have material interests in line with a more expansive affirmative state. Nevertheless, the political alliance was forged in the 1980s and proved to be powerful and fairly cohesive for over two decades.

Strategies against the Affirmative State, 1980–2008

Beginning with the election of Ronald Reagan, and continuing through the George W. Bush administration, neoliberal ideas defined much of the terrain

---

[8] The word *liberal* in neoliberalism refers to the meaning of this term in the nineteenth century, when liberalism was associated with individual rights and the free market. This is still the meaning of liberalism in much of the world. The United States is almost unique in associating the word *liberal* with progressive politics and support of the affirmative state.

of political debate in the United States. Even during the Clinton period in the 1990s these principles were operative, if perhaps in a somewhat softened way. It was Clinton, after all, who proclaimed that "the era of big government is over" and who supported deregulation of the banking and financial services sector in ways that helped create the conditions for the financial collapse of 2008. Of course, in practice, actual policies were often half-baked compromises between neoliberal principles and various kinds of political pressures; and certainly in many instances, otherwise very conservative politicians supported expensive government subsidies for various things when it suited their political interests. The strong support for agricultural subsidies by right-wing politicians in agricultural states and subsidies for the oil industry by politicians from oil-producing states are just two notorious examples. Still, despite considerable hypocrisy and inconsistency, the anti-state principles of neoliberalism did shape much of the political agenda for a quarter of a century.

Five clusters of policies have attempted to put into practice the core ideas of the neoliberal agenda:

1. *Cutbacks in publicly funded programs.* The simplest way of undermining the affirmative state is simply to reduce funding for its core programs. Less tax money spent on higher education means higher tuitions, so large public universities begin to look more like private institutions, seeking private endowments and grants. Many public universities currently receive less than 20 percent of their funding through direct state support. Top-tier public universities are not exempt from this trend: the University of Michigan at Ann Arbor receives only 16 percent of its revenue from direct state funding; the University of Wisconsin–Madison, 17 percent; the University of California, Berkeley, 12 percent; and the University of California, Los Angeles, only 7 percent.[9] Less money spent on public education makes it more likely that parents who can afford it will seek private alternatives. Less money spent on drug treatment programs and mental health services

---

[9] "University of Michigan Funding: A Snapshot" (University of Michigan, 2014); "Factbook 12–13: A Reference Guide to University of Wisconsin System Statistics and General Information" (University of Wisconsin System, 2013), table: "Budget Allocations by Institution and Source of Funds, 2012–13," p. 32; "2012–13 UC Berkeley Budget Plan" (University of California at Berkeley, 2012), table: "UC Berkeley Total," p. 4; "About UCLA" (University of California, Los Angeles. 2014), http://newsroom.ucla.edu/portal/ucla/about-ucla.aspx (accessed April 7, 2014).

means that the waiting lists grow long, and people either go without treatment or seek alternatives through private services and charity. And in all these cases, the deterioration of the services adds credibility to the accusation that the state cannot do things well.

2. *Deregulation.* A central mantra of the attack on the affirmative state is the need to reduce government regulation of the market. Regulations are attacked as increasing the cost of doing business, reducing competitiveness, and ultimately hurting everyone. It rarely happens that regulations are entirely eliminated, particularly because some regulations are so clearly in the interests of corporations themselves; even so, many sectors of the economy have become much less monitored and constrained by democratically imposed rules. Before the 1990s, banks were quite restricted in the kind of financial services they could offer. The deregulation of banking resulted in the vast expansion of opaque and risky investments. The deregulation of airlines ultimately led to a dramatic consolidation of airline companies, the complete domination of certain markets by single providers, and significant reductions in services to many smaller cities. As we will see in Chapter 20, the deregulation of broadcasting and mass media led to the elimination of local ownership of thousands of radio stations and the consolidation of huge media corporations controlling TV, newspapers, and radio. Now a single corporation often dominates multiple sources of news in a given market.

3. *Lax enforcement.* Rules and regulations of the state are not self-enforcing. They require government agencies to specify the details of the rules to be followed, gather information, monitor compliance, decide when an infraction matters, and so on. Without any change in the underlying legislation, a form of regulation can be gutted either by appointing administrators who change critical details of regulatory and enforcement policies or by reducing the funding and staffs to such an extent that the agency becomes incapable of effectively enforcing regulations. Both have occurred since the early 1980s. The critical agency for monitoring and enforcing laws about labor unions in the United States is the National Labor Relations Board (NLRB). This board certifies elections to form unions and responds to claims of abuses of employers. Since the Reagan administration, the leadership of the NLRB has generally been very hostile to unions, and the funding has been cut to the point that the delays in hearing grievances about abuses mean that employers almost never have to worry

about enforcement. Since the early 1980s, there has been a dramatic reduction in the number of inspectors for food safety. Some people argue that this situation has increased the risks of foodborne contaminations. The Occupational Health and Safety Administration (OSHA) cut its inspection staffs for workplace health and safety. It has been estimated that there are now so few OSHA inspectors that it would take fifty years for every workplace in America to be visited once. Fewer tax auditors in the Internal Revenue Service means less consistent enforcement of tax codes.

4. *Privatization.* The most straightforward strategy for undermining the affirmative state has been to shift certain tasks from the public to the private sphere. At one time in the United States, many municipalities directly owned their water treatment plants, electrical utilities, garbage collection, and many other utilities. The justification for this public ownership was that these were natural monopolies, so real competition was not possible and direct public ownership would be more efficient than private ownership. In the last decades of the twentieth century, these utilities have been mostly sold to private corporations. Many of the ordinary government administrative tasks— accounting, clerical work, computer services, processing applications for a wide range of services (passports and visas, welfare, Social Security)—have been outsourced to private firms. This outsourcing has reached the point that the capacity of the government to directly do this kind of ordinary administrative work has declined significantly. Although this change has been made in the name of increasing efficiency, often the motivation is avoiding union constraints because the public sector is much more heavily unionized than the private sector firms that take over state functions. In some parts of the United States, major highways have been partially privatized through long-term contracts to gather tolls and maintain the roadway. Private for-profit prisons have become an integral part of the prison system. Private corporations provide a wide range of services for the U.S. military, including prisons, interrogations, security, and convoys as well as purely support activities like food, canteens, and housing. In Iraq by 2008, the number of employees of private military corporations working with the U.S. military exceeded the number of American soldiers.

5. *Public-private partnerships in the delivery of social services.* One final, somewhat ambiguous strategy for weakening the affirmative state

goes under the rubric of public-private partnerships.[10] Sometimes instead of simply divesting themselves of certain responsibilities, private sector organizations are invited to be "partners" with government in providing services of various kinds. After the welfare reforms in 1996, in many states the actual administration of welfare services to the poor was run by private sector organizations. Some of these are nonprofit organizations, but others are ordinary for-profit firms that take over these state services. In the 1990s, Lockheed-Martin, one of the major corporations producing military armaments, took over a significant portion of the welfare services for the poor in Texas and a number of other states. Charter schools and various kinds of school voucher programs allow for public schools to be run by private organizations that sometimes include for-profit, market-driven education-service firms. In all these instances the private sector partners are nominally supervised by public agencies, but frequently such supervision is so lax that the service in question becomes much more like a private sector activity. The ambiguity in this strategy of weakening the affirmative state is that sometimes these partnerships open the door for genuine, democratic participation by communities that would otherwise be excluded and alienated from politics. When this happens, there is the potential for revitalizing democracy rather than undercutting it. We will examine this possibility in Chapter 24.

Taken together, these policies constituted a retreat of democracy and an enlargement of privatized ways of organizing social life. The retreat has never gone so far as to fully dismantle the affirmative state, but it has significantly weakened the regulatory capacity of the state and its ability to raise resources for public purposes.

Due to the quarter century of sustained attack of the affirmative state, when the balance of political forces began to shift in the mid-2000s, culminating in the defeat of the Republican Party in national elections in 2006 and 2008, supporters of a revitalized affirmative state faced serious obstacles to expanding the scope of public goods and collective problem solving. The issue was not, at its core, that the severity of the economic crisis of this

---

[10] For a good discussion of the relationship between public-private partnerships and the erosion of democracy, see Dorothy Holland, Donald Nonini, Catherine Lutz, et al., *Local Democracy Under Siege: Activism, Public Interests, and Private Politics* (New York: New York University Press, 2007).

period meant that the society could not "afford" expansive programs. The level of taxation in the United States is low enough when compared to other countries that there is no reason to believe that a higher tax equilibrium is impossible for strictly economic reasons. The problem was—and remains to this day—mainly political and institutional, not economic.

At the time of the first Obama election, the political coalition for decisively shifting priorities from private consumption and investment to collective needs and public goods was still relatively weak and fragmented, and no broad consensus for a longer-term strategy of high taxation for public purposes had been forged. Institutionally, the hollowing out of the state during the previous quarter century meant that the administrative capacity of the state had seriously weakened, undermining its ability to effectively gather information and run new programs. In this political context, every proposal for expanding the role of the state to deal with pressing public problems met with stiff resistance by conservative political forces. Even though the country was in the midst of the worst economic crisis since the 1930s, the attempt to stimulate the economy through modest government spending on infrastructure projects was denounced as reckless spending. The attempt at major reform of the health-care system was denounced as a government takeover of health care, even though it was based on what were originally Republican proposals for a system still largely reliant on private health insurance. By the second Obama administration, the forces opposed to taxation and the affirmative state had rallied, fueled by the anger and hysteria of the Tea Party, and effectively blocked virtually all new initiatives. The midterm elections in 2014 further consolidated the forces opposed to the affirmative state at the national level and in many state governments. It is unclear whether the United States has the political will and energy to rebuild state capacity and construct a more publicly weighted balance between the public and private division of the economic pie.

20

CORPORATE CONTROL OF THE MEDIA

So far in our discussion of democracy, we have focused directly on the institutions of the state itself: how elections are organized, how taxes are gathered, what kinds of policies are pursued and opposed, and how the functions of the state can be expanded or narrowed. But democracy is not just about what happens in the state. It also concerns a wide range of issues concerning what is often called civil society—the areas of social life outside of the state where people meet to discuss issues, form their political views, and join together for collective action. A central requirement for the health of democracy concerns the vibrancy of civil society, and a key issue for this vibrancy is the problem of information.

Few people would disagree that information is pivotal for a democratic, free society. When dictators seize power, one of the first things they do is seize the TV stations and close down opposition newspapers. As is often said, a free press is essential for a free society. More broadly, the way the media and mass communications—newspapers, magazines, television, radio, the arts, and so on—are owned, produced, and controlled has pervasive consequences for the character of public debate, for the attitudes people form toward social issues and social conflicts, and ultimately for the possibilities that various kinds of social change will occur in a democracy. How the mass media is controlled, therefore, is a fundamental problem for a democratic society.

At the heart of the problem of the media and democracy is the question of the ownership and control of the production and dissemination of news. However, other aspects of the media and communication—including movies, novels, music, theater, and television entertainment—are also critical for public debate and democracy. The arts are one of the most important ways of articulating issues of public concern and making them salient to democratic processes. Right after they close opposition newspapers, dictators take control of the arts. In this chapter we focus on issues surrounding the democratic press, but the analysis is also relevant to the broader question of the production and dissemination of ideas and art in a democratic society.

MARKETS AND THE MEDIA

Although everyone acknowledges that a "free" press is essential for a "free" society, there is considerable ambiguity about precisely what the word *free* means.[1] The standard view is that the "free" in *free press* means a press that is *free from government control*, and this, in turn, means a *free market* press. A free market press serves the interest of a free society, the reasoning goes, because market competition will guarantee an open arena for the exchange and dissemination of ideas. The metaphor of the market permeates such discussions: the free marketplace of ideas is a standard way of talking about open debate and unimpeded dissemination of opposing views. And, just as in the ordinary market of capitalist competition in material products, the free market press and the free marketplace of ideas are seen by many people as the best ways of ensuring that the best ideas survive the competition. This mechanism serves the public interest by maximizing the chance that lies and misinformation are exposed and that citizens can hear all sides of arguments and thus develop their own well-informed opinions on matters of public importance. In this view, the greatest threats to a free press are government authority, government control, and censorship.

In the following subsections, we discuss four basic problems with these standard arguments for the free market as the guarantor of a free press that serves the public interest.

Corporate Control of Media Content

The first problem centers on the simple and obvious fact that the owners of mass media companies have the power to control the content of what the media produces. "In commercial media," Robert McChesney writes, "owners hire, fire, set budgets and determine the overarching aims of the enterprise. Journalists, editors and media professionals who rise to the top of the hierarchy tend to internalize the values, both commercial and political, of media owners."[2]

---

[1] This discussion draws heavily from Robert McChesney, *Corporate Media and the Threat to Democracy* (New York: Seven Stories Press, 1997); *Rich Media, Poor Democracy: Communication Politics in Dubious Times* (New York: New Press, 1999); and *The Problem of the Media: U.S. Communications Politics in the Twenty-first Century* (New York: Monthly Review Press, 2004).

[2] McChesney, *The Problem of the Media*, p. 100.

The political views of the owners of a firm that produces lawn mowers are unlikely to have much effect on the nature of the lawn mowers produced, but the political views of the owners of newspapers and television networks are likely to matter a lot for the character of the information these firms produce and disseminate. The owners of media companies may, of course, abdicate that control or delegate such control to the people they hire. In principle they could give complete autonomy to editors and reporters to determine the character of the news. But owners and corporate executives generally have political views on the salient issues in the press, and because they have the right to influence the operation of the firms they own, they typically exercise broad control over the character of news reporting: which issues get dealt with and which are ignored; which "experts" are quoted and which are not; which sorts of explanations are taken seriously and which ones are dismissed.

Major newspapers and news broadcasts are produced by large and powerful corporations, and their owners are very wealthy. It should be no surprise to anyone that this business structure significantly affects the perspectives embodied in news reporting. News organizations are perfectly prepared to report particular scandals and abuses by corporations and wealthy individuals; but the conservative, pro-business ideological slant resulting from the capitalist character of news organizations ensures that overall, such news organizations are unlikely to report news that is broadly hostile to corporate capitalism and the American elite.[3]

Corporate Control of Media Markets

The second problem with the argument that the free market is the guarantor of a free press makes the first problem more serious: the argument assumes that the market for media products, especially news, is highly competitive. If in fact there were few barriers to entry to media markets, and

---

[3]Conservative talk-show radio and political analysts have relentlessly argued that the national media has a strong liberal bias. Though it is true that journalists tend to be relatively liberal, especially on social issues, according to McChesney (*The Problem of the Media*, p. 102) surveys show "that media owners and editorial executives vote overwhelmingly Republican." Journalists may be more liberal than their editors, but this does not get translated into a consistent liberal bias in actual news reporting, and certainly not into an anti-business bias. The popular impression that the press has an anti-business, left-wing bias should therefore not be understood as a credible position based on careful empirical research of actual news stories and reporting, but rather as a strategy of intimidation of the press by right-wing commentators, especially talk-show radio hosts.

people from all social classes could easily come together to create viable news organizations, then the pro-business bias of the mass market press would probably be weaker.

This might have been the situation during the nineteenth century, when dozens of newspapers competed with each other in major cities. It is certainly not the case today. Most cities in the United States have only one important newspaper, and most major newspapers are part of large newspaper chains owned by large corporations rather than by local people. The ownership of television news is even more concentrated; a very few corporations control all the major networks and cable news channels. Table 20.1 presents the seven largest media corporations in the United States. The biggest, Comcast, had 2011 revenues of $55.8 billion and media-related holdings that include television networks NBC and 24 stations in the NBC network, Telemundo, USA Network, SyFy, CNBC, MSNBC, Bravo, and Oxygen, as well as online media holdings that include MSNBC.com (50 percent stake), Hulu (32 percent stake), iVillage, and Fandango.

What about the Internet? The Internet is filled with news blogs and news sites, some of them with a fairly wide following. Occasionally some of these sites play an important role in breaking a news story. In the future, news gathering and reporting on the Internet could possibly act as a meaningful counterweight to corporate-dominated news organizations, but this has not happened yet. The problem with looking to the Internet to neutralize corporate domination of the news, however, is the extremely high cost of engaging in serious news gathering, investigating, and reporting. Internet news organizations that are unaffiliated with large capitalist corporations do not have access to the revenues needed for these pursuits.

Advertiser Control of Media Content

The third problem with the identification of the free press with the free market is that newspapers and television stations owned by capitalist corporations make money almost entirely from advertising. The central profit-making goal of owners, therefore, is to attract advertisers. Actually selling newspapers or attracting viewers matters mainly to the extent that readership and audience size are translated into attracting advertisers. This dependence on advertising has a number of systematic consequences for the production of news.

The marketing objective of the media is to be viewed by people *who are as attractive to advertisers as possible*, and in general this means that media

TABLE 20.1—Principal holdings of the seven largest media corporations

Corporation	2011 Revenues	Types of Media						Principal Holdings
		TV	Film	Publishing	Online	Radio	Other	
Comcast	$55.8 billion	X			X		X	NBCUniversal; 24 television stations and the NBC television network; Telemundo; USA Network; SyFy; CNBC; MSNBC; Bravo; Oxygen; MSNBC.com (50% stake); Hulu (32% stake); iVillage; Fandango.
Walt Disney Company	$40.8 billion	X	X	X		X	X	The ABC television network; ESPN, the Disney Channel, SOAPnet, A&E, and Lifetime; 277 radio stations, music– and book-publishing companies; film-production companies Touchstone, Miramax, and Walt Disney Pictures; Pixar Animation Studios; the cellular service Disney Mobile; and theme parks around the world.
News Corp.	$33.4 billion	X	X	X	X		X	Media holdings include the FOX Broadcasting Company; television and cable networks such as Fox, Fox Business Channel, National Geographic, and FX; print publications including the Wall Street Journal, the New York Post, and TV Guide; the magazines Barron's and SmartMoney; book publisher HarperCollins; film production companies 20th Century Fox, Fox Searchlight Pictures, and Blue Sky Studios; numerous websites including MarketWatch.com.
Time Warner, Inc.	$28.9 billion	X	X	X	X		X	Warner Brothers; Warner Brothers Pictures; New Line Cinema; Castle Rock; CW Network (50% stake); TBS; TNT; Cartoon Network; truTV; Turner Classic Movies; Boomerang; CNN; HLN; CNN International; HBO; Cinemax.
Viacom	$14.9 billion	X	X		X		X	Viacom Media Networks (160 cable channels including MTV, VH1, CMT, Logo, Nickelodeon, Comedy Central, TV Land, Spike TV, Tr3s, BET).
CBS	$14.2 billion	X	X	X	X	X	X	CBS, the CW—a joint venture between CBS Corporation and Warner Bros. Entertainment, Showtime Networks, Smithsonian Networks, and CBS Sports Network, CBS local television stations, CBS Television Studios, CBS Studios International and CBS Television Distribution, CBS Radio, publishing (Simon & Schuster), interactive media (CBS Interactive), music (CBS Records), licensing and merchandising (CBS Consumer Products), video/DVD (CBS Home Entertainment), motion pictures (CBS Films), and socially responsible media (EcoMedia).
CC Media Holdings	$6.2 billion					X	X	Clear Channel owns 866 radio stations (programs include the Rush Limbaugh Show, Glenn Beck, and the Sean Hannity Show); Fox Sports Radio; Fox News Radio; Australian Radio Network.

owners want their newspapers and television news programs to be consumed by affluent people who buy lots of stuff. The news is thus geared to the interests of the affluent, not the average person. As Robert McChesney, the leading academic critic of corporate domination of the media, put it, the media market is "predicated upon one dollar, one vote. Affluent people therefore have considerably more 'votes' in determining the course of the media system, while the poorest people are effectively disenfranchised."[4] News that is relevant to the "public interest" or "common good" is generally marginalized unless it is also of interest to affluent readers and viewers. Also, because the media depends on advertising, news that might be offensive to important advertisers is unlikely to be broadcast. Quite apart from any political biases the owners of the media might themselves have, their direct economic interests ensure that they will be concerned with not offending or alienating affluent consumers or advertisers.

Effects of Cost Cutting on Media Content

The final problem with a free press rooted in corporate capitalism centers on the role of cost cutting in profit-maximizing strategies of corporations. All organizations with budget constraints, not just capitalist corporations, have to worry about costs, but the problem of cost reduction becomes especially pressing in profit-maximizing corporations. When newspapers were a family-owned business, the owners could balance their desires for profits with their commitments to the newspaper and its public role. They had to cover their costs of production, but they did not have to maximize their profits. When a newspaper becomes part of a massive corporation owned by stock-owning investors with no particular commitment to any single kind of product, the bottom line becomes a much more pressing concern.

Cost-cutting pressures significantly affect the quality of news, even aside from the problem of specific ideological biases. One way of reducing costs is for news organizations to rely mainly on material from syndicated sources and celebrity journalists rather than in-house journalists. Robert McChesney explains the problem this way:

> To do effective journalism is expensive and corporate managers realize that the surest way to fatten profits is to fire editors and reporters and fill the news hole with inexpensive syndicated material and fluff. The result has been a sharp polarization among journalists with salaries and benefits

[4]McChesney, *The Problem of the Media*, p. 200.

climbing for celebrity and privileged journalists at the elite news media while conditions have deteriorated for the balance of the working press.[5]

Another way of reducing costs is for journalists to rely heavily on public relations documents, press releases, and news conferences as the primary source of news information. Reporting on artificially contrived news events becomes a substitute for investigating real events for the news. What, after all, is a press release? It is information carefully crafted by elites to present a particular view of what is happening. When newspapers rely primarily on such sources for the news, in effect news is being generated by elites in their interest rather than by reporters directly examining events. Robert McChesney estimates that public relations and press releases now account for somewhere between 40 and 70 percent of all "news" reports.

The drastic cost-cutting pressure contributes to a downward spiral within the newspaper business. The absorption of newspapers into the portfolio of large corporations increases the drive to maximize profits by cutting costs; a central strategy of cutting costs is to reduce staff drastically by laying off reporters and news analysts; this move reduces the quality of newspapers, making them less interesting and useful; that step then reduces the number of subscribers and makes the newspapers less attractive to advertisers; the reduction in advertising revenue increases the pressure of newspapers to cut costs; and so on. John Nichols and Robert McChesney put it this way:

> Mired in debt and facing massive losses, the managers of corporate newspaper firms seek to right the sinking ship by cutting costs, leading remaining newspaper readers to ask why they are bothering to pay for publications that are pale shadows of themselves. It is the daily newspaper death dance-cum-funeral march.[6]

By 2009 nearly every major newspaper in the country was in a state of financial crisis, many faced imminent bankruptcy, and a number of important regional papers had ceased publication.

Taken together, these four processes undermine the autonomy and effectiveness of the news media as the fourth estate of the political system. The free press is intended to serve the public interest by helping to create an

---

[5] McChesney, *Corporate Media and the Threat to Democracy*, p. 24.

[6] John Nichols and Robert W. McChesney, "The Death and Life of Great American Newspapers," *The Nation*, April 6, 2009.

informed citizenry. But reporters and editors, even when they personally believe in the professional ethics of neutrality and objectivity, are severely constrained by the interests and orientations of the owners and business executives of media corporations and the commercial advertisers that are their main source of profits. A truly free press must be free from the domination of any sources of concentrated power, and this includes the power of corporations as well as the power of the state.

DEREGULATION: THE CASE OF RADIO

All the issues we have been examining become worse as ownership of media outlets becomes concentrated in larger corporations. A striking example concerns the patterns of ownership over radio stations. When radio first began in the United States, it was not at all clear that it would be dominated by commercial broadcasters. The airwave broadcast spectrum had to be publicly regulated in one way or another—otherwise the radio signals of stations would constantly interfere with each other—but there were many possibilities for how this could be done. Selling or auctioning off the spectrum to private corporations was one possibility. Leasing the broadcast spectrum from the public was another. Significant portions of the spectrum could be reserved for public use.

In the early 1930s, when these issues were being actively debated, there were influential proponents of the idea that the spectrum should be allocated mainly to noncommercial broadcasters; and it was far from obvious that the optimal solution was to turn large parts of the spectrum into private property. Even in a capitalist country like the United States, after all, we do not turn into private property all the public resources that have potential commercial value. All navigable rivers, for example, are permanently retained as public property. Imagine what it would be like if particular stretches of the Mississippi River were sold off to private owners, who could then decide who could or could not use the river and at what cost.

In the United States these issues for the broadcast spectrum were initially resolved in the 1934 Communications Act, which basically privatized most of the airways but did so in a way that also affirmed the ongoing public character of the resource. Broadcasters were given renewable licenses for fixed terms that gave them exclusive use of specific parts of the radio spectrum, but they were also described as "trustees" who had to serve the "public interest" rather than as simple, outright owners who had full private property rights. Critically, the provisions of the original 1934

Communications Act severely restricted the number of radio stations a single firm could own in a given broadcasting market, as well as the total number of stations a firm could own across markets. The idea behind these restrictions was quite simple: concentrations of ownership would threaten the public functions of the airways and reduce local responsiveness and diversity.

These ownership rules remained largely intact until the Telecommunications Act of 1996. That act lifted nearly all restrictions on ownership. Historically, radio has been one of the most competitive segments of American media. In the early 1990s, no firm owned more than a dozen or so of the over 10,000 radio stations in the country, and no firm owned more than two radio stations in a single market. Following the Telecommunications Act, there was a truly massive elimination of locally owned and controlled radio stations. Within a decade after the restrictions were lifted, one radio station company—Clear Channel—owned some 1,200 stations nationwide. By 2011 Clear Channel, Sirius XM, CBS, and Cumulus, the four top companies owning radio stations, controlled nearly 45 percent of industry revenues nationwide (Figure 20.1).

Concentration of ownership is even higher when you look at local radio markets. In 2010 the four largest firms in local radio markets controlled

FIGURE 20.1—Concentration of revenues of radio station owners, 2011

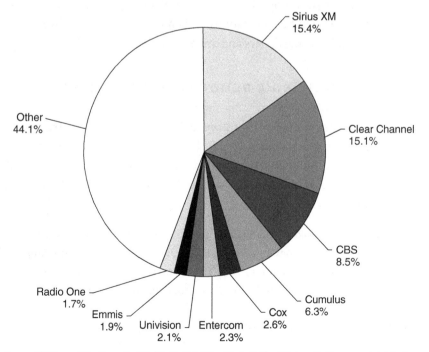

Source: Eli Noam, *Who Owns the World's Media?* (New York: Oxford University Press, 2015), table 18.5.

85.1 percent of revenues in small cities, 82.6 percent in medium cities, and 65.8 percent in large cities.[7] These companies are often not locally owned but are part of large national or regional chains of stations. As a consequence, radio programmers in corporate headquarters make the decision about what music to play across the country. Local news disappears from most radio stations. We are rapidly approaching the day when locally owned, community-oriented radio stations will virtually disappear.

It is important here to understand that this concentration of ownership is not the result of substantial technological or economic efficiencies in having hundreds of stations owned by a single corporation. It is cheaper for a few large corporations to produce automobiles than it is for every town to have its own automobile manufacturer. This principle, called an economy of scale, simply does not apply to radio. Owning and running a local radio station is not that expensive. The problem is getting access to an adequate revenue stream through advertising. With deregulation, big chains owning more powerful stations can monopolize the advertising and squeeze out smaller local stations. An owner of five hundred stations is not markedly more efficient than an owner of one in the actual running of a radio station. But a big chain is more efficient in attracting advertising, and this ability makes it very hard for the owner of a single station to compete. This is one reason that the rules for owning stations were heavily regulated: if people want a locally rooted system of radio broadcasting, then they must block large corporations from owning unlimited numbers of stations. When corporations take over, they suck up all the advertising dollars and drive local stations out of business.

REVITALIZING A DEMOCRATIC FREE PRESS

In the twenty-first century, the future existence of a vibrant, free press needed for a robust democracy cannot be taken for granted. Newspapers are in crisis. Dozens of papers have folded. The remaining newspapers have drastically cut their staffs. Here is how John Nichols and Robert McChesney described the crisis in early 2009:

> In a nutshell, media corporations, after running journalism into the ground, have determined that news gathering and reporting are not profit-making propositions. So they're jumping ship. The country's great regional dailies—the *Chicago Tribune*, the *Los Angeles Times*, the *Minneapolis Star Tribune*, the

[7]From Eli Noam, *Who Owns the World's Media?* (New York: Oxford University Press, 2015), table 18.6.

Philadelphia Inquirer—are in bankruptcy. Denver's *Rocky Mountain News* recently closed down, ending daily newspaper competition in that city. The owners of the *San Francisco Chronicle*, reportedly losing $1 million a week, are threatening to shutter the paper, leaving a major city without a major daily newspaper. Big dailies in Seattle (the *Times*), Chicago (the *Sun-Times*) and Newark (the *Star-Ledger*) are reportedly near the point of folding, and smaller dailies like the *Baltimore Examiner* have already closed. . . . Whole newspaper chains—such as Lee Enterprises, the owner of large and medium-size publications that for decades have defined debates in Montana, Iowa and Wisconsin—are struggling as the value of stock shares falls below the price of a single daily paper.[8]

Many of the most prominent national and regional papers used to have foreign news bureaus as well as bureaus in Washington. Many of these offices, too, have been closed. Radio news reporting, aside from National Public Radio and some independent, community-based stations, has almost disappeared. Television news has shrunk considerably, and in any case is controlled by some of the largest corporations in America. This configuration of power and organization of the press greatly weakens its role in fostering informed and engaged citizens in a democratic society.

So, what can be done? The starting point for seeking a solution is to recognize that a vibrant press engaged in serious journalism in the public interests is a special kind of *public good*.[9] A public good, as explained in our exploration of capitalist markets, is a good whose production has positive effects on society beyond the effects on the specific people who directly consume the good. Because of the way it strengthens democracy, a vibrant and healthy free press—free from both government control and domination by powerful corporations—benefits most people, even people who are not interested in the news, do not read newspapers, and remain politically passive. The capitalist market usually does a bad job of producing public goods because the profit-maximizing strategies of firms cannot give adequate weight to these positive, universal benefits. As a result, public goods require direct public support to be produced. This is as true for the press as it is for other public goods.

---

[8] Nichols and McChesney, "The Death and Life of Great American Newspapers."

[9] A pure public good, as discussed in Chapter 4, is a good that it is impossible to exclude people from consuming, whether or not they pay for the good in question. National defense and clean air are examples. The press is a combination of a public good and a private good: some of the benefits of a vibrant press go exclusively to those who directly consume the press, and some of the benefits affect everyone in the broader society.

Treating the free press as a public good goes back to the very founding of the American Republic. The U.S. Constitution explicitly gives Congress the power to establish post offices, and one of the very earliest acts of Congress was the Post Office Act of 1792. A central purpose of the postal service was precisely to provide public support for mass communication and subsidy for the press. Robert McChesney writes:

> The crucial debate in the 1792 Congress was how much to charge newspapers to be sent through the mails. All parties agreed that Congress should permit newspapers to be mailed at a price well below actual cost—to be subsidized—to encourage their production and distribution. Postal subsidies of newspapers would become perhaps the largest single expenditure of the federal government. In Congress, the range of debate was between those who wished to charge newspapers a nominal fee for postage and those who wanted to permit newspapers the use of the mails absolutely free of charge.

James Madison led the fight in Congress for completely free mailing privileges, calling even a token fee a "tax" on newspapers that was "an insidious forerunner of something worse."[10]

In the context of the times, this was really a massive subsidy that contributed significantly to the proliferation of newspapers and periodicals and their wide dissemination. According to the political scientist Timothy Cook, "Public policy from the outset of the American Republic focused explicitly on getting the news to a wide readership and chose to support news outlets by taking on costs of delivery and, through printers' exchanges, of production." The result was that by 1832, over 90 percent of post office traffic consisted of newspapers.[11]

So, government support explicitly designed to sustain a democratically energetic press in the public interest is not something new in American history. In the twenty-first century, however, the specific policies adopted in the late eighteenth century will hardly be adequate to the task (although, it should be said, subsidized postage for periodicals is still important for small presses). What we need are new policies of regulation and subsidy that deal

---

[10] McChesney, *The Problem of the Media*, p. 33.

[11] Timothy E. Cook, *Governing with the News: The News Media as a Political Institution* (Chicago: University of Chicago Press, 1988), p. 44; cited in McChesney, *Corporate Media and the Threat to Democracy*, pp. 33–34.

with the realities of the threat of concentrated corporate power to a genuinely free press. Here are four proposals that we feel would do much to reverse the erosion of democratic media in the public interest.

Reinstating Restrictions on Corporate Media Ownership

Reinstating ownership rules is, perhaps, the simplest thing to do. The regulations that restricted ownership of many radio stations and domination of specific regional mass media markets were weakened only in the last decades of the twentieth century as the neoliberal ideology of the unfettered free market became politically ascendant. Restoring restrictions on the degree to which concentrations of corporate power can be translated into control over media markets would be a first step in rebuilding a genuine free press.

Conservatives object to such restrictions on the grounds that these restrictions themselves constitute a violation of free speech. For many strong defenders of private property rights, the idea of free speech as a right of individuals equally applies to large corporations. Corporations are regarded as "legal persons" for a wide range of narrowly economic purposes, and many conservatives believe that this legal classification naturally entails that all rights we accord to individuals also apply to corporations. Regulating the right of a corporation to "speak" is the same as abridging the right of an individual to speak, and because owning the media is the necessary condition for being able to speak, restrictions on such ownership amount to a violation of fundamental rights of free speech.

These arguments rest on a fundamentally flawed understanding of the value of freedom. Corporations are not citizens. We do not allow them to vote in elections, nor can they be elected to public office. They are instruments of human action, and if their use in particular ways undermines the freedom of individuals and the prospects for democracy, then it is legitimate for these powers to be regulated.

Strengthening the Public Sector of the Mass Media

Nearly every country, including the United States, has some kind of public, noncommercial sector of broadcast media. In the United States this includes the Public Broadcasting Service television network and National Public Radio, along with a range of locally run, nonprofit community radio stations. Although PBS and NPR do receive some tax support, most of their funding comes from voluntary contributions by listeners and program underwriting by corporations and nonprofit foundations. Only about 15 percent of total funding comes from tax support, and even this level has been under attack by conservatives. In many other countries, direct government support for the public sector of broadcasting is much greater. The British Broadcasting Corporation, for example, is supported almost entirely by a direct license fee for the use of televisions. The cost is quite considerable—£145 in 2013 (around $220)—until the age of seventy-five, after which it is free. This license fee provides well over $3 billion per year in funding for the public sector of broadcasting.

There is no reason, in principle, that the United States could not levy a license fee for television use in order to fund the public sector of broadcasting. We already have taxes on telephone use, home ownership, hotel use, airport use, and many other amenities. Automobile owners have to pay an annual license fee to be allowed to drive their cars. Usually the rationale for such consumption-specific taxation is that it helps to support the public goods associated with the consumption. Even though it would be politically very difficult to pass a television use tax, it could do much to enhance the democratic potential of the broadcast media. In the absence of tax-supported funding, public broadcasting suffers from a classic free-rider problem: each potential contributor can enjoy public broadcasting even if they don't pay for it, so why make the sacrifice? If everyone thinks this way, no one contributes, and thus there is no funding. This is why taxes are needed for an expansive and effective public broadcast system. So long as public broadcasting relies on private contributions, it will occupy a relatively small niche in broadcast communication and will be under continual pressure to sacrifice some of its autonomy for corporate contributions.

Encouraging a Much Wider Range of Forms of Ownership of Media

Most media companies in the United States are privately owned and organized as capitalist firms. Many other forms of ownership are possible. Newspapers, radio stations, cable channels, and televisions could be owned by public bodies like universities, nonprofit corporations, community-based associations, and employee-owned cooperatives. Each of these forms has advantages and disadvantages, so a healthy media environment should have a good distribution of all of them. Newspapers that were owned and run by practicing journalists would be a particularly attractive component of such an ecology of organizational forms, because they would enable journalists to practice their craft in a much more autonomous way than when they work for newspapers controlled by capitalist firms.

The central problem faced by all these noncommercial forms is having access to the necessary financial resources to actually operate a press. If we are to create a pluralistic, democratic mass media that serves the public interest, we need to figure out a way to financially subsidize these endeavors.

Providing Public Subsidies without Public Control

In the United States there exists a convenient set of mechanisms for large and systematic public subsidies without the imposition of government control: the tax system. This is how we subsidize private charity: the tax deduction for charitable contributions that citizens get on their income tax returns is, in reality, a form of spending by the government directed at charities. The government provides the subsidy, but the individual taxpayer determines where the subsidy goes. All the state does is monitor that the rules are obeyed—that the charities are legitimate and have tax-exempt status and that the taxpayer actually made the contribution. This is public subsidy without public control.

The rationale for the tax deduction for charitable contributions is that charities constitute a public good. Having vibrant charitable organizations is one aspect of having a vibrant civil society in which citizens voluntarily form associations to solve problems and advance various kinds of collective purposes. A robust civil society is a public good: it makes for a more humane world with stronger communities and greater public connectedness. For a civil society to have these qualities, however, it is essential that the initiative for association and activity comes primarily from citizens freely associating with one another. This is where the great advantage of using tax subsidies for these public purposes lies: the tax deduction mechanism allows citizens to form the charitable organizations on the basis of their priorities and energies, but it still provides a way for tax resources to be funneled to those associations so that they can operate more effectively for the public good.

The problem with tax deductions as a mechanism for this purpose is that they have the side effect of making nonprofit organizations more dependent upon wealthy donors than on average citizens. In a tax deduction, the richer you are, the greater the tax subsidy the state provides for the organizations you donate to. If you have a high income with a marginal tax rate of 35 percent and you contribute $1,000 to a charity, the state subsidy for this donation is $350. If you have a low income with a 10 percent marginal tax rate, and you donate the same amount, the subsidy is only $100. This effect might not matter so much for many kinds of charities, but it would pose problems for a tax subsidy system for an autonomous free press.

There is an alternative device that still involves public subsidy without public control. It is called a tax credit. John Nichols and Robert McChesney describe a tax credit subsidy for newspapers this way:

> Let's give all Americans an annual tax credit for the first $200 they spend on daily newspapers. The newspapers would have to publish at least five times per week and maintain a substantial "news hole," say at least twenty-four broad pages each day, with less than 50 percent advertising. In effect, this means the government will pay for every citizen who so desires to get a free daily newspaper subscription, but the taxpayer gets to pick the newspaper— this is an indirect subsidy, because the government does not control who gets the money.[12]

In this kind of tax credit system, all citizens are on an equal footing in directing subsidies toward newspapers: everyone has $200 to spend (in the Nichols-McChesney proposal). In this way, it is very much like the democracy card proposal for public financing of elections discussed in Chapter 17. A tax credit system of subsidies for a free press would also mean that newspapers would no longer have to rely heavily on commercial advertising for their core revenues. This system would reduce the need to attract the kinds of readers that advertisers want. Again, this means that newspapers regard potential subscribers more like equal citizens.

Many specific details would have to be worked out for such a system of subsidies to newspapers to work effectively in the public interest. Should different kinds of news organizations be treated equally in the subsidy scheme, or should public subsidies be available only to newspapers that are run by nonprofit organizations? How narrowly or broadly should the ideas of "news" and "reporting" be in defining eligible publications? Should the subsidy be the same for local newspapers as it is for national papers? Should subscribers have to pay something out of their own pockets, or should the tax credit be designed to cover the entire subscription cost? What rules should govern the pay of the staff that receives these subsidies? These and other issues are important, but the basic principle is simple: just as in the case of other public goods that are essential for democracy, such as public education, unless there is a mechanism to provide meaningful collective subsidies to the press, the public good will be inadequately served.

[12] Nichols and McChesney, "The Death and Life of Great American Newspapers."

21

MILITARISM AND EMPIRE

Most Americans think of the military power of the United States in roughly the following way:

> The world is a dangerous place. There are war-making aggressive, hostile forces in the world, countries which oppress their own people and threaten others, as well as political movements that are prepared to use violence to get their way. We must oppose these threats to our national security. But we are not aggressors. We have a Department of Defense, not a Department of War. We use our military power to defend freedom, to defend democracy, to protect America, but not to dominate other countries and people. If sometimes serious problems arise from our use of military power, as in the Vietnam War or in the Iraq War, mostly these reflect bad judgment, poor information or inadequate understanding of the context rather than bad motives or malevolent goals. Even though we are not perfect, we are a moral force in the world and use our military power for moral purposes.

That is the dominant view of the American military. In this chapter we offer an alternative perspective on the character and role of the military in American society. We begin by presenting data on the empirical realities of military power in American society in the present and explain why these data suggest that the United States today is a militaristic society. We then present a brief sketch of the historical trajectory of American militarism from the early years of the republic to the present. This section is followed by an exploration of a range of possible explanations of contemporary American militarism. The chapter concludes with a discussion of the consequences of militarism for the future of American society and institutions.

THE REALITIES OF AMERICAN MILITARISM

Three stark facts about the reality of American military power stand in tension with the idealized view:

1. *The United States spends orders of magnitude more on the military than any other country.* As indicated in Figure 21.1, in 2012 military spending in the United States accounted for more than 40 percent of the world's total military spending. This is more than the next fifteen highest-spending countries in the world combined. It is 6.3 times more than the spending on the military in China, and 10.8 times more than in Russia. If we add to the U.S. figures the spending by the strongest allies of the United States—the NATO countries, Japan, South Korea, and

FIGURE 21.1—U.S. military spending and percentage of global spending compared with next 15 countries and rest of the world, 2012

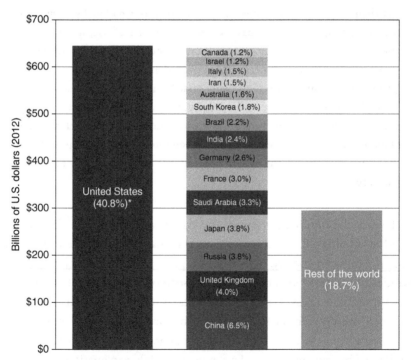

*U.S. figure includes funding for the Pentagon base budget, Department of Energy–administered nuclear weapons activities, and the war in Afghanistan.

Note: Percentage of world total spending in parentheses.

Source: Laicie Heeley, "U.S. Defense Spending vs. Global Defense Spending" (The Center for Arms Control and Non-Proliferation, April 24, 2013). Available at http://armscontrolcenter.org/issues /securityspending/articles/2012_topline_global_defense_spending/ (accessed April 9, 2014).

Australia—the total comes to over 60 percent of the entire world's military spending. The United States is not simply the world's only super-power; our military dwarfs that of all potential adversaries combined.

2. *The use of military power is a pervasive aspect of U.S. foreign policy.* More than any other country in the world today, the United States uses military power as a central instrument of national policy throughout the world. The threat of force and the actual use of force are frequent strategies in pursuit of what are perceived as U.S. interests. To facilitate this use of military power, at the beginning of the twenty-first century the United States had hundreds of military bases and installations all over the world (Figure 21.2). Official documents by the Department of Defense report 598 DoD facilities outside the United States and U.S. territories, covering a total of 39 countries.[1] Unofficial

FIGURE 21.2—U.S. military bases around the world, 2012

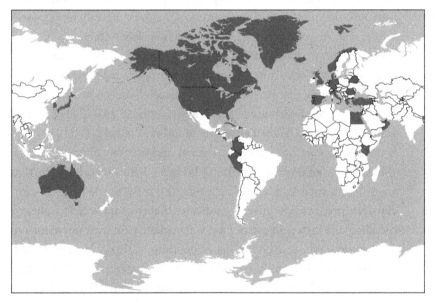

Sources: "Base Structure Report. Fiscal Year 2013 Baseline. A Summary of the Department of Defense's Real Property Inventory" (Department of Defense, 2013). Available at http://www.acq.osd .mil/ie/download/bsr/Base%20Structure%20Report%202013_Baseline%2030%20Sept%202012%20 Submission.pdf (accessed May 7, 2014). Map produced using Tableau Public. "General Analysis on US Military Expansion and Intervention," Global Policy Forum. Available at http://www.globalpolicy .org/us-military-expansion-and-intervention/general-analysis-on-us-military-expansion-and -intervention.html (accessed May 1, 2014).

[1] "Base Structure Report. Fiscal Year 2013 Baseline. A Summary of the Department of Defense's Real Property Inventory" (Department of Defense, 2013). Available at http:// www.acq.osd.mil/ie/download/bsr/Base%20Struc-ture%20Report%202013_Baseline%20 30%20Sept%202012%20Submission.pdf (accessed May 7, 2014).

accounts report at least 700 U.S. bases abroad, covering 130 countries and territories.[2]

It once was said that the sun never set on the British Empire. In the twenty-first century, it never sets on the U.S. military. The United States has directly used its troops to overthrow the governments of other countries or has attempted to do so more frequently than any other country since the end of World War II. The wars in Iraq and Afghanistan and the 2011 Libyan intervention are only the most recent examples. The United States also has frequently subsidized proxy military forces for these purposes when, for political reasons, it was difficult to use its own.

A partial list of the interventions since the end of World War II is given in Table 21.1. Some of these interventions involve the overthrow of democratic regimes (e.g., Iran, 1953; Guatemala, 1954; Dominican Republic, 1965; Chile, 1973). Others involve fighting insurgencies against authoritarian regimes that we supported (e.g., the Philippines, 1948; Vietnam, 1960–1975), or supporting insurgencies against regimes we opposed (Cuba, 1961; Angola, 1976–1992; Nicaragua, 1981–1990; Afghanistan, 1981–1988). In only two cases—the Korean War in 1951–1953 and the first Gulf War, 1990—was the United States responding to military aggression by a foreign state that had any plausible bearing on U.S. national security. The United States uses its military to impose its will around the world, not simply to defend itself from military attack.

3. *In the United States, the domestic economy and internal politics are deeply affected by the military.* The military budget constitutes a huge part of government spending, and of necessity, this reduces the flexibility for domestic programs. Figure 21.3 indicates that if we include in military spending the current cost of past wars (mainly interest payment on debt attributable to past military spending, military pensions, and Veterans Affairs spending), then for fiscal year 2012, total military spending was about 40 percent of the annual federal budget.[3] Because this has been the case, with some ups and downs, since around 1940,

---

[2] "General Analysis on US Military Expansion and Intervention," Global Policy Forum. Available at http://www.globalpolicy.org/us-military-expansion-and-intervention/general -analysis-on-us-military-expansion-and-intervention.html (accessed May 1, 2014).

[3] Estimating the amount of total military spending is not a straightforward matter; some military spending is hidden in nonmilitary agencies, and the attribution of costs of past wars is difficult. As a result, there are different overall estimates depending upon the precise methodology used.

TABLE 21.1—Partial list of U.S. military interventions, 1947–2014

Greece	1947–49	U.S. directs extreme right in civil war.
Philippines	1948–54	CIA directs war against Huk Rebellion.
Korea	1951–53	Korean War
Iran	1953	CIA overthrows democracy, installs shah.
Guatemala	1954	CIA directs overthrow of democratic government.
Lebanon	1958	Marine occupation against rebels
Vietnam	1960–75	Vietnam War
Laos	1962	Military buildup during guerrilla war
Cuba	1961	CIA-directed exile invasion fails.
Indonesia	1965	Over 500,000 killed in CIA-assisted army coup.
Dominican Rep.	1965–66	Marines land during election campaign.
Guatemala	1966–67	Green Berets intervene against rebels.
Cambodia	1969–75	Bombing
Laos	1971–73	U.S. directs South Vietnamese invasion.
Chile	1973	CIA-backed coup ousts elected Marxist president.
Angola	1976–92	CIA assists South African–backed rebels.
El Salvador	1981–92	Advisors, overflights aid anti-rebel war.
Nicaragua	1981–90	CIA directs exile (Contra) invasions.
Lebanon	1982–84	Marines expel PLO and back Phalangists.
Grenada	1983–84	Invasion 4 years after revolution ousts regime.
Iran	1984	Two Iranian jets shot down over Persian Gulf.
Libya	1986	Air strikes to topple nationalist government
Iran	1987–88	U.S. intervenes to protect Iraqi tankers in Iran war.
Panama	1989	Nationalist government ousted by 27,000 soldiers.
Kuwait	1991	First Gulf War
Somalia	1992–94	U.S.-led United Nations occupation during civil war.
Bosnia	1993–94	No-fly zone in civil war; downed jets, bombed Serbs.
Haiti	1994	Troops restore Aristide to office 3 years after coup.
Yugoslavia	1999	Heavy NATO air strikes after Serbia declines to withdraw from Kosovo.
Afghanistan	2001–?	Afghanistan War
Colombia	2003	U.S. special forces sent to rebel zone.
Iraq	2003–?	Iraq War
Liberia	2003	Brief involvement in peacekeeping force as rebels drove out leader.
Haiti	2004	Marines land after rebels oust elected President Aristide.
Pakistan	2005–?	CIA missile and air strikes made on suspected Taliban sites. Periodic drone strikes.
Somalia	2006	Special Forces advise Ethiopian invasion that topples Islamist government.
Syria	2008	Special Forces in helicopter raid village 5 miles from Iraq; kill 8 Syrian civilians.
Yemen	2009–?	Cruise missile attack on al-Qaeda kills 49 civilians. Yemeni military assaults on rebels. Periodic drone strikes.
Libya	2011	NATO coordinates air strikes and missile attacks against Qaddafi government during uprising by rebel army.

Source: List compiled by Zoltán Grossman; available at http://academic.evergreen.edu/g/grossmaz/interventions.html (accessed August 25, 2014).

FIGURE 21.3—Military spending as a proportion of the total "Federal Fund Budget," 2013 fiscal year

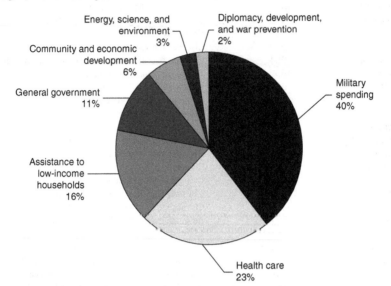

Note: Figures cover the $2,537,133,000,000 "federal fund" budget, which is the spending supported by income taxes, estate taxes, and other general revenues. Not included are trust funds, such as Social Security, Medicare, and highway trust funds, which are supported by dedicated revenues. Military spending includes the Pentagon budget and related programs with a military function, such as nuclear weapons production in the Department of Energy, and foreign military assistance (28%); interest on the federal debt accumulated from past Pentagon spending (7%); and care and benefits for veterans plus other costs and obligations from past wars (5%).

Source: "Where Do Our Income Tax Dollars Go?" (Friends Committee on National Legislation, 2013). Available at http://fcnl.org/assets/flyer/FCNL_Taxes13_final.pdf (accessed April 11, 2014).

the result has been a deep penetration of military spending in the U.S. economy. Particularly in the context of a state that has been reluctant to create jobs directly through public investment in the civilian economy, military spending, especially by awarding business contracts for military products and services, has become a principal way for the federal government to intervene in the economy. What's more, military spending is one of the main ways the government provides funding for research and development, which often has large spillovers for the civilian economy. The manufacture of weapons is also one of the few economic sectors in which the United States has a large positive trade balance, thus adding to the importance of military spending for the overall health of the economy. Whenever proposals are made to end particular weapons systems or close military bases, members of Congress from the affected region object on the grounds that doing so will harm the economy. Often they do not even bother to debate the issues, on grounds of military policy and efficiency. Political coalitions form around military spending for economic reasons, and the resulting political pressures further distort the role of the military in foreign policy.

These three facts suggest that the United States in the twenty-first century is not simply a society with a strong military; it has become a militaristic society. *Militarism* can be defined as a political and ideological orientation toward international affairs in which three conditions are present:

1. The use and threat of military power is a central strategy of international policy.
2. The military plays a pervasive role in the economic and political life of a country.
3. Military strength is the highest priority of government policy.

Militarism is not just the policy of a particular administration; it is institutionalized into our economic, political, and social structure. Over the past half century, American militarism has been built up by administrations led by both the Republican and Democratic parties. It is supported, although perhaps with differing fervor, by both parties; and the leadership of both parties advocates an American role in the world that depends on militarism. All American politicians in leadership roles argue that we must have a strong military that is flexible in ways that enable it to be deployed on short notice around the world. No viable presidential candidate can stand up and say, "The American military should be used exclusively for the defense of the United States against attack. We should dismantle bases abroad, and bring our troops home. Our military budget should be tailored entirely for defensive purposes.[4] If military action abroad is needed for humanitarian reasons, then this must be done by international authority, not by unilateral action of individual states." Such a position is completely outside of legitimate political discourse in the United States.

[4] In the 2008 presidential election, three marginal candidates took this position: Ralph Nader and Dennis Kucinich on the left, and Ron Paul on the libertarian right. Ron Paul's position was especially surprising to many people. He advocated cutting the military budget by two-thirds, closing all bases abroad, and ending the practice of global military interventions. His stance was in keeping with a consistent libertarian position that argues for a minimalist state providing for security only.

A SKETCH OF THE HISTORICAL TRAJECTORY
OF AMERICAN MILITARISM

Militarism was not always a prominent feature of American political culture.[5] At the founding of the United States, there was widespread objection to the idea of a standing army and great skepticism about the use of military power for national objectives. George Washington and James Madison expressed these worries in the early years of the Republic:

Washington: "Overgrown military establishments are under any form of government inauspicious to liberty, and are to be regarded as particularly hostile to Republican liberty."

Madison: "Of all enemies to public liberty, war is, perhaps, the most to be dreaded, because it comprises and develops the germ of every other. War is the parent of armies; from these proceed debts and taxes; and armies, debt and taxes are the known instrument for bringing the many under the domination of the few."[6]

Nearly two hundred years later, Dwight Eisenhower expressed the same worry in his famous farewell address:

This conjunction of an immense military establishment and a large arms industry is new in the American experience. . . . In the councils of government, we must guard against the acquisition of unwarranted influence . . . of the military industrial complex. The potential for the disastrous rise of misplaced power exists and will persist. We must never let the weight of this combination endanger our liberties or democratic processes. We should take nothing for granted.

Even more poignantly, he rejected militarism as a tolerable way of life:

Every gun that is made, every warship launched, every rocket fired signifies, in the final sense, a theft from those who hunger and are not fed, those who are cold and are not clothed. The world in arms is not spending money alone. It is spending the sweat of its laborers, the genius of its scientists, the

[5] This discussion draws heavily from Chalmers Johnson, *The Sorrows of Empire: Militarism, Secrecy, and the End of the Republic* (New York: Metropolitan Books, 2004).

[6] Ibid., pp. 39, 44–45.

hopes of its children. . . . This is not a way of life at all, in any true sense. Under the cloud of threatening war, it is humanity hanging from a cross of iron.[7]

Antimilitarism is thus also a current throughout American history. But right from the start, antimilitarism was challenged because of the importance of military power for the conquest of lands in North America itself. This more militaristic stance became crystallized early in the nineteenth century as manifest destiny—the belief that the United States, then in the eastern part of North America, had a natural right to expand westward to the Pacific Ocean. Military power was pivotal to this conquest: it was used initially for displacing indigenous people and, in the middle of the nineteenth century, for invading and taking over territory from Mexico—Texas and California. Most historians today acknowledge that the Mexican War of 1848 was a war of conquest initiated by the United States.

The key turning point for the emergence of a more coherently militarist state occurred at the end of the nineteenth century. The Spanish-American War launched the modern period of U.S. imperial wars and conquests, including the military suppression of resistance by conquered people. The Philippine resistance to American occupation (1901–1903), in which 200,000 Filipinos were killed, is the starkest example. The United States justified this suppression on the grounds of racial superiority and the need to liberate the Philippines from Spanish control. Ironically, this ideology contributed to the Japanese sense of entitlement to conquest as the right of great nations.

Before the Spanish-American War, the U.S. military was a somewhat chaotic, relatively underdeveloped organization; it was not really organized in such a way that it could be readily deployed for national purposes. This situation changed in the years leading up to World War I, during which time a modern military bureaucracy was created. It was modeled in some ways after what was seen as the most successful military organization at that time—that of Prussia.

Woodrow Wilson articulated what was to become the core ideology of the use of American military power, which Chalmers Johnson calls the ideology of crusades. The earliest example was Wilson's military expeditions to Mexico during the Mexican revolution to teach its leaders democracy. These interventions were justified on grounds of benevolence and

---

[7] Speech delivered before the American Society of Newspaper Editors, Washington, DC, April 16, 1953.

liberation. World War I was proclaimed "the war to end all wars," the war "to make the world safe for democracy." These lofty humanitarian goals were sincerely meant, even if they were always mixed with other motives.

After World War I there was a general military demobilization, and tendencies toward militarism were largely curtailed. During the first part of the Great Depression, the military was substantially neglected as the federal government built the institutions of the New Deal affirmative state. It was only during the late 1930s, as the threat of war with Germany and Japan grew, that a serious effort at building U.S. military capacity began.

World War II was a monumental military mobilization for the United States: this war was by far the most intense foreign military conflict in American history, and the most popular. Still, even after World War II there was a good chance of demilitarization; and briefly after the war, it looked like the military would be significantly reduced in scale and importance. The Cold War changed all that. The rivalry with the Soviet Union, fueled by virulent anti-Communism, created the context for definitively consolidating militarism as a core feature of American politics and society.

From the early 1950s to the present, the military has played an absolutely central role in government spending as well as the U.S. economy. Throughout this period, military spending was at least $380 billion per year in 2012 dollars; and in four instances, it shot up to over $500 billion: during the Korean War, the Vietnam War, the Reagan military buildup, and the Iraq and Afghan wars (Figure 21.4). Defense contracts are the single most important way that the government intervenes in the economy; they provide jobs, research, technical change, and economic stimulation. The livelihood of millions of Americans depends on military spending. And, ultimately, this means the economic well-being of many people depends on war: in the absence of war, it is almost impossible to maintain huge military spending over the long term, so the deep dependency of the economy on militarism itself promotes militarism.

This kind of massive military spending has significant corrupting effects on politics and economics. There can be no real competition in the contracting process because so few companies can really place bids, and thus military contracts are chronically plagued with inflated prices and huge amounts of fraud. The inspector general of the Pentagon reported in May 2001, even before the rapid expansion of military spending following 9/11, that something like a trillion dollars of spending on the Pentagon's books could not be traced. The massive scandals during the Iraq War by

FIGURE 21.4—Department of Defense budget, 1900–2013

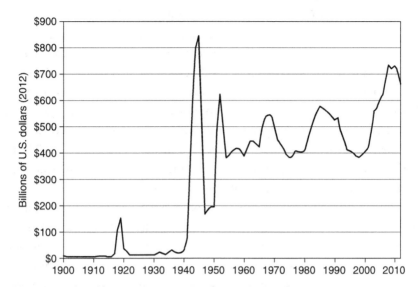

Source: 1900–1947: http://www.usgovernmentspending.com (accessed August 20, 2013); 1948–2013: National Defense Budget Estimates for FY 2014 (Washington, DC: U.S. Department of Defense, 2012), table 6.3.

Halliburton and other military contractors are recent instances in a long line of such looting of the public purse. Because military contracts are surrounded by secrecy under the shield of "national security" and "classified information," it is almost impossible to adequately monitor military spending.

Militarism became an organic part of American society in the decades of the Cold War. In the aftermath of the Cold War, a reversal of this trajectory might have seemed possible, and there were some signs of it happening. There was much talk in the 1990s of the "peace dividend" and how it might open up policies for a wide range of important public investments: environmental protection, energy transformation, high-speed rail, rebuilding infrastructure. Such prospects were cut off in the aftermath of 9/11, which led to an energetic reinvigoration of militarism in the name of fighting the war on terrorism. This reinvigoration was backed by an extreme version of the doctrine of the supremacy of American military might and the right of the United States to unilaterally decide when and where to intervene in the world on the basis of its own views of its national interest.

MOTIVATIONS FOR MILITARISM IN THE TWENTY-FIRST CENTURY: THE PROBLEM OF EMPIRE

The historical trajectory describes the development of our enormous military machine, its importance to the U.S. economy, and its use as a tool of foreign policy. But still, that analysis leaves critical questions unanswered: What are the real motives behind American militarism? Why does the United States so aggressively use its military power around the world?

There is no single, simple answer. We do not think it is possible to point to one overriding factor or motive and say, this explains American militarism. Most pervasive, durable features of a social system are supported through complex combinations of interests and motivations rather than some single overriding cause. These complex, interconnected motivations and interests help explain the broad political coalition behind militarism. When we say that militarism is an institution, we mean, in part, that it becomes self-perpetuating because the interests that support militarism are in significant ways generated and reinforced by militarism itself.

Analyzing the motivations and interests behind militarism is also complicated by the problem of ideology—the beliefs people hold about the world and how it works. For example, consider the problem of national security, one of the motives behind militarism. One view during the Cold War was that the Union of Soviet Socialist Republics (USSR) and other Communist countries would attack the United States militarily if they could. Communism was viewed by some people as an aggressive, militaristic force in the world that directly threatened capitalist democracies like the United States, so the only way to protect the United States was to have a very aggressive military capacity. The best defense is a strong offense, as the sports metaphor goes. Other people argued that we really had no reason to fear such attack; a policy of engagement, international cooperation, and strengthening of international institutions would be the best way to advance national security. These differences reflect, in part, different views about how the world works, and about what sorts of strategies will produce what sorts of outcomes. These are very difficult matters to sort out.

The problem of sorting out the underlying reasons and motivations for militarism is an especially pressing issue for the opponents to military aggression. Before the outset of the Iraq War, protesters in the run-up to the war held signs saying, "No Blood for Oil." This slogan implied a theory that a driving motivation for the war was the desire to control oil reserves in the Middle East. If that was indeed a central motive, then seeking ways of reducing American dependence on foreign oil by developing a new energy system would be part of antimilitarism initiatives. But if oil as such was more of a side issue, and if militarism is based on a broader motive for American global preeminence, then energy independence might not do much to undermine the structural foundations of militarism.

We believe that six different clusters of motivations play a role in sustaining American militarism. In different times and contexts, one or another of these may become preeminent and others become less important; but the long-term robustness of American militarism comes from the ways they interact.

Specific Economic Interests

The simplest motivation for using American military power abroad is that it serves specific economic interests of powerful sectors of American capitalism. There are certainly instances of this kind of motivation. In the 1920s, the United States sent the Marines on several occasions to small Central American countries to protect the interests of the United Fruit Company. In the 1950s, the United States overthrew the elected government in Guatemala, which was interested in land reform, as well as the government of Iran, which wanted to nationalize the oil industry.

In the twenty-first century, the strongest candidate for a narrow economic motivation for militarism is the desire to control crucial global resources, especially oil. The large oil companies are powerful corporations with great access to the heights of political power and, in some situations, considerable influence on public policy. The United States is highly dependent on foreign oil, and some people believe the only way to guarantee those supplies is for the United States to directly dominate the sources. This issue is likely to become ever more pressing in the next three or four decades, as oil supplies begin to be depleted and the demand for oil from rapidly industrializing countries like China increases. There are alternatives, of course, in the form of massive efforts to develop alternative energy supplies and conservation. However, such efforts would require more direct economic intervention by the state, and in any case they will take a long time to achieve. Meanwhile, it is essential to protect our sources of oil, the argument goes, and military force is one possible strategy for doing so.

The Defense of Global Capitalism

Large American-based corporations and wealthy individuals make investments all over the world. To do so, they need a global economic environment in which they have relatively open access to world markets and their investments are protected from confiscation by governments. One motivation for a large and effective military is that force can play a role in securing these conditions. In earlier periods of capitalist development, this was one of the central motivations for colonialism: colonial empires, forged through military conquest, provided access to markets and products for capitalists based in the home countries of colonial powers.

Colonialism more or less ended in the decades following World War II, but the need for a secure global environment for capitalist investment remained, and military power continued to play a role in creating and protecting that environment. In particular, American military power had an active part in opposing certain kinds of nationalist movements and revolutionary socialist movements in poor countries that posed a potential threat to global capitalism in general and American corporate interests in particular. The fact of the Chinese Revolution in 1949 and the earlier Russian Revolution raised the specter of more and more parts of the developing world seceding from world capitalism. One task of the American military, therefore, was to make this secession less likely by raising the costs of anticapitalist struggles and to decrease the likelihood that when revolutions did occur, they would be shining examples of alternatives. This kind of reasoning is often used to explain things like the war in Vietnam. The United States did not really have significant direct economic interests in Vietnam. Our concern was more that if an anticapitalist revolution succeeded there, and if it was successful in improving the lives of the people, then in the long term this would reduce the scope for global capitalism, and that in turn would harm American economic interests.

These first two motivations for militarism are often referred to as *empire* or *imperialism*: the use of military force to back the global economic interests and expansion of American capitalism.

National Security

National security is certainly one of the motivations for militarism. During the Cold War, many people believed that Communism in general and the Soviet Union in particular (and maybe China as well) did pose a real military threat to the United States. Even if the threat was not imminent—few careful analysts really feared a direct attack by the USSR—the fear was that over a long period of time, this military threat could grow. Some people believed that we needed to counter it with a fairly aggressive policy of military containment, which meant above all military intervention to prevent "the spread of Communism." During the Vietnam War, defenders of the war argued that it was better to fight the Communists in Southeast Asia than on the beaches of California. Even if most people thought this was overheated rhetoric, nevertheless it reflected a belief that Communist insurgencies in poor countries, backed by the Soviet Union and China to varying degrees, posed some kind of long-term threat to U.S. security. To counter this threat, it was sometimes necessary to support dictators and even overthrow democracies, but these actions were defended on the grounds of protecting the United States from future Communist aggression.

When the Cold War ended this threat disappeared, and with it an important prop to militarism. New threats, however, were soon found and crystallized in the War on Terror directed against Islamic fundamentalists. The attack on the World Trade Center became the anchor for the view that the United States was seriously threatened by a global network of malevolent, ruthless fanatics. Nightmare scenarios of biological weapons being released in large American cities, or small nuclear bombs carried in suitcases and being exploded, were taken seriously in the mass media and used to justify a renewed emphasis on the importance of military power for national security.

Distinct Interests of the Military-Industrial Complex

Militarism is, in significant ways, a self-perpetuating system. Once it is in place, large numbers of people with considerable economic power develop a strong stake in militarism itself. Cuts in military programs hurt powerful corporations. But they also hurt workers and communities, and these broader economic ramifications for ordinary people are very important: our national economy has become deeply dependent on this particular form of public spending. The result is that military contractors form a coalition with regional politicians and workers whose jobs are threatened by reductions in military spending and fight for military budgets. To justify such budgets, you need threats. Because the world is filled with so much uncertainty, threats are usually easy to find if it is in one's interest to do so.

It might be possible, of course, to replace all cuts in military spending with equivalent increases in job-creating civilian spending, so in principle many of the economic interests currently supported by militarism could be accommodated by alternatives. For a fraction of what it spends on the military, the federal government could, for example, build a national high-speed rail system to help with energy independence. It is easy to show that such spending would improve the quality of life and even improve American productivity far more than does military spending. Corporations currently receiving military contracts could receive high-speed rail contracts, and many of the workers in the defense sector could get jobs in the newly expanded civilian infrastructure sector.

This is what could happen in principle. In practice, demilitarization presents two large problems. First, there will inevitably be mismatches between the firms and individuals who lose out from a significant reduction in military spending and those who will gain from alternatives. Because it is generally clearer in advance who will lose than who will gain, political mobilization against demilitarization is likely to be stronger than mobilization for the alternative. Second, massive infrastructure projects, like a national high-speed rail system, pose a serious problem for political conservatives by affirming the legitimacy of the state's role in shaping the economic environment.

The beauty of military spending is that it is the one form of large-scale economic intervention by the state that can be defended by people opposed to government in general. A clear line exists between military spending and the wide range of other public goods we might care about: health care, transportation, energy, the environment. There is a kind of Pandora's box problem with large-scale civilian projects: once it becomes politically legitimate to do one sort of project, say high-speed rail, it is harder to object to other worthy civilian projects. Military spending does not have this problem. The result is that the alliance between economic interests connected to the military-industrial complex and the conservative political forces generally opposes civilian projects that would have an equivalent economic impact to military spending.

Ideological Crusades

Chalmers Johnson, a leading political scientist who studies international relations, argues that crusading has been part of the American global project for over a hundred years. The precise character of the crusade changes from time to time—spreading democracy, defending freedom, fighting

Communism—but at its core is the belief that the United States has a divine mission to spread its values and way of life around the world, not just because this is in its narrow national interests but also because it is the right thing to do—or, to use even stronger language, because America is doing God's work by extending American institutions globally. The Bush administration staked out this position starkly in a national security strategy document, saying that there is "a single sustainable model for national success . . . that is right and true for every person in every society. . . . The United States must defend liberty and justice because these principles are right and true for all people everywhere."[8] Of course, in the real world the ideas of liberty and justice are sharply contested, and what the United States means by these ideas is very different from what many others mean by them. Nevertheless, they serve as a moral justification for our actions.

It is easy to dismiss these kinds of moralistic claims as mere rationalizations, symbolic covers for actions whose driving motivations lie elsewhere. Particularly given the historical record of the United States in supporting dictators and overthrowing democracies when these are seen as serving important national interests, high-minded claims about fostering American ideals around the world do seem like cynical manipulations. Still, these ideals would not serve as a cover for other motives if they did not resonate strongly with many people. Even if they are not the primary motivations of elites in supporting militarism, the self-righteousness of moral crusades may increase the self-confidence of elites in pursuing militaristic goals and may help rally broader support.

Fueling a Politics of Fear

Militarism is one of the central foundations for what can be called the *politics of fear*. Political action is not only rooted in ideas; it is also connected to emotions. Love, fear, hate, anger, hope—all of these can serve as potential emotional underpinnings for politics. A politics of fear revolves around defending oneself from enemies, protecting oneself from danger and threats. It has a kind of primal potency; when fear rules, other things one might care about tend to be displaced. For this reason, throughout history political leaders have used the presence of a foreign threat (and sometimes domestic threat as well) as a way of building support and repressing dissent. This strategy is particularly effective when fear is successfully joined with anger and hate.

[8] Johnson, *The Sorrows of Empire*, p. 287.

Militarism fosters these emotions: it cultivates foreign threats; it identifies enemies who become objects of hate; and it fuels anger from the harms endured in conflicts. Dissenters who object to the priorities fostered by militarism are then deemed unpatriotic, perhaps even traitors. One of the motivations for militarism is fostering this kind of political culture.

CONSEQUENCES OF MILITARISM AND EMPIRE

Militarism is both a fact of life and a way of life in the United States at the beginning of the twenty-first century. Although Barack Obama was elected partially because of his early opposition to the Iraq War, he has continually reassured the American public that he fully supports a strong military and has demonstrated his willingness to use military force to advance foreign policy objectives. While he did end the decade-long wars in Afghanistan and Iraq, the U.S. military intervention in Libya and the widespread use of drone attacks in Pakistan, Yemen, and elsewhere indicate that the Obama administration did not depart in any fundamental way from this institutional configuration.

What can we expect for the future? Chalmers Johnson argues that if the kind of intensive militarism that has become part of the fabric of American society continues, four consequences are likely to follow: perpetual war, reduced democracy at home, degradation of information, and bankruptcy.

Perpetual War

Militarism generates war; it is not simply a response to war. The triumph of American militarism is likely to place the United States in a situation of nearly continuous warfare. With a massive and flexible military force in hand, the United States is much more likely to use the military option in the context of a conflict than if we had a purely defensive military posture. An aggressive, interventionist posture around the world provokes reactions in response to our interventions. This reaction is sometimes called *blowback*: terrorism is in part a response to militarism. This terrorism then provides justifications for further intervention and militarism.

Reduction in Democracy at Home

Militarism and imperialism erode democracy in many ways. Militarism brings with it an increasing concentration of power in the presidency, creating what has come to be called the imperial presidency. The imperial president can act with minimal accountability to Congress or the courts in the name of national security, elevating the powers of the president as the commander in chief of the armed forces to the status of broadly autonomous power over anything connected to foreign affairs. This concentration of power in the presidency has characterized both Democratic and Republican presidents in the era of militarism but was greatly intensified during the Bush administration, when a wide range of constitutional safeguards were violated on the grounds of autonomous presidential power. The Obama administration continued along this path through its widespread spying on American citizens, always in the name of national security.

Militarism also preempts other forms of state spending, and this in turn curtails the scope of democratic deliberation about the public good. As we argued in Chapter 17, a society is democratic to the extent that decisions on matters of collective importance are subjected to collective deliberation and democratic choice. Militarism threatens this principle in two ways: decisions over the use of the military are likely to be made in relatively undemocratic ways by elites operating behind closed doors, and militarism squeezes out other priorities.

More broadly, militarism undermines democratic political culture. Military priorities are bolstered by intensified fear, and people are more willing to give up civil liberties and democratic rights when they are afraid. In debates over domestic priorities, people can see their opponents as legitimate. Some people want a public health-care system, others want to maintain a private system; both are legitimate views within a political spectrum of debate. In a militarized context of debates over war and security, opponents to militarism are treated as unpatriotic on the grounds that they are putting the security of the nation at risk. The polarized good-versus-evil view of the world that is linked to militarism and the politics of fear corrodes the civility and mutual respect needed for democratic deliberation.

Degradation of Information

Militarism brings with it deception and misinformation. Deception becomes official policy. Of course, politics always involves misinformation; politicians distort information to their own political advantage all the time. The problem is much worse in the case of militarism because information is surrounded by strong mechanisms of official secrecy. Political leaders can distort the facts to fit their purposes and claim that what they are saying is based on classified information unavailable to the general public. The use of secrecy classifications makes it much harder for such lies to be revealed. The war on Iraq was a stunning example of this: lies and deception were a routine policy both in the run-up to the war and in the subsequent conduct of the war.

Bankruptcy

Historically, empires typically crumble because the overhead costs of running an empire become unsustainable. The central component of such costs is the military. The attempt by the United States to be the world's only global superpower is extraordinarily costly, both directly and indirectly: directly through the costs of maintaining a large military presence around the world and accounting for 40–50 percent of the global military spending; indirectly by neglecting investments in infrastructure and civilian technologies that would enhance productivity and strengthen the economy. The result has been both a massive government debt held partially by foreign governments and a massive trade deficit. These trends were greatly exacerbated by the financial crisis that began in 2008. It is only the global power of the United States that prevents this debt load from crashing down as it did in Russia in 1997 or Argentina in 2002. This situation cannot go on forever.

22

LABOR UNIONS

When people think about democracy in the United States, mostly they think about elections and about civil liberties enforced by the rule of law. We say a country is democratic when it has free and fair elections and when the basic liberties that make such elections possible exist—freedom of speech, freedom of association, and so on.

In this chapter and the next, we examine another face of democracy: the way democracy is rooted in the collective action of citizens outside the formal institutions of democratic government. We begin by exploring a central problem for a healthy democracy: how to create citizens who feel a sufficient sense of civic obligation and collective purpose to want to engage actively in political life. We then examine labor unions as a specific form of collective association that builds solidarities conducive to democratic participation.

THE PROBLEM

All democratic societies face a fundamental problem: So long as citizens live their lives as separate, discrete individuals, going their separate ways, acting exclusively as self-contained, self-interested individual persons, then the idea of democracy as "rule by the people" will be at best only a thin reality. People may vote in elections—although even for that, many people will ask themselves, "Why bother since my vote isn't going to make a difference?"—but beyond that, they will do little to create a "will of the people," let alone to help actually translate that will into real power. This is a problem in any society, but it is especially intense in a country like the United States with its very high levels of geographical mobility, highly competitive labor markets, anonymous suburbs, and a culture that emphasizes individualism. All these forces contribute to what some sociologists call an *atomized society*: a society made up of separate, isolated individuals rather than organic, integrated communities. As we have seen in our discussions of the free-rider problem, so long as people experience their lives in this way, they are very unlikely to join together to cooperate in collective efforts. Overcoming this problem requires building up a sense of meaningful solidarity among people: a sense that people have obligations to one another and that they are therefore willing to make sacrifices for collective goals. A vibrant democracy requires this kind of connectedness among citizens.

The question then becomes how to create this sense of solidarity and mutual obligation. How can this stronger sense of solidarity be generated in the face of a competitive, individualistic, market society? One crucial dimension of a solution lies in strengthening ways in which participating in collective associations can be deeply integrated into everyday life. What is needed is some kind of organic relationship between our lives as separate individuals and our lives as members of community of common interest.

Sociological discussions of these issues often talk about the importance of civil society. You can think of the problem this way: what we call a society can be broken down into a number of different overlapping spheres of social processes.[1] Think of these as different social settings in which people interact and cooperate for various purposes. Three such spheres are especially important:

1. *The economy* is the sphere in which we produce and buy things.
2. *The state* is the sphere in which we govern our collective affairs.
3. *Civil society* is the sphere in which we get together voluntarily in organizations to pursue common purposes.

These spheres are interconnected, and they affect one another. Here we are particularly concerned about the link between the state and civil society. A vibrant democracy depends in important ways on a vibrant civil society in which it is easy for people to form collective associations to pursue collective purposes.

Churches are, for many people, an important form of such voluntary association. It should be no surprise that at various times in history, churches

---

[1]Sociologists like to use words like *spheres* or *domains* to describe different aspects of society. Such spatial metaphors are always a bit misleading because these different aspects of social life intersect and overlap in all sorts of ways.

become important sources of collective association for political participation, whether they are Quaker churches involved in the abolitionist movement in the nineteenth century or peace movements in the twenty-first century, African American churches involved in the civil rights movement of the 1950s and 1960s, or evangelical Christian churches actively involved in conservative political movements around certain kinds of moral questions in the present. At some times in U.S. history, veterans' associations have been a crucial form of collective organization in civil society that has energized democracy. Unions are another important example of this kind of bottom-up, voluntary organization. And this is why unions matter for democracy and not simply for economic conditions of their members.

In this chapter, we begin by discussing briefly what unions are and how to think about them. That discussion is followed by a brief history of unions in America and the current state of affairs. The chapter concludes with an analysis of the political ramifications for democracy of the decline of unions. In the next chapter, we will examine other sorts of community and grassroots organizations that can contribute to democracy from below.

WHAT ARE LABOR UNIONS?

Many people think of labor unions as a kind of special interest group—workers looking out for their own narrow economic interests. Unions are portrayed as powerful organizations, often corrupt, that at best benefit their members at the expense of nonmembers and the society at large, and at worst really serve only the interests of union bosses. Most people interpret the dramatic decline of unions as indicating that American workers no longer want unions. Americans are individualistic; they believe in individual competition and think the best way to get ahead is on your own. If unions are no longer all that important, it is because workers have abandoned unions.

Many professional economists share this basic view. The free market works best, they argue, when there is no interference with purely voluntary exchanges. Unions get in the way of individual workers voluntarily making bargains with individual employers. Unions create rigidities in the market, in wage rates, in free choice, and in hiring decisions by employers—and all this inflexibility reduces efficiency and economic performance. In the end, the story goes, everyone is worse off because unions muck up the smooth functioning of the system.

We offer an alternative view of labor unions that stresses two main points. The first concerns the effect of unions on the distribution of economic power in a capitalist system; the second concerns the nature of political power and its relation to collective association in a democracy.

Economic Power

Workers as individuals are at an inherent disadvantage in bargaining with employers because they have fewer options than their employers. Power in a market depends on how many options each party has and how badly harmed each party is if they fail to make a deal. In most circumstances, an employer has many potential employees who can be hired for most jobs. Usually it hurts an employee more to be fired than it hurts an employer for an individual employee to quit, and this means that employers have more power than workers.

This imbalance of power in the labor market can be rectified in various ways. One main way is for the government to impose regulations on labor contracts that in one way or another reduce the ability of employers to dictate the terms of an agreement. All developed capitalist countries have such rules. Examples include minimum-wage rules, health and safety rules, and rules governing overtime and working hours. The assumption behind all such rules is that if left to their own devices, employers would offer jobs with unsafe working conditions that pay below the minimum wage and demand excessive working hours—and because of their vulnerability, some workers would be willing to accept such jobs. The rules are therefore designed to block employers from using their power advantage in labor markets to employ workers under the excluded conditions.

Unions are the second main way of rectifying the imbalance of power by creating some semblance of equality in bargaining over the employment contract. Where unions are strong, employers must come to a collective agreement with workers by bargaining with the union; otherwise, the employer will not have access to a labor force. This means that workers have a capacity to punish employers for failing to agree to a satisfactory contract by collectively refusing to work. This action is called a strike. Although an individual worker refusing to work generally does little harm to an employer, a collective refusal matters. The threat of that collective refusal, then, constitutes a new background condition for labor market bargaining. The results are contractual terms that are more favorable to workers.

This narrow economic benefit of unions for workers is called the wage premium for unionized workers. For example, the average annual earnings for a full-time, year-round unionized cashier was $23,173 in 2012—33 percent more than that for nonunionized cashiers. For janitors, unionization increased annual earnings 42 percent.[2] In 2012, even in this period of greatly diminished union power, unions continue to make a difference in the earnings of workers, especially low-wage workers.

Political Power

Most discussions of unions focus only on the issue of economic power and the impact of unions on the labor market. This is undoubtedly the main motivation for most people in joining a union, but it is by no means the only important role that unions play in society. In particular, unions have the potential to help forge more democratically engaged citizens. Isolated, atomized, individual citizens are likely to be a passive, apathetic political force. The problem of rational ignorance, as discussed in Chapter 17, makes people easy to manipulate and discourages participation. In the absence of strong solidarities, a sense of civic obligation is unlikely to flourish. The labor movement is one of the important forces that help individuals feel connected to one another in ways that make political activity seem relevant.

Labor unions foster democratic participation in two ways. First, unions contribute to what can be called *organic solidarities*. Unions are organizations that are embedded in one important setting in many people's lives—their workplaces. In countries with a vibrant labor movement, unions in the workplace organize all sorts of activities and help ordinary workers get involved in many collective decisions within work. Many European countries have workplace councils in which workers, through their unions, are involved in implementing health and safety regulations, monitoring working conditions, conducting grievance procedures, and participating in many other ways. When conflicts occur with management, individual workers are more likely to experience these as collective struggles rather than simply individual complaints. Through these activities, the interdependencies that exist within work can become solidarities, and these solidarities can facilitate greater involvement in broader democratic politics.

---

[2] These average annual earnings are calculated from average weekly earnings, assuming 52 weeks of work a year. The figures come from calculations based on the CPS ORG data set provided by the Economic Policy Institute.

A strong union movement does more than give people the kind of life experiences that affect their identities and build a sense of connectedness and solidarity. It also solves crucial organizational problems. Unions provide their members with information that helps mitigate the problem of rational ignorance about political issues, and they significantly lower the individual costs of active participation. Unions often become, as organizations, directly involved in political parties. In electoral campaigns this involvement helps parties solve the crucial problem of mobilizing people for electoral campaigning, both as voters and as volunteer campaign workers. A strong union movement can help provide the volunteer legwork for practical electoral activities, and in this way it counteracts the influence of money in campaigns. This is an important reason, where unions are strong, for higher voter participation rates and for public policies that tend to serve the wider interests of ordinary citizens rather than just elites.

Unions are certainly not the only kind of voluntary association that can play this role of building solidarities and facilitating democratic political participation. They do, however, have two big advantages over many other potential associations. First, they are closely tied to workplaces in which workers already have some solidarity through their interdependencies within work. Workplaces are themselves a cooperative community of interacting persons, and this structure provides a social basis for building deeper solidarities through conscious organization. Second, unions have the potential to be a mass movement—called the *labor movement*—because in contemporary capitalism, the vast majority of adults work for a living as employees, and most of these employees have no managerial authority within work. The labor movement has the potential to build broad and inclusive solidarities.

A SKETCH OF THE HISTORY AND FATE OF THE U.S. LABOR MOVEMENT

If unions are such wonderful associations for creating a more equal balance of power in labor markets and facilitating a more engaged citizenry in democratic politics, then why are they so weak in the United States? Figure 22.1 charts the trajectory of union membership from 1890 to 2013. Union membership rates in 2013 constituted 12.5 percent of the nonfarm-employed workforce. Unions are legal, and they seem to be a good thing, so why are there so few union members?

FIGURE 22.1—Union coverage in the United States, 1890–2013

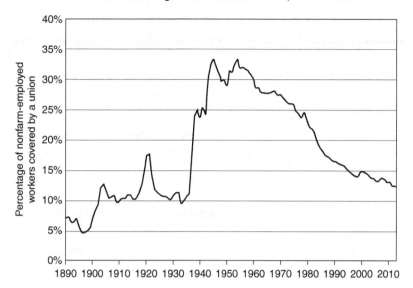

Source: 1890–1999 data: Joshua L. Rosenbloom, "Labor Unions," in *Historical Statistics of the United States, Earliest Times to the Present: Millennial Edition Online*, eds. Susan B. Carter, Scott Sigmund Gartner, Michael R. Haines, Alan L. Olmstead, Richard Sutch, and Gavin Wright (New York: Cambridge University Press, 2006); 2000–2013 data: Barry T. Hirsch and David A Macpherson, *I. U.S. Historical Tables*: "Union Membership, Coverage, Density and Employment, 1973–2013," http://www.unionstats.com/ (accessed April 30, 2014).

To understand this issue, we need to briefly sketch the history of the union movement in the United States and explain the conditions that make it relatively easy or difficult to actually form unions. Throughout the nineteenth century, the state and the courts were extremely antagonistic to unions. Unions were seen as a form of trade restraint that violated the core principles of laissez-faire capitalism. Basically, this situation reflected a conflict between two values: *freedom of association*, which would give people the right to form unions, and *freedom of voluntary exchange on markets*, which would prevent all forms of organized coercion in market contracting and thus would oppose unions. Until the reforms of the 1930s, the courts sided consistently with the second of these principles. A union going on strike was regarded as an organized conspiracy to coerce the legitimate owners of businesses to agree to contracts. The result was that strikes were often repressed violently by the police and the National Guard, sometimes resulting in loss of life.

This kind of legal environment made it difficult to form unions. The basic problem is the extreme vulnerability of organizers to repression and of union members to dismissal until a union becomes reasonably powerful;

but it is difficult to become powerful if a union cannot grow incrementally. For a union to be strong, it needs a high proportion of workers in a firm to be members; there is strength in numbers. But of necessity, all unions begin as weak organizations. When a union is weak, individuals are extremely vulnerable to reprisal from employers for joining a union. This makes it very hard for a union to grow slowly and incrementally *unless there are legal protections enforced by the state.*

A central problem in any labor movement is therefore creating a favorable legal framework for union organizing. Four legal protections are especially important:

1. Employees need protection against being fired or disciplined for joining a union.
2. Employees need protections against being fired while on strike.
3. There need to be fair rules for union recognition.
4. There need to be effective prohibitions against employers engaging in unfair tactics against a union.

And, of course, all these rules need to be effectively enforced and violations rapidly dealt with. Before the New Deal, none of these protections existed. Employers had nearly a free hand to do whatever they liked to block union drives.

The entire situation changed in the 1930s with the passage of New Deal labor law reforms. The key legislation was the National Labor Relations Act, commonly referred to as the Wagner Act, passed in 1935. The central elements of the act included the establishment of clear rights of workers to form unions, protections for organizing activities, and machinery for preventing employers from engaging in unfair practices and bad-faith bargaining. The act established the National Labor Relations Board (NLRB) to enforce these protections and investigate abuses.

The act signaled a major change in the attitude of the federal government about the legitimacy of collective organization by workers. Senator Wagner, the sponsor of the legislation, expressed this change in this way:

> There can no more be democratic self-government in industry without workers participating therein than there could be democratic government in politics without workers having the right to vote. . . . The right to bargain collectively is at the bottom of social justice for the worker, as well as

the sensible conduct of business affairs. The denial or observance of this right means the difference between despotism and democracy.[3]

Under the terms of the Wagner Act, the first step in forming a union is for organizers to get employees to sign cards saying that they want a union. When a majority of employees have signed these organizing cards, then the employer can either agree to the union or insist that a vote be taken to certify the union as a collective bargaining unit. After a union has been certified, employers have to meet with union representatives and engage in a process called *good-faith bargaining*. This bargaining ideally culminates in a contract—an agreement between the union and the employers. The contract is then voted on by union members. If no contract is agreed upon, then the union can go on strike to put pressure on the employer. During the strike, an employer can hire replacements—which unions call *scabs*—to work instead of the striking workers. Often employers hire immigrants for this and even recruit workers from poorer regions. Employers are not allowed to fire workers while on strike, but they also are not prevented from supplanting them with permanent replacements. A condition of settlement for successful strikes is always getting rid of the replacement workers.

With these rules in place and more or less effectively enforced, many successful organizing drives were launched from the mid-1930s to the early 1950s. The result was a rapid and dramatic expansion of unions.

This favorable legal framework for union organizing lasted only twelve years. In 1947, in the aftermath of the massive strike wave involving over 5 million workers and in the context of the growing anti-Communist hysteria of the emerging Cold War, the Wagner Act was drastically amended by legislation known as the Taft-Hartley Act. In the original Wagner Act, only potential abuses by employers were included in the list of unfair labor practices. The new act added a long list of prohibited actions by unions; these included wildcat strikes, solidarity or political strikes, and secondary boycotts, among other things.[4] The law also allowed states to pass what are called *right-to-work laws*. These laws prohibit unions from forcing all

---

[3] John W. Budd, *Employment with a Human Face: Balancing Efficiency, Equity, and Voice* (Ithaca, NY: Cornell University Press, 2004), p. 103.

[4] A secondary boycott is an organized attempt by a union to influence the actions of a business with which it has a dispute by putting pressure on a different business not directly involved in the dispute. An example would be a truck driver union refusing to deliver goods produced by a firm where workers are on strike to a store that is not on strike.

workers to join the union in a company that is unionized. This provision, in effect, allows individual workers to be free riders on the union dues paid by union members: the nonunion members get the benefits of a union without having to pay any of the costs. All the states in the Deep South rapidly passed such right-to-work laws, along with most other traditionally Republican states in the Midwest and Mountain regions.

These changes in the legal framework of unions significantly undermined efforts to expand union membership in existing unions and to form new unions. Equally important, there was a gradual erosion of the willingness of the NLRB to intervene energetically on the side of workers in labor disputes, particularly beginning in the 1980s with the ascendency of free market neoliberalism as the dominant political ideology. The response of unions to these changes was mostly defensive: adopting strategies to protect the union members in established unions rather than engage in aggressive drives to create new unions and expand membership. In many instances, in fact, it seemed to many observers that union strategies were mainly concerned with protecting the interests of union leaders rather than the rank and file, although such accusations were often simply expressions of anti-union sentiment.

Unionization in the private sector reached its peak in 1953 and has declined ever since. This decline was, at first, largely a direct reflection of strategic decisions of unions themselves. At the end of World War II, unions had a defined core of strength in a limited number of sectors: regulated industries (transportation, communication, and utilities), mining, commercial construction, and manufacturing. In ways the unions would later come to sorely regret, their membership was also heavily clustered in limited parts of the country: New England, the Upper Midwest and Great Lakes, and the West Coast, from Seattle to Los Angeles. The unions did not put much effort into organizing outside this core except in the public sector, in which a small explosion in new organizing occurred in the 1960s among civil servants working directly in government and among public sector teachers. What unions failed to do was attempt to expand membership into the rapidly growing private service sector or the growing South and other largely union-free areas. Still, even as the rest of the economy grew around them, and thus the share of the economy in which unions were prominent dropped, unions managed to maintain high densities within this core well into the late 1960s.

By the early 1970s, however, the uneasy truce between unions and employers, always confined to this core, was already breaking down. New competitive pressures from abroad highlighted union costs to employers. New technologies in mining, longshore work, and meatpacking were eroding union power. And a drumbeat of academic studies, often sponsored by business, was pointing out the excessive costs of regulation. Business was also changing its organization, becoming qualitatively more sophisticated and coordinated in attacking union power. The formation of the Business Roundtable and a revived U.S. Chamber of Commerce, among other developments, presaged what was to become a tough decade for unions. Those parts of the union core that were active in international trade especially felt the bite of new competitors. Major deregulatory initiatives succeeded in the industries of trucking and airline transportation and communications. And then, in the 1980s—with the election of Ronald Reagan—the government launched a major attack directly on unions, beginning with Reagan's decision to fire all unionized air traffic controllers in 1981 during a strike early in his administration. The result was a precipitous decline of unions even within its traditional core.

Since the early 1990s, there has been renewed effort in revitalizing the labor movement. There have been some successes in organizing previously unorganized sectors, most notably among some categories of service workers. There have also been initiatives to reinvigorate internal democracy within unions, although in general with uneven success. None of these efforts, however, has been robust enough to reverse the overall decline in union membership.

These efforts at reviving unions have occurred in a context in which labor law remains hostile to union organizing. Employers frequently go just up to the limits of the law—and often beyond—to intimidate workers, knowing that they face no meaningful penalties for violating even these weak laws. Over the years, employers have developed a sophisticated arsenal of strategies to combat unionization. Here is a partial list:

- Employers organize mandatory captive audience meetings that all workers must attend. They also often require repeated one-on-one meetings of supervisors with workers at which anti-union propaganda is presented.
- When a union drive occurs, employers regularly hire professional anti-union consultants to fight the union. These consultants train managers and supervisors in the best ways of discrediting unions.
- Employers make widespread threats to move businesses abroad if a union is certified. If there are immigrant workers in the firm, it is also

common to intimidate workers by threatening to notify the Immigration and Naturalization Service.

- Illegal firing and discrimination against workers who sign union cards are commonplace. In firms in which the employer engages in illegal forms of intimidation, it is very hard and expensive for workers to take employers to court and have the laws properly enforced. The process is cumbersome and time consuming, the fines are not serious, and the long delays in getting a decision effectively give power to employers to use illegal tactics. Many professional anti-union consultants, in fact, encourage employers to act illegally. This is why the issue of the efficient enforcement of labor laws and not simply the existence of laws on the books is so important. Nonenforcement is a deliberate strategy of the government, through understaffing and directives, not to pursue cases aggressively.

- Even after union victories, the consultants encourage continual, aggressive anti-union activity, delays, and the like to block contracts. Again, the passivity of the NLRB in enforcing the good-faith bargaining provisions of labor law is crucial here. Less than half the unions that win certification manage to negotiate a contract.

In the face of these strategies, by the beginning of the twenty-first century there was only one substantial sector in which unions remained fairly strong in the United States—the public sector. As indicated in Figure 22.2, in the period 1977–2013, within the private sector, union membership rates declined steadily from 21.7 percent of employees to only 6.7 percent, whereas public sector unionization remained fairly constant, fluctuating between 35 percent and 38 percent. In 2013, in fifteen states, over half of all public sector workers were unionized. The highest level was in New York, where just under 70 percent of public sector employees were members of a union.[5]

For many years conservatives had complained about the strength of unions in the public sector, but it was not until the political upheavals following the financial crisis of 2008 that aggressive attempts at attacking

---

[5] The lowest rate of public sector unionization in the United States in 2013 was in Mississippi, where only 4.9 percent of employees were unionized, followed by Wyoming and North Carolina at 9.7 percent. Generally the public sector unionization rates are above 40 percent in the Northeast, West Coast, and upper Midwest, and lowest in the South. Data are from Barry T. Hirsch and David A. Macpherson, "Union Membership and Coverage Database from the CPS," available at http://www.unionstats.com.

FIGURE 22.2—Public and private sector union density, 1977–2013

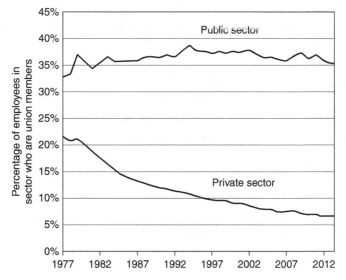

Source: Barry T. Hirsch and David A. Macpherson, "Union Membership and Coverage Database from the CPS," http://www.unionstats.com/ (accessed April 30, 2014). 1973–1981 data: the May Current Population Survey (CPS). 1983–2013 data: the CPS Outgoing Rotation Group (ORG) Earnings Files. There were no union questions in the 1982 CPS, so the figures for that year are interpolated. Sample includes wage and salary workers ages 16 and over.

public sector unions in places where they had been traditionally strong began to be successful. Perhaps the most well known of these attacks occurred in Wisconsin in 2011. In the 2010 statewide elections, the Republican Party gained control of both houses of the Wisconsin state legislature and the governor's office. Immediately after taking office, the new governor, Scott Walker, submitted a bill to the state legislature designed to severely undermine the viability of public sector unions in the state. Under the provisions of the bill, unions would be prohibited from bargaining over anything except pay increases up to the level of inflation—that is, they could never bargain for a real raise. Union dues also could no longer be gathered through automatic deductions from paychecks, and unions would be required to hold recertification elections every year in which a majority of relevant employees (not just of those voting) would have to vote for the union. This bill triggered massive, prolonged protests, including an occupation of the state capitol building by protesters for over two weeks and daily rallies and marches around the building sometimes involving over 100,000 people. Fourteen state senators left the state in order to prevent a quorum of senators needed for a vote on the bill. Eventually the bill passed. The result was a dramatic decline of public sector unionization in Wisconsin—from 53.5 percent in 2010 to 35.5 percent in 2013.

The only people clearly served by the collapse of unions are employers set against giving workers any real voice and power. Certainly the society is ill served by a deliberately adversarial system of labor relations. And certainly this does not come close to meeting the desire of workers for greater voice and say in the workplace. Richard Freeman and Joel Rogers, who conducted a systematic national survey of the workforce, explored a wide range of themes around attitudes toward work and workplace representation. They found that about a third of nonunion workers said they would vote for a union if given the opportunity, and virtually all existing union members said they would vote to retain their union in an election for union representation. Taking these two numbers together suggests that *in the absence of intimidation and other anti-union tactics*, the rate of unionization in the private sector in the United States would be around 44 percent.[6]

POLITICAL CONSEQUENCES
OF THE DECLINE OF UNIONS

Many commentators have examined the economic consequences of the decline of unions. For example, the decline of unions is often cited as one of the important trends that contributed to rising income inequality since the 1970s. Strong unions also tend to create broad sectoral norms on wage rates that reduce variation among nonmanagerial employees. Less attention has been given to the political effects of the decline of unions and the implications for American democracy.

Two things seem especially important: first, the impact of the decline of unions on the character of political participation of people in the working class, and second, the impact on the priorities and policies of the Democratic Party.

The decline of unions removes the most important associational basis for a coherent working-class electorate. Unions constitute a systematic associational counterweight to the competitive pressures of the market and the privatized lives within the working class. They provide the micro-context for linking the experiences workers have within their workplace to a form

---

[6] Richard B. Freeman and Joel Rogers, *What Workers Want* (Ithaca, NY: Cornell University Press, 1999; rev. ed., 2006).

of collective organization, and this is a crucial step in the process of becoming connected to political processes on a class basis. The issue here is not only that unions counteract the tendency for people to act in individualistic ways that fuel political apathy, but that unions help foster political identities in class terms. A strong union movement is essential both for increasing the political engagement of workers and for that engagement to have a distinctively working-class character.

It is entirely possible, after all, for workers to become politically engaged in ways quite disconnected to their class situations. Workers can be embedded in associational contexts in which their political identities are formed on the basis of religion or ethnicity or gun ownership or many other issues. Associations are critical to political participation, but class-based associations are only one of many. The decline of unions, then, has seriously eroded the basis for working-class politics.

In such a situation, two things are likely to happen. Many workers simply become disengaged from politics altogether. Politics seem remote and unconnected to their lives, and they feel no strong sense of civic obligation to participate in the rituals of democracy. That is one possibility. Another is that the workers become politically engaged through other kinds of associations. This is one explanation for the rise of working-class Republican voters mobilized around conservative social and moral values in the last decades of the twentieth century. With the decline of unions, the main remaining associations in which workers participated were churches; and because working-class churches tend to be socially conservative, this became the basis for a shift in political identity and loyalty among a segment of the working class. If unions had remained strong, then at least there would have been competing associational contexts for political engagement within the working class.

The decline in unions not only affects the way working-class political identities are formed; it also reduces pressures on the Democratic Party to support working-class interests. Both the Democratic Party and the Republican Party have to seek support from rich individuals and major corporations because of the financial exigencies of electoral campaigns. Unions since the 1930s constituted a counterweight to the role of money in shaping the political agenda of the Democratic Party. As we argued in Chapter 17 when discussing the resource constraint, groups of people can systematically influence politics in a democracy in two main ways—one is based on *willingness to pay*, the other on *willingness to act*. Corporations and wealthy individuals can affect politics in the first way. Unions are one of the main forces for facilitating the second way. The decline of unions means that their influence on Democratic Party agendas relative to the influence of large corporations has also declined.

This shift in the balance of organized forces in the Democratic Party helped push the party away from a political agenda anchored in the model of an affirmative state that was centrally concerned with inequality, poverty, and urban development to a party that shared with the Republicans an aversion to taxation and a commitment to much more relaxed regulation of the market. By the 1990s a Democratic president could announce the end of the era of big government. Reversing these trends by revitalizing the labor movement is a necessary condition for renewing American democracy. For that to happen in a sustainable way, basic changes in the legal environment for union activity are essential.

23

DEMOCRACY FROM BELOW

Citizens in the United States influence the decisions carried out by the state mainly by electing public officials to make those decisions. This is called *representative* democracy. Throughout American history, a second conception of democracy has influenced both the ideal of democracy as "rule by the people" and its practical realization: *direct* or *participatory* democracy, in which citizens are directly engaged in shaping public policy and its implementation. In this chapter, we explore this second face of democratic life. We begin by briefly examining the wide variety of forms that direct democracy takes in the United States. This section is followed by a more theoretical discussion of the problem of making and implementing public policies and the possibility for a new form of direct democracy, which we call *empowered participatory governance*. We then discuss two especially innovative examples of direct democracy in the revitalization of a blighted urban area in the city of Boston and recent experiments in municipal participatory budgeting. The chapter concludes with a discussion of the wider prospects for democracy from below in twenty-first-century America.

FORMS OF DIRECT CITIZEN PARTICIPATION IN DEMOCRACY

Direct citizen participation in democracy takes many different forms. Here are some important examples.

Juries

In a jury, the task of deciding court cases is handed over to ordinary citizens. Such decisions are a direct exercise of critical powers of the state—the power to decide on the guilt or innocence of people accused by the state of crimes and sometimes to decide on their punishments as well, and the power to resolve disputes among parties in civil cases. In many countries, such decisions are made by professionals employed by the state and trained in the law and judicial rules. In the United States, defendants and litigants have the option of choosing to have these decisions made by ordinary fellow citizens. This does not mean that juries invariably make reasonable decisions. Jurors can be heavily biased in various ways and can be manipulated by judges and attorneys. Nevertheless, where the jury system is strong and jurors feel a strong sense of civic obligation to act fairly, they embody the ideal of equality before the law that is central to democracy.

Initiatives and Referenda

Most laws in American democracy are passed in various kinds of legislatures—city councils, county boards, state legislatures, the U.S. Congress—by elected representatives. But in some states citizens have the right, if they can get a sufficient number of signatures on a petition, to have a proposed law put on a ballot, enabling citizens to vote directly for the proposed legislation (called an *initiative*) or to approve or reject a law passed by a legislative body (called a *referendum*). In some states, like California, Oregon, and Washington, hundreds of laws have been passed in this way.

Initiatives and referenda have been championed by people who believe that professional politicians are likely to be beholden to special interests and elites and that ordinary citizens are in a better position to vote for the public interest. Critics argue that direct citizen voting on laws is subject to the same kinds of distortions of money in politics that plague ordinary elections, particularly because initiatives and referenda are often on the ballot in special elections with very low turnout. The problems of rational ignorance that plague voting for candidates can be even more serious in voting for complex legislative measures because the cheap information voters receive through political ads tends to be simplistic. Initiatives and referenda are a form of direct democracy, but they can be easily manipulated by many of the forces that also distort representative democracy.

Open Public Hearings

Particularly in local political contexts, public hearings can be a vibrant way for the public to directly affect public policy. When a city council or a school board holds a public hearing on a controversial matter and hundreds of citizens line up to speak about the issues, it can be more difficult for the elected officials to make their decisions through backroom deals. Of course, public hearings can be packed by well-organized small groups that give the impression of much broader support for one side of an issue than actually exists. Public hearings can also sometimes be just a symbolic sideshow, window dressing to create the appearance of responsiveness. But they can also contribute to genuine public input that affects decisions of politicians who are prepared to listen and take them seriously.

Public Issue Campaigns

In a public issue campaign, citizens mobilize petitions, letter writing, telephone calls, and other means of communication to express their views on some specific issue to public officials. The general idea is that a well-organized campaign of this sort creates a sense of the strength and passion of public opinion on an issue. Elected officials want to be reelected, so they are particularly sensitive to instances of strongly held views because groups with passionate views are more likely to mobilize for or against them in electoral campaigns. This sensitivity to the potential of mobilized constituents also opens public issue campaigns to manipulation by well-financed groups, especially because contemporary communications technologies make it easy to organize millions of e-mails.

Social Protests

Throughout American history, people have engaged in public rallies and demonstrations, and sometimes civil disobedience, in an effort to shape public policy. Public protests potentially do a variety of things: they can bring to the attention of a passive public a moral issue that has not gotten sufficient attention, and thus contribute to changing public opinion; they can raise the specter of disruption and disorder, and thus force elites to take some kind of action; they can reaffirm to the protesters their sense of solidarity and purpose, and provide a context for recruiting new participants; they can demonstrate the seriousness of commitment of a particular constituency and thus, like public issue campaigns more generally, make elected officials concerned about reelection.

Some of the most fundamental political issues in American history have been heavily shaped by mass movements that engaged in a wide range of peaceful and disruptive protests. The abolition movement in the nineteenth century contributed to the rising sense of political crisis that culminated in the Civil War and the eventual end of slavery. The suffragette movement to obtain the vote for women was a key force that ultimately moved men to allow women to vote. The civil rights movement used illegal sit-ins in segregated facilities and mass marches to dramatize to the world the moral failings of racial oppression in the United States. These actions put tremendous pressure on the federal government to intervene in the Southern states and eventually to pass the civil rights legislation of the 1960s.

Protests have helped advance the political agendas of citizens in support of both progressive and conservative values. In the same era that suffragettes marched to achieve the right to vote, the Women's Christian Temperance Union marched to ban alcohol. Protest marches and rallies have played a central role for advocates of reproductive rights and also for opponents of abortion. An important feature of democracy provides that citizens can feel free to publicly demonstrate their views in vigorous ways regardless of their specific political views.

Protests and demonstrations have more than just political effects on the most visible stage of national politics. Many kinds of struggles over local political issues also involve public protests, sometimes with clear effects on policies. City councils are sometimes quite responsive to public demonstrations and picketing over zoning decisions and development projects. Universities introduced black studies programs in response to demands and demonstrations by African American students. Protests in the late 1990s on campuses over the use of sweatshop labor to produce university apparel led some universities to adopt labor codes of conduct in the contracts for such products. Countless other examples could be given.

Social protests can serve to advance the principles of equality and democracy, but they are also tools for highly motivated exclusionary groups to exert pressure on public officials. At times in American history, the Ku Klux Klan used social protests to enforce and extend laws of racial domination. Social protests by NIMBY movements (not in my backyard) have resulted in the placement of undesirable public facilities like toxic waste dumps close to vulnerable, disadvantaged populations who are less able to mount an effective protest. Though, on balance, public protests by social movements have almost certainly enhanced democracy in America, the record is not unequivocal.

Empowered Participatory Governance

Empowered participatory governance is the least familiar form in which direct democracy exists in the United States, and it has yet to be given a widely used label.[1] In empowered participatory governance, certain kinds of government activity that would otherwise be controlled by government bureaucracies or elected officials are delegated to decentralized bodies in which citizens directly participate in making the decisions.

The oldest form of this kind of governance in the United States is the New England town meeting. In the traditional New England town meeting, important local policy matters are decided not by an elected town council but by citizens in a meeting where they vote directly on things like local taxes, town spending, and town ordinances. As communities grew larger and more heterogeneous, and as issues of local government became more complex, this kind of direct democracy mostly disappeared. In the last decades of the twentieth century, however, new and innovative forms of empowered participatory governance have emerged. As we will see in the following sections, this kind of governance potentially creates opportunities for a much more deeply engaged process of democratic citizenship in solving pressing and difficult problems.

All these examples constitute forms of democracy from below, in which citizens attempt to directly influence the shape of public policies. Mostly they have the character of either having a very limited scope of action, as in juries, or of primarily being a way of applying periodic external pressure on the real centers of power. Only the last form, empowered participatory governance, constitutes a way of bringing citizens inside the decision-making process of government in a regular and ongoing way.

In the rest of this chapter, we explore these new forms of democracy from below. We begin by explaining how this kind of direct democracy can fit into a modern, complex political system. The key to this possibility lies in understanding the relationship between passing a law and implementing a public policy. This discussion is followed by an exploration of two examples of this new institutional form.

---

[1] The term *empowered participatory governance*, describing these kinds of institutional arrangements, was coined by Archon Fung and Erik Olin Wright in *Deepening Democracy: Institutional Innovations in Empowered Participatory Governance* (London and New York: Verso, 2003).

THE PROBLEM OF TURNING LEGISLATION
INTO FUNCTIONING POLICIES

The normal, simple way that most people think of democratic government is that laws get passed by elected legislatures and are then carried out by administrative organizations that implement the laws that have been passed. However, this simple idea faces an immediate problem: the so-called implementation of a law often involves creating a wide range of concrete rules and programs.

This is an issue even in cases where legislatures pass laws that seem straightforward and uncomplicated. Consider, for example, what happens when a law is passed to set the speed limit at 65 mph on highways. Here the administrative task of implementing the law is fairly straightforward: putting up speed limit signs and instructing police officers to enforce the limit. But even this case still involves issues in implementation that are not specified in the law itself: How strict or lax will the enforcement be? Will motorists be stopped if they are driving at 67 mph? 70 mph? 73 mph? How many police will patrol the highways, and what technologies will they use to measure driving speed? These decisions are made after the law is passed in the legislature and will determine how rigorously and effectively the rule is actually enforced. Anyone who has traveled through many states knows that in some places the speed limit is quite rigorously enforced, and in others you can consistently exceed the speed limit by fifteen miles per hour without worrying, even though the laws on the books are the same.

Many pieces of legislation pose enormously greater problems than speed limits, and the distinction between passing the legislation and implementing the actual policy begins to break down. Think of legislation that provides funding for urban redevelopment, public transportation, or education, or legislation that protects endangered species or regulates pollution. In these instances legislation creates a program with general guidelines and principles, but this is still very far from actual, functioning policies in the world.

The traditional way of solving this problem of implementation is to empower an administrative agency to create the detailed rules and programs and put them concretely into practice. *Bureaucracy* is the term used to describe this sort of approach. The style of implementation that corresponds to bureaucracy is often referred to as *command and control*. The procedure is this: At the top of the bureaucracy are political appointees who are responsible to the elected executive of the government—the president in the case of the federal government; governors in the state; mayors in cities. The political heads of the bureaucracy oversee the process of rule setting and implementation. Often they set up special advisory panels of experts to help with this rule-setting task. In some instances these panels include representatives of powerful interest groups, but sometimes they are just experts of one sort or another. Below this political directorate of the bureaucracy are professional, career civil servants who do most of the practical work. For example, in the case of the Endangered Species Act, these people include scientists responsible for studying the problem and identifying endangered species; field agents who monitor sites; and of course lots of the people we commonly call bureaucrats, who manage the paperwork involved in this whole endeavor.

This kind of system is called command and control because the rules are imposed from above by centralized command, and then the bureaucratic staff controls the practical implementation of these commands. There are lots of variations, of course, but this is the basic idea. This kind of structure is used in most policy areas: pollution control, health and safety regulation, welfare policy, public housing, parks and recreation, community development, and so on.

Suppose that legislation is passed to give cities funds for urban development projects to deal with the problem of deterioration and blight in parts of a city. The money can be used for a wide range of purposes, among them improving urban infrastructure like sewers, lighting, and streets; demolishing dilapidated buildings and providing subsidies of different sorts to build apartments or office buildings; renovating parks, libraries, and other public amenities; and improving public transportation. The question then becomes how the city decides precisely what sorts of things to do. Typically there is a planning office in the city, and often for big projects a special commission will be set up by the planning department to develop the basic contours of a long-term plan. This commission will consist of experts from the planning department, possibly other city officials, sometimes civic leaders of different sorts, and sometimes outside experts. Initial plans will be prepared and public hearings organized. Proposals for particular projects will be reviewed by the commission. Eventually a general plan is devised from this process and then specific projects are begun. The funds are allocated and the projects are monitored (more or less effectively) by city officials.

Democracy enters this bureaucratic process in three ways: First, the bureaucracy is accountable to the elected executive, and thus there is an electoral constraint on the policies implemented by the bureaucrats. Second, in at least some of the rule-setting and planning processes, public input is solicited, and sometimes this activity has a democratic character. And third, the bureaucracy is itself subject to rules and courts, so if you feel that a bureaucracy has implemented a rule that violates the principles of some law, you can sue the bureaucracy in court.

All these democratic constraints on bureaucracy are important; it is surely worse to live in a world where government bureaucracy cannot be challenged in courts, where there is no open public input into implementation decisions, and where the leadership of the bureaucracy is not accountable to elected officials. Still, the democratic constraints often seem quite weak. Many people see government bureaucracy as unresponsive and undemocratic. What is worse, due to the capacity of powerful interests and well-funded lobbyists to influence centralized bureaucracies, the process of policy implementation often gets captured by special interests. This situation further erodes the democratic character of a bureaucracy.

AN ALTERNATIVE:
EMPOWERED PARTICIPATORY GOVERNANCE

Empowered participatory governance is an alternative way of creating concrete implementations of legislation for some kinds of public policies. The basic idea is this: in many public policies, including national policies, the actual implementation of the policy can be significantly decentralized to quite local units in which ordinary citizens can become actively involved in working out the practical details of implementation. The idea here is not simply to remove certain policies from centralized bureaucracies, but to create new participatory mechanisms for citizens to become directly involved in policy formation and policy implementation. This system becomes more feasible when citizens have formed civic action groups to solve in practical ways the problems faced by their communities. The trick is to figure out institutional arrangements in which such civic associations can become actively linked to government administration in ways that genuinely empower them to shape the process of rule implementation and program development.

The United States has a long tradition of civic activism and voluntary association. The nineteenth-century French social commentator Alexis de Tocqueville saw this penchant for Americans to join voluntary associations as a defining characteristic of American society, one of the things that contributed to the vibrancy of our democracy. Such associations contributed to a dense, collectively organized civil society in the nineteenth century and into the twentieth.

Many sociologists believe—we think incorrectly—that participation in voluntary associations has sharply declined over the last fifty years and that this decline has led to a serious weakening of civil society in the United States.[2] Participation in certain traditional forms of association clearly has declined, especially in organizations like fraternal clubs and traditional civic associations. But there has also been a rise in a new kind of association: grassroots associations organized around particular social, environmental, and political issues. Often, these associations mainly protest policies and put pressure on public officials. This is certainly the traditional role that civic associations play in democracy. But in halting and uneven ways, they have also taken on a more energetic role in the actual process of governance.

The best way to understand what empowered participatory governance is all about is to look at particular examples in some detail. We will examine two examples—the Dudley Street Neighborhood Initiative and municipal participatory budgeting—and then discuss the broader implications of this kind of participation for a revitalization of American democracy.

THE DUDLEY STREET NEIGHBORHOOD INITIATIVE

The Dudley Street neighborhood, an area with about 23,000 residents, is located two miles from downtown Boston.[3] Demographically, it is a racially and ethnically diverse community made up primarily of African Americans, Hispanics, and Cape Verdeans. Only about 4 percent of residents are

---

[2] For discussions of the possible decline in civic associations in the United States, see Robert W. Putnam, *Bowling Alone* (New York: Simon and Schuster, 2000), and Theda Skocpol, *Diminished Democracy: From Membership to Management* (Norman, OK: University of Oklahoma Press, 2004).

[3] This account draws heavily from a superb account of the Dudley Street Neighborhood Initiative by Peter Medoff and Holly Sklar, *Streets of Hope: The Fall and Rise of an Urban Neighborhood* (Boston: South End Press, 1994), and from a documentary film, *Holding Ground*. For additional information on this experience, see the Dudley Street Neighborhood Initiative website, http://www.dsni.org.

white.[4] Economically, Dudley Street is one of the poorest neighborhoods in the city of Boston. Its unemployment and poverty rates are roughly twice as high as those for the city of Boston as a whole.

In the early 1980s, the Dudley Street neighborhood was also one of the physically most devastated parts of the city. Due to highly discriminatory urban housing policies in the 1960s and 1970s, chronic neglect by the city, and a persistent problem of arson, by 1985 roughly 21 percent of the parcels of land (1,300 parcels) in the area were vacant. The Boston Arson Prevention Commission argued in 1985 that much of this arson was probably the result of development interests wanting to displace people from the area. The commission wrote:

> Many of the buildings which have burned in this area [in 1985] were among the approximately ⅔ abandoned buildings which area residents would like to see developed by and for local, low-income residents. Other fires have occurred in buildings currently occupied by low-income tenants that appear destined for Condo Conversion. . . . It is obvious that this increase in serious fires in the Sav-Mor area [part of the Dudley Street neighborhood] is directly related to the increased speculation due to the [Boston Redevelopment Authority] Dudley Square Revitalization plan.[5]

The vacant lots became a dumping ground for all kinds of trash and garbage. Private contractors for city garbage collection routinely, but illegally, used some of the lots as trash transfer stations. Residents of Boston also dumped refuse in the area. Streets were littered with abandoned cars.

This was the context in which the Dudley Street Neighborhood Initiative was founded in 1985. A private foundation, the Riley Foundation, had been involved in making grants for projects in poor sections of Boston for some time. In 1984 it helped create the Dudley Advisory Group to formulate a broad development strategy for the area. This group had roughly thirty regular members from various community organizations and agencies connected to the area. The group met regularly to formulate proposals and create a clear agenda that would facilitate funding from the Riley Founda-

---

[4] Data are for the year 2000, reported in the "Dudley Neighborhood Profile," June 2003, prepared for the Urban Village Working Group, DSNI, available at http://www.dsni.org (accessed Sept. 16, 2009).

[5] Quoted in Medoff and Sklar, *Streets of Hope*, p. 68, from the City of Boston Arson Prevention Commission, *Report to the BRA on the Status of Arson in Dudley Square.*

tion and other sources. It formally renamed itself the Dudley Street Neighborhood Initiative (DSNI) in January 1985.

In February 1985, the DSNI organized a large public meeting to present its ideas to the community. The meeting organizers fully expected to be greeted enthusiastically by local residents. After all, they were proposing a broad agenda for improving the neighborhood and infusing significant funds into a variety of constructive community development projects. Instead, they were greeted with considerable skepticism and even hostility. Some of the neighborhood people at the meeting expressed deep resentment at being told what was best for their community by do-gooder outsiders. As one of the participants in the meeting declared, "Who the hell are you people and what do you want? . . . Who is Riley? Why should we trust you?"[6] Many people were especially incensed by the composition of the proposed twenty-three-member governing board of the DSNI, which was dominated by outsiders and had only four positions reserved for community members.

Many residents were extremely cynical about these kinds of lofty plans for neighborhood revitalization. They had heard such things before, but nothing much changed. For the Dudley Street neighborhood in 1985, this general cynicism had been intensified by the recent release of the city of Boston's own development plans for the area. As described by Peter Medoff and Holly Sklar, the Boston Redevelopment Authority's "Dudley Square Plan" was a classic urban development project that would lead to gentrification of housing and a large-scale displacement of existing low-income residents:

> The BRA proposed a "New Town" strategy with a $750 million complex of office towers, hotels, housing, historic parks and light manufacturing in the northern Dudley areas. The plan called for building high-, moderate- and low-income housing—with "home ownership opportunities for families with incomes as low as $20,000." That wasn't very low. Boston's median family income was only $22,000 in 1984. . . . Many saw the "New Town" strategy as the old "urban removal." . . . The BRA admitted that its strategy "could lead to displacement of existing residents, the gentrification of existing single-family neighborhoods, and jobs for 'new' residents at the expense of current residents."[7]

[6] Ibid., 53.

[7] Ibid., 51–52.

Given that the DSNI was dominated by educated white outsiders, it was perfectly reasonable for residents of the Dudley Street area to think that in some way the DSNI was part of this larger scheme.

In a situation like this, it might be reasonable to predict that the organizers of the meeting and the financial backers of the project would abandon their efforts, feeling that they were not wanted by the community. Instead, they acknowledged that they had screwed up by not involving ordinary members of the community from the start. So, instead of retreating, they proposed that the whole process be restarted on a new footing, led by a new governing board on which people directly elected by the community held most of the seats:

> There would be a 31-member board, with a resident majority   a minimum of 12 community members and 4 additional spots designated for residents. The multiracial, multiethnic character of DSNI was reaffirmed. Equal minimum representation was provided for the neighborhood's four major cultures—Black, Cape Verdean, Latino and White—rather than representation based simply numerically on Dudley's population. Equal minimum representation was chosen to strengthen collective action and underscore the common stake of all people in rebuilding Dudley. The Riley Foundation, the dollars behind DSNI at this point, never sought a seat on the board and, in keeping with the spirit of community control, it never occurred to the DSNI members to propose that they do.[8]

This restructuring resulted in the emergence of a community organization that was genuinely controlled by the members of the community and whose projects grew out of intense discussion within the community over their most pressing priorities.

At this point, the DSNI was already an interesting example of an inclusive community association working in a democratic manner to improve the conditions of life for people in a poor area of a large city. But it was not yet an instance of deepening democracy through empowered participatory governance, because it still had no systematic relationship to city government. This situation would change over the next several years.

Ray Flynn was elected mayor of Boston in 1984 after a bitter election campaign against a popular black politician, Mel King. In the aftermath of the election, Flynn was eager to find allies in the black community who could ease some of the racial tensions generated by the election. The DSNI suited this purpose well. Although Flynn probably did see the DSNI as a constructive effort to do something positive in one of the most blighted parts of the city, the level of city support was also clearly motivated by political considerations. The activists involved in the DSNI were not naïve about this situation, and there were concerns about being "used" by the city; but they still saw this as an opportunity to increase the real power of the association and its capacity to accomplish meaningful change.

The pivotal steps that consolidated a new kind of relationship with city government occurred in 1987 and 1988. Two things were especially important. The first was the adoption of a comprehensive strategy of participatory community planning to generate both a long-term vision for the revitalization of the community and an inventory of concrete plans for specific development projects. Participatory planning meant creating a community planning committee and holding a long series of community-wide meetings in which both visions and projects were discussed. The result of this process was the Dudley Street Neighborhood Comprehensive Revitalization Plan, which was subsequently adopted by the city as the official framework for future development of the community.

The second decisive development was a solution to the problem of how to control the 1,300 parcels of vacant land in the Dudley Street area. The disposition of this vacant land for constructive community purposes was critical for the revitalization plan. The city of Boston owned a significant number of these parcels, and many of the private parcels were delinquent in paying taxes to the city and in various stages of foreclosure, but much of the land remained in private hands. The question was, who would control the actual disposition of this land, and through what process could it be used for community development? The solution was dramatic, controversial, and unprecedented. It had two components: granting the DSNI the power of eminent domain (by the city) over the acquisition and disposition of the land, and creating a community land trust for the long-term ownership of the land.

At first the residents of the community were suspicious of the idea of the DSNI having the power of eminent domain. In the past, planning authorities had used eminent domain to displace people from their homes in order to demolish existing structures for purposes of "development." Often this process resulted in low-income housing being replaced by office buildings and luxury apartments. The DSNI was committed to development without displacement, and after all this was explained in a series of community meetings, the community enthusiastically embraced the idea of a community-controlled power of eminent domain.

The idea of community land trusts was completely unfamiliar to most people. Most people assume that ownership of buildings and ownership of land go together. What a community land trust does is break apart these two aspects of real estate. This enables the community to remove the pressures of the market from the land and therefore to exert significant control over the selling price of the buildings on that land. This process provides a way of building affordable subsidized housing and then ensuring that it remains affordable as it is bought and sold over time. The DSNI set up a new nonprofit association, Dudley Neighborhood Incorporated, as a community land trust authorized by the Boston Redevelopment Authority to acquire lots via the power of eminent domain.

By the end of 1988, these elements were in place. In the years that followed, the DSNI embodied the ideal of empowered participatory governance by involving members of the Dudley Street community in the actual exercise of power over a wide range of decisions concerning the use of resources and land. As summarized on the DSNI website, by 2008 over half of the 1,300 vacant lots had been rehabilitated for homes, gardens, parks, an orchard, playgrounds, schools, community centers, and a town commons. Over 400 new homes for low-income people had been built, and over 500 housing units were rehabilitated.[9] The demographic profile and economic conditions of the residents themselves had not changed much. Average incomes are still very low, and the community is still composed largely of minorities. But Dudley Street is no longer a blighted, disintegrated, crime-ridden community.

Of course, the scale of these projects would not have been possible without a great deal of outside funding, both from the government and from private foundations. However, the level of funding alone would not have generated such consistent positive changes on the ground. That outcome depended on the robust forms of participation and community empowerment through which these funds were used. Gus Newport, the executive director of the DSNI from 1988 to 1992, describes the process this way:

> The chief lesson from Dudley Street is that communities need to have complete control over the planning process. That doesn't mean that you can't use professionals. But you must remember that the people living there are

[9] Dudley Street Neighborhood Initiative, "History," http://www.dsni.org/history (accessed Sept. 15, 2014).

the experts. Community people are usually taken for granted. But here they look over everything and analyze it. They ask a lot of questions. Even people with little education. There are people with little education who have great ideas.[10]

MUNICIPAL PARTICIPATORY BUDGETING[11]

In the typical American city, city budgets are put together by the technical staff of the city's chief executive—usually a mayor—and then this bureaucratically constructed budget is submitted to the council for modification and ratification. The basic shape of the budget is determined by the political agenda of the mayor and other dominant political forces working with economists, engineers, city planners, and other technocrats. Many of the crucial decisions are made behind the scenes and often involve consultation with (and pressure from) powerful business interests. With some variations in the details, this is the way city budgets are determined in most places in the United States.

Now, imagine the following alternative: Instead of the city budget being formulated from the top down, suppose that the city is divided into a number of neighborhoods, and each neighborhood has a participatory budget assembly. Suppose also that there are a number of citywide budget assemblies on various themes of interest to the entire municipality—cultural festivals, for example, or public transportation. The mandate for the participatory budget assemblies is to formulate concrete budget proposals, particularly for infrastructure projects, and submit them to a citywide budget council. Any resident of the city can participate in the assemblies and vote on the proposals. They function rather like New England town meetings, except that they meet regularly over several months so that there is ample opportunity for proposals to be formulated and modified before being subjected to ratification. After ratifying these neighborhood and thematic budgets, the assemblies choose delegates to participate in the citywide budget

---

[10] Quoted by Jay Walljasper in "The Dudley Street Example," *Citizen at Large*, June 2000.

[11] Some of the passages in this account of participatory budgeting are taken from Erik Olin Wright, *Envisioning Real Utopias* (New York, Verso: 2010), p. 2. For a more detailed discussion, see Gianpaolo Baiocchi, *Militants and Citizens: The Politics of Participatory Democracy in Porto Alegre* (Stanford, CA: Stanford University Press, 2005).

council for a few months until a coherent, consolidated city budget is adopted.

This model is in fact the reality in the city of Porto Alegre, Brazil. Before it was instituted in 1989, few people would have thought that a participatory budget could work in a relatively poor city of more than 1.5 million people, in a country with weak democratic traditions plagued by corruption and political patronage. It constitutes a form of direct participatory democracy fundamentally at odds with the conventional way that social resources get allocated for alternative purposes in cities.

In the years since the invention of the participatory budget in Porto Alegre, several hundred cities around the world have tried some form of participatory budgeting. In 2009, an experiment in participatory budgeting was instituted in a city council district in the Forty-Ninth Ward of Chicago. The experiment was inspired by the experience in Brazil and other cities, but the actual design of the process was somewhat different. City council members in Chicago are each allocated a discretionary budget to use as they wish for projects in their district. Typically these funds are used in a highly reactive way, responding to complaints from constituents about one thing or another. As one might imagine, much of the money is used to repair potholes. In this district alone, the alderman decided that the use of the available funds would be determined through a participatory budget. Neighborhood assemblies were held, citizens volunteered to participate in committees to develop specific projects, and then a kind of fair was held in a public meeting space for other residents in the district to see displays about the alternative projects. Residents of the district then voted on projects by rank-ordering them, and projects were funded based on their relative popularity.

The alderman for the Forty-Ninth Ward, Joe Moore, reports that before the participatory budget experiment, most of the discretionary funds in his ward were used for street repairs. Through participatory budgeting, the types of projects funded diversified to include bike lanes, dog parks, community gardens, and murals. This outcome is not surprising. If the discretionary funds under the control of a political official are mainly allocated on the basis of individual complaints, then one expects things like street repairs to absorb most of the resources; but if residents have a chance to imagine together what is the best way to spend $1 million each year and then discuss alternatives and vote, projects that serve broader needs are likely to get more weight.

Since this initial effort in Chicago in 2009, this kind of limited participatory budgeting has been tried in a number of other city council districts in

Chicago, and starting in 2011, in New York City as well. In 2013 four districts in Chicago and eight districts in New York instituted participatory budgets for such discretionary funds. In New York City, following the election of a progressive mayor in 2014, participatory budgeting has been expanded to twenty-four districts, covering nearly half the population. Roughly $25 million will be allocated to projects developed through empowered community participation.

An even more dramatic use of participatory budgeting occurred in the California city of Vallejo in 2012. Vallejo is a city of a little over 100,000 people that was hit especially hard by the collapse of the housing bubble in 2008 and the subsequent economic crisis. As a result, the city went into bankruptcy proceedings in 2008. After much discussion and mobilization, a participatory budget procedure was implemented in 2012 as a way of involving citizens directly in the difficult task of constructing a city budget under conditions of severe budgetary cuts.

The city committed $3 million to the first year of participatory budgeting—almost a third of the revenue collected through a special citywide sales tax adopted in the aftermath of the city's bankruptcy. The design of Vallejo's participatory budget was put in the hands of a steering committee composed of local residents, who developed a rule book and oversaw each stage of the process. Over a period of nine months, hundreds of local residents attended assemblies and worked with city employees to develop project proposals for the ballot. While in other U.S. cities, participatory budgeting was used for discretionary budgets only in specific city council districts, it was a citywide process in Vallejo. More than 4,000 residents aged 16 and over turned out to cast their vote.

WIDER PROSPECTS FOR DEMOCRACY FROM BELOW

In the United States, the last quarter of the twentieth century was a period of general retreat from the democratic ideal of an affirmative state actively engaged in solving collective problems. One part of this retreat was the promotion of a wide variety of schemes to make various aspects of the state function more like markets. Sometimes this meant simply turning over to the private sector various state responsibilities, but at other times it involved creating public-private partnerships for carrying out public functions. Such partnerships had been in existence during the 1960s as a way of involving community groups and other associations of civil society in implementing public policy. Although in the neoliberal era such partnerships often reduced democratic accountability, sometimes they contributed to the expansion of opportunities for real democratic empowerment.

The Dudley Street Neighborhood Initiative and participatory budgeting are two examples of this empowerment, but there are many others. Here are just a few:

- The *Minneapolis Neighborhood Revitalization Program.* In the early 1990s, this program allocated $400 million in public funds for Minneapolis neighborhood groups to spend over a twenty-year period on a variety of improvement projects.[12] The level of energetic participation varied considerably across the city, but in at least some neighborhoods the citizens were actively involved in formulating plans and implementing projects.
- *Communities Organized for Public Service (COPS).* COPS is an affiliated program of the Industrial Areas Foundation in San Antonio.[13] Founded in 1974, it is one of the oldest projects of community-based participatory planning in the United States. Organizationally, it is a coalition of grassroots associations rooted in the Mexican American community in San Antonio. COPS organizes an elaborate series of meetings of residents in homes, churches, and schools to discuss projects they would like. Initially this is an open-ended discussion, which of course means that residents want many more projects done than are possible. But these initial discussions are still important for they make people aware of the range of projects that are needed. Once the list is formulated, the participants in these meetings begin an extended process of trimming, prioritizing, bargaining, discussing which projects to put off for the future, and so on. Those discussions take place in a variety of venues in which active citizen participation plays a vital role. The process culminates in a plan agreed upon by community leaders and city council representatives.
- *Community policing in Chicago.*[14] This is a very different example. The general idea of "community policing" is for police departments to

---

[12] Elena Fagotto and Archon Fung, "Empowered Participation in Urban Governance: The Minneapolis Neighborhood Revitalization Program," *International Journal of Urban and Regional Research* 30, no. 3 (September 2006): 638–55.

[13] For a discussion of COPS, see Mark Warren, *Dry Bones Rattling: Community Building to Revitalize American Democracy* (Princeton, NJ: Princeton University Press, 2001).

[14] Archon Fung, *Empowered Participation: Reinventing Urban Democracy* (Princeton, NJ: Princeton University Press, 2006).

operate in such a way that they cultivate closer, less antagonistic ties to people in the community. In Chicago in the 1990s, there was an attempt to enhance the quality of this engagement by creating regular community "beat meetings" in which residents could interrogate the police and help set concrete policing priorities for their neighborhood. Each month the police would then have to report to this participatory forum about what they had done in response to these priorities.

- *The Boston Youth Zone.* In January 2014, the city of Boston launched a novel participating budgeting plan in which $1 million was made available to fund projects developed by youth ages twelve to fifteen to improve the communities in which they live. These projects were developed by committees of young people who discussed priorities, worried about trade-offs, and worked out practical details in collaboration with city officials. The projects were then voted on by youth in these communities. Initially, there was considerable skepticism that the youth would not exercise good judgment and would use much of the money for frivolous projects. This was not the case. Funded projects included upgrades to the playground and picnic area in a park specifically designed to better serve children with disabilities; the creation of "Designated Free Wall Space" for graffiti writers and artists; Chromebooks for high schools in underserved parts of Boston; security cameras for a family park; and various other improvements for parks in poor sections of the city.[15]

Many other examples could be given. And, of course, many more examples could be given of failed attempts at creating forms of direct community democratic empowerment. It is impossible to take a real census of such initiatives so that we could measure the rate of success, but almost certainly the vast majority of attempts at building democratic empowerment from below fail. This outcome is hardly surprising because most such initiatives occur against a hostile, unsupportive background. But even when there is some real support from the centers of power, building this kind of community democratic capacity may be difficult. Peter Medoff and Holly Sklar, in reflecting on the lessons from the tremendous success of the Dudley Street process, wrote:

---

[15] For details on this project, visit http://www.cityofboston.gov/youthzone/youthlead thechange/.

Communities that are unorganized, have forged little or no consensus as to what they want to see done and have not yet identified resources to bring to the table cannot be expected to participate as equal partners with government and private sector leaders. . . . The result of this premature partnership is almost always failure.

To forge effective partnership the community must be organized well enough to be an equal partner at the table, not a junior partner. It must participate out of strength, so that it can pursue its own agenda and not be suffocated or co-opted by the agenda of others. . . .

Though Boston city officials claim to have developed partnerships with other neighborhoods based on the DSNI precedent, the results have been mixed at best because no other neighborhood has yet won the community control necessary to make that kind of partnership work.[16]

For these innovative forms of empowered participatory democracy from below to flourish, it is essential to have autonomous, representative community organizations in civil society capable of sustaining the arduous process of participatory planning. If such associations do not exist, and if progressive city officials are serious about democracy from below, then in Medoff and Sklar's words, they need to give "the community time and resources to organize itself and to create a representative community organization."[17] City officials are rarely interested in fostering this kind of autonomous popular power, so expanding the possibility of democracy from below almost always depends on the vision, commitment, and skills of activists to build such capacity through community struggles and confrontations with local centers of power.

[16] Medoff and Sklar, *Streets of Hope*, pp. 276–77.

[17] Ibid., 277.

Conclusion

24

POSSIBLE FUTURES

History is full of surprises. We like to think we live in a predictable world, a world with enough stability and regularity that we know pretty well what things will be like in the near future so that we can make sensible plans. Some things we can predict confidently. We can predict with a high level of confidence, for example, that in the year 2032 there will be a presidential election in the United States. We are confident about this because we believe it is extremely unlikely that the four-year election cycle "rules of the game" for choosing presidents, which has been in place for over two hundred years, will change.

Other kinds of predictions are less certain. Students in universities today mostly believe that investing time and resources in a college education will get them a pretty good job when they graduate—certainly a better job than they would get if they had not gone to college. On this basis, these students make decisions now in anticipation of a future in which the rules of the game will be operating in more or less the same way they are today. This is what many college freshmen believed in 1928 at the height of the economic boom of the 1920s. By the time they graduated in 1932, the stock market had crashed, unemployment rates were around 25 percent, and it was extremely difficult to find jobs. In four years we went from one of the biggest booms to the worst economic crisis in American history. Could this happen again?

History is full of surprises for the fate of societies, not just individuals. Consider the following. Let us go back in history a century or so to 1910 and then examine important things that happened in the world in fifteen-year intervals from then to the present. At the beginning of each of these intervals, ask yourself the following question: would anyone at the beginning of the period, looking forward only fifteen years, have remotely anticipated the shocking, extraordinary, often world-shattering things that happened in the short future they faced?

1910–1925: World War I and the Russian Revolution; first commercial radio broadcasting

1925–1940: From the economic boom of the Roaring Twenties with an unshakable, large Republican majority to the stock market crash, the Great Depression, and the New Deal

1940–1955: World War II and the atomic bomb; the Cold War; first commercial television broadcasts

1955–1970: The civil rights movement; the end of segregation in the South; the student movement and hippies of the 1960s; the mass antiwar movement; assassinations of several prominent political figures

1970–1985: The first U.S. defeat in a war; the impeachment of Nixon; the sharp move of national politics to the right in the United States and the UK; personal computers

1985–2000: The collapse of the Soviet Union and the end of Communism and the Cold War; the creation of e-mail and the Internet

2000–2015: 9/11 and the War on Terror; the electoral triumph of the most extreme, ideologically right-wing political coalition in modern U.S. history controlling both Congress and the executive branch; the election of the first black president with initially strong Democratic Party majorities in both houses of Congress

2015–2030: Unknown

So, if history is any guide at all, we should expect the unexpected. In all likelihood, the fifteen years from 2015 to 2030 will witness monumental, unanticipated disjunctures and transformations. This can be a source of both fear and hope: fear, because sometimes these disjunctures have constituted catastrophes of human suffering and despair; hope, because they sometimes open up new possibilities for human freedom and flourishing.

Many possible futures are thus contained in the present. Do any of these have the potential to dramatically solve some of the problems we have touched on in this book? Can we envision a future in which the destructive effects of markets are tamed, poverty and inequality are significantly reduced, urban spaces are revitalized, global warming is contained, and democracy is deepened? We think the answer is yes, but whether we as a society will actually be able to realize this kind of future depends on the historical surprises we will encounter, and also—crucially—on how we respond to those surprises. And this is where the ideas of this book could be of some relevance.

If we could guide our national response to the opportunities for institutional change that the surprises of the future open up, what would we recommend? At the core of our perspective on what should be done is the question of democracy. More specifically, the central idea is that democracy needs to be both *extended* and *deepened*.

EXTENDING DEMOCRACY

Democratic practices need to be extended from the sphere of conventional politics to the economy and other arenas of social life. In a true and robust democracy, the scope of democracy extends to all issues that affect our common life as members of society. This does not mean that in a democracy the state intrudes into all aspects of personal life. Individual freedom and autonomy are also deep values in a democracy; people should have control over decisions that affect their own lives as separate persons. The problem, as we discussed in Chapter 17, is that there is no hard-and-fast, unambiguous boundary between decisions that affect only the person making the decision and decisions that have broader ramifications for the lives of others. This means that the politically recognized boundary between the public and the private—between the realm of issues subject to democratic control and the realm of decisions left to individual persons—will always be contested. There will always be disagreements about how to deal with the balance and trade-offs between individual autonomy and collective responsibility. There can be no once-and-for-all, absolute answer to the question of what decisions should be made through a democratic collective process and which should be left up to individuals as private matters. This decision itself needs to be made through democratic means.

So, we cannot draw a bright line between the public and the private. What we can say with confidence is that the rules of the game of American institutions create a far too restrictive arena for democratic deliberation with respect to the capitalist economy. The *private* in *private property* receives too much weight and presents too many barriers to democratic control. The result is a form of hypercapitalism that generates huge inequalities, perpetuates poverty, underproduces all sorts of public goods, and generally devalues the common good of the many relative to the private advantage of the few. These problems can be solved only by a significant extension of democracy. For such an extension of democracy to be meaningful, a wide range of changes in American institutions need to occur.

Refining the Boundary between Democratic Regulation and Private Rights in the Market

Even in the era of neoliberalism, with the triumphant calls for deregulation of markets and unfettering the entrepreneurial spirit, markets in American capitalism have never really became fully free. The rights of owners to use and dispose of their property just as they pleased are always curtailed by publicly enforced rules. Nevertheless, there has been a retreat of the democratic affirmative state from regulation of the capitalist economy beginning in the early 1980s. The results have been disastrous: the financial collapse of 2008; the massive rise in inequality; the erosion of the manufacturing capacity of the United States; the growth of low-wage, low-skill jobs; and the overall polarization of the job structure. These consequences can be reversed only by a reconstruction of the affirmative state on a new footing, and this means extending the reach of democratic regulation much more deeply into private property and the market.

Massive Public Investment in Public Transportation Infrastructure

The automobile-based urban transportation system in the United States creates tremendous negative externalities that can be countered only through public regulation and investment. Automobile drivers need to pay the true costs of driving cars, which includes estimated costs for future generations, and public transportation systems need to be dramatically expanded to make them an attractive alternative to private cars. A meaningful expansion of public transportation necessarily means large tax subsidies for the price of public transportation rides. Such subsidies should not be regarded as a way of creating *artificially* cheap public transportation that unfairly competes with cars, but rather as a way of embodying the true value to society of public transportation in the price of a ticket. Although individual choices of modes of transportation for any given trip would remain a private matter, the transportation environment within which those private choices are made needs to be deliberately constructed through democratic processes.

Public Control over Energy Development

Energy choices need to be part of public deliberation and democratic decisions, not simply the result of private choices by individuals and corporations. Such public control is essential if we are to combat global warming as well as contend with the long-term depletion of currently available energy resources. Democratic control over energy choices implies a diverse set of policies. First, significant resources need to be allocated to the research and development of clean energy sources. Because the payoffs from much of this research are long term, this effort must be heavily led by public funding. Second, the price of different energy sources needs to reflect the long-term, negative externalities of their use; this means, especially, a dramatic increase in the tax on gasoline. Third, large-scale retrofitting of buildings is needed to make them energy efficient. This retrofitting also needs to be driven by public choice with appropriate subsidies and incentives rather than simply by the market.

Creating a Genuine Public Health Care System

The capitalist market has proven to be an inadequate mechanism for producing high-quality, universally accessible health care. Rather than having a basically private system of health care delivery with public provision filling gaps and subsidizing private insurance to make it affordable to all, we need a public system that comprehensively provides health care for all and in which private provision exists only in ways allowed by democratic public choice. Such a universal, public health care system need not at all imply a national health care system run and administered by a centralized bureaucracy. A public, democratically coordinated health care system is consistent with a highly decentralized system in which the actual provision of services is organized in a wide variety of ways: community-based clinics, cooperatives run by health-care professionals, nonprofit foundations, solo practitioners, municipalities, and so on. The key issues are to provide the funding through collective resources—taxation—and set the rules through democratic processes rather than markets.

Extending Labor Market and Workplace Regulation

In all capitalist democracies, the democratic state intervenes systematically in the seemingly private agreements made between employers and employees in the form of the labor contract. In effect, this means that many of the choices made in those agreements are seen as matters of public concern: the health and safety conditions in the workplace; the number of hours worked per day or per week; the minimum wage levels; the kinds of punishments the employer can impose on employees; the permissible criteria the employer can use in promotions, or indeed even in hiring (i.e., discrimination in various forms is illegal); and so on. So, even in the hypercapitalism of the United States, the boundary between public and private within labor markets and workplaces is already relatively permeable and offers a significant scope for public intervention.

This scope needs to be widened if democratic principles are to be fully realized. Minimum wages need to be adjusted to be living wages. Impediments to unionization need to be removed so that workers can more easily form collective organizations to pursue their interests. Health and safety regulations need to be strengthened and, even more important, aggressively enforced.

A much more controversial issue concerns the rights of workers to participate in the governance of corporations. In the United States workers have no such rights: management has the right to exclude nonmanagerial employees from any role whatsoever in corporate decision making. This right, defenders of the authoritarian corporation argue, follows from the fact that the corporation is privately owned, and the owners have the right to tell everyone they employ what to do. Managers are simply delegated by the owners to exercise these powers. This argument directly violates the central value of democracy, which says that people have a fundamental right to participate in decisions that affect their lives. Because many decisions within corporations have profound ramifications for the lives of their employees, democratic rights of participation in the governance of firms should be extended to employees. There is no legitimate reason why firms should be run as dictatorships any more than states should be run this way. People can invest financial resources in corporations and thereby earn a rate of return on their investment, and still on democratic principles all *stake*-holders in the firm—all people whose lives are directly affected by those decisions in a significant way—and not just *stock*holders, should have meaningful representation on the board of directors of the firm.

Expanding Public Sector Employment

In the United States there is a general presumption that employment should be organized by the market rather than directly by the state. Only essential tasks that fail to be done efficiently in the market are candidates for public sector employment. There is an alternative way of thinking about this issue: consider all the needs that have to be met through economic activity and ask, which of these are best done by the market and which are better done by public employment? No priority should be given to the market over public employment; the focus should be on determining what needs doing and then seeing how best to organize it. Many important tasks that need to be done simply will not be provided sufficiently through the market: good-quality, affordable child care services; eldercare services, especially those directed at enabling the frail elderly to stay in their homes and communities; preschool education; adult education and lifelong skill upgrading; and health-care services. These needs have to be provided substantially through public sector employment or various forms of publicly funded employment if they are to be provided well.

Taxation and Redistribution Policies That Counter the Inegalitarian Effects of Markets

Finally, to be effectively extended in any of the ways we have discussed, democracy needs to be extended into the realm of income distribution. The view that income generated in the market is somehow intrinsically private income acts as a significant constraint on the capacity of democratic decision making to allocate resources to public purposes. As we argued in Chapter 19 on taxation, the total economic pie in a complex economy is generated through an extended process of social cooperation. This pie then needs to be divided—distributed—to different purposes. In a market economy, taxation is the principal way we divide the pie between public and private uses. Increasing taxation fundamentally means increasing the scope for democratic deliberation over how best to use our resources.

John Kenneth Galbraith, one of the most publicly influential economists in the second half of the twentieth century, commented in his book *The Affluent Society* that the United States was characterized by private affluence and public squalor, dirty streets and clean houses. This is a chronic problem in a society within which the private choices of individuals and corporations in the market are privileged over collective choices of citizens and communities in the public sphere. Building a vigorous, affirmative state by extending democracy into domains currently dominated by the market is an essential part of the solution.

DEEPENING DEMOCRACY

Unless democracy is also *deepened*, then extending the role of the state in an affirmative direction simply means extending the role of centralized bureaucracy. This is the specter that political conservatives always invoke against efforts at extending the scope of the democratic affirmative state. Do you want the government controlling your life? Do you want bureaucrats in Washington deciding on your health care? Part of the appeal in extending the "free" market is precisely its promise of preventing heavy-handed, centralized bureaucracies from dominating our lives.

As we have argued throughout this book, the free market, at best, provides only a limited basis for people to control their own lives and destinies. The problem is that many aspects of our lives are deeply shaped by the choices and actions of other people, especially people in control of large corporations operating in capitalist markets. "Democracy" is the name we give to a society whose people really do have the power to control their own lives and destinies, but this means putting the market in its place rather than letting the market itself insulate vast realms of important decisions from collective deliberation and choice.

Still, the fact remains that expanding the scope and jurisdiction of the state is no guarantee at all for enhancing democracy. What we want is not intensified *bureaucratization* of social life, but intensified *democratization*. Deepening democracy basically means strengthening the ways in which ordinary citizens effectively participate in democratic politics and subordinate the machinery of the state to their collective purposes. Such a real deepening of democracy entails a number of difficult institutional transformations.

Striving for Political Equality

The goal of political equality is of fundamental importance: to realize the goals of democracy requires achieving the greatest possible equality in people's ability to participate in public deliberations and collective choices. This, of course, means removing formal legal obstacles to participation; but just as important, meaningful political equality requires a considerable equalization of resources. Vast material inequality in life conditions is itself a source of inequalities in real freedom and access to political power. Both the levels of extreme poverty in the United States and the levels of extraordinary wealth are inconsistent with genuine political equality. Here the issue is not whether such economic inequality is unfair or unjust, but whether it subverts the necessary conditions for meaningful political equality. It does.

In this book we have discussed a range of remedies for the economic inequalities in American society: public jobs programs and lifelong education and skill formation programs can reduce inequalities in access to good jobs; more progressive tax policies combined with income subsidy programs, including potentially universal basic income, can reduce income inequality; comparable worth is a remedy for gender inequalities in earnings resulting from sex typing of jobs. In these and other ways, democracy requires countering the spontaneous inequalities generated by capitalist markets.

Reducing the Role of Private Money in Politics

Given that large inequalities in private incomes will remain a characteristic of American capitalism for the foreseeable future, it becomes especially important to somehow block the translation of private economic power into political power. One central aspect of this problem is limiting the role of private money in politics. Of course, elections are expensive, especially in large jurisdictions, and any viable public system of financing elections will be costly. To really drive private money out of elections will require something like Bruce Ackerman's proposal for democracy cards (discussed in Chapter 18), which would certainly cost billions of tax dollars a year. Given the stakes, this is cheap. Without such reforms, private wealth will continue to disproportionately influence the elections for public office.

Reforming the Electoral Rules of the Game

The existing electoral rules in the United States guarantee a political duopoly of the two major parties. Minority political voices are marginalized, and both major parties firmly support the interests of corporate capitalism. A wide range of alternative electoral rules could be used to open up the political arena; these include various schemes of proportional representation, two-round run-offs, and instant run-offs.

Revitalizing the Labor Unions

The collapse of the American labor movement has not only weakened the capacity of employees to bargain with their employers, but it has deeply eroded the most important collective association of working people capable of giving them an effective democratic voice. Revitalizing the labor movement requires significant changes in the existing rules that regulate labor unions as well as the patterns of enforcement of those rules.

Democratic Innovation

Ultimately a robust, deep democracy must be based on the active, ongoing participation of ordinary citizens in governance. It is important, of course, that elections be vigorously and fairly contested. But democracy needs more than just fair elections; it needs a wide range of ways for citizens to actively participate in the governance of their society. This task necessarily requires serious forms of decentralization, for it is above all in local contexts where people live and work that most people have the possibility of being directly involved in democratic processes. Decentralization is not, however, the same as privatization, in which the state sheds its responsibilities in favor of the market. Decentralization means locating sites of participatory problem solving where the problems lie and then empowering citizens to become directly involved in the decision-making process. Without such participation and real citizen empowerment, decentralization can simply be a cover for reducing the capacity of the state to act in the collective interest.

REALIZING AMERICAN IDEALS

We began this book by laying out what we felt were a core set of American ideals anchored in the values of freedom, prosperity, efficiency, fairness, and democracy. These values are only imperfectly realized in American institutions as they exist at the beginning of the twenty-first century.

Freedom is embodied in the ability of people to make choices in the market, but because of the huge inequalities generated by the market, such freedom is very unequally distributed. Prosperity is reflected in the high material standard of living of many people in the United States; however, the continued exclusion of a significant part of the population from real access to this standard of living means that we fall far short of the ideal of prosperity for all. Additionally, the culture of obsessive private consumerism undermines the connection between prosperity and the quality of life. American capitalism does promote certain forms of efficiency, but because of the chronic and inherent problems of negative externalities and concentrations of economic power, capitalist markets also produce inefficient outcomes that generate great harms to our collective well-being. Progress on fairness has been substantial through the elimination of many blatant forms of sexism and racism in the last half of the twentieth century, yet life opportunities remain grossly unequal. No one can regard the severe poverty experienced by many American children as in any way just or fair. And finally, democracy and its associated freedoms remain central features of the American political system, yet the large disparities of power among citizens violate the basic democratic principle of political equality, and the restrictions on the scope of state activity undermine the extent to which the society is democratically governed. These are the realities of how American society really works.

These realities, however, are not destinies. They are the result of past struggles over how American institutions should be organized, struggles in which some visions prevailed and others were defeated. The result of those struggles has been the complex institutional configuration we call American society, a configuration that from time to time will be subjected to new struggles and transformations. At those times, people will be called upon to make choices concerning these values—in the ballot box, in support for various kinds of social movements, in conflicts within workplaces and other institutions.

Extending and deepening democracy is one possible direction the transformations could take. This outcome would not automatically solve the pressing social and economic problems of American society, but it would create a context within which creative solutions become much more achievable because the constraints on what can be done are weakened. And this just might make possible a surprising future: an American society that is fairer and more democratic, an America whose economy advances the common good and extends the promise of real freedom to all, an America that finally realizes its potential and lives up to its ideals.

CREDITS

Figure 5.11: Figure from "Rising Seas Will Affect Major U.S. Coastal Cities by 2100" by Mari N. Jensen. *UA News*, 2/15/2011. Figure by Jeremy Weiss. Reprinted by permission of Jeremy Weiss, University of Arizona. See also: Strauss, B.H., R. Ziemlinski, J.L. Weiss, and J.T. Overpeck. 2012. Tidally-adjusted estimates of topographic vulnerability to sea level rise and flooding for the contiguous United States. *Environmental Research Letters* 7: 014033 10.1088/1748-9326/7/1/014033.

Figure 8.5: Figure "Spending on Health Insurance Administration per Capita 2011," from *The Commonwealth Fund* 2013 *International Health Policy Survey in Eleven Countries*, by Robin Osborn & Cathy Schoen, November 2013. Used by permission of the Commonwealth Fund.

Figure 8.6: Figure "Insurance Complexity and Restrictions Create Concerns for Patients and Doctors," from *The Commonwealth Fund* 2013 *International Health Policy Survey in Eleven Countries*, by Robin Osborn & Cathy Schoen, November 2013. Used by permission of the Commonwealth Fund.

Figure 8.10: Figure "Experienced Cost Related Access Problem," from "Access, Affordability, and Insurance Complexity Are Often Worse in the United States Compared to 10 Other Countries," by C. Schoen, R. Osborn, D. Squires, and M.M. Doty. *Health Affairs Web First*, November 14, 2013. Used by permission of the Commonwealth Fund.

Figure 8.13: Figure "Overall Views of Health Care System, 2013," from *The Commonwealth Fund* 2013 *International Health Policy Survey in Eleven Countries*, by Robin Osborn & Cathy Schoen, November 2013. Used by permission of the Commonwealth Fund.

Figure 9.6: Figure 7-1: Growth of Six Big Banks" from 13 *Bankers: The Wall Street Takeover and the Next Financial Meltdown* by Simon Johnson, copyright © 2010 by Simon Johnson and James Kwak. Used by permission of Sagalyn Literary Agency and by permission of Pantheon Books, an imprint of the Knopf Doubleday Publishing Group, a division of Random House LLC. All rights reserved.

Figure 13.16: Figure 2 from "Building a Better America—One Wealth Quintile at a Time," by Michael I. Norton and Dan Ariely. *Perspectives on Psychological Science*, 6 (1), pp. 9–12. Copyright © 2011 by Association for Psychological Science. Reprinted by Permission of SAGE Publications.

Figure 13.17: Figure 1 from "Building a Better America—One Wealth Quintile at a Time," by Michael I. Norton and Dan Ariely. *Perspectives on Psychological Science*, 6 (1), pp. 9–12. Copyright © 2011 by Association for Psychological Science. Reprinted by Permission of SAGE Publications.

INDEX